The Legal and Ethical Environment of Business

Timothy L. Fort

Everleigh Chair in Business Ethics,
Professor of Business Law and Ethics
Kelley School of Business, Indiana University

Stephen B. Presser

Raoul Berger Professor of Legal History, Emeritus
Professor of Business Law, Kellogg School of Management,
Northwestern University

444 Cedar Street, Suite 700
St. Paul, MN 55101
1-877-888-1330

Printed in the United States of America

ISBN: 978-1-68328-549-6

To Susan Graff and to Nancy Nerad

Preface

WHY IS IT that although the two of us have been teaching Business Law for a combined sixty years, we excitedly walk into each class? It is true that we both love to teach, but our experience hardly seems the exception. Indeed, nearly every Business Law professor we have ever met has the same experience.

Part of the answer might lie in the reaction students have to the course. To be sure, there will always be a student here and there who doesn't view a Legal Environment of Business or a Business Organizations course as his or her favorite. There are quite a few more who have doubts about the course until their first day. Yet, by and large, students also find these courses to be among the most interesting—and useful—they take. Students expect business law to be dull, uninspiring, and, in short, boring. What we and many of our business law colleagues seek to do, however, is to show that business law is about human drama. It is about yearning, emotion, and even revenge. It is, we believe, as fascinating as is the human race itself. Seeing our students begin to sense that, and seeing student skepticism transform into unexpected enthusiasm is, for want of a better word, fun.

The regulation of the business organization by law is America's great contribution to world jurisprudence. And, of course, as David Dudley Field remarked in 1859, as Americans, law is our only sovereign. We have no monarchy, we have no aristocracy, we have no established church. It is the law and the Constitution which holds this republic together, and as Americans we do really believe that ours should be a government of laws, not men (or women), and that our conduct should be guided by a benevolent rule of law. For Americans then, the study of law is not just the story of legal doctrine. It is history. It is philosophy. It is analysis. It is critical thinking. It is communication. It is politics. It is ethics. It is drama. It is even art. How could one not be excited about having the privilege to teach it?

Law touches on so many different parts of our lives that it is, after all, easy to relate to any person's—any student's—daily experience. Students have seen, and sometimes been, the careless driver. They've seen, and sometimes experienced, discrimination. They have had contracts breached and they have wondered if they are really bound to their promises, given their idiosyncratic circumstances. They wonder about how to reign in giant corporations, unruly agents and misguided principals, and they may have even wondered which of the myriad business forms would best suit their entrepreneurial ideas.

We have tried to construct a business law text which captures what we believe to be the intrinsic interest and the immediacy of law. This book has been assembled in a manner that allows the instructor to immerse students in the complex business of business law a bit more fully than can be done in some good business law textbooks that we do admire. We allow cases to run a little longer, believing that in doing so, critical thinking can better emerge within the confines of the richness of the case itself; so too can ethics. In photographs, notes, graphs, and questions, we try also to connect the dots between the law and current events, art, history, and politics.

The collaboration that produced this text is more than three decades long. It dates back to a cold Chicago January day in 1981 when a young law student named Tim Fort sat in Professor Presser's American Legal History course at Northwestern University School of Law, and on the second day of class found himself being grilled on topics pertaining to England's Sir Edward Coke and the relationship between law and religion. (You will see that the same subject matter begins this textbook.) Our relationship developed over the years, as Presser was one of Fort's supervisors during his work toward an unusual PhD in law, management, and theology. We have continued to teach in both management and law schools, and have found this opportunity to work as co-authors to be one of the true high points of our careers.

There are several people we would like to acknowledge. Jim Cahoy has been our terrific editor at West Academic Publishing who has fostered this book and kept us on task, always with grace, humor and enthusiasm. Carol Logie, the creative talent who put this book together, has been fantastic, crafting something truly unusual for a law text, an aesthetically superb book. We are grateful to both of them.

Professor Presser would like to thank his research assistants William O'Hara, Andreas Havajias, and Tiffany Chu, all of whom, in the summer of 2013, drafted large chunks of chapters, and all of whom served as valuable sounding boards for the materials on agency, partnership, LLCs, and corporations. Professor Presser's longtime faculty assistant, Tim Jacobs, performed his usual invaluable services.

Professor Fort would like to thank his research assistants, Lauren Chan and William LeBas at George Washington University School of Law and Jason Allen at the Mauer School of Law at Indiana University. He would also like to recognize four undergraduate students who, as an independent study, took up the challenge to propose graphics, photos, and other art that might capture the attention of students: Amna Bibi, Christopher Oman, Siddhi Salvi, and Danielle Stacey. Finally, Lisa Corneleo did tremendous service to us in editing the second edition (the previous edition was titled *Business Law*).

Our hope, in assembling these materials, is that those using them will help us, in future editions, better to meet their needs. We welcome any and all suggestions for improvement, and humbly take responsibility for any errors, omissions, or lapses which inevitably creep into such a bold undertaking.

— Stephen B. Presser
Asheville, NC

— Timothy L. Fort
Bloomington, IN

About the Authors

STEPHEN PRESSER is the Raoul Berger Professor of Legal History, Emeritus, at Northwestern University School of Law, and a Professor of Business Law at Northwestern's Kellogg School of Management, with an appointment in the Management and Strategy Department. He is the co-author of a legal history casebook, the author of a corporations casebook, and the author of a treatise on the law of shareholder liability for corporate debts.

Presser is a graduate of Harvard College and Harvard Law School, and has frequently been an invited witness before committees of the U.S. Senate and House of Representatives on issues of constitutional law. He has been teaching courses on business organizations to law students and to management students for the last three decades. A course he created for Kellogg, "Law and the Manager," is one of the most popular of Kellogg's highly-ranked Executive Masters of Business Administration program. He is the recipient of many teaching awards from Kellogg and from the Law School, and has twice been a Fulbright Senior Scholar at University College, London.

TIMOTHY FORT holds the Everleigh Chair in Business Ethics and is Professor of Business Law and Ethics at the Kelley School of Business at Indiana University. His primary research identity pertains to issues of ethical corporate culture and the relationship between ethical business and sustainable peace. He has authored six major research books published by Oxford, Cambridge, Yale, and Stanford University Presses. His *Business, Integrity and Peace* and *Diplomat in the Corner Office* both won the Best Book Award from the Academy of Management's Social Issues in Business Section. He has also authored two textbooks in the field of business ethics.

Fort holds his PhD from Northwestern University, where he also received his JD. His M.A. and B.A. are from the University of Notre Dame. He has received research awards from The Academy of Management, the Society of Business Ethics, and The Academy of Legal Studies of Business and has served on the editorial board of *The Academy of Management Review*, *Business Ethics Quarterly*, and *The American Business Law Journal*. He has also won teaching awards and recognition at the Doctoral, Executive, MBA, and undergraduate levels.

TABLE OF CONTENTS

The Legal and Ethical Environment of Business

Ethical, Historical and Philosophical Foundations

Perhaps it may seem strange to begin a Business Law textbook with ethics, but it should not. Underlying any government and its laws is a philosophy. The philosophy may be rudimentary: a strong man has power and enforces his will on others because what is powerful is what is right. It may be a Confucian understanding of the right relationships that exist among human beings and how government educates, is informed by, and enforces those relationships. It may be based on notions on the inalienable human rights that are self-evident, government justified by the consent of the governed rather than through the projection of power, both joined with a mixed view of human nature so that governmental authority is limited.

The founders of the United States deeply immersed themselves in the political philosophies of the times, of those found in antiquity, and even from religion. They founded a system grounded in Enlightenment notions drawn from philosophers such as Locke and Montesquieu. They dwelled on the notion of a social contract, existing at least since Plato and given then-current reformation by Hobbes, Rousseau and Locke. Locke's notions of rights to life, liberty and property found their way into both the Declaration of Independence and into the Constitution.

The Constitutional and legal commitments to the rights of man, to judicial review and separation of powers, and to equality and freedom among others, then found their way into the legal system from philosophical sources and debates about them. Notions of justice were not simply ways to describe a system—"the Justice system"—but were a part of a dialogue about ethics and morality as well. Corruption was not a designation of bribery per se, but of a commitment to make an entire system of government one based on the rule of law rather than on the basis of favoritism.

These social contract kinds of championed the dignity of human beings and, especially as articulated through *The Federalist Papers*, logically required institutional structures. That social contract tradition has continued philosophically, such as through the work of John Rawls in the 20th Century and into the field of business ethics through the work of Thomas Donaldson and Thomas Dunfee. Notions of the inherent value of human beings, their rights and their dignity, were also articulated by Immanuel Kant, writing exactly at the time of the formative years of the U.S. Kant's work has been enormously influential in philosophy ever since and has been relied upon by businesses ethicists such as Ed Freeman, Patricia Werhane, and Norman Bowie.

Jeremy Bentham, also writing at this time and later, John Stuart Mill, articulated the utilitarian—or majoritarian—notions of creating the greatest good for the greatest number, with joins notions of Kantian Rights and Rawlsian Justice to stand as the triumvirate of contemporary philosophical approaches to stakeholder holder theory of the firm.

Yet again writing at the same time of the formative years of the United States was the moral philosopher, Adam Smith. Smith's work is often misinterpreted to be represented that no one needs to consider society; just one's own self-interest. That's not exactly what he said; he also situated his framework with the context of a sense of moral citizenship, even among business people. At the same time, he did articulate a philosophy that justified the pursuit of self-interest and wealth with a confidence that an invisible hand would provide social benefits. That position, added onto by multiple economists including Milton Friedman and F.A. Hayek, forms the basis of today's shareholder theory of the firm.

Finally, the well-chronicled observer of early America, Alexis de Tocqueville, also commented upon the ways in which religious sentiments hemmed in excessive self-interest. That need for virtue was emphasized by founders as spiritually diverse as George Washington, Benjamin Franklin, Thomas Jefferson and John Adams. Laws simply were not enough, though the founders also believed them to be essential. Also essential were the inculcation of civic virtue, a theme extended philosophically since then, perhaps most prominently in recent times by Alasdair MacIntyre and, in the field of business ethics by Robert Solomon and Ed Hartman. Indeed, joining shareholder theory and stakeholder theory is virtue theory as the three leading business ethics frameworks.

This history is worth recounting because the legal system you will study in this book and in your class is based on the philosophical foundations that also drive contemporary business ethics. Yet rather than refer back to those classic formulations of these philosophical traditions, there is abundant, extant, and contemporary formulations and applications of them directly to the field of business today. Thus, throughout the book, we will be considering the laws that arise from these traditions and also, in each chapter, challenge you to think through anew how those same foundations help us to consider the ethical dimensions of business activities as well.

On the one hand, the idea of businesses having ethical obligations is very old. Legal historian Reuven Avi-Yonah has shown that social obligations of business, grounded in the law, date back to Roman antiquity.[1] In early American legal history, one could only obtain a corporate charter if a legislature determined that the corporate purpose served some kind of public good. In smaller towns and urban neighborhoods around the country, the currency of a businessperson very much depended on the extent to which that person was a leading citizen in the community.

For a variety of reasons, the connection between ethical, social engagement of businesses and their profit-making function became perceived to be more tenuous. Part of that reason may have been because the rise of large corporations made it difficult for any one person in the organization, except perhaps the CEO, to see her own obligations extended beyond her job performance. One of the prominent philosophers of the twentieth century, Alasdair MacIntyre, has decried "managerialism" that does not ask ultimate questions of whether a business action is bad or good, but simply whether one has completed one's job description.[2]

Liquid markets also play a role because today, a stockholder who has a computer can change positions in the market a dozen or more times a day. Many academic studies—and meta-studies of those studies—conclude that there is a slight correlation between good ethics/social performance and good business/financial performance.[3] But those studies look at long-term business performance. In the long term, concepts such as reputation, goodwill, and social capital have genuine economic value. In the short term, it is much harder to calculate the value of goodwill when determining the company's quarterly forecast on which basis shareholders will make decisions to buy and sell, as well as to retain or fire a CEO.

A third factor has been the rise, both in law and in business, of an economics movement, primarily drawing on the Chicago School of Economics, that sidelines notions of corporate responsibility. As Milton Friedman argued, a CEO who spends corporate assets on philanthropic purposes commits theft: stealing shareholder money. Unless that philanthropy leads to a measurable economic benefit (which Friedman acknowledges could happen) then executives should maximize profit and let the shareholders choose what to do with their own money. Similar economic models, especially within finance, have developed precise statistics models that measure mechanisms that enhance profitability while leaving hard-to-measure issues of ethics and social goods out of the equation.

---

1 See, Reuven S. Avi-Yonah, *The Cyclical Transformations of the Corporate Form* (2005).

2 *See*, Alasdair MacIntyre *After Virtue* 75 (2007).

3 *See*, Joshua D. Margolis, Hillary Anger Elfenbein, and James P. Walsh, *Do Well by Doing Good? Don't Count on It* 86.1 *Harvard Business Review* 19 (Jan. 2008).

These factors triggered a reaction. Depending on where one begins the history, that reaction could be located in a famous debate between Adolf Berle and E.M. Dodd in the *Harvard Law Review* where they debated whether corporate leaders should manage for the benefit of the shareholders or for the benefit of the general public.[4] In the 1960s, one began to see studies by academics of what businesspeople say about ethics.[5] In the 1970s, in the aftermath of political scandals such as Watergate and then with corporate scandals like the bribery scandals of Lockheed (see William Hartung, *Prophets of War: Lockheed Martin and the Making of the Military-Industrial Complex* 115 (2011)), public and institutional pressure built on business schools to address ethical issues.

In the 1980s, that gave rise to the major effort of philosophers entering into business schools who took classic philosophical frameworks and applied them to business. This included scholars such as Ed Freeman, who brought to life the idea of Stakeholder Theory, a play on the more traditional focus on Shareholders. Following principles of the German philosopher, Immanuel Kant, Freeman argued that all people should be treated as ends, not as means to an end (a corollary of Kant's Categorical Imperative), and so, businesses should not look at employees as "labor inputs," but as flesh-and-blood beings with dignity to be treated as an end. The same logic applied to anyone else who was affected by a corporate action (Freeman's definition of a stakeholder). Kant was also followed by those who advocated for a human rights standard within business. Some such philosophers have already been mentioned in this book, such as Patricia Werhane. Thomas Donaldson invoked the work of social contractarian John Rawls and argued for a meta-bargain between businesses and society with businesses owing obligations to society in exchange for its existence. Donaldson later partnered with Thomas Dunfee to expand that social contract to consider not only philosophical social contracts, but practical, political, and legal social contracts that already exist around the world. Robert Solomon and Edwin Hartman drew on Aristotle to argue for a virtue-based philosophy of business ethics and a community-based one, respectively. William Frederick drew upon naturalist notions and applied them to business to create a more pragmatic version of business ethics; drawing on different sources, Richard De George similarly articulated a pragmatic model.

Though these rich formulations were being developed, notions of ethics and social responsibility were fairly marginalized in business schools until the mid-to-late 1990s. At that point, more scandals erupted, especially just after the turn of the century with Enron, Worldcom, and others. This placed more pressure on business schools. Their accrediting body, the AACSB, responded with a requirement that all business schools have some method of teaching ethics. Perhaps more influentially,

---

4 A.A. Berle, *Corporate Powers as Powers in Trust* 44 Harv. L. Rev 1049 (1931); E. Merrick Dodd, *For Whom are Corporate Managers Trustees* 45 Harv. L. Rev. 1145 (1932).

5 *See*, Raymond Baumhart *Ethics is Business* (1968).

cell phones and the Internet appeared. When those technological tools became available, it became quickly apparent that a corporate indiscretion could be captured on a hand-held cell phone and placed for worldwide view on the Internet within a matter of seconds.

Suddenly corporations realized that actions matter, just as they might for a business in a small town or in an urban neighborhood. Corporations began to create public relations departments that focused on issues of corporate responsibility. Perhaps as or more importantly, business school students drove the faculty and deans to address the issue of ethics, corporate social responsibility, and environmental responsibility. Thus, by 2005 or so, business schools had been pushed by students and businesses to address corporate responsibility issues by technology, scandals, and accrediting bodies. One more thing added to this mix, the previously mentioned Federal Sentencing Guidelines. By 2005, studies were showing that paper programs and legal-only based compliance programs were ineffective. Amendments to the Guidelines were, in light of the scandals of Enron and others, requiring that attention be given to "organizational culture" and "ethics."

With this history in mind, one has an answer to the question of why a company would bother to undertake an ethics initiative or social responsibility project. One reason is economic. No less an authority than former Federal Reserve Chairman Alan Greenspan testified before Congress that in today's economy, the only thing a business may bring to the market is its reputation; if that reputation is damaged, so is the company.[6] Protection of reputation has become a vital issue of today's modern businesses whether in the form of a public relationship campaign, partnering with an NGO to address social ills, or hiring employees or consultants to "scrub" damaging statements about the company placed on the Internet.

The economic calculus is not merely that of damage control. It also brings with it opportunity. Some firms seek to differentiate themselves in the market by appealing to a segment that values identifiable corporate reputation. Ben and Jerry's ice cream was the forerunner of this, but today that niche—and it can be a big niche—is filled with companies such as Whole Foods, Timberland, and Starbucks. Without canonizing these companies, other companies have had more mixed results in achieving this niche, but their effort in trying to do so is indicative of the value reputation has in today's market. Thus, one sees extractives such as Chevron, Shell, and even Exxon touting their corporate social responsibility programs, even though each has been the target of major, public demonization in the not-so-recent past. Diamond companies, such as Tiffany's and DeBeers, embraced a certification program (the Kimberly Protocol) that attempted to assure a customer that diamonds were not mined with the assistance of child soldiers. Wal-Mart gets hammered in the press for its labor practices one day and then is touted for its environmental programs the next. Johnson & Johnson was one of the great champions of ethical conduct

6 Alan Greenspan, *The Assault on Integrity*, 2.8 *The Objectivist Newsletter* 31(1963).

in the 1980s, but its reputation suffered under continuous recalls and lawsuits so much that its shareholders filed a derivative lawsuit demanding that the board of directors bring the company back to its moral roots. In short, companies today see an opportunity to maintain or gain market share by being a company that seeks to do good while also doing well.

These considerations spill over into two other reasons for why a company might take ethics and social responsibility seriously. Legal reasons also are important. Companies get sued for breaches of conduct. To get out ahead of potential litigation, one might adopt an ethically driven policy. Studies also show that sexually harassing workplaces, for instance, tend to be less productive. After all, the harasser isn't working; he is harassing. And targets of the harassment aren't working either; they are trying to get away from the harasser. Neither lends itself to economic productivity.[7]

That leads to a third reason for why one might bother: identity reasons. Continuing with the sexual harassment example, most companies would prefer not to be known as the sexual harassment company. It also leads to some of the earlier examples of wanting to be known as a clean diamond company or a shoe company that gives its employees forty hours a year off from work to do volunteer work in the community (as Timberland does). In an Internet age where reputation is important, so is identity. Indeed, companies recruit on the basis of their identity and so if a company does not consistently manage with that identity in mind, it can have an impact on the morale of the employees recruited to work in "that kind" of company.

A final reason to bother with ethical issues is simply a moral one. At the end of the day, human beings, even at work, have moral sentiments. They have a hardwired desire to want to help those in need and they take pride, even joy, in treating others well. At times, organizational incentives do not reward such actions; they may even punish such considerations. But there is an aspect of human nature that wants to be proud of the ethical content of the work one does.

Even today, the law is hardly value-neutral. Indeed, in some ways, this entire book about the legal environment of business can be examined from the standpoint as a book about ethics and philosophy. To make this historical foundation relevant—and because increasingly many business law professors integrate ethics into their courses and sometimes teach courses designated as both ethics and law courses—we choose to begin this book with a chapter that provides a decision-making model for business actions

7 *See*, Roy Whitehead, Jr. and Walter Block, *Sexual Harassment in the Workplace: A Property Rights Perspective* 4 J. L. & Fam. Stud. 229, 243 (2002).

CHAPTER

1

Introduction to Ethical Decision-Making

Ethics is subjective but it is not only subjective. A sound decision-making process overcomes the biases we have to allow decisions that are less idiosyncratic. By setting out the steps of a decision and by applying leading scholarship to decisions, we can make it less likely that we will make decisions blinded by our biases. Learning a six-step decision making process in which one applies three leading, contemporary business ethics frameworks is the aim of this chapter of the book.

David Messick, a now-retired ethics professor at the Kellogg School of Business at Northwestern University, has argued that empirical studies demonstrate that we value our own self-interest over the well-being of others. There is nothing too surprising about that finding, but it is one that does create issues for the decisions we make. The more we are biased toward our own self-interest, the more we are likely to rationalize any decision we make and often demonize another person's actions if they annoy us.

Professor LaRue Hosmer

Thus, an aim of a decision-making process is to make better, more objective decisions. The model I follow tracks heavily with that of Professor LaRue Hosmer, taught ethics at the University of Michigan Business School for many years. There are other models, but they tend to aim toward the same objective and pose similar questions and steps.

I. An Introduction to the Six-Step Process

DECISION-MAKING PROCESSES attempt to mute biases that we have so that we can make decisions more rationally and defend our reasoning more clearly. Ethics is not unique in this. In a Strategy or Marketing class, it is not enough to simply say that your gut feeling tells you to adopt a certain new marketing effort or corporate strategy. Gut feelings are important, but a company goes through a process to determine best strategies, marketing and human resources approaches. They do this so that they make better decisions. Once they are made, a process allows others to better understand why they are made rather than simply being told that the decision came from the CEO's gut instincts (though that does happen sometimes).

It is a bit strange, then, when people say that ethics can't be taught or that they are simply subjective intuitions or traits of personal character that either one has or one doesn't have. Of course, there are intuitions in ethics, just as there are intuitions in Strategy. Of course, some people have traits that lend themselves well to making ethical decisions in Marketing. But decisions can be made better and are better explained when one tries to apply a reasoning process to dilemmas. That is as true of ethics as it is of anything else.

There is another anomaly about ethics: it is personal and it is private. Well, yes, sort of, and so what? Ethics are personal. They comprise decisions about who we are as human beings, what we value, what we stand for, and how we are identified to the world. There certainly is a personal dimension to ethics, but is ethics private? In one sense, it is absurd to think that it is. Ethics are about how we treat other people, so how could interacting with other people be considered private? Ethics are always about some degree of public interaction where we ask how others should be treated. Ethics cannot be purely private. A follow up response, however, requires us to consider how big of a circle we are thinking of when talking about ethics. Ethical conduct is crucial to a relationship with a significant other. There is privacy in that relationship, but it is not purely private. The wider we draw the circle—to friends, to community, to a business, to a nation, to the human race, to the ecosystem—the more questions are raised of just how private or public our decisions are. As we draw those circles, some things are indeed private. But they are never purely private.

So what? What if they are personal and what if they are a mix of private and public? Even if that is true, we human beings don't simply sit around and let other people do whatever they want to do. Or, when we do see such inaction, we can get pretty disgusted. None of us would say, well, Adolf Hitler had his moral views and they are personal and private to him and so we should not do anything as he kills six million Jews. That would be an absurd moral position. When we see such things, we react. We do not allow anyone to do whatever he or she please when such actions negatively impact others. So even if there are degrees of personal conduct and of private conduct, there are limits too. Defining what those limits are is tough stuff. But I want to be certain to disabuse you of some of these dismissive—and frankly, thoughtless—rules of thumb that some will toss out to argue that ethics is so different from any other subject in a business or law school that it cannot be taught.

With this in mind, let's look at the decision-making model. The six steps of Hosmer's moral reasoning process ("HMRP") are as follows:

1. Identify the Moral Issue
2. Identify Additional Facts Helpful to Making a Decision
3. Identify the Alternatives Available to Apply to the Problem
4. Identify the Personal Impacts to the Decision Maker
5. Apply Three Leading Contemporary Theories of Business Ethics: Shareholder, Stakeholder, and Virtue
6. Conclude With a Decision

A. HMRP STEP ONE: IDENTIFY THE MORAL PROBLEM

A quick and dirty way of identifying the moral issue is asking who has been harmed and whether they have been harmed in a significant way. Of course, people are harmed all the time. People lose all the time. It's one thing to lose; it's another thing to create an ethical dilemma. Just because your favorite team loses a game, or you lose a job or another company or another individual wins a bid does not mean that there is an ethical dilemma. In a capitalist society, there are winners and losers. Fair or not, the free market system is the one we find ourselves in, and this decision-making framework assumes that to be the case.

In identifying a moral issue, one is looking at a situation where there has been harm to a vulnerable party who has been unable to protect him or herself particularly well. For instance, we will see a case in the next chapter where there was a depletion of well water for an agricultural plant to operate in Mexico. Residents had previously been able to get clean drinking water by drilling sixty feet deep, but with the depletion, one had to drill 450 feet deep. As a result, children now drink sewage with human waste in it. And so when a five-year old asks, "Daddy, can I have a drink of water?" the father will have to give him human waste to drink. That constitutes a moral dilemma.

In another famous case, orphaned street children sniffed glue in Central America. It may be true that their parents have the primary responsibility to make sure their kids aren't sniffing glue. It is also probably true that the government and the society has a responsibility to make sure that those kids are cared for and not just left on the street where they end up sniffing the glue in order to relieve hunger pangs and to make them high and to give a bit of relief in an otherwise pretty dreary existence. But this does not preclude a tertiary responsibility, a third level of responsibility held by companies doing business in the area, whose product is what the children sniff. The only thing standing between the children sniffing glue and sniffing his or her brains out and potentially dying is what the company chooses to do.

The moral issue can be stated in a sentence or two. There could be twenty moral harms in a given case. Picking one doesn't mean that that's necessarily the only one that has been brought up in a particular case, but this step provides a focus for an evaluation.

B. HMRP STEP TWO: ADDITIONAL FACTS

Business students and businesspeople tend to do quite well in finding many additional facts and identifying questions that they want to have answers to before they make a conclusion. That's healthy. One of the best things you can do in making an ethical analysis is to find additional facts so that you're not gossiping. This step thus becomes the opportunity to recognize the additional facts that would be helpful to know. One still must often make a decision based on insufficient information; life tends to require that. But this is an opportunity to identify three or four additional facts that would be helpful to know in making a moral decision. Of course, these facts need to be relevant. Additional facts need not be determinative, but they do need to be germane.

C. HMRP STEP THREE: AVAILABLE ALTERNATIVES

Step three looks at additional alternatives. Sometimes, we may think of an ethical issue as an either-or choice. You must either do the saintly thing or risk selling your soul. Frequently there are a lot of options in between. When H.B. Fuller was faced with street children sniffing its shoe-repair glue in Honduras, the company could have bookend choices: get out of the market or continue to sell the product as is. Yet, there were many alternatives Fuller could pursue. It could fund social service agencies to help the kids, place better warning labels so the kids recognize the danger of the product even if they even they were illiterate, or conduct additional research and development to have a safer product. Thus, between the bookends, one finds alternatives.

D. HMRP STEP FOUR: IDENTIFY PERSONAL IMPACTS

Personal impacts are not the impacts on the various human beings that are affected by a corporate decision. That's what stakeholder theory is about. Personal impacts apply to the following: Assume that you are in the position of being the decision-maker or a person who's making a recommendation to the decision-maker. In that position, what are the consequences to you as a person and what are the consequences to your career resulting from the decision you make? Recognize that from a career standpoint, it can cut both ways. If the company thinks that you spend too much money in order to head off an ethical problem, you may be viewed as a profligate spender who has no business in the tough world of being a manager and may therefore lose your career track or be fired.

On the other hand, if you ignore the problem, things could go the opposite way: you could become the scapegoat. One can imagine an executive saying, "You know, if Tim had told me there was a problem, I would have done something about it. He stayed quiet, he's to blame." So recognize that in many situations, the personal impacts could go in a couple of different directions.

In addition to this career issue, there are personal impacts that relate to your conscience and well-being. These personal impacts have become clichés. The problem with a cliché is that it has enough truth in it to bear repeating, which is why it gets repeated, which is how it becomes a cliché. While I prefer not to perpetuate clichés, let me repeat them one more time.

The first one is the newspaper approach. Are you comfortable with having your proposed action being reported in a newspaper of wide circulation: *The Washington Post*, *The New York Times*, *The Wall Street Journal*, *Le Monde*, or whatever the paper of importance is to you? A variation of this test is the loved one test. There is a wonderful book that was written several years ago by Yale Law Professor Amy Chua, entitled *World on Fire*. Professor Chua interviewed many executives around the world. One executive told Professor Chua that he would never tell his family what he did during the day. Well, if you can't tell your family what you're doing during the day because you're embarrassed by what you do, maybe there's a problem with what you're doing.

The final variation is the tombstone test. What would you like to have said about you on your tombstone or your gravestone? What kind of a person will you be remembered as?

E. HMRP STEP FIVE: APPLY THREE MORAL FRAMEWORKS

Professor Hosmer's Step Five applies ten ethical principles drawn from thousands of years of philosophy. The modification is to reduce these to three leading, contemporary business ethics frameworks which capture the historical philosophies and place them into a business application.

Shareholder Theory: The correct way to state the legal duty of managers to shareholders is that managers should carry out the lawful directives of shareholders. As we will see in the latter chapters of this book, this statement is a simple one of agency law. Shareholder are the principals and agents are the managers. To be sure, shareholders will be interested in profit. But shareholders may also hold non-economic directives as well such as adhering to standards of journalistic excellence, or employing a percentage of individuals with disabilities, or commitment one's business to fostering peace. There are companies that do each of these things and if their shareholders are comfortable with these objectives, there is nothing illegal about them. So, don't just assume that the only thing that matters in a corporation is profit; there may be more. Moreover, what is in the short-term interest of the shareholders and what is in the long-term interest may be two different things, even just in terms of making money. Finally, because corporations are creatures of the law, they should obey the laws that govern them. In using the term "corporations" the same principles apply to any business, so keep that in mind in looking at these cases.

Stakeholder Theory: Derived from Kantian principles of human dignity, the stakeholder position is that businesses should be run for the benefit of anyone affected by the action because we ourselves would like to be treated as an end rather than a means to an end. To prioritize what stakeholders to consider, evaluate whether a basic right has been affected; whether vulnerable parties are protected; and whether there is a way to great a greater good for a greater number. This framework can be elaborated and is in detail in Timothy Fort's *The Vision of the Firm*, but these abbreviated versions of these frameworks, (Rights, Justice and Utilitariansim) comprise the leading contemporary theories of business ethics.

Virtue Theory: Rather than just considering what duties people in business might have (both shareholder and stakeholder theories are deontological theories of ethics), virtue theory asks what would be exemplary. Because people seem to think that everyone has different virtues, you might take time to "elect" the virtues that a class thinks are most important. After doing that, one then has a list of virtues that can be defined and applied to the cases at hand.

F. HMRP STEP SIX: CONCLUSION

Step six calls for a conclusion. This could be to choose the Justice approach in the Stakeholder Theory. It could be to choose maximizing profitability in the short term. It could be a mix of a variety of the frameworks. For example, one would design a solution based on respecting rights and protecting the vulnerable because in the long term, such attention is going to create the greatest good for the greatest number, which will also equate with long-term shareholder value.

Every year, studies report that a large percentage of people think that they themselves are highly ethical, while they also think that a large percentage of the rest of the world is not.[1] It's hard to square those two observations except to note that we

1 Ann E. Tenbrusnel et al., *The Ethical Mirage: A Temporal Explanation as to Why We Aren't as Ethical as We*

are biased and we deceive ourselves. We need something to keep ourselves honest. A framework such as Hosmer's helps us do just that and will help us to make better ethical decisions in business.

II. Two Famous Legal Cases

Dodge v. Ford Motor Co., et al.

204 Mich. 459, 170 N.W. 668 (1919)

Ostrander, CJ.

* * *

When plaintiffs made their complaint and demand for further dividends, the Ford Motor Company had concluded its most prosperous year of business. The demand for its cars at the price of the preceding year continued. It could make and could market in the year beginning August 1, 1916, more than 500,000 cars. Sales of parts and repairs would necessarily increase. The cost of materials was likely to advance, and perhaps the price of labor; but it reasonably might have expected a profit for the year of upwards of $60,000,000. It had assets of more than $132,000,000, a surplus of almost $112,000,000, and its cash on hand and municipal bonds were nearly $54,000,000. Its total liabilities, including capital stock, was a little over $20,000,000. It had declared no special dividend during the business year except the October, 1915, dividend. It had been the practice, under similar circumstances, to declare larger dividends. Considering only these facts, a refusal to declare and pay further dividends appears to be not an exercise of discretion on the part of the directors, but an arbitrary refusal to do what the circumstances required to be done. These facts and

Henry Ford, top; John and Horace Dodge, bottom.

Think We Are (2007).

others call upon the directors to justify their action, or failure or refusal to act. In justification, the defendants have offered testimony tending to prove, and which does prove, the following facts: It had been the policy of the corporation for a considerable time to annually reduce the selling price of cars, while keeping up, or improving, their quality. As early as in June, 1915, a general plan for the expansion of the productive capacity of the concern by a practical duplication of its plant had been talked over by the executive officers and directors and agreed upon; not all of the details having been settled, and no formal action of directors having been taken. The erection of a smelter was considered, and engineering and other data in connection therewith secured. In consequence, it was determined not to reduce the selling price of cars for the year beginning August 1, 1915, but to maintain the price and to accumulate a large surplus to pay for the proposed expansion of plant and equipment, and perhaps to build a plant for smelting ore. It is hoped, by Mr. Ford, that eventually 1,000,000 cars will be annually produced. The contemplated changes will permit the increased output.

The plan, as affecting the profits of the business for the year beginning August 1, 1916, and thereafter, calls for a reduction in the selling price of the cars. It is true that this price might be at any time increased, but the plan called for the reduction in price of $80 a car. The capacity of the plant, without the additions thereto voted to be made (without a part of them at least), would produce more than 600,000 cars annually. This number, and more, could have been sold for $440 instead of $360, a difference in the return for capital, labor, and materials employed of at least $48,000,000. In short, the plan does not call for and is not intended to produce immediately a more profitable business, but a less profitable one; not only less profitable than formerly, but less profitable than it is admitted it might be made. The apparent immediate effect will be to diminish the value of shares and the returns to shareholders.

It is the contention of plaintiffs that the apparent effect of the plan is intended to be the continued and continuing effect of it, and that it is deliberately proposed, not of record and not by official corporate declaration, but nevertheless proposed, to continue the corporation henceforth as a semi-eleemosynary institution and not as a business institution. In support of this contention, they point to the attitude and to the expressions of Mr. Henry Ford. Mr. Henry Ford is the dominant force in the business of the Ford Motor Company. No plan of operations could be adopted unless he consented, and no board of directors can be elected whom he does not favor. One of the directors of the company has no stock. One share was assigned to him to qualify him for the position, but it is not claimed that he owns it. A business, one of the largest in the world, and one of the most profitable, has been built up. It employs many men, at good pay.

'My ambition,' said Mr. Ford, 'is to employ still more men, to spread the benefits of this industrial system to the greatest possible number, to help them build up their lives and their homes. To do this we are putting the greatest share of our profits back in the business.'

'With regard to dividends, the company paid sixty percent. on its capitalization of two million dollars, or $1,200,000, leaving $58,000,000 to reinvest for the growth of the company. This is Mr. Ford's policy at present, and it is understood that the other stockholders cheerfully accede to this plan.'

He had made up his mind in the summer of 1916 that no dividends other than the regular dividends should be paid, 'for the present.'

> 'Q. For how long? Had you fixed in your mind any time in the future, when you were going to pay—
>
> A. No.
>
> 'Q. That was indefinite in the future?
>
> A. That was indefinite; yes, sir.'

The record, and especially the testimony of Mr. Ford, convinces that he has to some extent the attitude towards shareholders of one who has dispensed and distributed to them large gains and that they should be content to take what he chooses to give. His testimony creates the impression, also, that he thinks the Ford Motor Company has made too much money, has had too large profits, and that, although large profits might be still earned, a sharing of them with the public, by reducing the price of the output of the company, ought to be undertaken. We have no doubt that certain sentiments, philanthropic and altruistic, creditable to Mr. Ford, had large influence in determining the policy to be pursued by the Ford Motor Company—the policy which has been herein referred to.

It is said by his counsel that—

> 'Although a manufacturing corporation cannot engage in humanitarian works as its principal business, the fact that it is organized for profit does not prevent the existence of implied powers to carry on with humanitarian motives such charitable works as are incidental to the main business of the corporation.'

And again:

> 'As the expenditures complained of are being made in an expansion of the business which the company is organized to carry on, and for purposes within the powers of the corporation as hereinbefore shown, the question is as to whether such expenditures are rendered illegal because influenced to some extent by humanitarian motives and purposes on the part of the members of the board of directors.'

Let's stop here for a moment. With the facts of this case set out, who do you think won this case? Who do you think should have won this case? The first question is a descriptive one: As a matter of prediction, what do you think the Court decided? The second question in an ethical one: Regardless of what the Court actually decided, what do you think the Court should have decided? Think about this for a few moments and then proceed on to see the results.

The difference between an incidental humanitarian expenditure of corporate funds for the benefit of the employees, like the building of a hospital for their use and the employment of agencies for the betterment of their condition, and a general purpose and plan to benefit mankind at the expense of others, is obvious. There should be no confusion (of which there is evidence) of the duties which Mr. Ford conceives that he and the stockholders owe to the general public and the duties which in law he and his codirectors owe to protesting, minority stockholders. A business corporation is organized and carried on primarily for the profit of the stockholders. The powers of the directors are to be employed for that end. The discretion of directors is to be exercised in the choice of means to attain that end, and does not extend to a change in the end itself, to the reduction of profits, or to the nondistribution of profits among stockholders in order to devote them to other purposes.

There is committed to the discretion of directors, a discretion to be exercised in good faith, the infinite details of business, including the wages which shall be paid to employes, the number of hours they shall work, the conditions under which labor shall be carried on, and the price for which products shall be offered to the public.

It is said by appellants that the motives of the board members are not material and will not be inquired into by the court so long as their acts are within their lawful powers. As we have pointed out, and the proposition does not require argument to sustain it, it is not within the lawful powers of a board of directors to shape and conduct the affairs of a corporation for the merely incidental benefit of shareholders and for the primary purpose of benefiting others, and no one will contend that, if the avowed purpose of the defendant directors was to sacrifice the interests of shareholders, it would not be the duty of the courts to interfere.

We are not, however, persuaded that we should interfere with the proposed expansion of the business of the Ford Motor Company. In view of the fact that the selling price of products may be increased at any time, the ultimate results of the larger business cannot be certainly estimated. The judges are not business experts. It is recognized that plans must often be made for a long future, for expected competition, for a continuing as well as an immediately profitable venture. The experience of the Ford Motor Company is evidence of capable management of its affairs. It may be noticed, incidentally, that it took from the public the money required for the execution of its plan, and that the very considerable salaries paid to Mr. Ford and to certain executive officers and employes were not diminished. We are not satisfied that the alleged motives of the directors, in so far as they are reflected in the conduct of the business, menace the interests of shareholders. It is enough to say, perhaps, that the court of equity is at all times open to complaining shareholders having a just grievance.

Assuming the general plan and policy of expansion and the details of it to have been sufficiently, formally, approved at the October and November, 1917, meetings of directors, and assuming further that the plan and policy and the details agreed upon were for the best ultimate interest of the company and therefore of its shareholders, what does it amount to in justification of a refusal to declare and pay a special dividend or dividends? The Ford Motor Company was able to estimate with nicety its income and profit. It could sell more cars than it could make. Having ascertained what it would cost to produce a car and to sell it, the profit upon each car depended upon the selling price. That being fixed, the yearly income and profit was determinable, and, within slight variations, was certain.

Defendants say, and it is true, that a considerable cash balance must be at all times carried by such a concern. But, as has been stated, there was a large daily, weekly, monthly receipt of cash. The output was practically continuous and was continuously, and within a few days, turned into cash. Moreover, the contemplated expenditures were not to be immediately made. The large sum appropriated for the smelter plant was payable over a considerable period of time. So that, without going further, it would appear that, accepting and approving the plan of the directors, it was their duty to distribute on or near the 1st of August, 1916, a very large sum of money to stockholders.

In reaching this conclusion, we do not ignore, but recognize, the validity of the proposition that plaintiffs have from the beginning profited by, if they have not lately, officially, participated in, the general policy of expansion pursued by this corporation. We do not lose sight of the fact that it had been, upon an occasion, agreeable to the plaintiffs to increase the capital stock to $100,000,000 by a stock dividend of $98,000,000. These things go only to answer other contentions now made by plaintiffs, and do not and cannot operate to estop them to demand proper dividends upon the stock they own. It is obvious that an annual dividend of 60 percent. upon $2,000,000, or $1,200,000, is the equivalent of a very small dividend upon $100,000,000, or more.

The decree of the court below fixing and determining the specific amount to be distributed to stockholders is affirmed.

Does the result of this case surprise you or confirm the prediction you made at the midpoint of its presentation above? In my 25-plus years of teaching this case, slightly more than half of the students reading this case expected Ford to win. Henry

Ford, after all, was the majority shareholder and the CEO of the company. If he decided to do something, it would be done. Students also argue that Ford's philosophy seems fairly contemporary and wise. He is executing an approach that will result in more market share (or as the auto industry was in its infancy, assure that Ford's large market share would be maintained). Paying employees more also played into another Ford policy of paying his workers enough to be able to purchase the product they produced. So slightly more than half of my students have been very surprised with the result.

Those who weren't surprised advanced two reasons. The first was a rationale based on reverse engineering: there is a Dodge Motor Company so they probably got the dividend to help fund their own company. The second was more philosophical: shareholders rule.

What was your reaction to the way the case came out, both as a matter of prediction—i.e. who won the case—and do you think the Court made the right decision?

Dodge v. Ford's emphasis on the duty of managers to its shareholders has been a staple of shareholder advocates for decades. Indeed, it would be a foolish executive who would ignore his/her obligations to the shareholders. But just when one would think that shareholder theory is a simple, straight-forward set of duties from management to shareholders to maximize shareholder value, along comes the Chicago Cubs to confuse things.

Shlensky v. Wrigley

95 Ill.App.2d 173, 237 N.E.2d 776 (1968)

Sullivan J.

This is an appeal from a dismissal of plaintiff's amended complaint on motion of the defendants. The action was a stockholders' derivative suit against the directors for negligence and mismanagement. The corporation was also made a defendant. Plaintiff sought damages and an order that defendants cause the installation of lights in Wrigley Field and the scheduling of night baseball games.

Plaintiff is a minority stockholder of defendant corporation, Chicago National League Ball Club (Inc.), a Delaware corporation with its principal place of business in Chicago, Illinois. Defendant corporation owns and operates the major league professional baseball team known as the Chicago Cubs. The corporation also engages in the operation of Wrigley Field, the Cubs' home park, the concessionaire sales during Cubs' home games, television and radio broadcasts of Cubs' home games, the leasing of the field for football games and other events and receives its share, as visiting team, of admission moneys from games played in other National League stadia. The individual defendants are directors of the Cubs and have served for varying periods of years. Defendant Philip K. Wrigley is also president of the corporation and owner of approximately 80% of the stock therein.

Plaintiff alleges that since night baseball was first played in 1935 nineteen of the twenty major league teams have scheduled night games. In 1966, out of a total of 1620 games in the major leagues, 932 were played at night. Plaintiff alleges that every member of the major leagues, other than the Cubs, scheduled substantially all of its home games in 1966 at night, exclusive of opening days, Saturdays, Sundays, holidays and days prohibited by league rules. Allegedly this has been done for the specific purpose of maximizing attendance and thereby maximizing revenue and income.

The Cubs, in the years 1961–65, sustained operating losses from its direct baseball operations. Plaintiff attributes those losses to inadequate attendance at Cubs' home games. He concludes that if the directors continue to refuse to install lights at Wrigley Field and schedule night baseball games, the Cubs will continue to sustain comparable losses and its financial condition will continue to deteriorate.

Plaintiff alleges that, except for the year 1963, attendance at Cubs' home games has been substantially below that at their road games, many of which were played at night.

Plaintiff compares attendance at Cubs' games with that of the Chicago White Sox, an American League club, whose weekday games were generally played at night. The weekend attendance figures for the two teams was similar; however, the White Sox week-night games drew many more patrons than did the Cubs' weekday games.

Plaintiff alleges that the funds for the installation of lights can be readily obtained through financing and the cost of installation would be far more than offset and recaptured by increased revenues and incomes resulting from the increased attendance.

Plaintiff further alleges that defendant Wrigley has refused to install lights, not because of interest in the welfare of the corporation but because of his personal opinions 'that baseball is a 'daytime sport' and that the installation of lights and night baseball games will have a deteriorating effect upon the surrounding neighborhood.' It is alleged that he has admitted that he is not interested in whether the Cubs would benefit financially from such action because of his concern for the neighborhood, and that he would be willing for the team to play night games if a new stadium were built in Chicago.

Plaintiff alleges that the other defendant directors, with full knowledge of the foregoing matters, have acquiesced in the policy laid down by Wrigley and have permitted him to dominate the board of directors in matters involving the installation of lights and scheduling of night games, even though they knew he was not motivated by a good faith concern as to the best interests of defendant corporation, but solely by his personal views set forth above. It is charged that the directors are acting for a reason or reasons contrary and wholly unrelated to the business interests of the corporation; that such arbitrary and capricious acts constitute mismanagement and waste of corporate assets, and that the directors have been negligent in failing to exercise reasonable care and prudence in the management of the corporate affairs.

Let's stop here again as we did with the *Dodge v. Ford* case with the same two questions. Who do you think won the case? Who do you think should have won the case? Take a moment to think about those questions and then continue on with the case.

The question on appeal is whether plaintiff's amended complaint states a cause of action. It is plaintiff's position that fraud, illegality and conflict of interest are not the only bases for a stockholder's derivative action against the directors. Contrariwise, defendants argue that the courts will not step in and interfere with honest business judgment of the directors unless there is a showing of fraud, illegality or conflict of interest.

* * *

Plaintiff argues that the allegations of his amended complaint are sufficient to set forth a cause of action under the principles set out in Dodge v. Ford Motor Co., 170 N.W. 668 (Mich.). In that case plaintiff, owner of about 10% Of the outstanding stock, brought suit against the directors seeking payment of additional dividends and the enjoining of further business expansion. In ruling on the request for dividends the court indicated that the motives of Ford in keeping so much money in the corporation for expansion and security were to benefit the public generally and spread the profits out by means of more jobs, etc. The court felt that these were not only far from related to the good of the stockholders, but amounted to a change in the ends of the corporation and that this was not a purpose contemplated or allowed by the corporate charter.

* * *

Plaintiff in the instant case argues that the directors are acting for reasons unrelated to the financial interest and welfare of the Cubs. However, we are not satisfied that the motives assigned to Philip K. Wrigley, and through him to the other directors, are contrary to the best interests of the corporation and the stockholders. For example, it appears to us that the effect on the surrounding neighborhood might well be considered by a director who was considering the patrons who would or would not attend the games if the park were in a poor neighborhood.

Furthermore, the long run interest of the corporation in its property value at Wrigley Field might demand all efforts to keep the neighborhood from deteriorating. By these thoughts we do not mean to say that we have decided that the decision of the directors was a correct one. That is beyond our jurisdiction and ability. We are merely saying that the decision is one properly before directors and the motives alleged in the amended complaint showed no fraud, illegality or conflict of interest in their making of that decision.

While all the courts do not insist that one or more of the three elements must be present for a stockholder's derivative action to lie, nevertheless we feel that unless the conduct of the defendants at least borders on one of the elements, the courts should not interfere. The trial court in the instant case acted properly in dismissing plaintiff's amended complaint.

We feel that plaintiff's amended complaint was also defective in failing to allege damage to the corporation. The well pleaded facts must be taken as true for the purpose of judging the sufficiency of the amended complaint. However, one need not accept conclusions drawn by the pleader. Furthermore, pleadings will be construed most strongly against the pleader prior to a verdict or judgment on the merits.

There is no allegation that the night games played by the other nineteen teams enhanced their financial position or that the profits, if any, of those teams were directly related to the number of night games scheduled. There is an allegation that the installation of lights and scheduling of night games in Wrigley Field would have resulted in large amounts of additional revenues and incomes from increased attendance and related sources of income. Further, the cost of installation of lights, funds for which are allegedly readily available by financing, would be more than offset and recaptured by increased revenues. However, no allegation is made that there will be a net benefit to the corporation from such action, considering all increased costs.

Plaintiff claims that the losses of defendant corporation are due to poor attendance at home games. However, it appears from the amended complaint, taken as a whole, that factors other than attendance affect the net earnings or losses. For example, in 1962, attendance at home and road games decreased appreciably as compared with 1961, and yet the loss from direct baseball operation and of the whole corporation was considerably less.

The record shows that plaintiff did not feel he could allege that the increased revenues would be sufficient to cure the corporate deficit. The only cost plaintiff was at all concerned with was that of installation of lights. No mention was made of operation and maintenance of the lights or other possible increases in operating costs of night games and we cannot speculate as to what other factors might influence the increase or decrease of profits if the Cubs were to play night home games.

[P]laintiff's allegation that the minority stockholders and the corporation have been seriously and irreparably damaged by the wrongful conduct of the defendant directors is a mere conclusion and not based on well pleaded facts in the amended complaint.

Finally, we do not agree with plaintiff's contention that failure to follow the example of the other major league clubs in scheduling night games constituted negligence. Plaintiff made no allegation that these teams' night schedules were profitable or that the purpose for which night baseball had been undertaken was fulfilled. Furthermore, it cannot be said that directors, even those of corporations that are losing money, must follow the lead of the other corporations in the field. Directors are elected for their business capabilities and judgment and the courts cannot require them to forgo their judgment because of the decisions of directors of other companies. Courts may not decide these questions in the absence of a clear showing of dereliction of duty on the part of the specific directors and mere failure to 'follow the crowd' is not such a dereliction. For the foregoing reasons the order of dismissal entered by the trial court is affirmed.

Both *Dodge v. Ford* and *Wrigley v. Shlensky* are shareholder cases. The *Dodge* case is more of a corporate governance case. That is, courts have no difficulty looking at property and deciding who owns it. They do such things all the time. In this case, Ford Motor Company had built up a substantial amount of cash and, as a matter of corporate governance, the principals (the shareholders) have a strong argument that they are entitled to their portions of that property. On the other hand, the *Wrigley* case is more of a strategy case. Relying on the business judgment rule, the court is saying that as long as there is a plausible reason for executive's strategies, the courts will not interfere. If shareholders don't like the strategy, they can invest elsewhere, but a long-term strategy, which builds in seemingly non-economic values, can still be upheld. Both of these cases are good law and so it is worth keeping in mind that "managing for the shareholders" is not as clear cut as one might think.

There are stakeholder aspects to these cases as well. Wrigley clearly was concerned about his customers, to make sure they didn't leave the park late at night into (what was then) a not-so-safe area around the ballpark (with little parking). He also wanted to build a long-term family brand image around the Cubs and Wrigley Field. Finally, he had concerns about the impact of late night games on the local community. Thus, one could characterize Wrigley's strategy as a stakeholder strategy.

One could do the same with respect to Henry Ford who proposed to lower the price of cars and to increase his employees' wages. This would help both customers and employees, two key stakeholder groups. It might also help the shareholders if, by doing so, he had more productive and loyal workers and grabbed more market share. But because the court was focused on accumulated profits (and also because 1919 was different than 1970 in terms of courts' review of property rights), short-term shareholder interests prevailed.

One could analyze these cases according to the virtues of honesty, accountability, creativity, loyalty, diligence and other virtues to assess the actions of the participants in the case.

In short, the laws you will learn in this book and in your course are laden with normative considerations. Thus, it is worth asking, at the end of each case, whether the case was decided fairly or not. Do you agree with the opinion of the court? Is there a better result? What are the values that underlie the opinion?

In addition, one can use the Hosmer framework, and in particular, the theories of shareholder, stakeholder, and virtue, in order to analyze the participants of these cases. In fact, over the years, many ethics have written research papers that come out of law cases and, with additional research, written extensive papers on these topics.

As a way to promote this integration of law and ethics, bundled with this textbook is *Ethics Vignettes*. These provide summaries of cases on ethical issues ranging across multiple disciplines found in business schools and also across various industries. A very large number of these vignettes are law cases, which provide a ready stepping-off point for the integration of law and ethics. Others come from regulatory or media sources and area also readily amenable to the analytical tool provided in this chapter. At the end of each chapter, there will be references to *Ethics Vignettes* and cases that can be discussed as an ethics as well as a legal case.

NOTES AND QUESTIONS

1. **WHEN YOU THINK** of the American legal system, what values do you see? Are they different from what you think they were historically? What, if anything, might improve them? In what respect to you think the legal system is fair or not? What about other legal systems with which you might be familiar?

2. **AFTER THINKING ABOUT** *Dodge v. Ford* and *Wrigley v. Shlensky*, how do you think those cases should have been decided? Why? What values underlie those decisions? Are they good values to apply today? Can you reconcile why these two seemingly different cases might be consistent with each other?

3. **THINK OF AN** example of a business that you think acted badly and one that you think acted well. How does the Hosmer process help you articulate why one can be described as bad and why the other can be described as good?

CHAPTER

2

Constitutional Issues Relevant to Business

Had it not been for businesspeople, there might never have been a U.S. Constitution. The idea of limited government was rare at the time of the founding of the United States. Royal monarchies were the norm rather than constitutional democracies. Even when democracy sought to take root, such as in the French Revolution—which occurred after the American Revolution and was contemporaneous with the writing of the Constitution—democracy gave way to the French Reign of Terror shortly thereafter, and then to Napoleon Bonaparte.

■ KING JOHN OF ENGLAND SIGNS THE MAGNA CARTA; ENGLAND, 1215.

The roots of the U.S. Constitution trace more to England, where the notion of limitations on government power started much earlier. In the 1215 *Magna Carta*, the English King was restricted from punishing "freemen" through rule of law protections. These freemen were the businessmen of the time; feudal barons who had acquired their own strength that the King was forced to recognize. Nearly four hundred years later, Lord Coke, serving as Chief Justice of the Court of Common Pleas, ruled that the King was subject to the laws and did not supersede law through divine right. To have a sense of the language and origins of these limitations, here are excerpts from the *Magna Carta* and from Coke's ruling in Dr. Bonham's Case.

excerpt

SIR EDWARD COKE
CHIEF JUSTICE OF
THE KING'S BENCH,
(1552–1634).

"No Freeman shall be taken or imprisoned, or be disseised of his Freehold, or Liberties, or free Customs, or be outlawed, or exiled, or any other wise destroyed; nor will We not pass upon him, nor condemn him, but by lawful judgment of his Peers, or by the Law of the Land. We will sell to no man, we will not deny or defer to any man either Justice or Right.

—*Magna Carta*. § XXIX

And it appears in our books, that in many cases, the common law will *(d)* controul Acts of Parliament, and sometimes adjudge them to be utterly void: for when an Act of Parliament is against common right and reason, or repugnant, or impossible to be performed, the common law will controul it, and adjudge such Act to be void [. . .]."

—*Dr. Bonham's Case*, 8. Co. Rep. 133b.

This history produced a view of government where rule of law was valued and in which government power was limited. In such a system, individual freedom and liberty flourished. After the American Revolution, the first "Constitution" came in the form of the "Articles of Confederation." The Articles took this notion of freedom from centralized authority and the value of human liberty to such an extreme that the thirteen original colonies found themselves economically bankrupt and militarily vulnerable. And so the debates began, most prominently in **The Federalist Papers**, as to the proper balance of governmental authority, states' rights, and individual liberty.

■ THE FEDERALIST PAPERS ARE A SERIES OF 85 ARTICLES AND ESSAYS AUTHORED BY JAMES MADISON, ALEXANDER HAMILTON, JOHN JAY PROMOTING RATIFICATION OF THE UNITED STATES CONSTITUTION.

Those debates gave rise to the U.S. system of government featuring three branches: **Executive** (i.e. the President), **Legislative** (i.e. the Congress), and **Judicial** (i.e. the Court system, culminating with the Supreme Court). As a partial explanation for why government can sometimes be slow to act, the rationale for the three-branch system was explicit: each branch would check the other branches and prevent the accumulation of excessive power. Institutional conflict was part of the plan.

Citizens had a say too, though voting had limitations. Initially the definition of who was a citizen empowered to vote meant white, property-owning males. Often, individual citizens did not directly elect statewide or national leaders. Citizens elected legislators, who would then cast votes for the President (the origin of the Electoral College) or Senators. So while citizens did vote, direct popular voting for many major offices did not occur.

The Constitution has been hailed as masterpiece of these kinds of checks and balances and, of course, the exact nature of the balancing has changed over the years. First among those changes was the protection of rights through the Bill of Rights, which created protection against the majority rule of individual and state rights. Over time the right to vote was extended, slavery and segregation ended, and many different doctrines and legal approaches waxed and waned. Yet core to all these developments have been basic principles of limited government, individual rights, and equal justice. Political debates for over two centuries have considered both the proper balance to effectuate the core principles of the Constitution and also the proper touchstones to anchor those debates, such as Courts adhering more to the original intent of the Founders versus viewing the Constitution as an organically evolving document.

I. The Notion of "Limited Government"

SO WHAT EXACTLY does limited government mean? It includes at least four facets: **Federalism and State Powers; Separation of Powers; Judicial Review**, and **Individual Rights.** Each of these has a particular application for business.

A. FEDERALISM AND STATE POWERS

The authors of the Constitution sought to strengthen the national government while also retaining as many state powers as possible. Indeed, the formulation is that the federal government only has those powers designated to it by the Constitution. If such a specific designation has not been made, then the states retain powers. The notion of Federalism, at its heart, recognizes power of both a central authority—the national government—and also state authority, which includes the states themselves of course, but also the many municipalities, counties, and other local governments.

The exercise of certain constitutional powers as interpreted by the Supreme Court has led to a strong central government. Some of these provisions or doctrines includes:

1. *The Supremacy Clause:* The Courts have held that in the case where there is a conflict between federal law and state law, the federal law "preempts" and overrides the state law. This is why there is only, for instance, a federal bankruptcy system as opposed to each state having its own bankruptcy system or why there is one nuclear regulatory system.

2. *The Necessary and Proper Clause:* Courts have interpreted Article 1, Section VIII of the Constitution as authorizing Congress to create laws

reasonably related to its enumerated duties. This provides a window for Congress to increase its authoritative reach.

3. ***The Commerce Clause:*** Congress has always had the authority to regulate interstate commerce, but the definition of interstate commerce has expanded dramatically through court decisions so that now, laws enacted via the Commerce Clause tend to be very difficult to overturn.

4. ***Taxing and Spending:*** It is central to government that it may impose taxes and spend. Over the history of the United States, that taxing and spending power has grown and become a strong source for federal power.

This list is not exhaustive, but it gives a sense of the fact that the authority of the federal government has expanded through history. That expansion frequently has economic impact.

B. SEPARATION OF POWERS

By setting up a system of checks and balances—implemented by the institutional framework of separation of powers—the framers of the Constitution guaranteed obstacles to government action. This does not mean that the government cannot move quickly; it certainly can during national security emergencies or when domestic issues demand swift action. After the economic scandals of Enron, WorldCom and others, Congress quickly enacted the Sarbanes-Oxley law, a complicated law promptly signed into law by the President.

Having said this, only Congress can pass a law; with two houses (the House of Representatives and the Senate), this can be difficult. The President must then sign the law, which is then subject to judicial review by the Court system. There are some exceptions, such as Presidential Executive Orders, but Presidents do not have fiat to do anything the want.

The framers of the Constitution, especially those such as James Madison and Thomas Jefferson (though Jefferson was in France at the time of the Constitution's writing and was skeptical of it) worried that the power of the government to accomplish good also equipped it with the power for more nefarious usage. Given their history of concerns over executive power, the failure of the weak Articles of Confederation, and the commitment to a rule of law approach that required judicial review, the framers sought to pit naturally occurring political ambitions (in each branch of government) against each other to protect individual liberties.

C. JUDICIAL REVIEW

Judicial review was one of the key checks on all branches of government, including not only the executive and legislative but also courts themselves and actions of states, too. That especially became the case over time as the power and authority of the Supreme Court grew. Legal philosopher Michael Perry has written about the advantages of creating law with an eye toward history: "when consulting a rule, we consult with the dead and by doing so enrich the quality of our conversation."[1] Courts do this as part of their work. They consult past experience and precedent to determine whether a law passes Constitutional or other muster, and they act, for better or for worse, as a pressure against the powers of a Congress or President.

D. INDIVIDUAL RIGHTS

As already suggested, a key reason for all the above limitations of governmental power is the protection of individual rights and liberties. But limitations on governmental powers based on the Constitution were not enough to satisfy many of the framers. Thus to clarify and to strengthen the rights possessed by the people, the framers agreed that immediately after the adoption of the Constitution by the states, there would be a Bill of Rights added to it, specifying rights to worship, speak, and assemble freely; to avoid self-incrimination; and to bear arms. These rights are crucial to the American experience and it is worth setting them out:

The Bill of Rights

I

AMENDMENT I: Congress shall make no law respecting an establishment of religion, or prohibiting the free exercise thereof; or abridging the freedom of speech, or of the press; or the right of the people peaceably to assemble, and to petition the Government for a redress of grievances.

II

AMENDMENT II: A well regulated Militia, being necessary to the security of a free State, the right of the people to keep and bear Arms, shall not be infringed.

III

AMENDMENT III: No Soldier shall, in time of peace be quartered in any house, without the consent of the Owner, nor in time of war, but in a manner to be prescribed by law.

1 Michael H. Perry; *Morality, Politics, and Law*; 37 (1988).

IV

AMENDMENT IV: The right of the people to be secure in their persons, houses, papers, and effects, against unreasonable searches and seizures, shall not be violated, and no Warrants shall issue, but upon probable cause, supported by Oath or affirmation, and particularly describing the place to be searched, and the persons or things to be seized.

V

AMENDMENT V: No person shall be held to answer for a capital, or otherwise infamous crime, unless on a presentment or indictment of a Grand Jury, except in cases arising in the land or naval forces, or in the Militia, when in actual service in time of War or public danger; nor shall any person be subject for the same offence to be twice put in jeopardy of life or limb; nor shall be compelled in any criminal case to be a witness against himself, nor be deprived of life, liberty, or property, without due process of law; nor shall private property be taken for public use, without just compensation.

VI

AMENDMENT VI: In all criminal prosecutions, the accused shall enjoy the right to a speedy and public trial, by an impartial jury of the State and district wherein the crime shall have been committed, which district shall have been previously ascertained by law, and to be informed of the nature and cause of the accusation; to be confronted with the witnesses against him; to have compulsory process for obtaining witnesses in his favor, and to have the Assistance of Counsel for his defence.

VII

AMENDMENT VII: In Suits at common law, where the value in controversy shall exceed twenty dollars, the right of trial by jury shall be preserved, and no fact tried by a jury, shall be otherwise reexamined in any Court of the United States, than according to the rules of the common law.

VIII

AMENDMENT VIII: Excessive bail shall not be required, nor excessive fines imposed, nor cruel and unusual punishments inflicted.

IX

AMENDMENT IX: The enumeration in the Constitution, of certain rights, shall not be construed to deny or disparage others retained by the people.

X

AMENDMENT X: The powers not delegated to the United States by the Constitution, nor prohibited by it to the States, are reserved to the States respectively, or to the people.

II. Federal Government Powers

A. COMMERCE POWER

Does growing some corn in your backyard to eat at your own dinner table constitute interstate commerce? In an important 1942 case, *Wickard v. Filburn*, the Supreme Court said yes. As a way to try to create supports for farmers' prices, Congress established limits on the amount of wheat, among other crops, that could be grown. Mr. Filburn grew some extra wheat, not for sale in the marketplace, but simply to use for food in his own house. Filburn lost the case because the Supreme Court said that Congress had the power to regulate interstate commerce and Filburn's act was interstate commerce. If an activity substantially affects interstate commerce, then Congress can regulate it and if growing some wheat in your own backyard for your own use is by definition interstate commerce, then the range of Congressional authority is vast.

FEDERAL INTERSTATE TRAVEL REGULATIONS WERE CITED AS THE BASIS FOR ENDING RACIAL DISCRIMINATION BY STATES AT HOTELS AND MOTELS IN THE U.S.

A tremendous number of laws have been passed pursuant to the commerce clause. These include transactions that clearly have a direct impact on commerce, such as trademarks, labor and employment rights, environmental laws, consumer protection and others. It also includes issues one might think are more related to other principles of fairness and equality. For example, the landmark 1964 Civil Rights Act was passed pursuant to the Commerce Clause. Key provisions of this and other Civil Rights Acts made it illegal for businesses to discriminate on the basis of skin color and other attributes. The following case shows the use of the Commerce Clause with respect to racial classifications.

Image: Atlanta Time Machine

Heart of Atlanta Motel v. United States

379 U.S. 803 (1964)

MR. JUSTICE CLARK delivered the opinion of the Court. . .

1. The Factual Background and Contentions of the Parties.

Appellant owns and operates the Heart of Atlanta Motel which has 216 rooms available to transient guests. . . .It is readily accessible to interstate highways 75 and 85 and state highways 23 and 41. Appellant solicits patronage from outside the State of Georgia through various national advertising media, including magazines of national circulation; it maintains over 50 billboards and highway signs within the State, soliciting patronage for the motel; it accepts convention trade from outside Georgia and approximately 75% of its registered guests are from out of State. Prior to passage of the Act the motel had followed a practice of refusing to rent rooms to Negroes, and it alleged that it intended to continue to do so. In an effort to perpetuate that policy this suit was filed.

The appellant contends that Congress in passing this Act exceeded its power to regulate commerce under [the Commerce Clause] . . . The appellees counter that the unavailability to Negroes of adequate accommodations interferes significantly with interstate travel, and that Congress, under the Commerce Clause, has power to remove such obstructions and restraints

* * *

2. *The History of the Act.*

Congress first evidenced its interest in civil rights legislation in the Civil Rights or Enforcement Act of April 9, 1866. There followed four Acts, with a fifth, the Civil Rights Act of March 1, 1875, culminating the series. In 1883 this Court struck down the public accommodations sections of the 1875 Act in the *Civil Rights Cases*, 109 U.S. 3. No major legislation in this field had been enacted by Congress for 82 years when the Civil Rights Act of 1957 became law. It was followed by the Civil Rights Act of 1960. Three years later, on June 19, 1963, the late President Kennedy called for civil rights legislation in a message to Congress to which he attached a proposed bill. Its stated purpose was

> 'to promote the general welfare by eliminating discrimination based on race, color, religion, or national origin in * * * public accommodations through the exercise by Congress of the powers conferred upon it * * * to enforce the provisions of the fourteenth and fifteenth amendments, to regulate commerce among the several States, and to make laws necessary and proper to execute the powers conferred upon it by the Constitution.'

Bills were introduced in each House of the Congress, embodying the President's suggestion, one in the Senate [. . .] and one in the House [. . .]. However, it was not until July 2, 1964, upon the recommendation of President Johnson, that the Civil Rights Act of 1964, here under attack, was finally passed.

* * *

3. Title II of the Act.

This Title is divided into seven sections beginning with § 201(a) which provides that:

> 'All persons shall be entitled to the full and equal enjoyment of the goods, services, facilities, privileges, advantages, and accommodations of any place of public accommodation, as defined in this section, without discrimination or segregation on the ground of race, color, religion, or national origin.'

There are listed in § 201(b) four classes of business establishments, each of which 'serves the public' and 'is a place of public accommodation' within the meaning of § 201(a) 'if its operations affect commerce, or if discrimination or segregation by it is supported by State action.' The covered establishments are:

> '(1) any inn, hotel, motel, or other establishment which provides lodging to transient guests, other than an establishment located within a building which contains not more than five rooms for rent or hire and which is actually occupied by the proprietor of such establishment as his residence;
>
> '(2) any restaurant, cafeteria * * * (not here involved);
>
> '(3) any motion picture house * * * (not here involved);
>
> '(4) any establishment * * * which is physically located within the premises of any establishment otherwise covered by this subsection, or * * * within the premises of which is physically located any such covered establishment * * * (not here involved).'

. . .

4. Application of Title II to Heart of Atlanta Motel.

It is admitted that the operation of the motel brings it within the provisions of § 201(a) of the Act and that appellant refused to provide lodging for transient Negroes because of their race or color and that it intends to continue that policy unless restrained.

The sole question posed is, therefore, the constitutionality of the Civil Rights Act of 1964 as applied to these facts. The legislative history of the Act indicates that Congress based the Act on § 5 and **the Equal Protection Clause of the Fourteenth Amendment** as well as its power to regulate interstate commerce under Art. I, § 8, cl. 3, of the Constitution.

* * *

7. The Power of Congress Over Interstate Travel.

The power of Congress to deal with these obstructions depends on the meaning of the **Commerce Clause.** Its meaning was first enunciated 140 years ago by the great Chief Justice John Marshall in *Gibbons v. Ogden*, (1824), in these words:

> **'The subject to be regulated is commerce; and * * * to ascertain the extent of the power, it becomes necessary to settle the meaning of the word. The counsel for the appellee would limit it to traffic, to buying and selling, or the interchange of commodities * * * but it is something more: it is intercourse * * * between nations, and parts of nations, in all its branches, and is regulated by prescribing rules for carrying on that intercourse.**
>
> 'To what commerce does this power extend? . . .
>
> 'It is the power to regulate; that is, to prescribe the rule by which commerce is to be governed. This power, like all others vested in Congress, is complete in itself, may be exercised to its utmost extent, and acknowledges no limitations, other than are prescribed in the constitution. * * * If, as has always been understood, the sovereignty of Congress * * * is plenary as to those objects (specified in the Constitution), the power over commerce * * * is vested in Congress as absolutely as it would be in a single government, having in its constitution the same restrictions on the exercise of the power as are found in the constitution of the United States. The wisdom and the discretion of Congress, their identity with the people, and the influence which their constituents possess at elections, are, in this, as in many other instances, as that, for example, of declaring war, the sole restraints on which they have relied, to secure them from its abuse. They are the restraints on which the people must often rely solely, in all representative governments.

"ONE NEED ONLY examine the evidence which we have discussed above to see that Congress may—as it has—prohibit racial discrimination by motels serving travelers, however 'local' their operations may appear."

In short, the determinative test of the exercise of power by the Congress under the Commerce Clause is simply whether the activity sought to be regulated is 'commerce which concerns more States than one' and has a real and substantial relation to the national interest.

. . .

It is said that the operation of the motel here is of a purely local character. **But, assuming this to be true, '(i)f it is interstate commerce that feels the pinch, it does not matter how local the operation which applies the squeeze.'**

'The power of Congress over interstate commerce is not confined to the regulation of commerce among the states. It extends to those activities intrastate which so affect interstate commerce or the exercise of the power of Congress over it as to make regulation of them appropriate means to the attainment of a legitimate end, the exercise of the granted power of Congress to regulate interstate commerce.

Thus the power of Congress to promote interstate commerce also includes the power to regulate the local incidents thereof, including local activities in both the States of origin and destination, which might have a substantial and harmful effect upon that commerce. One need only examine the evidence which we have discussed above to see that Congress may—as it has—prohibit racial discrimination by motels serving travelers, however 'local' their operations may appear.

. . .

We, therefore, conclude that the action of the Congress in the adoption of the Act as applied here to a motel which concededly serves interstate travelers is within the power granted it by the Commerce Clause of the Constitution, as interpreted by this Court for 140 years. It may be argued that Congress could have pursued other methods to eliminate the obstructions it found in interstate commerce caused by racial discrimination. But this is a matter of policy that rests entirely with the Congress not with the courts. How obstructions in commerce may be removed—what means are to be employed—is within the sound and exclusive discretion of the Congress. It is subject only to one caveat-that the means chosen by it must be reasonably adapted to the end permitted by the Constitution. We cannot say that its choice here was not so adapted. The Constitution requires no more.

Affirmed.

It may seem surprising that the Commerce Clause was the key Constitutional principle used to attack racial discrimination, yet the Heart of Atlanta case demonstrates the power of the Commerce Clause and the impact it has had.

The flip side of the Commerce Clause coin considers what states can do to regulate commerce. If the federal government can regulate most anything pursuant to the Commerce Clause, is there anything left for a state to regulate? Or, does federal power preempt any kind of state action? The answer is that states can regulate businesses as well, but they cannot pass regulations that unduly burden interstate commerce. The courts use a balancing approach to try to achieve this goal. The test asks if the state regulation is necessary and important to a state objective (such as the health and safety of its citizens), if the burden the regulation places on interstate commerce is reasonable, and whether or not the legislation is actually making an effort to favor a local industry over interstate commerce.

The last part of that test is particularly important. Many times a state legislature or local government will seek to pass a law that favors a local business. The executives of the business may be important community leaders or even contributors to campaigns. The employees are the friends, neighbors and voters in the community and strengthening their job security via a thriving business has local benefits. Of course the legislature will not be so obvious as to say "buy from company X," but the impact of the legislation may be exactly that. So the courts will look closely at the impact of state and local legislation to determine whether or not it does, in fact, intrude on interstate commerce.

For example, in a 1970 case, *Pike v. Bruce Church, Inc.*, the U.S. Supreme Court struck down an attempt of the State of Arizona to pack cantaloupes within the state. A company had spent more than $3,000,000 developing 6,400 acres of arid land for agricultural use and ended up producing a product recognized as being very high quality. Because cantaloupes need to get from field to dinner table quickly to prevent spoilage, the company located a packing facility thirty miles away. The problem was that the facility was across the border in California. Arizona wanted to retain production facilities within the State for a variety of reasons, including making sure that Arizona produce—especially high quality produce—was not stamped as a California product and because retaining packing facilities within the state helped employ Arizonans. Thus, the relevant Arizona agency stopped the company from shipping its crop to the California facility, thereby putting $700,000 of produce at risk of never being sold.

IN 1970, THE U.S. SUPREME COURT STRUCK DOWN AN ATTEMPT OF THE STATE OF ARIZONA TO PACK CANTALOUPES WITHIN THE STATE.

The Supreme Court said that such a regulation went too far. It recognized that Arizona did have legitimate interest in making sure to protect the brand of its state's products and to provide employment for people. But citing previous cases, Justice Stewart's opinion held that this was too great of a burden to place on the company and on interstate commerce.

Beyond the balancing tests to determine whether states impact interstate commerce, other laws are more straightforward. States cannot tax imports into the country because that is a power specifically reserved to Congress by the Constitution. Taxation itself has limits. All states impose some taxation whether on real estate, sales, or income, but states still must be careful that their taxing does not intrude into interstate commerce. Imposing an income tax on a state resident will not create such a burden, nor will a tax on real estate or sales of real estate. But a sales tax, especially in this Internet age, could create a substantial effect on interstate commerce, and a tax on income earned in the state by a non-resident may raise a question as well.

There is no better exemplar of Internet commerce—and the ability to transcend borders through the sales of all kinds of different goods, than Amazon.com. Thus, it is not surprising that Amazon.com's business model would lead to questions of exactly which states are able to tax and for what reasons. The following case looks at that issue in a dispute between Amazon.com and New York.

Amazon.com, LLC v. New York State Dept. of Taxation and Finance

81 A.D. 3d. 183, 913 N.Y.S.2d 129 (1st Dep't 2010)

Nardelli, J.

. . .

Plaintiff Amazon.com, LLC, is a limited liability company incorporated in Delaware, and Amazon Services, LLC is a limited liability company incorporated in Nevada. Neither has offices, employees or property in New York. New York residents order products from Amazon solely through its Web site. Amazon does not have any in-state representatives in New York to assist customers in placing orders, and all technical support telephone calls or e-mails are handled by Amazon's representatives located outside of New York. Products sold by Amazon are shipped directly to customers from fulfillment centers located outside New York.

Amazon, however, has developed a program using entities known as Associates which it allows hundreds of thousands of independent third parties located around the world, many of which have provided Amazon with New York addresses, to advertise the Web site "Amazon.com" on their own Web sites. Visitors to the Affiliates' Web sites can click on the link and immediately be redirected to Amazon.com. If the visitor ends up making a purchase from Amazon on the Amazon.com Web site—and only in that event—the Associate is paid a commission. Any purchase made by the visitor takes place solely with Amazon, and all customer inquiries are handled only by Amazon, its corporate affiliates, or other sellers without any involvement of the Associate.

In the standard operating agreement which governs the relationship between Amazon and its Associates, Amazon expressly disavows any control over their activities or Web site content, except to state that Associates are prohibited from "misrepresent[ing] or embellish[ing]" the relationship between themselves and Amazon.

. . .

On this appeal Amazon raises three challenges to the statute. It does not pursue its facial claims with the Commerce Clause, but argues that, as applied to it, the statute is unconstitutional because it lacks a "substantial nexus" within the State. Amazon also argues that the statute violates the **Due Process Clause** because, facially and as applied, it enacts an irrational and irrefutable presumption, and is also vague.

It lastly argues that the statute violates the **Equal Protection Clause** because it targets Amazon, one of the world's largest Internet retailers, in bad faith.

. . .

[The Commerce Clause] of the U.S. Constitution expressly authorizes Congress to "regulate Commerce with foreign Nations, and among the several States." While the Constitution "says nothing about the protection of interstate commerce in the absence of any action by Congress . . . the Commerce Clause is more than an affirmative grant of power; it has a negative sweep as well." "'[B]y its own force', [it] prohibits certain state actions that interfere with interstate commerce."

In *Moran Towing Corp.*, the Court of Appeals outlined the four-prong test for determining whether a state tax violates the Commerce Clause. The court stated that the tax will be upheld " '[1] when the tax is applied to an activity with a substantial nexus with the taxing State, [2] is fairly apportioned, [3] does not discriminate against interstate commerce, and [4] is fairly related to the services provided by the State'." As was the situation in Moran, the challenge to the tax in this case only implicates the first prong, i.e., whether the activity involved has a substantial nexus with the taxing State.

The *sine qua non* for the finding that a party has a substantial nexus with New York, and is thus required to collect sales or use taxes, is that it have a physical presence within the state. Nevertheless, "[w]hile a physical presence of the vendor is required, it need not be substantial. "While it must constitute more than a 'slightest presence' "it may be manifested by the presence in the taxing State of the vendor's property or the conduct of economic activities in the taxing State performed by the vendor's personnel or on its behalf."

* * *

Our analysis leads us to the conclusion that on its face the statute does not violate the Commerce Clause. It imposes a tax collection obligation on an out-of-state vendor only where the vendor enters into a business-referral agreement with a New York State resident, and only when that resident receives a commission based on a sale in New York. The statute does not target the out-of-state vendor's sales through agents who are not New York residents. Thus, the nexus requirement is satisfied.

Of equal importance to the requirement that the out-of-state vendor have an in-state presence is that there must be solicitation, not passive advertising. While Tax Law § 1101(3)(8)(vi) creates the presumption that the in-state agent will solicit, it provides the out-of-state vendor with a ready escape hatch or safe harbor. The vendor merely has to include in its contract with the in-state vendor a provision prohibiting the in-state representative from "engaging in any solicitation activities in New York State that refer potential customers to the seller," and the in-state representative must provide an annual certification that it has not engaged in any prohibited solicitation activities as outlined in the memorandum. Thus, an in-state resident which merely acts as a conduit for linkage with the out-of-state vendor will be presumed to have not engaged in activity which would require the vendor to collect sales taxes. Presumably, there are vendors which will be able to execute the annual certification without fear of making a misrepresentation.

On the other hand, the State has a legitimate basis to conclude that many other in-state representatives will engage in direct solicitation, rather than mere advertising. For instance, a document prepared by Amazon explaining the benefits of joining the Associates' program, states, in pertinent part, "Our compensation philosophy is simple: reward Associates for their contributions to our business in unit volume and growth. Amazon is a fast growing business and we want our Associates to grow with us." The overview document goes on to state, "The Performance structure allows you to earn higher fees when you generate a sufficient volume of referrals that result in sales at Amazon.com during a month. *The higher your referrals, the greater your earnings will be.*"

Clearly, Amazon's program, reasonably, is not designed for the passive advertiser, but seeks growth by reliance upon representatives who will look to solicit business. The obligations imposed by the state to collect the tax only arise when the paradigm shifts from advertising to solicitation. Thus, until such time as the out-of-state vendor produces a certification from every one of its New York representatives that they have not engaged in solicitation, the facial challenge based upon the Commerce Clause must fail, since there is a set of circumstances under which the statute would be valid, i.e., when a New York representative uses some form of proactive solicitation which results in a sale by Amazon, and a commission to the representative; and the representative has an in-state presence sufficient to satisfy the substantial nexus test.

. . .

Especially given the porousness of geographical boundaries today, it is difficult to determine the dividing lines between what regulation of intrastate commerce is acceptable and at what point state regulation encroaches on Congress's authority over interstate commerce. Yet, as the Amazon case and those cited just before the presentation of the case demonstrate, there are lines that the courts are willing to draw. There is almost no line, however, defining the extent of Congressional authority over commerce.

B. TAXING AND SPENDING POWER

The federal government's authority to tax is well-established and extensive. The limitations on it primarily pertain to making sure that any duties or excise taxes are uniform throughout the country and that there are no import duties on any state. Also, Congress is limited in specifying a group on whom a tax would be levied. For example, Congress cannot impose a tax on anyone who is a chief executive officer of a company or who is a Hollywood star or a professional athlete. Any taxes must be neutrally framed.

Congress also has extensive spending power. In many instances this seems innocuous. Of course, Congress uses tax revenue to pay the nation's bills—but its spending power can also be used to achieve other regulatory aims or promulgate legislation. State and local governments often depend—often heavily so—on money from the federal government. Grants from the federal to state and local governments are examples of spending. This provides leverage to extract commitments from recipients to use the money only in accordance with the policies specified by the federal government. If states don't want to take the federal money and be obligated to follow federal policies, they are free to do so. However, often federal government funds are crucial to state and local projects. In this way, federal policies extend beyond Congressional legislation.

An example is that Congress has withheld highway construction money from states if they do not establish certain speed limits. It would be difficult, if not impossible, for Congress to establish a national speed limit, but it can achieve the same result by simply stating that the federal government will not provide money if the states fail to adhere to certain policies. Funding for similar projects could also be made contingent on the drinking age in each state. The following case illustrates this kind of Congressional approach.

South Dakota v. Dole

483 U.S. 203 (1987)

CHIEF JUSTICE REHNQUIST delivered the opinion of the Court.

Petitioner South Dakota permits persons 19 years of age or older to purchase beer containing up to 3.2% alcohol. In 1984 Congress enacted 23 U.S.C. § 158, which directs the Secretary of Transportation to withhold a percentage of federal highway funds otherwise allocable from States "in which the purchase or public possession . . . of any alcoholic beverage by a person who is less than twenty-one years of age is lawful." The State sued in United States District Court seeking a declaratory judgment that [the statute] violates the constitutional limitations on congressional exercise of the spending power and violates the Twenty-first Amendment to the United States Constitution. The District Court rejected the State's claims, and the Court of Appeals for the Eighth Circuit affirmed.

* * *

These arguments present questions of the meaning of the Twenty-first Amendment, the bounds of which have escaped precise definition. Despite the extended treatment of the question by the parties, however, we need not decide in this case whether that Amendment would prohibit an attempt by Congress to legislate directly a national minimum drinking age. Here, Congress has acted indirectly under its spending power to encourage uniformity in the States' drinking ages. As we explain below, **we find this legislative effort within constitutional bounds even if Congress may not regulate drinking ages directly.**

The [Taxing and Spending Clause of the] Constitution empowers Congress to "lay and collect Taxes, Duties, Imposts, and Excises, to pay the Debts and provide for the common Defence and general Welfare of the United States." Incident to this power, Congress may attach conditions on the receipt of federal funds, and has repeatedly employed the power "to further broad policy objectives by conditioning receipt of federal moneys upon compliance by the recipient with federal statutory and administrative directives." The breadth of this power was made clear in *United States v. Butler,* where the Court, resolving a longstanding debate over the scope of the Spending Clause, determined that "the power of Congress to authorize expenditure of public moneys for public purposes is not limited by the direct grants of legislative power found in the Constitution." Thus, objectives not thought to be within Article I's "enumerated legislative fields," may nevertheless be attained through the use of the spending power and the conditional grant of federal funds.

The spending power is of course not unlimited, but is instead subject to several general restrictions articulated in our cases. The first of these limitations is derived from the language of the Constitution itself: the exercise of the spending power must

be in pursuit of "the general welfare." In considering whether a particular expenditure is intended to serve general public purposes, courts should defer substantially to the judgment of Congress. Second, we have required that if Congress desires to condition the States' receipt of federal funds, it "must do so unambiguously . . . , enabl[ing] the States to exercise their choice knowingly, cognizant of the consequences of their participation." Third, our cases have suggested (without significant elaboration) that conditions on federal grants might be illegitimate if they are unrelated "to the federal interest in particular national projects or programs." Finally, we have noted that other constitutional provisions may provide an independent bar to the conditional grant of federal funds.

South Dakota does not seriously claim that § 158 is inconsistent with any of the first three restrictions mentioned above. We can readily conclude that the provision is designed to serve the general welfare, especially in light of the fact that "the concept of welfare or the opposite is shaped by Congress [. . .]." Congress found that the differing drinking ages in the States created particular incentives for young persons to combine their desire to drink with their ability to drive, and that this interstate problem required a national solution. The means it chose to address this dangerous situation were reasonably calculated to advance the general welfare. The conditions upon which States receive the funds, moreover, could not be more clearly stated by Congress. And the State itself, rather than challenging the germaneness of the condition to federal purposes, admits that it "has never contended that the congressional action was . . . unrelated to a national concern in the absence of the Twenty-first Amendment." Indeed, the condition imposed by Congress is directly related to one of the main purposes for which highway funds are expended-safe interstate travel. This goal of the interstate highway system had been frustrated by varying drinking ages among the States. A Presidential commission appointed to study alcohol-related accidents and fatalities on the Nation's highways concluded that the lack of uniformity in the States' drinking ages created "an incentive to drink and drive" because "young persons commut[e] to border States where the drinking age is lower." By enacting § 158, Congress conditioned the receipt of federal funds in a way reasonably calculated to address this particular impediment to a purpose for which the funds are expended.

. . .

Here Congress has offered relatively mild encouragement to the States to enact higher minimum drinking ages than they would otherwise choose. But the enactment of such laws remains the prerogative of the States not merely in theory but in fact. Even if Congress might lack the power to impose a national minimum drinking age directly, we conclude that encouragement to state action found in § 158 is a valid use of the spending power. Accordingly, the judgment of the Court of Appeals is *Affirmed.*

The spending and taxing authority of Congress, and not the Commerce Clause, was identified as the Constitutional justification for the 2010 Health Care Bill (The Patient Protection and Affordable Care Act). As the case was pending resolution by the U.S. Supreme Court, some wondered whether the Court would rely on the Commerce Clause to substantiate the law's requirement that individuals acquire coverage or face a tax. Instead, the Court looked to the tax and spending power as another way to justify what is sometimes called "Obamacare." Chief Justice Roberts explained his majority opinion in *National Federation of Independent Businesses v. Sebelius*:

> The Court today holds that our Constitution protects us from federal regulation under the Commerce Clause so long as we abstain from the regulated activity. But from its creation, the Constitution has made no such promise with respect to taxes.
>
> . . . Tax incentives already promote, for example, purchasing homes and professional educations. Sustaining the **mandate** as a tax depends only on whether Congress *has* properly exercised its taxing power to encourage purchasing health insurance, not whether it *can*. Upholding the individual mandate under the Taxing Clause thus does not recognize any new federal power. It determines that Congress has used an existing one.
>
> . . . Congress's ability to use its taxing power to influence conduct is not without limits. A few of our cases policed these limits aggressively, invalidating punitive exactions obviously designed to regulate behavior otherwise regarded at the time as beyond federal authority. More often and more recently we have declined to closely examine the regulatory motive or effect of revenue-raising measures. We have nonetheless maintained that **"'there comes a time in the extension of the penalizing features of the so-called tax when it loses its character as such and becomes a mere penalty with the characteristics of regulation and punishment.'"**
>
> . . . **[A]lthough the breadth of Congress's power to tax is greater than its power to regulate commerce, the taxing power does not give Congress the same degree of control over individual behavior.** Once we recognize that Congress may regulate a particular decision under the Commerce Clause, the Federal Government can bring its full weight to bear. Congress may simply command individuals to do as it directs. An individual who disobeys may be subjected to criminal sanctions. Those sanctions can include not only fines and imprisonment, but all the attendant consequences of being branded a criminal: deprivation of otherwise protected civil rights, such as the right to bear arms or vote in elections; loss of employment opportunities; social

> stigma; and severe disabilities in other controversies, such as custody or immigration disputes.
>
> By contrast, Congress's authority under the taxing power is limited to requiring an individual to pay money into the Federal Treasury, no more. If a tax is properly paid, the Government has no power to compel or punish individuals subject to it. We do not make light of the severe burden that taxation—especially taxation motivated by a regulatory purpose—can impose. **But imposition of a tax nonetheless leaves an individual with a lawful choice to do or not do a certain act, so long as he is willing to pay a tax levied on that choice. The Affordable Care Act's requirement that certain individuals pay a financial penalty for not obtaining health insurance may reasonably be characterized as a tax. Because the Constitution permits such a tax, it is not our role to forbid it, or to pass upon its wisdom or fairness.**

Thus, Congress has these three major tools it can use to regulate private industry as well as, of course, governmental affairs: the Commerce Clause, the Taxing Power and the Spending Power. A tremendous amount of regulatory activity (at least as it relates to the private sector) comes from these three sources. Of course, Congress has considerably more tools at its disposal to pass legislation than these three. Another crucial tool to which the Courts give considerable (though not unfettered) deference arises in issues of national security.

C. NATIONAL SECURITY POWER

Fundamental to any government, including that of the United States, is the obligation to keep the country safe. The U.S. is hardly alone in this respect. The essence of national sovereignty is the capacity to control a country's borders and to control violence; that is, to make sure the people in the country are safe. Security issues are thus central to any government and certainly to the United States.

At the same time, the framers of the Constitution were also aware that a strong executive could use national security concerns as a way to increase power. For that reason, the Constitution insures that Congress—not the President—declares war. Moreover, because Congress holds the spending power—as reviewed above—Congress could cut off funding for military actions if they prove to be unpopular. These are classic examples of the Constitution's effort to check power and balance the power of any one branch against the other.

Presidents, however, tend to find ways to expand power for more "limited" purposes that all-out war. Just how far they can push their executive power is a question that has caused great controversy over the years. It's not sufficient for a President to simply say that a government act is justified by national security reasons. If there is a national security threat, the Congress and the President have significant powers to enact legislation to protect the country. In *Youngstown Sheet & Tube Co. v. Sawyer,* also known as "The Steel Seizure Case," Justice Jackson's concurrence famously elaborates a three-part test discussing the abilities of the President and Congress to act collectively and separately.

Youngstown Sheet & Tube Co. v. Sawyer

343 U.S. 579 (1952)

Mr. Justice Black delivered the opinion of the Court.

. . . In the latter part of 1951, a dispute arose between the steel companies and their employees over terms and conditions that should be included in new collective bargaining agreements. Long-continued conferences failed to resolve the dispute. On December 18, 1951, the employees' representative, United Steelworkers of America, C.I.O., gave notice of an intention to strike when the existing bargaining agreements expired on December 31. The Federal Mediation and Conciliation Service then intervened in an effort to get labor and management to agree. This failing, the President on December 22, 1951, referred the dispute to the Federal Wage Stabilization Board to investigate and make recommendations for fair and equitable terms of settlement. This Board's report resulted in no settlement. On April 4, 1952, the Union gave notice of a nation-wide strike called to begin at 12:01 a.m. April 9. The indispensability of steel as a component of substantially all weapons and other war materials led the President to believe that the proposed work stoppage would immediately jeopardize our national defense and that governmental seizure of the steel mills was necessary in order to assure the continued availability of steel. Reciting these considerations for his action, the President, a few hours before the strike was to begin, issued [the executive order at issue here]. The order directed the Secretary of Commerce to take possession of most of the steel mills and keep them running. The Secretary immediately issued his own possessory orders, calling upon the presidents of the various seized companies to serve as operating managers for the United States. They were directed to carry on their activities in accordance with regulations and directions of the Secretary. The next morning the President sent a message to Congress reporting his action. Twelve days later he sent a second message. Congress has taken no action.

* * *

The President's power, if any, to issue the order must stem either from an act of Congress or from the Constitution itself. There is no statute that expressly authorizes

"Our national security and our chances for peace depend on our defense production. Our defense production depends on steel . . . I have no doubt that if our defense program fails, the danger of war, the possibility of hostile attack, grows that much greater. I would not be faithful to my responsibilities as President if I did not use every effort to keep this from happening."

—PRESIDENT HARRY TRUMAN

"The President's power, if any, to issue the order must stem either from an act of Congress or from the Constitution itself. There is no statute that expressly authorizes the President to take possession of property as he did here."

—JUSTICE HUGO BLACK

"Harry S. Truman" by Frank Gatteri, U.S. Army Signal Corps., courtesy of the Truman Library.

the President to take possession of property as he did here. Nor is there any act of Congress to which our attention has been directed from which such a power can fairly be implied. Indeed, we do not understand the Government to rely on statutory authorization for this seizure. There are two statutes which do authorize the President to take both personal and real property under certain conditions. However, the Government admits that these conditions were not met and that the President's order was not rooted in either of the statutes. The Government refers to the seizure provisions of one of these statutes (§ 201(b) of the Defense Production Act) as "much too cumbersome, involved, and time-consuming for the crisis which was at hand."

Moreover, the use of the seizure technique to solve labor disputes in order to prevent work stoppages was not only unauthorized by any congressional enactment; prior to this controversy, Congress had refused to adopt that method of settling labor disputes. When the Taft-Hartley Act was under consideration in 1947, Congress rejected an amendment which would have authorized such governmental seizures in cases of emergency. Apparently it was thought that the technique of seizure, like that of compulsory arbitration, would interfere with the process of collective bargaining. Consequently, the plan Congress adopted in that Act did not provide for seizure under any circumstances. Instead, the plan sought to bring about settlements by use of the customary devices of mediation, conciliation, investigation by boards of inquiry, and public reports. In some instances temporary injunctions were authorized to provide cooling-off periods. All this failing, unions were left free to strike after a secret vote by employees as to whether they wished to accept their employers' final settlement offer.

It is clear that if the President had authority to issue the order he did, it must be found in some provisions of the Constitution. And it is not claimed that express constitutional language grants this power to the President. The contention is that presidential power should be implied from the aggregate of his powers under the Constitution. Particular reliance is placed on provisions in Article II which say that "the executive Power shall be vested in a President * * *"; that "he shall take Care that the Laws be faithfully executed"; and that he "shall be Commander in Chief of the Army and Navy of the United States."

The order cannot properly be sustained as an exercise of the President's military power as Commander in Chief of the Armed Forces. The Government attempts to do so by citing a number of cases upholding broad powers in military commanders engaged in day-to-day fighting in a theater of war. Such cases need not concern us here. Even though 'theater of war' be an expanding concept, we cannot with faithfulness to our constitutional system hold that the Commander in Chief of the Armed Forces has the ultimate power as such to take possession of private property in order to keep labor disputes from stopping production. This is a job for the Nation's lawmakers, not for its military authorities.

JUSTICE HUGO BLACK, by Harris & Ewing. Courtesy of the U.S. Library of Congress Prints and Photographs.

Nor can the seizure order be sustained because of the several constitutional provisions that grant executive power to the President. In the framework of our Constitution, the President's power to see that the laws are faithfully executed refutes the idea that he is to be a lawmaker. The Constitution limits his functions in the lawmaking process to the recommending of laws he thinks wise and the vetoing of laws he thinks bad. And the Constitution is neither silent nor equivocal about who shall make laws which the President is to execute. The first section of the first article says that "All legislative Powers herein granted shall be vested in a Congress of the United States * * * ." After granting many powers to the Congress, Article I goes on to provide that Congress may "make all Laws which shall be necessary and proper for carrying into Execution the foregoing Powers and all other Powers vested by this Constitution in the Government of the United States, or in any Department or Officer thereof."

The President's order does not direct that a congressional policy be executed in a manner prescribed by Congress—it directs that a presidential policy be executed in a manner prescribed by the President. The preamble of the order itself, like that of many statutes, sets out reasons why the President believes certain policies should be adopted, proclaims these policies as rules of conduct to be followed, and again, like a statute, authorizes a government official to promulgate additional rules and regulations consistent with the policy proclaimed and needed to carry that policy into execution. **The power of Congress to adopt such public policies as those proclaimed by the order is beyond question.** It can authorize the taking of private property for public use. It can makes laws regulating the relationships between employers and employees, prescribing rules designed to settle labor disputes, and fixing wages and working conditions in certain fields of our economy. The Constitution did not subject this law-making power of Congress to presidential or military supervision or control.

It is said that other Presidents without congressional authority have taken possession of private business enterprises in order to settle labor disputes. But even if this be true, Congress has not thereby lost its exclusive constitutional authority to make laws necessary and proper to carry out the powers vested by the Constitution "in the Government of the United States, or in any Department or Officer thereof."

The Founders of this Nation entrusted the law making power to the Congress alone in both good and bad times. It would do no good to recall the historical events, the fears of power and the hopes for freedom that lay behind their choice. Such a review would but confirm our holding that this seizure order cannot stand.

The judgment of the District Court is affirmed.

Of course, national security concerns can be a significant source for executive as well as congressional power. If the country is attacked or if there is an immediate threat to an ally, Presidents need to be able to act quickly while Congress prepares to debate war resolutions. Yet, even as we see expansions of presidential power in military affairs overseas and both executive and congressional authority in the aftermath of terrorist attacks, the courts do carefully examine expansions of authority domestically, as the previous case demonstrates.

III. Business-Specific Individual Rights

A. PROPERTY RIGHTS

The right to own individual property was a core belief of the founders of the country. The Bill of Rights provides explicit protection of the right to own property without interference from the government. The Fifth Amendment tends to be most famous for its right against self-incrimination. One hears defendants in a criminal case say that they refuse to answer a question (from a prosecutor or a Congressional inquiry) on the grounds that their answer might tend to incriminate them. But the Fifth Amendment also has the **Takings Clause.**

> No person shall be held to answer for a capital, or otherwise infamous crime, unless on a presentment or indictment of a Grand Jury, except in cases arising in the land or naval forces, or in the Militia, when in actual service in time of War or public danger; nor shall any person be subject for the same offence to be twice put in jeopardy of life or limb; nor shall be compelled in any criminal case to be a witness against himself, nor be deprived of life, liberty, or property, without due process of law; nor shall private property be taken for public use, without just compensation. (U.S.C. Const. Amend. V.)

The Takings Clause prevents government from seizing one's property unless certain procedures are met. Those procedures entail the government's **eminent domain** powers. Generally, the government is not able to take away an individual's property. This goes back to principles emanating from ancient England and the insistence of businessmen that the king did not have unlimited power, especially not power to take away businessmen's property. Yet there are times and places where there is a public interest in private land being made to serve a larger, societal benefit. That is where the power of eminent domain comes into play.

Let's say that the government wants to build a new highway. The government cannot simply take away your land or your house to build a road through it. At the same time, the government's civil engineers have undoubtedly conducted studies so they have a plan for the most efficient (i.e. easier to build with less material) road after taking into account safety concerns (i.e. that the road does not curve wildly all over the place). All of this is based on which landowners have agreed to sell their homes and which landowners have refused to sell. Pursuant to the power of eminent domain, the government can build the road, but it must provide just compensation to the landowner for taking the land. The following case provides a traditional example of the interaction between the protections of the Takings Clause and the government's power of eminent domain.

Berman v. Parker

348 U.S. 26 (1954)

MR. JUSTICE DOUGLAS delivered the opinion of the Court.

. . . Congress made a 'legislative determination' that 'owing to technological and sociological changes, obsolete lay-out, and other factors, conditions existing in the District of Columbia with respect to substandard housing and blighted areas, including the use of buildings in alleys as dwellings for human habitation, are injurious to the public health, safety, morals, and welfare, and it is hereby declared to be the policy of the United States to protect and promote the welfare of the inhabitants of the seat of the Government by eliminating all such injurious conditions by employing all means necessary and appropriate for the purpose'.

Section 2 goes on to declare that acquisition of property is necessary to eliminate these housing conditions.

* * *

The first project undertaken under the Act relates to Project Area B in Southwest Washington, D.C. In 1950 the Planning Commission prepared and published a comprehensive plan for the District. Surveys revealed that in Area B, 64.3% of the dwellings were beyond repair, 18.4% needed major repairs, only 17.3% were satisfactory; 57.8% of the dwellings had outside toilets, 60.3% had no baths, 29.3% lacked electricity, 82.2% had no wash basins or laundry tubs, 83.8% lacked central heating. In the judgment of the District's Director of Health it was necessary to redevelop Area B in the interests of public health. The population of Area B amounted to 5,012 persons, of whom 97.5% were Negroes.

The plan for Area B specifies the boundaries and allocates the use of the land for various purposes. It makes detailed provisions for types of dwelling units and provides that at least one-third of them are to be low-rent housing with a maximum rental of $17 per room per month.

After a public hearing, the Commissioners approved the plan and the Planning Commission certified it to the Agency for execution. The Agency undertook the preliminary steps for redevelopment of the area when this suit was brought.

Appellants own property in Area B at 712 Fourth Street, S.W. It is not used as a dwelling or place of habitation. A department store is located on it. Appellants object to the appropriation of this property for the purposes of the project. They claim that their property may not be taken constitutionally for this project. It is commercial, not residential property; it is not slum housing; it will be put into the project under the management of a private, not a public, agency and redeveloped for private, not public, use. That is the argument; and **the contention is that appellants' private property is being taken contrary to two mandates of the Fifth Amendment—(1) 'No person shall * * * be deprived of * * * property, without due process of law'; (2) 'nor shall private property be taken for public use, without just compensation.'** To take for the purpose of ridding the area of slums is one thing; it is quite another, the argument goes, to take a man's property merely to develop a better balanced, more attractive community. **The District Court, while agreeing in general with that argument, saved the Act by construing it to mean that the Agency could condemn property only for the reasonable necessities of slum clearance and prevention, its concept of 'slum' being the existence of conditions 'injurious to the public health, safety, morals and welfare.'**

. . . Public safety, public health, morality, peace and quiet, law and order-these are some of the more conspicuous examples of the traditional application of the police power to municipal affairs. Yet they merely illustrate the scope of the power and do not delimit it. Miserable and disreputable housing conditions may do more than spread disease and crime and immorality. They may also suffocate the spirit by reducing the people who live there to the status of cattle. They may indeed make living an almost insufferable burden. They may also be an ugly sore, a blight on the community which robs it of charm, which makes it a place from which men turn. The misery of housing may despoil a community as an open sewer may ruin a river.

We do not sit to determine whether a particular housing project is or is not desirable. The concept of the public welfare is broad and inclusive. The values it represents are spiritual as well as physical, aesthetic as well as monetary. It is within the power of the legislature to determine that the community should be beautiful as well as healthy, spacious as well as clean, well-balanced as well as carefully patrolled. In the present case, the Congress and its authorized agencies have made determinations that take into account a wide variety of values. It is not for us to reappraise them. If those who govern the District of Columbia decide that the Nation's Capital should be beautiful as well as sanitary, there is nothing in the Fifth Amendment that stands in the way.

Once the object is within the authority of Congress, the right to realize it through the exercise of eminent domain is clear. For the power of eminent domain is merely the means to the end. Once the object is within the authority of Congress, the means by which it will be attained is also for Congress to determine. Here one of the means chosen is the use of private enterprise for redevelopment of the area. Appellants argue that this makes the project a taking from one businessman for the benefit of another businessman. But the means of executing the project are for Congress and Congress alone to determine, once the public purpose has been established. The public end may be as well or better served through an agency of private enterprise than through a department of government-or so the Congress might conclude. We cannot say that public ownership is the sole method of promoting the public purposes of community redevelopment projects. What we have said also disposes of any contention concerning the fact that certain property owners in the area may be permitted to repurchase their properties for redevelopment in harmony with the overall plan. That, too, is a legitimate means which Congress and its agencies may adopt, if they choose.

"IF OWNER AFTER OWNER were permitted to resist these redevelopment programs on the ground that his particular property was not being used against the public interest, integrated plans for redevelopment would suffer greatly."

In the present case, Congress and its authorized agencies attack the problem of the blighted parts of the community on an area rather than on a structure-by-structure basis. That, too, is opposed by appellants. They maintain that since their building does not imperil health or safety nor contribute to the making of a slum or a blighted area, it cannot be swept into a redevelopment plan by the mere dictum of the Planning Commission or the Commissioners. The particular uses to be made of the land in the project were determined with regard to the needs of the particular community. **The experts concluded that if the community were to be healthy, if it were not to revert again to a blighted or slum area as though possessed of a congenital disease, the area must be planned as a whole. It was not enough, they believed, to remove existing buildings that were insanitary or unsightly. It was important to redesign the whole area so as to eliminate the conditions that cause slums—the overcrowding of dwellings, the lack of parks, the lack of adequate streets and alleys, the absence of recreational areas, the lack of light and air, the presence of outmoded street patterns. It was believed that the piecemeal approach, the removal of individual structures that were offensive, would be only a palliative. The entire area needed redesigning so that a balanced, integrated plan could be developed for the region, including not only new homes but also schools, churches, parks, streets, and shopping centers. In this way it was hoped that the cycle of decay of the area could be controlled and the birth of future slums prevented. Such diversification in future use is plainly relevant to the maintenance of the desired housing standards and therefore within congressional power.**

* * *

The rights of these property owners are satisfied when they receive that just compensation which the Fifth Amendment exacts as the price of the taking.

The judgment of the District Court, as modified by this opinion, is *Affirmed.*

Taking private property for a public project such as the building of an interstate highway or for a sewage project is one thing. Tensions rise, though, when the government exercises the power of eminent domain for a project that will make private businesses owners more money.

Indeed, some commentators have argued that the Takings Clause protects against other kinds of government actions as well. For example, some have argued that the primarily responsibility of corporations is to maximize profit for their shareholders. The Takings Clause does more than simply promote profit, but even if we follow that assumption, legislation that permits managers to take into account the impact of corporate actions on non-shareholder constituents might be considered unconstitutional Takings. The academic or philosophical version of the consideration of non-shareholder constituents is called **Stakeholder Theory**, and the legal analogues are the **Corporate Constituency Statutes**. The excerpt from the following law review article by Lynda Oswald sets out this argument:

> Shareholders have a property interest in their shares, for the shares simply represent their ownership of the corporation. It seems almost axiomatic that constituency statutes—at least to the extent that they are ever exercised (and more likely to the extent that a legitimate threat of exercise exists)—work a very real diminution in the shareholders' interests in their corporation. If managers need no longer act in the best interests of the shareholders, and indeed are permitted to explicitly and deliberately act contrary to those interests, the value of the shareholders' ownership interest in the corporation is reduced, for their claim to residual earnings is weakened. Such statutes cannot be justified as legitimate police power regulations because the complete absence of standards and enforcement mechanisms that uniformly characterizes these statutes makes it clear that the promotion of the common good was neither the motivating factor for legislative action nor the certain outcome of corporate exercises of such statutes [. . .] A very large chunk of societal wealth is thereby rendered bereft of constitutional protection and subject to virtually unlimited state control. Lynda J. Oswald, *Shareholders v. Stakeholders: Evaluating Corporate Constituency Statutes Under the Takings Clause*, 24 J. Corp. L. 1, 2-3 (1998).

B. COMMERCIAL SPEECH AND OTHER FIRST AMENDMENT RIGHTS

First Amendment freedoms are perhaps the most well known aspects of the Constitution and its Bill of Rights. Everyone knows that they have the right to speak freely. Everyone has an opinion. Americans also have the right to practice a religion of their choosing and to assemble together. The First Amendment guarantees a free press. These freedoms are central to this country's identity.

Most of the litigation surrounding First Amendment rights concerns just how far these freedoms extend. Are there any limits? Can government restrict these freedoms? If so, how would they do it? What tests must a government meet? No freedom can be completely unencumbered. The right to speak freely does not give a person the right to yell "fire" in a crowded theater (As Justice Holmes famously observed, "[t]he most stringent protection of free speech would not protect a man in falsely shouting fire in a theatre and causing a panic."). The first half of the "free exercise clause"—the portion of the First Amendment that guarantees freedom of religion, states that Congress should not pass laws establishing any kind of preferred religion. While the lines on this "Establishment Clause" have been very difficult to draw, what is reasonably clear is that in order to provide freedom of religious belief, one has to also place limits on the reliance on religious belief—or at least religious action.

Businesses do not face First Amendment issues as frequently as does government. After all, the Constitution is aimed at restricting governmental power rather than business power *per se*. Nevertheless, there are times and places where cases arise.

Continuing with the example of freedom of religion, Title VII of the Civil Rights Act of 1964 (42 U.S.C. § 2000 *et. seq.*) passed under the Commerce Clause, requires that businesses provide "reasonable accommodations" for people to exercise their religion freely, even if this means at work. As the next case illustrates, these issues have caused increasing conflicts for Muslims in the workplace in the aftermath of September 11, 2001.

E.E.O.C. v. Alamo Rent-A-Car, LLC.

432 F. Supp.2d 1006 (D. Ariz. 2006)

Silver, District Judge

Bilan Nur is a Muslim woman who immigrated to the United States from Somalia in 1998. Alamo hired Ms. Nur as a rental agent in November 1999 for a rental agency location on East Washington Street in Phoenix, Arizona. In this position, Ms. Nur rented cars to customers, accepted payment, and answered the telephone; her duties required interaction with clients. Until the events which led to her termination, Ms. Nur's job performance was "fine." While Ms. Nur was employed by Alamo, the company had in effect a "Dress Smart Policy" which promoted a favorable first impression with customers, and expressly prohibited employees from wearing certain clothing and accessories, for example, the wearing of more than one earring, open toe shoes, and half-grown beards. Plaintiff states that the Policy did not expressly prohibit the wearing of head coverings; Alamo counters that the Policy prohibits the wearing of any "garment or item of outer clothing not specifically mentioned in the policy. . . . "

The Muslim holiday of Ramadan began on November 16, 2001. At some point in November 2001, Plaintiff spoke to Alamo's "City Manager" Victor Bellavia and requested permission to wear a head covering at work during the Ramadan holiday. Mr. Bellavia contacted Alamo's Human Resource Manager for the Western Region, Heather Phillips, about Ms. Nur's request for an accommodation to wear a head covering during Ramadan. Ms. Phillips instructed Bellavia that Plaintiff would be allowed to wear a head covering at work in the back of the office, but that she would need to remove the head covering while at the rental counter. Alamo did not excuse Ms. Nur from working at the rental counter during Ramadan.

On December 1, 2001, an Alamo manager, Herman Schilling wrote Ms. Nur a "Counselling [*sic*] Review," which stated: "You had previously been told by the City Manager that you are not allowed to wear a hat or head covering in your position at work. When I arrived at work this morning you were wearing a veil over your hair and I told you to clock-out and discuss with the City Manager on Sunday." The next day, December 2, 2001, Ms. Nur received another Counseling Review, pursuant to which she was suspended and advised: "You had been previously informed by the city manager that you are not allowed to wear a hat or head covering in your position at work. You were wearing a veil over your hair this morning. You were sent home yesterday for the same violation and will be sent home again today. You need to discuss this issue with the city manager tomorrow." The next day (December 3, 2001), Ms. Nur again received a counseling review. In this review, Mr. Bellavia and LaShunda Brown advised Ms. Nur: "Bilan you have been verbally warned on several different occassion [*sic*] reguarding [*sic*] your work uniform. You were also sent home on 12/01–12/02 for failing to comply with company policy. You are been [*sic*] suspended pending investigation. You are to return on 12/6/01, 8:30 am, to meet with the City Manager."

. . . Alamo terminated Ms. Nur's employment on December 6, 2001 for violation of company rules. The termination form indicates that Ms. Nur was not eligible for re-hire.

* * *

"[I]t is entirely appropriate, indeed necessary, for a court to engage in analysis of the sincerity—as opposed, of course to the verity—of someone's religious beliefs in . . . the Title VII context." Viewed in the light most favorable to Alamo, however, the evidence does not support the existence of a material factual issue regarding the sincerity of Ms. Nur's religious belief at the time of her termination. During Ramadan 2001, Ms. Nur continued to wear a head covering despite warnings from her supervisors that she would be subjected to progressive disciplinary action, and then was terminated because Alamo concluded she had repeatedly violated its official dress policy. Ms. Nur's actions strongly "demonstrate that [s]he attached the utmost religious significance" to her belief that her religion required her to cover her head during Ramadan.

Assistant City Manager Sal Vargas testified that he required Plaintiff to remove her head covering during Ramadan in 2000, which he stated she did do without raising any objection, religious or otherwise. Alamo contends that this fact raises a question about whether Ms. Nur's belief was sincere in 2001. An analysis of the sincerity of Ms. Nur's belief should "be measured by the employee's words and conduct at the time the conflict arose between the belief and the employment requirement." In the Complaint, the EEOC alleges that Alamo discriminated against Ms. Nur with regard to her assertion of her religious belief in November and December 2001, not in 2000. Although there is a dispute of fact regarding whether Ms. Nur was permitted to wear a head covering during Ramadan in 1999 and 2000, that dispute is not relevant to the sincerity of Ms. Nur's belief in the Fall of 2001, when Ms. Nur's assertions of religious belief led to her termination. Alamo further contends that because in 2001 Ramadan began on November 16, and because Alamo asserts that Ms. Nur did not raise the head covering issue with Mr. Bellavia until November 20, this is evidence that might lead a fact finder to infer that Ms. Nur did not wear a head covering at work during the first few days of Ramadan 2001, i.e., between November 16 and November 20. Similarly, Alamo suggests that because Ms. Nur was not first disciplined until December 1, 2001, 15 days into the Ramadan holiday, a reasonable fact finder might infer that Plaintiff had acted consistently with the accommodation Alamo offered prior to December 1, thus eroding Plaintiff's claim that Ms. Nur's religious belief was sincere.

These inferences are not reasonable in the factual context before the Court. Plaintiff testified that when Ramadan began, she started to wear a scarf at work. There is nothing in the record demonstrating that Plaintiff did not wear a head covering at work during Ramadan 2001. The record includes deposition testimony of both Victor Bellavia and LaShunda Brown, who supervised Ms. Nur. Neither Bellavia nor Brown testified that Ms. Nur did not wear a head covering during Ramadan in 2001. In fact, Victor Bellavia's December 3, 2001 memorandum to the file states that "[w]hen the Holiday started [Ms. Nur] insisted on having her head covered." LaShunda Brown testified that Ms. Nur advised her that she wanted to wear a head covering "during Ramadan until after Ramadan was over." The sort of speculation in which Alamo invites the fact finder to indulge does not create a factual dispute for purposes of summary judgment. "When the moving party has carried its burden [for summary judgment], its opponent must do more than simply show that there is some metaphysical doubt as to the material facts."

. . . Alamo must demonstrate that it made "some initial step to reasonably accommodate the religious belief" of Ms. Nur (or show that no reasonable accommodation was possible without undue burden). This obligation requires, at a minimum, that the employer "negotiate with the employee in an effort reasonably to accommodate the employer's religious belief." The accommodation Alamo offered Ms. Nur was that "she would be allowed to wear [a head covering] when she was in the back office . . . but when she went to the rental counter to rent cars in the front of the office, she would have to remove it." It is undisputed that the accommodation Alamo offered Ms. Nur required her to remove her head covering during Ramadan when she served clients but still required her to serve clients, making it impossible for Ms. Nur to avoid removing her head covering at work. Accordingly, Alamo's proposal would have failed to accommodate Ms. Nur's religious conflict, and was not a reasonable accommodation. Thus, Alamo failed to uphold its burden to attempt to accommodate Ms. Nur's beliefs, and was left with the alternative burden to show that permitting Ms. Nur to wear a head covering during Ramadan while dealing with clients would impose an undue hardship.

* * *

Alamo fails to support its assertion of undue burden with anything other than speculation, which is not a basis to establish a genuine issue of material fact. Victor Bellavia testified that it would not have cost Alamo any money to allow Ms. Nur to wear a head scarf while serving customers. Mr. Bellavia did state that allowing Ms. Nur to wear a head covering might have affected the efficiency of Alamo's operations by opening the door for other employees to violate the company uniform policy. Bellavia stated that "[t]he only burden I see is other people wanting to break the uniform policy." However, Mr. Bellavia did not believe that allowing Ms. Nur to wear a head covering at the rental counter would affect the impression she would make on customers, or would it negatively impact customer expectations concerning the level of service or quality of the product they would receive, or otherwise create any type of negative expectations with customers. * * *

Alamo has not presented genuine issues of material fact concerning either EEOC's *prima facie* case of religious discrimination or Alamo's burden to show that it offered to reasonably accommodate Ms. Nur's religious beliefs or that it could not accommodate those beliefs without undue hardship. Summary judgment has been granted in favor of EEOC on the question of liability.

It is, of course, true that the very first words of the First Amendment suggest a barrier between church and state though the metaphor of a wall of separation between the two came later in a letter from Thomas Jefferson. Yet the First Amendment's first sentence also guarantees the freedom for people to practice their religion. Because that freedom almost inevitably means that one person's faith might well bump into another person's beliefs, cases such as the above one can be expected. That means businesses, for better or for worse, have to learn how to accommodate varying religious beliefs and practices, especially in a globalized, diverse workforce..

At the time of the framing of the Constitution, the "press" were comprised of small entrepreneurs, if business people at all. The Bill of Rights was aimed to protect individuals and their expressions, and included rights to freedom of speech, religion and association, as well as freedom to publish news and opinions. Over time, many of these rights have been extended to large businesses as well.

Indeed, these days most members of the press are corporations. CNN, *The Washington Post*, and *The Huffington Post* are also businesses that seek to be profitable in the practice of journalism. The press frequently has to be aggressive in seeking stories; often people want to hide the truth. Are there restrictions on how far the press can go (in its exercise of the First Amendment Freedom of the Press) with respect to investigating and reporting on government activities? How about with respect to an individual? The following case is often considered one of the most important First Amendment cases ever decided by the Supreme Court.

New York Times v. U.S.

403 U.S. 713 (1971)

PER CURIAM.

Mr. Justice BLACK, with whom Mr. Justice DOUGLAS joins, concurring. I adhere to the view that the Government's case against the Washington Post should have been dismissed and that the injunction against the *New York Times* should have been vacated without oral argument when the cases were first presented to this Court. I believe that every moment's continuance of the injunctions against these newspapers amounts to a flagrant, indefensible, and continuing violation of the First Amendment. Furthermore, after oral argument, I agree completely that we must affirm the judgment of the Court of Appeals for the District of Columbia Circuit and reverse the judgment of the Court of Appeals for the Second Circuit for the reasons stated by my Brothers DOUGLAS and BRENNAN. In my view it is unfortunate that some of my Brethren are apparently willing to hold that the publication of news may sometimes be enjoined. Such a holding would make a shambles of the First Amendment.

'THE PEOPLE shall not be deprived or abridged of their right to speak, to write, or to publish their sentiments; and the freedom of the press, as one of the great bulwarks of liberty, shall be inviolable.'

Our Government was launched in 1789 with the adoption of the Constitution. The Bill of Rights, including the First Amendment, followed in 1791. Now, for the first time in the 182 years since the founding of the Republic, the federal courts are asked to hold that the First Amendment does not mean what it says, but rather means that the Government can halt the publication of current news of vital importance to the people of this country.

In seeking injunctions against these newspapers and in its presentation to the Court, the Executive Branch seems to have forgotten the essential purpose and history of the First Amendment. When the Constitution was adopted, many people strongly opposed it because the document contained no Bill of Rights to safeguard certain basic freedoms. They especially feared that the new powers granted to a central government might be interpreted to permit the government to curtail freedom of religion, press, assembly, and speech. In response to an overwhelming public clamor, James Madison offered a series of amendments to satisfy citizens that these great liberties would remain safe and beyond the power of government to abridge. Madison proposed what later became the First Amendment in three parts, two of which are set out below, and one of which proclaimed: 'The people shall not be deprived or abridged of their right to speak, to write, or to publish their sentiments; and the freedom of the press, as one of the great bulwarks of liberty, shall be inviolable.' The amendments were offered to curtail and restrict the general powers granted to the Executive, Legislative, and Judicial Branches two years before in the original Constitution. The Bill of Rights changed the original Constitution into a new charter under which no branch of government could abridge the people's freedoms of press, speech, religion, and assembly. Yet the Solicitor General argues and some members of the Court appear to agree that the general powers of the Government adopted in the original Constitution should be interpreted to limit and restrict the specific and emphatic guarantees of the Bill of Rights adopted later. I can imagine no greater perversion of history. Madison and the other Framers of the First Amendment, able men that they were, wrote in language they earnestly believed could never be misunderstood: 'Congress shall make no law * * * abridging the freedom * * * of the press * * * .' Both the history and language of the First Amendment support the view that the press must be left free to publish news, whatever the source, without censorship, injunctions, or prior restraints.

In the First Amendment the Founding Fathers gave the free press the protection it must have to fulfill its essential role in our democracy. The press was to serve the governed, not the governors. The Government's power to censor the press was abolished so that the press would remain forever free to censure the Government. The press was protected so that it could bare the secrets of government and inform the people. Only a free and unrestrained press can effectively expose deception in government. And paramount among the responsibilities of a free press is the duty to prevent any part of the government from deceiving the people and sending them off to distant lands to die of foreign fevers and foreign shot and shell. In my view, far from deserving condemnation for their courageous reporting, the New York Times, the Washington Post, and other newspapers should be commended for serving the purpose that the Founding Fathers saw so clearly. In revealing the workings of government that led to the Vietnam war, the newspapers nobly did precisely that which the Founders hoped and trusted they would do.

* * *

Individuals may have a right to speak freely but do corporations have the same right? That becomes especially interesting when giant corporations are themselves newspapers or television stations who are interested in both profit and journalism, noted in the case above.

Yet even beyond companies such as the *Wall Street Journal* or NBC, companies have been held to have rights too. Cases on their First Amendment rights tend to revolve around two kinds of issues. One is with respect to marketing of products. Companies do not have the latitude to say what they wish as do citizens participating in everyday life or the political sphere.

For instance, except with respect to violating an established law such as campaign financial disclosures, there are no laws that punish a politician for lying on the campaign trail. The antidote is not prosecution, but debate. Corporations marketing products do not have the same freedom. They may be able to exaggerate about a product, but they cannot lie about it. The following case demonstrates an example of these kinds of issues.

Friedman v. Rogers

440 U.S. 1 (1971)

Mr. Justice Powell delivered the opinion of the Court.

The Texas Legislature approved the Texas Optometry Act (Act) in 1969, repealing an earlier law governing the practice of optometry in the State. Section 2.01 of the Act establishes the Texas Optometry Board (Board) and § 2.02 prescribes the qualifications for Board members. The Board is responsible for the administration of the Act, and has the authority to grant, renew, suspend, and revoke licenses to practice optometry in the State. The Act imposes numerous regulations on the practice of optometry, and on several aspects of the business of optometry. Many of the Act's business regulations are contained in § 5.13, which restricts fee splitting by optometrists and forbids an optometrist to allow his name to be associated with any optometrical office unless he is present and practicing there at least half of the hours that the office is open or half of the hours that he practices, whichever is less. Section 5.13(d), at issue here, prohibits the practice of optometry under an assumed name, trade name, or corporate name.

The dispute in this case grows out of the schism between "professional" and "commercial" optometrists in Texas. Although all optometrists in the State must meet the same licensing requirements and are subject to the same laws regulating their practices, they have divided themselves informally into two groups according to their divergent approaches to the practice of optometry. Rogers, an advocate of the commercial practice of optometry and a member of the Board, commenced this action by filing a suit against the other five members of the Board. He sought declaratory and injunctive relief from the enforcement of § 2.02 of the Act, prescribing the composition of the Board, and § 5.13(d) of the Act, prohibiting the practice of optometry under a trade name.

Section 2.02 of the Act requires that four of the six members of the Board must be members of a state organization affiliated with the American Optometric Association (AOA). The only such organization is the Texas Optometric Association (TOA), membership in which is restricted to optometrists who comply with the Code of Ethics of the AOA. Rogers and his fellow commercial optometrists are ineligible for membership in TOA because their business methods are at odds with the AOA Code of Ethics. In his complaint, Rogers alleged that he is deprived of equal protection and due process because he is eligible for only two of the six seats on the

Board, and because he is subject to regulation by a Board composed primarily of members of the professional faction. Regarding § 5.13(d), Rogers alleged that while the section prohibits optometrists from practicing under trade names, the prohibition is not extended to ophthalmologists. Rogers claimed that this disparity of treatment denies him the equal protection of the laws, as he is denied the right to conduct his optometrical practice as he has in the past under the name "Texas State Optical."

* * *

In holding that § 5.13(d) infringes First Amendment rights, the District Court relied primarily on this Court's decisions in *Bates v. State Bar of Arizona and Virginia Pharmacy Board v. Virginia Citizens Consumer Council.* A trade name is a form of advertising, it concluded, because after the name has been used for some time, people "identify the name with a certain quality of service and goods." If found specifically "that the Texas State Optical [TSO] name has come to communicate to the consuming public information as to certain standards of price and quality, and availability of particular routine services," and rejected the argument that the TSO name misleads the public as to the identity of the optometrists with whom it deals. Balancing the constitutional interests in the commercial speech in question against the State's interest in regulating it, the District Court held that the prohibition of the use of trade names by § 5.13(d) is an unconstitutional restriction of the "free flow of commercial information."

* * *

In both *Virginia Pharmacy* and *Bates*, we were careful to emphasize that "[s]ome forms of commercial speech regulation are surely permissible." For example, restrictions on the time, place, or manner of expression are permissible provided that "they are justified without reference to the content of the regulated speech, that they serve a significant governmental interest, and that in so doing they leave open ample alternative channels for communication of the information." Equally permissible are restrictions on false, deceptive, and misleading commercial speech.

* * *

Once a trade name has been in use for some time, it may serve to identify an optometrical practice and also to convey information about the type, price, and quality of services offered for sale in that practice. In each role, the trade name is used as part of a proposal of a commercial transaction. Like the pharmacist who desired to advertise his prices in *Virginia Pharmacy*, the optometrist who uses a trade name "does not wish to editorialize on any subject, cultural, philosophical, or political. He does not wish to report any particularly newsworthy fact, or to make generalized observations even about commercial matters." His purpose is strictly business. The use of trade names in connection with optometrical practice, then, is a form of commercial speech and nothing more.

A trade name is, however, a significantly different form of commercial speech from that considered in *Virginia Pharmacy* and *Bates*. In those cases, the State had proscribed advertising by pharmacists and lawyers that contained statements about the products or services offered and their prices. These statements were self-contained and self-explanatory. Here we are concerned with a form of commercial speech that has no intrinsic meaning. A trade name conveys no information about the price and nature of the services offered by an optometrist until it acquires meaning over a period of time by associations formed in the minds of the public between the name and some standard of price or quality. Because these ill-defined associations of trade names with price and quality information can be manipulated by the users of trade names, there is a significant possibility that trade names will be used to mislead the public.

"**A TRADE NAME** frees an optometrist from dependence on his personal reputation to attract clients, and even allows him to assume a new trade name if negligence or misconduct casts a shadow over the old one."

The possibilities for deception are numerous. The trade name of an optometrical practice can remain unchanged despite changes in the staff of optometrists upon whose skill and care and public depends when it patronizes the practice. Thus, the public may be attracted by a trade name that reflects the reputation of an optometrist no longer associated with the practice. A trade name frees an optometrist from dependence on his personal reputation to attract clients, and even allows him to assume a new trade name if negligence or misconduct casts a shadow over the old one. By using different trade names at shops under his common ownership, an optometrist can give the public the false impression of competition among the shops. The use of a trade name also facilitates the advertising essential to large-scale commercial practices with numerous branch offices, conduct the State rationally may wish to discourage while not prohibiting commercial optometrical practice altogether.

The concerns of the Texas Legislature about the deceptive and misleading uses of optometrical trade names were not speculative or hypothetical, but were based on experience in Texas with which the legislature was familiar when in 1969 it enacted § 5.13(d). The forerunner of § 5.13(d) was adopted as part of a "Professional Responsibility Rule" by the Texas State Board of Examiners in Optometry in 1959. In a decision upholding the validity of the Rule, the Texas Supreme Court reviewed some of the practices that had prompted its adoption. One of the plaintiffs in that case, Carp, operated 71 optometrical offices in Texas under at least 10 different trade names. From time to time, he changed the trade names of various shops, though the licensed optometrists practicing in each shop remained the same. He purchased the practices of other optometrists and continued to practice under their names, even

though they were no longer associated with the practice. In several instances, Carp used different trade names on offices located in close proximity to one another and selling the same optical goods and services. The offices were under common management, and had a common staff of optometrists, but the use of different trade names facilitated advertising that gave the impression of competition among the offices.

The Texas court found that Carp used trade names to give a misleading impression of competitive ownership and management of his shops. It also found that Rogers, a party to this suit and a plaintiff in *Carp*, had used a trade name to convey the impression of standardized optometrical care. All 82 of his shops went under the trade name "Texas State Optical" or "TSO," and he advertised "scientific TSO eye examination[s]" available in every shop. The TSO advertising was calculated as well, the court found, to give "the impression that [Rogers or one of his brothers] is present at a particular office. Actually they have neither been inside nor seen some of their eighty-two offices distributed generally over Texas." Even if Rogers' use and advertising of the trade name were not in fact misleading, they were an example of the use of a trade name to facilitate the large-scale commercialization which enhances the opportunity for misleading practices.

It is clear that the State's interest in protecting the public from the deceptive and misleading use of optometrical trade names is substantial and well demonstrated. We are convinced that § 5.13(d) is a constitutionally permissible state regulation in furtherance of this interest.

A second kind of speech case involves corporations participating in political speech. For many years, Courts have ruled that corporations are "persons" within the eyes of the law with respect to many legal issues. Corporations can own property. They can enter into contracts. They can sue in court and they can be sued. They can lobby Congress for passage of certain legislation. So could they then also participate, as persons, in political campaigns? In the controversial *Citizens United v. Federal Election Commission*, 558 U.S. 310 (2010), Justice Kennedy, writing for the Supreme Court, announced that corporations could provide unlimited donations.

> Our Nation's speech dynamic is changing, and informative voices should not have to circumvent onerous restrictions to exercise their First Amendment rights. Speakers have become adept at presenting citizens with sound bites, talking points, and scripted messages that dominate the 24–hour news cycle. Corporations, like individuals, do not have monolithic views. On certain topics corporations may possess valuable expertise, leaving them the best equipped to point out errors or fallacies in speech of all sorts, including the speech of candidates and elected officials.

> Rapid changes in technology—and the creative dynamic inherent in the concept of free expression—counsel against upholding a law that restricts political speech in certain media or by certain speakers. Today, 30–second television ads may be the most effective way to convey a political message. Soon, however, it may be that Internet sources, such as blogs and social networking Web sites, will provide citizens with significant information about political candidates and issues. Yet, § 441b [a statute prohibiting campaign contributions from corporations and unions] would seem to ban a blog post expressly advocating the election or defeat of a candidate if that blog were created with corporate funds. The First Amendment does not permit Congress to make these categorical distinctions based on the corporate identity of the speaker and the content of the political speech. *Citizens United v. Fed. Election Comm'n*, (2010)

Citizens United was very controversial at the time of the decision and continues to be so. By protecting corporate contributions to political campaigns, it has unleashed a massive amount of money into the campaign process. While there have been expensive campaigns for many years—and many television commercials at election time—the opening of corporate coffers to contribute to campaigns has provided money to air even more of these commercials. Some warn that the size of corporate contributions make it impossible for the average citizen to have an impact on elections, though because corporations themselves have different interests, others point out that corporate funds might combat each other. However this debate plays out, the decision in this case has had a major impact on contemporary political campaigns.

C. DUE PROCESS

There are two kinds of due process rights: **substantive** and **procedural. Substantive due process** recognizes certain rights as particularly in need of court protection. These can be confusing terms. Like **procedural due process**, substantive due process arises from the Fourteenth Amendment prohibition that the states may not deprive a person of life, liberty, or property without due process of law. This protection had been guaranteed by the federal government under the Fifth Amendment, but the Fourteenth Amendment, which came in the aftermath of the Civil War, essentially authorized the courts to review actions of the individual states on due process terms as well.

The theory of substantive due process is that there are certain rights that require particular attention and protection. Thus, if a court finds that these individual rights have been threatened by state action, the courts will apply a rigorous standard of review and demand a high level of justification from the state in order to uphold the restriction. The courts determine what rights deserve constitutional protection. Under the **incorporation doctrine**, courts determine which of the First Amendment rights have this unique importance. After the ratification of the Fourteenth Amendment, substantive due process cases arose only in a few areas, most prominently with respect to property rights.

Indeed, substantive due process claims were used to strike down many attempts at economic regulation. The most infamous case involving economic, substantive due process was the *Lochner* case, which invalidated New York's maximum work-hours requirement for bakers and ushered in an era of *laissez-faire* economic regulation. It is important to note that the Supreme Court no longer regards substantive due process in the same way, and that it effectively overruled *Lochner* in the 1937 case, *West Coast Hotel v. Parrish.*

Today the substantive due process approach has its main importance in cases related to privacy. In the famous case of *Griswold v. Connecticut*, 1965, four of the seven justices grounded their approach to finding a right to privacy (which is not specifically identified in the Constitution) in this substantive due process/fundamental rights area. And the *Griswold* case was the key precedent for the 1973 *Roe v. Wade* decision. Here are some excerpts from those opinions. What is important to recognize is how privacy is "found" by the courts and then developed to have a particular importance.

excerpts

GRISWOLD V. CONNECTICUT:

"The foregoing cases suggest that specific guarantees in the Bill of Rights have penumbras, formed by emanations from those guarantees that help give them life and substance. Various guarantees create zones of privacy. The right of association contained in the penumbra of the First Amendment is one, as we have seen. The Third Amendment in its prohibition against the quartering of soldiers 'in any house' in time of peace without the consent of the owner is another facet of that privacy. The Fourth Amendment explicitly affirms the 'right of the people to be secure in their persons, houses, papers, and effects, against unreasonable searches and seizures.' The Fifth Amendment in its Self-Incrimination Clause enables the citizen to create a zone of privacy which government may not force him to surrender to his detriment.

The Ninth Amendment provides: 'The enumeration in the Constitution, of certain rights, shall not be construed to deny or disparage others retained by the people.'

We deal with a right of privacy older than the Bill of Rights—older than our political parties, older than our school system. Marriage is a coming together for better or for worse, hopefully enduring, and intimate to the degree of being sacred. It is an association that promotes a way of life, not causes; a harmony in living, not political faiths; a bilateral loyalty, not commercial or social projects. Yet it is an association for as noble a purpose as any involved in our prior decisions.

— *Griswold v. Connecticut,* 381 U.S. 479, 85 S.Ct. 1678 (1965).

ROE V. WADE:

"This **right of privacy**, whether it be founded in the Fourteenth Amendment's concept of personal liberty and restrictions upon state action, as we feel it is, or, as the District Court determined, in the Ninth Amendment's reservation of rights to the people, is broad enough to encompass a woman's decision whether or not to terminate her pregnancy. The detriment that the State would impose upon the pregnant woman by denying this choice altogether is apparent. Specific and direct harm medically diagnosable even in early pregnancy may be involved. Maternity, or additional offspring, may force upon the woman a distressful life and future. Psychological harm may be imminent. Mental and physical health may be taxed by child care. There is also the distress, for all concerned, associated with the unwanted child, and there is the problem of bringing a child into a family already unable, psychologically and otherwise, to care for it. In other cases, as in this one, the additional difficulties and continuing stigma of unwed motherhood may be involved. All these are factors the woman and her responsible physician necessarily will consider in consultation.

— *Roe v. Wade,* 410 U.S. 113, 93 S.Ct. 705 (1973) holding modified by *Planned Parenthood of S.E. Pennsylvania v. Casey*, 505 U.S. 833, 112 S.Ct. 2791 (1992).

The second kind of due process is **procedural due process.** As its name indicates, it focuses on the processes that a government must go through in order to take away a person's right to life, liberty or property. Many of these cases pertain to criminal prosecutions, where there exist due process rights to an attorney, notice that charges (or a lawsuit in a civil case) have been filed against you, a standard that the laws are not too vague (so that one can understand them), and decisions that are supported by evidence.

Typically a procedural due process claim must meet three criteria: there must be a deprivation, that deprivation must involve "life, liberty, or property," and it must be without due process of law. One of the most recent and surprising articulations of procedural due process was in the context of excessive punitive damage awards. In *State Farm v. Campbell*, the court considered a $145 million dollar punitive award against an insurance company, an amount that far exceeded the compensatory damages suffered by the plaintiffs in a car accident.

State Farm Mutual Insurance Co. v. Campbell

538 U.S. 408 (2003)

JUSTICE KENNEDY delivered the opinion of the Court.

* * *

The courts awarded punitive damages to punish and deter conduct that bore no relation to the Campbells' harm. A defendant's dissimilar acts, independent from the acts upon which liability was premised, may not serve as the basis for punitive damages. A defendant should be punished for the conduct that harmed the plaintiff, not for being an unsavory individual or business. Due process does not permit courts, in the calculation of punitive damages, to adjudicate the merits of other parties' hypothetical claims against a defendant under the guise of the **reprehensibility analysis**, but we have no doubt the Utah Supreme Court did that here. Punishment on these bases creates the possibility of multiple punitive damages awards for the same conduct; for in the usual case nonparties are not bound by the judgment some other plaintiff obtains.

* * *

[W]e have been reluctant to identify concrete constitutional limits on the ratio between harm, or potential harm, to the plaintiff and the punitive damages award. We decline again to impose a bright-line ratio which a punitive damages award cannot exceed. **Our jurisprudence and the principles it has now established demonstrate, however, that, in practice, few awards exceeding a single-digit ratio between punitive and compensatory damages, to a significant degree, will satisfy due process. In *Haslip*, in upholding a punitive damages award, we concluded that an award of more than four times the amount of compensatory damages might be close to the line of constitutional impropriety. We cited that 4-to-1 ratio again in *Gore*. The Court further referenced a long legislative history, dating back over 700 years and going forward to today, providing for sanctions of double, treble, or quadruple damages to deter and punish. While these ratios are not binding, they are instructive.** They demonstrate what should be obvious: Single-digit multipliers are more likely to comport with due process, while still achieving the State's goals of deterrence and retribution, than awards with ratios in range of 500 to 1, or, in this case, of 145 to 1.

* * *

The compensatory award in this case was substantial; the Campbells were awarded $1 million for a year and a half of emotional distress. * * *

The punitive award of $145 million, therefore, was neither reasonable nor proportionate to the wrong committed, and it was an irrational and arbitrary deprivation of the property of the defendant. The proper calculation of punitive damages under the principles we have discussed should be resolved, in the first instance, by the Utah courts.

The judgment of the Utah Supreme Court is reversed, and the case is remanded for further proceedings not inconsistent with this opinion.

It is so ordered.

[Separate dissenting opinions by Scalia and Ginsburg omitted.]

This is a novel case and effort at reigning in damage awards. By using due process as a tool, courts now have provided a weapon for defendants who lose a court case to limit the damages that can be imposed against them.

D. EQUAL PROTECTION ISSUES

Also in the Fourteen Amendment lies the equal protection clause. Indeed, it appears immediately after the due process clause just discussed.

> "All persons born or naturalized in the United States, and subject to the jurisdiction thereof, are citizens of the United States and of the State wherein they reside. No State shall make or enforce any law which shall abridge the privileges or immunities of citizens of the United States; nor shall any

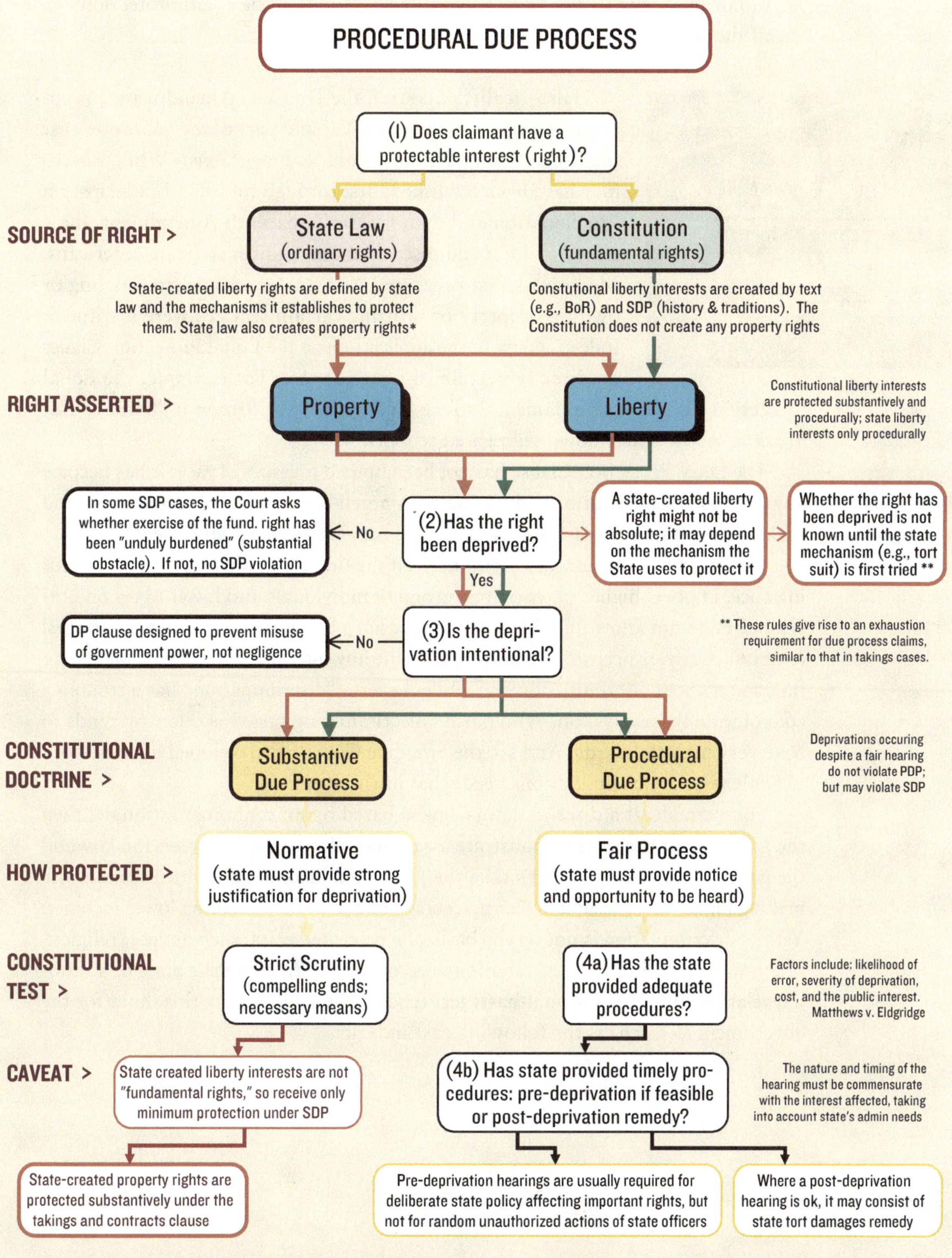

* States create liberty/property rights either through positive law or by creating a reasonable expectation that an interest will be protected

State deprive any person of life, liberty, or property, without due process of law; nor deny to any person within its jurisdiction the equal protection of the laws."

■ THE INSCRIPTION ABOVE THE ENTRANCE OF THE UNITED STATES SUPREME COURT WAS INSPIRED BY THE 14TH AMENDMENT EQUAL PROTECTION CLAUSE.

Historically, of course, the Fourteen Amendment was enacted as a result of the Civil War and part of the guarantee that the institution of slavery would no longer exist. While slavery may have been abolished, first through the 1863 Emancipation Proclamation and then via the Thirteenth Amendment, these efforts did not end discrimination against African Americans. Many laws that prevented African Americans from voting or owning property or utilizing certain services were instituted. Indeed, many of the applications of the Equal Protection Clause do directly pertain to issues of race. For example, the Equal Protection Clause was fundamental to the landmark, 1954 *Brown v. Board of Education*, which struck down segregated schools.

The Equal Protection Clause has not been limited to issues of race. It has become a widely used Constitutional doctrine with an elaborate matrix of variables and various constitutional standards for decision-making and judicial review.

Governments, of course, discriminate all the time. A graduated income tax for instance, imposes higher taxes on one group of individuals and lower taxes on others. States do not allow individuals under the age of sixteen (sometimes other ages) to obtain a drivers license. It is hard to imagine any institution or individual able to function without discrimination and while the term "discrimination" has a troubling connotation these days, one who has a "discriminating taste" is one who tends to have very high standards. And so, the Supreme Court has developed a framework to analyze what discriminations need what justifications.

For example, if a discriminatory law is based on an economic rationale, then the government needs to demonstrate a rational relationship between the law and the government objective. Let's take the graduated income tax, which taxes those making higher incomes at a higher percentage rate than those making lower incomes. Yet the discrimination is not on the basis of a protected class, such as race, religion, or ethnic origin. So the discrimination need only be justified on the basis of a rational relationship. This **rational-basis test** tends to be a fairly easy threshold for the government to reach, as the following case indicates.

F.C.C. v. Beach Communications, Inc.

508 U.S. 307 (1993)

JUSTICE THOMAS delivered the opinion of the Court.

* * *

Respondents Beach Communications, Inc., Maxtel Limited Partnership, Pacific Cablevision, and Western Cable Communications, Inc.—SMATV [satellite master antenna television] operators that would be subject to franchising under the Cable Act as construed by the Commission—petitioned the Court of Appeals for review. The Court of Appeals rejected respondents' statutory challenge to the Commission's interpretation, but a majority of the court found merit in the claim that § 602(7) violates the implied equal protection guarantee of the Due Process Clause. In the absence of what it termed "the predominant rationale for local franchising" (use of public rights-of-way), the court saw no rational basis "[o]n the record," and was "unable to imagine" any conceivable basis, for distinguishing between those facilities exempted by the statute and those SMATV cable systems that link separately owned and managed buildings. The court remanded the record and directed the FCC to provide "additional 'legislative facts' " to justify the distinction.

A report subsequently filed by the Commission failed to satisfy the Court of Appeals. The Commission stated that it was "unaware of any desirable policy or other considerations . . . that would support the challenged distinctions," other than those offered by a concurring member of the court. The concurrence had believed it sufficient that Congress *could* have reasoned that SMATV systems serving separately owned buildings are more similar to traditional cable systems than are facilities serving commonly owned buildings, in terms of the problems presented for consumers and the potential for regulatory benefits. In a second opinion, the majority found this rationale to be "a naked intuition, unsupported by conceivable facts or policies," and held that "the Cable Act violates the equal protection component of the Fifth Amendment, insofar as it imposes a discriminatory franchising requirement," The court declared the franchise requirement void to the extent it covers respondents and similarly situated SMATV operators.

Because the Court of Appeals held an Act of Congress unconstitutional, we granted *certiorari*. We now reverse.

II

Whether embodied in the Fourteenth Amendment or inferred from the Fifth, equal protection is not a license for courts to judge the wisdom, fairness, or logic of legislative choices. In areas of social and economic policy, a statutory classification that neither proceeds along suspect lines nor infringes fundamental constitutional rights must be upheld against equal protection challenge if there is any reasonably conceivable state of facts that could provide a rational basis for the classification. Where there are "plausible reasons" for Congress' action, "our inquiry is at an end." This standard of review is a paradigm of judicial restraint. "The Constitution presumes that, absent some reason to infer antipathy, even improvident decisions will eventually be rectified by the democratic process and that judicial intervention is generally unwarranted no matter how unwisely we may think a political branch has acted."

On rational-basis review, a classification in a statute such as the Cable Act comes to us bearing a strong presumption of validity, and those attacking the rationality of the legislative classification have the burden "to negative every conceivable basis which might support it," Moreover, because we never require a legislature to articulate its reasons for enacting a statute, it is entirely irrelevant for constitutional purposes whether the conceived reason for the challenged distinction actually motivated the legislature. Thus, the absence of " 'legislative facts' " explaining the distinction "[o]n the record," has no significance in rational-basis analysis. In other words, a legislative choice is not subject to courtroom fact-finding and may be based on rational speculation unsupported by evidence or empirical data. "'Only by faithful adherence to this guiding principle of judicial review of legislation is it possible to preserve to the legislative branch its rightful independence and its ability to function.'"

* * *

Applying these principles, we conclude that the common-ownership distinction is constitutional. There are at least two possible bases for the distinction; either one suffices. First, Congress borrowed § 602(7)(B) from pre-Cable Act regulations, and although the existence of a prior administrative scheme is certainly not necessary to the rationality of the statute, it is plausible that Congress also adopted the FCC's earlier rationale. Under that rationale, common ownership was thought to be indicative of those systems for which the costs of regulation would outweigh the benefits to consumers. Because the number of subscribers was a similar indicator, the Commission also exempted cable facilities that served fewer than 50 subscribers. ***

This regulatory-efficiency model, originally suggested by Chief Judge Mikva in his concurring opinion, provides a conceivable basis for the common-ownership exemption. A legislator might rationally assume that systems serving only commonly owned or managed buildings without crossing public rights-of-way would typically be limited in size or would share some other attribute affecting their impact on the welfare of cable viewers such that regulators could "safely ignor[e]" these systems.

Respondents argue that Congress did not intend common ownership to be a surrogate for small size, since Congress simultaneously rejected the FCC's 50–subscriber exemption by omitting it from the Cable Act. Whether the posited reason for the challenged distinction actually motivated Congress is "constitutionally irrelevant," and, in any event, the FCC's explanation indicates that both common ownership and number of subscribers were considered indicia of "very small" cable systems. Respondents also contend that an SMATV operator could increase his subscription base and still qualify for the exemption simply by installing a separate satellite dish on each building served. The additional cost of multiple dishes and associated transmission equipment, however, would impose an independent constraint on system size.

Furthermore, small size is only one plausible ownership-related factor contributing to consumer welfare. Subscriber influence is another. Where an SMATV system serves a complex of buildings under common ownership or management, individual subscribers could conceivably have greater bargaining power vis-à-vis the cable operator (even if the number of dwelling units were large), since all the subscribers could negotiate with one voice through the common owner or manager. Such an owner might have substantial leverage, because he could withhold permission to operate the SMATV system on his property. He would also have an incentive to guard the interests of his tenants. Thus, there could be less need to establish regulatory safeguards for subscribers in commonly owned complexes. Respondents acknowledge such possibilities, and we certainly cannot say that these assumptions would be irrational.

There is a second conceivable basis for the statutory distinction. Suppose competing SMATV operators wish to sell video programming to subscribers in a group of contiguous buildings, such as a single city block, which can be interconnected by wire without crossing a public right-of-way. If all the buildings belong to one owner or are commonly managed, that owner or manager could freely negotiate a deal for all subscribers on a competitive basis. But if the buildings are separately owned and managed, the first SMATV operator who gains a foothold by signing a contract and installing a satellite dish and associated transmission equipment on one of the buildings would enjoy a powerful cost advantage in competing for the remaining subscribers: He could connect additional buildings for the cost of a few feet of cable, whereas any competitor would have to recover the cost of his own satellite headend facility. Thus, the first operator could charge rates well above his cost and still undercut the competition. This potential for effective monopoly power might theoretically justify regulating the latter class of SMATV systems and not the former.

III

The Court of Appeals quite evidently believed that the crossing or use of a public right-of-way is the only conceivable basis upon which Congress could rationally require local franchising of SMATV systems. As we have indicated, however, there are plausible rationales unrelated to the use of public rights-of-way for regulating cable facilities serving separately owned and managed buildings. The assumptions underlying these rationales may be erroneous, but the very fact that they are "arguable" is sufficient, on rational-basis review, to "immuniz[e]" the congressional choice from constitutional challenge.

The judgment of the Court of Appeals is *reversed*, and the case is *remanded* for further proceedings consistent with this opinion.

So ordered.

When it comes to equal protection, the classification of the interest involved makes all the difference in the world. If there is "discrimination" on the basis of an economic category, the rational basis test applies and the legislation in question is generally upheld. Common observation supports this. A graduated income tax rate is, by definition, discriminatory against those who make more money: they have to pay a higher rate of tax. Yet such classifications based on economics are nearly always upheld.

Not all discriminations, however, are so benign, as is the case when a governmental action impacts a suspect class. Suspect classes have been identified as those pertaining to race, religion, and ethnic origin. If the government passes a law that discriminates on these classifications, the Courts demand that the government provide a "compelling state interest" to justify the discrimination. Just as the rational relationship test is relatively easy to pass, the compelling state interest test is very difficult for a state to pass.

Indeed, one of the very few cases where the courts have upheld such a discrimination has been in issues of national security and in retrospect, some of these cases might be decided differently today. For instance, the following case involved the constitutionality of an executive order that placed Japanese- American in internment camps during World War II. The case also marks one of the first applications of the strict scrutiny test and relates to the earlier discussion of the President's power in a time of emergency.

Korematsu v. United States

323 U.S. 214 (1944)

Mr. Justice Black delivered the opinion of the Court.

The petitioner, an American citizen of Japanese descent, was convicted in a federal district court for remaining in San Leandro, California, a 'Military Area', contrary to Civilian Exclusion Order No. 34 of the Commanding General of the Western Command, U.S. Army, which directed that after May 9, 1942, all persons of Japanese ancestry should be excluded from that area. No question was raised as to petitioner's loyalty to the United States. The Circuit Court of Appeals

Dissent on the Court

"We uphold the exclusion order as of the time it was made and when the petitioner violated it. In doing so, we are not unmindful of the hardships imposed by it upon a large group of American citizens. But hardships are part of war, and war is an aggregation of hardships."

—JUSTICE HUGO BLACK

"Racial discrimination in any form and in any degree has no justifiable part whatever in our democratic way of life. It is unattractive in any setting, but it is utterly revolting among a free people who have embraced the principles set forth in the Constitution of the United States. All residents of this nation are kin in some way by blood or culture to a foreign land. Yet they are primarily and necessarily a part of the new and distinct civilization of the United States. They must, accordingly, be treated at all times as the heirs of the American experiment, and as entitled to all the rights and freedoms guaranteed by the Constitution."

—JUSTICE WILLIAM FRANCIS MURPHY

< Fred Toyosaburo Korematsu, photo courtesy of Karen Korematsu and the Fred T. Korematsu Institute

affirmed, and the importance of the constitutional question involved caused us to grant *certiorari*.

It should be noted, to begin with, that all legal restrictions which curtail the civil rights of a single racial group are immediately suspect. That is not to say that all such restrictions are unconstitutional. It is to say that courts must subject them to the most rigid scrutiny. Pressing public necessity may sometimes justify the existence of such restrictions; racial antagonism never can.

In the instant case prosecution of the petitioner was begun by information charging violation of an Act of Congress, [. . .] which provides that:

> " * * * whoever shall enter, remain in, leave, or commit any act in any military area or military zone prescribed, under the authority of an Executive order of the President, by the Secretary of War, or by any military commander designated by the Secretary of War, contrary to the restrictions applicable to any such area or zone or contrary to the order of the Secretary of War or

> any such military commander, shall, if it appears that he knew or should have known of the existence and extent of the restrictions or order and that his act was in violation thereof, be guilty of a misdemeanor and upon conviction shall be liable to a fine of not to exceed $5,000 or to imprisonment for not more than one year, or both, for each offense."

Exclusion Order No. 34, which the petitioner knowingly and admittedly violated was one of a number of military orders and proclamations, all of which were substantially based upon Executive Order [. . .]. That order, issued after we were at war with Japan, declared that "the successful prosecution of the war requires every possible protection against espionage and against sabotage to national-defense material, national-defense premises, and national-defense utilities. * * * "

Here, as in *Hirabayashi*, *supra*, " * * * we cannot reject as unfounded the judgment of the military authorities and of Congress that there were disloyal members of that population, whose number and strength could not be precisely and quickly ascertained. We cannot say that the war-making branches of the Government did not have ground for believing that in a critical hour such persons could not readily be isolated and separately dealt with, and constituted a menace to the national defense and safety, which demanded that prompt and adequate measures be taken to guard against it."

Like curfew, exclusion of those of Japanese origin was deemed necessary because of the presence of an unascertained number of disloyal members of the group, most of whom we have no doubt were loyal to this country. It was because we could not reject the finding of the military authorities that it was impossible to bring about an immediate segregation of the disloyal from the loyal that we sustained the validity of the curfew order as applying to the whole group. In the instant case, temporary exclusion of the entire group was rested by the military on the same ground. The judgment that exclusion of the whole group was for the same reason a military imperative answers the contention that the exclusion was in the nature of group punishment based on antagonism to those of Japanese origin. That there were members of the group who retained loyalties to Japan has been confirmed by investigations made subsequent to the exclusion. Approximately five thousand American citizens of Japanese ancestry refused to swear unqualified allegiance to the United States and to renounce allegiance to the Japanese Emperor, and several thousand evacuees requested repatriation to Japan.

We uphold the exclusion order as of the time it was made and when the petitioner violated it. In doing so, we are not unmindful of the hardships imposed by it upon a large group of American citizens. But hardships are part of war, and war is an aggregation of hardships. All citizens alike, both in and out of uniform, feel the impact of war in greater or lesser measure. Citizenship has its responsibilities as well as its privileges, and in time of war the burden is always heavier. Compulsory exclusion of large groups of citizens from their homes, except under circumstances of

■ THOUSANDS OF JAPANESE AMERICANS WERE INTERNED AT THE CAMP IN MANZANAR, CALIFORNIA, MAY 1942.

Photo: Dorothea Lange. Prints and Photographs Division, Library of Congress.

direst emergency and peril, is inconsistent with our basic governmental institutions. But when under conditions of modern warfare our shores are threatened by hostile forces, the power to protect must be commensurate with the threatened danger.

* * *

It is said that we are dealing here with the case of imprisonment of a citizen in a concentration camp solely because of his ancestry, without evidence or inquiry concerning his loyalty and good disposition towards the United States. Our task would be simple, our duty clear, were this a case involving the imprisonment of a loyal citizen in a concentration camp because of racial prejudice. Regardless of the true nature of the assembly and relocation centers-and we deem it unjustifiable to call them concentration camps with all the ugly connotations that term implies-we are dealing specifically with nothing but an exclusion order. To cast this case into outlines of racial prejudice, without reference to the real military dangers which were presented, merely confuses the issue. Korematsu was not excluded from the Military Area because of hostility to him or his race. He was excluded because we are at war with the Japanese Empire, because the properly constituted military authorities feared an invasion of our West Coast and felt constrained to take proper security measures, because they decided that the military urgency of the situation demanded that all citizens of Japanese ancestry be segregated from the West Coast temporarily, and finally, because Congress, reposing its confidence in this time of war in our military leaders-as inevitably it must-determined that they should have the power to do just this. There was evidence of disloyalty on the part of some, the military authorities considered that the need for action was great, and time was short. We cannot-by availing ourselves of the calm perspective of hindsight-now say that at that time these actions were unjustified.

Affirmed.

It is hard to find many other cases in which discrimination based on race and ethnicity have been upheld, at least since the mid-twentieth century. In cases of racially-based discrimination, the court asks if there is a compelling state interest to justify the classification rather than whether there was a rational basis for the decision. The compelling state interest test is a much higher standard that is difficult to meet.

There was both legislative and judicial reaction to the Japanese Internment cases. In the mid-1980s, Korematsu brought a petition for *coram nobis*, requesting that the court vacate his earlier conviction based on allegations of earlier government misconduct and suppression of evidence. Judge Patel, the district judge in the case, granted the plaintiff's petition and reminded future judges and lawmakers of their constitutional duties in the trying times of war. He wrote,

> As historical precedent [this case] stands as a constant caution that in times of war or declared military necessity our institutions must be vigilant in protecting constitutional guarantees. It stands as a caution that in times of distress the shield of military necessity and national security must not be used to protect governmental actions from close scrutiny and accountability. It stands as a caution that in times of international hostility and antagonisms that our institutions, legislative, executive, and judicial, must be prepared to exercise their authorities to protect all citizens from the petty fears and prejudices that are so easily aroused.

Executive responses began with President Ford's 1976 repeal of Roosevelt's executive order, which began the initial internment. George H.W. Bush also apologized during his presidency saying, "We can never fully right the wrongs of the past. But we can take a clear stand for justice and recognize that serious injustices were done to the Japanese Americans during World War II." Congress also responded with the passage of the Civil Liberties Act of 1988, which provided surviving internees with reparations.[2]

Increasingly, issues of gender and sexual orientation have been brought to the courts under Equal Protection claims; however, they receive slightly different levels of scrutiny—sometimes known as intermediate scrutiny—than other classifications like those based on race or natural origin, which are reviewed under strict scrutiny. To date these have been evaluated under a "substantial interest test" or intermediate scrutiny test, akin to the standards courts apply in Commercial Speech tests. The government must justify its actions by more than a rational interest, but not as dauntingly as a compelling or strict scrutiny interest. The following two cases illustrate the tests the court employs in gender and sexual orientation cases.

Sometimes the government may pass a law that, on its face, is discriminatory, as some of the cases set out above exemplify. At other times, the language of the statute is neutral on its face, but has a **disparate impact.** In other words, one would not read the statute and conclude that it is biased, but as it is applied, that is exactly what the effect is. The courts become especially interested in such cases if the disparate impact pertains to a suspect class. Typically, these claims also arise in the Title VII context (that is, pertaining to discriminatory acts based on race, religion, color, national origins and gender) and courts have developed different tests to determine the scope of the "impact" and the nature of the disparate treatment. The following case shows one of the Supreme Court's most recent analyses of the disparate impact doctrine.

Ricci v. DeStefano

557 U.S. 557 (2009)

JUSTICE KENNEDY delivered the opinion of the Court.

In the fire department of New Haven, Connecticut—as in emergency-service agencies throughout the Nation—firefighters prize their promotion to and within the officer ranks. An agency's officers command respect within the department and in the whole community; and, of course, added responsibilities command increased salary and benefits. Aware of the intense competition for promotions, New Haven, like many cities, relies on objective examinations to identify the best qualified candidates.

In 2003, 118 New Haven firefighters took examinations to qualify for promotion to the rank of lieutenant or captain. Promotion examinations in New Haven (or City) were infrequent, so the stakes were high. The results would determine which

---

2 For a detailed history of judicial, executive and legislative responses to the cases and Japanese Internment in general, consult Yamamoto, Chon, Izumi, Kang and Wu, *Rights, Race and Reparation: Law and the Japanese American Internment* (2001).

firefighters would be considered for promotions during the next two years, and the order in which they would be considered. Many firefighters studied for months, at considerable personal and financial cost.

When the examination results showed that white candidates had outperformed minority candidates, the mayor and other local politicians opened a public debate that turned rancorous. Some firefighters argued the tests should be discarded because the results showed the tests to be discriminatory. They threatened a discrimination lawsuit if the City made promotions based on the tests. Other firefighters said the exams were neutral and fair. And they, in turn, threatened a discrimination lawsuit if the City, relying on the statistical racial disparity, ignored the test results and denied promotions to the candidates who had performed well. In the end the City took the side of those who protested the test results. It threw out the examinations.

Certain white and Hispanic firefighters who likely would have been promoted based on their good test performance sued the City and some of its officials. Theirs is the suit now before us. The suit alleges that, by discarding the test results, the City and the named officials discriminated against the plaintiffs based on their race, in violation of both Title VII of the Civil Rights Act of 1964 and the Equal Protection Clause of the Fourteenth Amendment. The City and the officials defended their actions, arguing that if they had certified the results, they could have faced liability under Title VII for adopting a practice that had a disparate impact on the minority firefighters. The District Court granted summary judgment for the defendants, and the Court of Appeals affirmed.

We conclude that race-based action like the City's in this case is impermissible under Title VII unless the employer can demonstrate a strong basis in evidence that, had it not taken the action, it would have been liable under the disparate-impact statute. The respondents, we further determine, cannot meet that threshold standard. As a result, the City's action in discarding the tests was a violation of Title VII. In light of our ruling under the statutes, we need not reach the question whether respondents' actions may have violated the Equal Protection Clause.

* * *

The CSB's decision not to certify the examination results led to this lawsuit. The plaintiffs—who are the petitioners here—are 17 white firefighters and 1 Hispanic firefighter who passed the examinations but were denied a chance at promotions when the CSB refused to certify the test results. They include the named plaintiff, Frank Ricci, who addressed the CSB at multiple meetings.

* * *

Petitioners allege that when the CSB refused to certify the captain and lieutenant exam results based on the race of the successful candidates, it discriminated against them in violation of Title VII's disparate-treatment provision. The City counters that its decision was permissible because the tests "appear[ed] to violate Title VII's disparate-impact provisions."

Our analysis begins with this premise: The City's actions would violate the disparate-treatment prohibition of Title VII absent some valid defense. All the evidence demonstrates that the City chose not to certify the examination results because of the statistical disparity based on race—i.e., how minority candidates had performed when compared to white candidates. As the District Court put it, the City rejected the test results because "too many whites and not enough minorities would be promoted were the lists to be certified." Without some other justification, this express, race-based decision making violates Title VII's command that employers cannot take adverse employment actions because of an individual's race.

THE DECISION IN FAVOR OF THE "NEW HAVEN 20" PROVOKED DEBATE ABOUT RACE-BASED ACTIONS THAT CONTINUES TO IMPACT TITLE VII CASES TO THIS DAY.

Cartoon: Bob Englehart

* * *

The racial adverse impact here was significant, and petitioners do not dispute that the City was faced with a *prima facie* case of disparate-impact liability. On the captain exam, the pass rate for white candidates was 64 percent but was 37.5 percent for both black and Hispanic candidates. On the lieutenant exam, the pass rate for white candidates was 58.1 percent; for black candidates, 31.6 percent; and for Hispanic candidates, 20 percent. The pass rates of minorities, which were approximately one-half the pass rates for white candidates, fall well below the 80-percent standard set by the EEOC to implement the disparate-impact provision of Title VII. Based on how the passing candidates ranked and an application of the "rule of three," certifying the examinations would have meant that the City could not have considered black candidates for any of the then-vacant lieutenant or captain positions.

Based on the degree of adverse impact reflected in the results, respondents were compelled to take a hard look at the examinations to determine whether certifying the results would have had an impermissible disparate impact. The problem for respondents is that a *prima facie* case of disparate-impact liability—essentially, a threshold showing of a significant statistical disparity, and nothing more—is far from a strong basis in evidence that the City would have been liable under Title VII had it certified the results. That is because the City could be liable for disparate-impact discrimination only if the examinations were not job related and consistent with business necessity, or if there existed an equally valid, less-discriminatory alternative that served the City's needs but that the City refused to adopt. We conclude there is no strong basis in evidence to establish that the test was deficient in either of these respects. We address each of the two points in turn, based on the record developed by the parties through discovery—a record that concentrates in substantial part on the statements various witnesses made to the CSB.

* * *

On the record before us, there is no genuine dispute that the City lacked a strong basis in evidence to believe it would face disparate-impact liability if it certified the examination results. In other words, there is no evidence—let alone the required strong basis in evidence—that the tests were flawed because they were not job related or because other, equally valid and less discriminatory tests were available to the City. Fear of litigation alone cannot justify an employer's reliance on race to the detriment of individuals who passed the examinations and qualified for promotions. The City's discarding the test results was impermissible under Title VII, and summary judgment is appropriate for petitioners on their disparate-treatment claim.

* * *

As we have discussed at length, the process was open and fair. The problem, of course, is that after the tests were completed, the raw racial results became the predominant rationale for the City's refusal to certify the results. The injury arises in part from the high, and justified, expectations of the candidates who had participated in the testing process on the terms the City had established for the promotional process. Many of the candidates had studied for months, at considerable personal and financial expense, and thus the injury caused by the City's reliance on raw racial statistics at the end of the process was all the more severe. Confronted with arguments both for and against certifying the test results—and threats of a lawsuit either way—the City was required to make a difficult inquiry. But its hearings produced

no strong evidence of a disparate-impact violation, and the City was not entitled to disregard the tests based solely on the racial disparity in the results.

Our holding today clarifies how Title VII applies to resolve competing expectations under the disparate-treatment and disparate-impact provisions. If, after it certifies the test results, the City faces a disparate-impact suit, then in light of our holding today it should be clear that the City would avoid disparate-impact liability based on the strong basis in evidence that, had it not certified the results, it would have been subject to disparate-treatment liability.

. . . The judgment of the Court of Appeals is reversed, and the cases are remanded for further proceedings consistent with this opinion.

Some have argued that cases like these show that in some instances, to solve a lawsuit, you end up buying another one. In other words, no matter what the city chose to do, it would anger a group that might sue the city on the grounds of discrimination because of a disparate impact. Indeed, these kinds of cases show little sign of easing up in the foreseeable future.

NOTES AND COMMENTS on the Legal Environment of Business

1. **MOST STUDENTS FIND** Constitutional Law the easiest area of law to follow because it is so regularly part of the news. While many courts consider constitutional law issues, especially at the Federal level, the U.S. Supreme Court garners most of the attention. The Supreme Court begins its "year" in October and renders its decision in late Spring/early Summer, especially in June, a calendar that fits nicely into the usual academic year. Try to follow the Supreme Court as it decides what cases to hear, as attorneys for each side make oral arguments, and even as commentators try to determine the outcome of a case based on the questions posed by the Justices. In addition to major national newspapers like *the New York Times* or *Washington Post,* some good sources are *www.scotusblog.com, twitter.com/USSupremeCourt, and www.supremecourt.gov.*

2. **AN ONGOING DEBATE** concerning Constitutional interpretation focuses on whether justices should apply the original intent of the framers of the Constitution or whether one should read the Constitution as a developing document. Of course, there are shades of interpretation in between. What do you think is the best way to apply the Constitution to today's issues?

3. **IN CHAPTER FOUR,** you will see that President Franklin Roosevelt considered asking Congress to change the number of justices from nine to a higher number. What do you think the number of justices on the Court should be and why?

4. **THE PRESIDENT NOMINATES** individuals to serve on the Supreme Court and the Senate must approve the nominee. Controversies about choices are not new, but in recent years, especially since the 1987 nomination by President Reagan of Robert Bork, the nomination process has featured highly partisan battles with attempts to uncover anything detrimental to a nominee that would preclude a nomination. Thus, questions about whether a nominee had paid social security taxes on a nanny, one whether the nominee had ever used marijuana, or even what videos the nominee checked out of a video stores have been used to question a nominee's credential. What do you believe is relevant to determine whether a nominee is qualified to serve or the Court or not? What allegations go too far? Where would you draw the line?

NOTES AND COMMENTS on the Ethical Environment of Business

MANY OF THE philosophical precepts that guide contemporary business ethics arose from the same sources that guided the establishment of the United States Constitution. The framers of the Constitution studied concepts of the social contract running from Plato to Hobbes, Rousseau and Locke and finding their way into contemporary ethics of John Rawls and, in business ethics, to the work of Thomas Donaldson and Thomas Dunfee. Notions of the importance of individual rights gave rise to the Bill of Rights and, today, animate rights-based theories by business ethics scholars such as Patricia Werhane. Debates over the nature of human beings and even conceptions of nature and God through Deism today find currency in naturalistic business ethics theories drawn from scholars such as William Frederick. A utilitarian emphasis on majority rule today informs cost-benefit and wider win-win stakeholder analysis. The importance of virtue was crucial to the framers and today is articulated in the field of business ethics by scholars such as Robert Solomon and Ed Hartman.

We have already seen the importance of process in determining the fairness of ethical practices. To repeat earlier chapters, evidence demonstrates that people can adapt to different ethical styles and framing as long as there is notice of what the style and framings are and that they are evenhandedly implemented. Here we see direct corollaries with due process guarantees from the Constitution. The founders were concerned about the power of government to lay taxes and, again as cases in this chapter show, that concern over the fair implementation of taxes remains a concern among businesses today.

So, read through the cases of this chapter with the following questions: Is the decision reached by the court fair? Why or why not? Could the decision have been made more fairly? What would that have looked like? What principles, from the Constitution itself, might you rely on in arguing for better or different results or for a more compelling argument than what the courts provide?

Prior to the 2006 Super Bowl, much was made of the opposing coaches: Tony Dungy of the Indianapolis Colts and Lovie Smith of the Chicago Bears. It was the first time both Super Bowl teams were led by African-American coaches, but the two shared something else. Each of them rely heavily on their spiritual beliefs to guide the coaching philosophy. Officially, as long as there is no discrimination involved, there is no separation of corporation and religion as there is with respect to government. Should there be? Should a leader of an organization, whether a business or a sports team or anyone else, rely on their religious beliefs to inform their leadership? Why or why not? Would you prefer that they at least not talk about their beliefs even if they consider those beliefs to be important? Or does that risk being dishonest? Is it better to be open about who you are as a person and talk about one's beliefs? Or, does that risk offending or threatening others with whom the leader works? The First Amendment does guarantee freedom of religion; in what ways, if any, does this extend to the workplace, especially if the ethical values in the workplace are founded in spirituality?

Chapter 7 features an article about the ethics of government use of data. This article looks at privacy issues. As we have seen, under notions of substantive due process, courts have found that there is a Constitutional right to privacy. If that is the case, then exactly what use, if any, should government make use of data that intrudes on privacy rights? Where would you draw the line? Extending these discussions further, to what extent do you believe that businesses shoud be able to use private data of consumers in order to make more effective marketing decisions and pitches? Or does the right to privacy extend from protection from government to protection from business? Where would you draw the line in such cases?

Finally, with respect to issues of eminent domain, Chapter 10 features an article: *A Close Look at Stadium Subsidies*. Whether through the condemnation of property or spending tax dollars on private stadiums, how heavily should government support business? Are stadium subsidies fair? Should business, following stakeholder theory, consider the impact of the use of taxpayer money and, forgo it unless the company can show tangible benefits to a stakeholder? What might those benefits be? Or, following shareholder theory, should a business try to get as much money from the government, whether through extra spending or through eminent domain, in support of its work?

The Constitution's notions of justice, rights, majority rule, rights to property, due process, and more continue throughout this book and through the ethical environment of business as well. Drawing on Constitutional philosophy does not mean that one is equating being legal and being ethical. Instead, the point is that the underlying philosophies of the Constitution and contemporary business ethics share much and in common and so one can use the understanding of the Constitution in order to help frame issues and make ethical decisions as well.

CHAPTER

3

The Common Law System and Comparative Alternatives

The United States, like many countries with an historical linkage to England, has a common law system. This means that judges play a very strong role in determining the content of the law. In theory, judges are not supposed to do this; they are supposed to interpret, clarify, and apply the law, but given the structure of the common law system itself, even the most reticent judge will end up making some law. In interpreting, clarifying, and applying the law judges have the power to shape the way it affects the community. Supreme Court Justice Antonin Scalia once described the role of the common law judge as, "playing king—devising, out of the brilliance of one's own mind, those laws that ought to govern mankind."[1]

Most countries follow the civil law system, which does not give the same legal authority to judicial precedence. However, both the United States and the United Kingdom are common law countries. In some cases, countries with a common law system lack a constitution. England, for example, does not have a formal constitution, although others, such as the United States, Australia and India do.

As we will see throughout this book, legislatures have the primary responsibility to make law and, through delegation, administrative agencies as well. For example, in the United States, Congress grants, through legislation, certain authorities to the

1 Antonin Scalia, "*Common-Law Courts in a Civil-Law System: The Role of United States Federal Courts in Interpreting the Constitution and Laws.*" *The Tanner Lectures on Human Values, delivered at Princeton University, March 8-9, 1995.*

Food and Drug Administration (FDA) and using those authorities, the FDA can enact regulations that are binding on the people as law. The Executive of the country or state also plays a role in this, not only with respect to enforcing laws (which always has some degree of discretion) but through executive orders as well.

While courts do not have the ability to draft new legislation as Congress does, administrative agencies and the Executive of a country, judges in a common law system can have just as much influence in law-making because of their discretion in interpreting and applying the laws. No court better exemplifies this influence in law-making than the Supreme Court of the United States. The Supreme Court has the authority to review and determine constitutional issues, and thus it has the power to overturn legislation that it finds unconstitutional. In *Roe v. Wade*, 410 U.S. 113 (1973), the Supreme Court found Texas criminal abortion statutes prohibiting abortions at any stage of pregnancy except to save the life of the mother to be unconstitutional. Instead, the Court decided that states only have the power to regulate abortion procedures past the first trimester of pregnancy. Because the Supreme Court is the highest court in the United States, and the United States is a common law society, any challenge to state abortion laws would have to follow the precedent set in *Roe v. Wade*. Thus, with this decision, the Supreme Court effectively legalized all abortions during the first trimester of pregnancy.

IN A COMMON LAW SYSTEM, any citizen (and some non-citizens) can bring a case to court to determine a legal issue without waiting for a legislature to enact or amend a law, as is the case in civil law societies.

I. The Common Law System

IN A COMMON LAW SYSTEM, any citizen (and some non-citizens) can bring a case to court to determine a legal issue without waiting for a legislature to enact or amend a law, as is the case in civil law societies. This keeps an open, fluid legal system ongoing to change and development. It also enhances individual liberty by keeping in the hands of the individual the opportunity for a grievance to be heard and resolved. Common law systems, particularly that of the United States, also rely on the jury system. Not all cases are heard by juries, but many are. The United States is one of the few countries that uses juries regularly. The idea behind juries is that cases should be heard by one's peers and not decided by specialists, so as to check against state power and add legitimacy to legal decisions. This is a strong egalitarian value that further harmonizes the common law system and democracy (though not all democracies utilize the common law system).

At the same time, the common law system has its drawbacks as well. The very nature of individuals being able to file suit means that there is a chance for a lot of lawsuits to be filed. That can clog the system. Indeed, one of the complaints about the system is its slowness. Even in criminal proceedings, when a person's liberty is at stake, it can take up to eight years as it did in *State v. Patin*, for a case to go to trial without the court violating the defendant's constitutional right to a speedy trial.

State v. Patin

95 So. 3d 542 (La. Ct. App. 4th Cir. 2012)

TERRI F. LOVE, JUDGE.

FACTS

Patin and Thomas were charged with shooting Christopher McCrory, Malcolm Green, and Troy Steen on Parc Brittany Court on December 23, 2001. McCrory died as a result of the shooting. Patin became a suspect, and on December 26, 2001, Patin surrendered to the police. Thomas, his brother, accompanied him to the police station and gave a statement. He and Patin were both arrested for the murder. On February 28, 2012, a grand jury returned an indictment charging both of them for the first degree murder of McCrory. They pled not guilty at their arraignment on March 6, 2002. The case was reset for determination of counsel for both defendants, and both defendants appeared with counsel on May 10, 2002. The court held motion hearings on June 14 and July 10, 2002, and at the conclusion of the latter hearing, the court denied the motions to suppress. The court set trial for August 13, 2002.

The matter was reset several times, and on April 20, 2009, the State amended the indictment to charge Thomas and Patin with second degree murder. Counsel for Thomas withdrew; new counsel enrolled in July and filed a motion to sever the trials of Thomas and Patin. The matter was reset several more times, and on August 31, Patin filed a motion to quash the indictment. The court heard the matter on September 10 and denied the motion on statutory grounds. The court held open the opportunity for an evidentiary hearing on each defendants' constitutional claim. On October 28, 2009, after denying the defendants' motion for an evidentiary hearing, the court denied both motions to quash. The court set a trial date of February 1, 2010. Both defendants objected and noted their intent to seek writs, and the court granted the defendants until November 30. On January 4, 2010, the court set the matter for January 13 for the State to indicate which defendant it intended to try first. On January 13, the State elected to try Patin first, and the court ruled that all dates previously set were to remain in effect.

This court granted both Patin's and Thomas' writ applications, vacated the court's denial of their motions to quash, and remanded the cases with the instructions to allow the defendants to present evidence on the issue of prejudice from the delay in going to trial.

On remand, the court heard the matter on February 4, 2010. At the conclusion of the hearing, the court granted both motions to quash only on the issue of the violation of the defendants' constitutional right to speedy trial. The State noted its intent to appeal, and the court stayed the release of the defendants to allow the State time to file its appeal. On February 10, the court denied the defendants' motion for release pending the State's appeal. Both defendants sought writs, which this court granted, ordering the defendants' release. However, the Supreme Court reversed this court's release, ordering a stay of their release until further orders from that Court. The Court then ordered the State to file its appeal "forthwith" and this court to give the State's appeal expedited consideration.

Thomas filed a writ in this court seeking reversal of the trial court's denial of his motion to quash on statutory speedy trial grounds. This court denied writs, noting that it did not have jurisdiction to consider the application because of the State's pending appeal. Thomas sought relief in the Supreme Court. The Court granted the writ. The Court also directed this court to give the appeal expedited consideration. Patin, however, did not seek review of the trial court's denial of his motion to quash on statutory grounds.

On remand, a jury found Thomas not guilty on October 7, 2010. On October 18, 2010, the State amended the bill of indictment to charge Patin with manslaughter, and Patin pled guilty as charged, reserving his right to appeal the trial court's denial of his motion to quash. The court sentenced him to serve ten years at hard labor and granted his motion for appeal.

OPINION

Appellant contends his constitutional right to a speedy trial has been violated because over eight years elapsed between the filing of the first indictment and the filing of his motion to quash. This issue was raised, fully discussed, and rejected by this court in the State's prior appeal of the trial court's granting of the motion to quash. For this reason, the State argues that this issue should not be considered in this appeal, citing the "law of the case" doctrine.

. . . The "law of the case" doctrine applies to all prior rulings or decisions of an appellate court or the Supreme Court in the same case, not merely those arising from the full appeal process. This policy applies to parties who were parties to the case when the former decision was rendered and who thus had their day in court. The reasons for the "law of the case" doctrine is to avoid relitigation of the same issue; to promote consistency of result in the same litigation; and to promote efficiency and fairness to both parties by affording a single opportunity for the argument and decision of the matter at issue.

. . . Considering that this court has already found that Appellant Patin's constitutional right to a speedy trial has not been violated, and he has presented no new evidence to dispute this ruling, this court will not reconsider this matter under the "law of the case" doctrine.

Appellant Patin also argues that his statutory right to a speedy trial has been violated because the State failed to bring him to trial within the statutory limits. . . . In cases in which there is interruption, the time limitations set forth in La.C.Cr.P. art. 578 start anew. Once the time limitations . . . have expired, the trial court shall dismiss the charge upon the defendant's filing of a motion to quash the bill . . . Nonetheless, according to La.C.Cr.P. art. 580, once a defendant files a motion to quash "or other preliminary plea," the time limitations are suspended until the court rules on the motion, "but in no case shall the state have less than one year after the ruling to commence trial."

In addition, this court has held that the delays caused by Hurricane Katrina constituted a "cause beyond the control of the State" which interrupted the time periods. . . . This court set June 5, 2006, as the date upon which interruption based upon Hurricane Katrina ended.

In the case at hand, the grand jury returned the indictment on October 17, 2002. Appellant Patin filed his first motion to quash the indictment on October 30, 2002, thereby suspending the three-year prescriptive period to bring him to trial. He also filed a motion to adopt for all defendants any pleadings filed by any defendant. The court denied the motion to quash on January 27, 2003, thereby giving the State at least until January 27, 2004 to try him. On July 22, 2003, Appellant filed a second motion to quash, which again suspended the time period. There is no evidence in the record that the court ruled on that particular motion, but on August 20, 2003, Appellant moved to continue his trial. The motion was granted, and at that point, the State had until at least August 20, 2004 to try him. On January 30, 2004, Appellant Patin joined the State in a motion to continue his trial, giving the State until at least January 30, 2005 to try him. On April 20, 2004, Appellant Patin again moved to continue trial, thereby granting the State until April 20, 2005, to try him. Appellant subsequently moved to continue trial on June 17, 2004, and then on January 21, 2005, he joined in a motion to continue trial, giving the State until at least January 21, 2006, to try him. Appellant Patin again moved to continue the trial on March 11, 2005, giving the State until March 11, 2006, to try him.

> **"THE DEFENDANTS have been incarcerated for almost nine years. This delay, even though partially attributable to actions of the public defender's office and a disaster . . . is simply unacceptable in a criminal justice system based upon a presumption of innocence until proven guilty."**
>
> — Dissent of Judge Lombard

Hurricane Katrina struck New Orleans on August 29, 2005, and the time limitations of La.C.Cr.P. art. 578 were interrupted . . . Regarding the constitutional speedy trial claim, and on remand from this court's ruling, the trial court held an evidentiary hearing on February 4, 2010. At the conclusion of which it granted Appellant's and Thomas' motions to quash based upon constitutional grounds. Again, the State could not try the appellant, and it appealed this ruling. This court reversed the quashing of the bill of information on June 27, 2010. This gave the State until June 27, 2011, to try Appellant. In early October 2010, the Appellant Patin filed more preliminary motions, which the court denied on October 14, 2010.

Appellant subsequently pled guilty . . . **This court fully considered Appellant Patin's constitutional right to speedy trial claim in the 2010 appeal, and he has presented no new evidence to show that this court erred in its 2010 ruling. Thus, pursuant to the "law of the case" doctrine, this court's previous ruling will not be considered. Additionally, we find that Appellant Patin's statutory speedy trial claim has no merit. . . .** Accordingly, the findings of the trial court are affirmed.

In this case, the defendant's right to a speedy trial was not considered violated after over eight years of pre-trial delays because under Louisiana state law, in cases where there is an interruption, the statutory time limitations for right to a speedy trial start anew. Furthermore, the "law of the case" doctrine precludes a court from reviewing an issue in a case that has been previously decided by that court or by a higher court. A defendant can't keep delaying trials and then complain that s/he didn't get a speedy trial.

With many cases, and many heard by juries, there is a fear of unpredictability that makes planning in a business context difficult.. If one knows what the law is, one can make plans for how to arrange one's business decisions. If the law is unpredictable, it is difficult to make such plans.

In 2012, the U.S. Court of Appeals D.C. Circuit handed down a much anticipated decision that had the potential to adversely affect many small businesses. *AKM, LLC dba Volks Constructors v. Secretary of Labor,* 675 F.3d 752 (2012), arose from a citation from the Occupational Safety and Health Administration for an employer's improper recording of workplace injuries that occurred as many as five years earlier. The statute of limitations on such citations was previously understood to be six months from the occurrence of a violation.

The importance of precedent tries to address some of these downsides. The Latin term for precedent, *stare decisis*, means: Let the decision stand. In other words, once a court has decided a case, other similar cases in that jurisdiction should be decided the same way. If a court in one jurisdiction determines that a person driving a car over the speed limit is liable for damages when the car injures a pedestrian, a case involving another driver who injures a pedestrian while driving over the speed limit will be decided the same way.

However, there are different degrees of legal authority when it comes to cases providing precedent. There is mandatory authority and persuasive authority. **Mandatory authority** applies in cases where the legal issue has already been decided by a higher court in that jurisdiction or by the Supreme Court of the United States. For example, a trial court in Los Angeles must follow the legal precedent set by the Second District Court of Appeals in California, and the Court of Appeals in California must follow the decisions of the Supreme Court of California. So if the

Supreme Court of California has determined liability for that driver who hit a pedestrian, then when a similar case comes up in the Los Angeles County Court, the judge there will be guided by that precedent. In California, as with the other states, the court process typically begins with a trial court with appeal rights to higher courts.

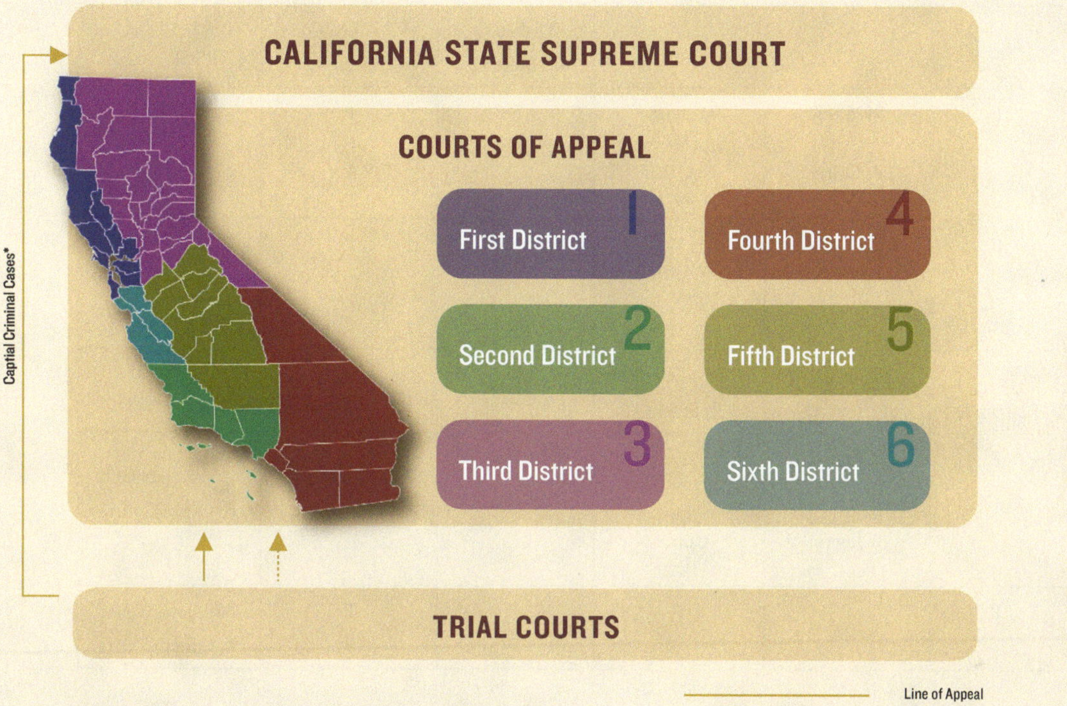

* Death Penalty cases are automatically appealed form the superior court to the Supreme Court

On a state-to-federal level, because of the separation of powers between state and federal law, decisions from federal courts are not binding on state courts unless the legal issue is pertaining to federal law. Similarly, state court decisions on issues of state law are mandatory authority for federal courts interpreting state law.

Persuasive authority is not binding. Generally speaking, persuasive authority tends to come from the same jurisdiction and the higher up the court, the more persuasive the authority. However, decisions by lower courts within the same jurisdiction can also be considered persuasive. On a federal level, District Court decisions from different districts are not binding on one another but are considered very persuasive. For example, if a case is pending in the Eighth District and the Third District has been known to hand down consistent decisions on antitrust cases, a judge from the Eighth District may find a Third District opinion to be very persuasive.

The following chart provides an easy way of determining when authority is mandatory and when it is persuasive:

Mandatory or Persuasive Authority?

	COURT AFFECTED BY DECISION					
Court Issuing Decision	US Supreme	Federal Appeals	Federal District	State Supreme	State Appellate	State Trial
US Supreme	M	M	M	M: Fed Q P: State Q	M: Fed Q P: State Q	M: Fed Q P: State Q
Federal Appellate	P	M: Same Circuit P: Other Courts	M: Same Circuit P: Other Courts	P	P	P
Federal District	P	P	M: Same District P: Other Courts	P	P	P
STATE SUPREME	M : Fed Q P: State Q	M : Fed Q P: State Q	M : Fed Q P: State Q	M	M	M
STATE APPELLATE	P	M: Same State Appellate Ct P: Other Courts	M: Same State Appellate Ct P: Other Courts	P	M: Same State Appellate Ct P: Other Courts	M: Same State Appellate Ct P: Other Courts
State Trial	P	P	P	P	P	M: Same Court P: Other Courts

In the United States, the American Law Institute publishes a collection of rules that reflect modern common law, called the Restatements. The Restatements cover many areas of law, including torts, contracts, agency, property, and foreign relations of the United States. While courts are not bound by the Restatements, as they reflect the case law of the majority of states, many courts tend to consider the Restatements persuasive authority. It is also interesting to note that the Restatements are drafted by a community of lawyers, judges and scholars, meaning lawyers and legal scholars also have the ability to influence the development of law. While the Restatements are often based on precedent from the majority of states, its drafters also suggest new rules that reflect developments or changes in the legal field.

Precedent in our legal system serves several interests. One is that it does make the law more predictable. If one knows what the law is concerning a situation, then one can know the likely consequences of one's actions. This predictability promotes another interest, which is fairness. As any three year old will realize (and verbally assert), it is manifestly unfair if she gets in trouble for doing the same thing that her sibling just got away with. In a legal setting the sentiment is the same: factually similar cases should be decided similarly. A final interest promoted by precedent is efficiency. This partners with predictability, in that one can efficiently and knowingly undertake actions that accord with the law. In the following case, the Supreme Court found that in the absence of legislation applicable to a particular industry, the parties are entitled to the benefits of *stare decisis*.

Flood v. Kuhn

407 U.S. 258 (1972)

BACKGROUND

Curtis Charles Flood, a professional baseball player was 'traded' to another team without his previous knowledge or consent. Flood brought this antitrust suit after being refused the right to make his own contract with another major league team, which is not permitted under the reserve system. The District Court rendered judgment in favor of defendants, and the Court of Appeals affirmed.

The District Court trial took place in May and June 1970. An extensive record was developed. In an ensuing opinion, Judge Cooper first noted that:

> 'Plaintiff's witnesses in the main concede that some form of reserve on players is a necessary element of the organization of baseball as a league sport, but contend that the present all-embracing system is needlessly restrictive and offer various alternatives which in their view might loosen the bonds without sacrifice to the game. . . .
>
> 'Clearly the preponderance of credible proof does not favor elimination of the reserve clause. With the sole exception of plaintiff himself, it shows that even plaintiff's witnesses do not contend that it is wholly undesirable; in fact they regard substantial portions meritorious. . . .'

He then held that *Federal Baseball Club v. National League*, (1922), and *Toolson v. New York Yankees, Inc.*, (1953), were controlling; that it was not necessary to reach the issue whether exemption from the antitrust laws would result because aspects of baseball now are a subject of collective bargaining; that the plaintiff's state-law claims, those based on common law as well as on statute, were to be denied because baseball was not 'a matter which admits of diversity of treatment,'; that the involuntary servitude claim failed because of the absence of 'the essential element of this cause of action, a showing of compulsory service,' and that judgment was

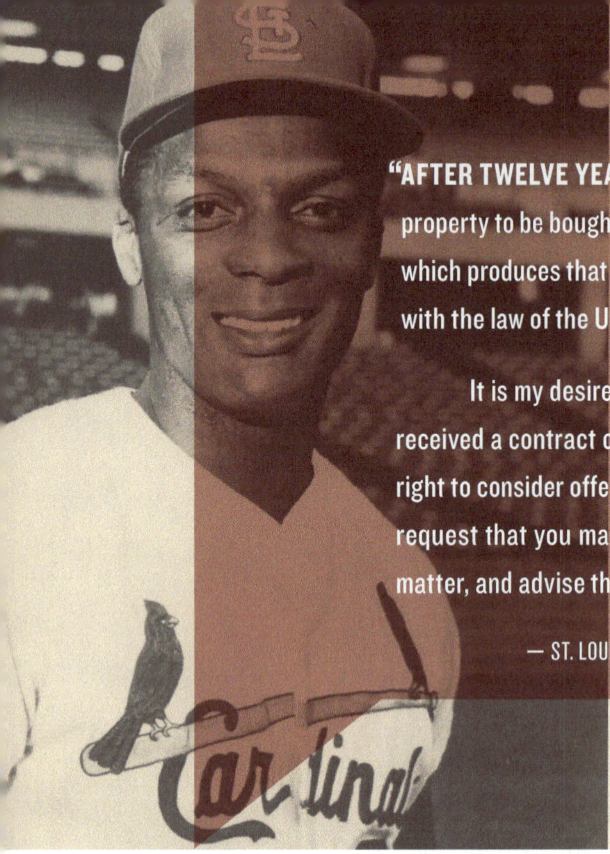

"**AFTER TWELVE YEARS** in the Major Leagues, I do not feel that I am a piece of property to be bought and sold irrespective of my wishes. I believe that any system which produces that result violates my basic rights as a citizen and is inconsistent with the law of the United States and of several States.

It is my desire to play baseball in 1970, and I am capable of playing. I have received a contract offer from the Philadelphia Club, but I believe that I have the right to consider offers from other clubs before making any decisions. I, therefore, request that you make known to all the Major League Clubs my feelings in this matter, and advise them of my availablility for the 1970 season."

— ST. LOUIS CARDINAL CURT FLOOD TO BOWIE KUHN, COMMISSIONER OF BASEBALL IN 1969

to be entered for the defendants. Judge Cooper included a statement of personal conviction to the effect that 'negotiations could produce an accommodation on the reserve system which would be eminently fair and equitable to all concerned' and that 'the reserve clause can be fashioned so as to find acceptance by player and club.'

On appeal, the Second Circuit felt 'compelled to affirm.' It regarded the issue of state law as one of first impression, but concluded that the Commerce Clause precluded its application. Judge Moore added a concurring opinion in which he predicted, with respect to the suggested overruling of *Federal Baseball* and *Toolson*, that 'there is no likelihood that such an event will occur.'

HOLDING

Mr. Justice Blackmun

In view of all this, it seems appropriate now to say that:

1. Professional baseball is a business and it is engaged in interstate commerce.

2. With its reserve system enjoying exemption from the federal antitrust laws, baseball is, in a very distinct sense, an exception and an anomaly. *Federal Baseball* and *Toolson* have become an aberration confined to baseball.

3. Even though others might regard this as 'unrealistic, inconsistent, or illogical,' . . . the aberration is an established one, and one that has been recognized not only in *Federal Baseball* and *Toolson*, but in *Shubert*, *International Boxing*, and *Radovich*, as well, a total of five consecutive cases in this Court. It is an aberration that has been with us now for half a century, one heretofore deemed fully entitled to the benefit of *stare decisis*, and one that has survived the Court's expanding concept of interstate commerce. It rests on a recognition and an acceptance of baseball's unique characteristics and needs.

4. Other professional sports operating interstate-football, boxing, basketball, and, presumably, hockey and golf-are not so exempt.

5. The advent of radio and television, with their consequent increased coverage and additional revenues, has not occasioned an overruling of *Federal Baseball* and *Toolson*.

6. The Court has emphasized that since 1922 baseball, with full and continuing congressional awareness, has been allowed to develop and to expand unhindered by federal legislative action. Remedial legislation has been introduced repeatedly in Congress but none has ever been enacted. The Court, accordingly, has concluded that Congress as yet has had no intention to subject baseball's reserve system to the reach of the antitrust statutes. This, obviously, has been deemed to be something other than mere congressional silence and passivity.

7. The Court has expressed concern about the confusion and the retroactivity problems that inevitably would result with a judicial overturning of *Federal Baseball*. It has voiced a preference that if any change is to be made, it come by legislative action that, by its nature, is only prospective in operation.

. . .

We continue to be loath, 50 years after *Federal Baseball* and almost two decades after *Toolson*, to overturn those cases judicially when Congress, by its positive inaction, has allowed those decisions to stand for so long and, far beyond mere inference and implication, has clearly evinced a desire not to disapprove them legislatively.

. . . The conclusion we have reached makes it unnecessary for us to consider the respondents' additional argument that the reserve system is a mandatory subject of collective bargaining and that federal labor policy therefore exempts the reserve system from the operation of federal antitrust laws.

We repeat for this case what was said in *Toolson*:

> 'Without re-examination of the underlying issues, the (judgment) below (is) affirmed on the authority of *Federal Baseball Club of Baltimore v. National League of Professional Baseball Clubs*, *supra*, so far as that decision determines that Congress had no intention of including the business of baseball within the scope of the federal antitrust laws.'

And what the Court said in *Federal Baseball* in 1922 and what it said in *Toolson* in 1953, we say again here in 1972: the remedy, if any is indicated, is for congressional, and not judicial, action.

The judgment of the Court of Appeals is affirmed.

This case demonstrates the reluctance of courts to overturn precedent. Unless there is a strong reason the precedent is no longer just, the courts are likely to rule the same way they have in the past and defer any changes in the law to the legislature. Yet there are times and places where the courts will differentiate among cases to chip away at precedent.

Change and development in the law occurs because no two cases are exactly alike. There will always be cases arising with sets of unique factual details that provide room for courts to distinguish a new case before it from past precedent. One might think, for example, that because of the Court's ruling in *Flood,* all baseball-related activities are also exempt from antitrust considerations. After all, the unwillingness of the *Flood* court to interfere with the antitrust exemptions established by Congress and the Court's insistence that any changes to those exemptions need to be done by Congress and not the Courts, seems to suggest that baseball is in a category by itself. Yet the following case shows the willingness of judges to distinguish from one case to another so that different sets of rules might be applicable.

Butterworth v. Nat'l League of Professional Baseball Clubs

644 So. 2d 1021 (Fla. 1994)

HARDING, JUSTICE

FACTS

This case arose from the unsuccessful attempt of a group of investors to purchase the San Francisco Giants Major League Baseball franchise and relocate it to Tampa Bay, Florida. After the baseball owners voted against approval of the sale to the Tampa investors and the Giants owner signed a contract to sell the franchise to a group of San Francisco investors, Florida Attorney General Robert Butterworth (Attorney General) issued antitrust civil investigative demands (CIDs) to the National League of Professional Baseball Clubs and its president William D. White (National League) pursuant to section 542.28, Florida Statutes (Supp.1992). According to the CIDs, the specific focus of the investigation was "[a] combination or conspiracy in restraint of trade in connection with the sale and purchase of the San Francisco Giants baseball franchise."

* * *

OPINION

We have for review *Butterworth v. National League of Professional Baseball Clubs* (1993), in which the Fifth District Court of Appeal certified the following question to be one of great public importance:

> **Does the antitrust exemption for baseball recognized by the United States Supreme Court in *Federal Baseball Club of Baltimore, Inc. v. National League of Professional Baseball Clubs* (1922) and its progeny exempt all decisions involving the sale and location of baseball franchises from federal and Florida antitrust law?**

We answer the certified question in the negative and quash the decision below because we find that baseball's antitrust exemption extends only to the reserve system.

The United States Supreme Court originally recognized some form of antitrust law exemption for baseball in *Federal Baseball Club, Inc. v. National League of Professional Baseball Clubs*, (1922). That case involved an antitrust action by a baseball club of the Federal League against the National League and the American League, alleging a conspiracy to monopolize the baseball business. The Supreme Court concluded that the federal antitrust laws were inapplicable because the business at issue, "giving exhibitions of base ball," did not involve interstate commerce. Although the Supreme Court reaffirmed that exemption in the subsequent case of *Toolson v. New York Yankees, Inc.*, (1953), it did so "[w]ithout re-examination of the underlying issues." Instead, the Supreme Court affirmed the judgments of the courts of appeals in three consolidated cases brought against baseball owners on the authority of *Federal Baseball*, "so far as that decision determines that Congress had no intention of including the business of baseball within the scope of the federal antitrust laws." The Supreme Court noted that Congress "has not seen fit to bring such business under [the antitrust] laws by legislation" and concluded that any such application "should be by legislation." In a later case, the Supreme Court described *Toolson* as "a narrow application of the rule of *stare decisis*." *United States v.*

Shubert (1955) (finding that business built around the performance of local theatrical productions is subject to antitrust laws).

In response to attempts to extend the reasoning of *Federal Baseball* beyond the context of baseball, the Court specifically limited the antitrust exemption to "the business of organized professional baseball."

The Supreme Court directly addressed the baseball exemption for the third and most recent time in *Flood v. Kuhn*, (1972). In *Flood*, a player challenged professional baseball's reserve system, whereby the player was traded to another franchise without his knowledge or consent. The Supreme Court affirmed the lower court's judgment dismissing the complaint based upon the controlling authority of *Federal Baseball* and *Toolson*. The Supreme Court also made a number of findings, including the following: professional baseball is a business engaged in interstate commerce; the exemption from antitrust laws is an exception, an anomaly, and an aberration confined to baseball; the exemption is an established one that is entitled to the benefits of *stare decisis;* and any change in the exemption should come through legislative action and should be prospective only in operation.

Based upon the Supreme Court's trilogy of baseball cases, baseball clearly enjoys some form of exemption from antitrust laws. However, there is some disagreement as to the scope of that exemption.

The parties in the instant case view the parameters of the exemption from equally differing perspectives. The Attorney General contends that the exemption only applies to the reserve clause system. The National League asserts that the exemption applies broadly to "the business of baseball," which includes decisions regarding the sale and location of franchises.

Several federal courts have interpreted the scope of the exemption broadly. For example, the United States Court of Appeals for the Seventh Circuit concluded that the "Supreme Court intended to exempt the business of baseball, not any particular facet of that business, from the federal antitrust laws."

However, in a recent decision involving two Pennsylvania citizens who were part of the same investment group as the Tampa Bay investors in the instant case the United States District Court for the Eastern District of Pennsylvania stated that the "antitrust exemption created by *Federal Baseball* is limited to baseball's reserve system. After an extensive analysis of the Supreme Court's baseball trilogy, the *Piazza* court concluded that *Flood* invalidated the rule *stare decisis* of *Federal Baseball* and *Toolson* and left only the result *stare decisis* under the facts of the case, namely the exemption of baseball's reserve system from federal antitrust law.

Even though the *Piazza* court is the only federal court to have interpreted baseball's antitrust exemption so narrowly, the language of the *Flood* opinion supports such an interpretation. In *Flood*, the Supreme Court itself characterized the trilogy of cases in this manner: "For the third time in 50 years the Court is asked specifically to rule that professional baseball's reserve system is within the reach of the federal antitrust laws." In discussing the reasons why the Supreme Court followed *Federal*

***Baseball* in *Toolson*, the Court cited baseball's development between 1922 and 1953 "upon the understanding that the reserve system was not subject to existing federal antitrust laws." In listing its eight findings regarding baseball and the exemption, the Court twice described the exemption as applying to the "reserve system." First, in concluding that baseball's status is "an exception and an anomaly" and that "*Federal Baseball* and *Toolson* have become an aberration confined to baseball," the Court described baseball's "reserve system [as] enjoying exemption from federal antitrust laws." Second, the Court concluded that "Congress as yet has had no intention to subject baseball's reserve system to the reach of the antitrust statutes."**

The Supreme Court also rejected the rationale of *Federal Baseball* when it stated that "professional baseball is a business . . . engaged in interstate commerce." The *Piazza* opinion includes a thorough analysis of what this rejection of the analytical underpinnings of *Federal Baseball* means to the precedential value of *Federal Baseball and Toolson.* The court concluded that those cases have no precedential value beyond the particular facts involved, i.e., the reserve clause. The *Piazza* court also noted that the other federal cases which have construed the exemption broadly have not engaged in such an analysis of the Supreme Court's baseball trilogy.

In *Finley*, the Seventh Circuit Court of Appeals rejected the plaintiff's argument that the exemption applies only to the reserve system. The plaintiff argued that the Supreme Court's references to the reserve system in *Flood* supported a narrow interpretation of the exemption. Despite the references in *Flood* to the reserve system, the *Finley* court concluded that the language in the three baseball cases and *Radovich* shows that "the Supreme Court intended to exempt the business of baseball, not any particular facet of that business, from the federal antitrust laws." The United States District Court for the Eastern District of Louisiana agreed with the *Finley* court's interpretation of the baseball exemption and rejected the "cramped view" of the *Piazza* court, even though it found the "reasoning impressive."

There is no question that *Piazza* is against the great weight of federal cases regarding the scope of the exemption. However, none of the other cases have engaged in such a comprehensive analysis of *Flood* and its implications. In fact, many of the cases simply state that baseball is exempt and cite to one or more of the baseball trilogy without any discussion at all. Although the *Finley* opinion does contain analysis and discussion, the court simply cites "business of baseball" language from the baseball trilogy and disregards the Supreme Court's references in *Flood* to the reserve system and its own characterization of the exemption as involving the reserve system. Moreover, *Finley* contains no analysis of what implications the *Flood* findings have on the precedential value of *Federal Baseball* and *Toolson.*

The Supreme Court's "Baseball Trilogy"

BasebalL's Antitrust exEmption was established through decisions in three supreme court cases:

- *Federal Baseball Club of Baltimore, Inc. v. National League of Professional Baseball Clubs*
- *Toolson v. New York Yankees*
- *Flood v. Kuhn*

The Supreme Court's determination in *Flood* that professional baseball "is engaged in interstate commerce," directly contradicts the determination in *Federal*

Baseball that baseball exhibitions are "purely state affairs" and thus do not constitute "commerce among the States." This rejection of the very reason that the Court recognized such an exemption in *Federal Baseball* seriously undercuts the precedential value of both *Federal Baseball* and *Toolson*. **Based upon the language and the findings in *Flood*, we come to the same conclusion as the *Piazza* court: baseball's antitrust exemption extends only to the reserve system.**

Accordingly, we answer the certified question in the negative, quash the decision below, and remand this case for proceedings consistent with this opinion.

While plaintiffs in previous antitrust cases involving professional baseball could not prevail in court because of the antitrust exemption for professional baseball, the Florida Supreme Court found differently in this case because the business in question was not the business of baseball (aka the "reserve system") but instead a facet of that business—the sale and purchase of a franchise.

Sometimes, a court will distinguish a case on the basis of law. That is, the court doesn't try to say that the case before the court provides a different set of facts than what has been controlled by previous precedent, but instead that the underlying law of the particular case might itself need to change. This is particularly true when an older or outdated law is being relied upon. Over the years, a series of other cases may have chipped away at various principles that, together, had been the basis for a previous decision. But with weakened precedent, the time may finally come for the case to be overturned on the basis of an interpretation of current law.

Lawrence v. City of New York

82 A.D.2d 485, 447 N.Y.S.2d 506 (2d Dep't 1981)

BACKGROUND

On February 2, 1971, plaintiff was employed as a fireman by the New York City Fire Department. While on a break in the backyard of premises where he and other fire fighters had been fighting a fire in the building thereon, plaintiff was struck by a couch pushed or thrown from the building. On or about February 8, 1972, plaintiff brought the within action against the appellant City of New York (hereinafter the city).

Although there was some evidence respecting the failure of the city to have had a lookout stationed on the ground below in preparation for defenestration of smoldering items that might reignite the building, the thrust of plaintiff's case at the trial, limited to the issue of liability, was directed toward the alleged negligence of those who threw or pushed the couch from the building.

At the end of the trial, the jury, in response to interrogatories, held that the negligence of the city had been the proximate cause of the accident, and that plaintiff had not been guilty of contributory negligence nor had he assumed the risk of the incident which caused the injuries.

. . .

The rule that the employer is not liable for injuries caused solely by the negligence of a servant was first promulgated in England in 1837. Shortly thereafter it became recognized in the United States as well. One of the bases for the **fellow-servant rule** was that it would promote the safety of the public and all servants to make each one watchful of the conduct of others for his own protection. While such reason and others might have been appropriate to small enterprises and shops because of the close contact and acquaintance one workman had with the others, they had little validity in the industrial area where one employee might be injured by the negligence of a co-employee whom he had never seen. According to one writer, the explanation of the rule probably lay in the highly individualistic viewpoint of courts in common law, and their desire to encourage industrial undertakings by making the burden upon employers as light as possible.

"THE FELLOW-SERVANT RULE" was a rule of tort law created in the mid-nineteenth century. It carved out an exception to the well-established rule of *respondeat superior*, and relieved employers of liability for injuries negligently inflicted by any employee upon a "fellow servant." The rule did not exist until 1837, when it was first pronounced in England by Lord Abinger in *Priestley v. Fowler*. In 1842 Chief Justice Lemuel Shaw of Massachiusetts gave the rule its American reception and rationale in the leading case of *Farwell v. Boston & Worcester Rail Road*. By 1880 the rule, in one form or another, was so firmly entrenched in nearly every American jurisdiction that late nineteenth-century treatise writers warned legislatures and courts against tampering with "a rule of the common law, based upon the wisdom and precedents of the ages."

–*The Creation of a Common Law Rule: The Fellow-Servant Rule, 1837-1860; University of Pennsylvania Law Review Vol. 139:579.*

Although it is true that slow progress toward imposition of liability upon an employer occurred as a result of decisions in common law cases, the impetus in that direction was greatly accelerated by the passage of workers' compensation acts. In fact it has been held that the fellow-servant rule practically disappeared with workers' compensation.

However, workers' compensation acts, at least in the earlier years, have been held not to cover the injuries of many categories of employees, such as farm laborers. In the absence of remedial legislation, such as workers' compensation laws, courts in many jurisdictions concluded that an employee's action against his employer was still subject, *inter alia*, to the fellow-servant rule defense.

In this State, although it has been held that a New York City policeman and a New York City fireman are not entitled to benefits under the Workers' Compensation Law, the absence of such coverage was not used as a basis for upholding the fellow-servant rule against a member of the city's uniformed officers. Rather . . . a majority of the Justices of this court hearing the appeal, in applying the fellow-servant rule, did not refer to the absence of Workers' Compensation coverage for the injured policeman . . .

. . . However, the Court of Appeals reversed this court's order dismissing the complaint under the fellow-servant rule and reinstated the trial court's judgment in favor of plaintiff. In rejecting the applicability of the fellow-servant doctrine, JUDGE FULD, writing for the majority, stated that the purpose of section 50-a of the General Municipal Law was to impose liability upon the city for the negligent operation of vehicles by police officers and other municipal officers and thereby overcome the hardship visited upon those who, injured by such negligence, would otherwise be without remedy. According to the majority there was no reason for not extending the relief afforded private persons under 50-a to the police driver's fellow officers as well, since the Legislature had not provided for their exclusion from the provisions of 50-a.

Of particular significance with respect to the case at bar is the strong criticism of the fellow-servant rule found in JUDGE FULD's majority opinion in *Poniatowski*:

> "The inherent injustice of a rule which denies a person, free of fault, the right to recover for injuries sustained through the negligence of another over whose conduct he has no control merely because of the fortuitous circumstance that the other is a fellow officer is manifest. Dean Prosser has characterized the fellow-servant rule as 'wicked' (Prosser, *Torts* [2d ed., 1955], p. 383), and one court has described it as resulting in 'gross injustice' and as 'callous to human rights'. This may well suggest the desirability of abolishing the rule but we leave decision of that question to the future."

As is evident from both the majority and dissenting opinions of the Court of Appeals in *Poniatowski*, all seven members of this State's highest tribunal had severe reservations about the viability of the fellow-servant rule in this era. However, since the majority believed that the rule was not applicable in that case because of the provisions of section 50-a of the General Municipal Law, it left for the future the decision as to whether the rule should be abolished. We strongly believe that such "future" has arrived in the case at bar.

In our opinion this bench has three options, (1) it may determine that the fellow-servant rule is not applicable under an exception to the rule and thus sustain plaintiff's verdict; or (2) it may apply the rule and thus nonsuit the plaintiff; or (3) it may hold that the fellow-servant rule is no longer viable and thus affirm the order and sustain plaintiff's verdict.

With respect to the first two options, it has been stated that because of the great injustice stemming from the application of the fellow-servant rule, courts have been astute to engraft upon it so many modifications that little is left of its original import. It has also been noted that courts have carved out so many exceptions to the applicability of the rule that many have come to be considered as part of the original rule. Amongst the multitudinous number of exceptions to the rule are the nondelegable duty to furnish a safe place to work, the duty to instruct and to warn, the "vice principal rule," the "superior servant rule," the "different department rule," the "dangerous agency rule," *ad infinitum.*

In our opinion it is both illogical and self-defeating to continue a practice of engrafting exception after exception upon a flawed rule of law, which was founded not on natural justice but on an absurd and disingenuous public policy, and which has been universally discredited almost from its inception. Such action might well be compared to the engrafting of roses upon a large weed in the vain hope that the latter will no longer constitute both a threat to beneficial growth in the garden and an eyesore to the landscape. Creating exceptions to the rule does not destroy its lamented and unwanted existence, but instead leaves it readily available for judicial decisions shocking to society's sense of justice.

"THE THEORY . . . that public policy requires that servants, injured as a result of the negligence of a co-servant, should have no remedy against their masters, because the absence of any remedy will make them more careful of their own safety than they would otherwise be, not only is untenable but is fallacious."

With respect to the rule itself, the theory upon which it is based, i.e., that public policy requires that servants, injured as a result of the negligence of a co-servant, should have no remedy against their masters, because the absence of any remedy will make them more careful of their own safety than they would otherwise be, not only is untenable but is fallacious. Unlike the relation of the master with a third person which is one of arm's length, the servant is obligated to the former under a bond of fidelity and loyalty. Under the fellow-servant rule the servant, in addition, must be endowed with a prescience and ultra sensory perception in order to forewarn him of the careless propensities of his working counterparts.

> "[I]t is indeed strange that we should go on holding that the master is liable to everyone else in the world for the negligent acts of the employee whom he selects, while acting within the scope of his employment, except to the fellow-servant or employee, who is usually more apt to be injured than any member of the general public, and who has usually, by the master's orders, been subject to the peril of such negligence on the part of his fellow servant, in the selection of which fellow servant the injured servant had no voice whatever. Such a doctrine shocks our sense of justice. *The general rule of respondeat superior should not any longer contain an exception which is so callous to human rights.*"

Accordingly, I conclude that the fellow-servant rule is no longer viable in this State and is hereby abrogated.

The order of the trial court, therefore, should be affirmed insofar as appealed from, without costs or disbursements.

Because courts value precedent, they will work diligently to decide cases without overturning previous rulings. Yet as *Lawrence* shows, the compilation of exceptions and variances from a case's rulings can ultimately erode precedent to the extent that there is no precedent remaining. In such instances, the courts will recognize that there is no point to continue to rely on the precedent of an outdated case.

Finally, there are times when a past law is viewed as simply being morally wrong or outdated. In such cases, a high court may strike down a law and establish a new line of precedent. A classic example of this occurred in the following case: *Brown v. Board of Education.*

Brown v. Board of Ed. of Topeka, Shawnee County, Kan.

347 U.S. 483 (1954)

These cases come to us from the States of Kansas, South Carolina, Virginia, and Delaware. They are premised on different facts and different local conditions, but a common legal question justifies their consideration together in this consolidated opinion.

In each of the cases, minors of the Negro race, through their legal representatives, seek the aid of the courts in obtaining admission to the public schools of their community on a nonsegregated basis. In each instance, they have been denied admission to schools attended by white children under laws requiring or permitting segregation according to race. This segregation was alleged to deprive the plaintiffs of the equal protection of the laws under the Fourteenth Amendment. In each of the cases other than the Delaware case, a three-judge federal district court denied relief to the plaintiffs on the so-called 'separate but equal' doctrine announced by this Court in *Plessy v. Ferguson*. Under that doctrine, equality of treatment is accorded when the races are provided substantially equal facilities, even though these facilities be separate. In the Delaware case, the Supreme Court of Delaware adhered to that doctrine, but ordered that the plaintiffs be admitted to the white schools because of their superiority to the Negro schools.

The plaintiffs contend that segregated public schools are not 'equal' and cannot be made 'equal,' and that hence they are deprived of the equal protection of the laws. Because of the obvious importance of the question presented, the Court took jurisdiction. Argument was heard in the 1952 Term, and reargument was heard this Term on certain questions propounded by the Court.

MR. CHIEF JUSTICE WARREN

In the first cases in this Court construing the Fourteenth Amendment, decided shortly after its adoption, the Court interpreted it as proscribing all state-imposed discriminations against the Negro race. The doctrine of "separate but equal" did not make its appearance in this court until 1896 in the case of *Plessy v. Ferguson*, involving not education but transportation. American courts have since labored with the doctrine for over half a century. * * *

In the instant cases, that question is directly presented. Here, unlike *Sweatt v. Painter*, there are findings below that the Negro and white schools involved have been equalized, or are being equalized, with respect to buildings, curricula, qualifications and salaries of teachers, and other 'tangible' factors. Our decision, therefore, cannot turn on merely a comparison of these tangible factors in the Negro and white schools involved in each of the cases. We must look instead to the effect of segregation itself on public education.

In approaching this problem, we cannot turn the clock back to 1868 when the Amendment was adopted, or even to 1896 when *Plessy v. Ferguson* was written. We must consider public education in the light of its full development and its present place in American life throughout the Nation. Only in this way can it be determined if segregation in public schools deprives these plaintiffs of the equal protection of the laws.

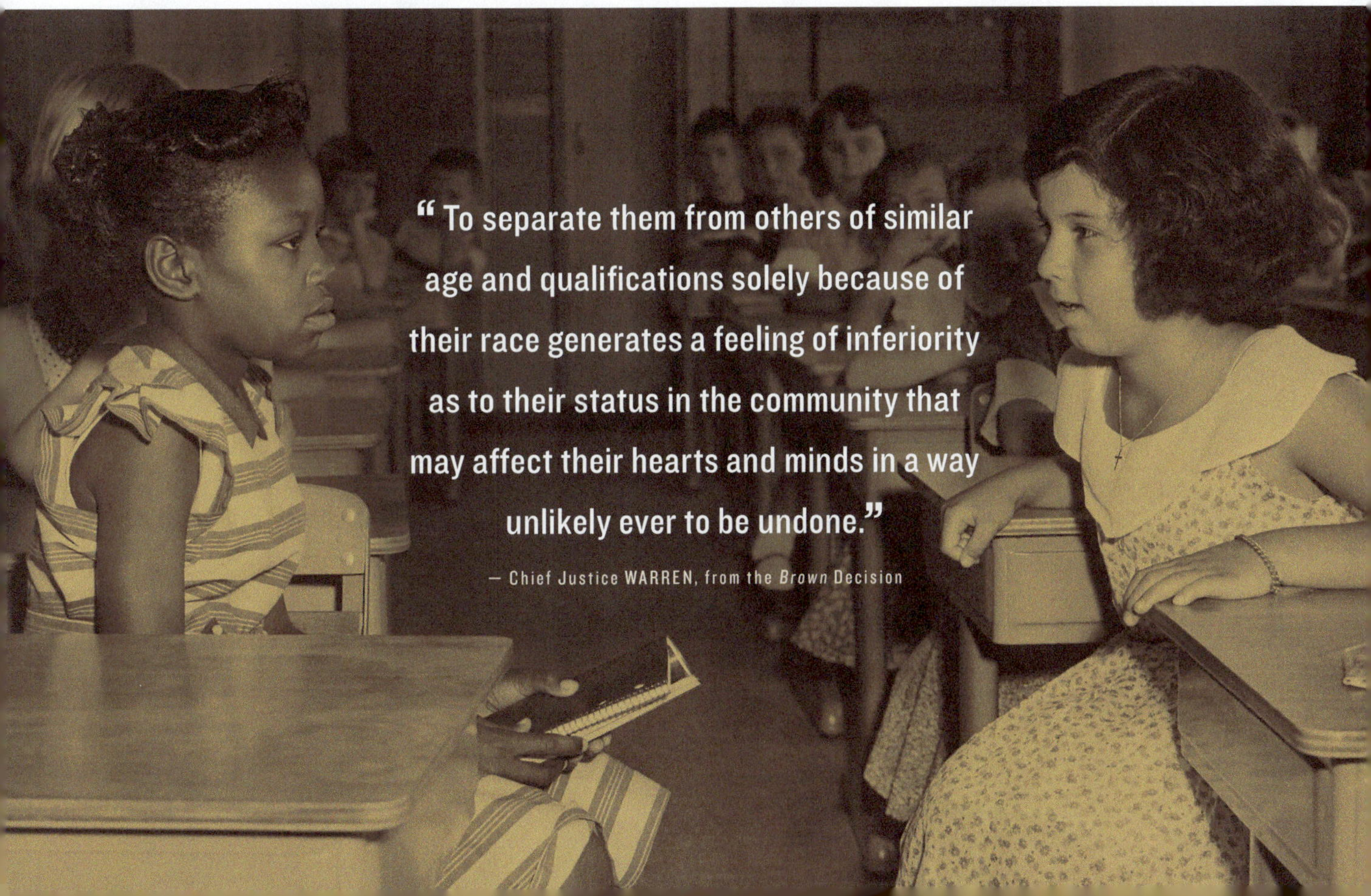

Today, education is perhaps the most important function of state and local governments. Compulsory school attendance laws and the great expenditures for education both demonstrate our recognition of the importance of education to our democratic society. It is required in the performance of our most basic public responsibilities, even service in the armed forces. It is the very foundation of good citizenship. Today it is a principal instrument in awakening the child to cultural values, in preparing him for later professional training, and in helping him to adjust normally to his environment. In these days, it is doubtful that any child may reasonably be expected to succeed in life if he is denied the opportunity of an education. Such an opportunity, where the state has undertaken to provide it, is a right which must be made available to all on equal terms.

We come then to the question presented: Does segregation of children in public schools solely on the basis of race, even though the physical facilities and other 'tangible' factors may be equal, deprive the children of the minority group of equal educational opportunities? We believe that it does.

In *Sweatt v. Painter*, in finding that a segregated law school for Negroes could not provide them equal educational opportunities, this Court relied in large part on 'those qualities which are incapable of objective measurement but which make for greatness in a law school.' In *McLaurin v. Oklahoma State Regents*, the Court, in requiring that a Negro admitted to a white graduate school be treated like all other students, again resorted to intangible considerations: ' * * * his ability to study, to engage in discussions and exchange views with other students, and, in general, to learn his profession.' Such considerations apply with added force to children in grade and high schools. To separate them from others of similar age and qualifications solely because of their race generates a feeling of inferiority as to their status in the community that may affect their hearts and minds in a way unlikely ever to be undone. The effect of this separation on their educational opportunities was well stated by a finding in the Kansas case by a court which nevertheless felt compelled to rule against the Negro plaintiffs:

> 'Segregation of white and colored children in public schools has a detrimental effect upon the colored children. The impact is greater when it has the sanction of the law; for the policy of separating the races is usually interpreted as denoting the inferiority of the negro group. A sense of inferiority affects the motivation of a child to learn. Segregation with the sanction of law, therefore, has a tendency to (retard) the educational and mental development of Negro children and to deprive them of some of the benefits they would receive in a racial(ly) integrated school system.'

Whatever may have been the extent of psychological knowledge at the time of *Plessy v. Ferguson*, this finding is amply supported by modern authority. Any language in *Plessy v. Ferguson* contrary to this finding is rejected.

We conclude that in the field of public education the doctrine of 'separate but equal' has no place. Separate educational facilities are inherently unequal. Therefore, we hold that the plaintiffs and others similarly situated for whom the actions have been brought are, by reason of the segregation complained of, deprived of the equal protection of the laws guaranteed by the Fourteenth Amendment.** This disposition makes unnecessary any discussion whether such segregation also violates the Due Process Clause of the Fourteenth Amendment.

Brown stands as landmark case in U.S. history and marks a rare occasion where the courts hold that a previous decision no longer should stand. As we have seen, courts tend not to be this dramatic, but there are times and places when courts do simply overturn previous decisions.

As seen in *Butterworth v. National League of Professional Baseball Clubs* (1994), *Lawrence v. City of* New *York*, (1981), and *Brown v. Board of Ed. of Topeka, Shawnee County, Kan.* (1954), the common law system in the U.S. provides not only predictability in legal disputes, but also the flexibility for law to evolve with society.

II. Contemporary Comparative Alternatives

CIVIL LAW IS A PRIMARY ALTERNATIVE to the common law system, and its reach is vast. Much of its reach stems from European colonization, apart from England, which follows the common law system. Civil law societies include France, Spain, Portugal, and the Netherlands. If one looks to where those countries colonized, including Latin America, one often finds a civil law tradition. Even in the United States, Louisiana continues to follow a civil law system because of its history as a French settlement.

In a civil law system, judges look only to statutory authority and apply their interpretation of a statute to the facts of a case; prior decisions do not have the binding authority they possess in a common law system. While it may seem like it would be more efficient for judges to apply a single authority to an issue at hand, statutes can be difficult to interpret because of the inherent ambiguity of language, and many different decisions may be reasonably handed down on one legal issue. This makes cases in civil law systems more unpredictable than in common law systems. Another important distinction is the way judges analyze law in the different systems. Judges in civil law societies (particularly in Europe) tend to extrapolate theory from codified laws and use deductive reasoning to come to an appropriate judgment on a case-by-case basis.

Some courts in civil law societies can actually strike down a codified law. Over fifty countries, including Germany, Italy and France have constitutional courts that operate separately from the rest of their courts. Constitutional courts have a monopoly over constitutional review of law and if a codified law is found to be unconstitutional, this specialized court may actually nullify it. In the common law system of the United States, the Supreme Court can only declare a law unconstitutional and choose to not apply it to the case at hand, but it is up to the legislature to amend or nullify it.

Below is an excerpt from the German Law Journal[2], describing an infamous case heard in the German constitutional court concerning the constitutionality of life imprisonment:

> In the *Life Imprisonment Case* from 1977, the First Senate of the *Bundesverfassungs-gericht* (German Federal Constitutional Court) was confronted with a challenge to the constitutionality of a sentence of life-long imprisonment without the possibility of parole. Among other asserted constitutional violations the applicant claimed that this complete exclusion from society violated the right to human dignity guaranteed by Article 1 of the Basic Law. The ordinary courts disagreed. Having considered the legislative history behind the framer's abolition of the death penalty, the ordinary courts concluded that the justifications offered in the *Parlamentarisches Rat* (1948 West German constitutional convention) in support of the abolition of capital punishment did not preclude life imprisonment as a substitute.
>
> The First Senate of the Constitutional Court rejected the ordinary courts' interpretive analysis, invoking a standard reminiscent of the American "evolving standard of decency" from the Supreme Court's Eighth Amendment jurisprudence. The Senate explained: "Neither original history nor the ideas and intentions of the framers are of decisive importance . . . Since the adoption of the Basic Law [constitution], our understanding of the content, function, and effect of basic rights has deepened . . . Current attitudes are important in assessing the constitutionality of life imprisonment."
>
> Thus, freed from the shackles of original intent, the Senate began its analysis with the dramatic proposition that "the free human person and his [or her] dignity are the highest values of the constitutional order." From this foundational value the Court extracted the principle that "it is contrary to human dignity to make persons the mere tools of the state" in the context of criminal justice policy, that the state "cannot turn the offender into an

2 Russell Miller, *The Shared Transatlantic Jurisprudence of Dignity, 4 German Law Journal 9, 929 (2003), available at http://www.germanlawjournal.com/pdfs/Vol04No09/PDF_Vol_04_No_09_925-934_SI_Miller.pdf.*

> object of crime prevention to the detriment of his constitutionally protected right to social worth and respect." The Court explained that life imprisonment without the possibility of parole violated the constitutional value that holds that every prisoner must possess some hope of regaining his or her freedom: "A sentence of life imprisonment cannot be enforced humanely if the prisoner is denied *a priori* any and every possibility of returning to freedom . . . The condemned criminal must be given the chance, after atoning for his crime, to reenter society."
>
> Shortly after the Constitutional Court's ruling the *Bundestag* (federal parliament) amended Germany's *Strafgesetzbuch* (criminal code) to authorize courts to suspend a life sentence when the situation warranted the offender's release from prison. In determining whether or not to release a person sentenced to life imprisonment, the amendments to the statute required courts to consider the personality of the offender, his or her behavior in prison, the circumstances of the crime, and his or her capacity to lead a normal life outside prison. These are statutory terms of human dignity, the idea that respect for human dignity particularly requires consideration of the offender's background and the circumstances of his or her crime.

There are some differences between civil law systems and common law systems in terms of the substance of legislation. Governments in a civil law country have a greater range of authority to step into a contractual situation to protect the fairness to either party or to protect the interests of the country as a whole. In common law systems there is a much greater freedom of contract. Whatever two parties decide to include in a contract tends to be enforced unless it violates a law. But in civil law countries the parties do not have to be quite as specific and can rely upon the overarching laws to fill in the blanks of a contractual agreement. Below is a contract law case from France. At issue is a clause in the contract limiting the liability of a transport company.

Case Société Chronopost v. Société Banchereau

Bull. Civ. 2002.IV, no. 121, p.129

Given that according to the decision under attack, rendered after remand following the quashing of an earlier decision (22 October 1996, Bull. civ., IV, no. 261), the Banchereau company handed certain documents to the Société Française de Messagerie Internationale (SFMI) addressed to the national office of butchers, meat producers and farmers in order to bid for an allocation of meat, and that since the documents were not delivered the day following their dispatch in breach of SFMI's undertaking, Banchereau was unable to bid for an allocation; that when Banchereau sued SFMI for damages as compensation for the harm it suffered, SFMI invoked the term of the contract which limited its liability to the cost of the carriage;

On the first ground of the application for review:

Given that Chronopost, successor to SFMI, criticises the judgment below for holding that the obligation it undertook was one "de résultat" or guarantee, whereas, it maintains, although the judges have a sovereign power to interpret contracts containing several terms which must be read together, it is on condition that it takes all such terms into account, and that in simply disregarding the term in Chronopost's general conditions of business that Chronopost will use every effort to deliver its clients' packages within the time laid down, which is characteristic of a mere obligation "de moyens", the court below misinterpreted the contract in breach of article 1134 Code civil;

But given that the court of appeal merely applied the law laid down by the Court of Cassation, this criticism is unacceptable;

But on the second ground of the application for review:

In view of article 1150 Code civil, article 8(II) of the Law of 30 December 1982 (Law no. 82-1153) and articles 1 and 15 of the rules of the contract for the carriage of packages, established by the decree of 4 May 1988, which is applicable:

Given that in declaring that because the contract here contained a specific obligation guaranteeing timeous delivery which could be relied on it was not a contract for the carriage of packages and that in consequence the general law of carriage was inapplicable;

Given that its holding that the clause limiting the carrier's liability was to be treated as not written entails that the statutory limit of compensation, avoidable only on proof of gross negligence on the part of the carrier, falls to be applied, the court of appeal's decision violated the texts cited above;

For these reasons QUASHES the decision of the Court of Appeal of Caen dated 5 January 1999 and remands the case to the Court of Appeal of Rouen. *Com, 9 July 2002, Bull IV no 121.*

The solution put forward by this judgment has formed the subject of numerous criticisms by legal writers; it has been pointed out that the Rouen court of appeal, which received the court file on the reference back after quashing still did not reach a decision, and that neither the lower courts nor the Cour de Cassation have had to do so since. Without returning expressly to the principle laid down by the commercial chamber on October 22, 1996 (this case is concerned with the same affair, with the same parties: the judgment is called "Chronopost"), the judgment of September 9 reduces this solution to much more modest proportions. It substitutes for the clause restricting liability which is nullified (a solution expressly maintained) application of the *droit commun* of carriage which provides in this case for a legal ceiling of indemnification which corresponds to the total amount of sums provided for in the clause restricting liability. The Cour de Cassation in effect considers that nullity of a clause restrictive of liability which is judged to be abusive and therefore nullified, entails, unless there is grave fault on the part of the carrier, a return not to the rules of the *droit commun* as the judges at first instance had considered, but application of the provisions of the *droit commun* of carriage. (A clause contradicting the very essence of a contract—and only such a clause—should be nullified leaving all the other provisions of the contract in existence, including those referring to a contract type capable of having the effect of restricting indemnification of the other contracting party in the same way as the annulled clause would do). However, it should be noted that this solution only applies to cases where a legal ceiling exists to indemnification which prevents return to the application of the rules of the *droit commun*; and that proof of a grave fault on the part of the other contracting party would in all circumstances entail return to the *droit commun* of contractual liability.[3]

This case has a different feel to it than the ones we have seen so far in this book. Civil law courts tend to be driven more by governmental assessment of a case than by individual parties moving the case along through their own motions and decisions. This, along with a different sense of the importance of precedent and the reliance on comprehensive legal statutes, makes for a different court room—and decision—dynamic.

There are also specific concepts that apply in most civil law countries. One is called "force majeure." This is a principle that eliminates an obligation to perform a contract because of an unpredictable event, such as an earthquake or a hurricane.

Though not necessarily a feature of civil law, per se, bankruptcy in civil law countries tends to result in liquidation of a company rather than a reorganization (as is common in the U.S. and U.K). Consistent with their friendliness to commercial affairs, common law countries tend to have a wider range of security interests that facilitate new forms of business activities than in civil law countries. While the distinction between common and civil law countries is commonly made, it is worth noting the range of systems utilized by the largest economic actors. Appendix A sets out a comparative chart that summarizes some of these differences.

3 Bull. Civ. 2002.IV, no. 121, p.129 *Case Société Chronopost v. Société Banchereau*, translated by Tony Weir, University of Texas, © Professor B. S. Markesinis, available at http://www.utexas.edu/law/academics/centers/transnational/work_new/french/case.php?id=1154.

NOTES AND COMMENTS on the Legal Environment of Business

1. **AS A BUSINESS STUDENT,** do you believe that the common law system or a civil law system is more conducive to commerce? What strengths and weaknesses does each have? To be sure, most systems we see are hybrids with a mix of both. As you think about planning a business or operating a business, what features of each attract or concern you?

2. **HAS LIVING IN THE SYSTEM** of your native country influenced the way you think about deciding issues personally or in a group setting (such as a sorority or fraternity)? For example, does the Constitutional adage "innocent until proven guilty" influence the way you look at issues of right and wrong?

3. **DOES PRECEDENT CREATE** a good balance of predictability with change or does it unduly inhibit legal changes that match a dynamic business world? Many business people argue strongly both ways, saying on the one hand, that the predictability of precedent allows for good strategic planning, while on the other hand, some argue that law becomes too slow to respond to a changing world. What do you think?

NOTES AND COMMENTS on the Ethical Environment of Business

LIKE ANY COMPLEX topic, ethics can be divided in several different ways. One helpful division is that of making decisions and the other is preventing dilemmas from arising in the first place. The latter is proactive and is involved with building cultures and communities as well as forming the character of individuals and their habits and dispositions.

The common law's emphasis on precedent helps with the preventive, proactive aspect because it provides a sense of predictability and stability. Once one has a sense of how the legal system will handle a case, one has guidelines that inform behaviors.

This is true within organizations as well. Many studies show that there is not one magical ethical style that employees believe must be adopted in order for ethical conduct to flourish; instead, employees want to know what the rules of an organization are and then desire that those rules are applied even-handedly. The fairness of the procedure is as important as any particular principle. Or, to phrase it otherwise, fairness is often about process.

With this emphasis on procedural fairness in mind, the common law system has much to teach us about ethics. The common law system sets up a process of how disputes are going to be handled. Through the decisions that are made by courts, predictability, stability and guidance are provided,

While procedural fairness is important, flexibility is as well. Here again, the common law system has much to teach us in that every case is a little bit different. There may be precedents that control a topic, but there can also be exceptions, variations, and new developments that make each case unique. Thus, the common law provides flexibility and growth as well as stability and predictability. We have seen this balance between flexibility and predictability throughout this chapter and they provide a model not only for how the law develops, but how ethical principles can evolve within a business as well.

These are simple observations, but they also are helpful when one is considering how to make ethical decisions or to create ethical business cultures. Process is important. So are predictability and stability. So too is flexibility.

Accompanying this text is the e-book, *Ethics Vignettes*. While there are several cases that may provide interesting augmented discussion about ethical principles, two are worth starting with. The first one is the famous case about the Ford Pinto, the *Grimshaw* case in Chapter 2. In this case, Ford engineers and accountants has read previous court cases carefully and concluded that it was cheaper to pay wrongful death suit, arising from the Pinto crashes, than to equip each Pinto with a very inexpensive part. The Ford engineers and accountants made this calculation based on an assessment of previous court cases; in other words, based on precedent. What they did not expect is that once jurors discovered that these calculations were made, the damage awards increased dramatically beyond what was expected as jurors vented their anger on these kinds of calculations.

In reading this case, one question to ask is why Ford did what they did and how do you access their ethical principles. A second question is how does an analysis of this case—of issues of predictability, stability, and flexibility—help us understand how to make decisions about human life and limb and about using cost-benefit analysis.

Another case from Chapter 2 worth reviewing is the EEOC case against Capital Healthcare Solutions. This case looks at issues of disability discrimination. Here too, one can have a good discussion about the ethics—or lack thereof—of disability discrimination, but it is also worth reflecting on the process of how these kinds of decisions by both the EEOC and by the court are made.

Turning back to the cases in this chapter provides ample opportunity for discussion of ethics issues as well. For example, how far do you think a person should be able to go in order to delay a trial as was discussed in the *Patin* case? Why is there a right to a speedy trial in the first place? Do you think Patin was justified in trying to delay the case? At what point does legal maneuvering cross the line?

Looking at the baseball cases, why should players be restricted from moving from team to team in the first place? Is there any other field, other than sports, that precludes a person from working wherever they wish, as objected to in the *Flood* case? Why should sports generally and baseball specifically be different? Even assuming that players can be restricted in their movement, do you agree that the business of baseball, as in the *Butterworth* case, is different than the restriction of players' issue? Why or why not?

Finally, turning to the way in which precedent can be changed, do you agree that the decision in *Lawrence* is a good one? Should employees be able to sue their employers more freely and not be restricted by (now overturned) laws like the fellow-servant rule or even with respect to workers compensation? And lastly, do you think that the *Brown* case was decided correctly, to overturn the notion of separate but equal?

As you can see both from the *Ethics Vignettes* material as well as from the cases themselves, legal issues are frequently saturated with questions of values. That is worth keeping in mind as you work your way through the book and class.

CHAPTER

4

Jurisdiction and the Elements to a Trial

Lawsuits can't take place unless certain procedural elements are met. Suppose you're driving to school in New Jersey and suddenly a deer appears in the road. You try to hit the brakes on your car, and they just don't respond.

You end up veering off the road to avoid the deer and hit a tree, sustaining serious injuries. As a result of your injuries, you have incurred thousands of dollars of medical bills and still feel pain in your legs when you walk. To recover for your injuries, you want to sue the Michigan car manufacturer that put defective brakes in your car.

You may have a strong products liability case, but finding the applicable products liability law and establishing that the car manufacturer owed a duty to produce non-defective brakes is only a tiny portion of the battle. You will first have to establish jurisdiction over the Michigan company, find the right venue to bring your case, properly serve the car manufacturer, and sufficiently plead your case. Once all of those elements are satisfied, you can proceed to trial. At trial you must then abide by the requirements of trial procedure, which can include depositions, discovery, and presenting witness testimony. If at any point along the way you fail to abide by the procedural laws governing a trial, a judge may dismiss your case—and in the worst case, you and your attorney may be subject to sanctions. But let's say you satisfy all the elements of a trial and either a judge or a jury finds in your favor. It is almost guaranteed that the car company will file a motion for a new trial or appeal the final judgment. If either is granted, you must then follow post-trial procedures and argue your case all over again.

As you can see, understanding the procedural elements of the law and a trial is just as important if not more important than the substantive law, and it is certainly more cumbersome. The first element any plaintiff will have to satisfy in a lawsuit is establishing jurisdiction—you can't sue the car manufacturer in any court you please. The court must have personal jurisdiction over the defendant or **in rem jurisdiction** over the property in dispute, and subject matter jurisdiction over the type of dispute.

I. Jurisdiction and Long-Arm Statutes

A. JURISDICTION OF THE COURT

In total, there are 52 court systems in the United States and every court system has its own rules of civil and criminal procedure. Each state, plus the District of Columbia, has its own court system—these make up the state courts. State courts have jurisdiction over substantive state law matters, disputes arising in the state, and persons in the state. Then there is the federal court system. There are 94 federal judicial districts; at least one in each state, plus the federal circuit courts, which serve as the courts of appeal for decisions made by the district courts. Federal courts are organized by districts and each state is designated a federal district court or circuit court. For example, Alabama, Georgia and Florida make up the 11th Circuit, while Wisconsin, Illinois and Indiana make up the 7th Circuit.

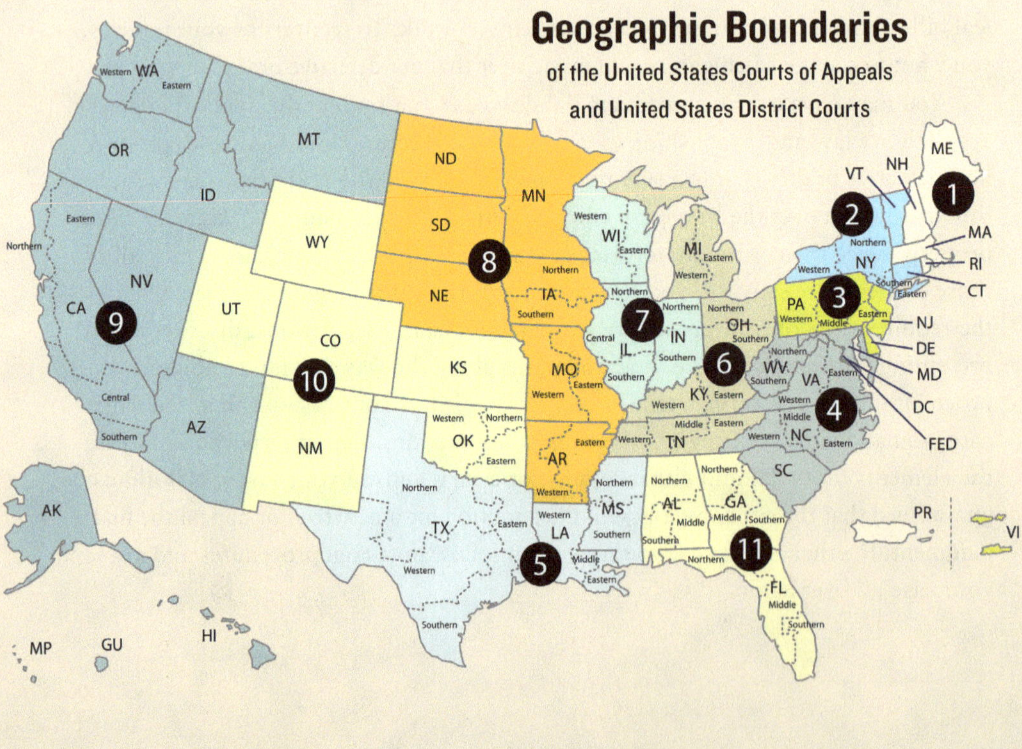

Federal courts have jurisdiction over substantive federal law matters, also known as federal question jurisdiction, and cases that involve citizens of two different states, also known as diversity jurisdiction. A party can also bring a case into the federal court system if the amount in controversy exceeds $75,000.

Within each court system are trial courts, where cases are first brought, and appellate courts, where trial court decisions are appealed. Trial courts are fact-finding courts, meaning they serve the dual purpose of analyzing both the evidence (facts) presented and the applicable law. Appellate courts, however, do not generally make determinations about the factual elements of a case and consider only the legal questions. Trial court cases are reviewed for legal error and the appellate court will not accept new evidence or retry the case. When a motion for a new trial is granted, it is tried anew in state trial court, not the appellate court.

Two trial courts that can have nationwide jurisdiction over their specialized subject matter are the Court of International Trade, located in New York City, and the U.S. Court of Federal Claims in Washington, D.C. The Court of International Trade hears cases involving international trade and customs issues, while the Court of Federal Claims hears cases where the plaintiff is suing the United States for money damages, disputes over federal contracts, and unlawful takings of private property by the U.S. government (which you will learn more about in Chapter 6).

In addition to trial courts and appellate courts, there are also courts of limited jurisdiction. These courts try minor criminal cases and some civil disputes. Courts of limited jurisdiction usually deal with specialized matters, like tax courts, small claims courts, traffic courts, and probate courts. Courts of limited jurisdiction are used for matters which occur frequently, involve small amounts of money, address minor damages, and are best handled by judges familiar with the specific laws. Parties can often represent themselves in courts of limited jurisdiction and therefore do not require attorneys. When decisions of these courts are appealed, the case is tried *de novo* (a new trial, complete with fact-finding) in trial court.

B. PERSONAL JURISDICTION

There are several ways a court can establish personal jurisdiction over a defendant. The first and simplest way is for a defendant to consent to the jurisdiction of the court. At the state level, rules governing personal jurisdiction vary, so it is very important to become familiar with the applicable rules of the state in which you want to bring a case. At the federal level, a court can establish personal jurisdiction over a defendant who enters a general appearance to subject himself to unlimited jurisdiction or one who fails to assert a defense outlined in the Federal Rules of Civil Procedure, FR 12(b)(2)-(5). Failure of a defendant to assert the defense of no personal jurisdiction actually constitutes consent.

Another way for the court to obtain personal jurisdiction over a defendant is if the defendant resides in the forum—the state or district in which the court is located. It is important to note here that contracts will often contain clauses called "forum selection clauses" which require disputes to be settled in a specified forum. Many times contract clauses addressing disputes will opt for alternative dispute resolution mechanisms (most commonly, arbitration). In some cases, the party drafting the contract or the party with more power in the deal-making will insert an arbitration clause that requires the dispute to be settled in a remote location, such as France, to make it unaffordable and undesirable for the other party to bring a dispute. It is an interesting exercise to look through the routine contracts you sign—with your cable provider, cell phone company, even your landlord—to see the forum selection for dispute resolution. You may be surprised by how impractical or seemingly random some of them are.

A residence is considered the state where a person has the intent to remain indefinitely, and an individual's residence can only be changed by establishing a new domicile. Intent to remain can be evidenced by where a defendant pays taxes and votes. When the defendant is a company, the residence of the company is the place of its incorporation. In *Milliken v. Meyer*, a 1940 U.S. Supreme Court case, a state was able to exercise jurisdiction over a temporarily absent citizen because it was shown that the defendant was still enjoying the privileges and protections of being a citizen of the state.

Another way of establishing personal jurisdiction over a defendant is physical presence within the state or district. A defendant is subject to jurisdiction if personally served within the relevant territory, even if he or she is not a citizen of the state. The following case is a landmark case on personal jurisdiction through physical presence.

Pennoyer v. Neff

95 U.S. 714 (1877)

This is an action to recover the possession of a tract of land, of the alleged value of $15,000, situated in the State of Oregon . . . . The defendant claims to have acquired the premises under a sheriff's deed, made upon a sale of the property on execution issued upon a judgment recovered against the plaintiff in one of the circuit courts of the State. The case turns upon the validity of this judgment.

It appears from the record that the judgment was rendered in February, 1866, in favor of J. H. Mitchell, for less than $300, including costs, in an action brought by him upon a demand for services as an attorney; that, at the time the action was commenced and the judgment rendered, the defendant therein, the plaintiff here, was a non-resident of the State that he was not personally served with process, and did not appear therein; and that the judgment was entered upon his default in not answering the complaint, upon a constructive service of summons by publication.

The Code of Oregon provides for such service when an action is brought against a non-resident and absent defendant, who has property within the State. It also provides, where the action is for the recovery of money or damages, for the attachment of the property of the non-resident. And it also declares that no natural person is subject to the jurisdiction of a court of the State, 'unless he appear in the court, or be found within the State, or be a resident thereof, or have property therein; and, in the last case, only to the extent of such property at the time the jurisdiction attached.' Construing this latter provision to mean, that, in an action for money or damages where a defendant does not appear in the court, and is not found within the State, and is not a resident thereof, but has property therein, the jurisdiction of the court extends only over such property, the declaration expresses a principle of general, if not universal, law. The authority of every tribunal is necessarily restricted by the territorial limits of the State in which it is established. Any attempt to exercise authority beyond those limits would be deemed in every other forum, as has been said by this court, in illegitimate assumption of power, and be resisted as mere abuse.

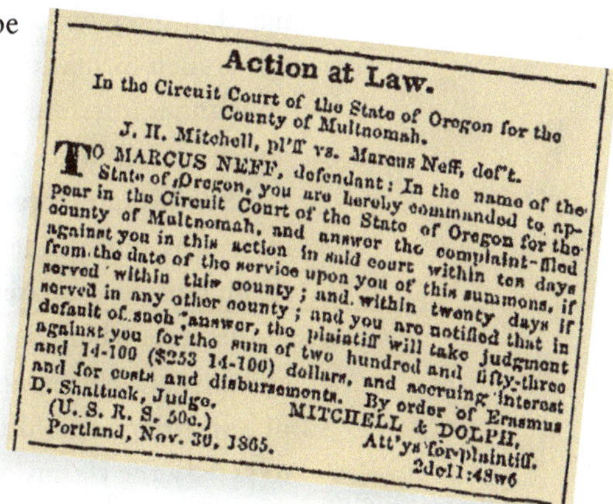

Action at Law.

In the Circuit Court of the State of Oregon for the County of Multnomah.

J. H. Mitchell, pl'ff vs. Marcus Neff, def't.

TO MARCUS NEFF, defendant: In the name of the State of Oregon, you are hereby commanded to appear in the Circuit Court of the State of Oregon for the county of Multnomah, and answer the complaint filed against you in this action in said court within ten days from the date of the service upon you of this summons, if served within this county; and within twenty days if served in any other county; and you are notified that in default of such answer, the plaintiff will take judgment against you for the sum of two hundred and fifty-three and 14-100 ($253 14-100) dollars, and accruing interest and for costs and disbursements. By order of Erasmus D. Shattuck, Judge.

(U. S. R. S. 50c.) MITCHELL & DOLPH,

Portland, Nov. 30, 1865. Att'ys for plaintiff.

2dc11:48w6

A COPY OF THE NOTICE ATTEMPTING TO PROVIDE MARCUS NEFF WITH SUBSTITUTED SERVICE, PRINTED IN THE *PACIFIC CHRISTIAN ADVOCATE*, ON SAT., DEC. 2, 1865 AND DEC. 9, 1865.

...

The several States of the Union are not, it is true, in every respect independent, many of the right and powers which originally belonged to them being now vested in the government created by the Constitution. But, except as restrained and limited by that instrument, they possess and exercise the authority of independent States, and the principles of public law to which we have referred are applicable to them. One of these principles is, that every State possesses exclusive jurisdiction and sovereignty over persons and property within its territory. As a consequence, every State has the power to determine for itself the civil *status* and capacities of its inhabitants; to prescribe the subjects upon which they may contract, the forms and solemnities with which their contracts shall be executed, the rights and obligations arising from them, and the mode in which their validity shall be determined and their obligations enforced; and also the regulate the manner and conditions upon which property situated within such territory, both personal and real, may be acquired, enjoyed, and transferred. The other principle of public law referred to follows from the one mentioned; that is, that no State can exercise direct jurisdiction and authority over persons or property without its territory. The several States are of equal dignity and authority, and the independence of one implies the exclusion of power from all others. And so it is laid down by jurists, as an elementary principle, that the laws of one State have no operation outside of its territory, except so far as is allowed by comity; and that no tribunal established by it can extend its process beyond that territory so as to subject either persons or property to its decisions. 'Any exertion of authority of this sort beyond this limit,' says Story, 'is a mere nullity, and incapable of binding such persons or property in any other tribunals.'

But as contracts made in one State may be enforceable only in another State, and property may be held by non-residents, the exercise of the jurisdiction which every State is admitted to possess over persons and property within its own territory will often affect persons and property without it. To any influence exerted in this way by a State affecting persons resident or property situated elsewhere, no objection can be justly taken; whilst any direct exertion of authority upon them, in an attempt to give ex-territorial operation to its laws, or to enforce an ex-territorial jurisdiction by its tribunals, would be deemed an encroachment upon the independence of the State in which the persons are domiciled or the property is situated, and be resisted as usurpation.

Thus the State, through its tribunals, may compel persons domiciled within its limits to execute, in pursuance of their contracts respecting property elsewhere situated, instruments in such form and with such solemnities as to transfer the title, so far as such formalities can be complied with; and the exercise of this jurisdiction in no manner interferes with the supreme control over the property by the State within which it is situated.

So the State, through its tribunals, may subject property situated within its limits owned by non-residents to the payment of the demand of its own citizens against them; and the exercise of this jurisdiction in no respect infringes upon the sovereignty of the State where the owners are domiciled. Every State owes protection to its own citizens; and, when non-residents deal with them, it is a legitimate and just exercise of authority to hold and appropriate any property owned by such non-residents to satisfy the claims of its citizens. It is in virtue of the State's jurisdiction over the property of the non-resident situated within its limits that its tribunals can inquire into that non-resident's obligations to its own citizens, and the inquiry can then be carried only to the extent necessary to control the disposition of the property. If the non-resident have no property in the State, there is nothing upon which the tribunals can adjudicate.

. . .

One caveat to using physical presence to obtain personal jurisdiction is that the defendant cannot be tricked into coming into the state. In *Tickle v. Barton* (1956), the plaintiff's lawyer tricked the defendant into coming into the state by calling Barton and telling him that he was invited to a football banquet that did not really exist.

Once Barton arrived in the state, the plaintiff's lawyer served Barton with process. The court held that because the lawyer used false representation to lure Barton into the state and Barton would not have come into that jurisdiction if the lawyer had disclosed his identity and real purpose, the service of process was invalid and there was no personal jurisdiction. Again, note how important it is to follow the rules of procedure—Tickle's case against Barton for injuries in an automobile accident could no longer proceed because of an error in the service of process against the defendant.

As seen in the opinions of *Pennoyer and Tickle*, purposeful availment of the protections and privileges of a state, as well as purposeful presence in a state, are enough to establish personal jurisdiction over a defendant. The purposeful presence test was highlighted in a case where a passenger on a plane was served while passing over Arkansas. In *Grace v. Macarthur* (1959), the defendant was not tricked into being in Arkansas, as he purposefully boarded the plane which would pass through Arkansas. The Supreme Court held that because the airspace above a state is still considered the territory of the state, the defendant's presence in the airplane going over Arkansas was sufficient physical presence and this form of service was valid.

Thinking about the presence of corporations can be tricky. Because the personality of a corporation is a fiction and just a legal tool, it is difficult to determine the purpose or intent of a corporation, its physical presence, and what constitutes an arm of the corporation. Therefore, the courts established a much-needed test in the *International Shoe* case—one of the most important cases to know when thinking about personal jurisdiction of corporations. To establish jurisdiction over corporations, one must look to the activities carried out on its behalf by those who are authorized to act for it.

International Shoe Co. v. State of Wash., Office of Unemployment Compensation and Payment

326 U.S. 310 (1945)

* * *

The facts . . . are not in dispute. Appellant is a Delaware corporation, having its principal place of business in St. Louis, Missouri, and is engaged in the manufacture and sale of shoes and other footwear. It maintains places of business in several states, other than Washington, at which its manufacturing is carried on and from which its merchandise is distributed interstate through several sales units or branches located outside the State of Washington.

Appellant has no office in Washington and makes no contracts either for sale or purchase of merchandise there. It maintains no stock of merchandise in that state and makes there no deliveries of goods in intrastate commerce. During the years from 1937 to 1940, now in question, appellant employed eleven to thirteen salesmen under direct supervision and control of sales managers located in St. Louis. These salesmen resided in Washington; their principal activities were confined to that state; and they were compensated by commissions based upon the amount of their sales. The commissions for each year totaled more than $31,000. Appellant supplies its salesmen with a line of samples, each consisting of one shoe of a pair, which they display to prospective purchasers. On occasion they rent permanent sample rooms, for exhibiting samples, in business buildings, or rent rooms in hotels or business buildings temporarily for that purpose. The cost of such rentals is reimbursed by appellant.

The authority of the salesmen is limited to exhibiting their samples and soliciting orders from prospective buyers, at prices and on terms fixed by appellant. The salesmen transmit the orders to appellant's office in St. Louis for acceptance or rejection, and when accepted the merchandise for filling the orders is shipped f.o.b. from points outside Washington to the purchasers within the state. All the merchandise shipped into Washington is invoiced at the place of shipment from which collections are made. No salesman has authority to enter into contracts or to make collections.

■ THE INTERNATIONAL SHOE FACTORY BUILDING IN ST. LOUIS, MISSOURI. *Photo: Stephen McCaffrey*

The Supreme Court of Washington was of opinion that the regular and systematic solicitation of orders in the state by appellant's salesmen, resulting in a continuous flow of appellant's product into the state, was sufficient to constitute doing business in the state so as to make appellant amenable to suit in its courts. But it was also of opinion that there were sufficient additional activities shown to bring the case within the rule frequently stated, that solicitation within a state by the agents of a foreign corporation plus some additional activities there are sufficient to render the corporation amenable to suit brought in the courts of the state to enforce an obligation arising out of its activities there. The court found such additional activities in the salesmen's display of samples sometimes in permanent display rooms, and the salesmen's residence within the state, continued over a period of years, all resulting in a substantial volume of merchandise regularly shipped by appellant to purchasers within the state. The court also held that the statute as applied did not invade the constitutional power of Congress to regulate interstate commerce and did not impose a prohibited burden on such commerce.

Historically the jurisdiction of courts to render judgment **in personam** is grounded on their de facto power over the defendant's person. Hence his presence within the territorial jurisdiction of court was prerequisite to its rendition of a judgment personally binding him. But now that the **capias ad respondendum** has given way to personal service of summons or other form of notice, due process requires only that in order to subject a defendant to a judgment *in personam*, if he be not present within the territory of the forum, he have certain minimum contacts with it such that the maintenance of the suit does not offend 'traditional notions of fair play and substantial justice.'

Since the corporate personality is a fiction, although a fiction intended to be acted upon as though it were a fact, it is clear that unlike an individual its 'presence' without, as well as within, the state of its origin can be manifested only by activities carried on in its behalf by those who are authorized to act for it. . . . 'Presence' in the state in this sense has never been doubted when the activities of the corporation there have not only been continuous and systematic, but also give rise to the liabilities sued on, even though no consent to be sued or authorization to an agent to accept service of process has been given. Conversely it has been generally recognized that the casual presence of the corporate agent or even his conduct of single or isolated items of activities in a state in the corporation's behalf are not enough to subject it to suit on causes of action unconnected with the activities there. To require the corporation in such circumstances to defend the suit away from its home or other jurisdiction where it carries on more substantial activities has been thought to lay too great and unreasonable a burden on the corporation to comport with due process.

. . . It is evident that the criteria by which we mark the boundary line between those activities which justify the subjection of a corporation to suit, and those which do not, cannot be simply mechanical or quantitative. The test is not merely, as has sometimes been suggested, whether the activity, which the corporation has seen fit to procure through its agents in another state, is a little more or a little less. Whether due process is satisfied must depend rather upon the quality and nature of the activity in relation to the fair and orderly administration of the laws which it was the purpose of the due process clause to insure . . .

But to the extent that a corporation exercises the privilege of conducting activities within a state, it enjoys the benefits and protection of the laws of that state. The exercise of that privilege may give rise to obligations; and, so far as those obligations arise out of or are connected with the activities within the state, a procedure which requires the corporation to respond to a suit brought to enforce them can, in most instances, hardly be said to be undue.

Applying these standards, the activities carried on in behalf of appellant in the State of Washington were neither irregular nor casual. They were systematic and continuous throughout the years in question. They resulted in a large volume of interstate business, in the course of which appellant received the benefits and protection of the laws of the state, including the right to resort to the courts for the enforcement of its rights. The obligation which is here sued upon arose out of those very activities. It is evident that these operations establish sufficient contacts or ties with the state of the forum to make it reasonable and just according to our traditional conception of

fair play and substantial justice to permit the state to enforce the obligations which appellant has incurred there. Hence we cannot say that the maintenance of the present suit in the State of Washington involves an unreasonable or undue procedure.

We are likewise unable to conclude that the service of the process within the state upon an agent whose activities establish appellant's 'presence' there was not sufficient notice of the suit, or that the suit was so unrelated to those activities as to make the agent an inappropriate vehicle for communicating the notice. It is enough that appellant has established such contacts with the state that the particular form of substituted service adopted there gives reasonable assurance that the notice will be actual. Nor can we say that the mailing of the notice of suit to appellant by registered mail at its home office was not reasonably calculated to apprise appellant of the suit.

Only a word need be said of appellant's liability for the demanded contributions of the state unemployment fund. The Supreme Court of Washington, construing and applying the statute, has held that it imposes a tax on the privilege of employing appellant's salesmen within the state measured by a percentage of the wages, here the commissions payable to the salesmen. This construction we accept for purposes of determining the constitutional validity of the statute. The right to employ labor has been deemed an appropriate subject of taxation in this country and England, both before and since the adoption of the Constitution. And such a tax imposed upon the employer for unemployment benefits is within the constitutional power of the states. . . . The state thus has constitutional power to lay the tax and to subject appellant to a suit to recover it. The activities which establish its 'presence' subject it alike to taxation by the state and to suit to recover the tax.

Affirmed.

On the basis of this case and others, a business can fairly easily be pulled into a jurisdiction outside of its home base given the contacts it may have in another state. This possibility is magnified even more today with the ease of moving across borders in the Internet age.

No state has jurisdiction over people and property outside the state, unless the claim arises out of minimum contacts with the state and the suit does not offend "traditional notions of fair play and substantial notice" of Due Process. The case above resulted in the modern day two-prong test for personal jurisdiction: minimum contacts plus fairness.

In some cases, jurisdiction can be extended to nonresidents who cannot be found and served in the jurisdiction's territory. This is made possible through **long-arm statutes.** When exercising personal jurisdiction under a long-arm statute, courts must ask (1) whether there is a state statute that authorizes it to exercise personal jurisdiction under the circumstances, and (2) whether it would be constitutional under the due process clause to do so. Because long-arm statutes are intended to reach to the limits of due process, the specific categories of jurisdiction conveyed by the long-arm statute are to be interpreted as liberally as the due process clause will allow.

The courts must consider a defendant's general activity within the state, the commission of any of a series of enumerated acts within the state, or the commission of a certain act outside the state causing consequences within it. In *Gray v. American Radiator and Standard Sanitary Corps*, (1961), the court held that personal service outside the state was valid on a safety valve manufacturer in Ohio where the only injury occurred in Illinois. The valve was integrated into a water heater in Pennsylvania and exploded in Illinois, and the Illinois long arm statute read: "a nonresident who, either in person or thorough an agent, commits a tortuous, or wrongful act within this State submits to its jurisdiction." Furthermore, agency and consent to service can be appointed or implied by an action. In *Hess v. Pawloski*, (1927), the Supreme Court upheld a Massachusetts statute that said driving on state roads implied consent to service of process by the state registrar.

Ultimately, the courts have tended to look to any purposeful availment of a state's privileges and protections, and the foreseeability of harm. What that means is that if a defendant seems to be asking for the protection of a state even though he does not reside there, the same defendant can't complain about that state holding the defendant accountable if it is likely that the defendant's actions harmed someone. These two elements are highlighted in the Supreme Court's opinion in the following landmark case.

Worldwide Volkswagen Corp. v. Woodson

444 U.S. 286 (1980)

Respondents Harry and Kay Robinson purchased a new Audi automobile from petitioner Seaway Volkswagen, Inc. (Seaway), in Massena, N.Y., in 1976. The following year the Robinson family, who resided in New York, left that State for a new home in Arizona. As they passed through the State of Oklahoma, another car struck their Audi in the rear, causing a fire which severely burned Kay Robinson and her two children.

The Robinsons subsequently brought a products-liability action in the District Court for Creek County, Okla., claiming that their injuries resulted from defective design and placement of the Audi's gas tank and fuel system. They joined as defendants the automobile's manufacturer, Audi NSU Auto Union Aktiengesellschaft (Audi); its importer Volkswagen of America, Inc. (Volkswagen); its regional distributor, petitioner World-Wide Volkswagen Corp. (World-Wide); and its retail dealer, petitioner Seaway. Seaway and World-Wide entered special appearances, claiming that Oklahoma's exercise of jurisdiction over them would offend the limitations on the State's jurisdiction imposed by the Due Process Clause of the Fourteenth Amendment.

The facts presented to the District Court showed that World-Wide is incorporated and has its business office in New York. It distributes vehicles, parts, and accessories, under contract with Volkswagen, to retail dealers in New York, New Jersey, and Connecticut. Seaway, one of these retail dealers, is incorporated and has its place of business in New York. Insofar as the record reveals, Seaway and World-Wide are fully independent corporations whose relations with each other and with Volkswagen and Audi are contractual only. Respondents adduced no evidence that either World-Wide or Seaway does any business in Oklahoma, ships or sells any products to or in that State, has an agent to receive process there, or purchases advertisements in any media calculated to reach Oklahoma. In fact, as respondents' counsel conceded at oral argument, there was no showing that any automobile sold by World-Wide or Seaway has ever entered Oklahoma with the single exception of the vehicle involved in the present case.

Despite the apparent paucity of contacts between petitioners and Oklahoma, the District Court rejected their constitutional claim and reaffirmed that ruling in denying petitioners' motion for reconsideration.[5] Petitioners then sought a writ of prohibition in the Supreme Court of Oklahoma to restrain the District Judge, respondent Charles S. Woodson, from exercising *in personam* jurisdiction over them. They renewed their contention that, because they had no "minimal contacts," with the State of Oklahoma, the actions of the District Judge were in violation of their rights under the Due Process Clause.

The Supreme Court of Oklahoma denied the writ, holding that personal jurisdiction over petitioners was authorized by Oklahoma's "long-arm" statute. Although the court noted that the proper approach was to test jurisdiction against both statutory and constitutional standards, its analysis did not distinguish these questions, probably because [the long-arm statute] has been interpreted as conferring jurisdiction to the limits permitted by the United States Constitution.

As has long been settled, and as we reaffirm today, a state court may exercise personal jurisdiction over a nonresident defendant only so long as there exist "minimum contacts" between the defendant and the forum state. The concept of minimum contacts, in turn, can be seen to perform two related, but distinguishable, functions. It protects the defendant against the burdens of litigating in a distant or inconvenient forum. And it acts to ensure that the States through their courts, do not reach out beyond the limits imposed on them by their status as coequal sovereigns in a federal system.

The protection against inconvenient litigation is typically described in terms of "reasonableness" or "fairness." We have said that the defendant's contacts with the forum State must be such that maintenance of the suit "does not offend 'traditional notions of fair play and substantial justice.'" . . . The limits imposed on state jurisdiction by the Due Process Clause, in its role as a guarantor against inconvenient litigation, have been substantially relaxed over the years. As we noted . . . this trend is largely attributable to a fundamental transformation in the American economy:

> "Today many commercial transactions touch two or more States and may involve parties separated by the full continent. With this increasing nationalization of commerce has come a great increase in the amount of business conducted by mail across state lines. At the same time modern transportation and communication have made it much less burdensome for a party sued to defend himself in a State where he engages in economic activity."

The historical developments . . . of course, have only accelerated in the generation since that case was decided.

Nevertheless, we have never accepted the proposition that state lines are irrelevant for jurisdictional purposes, nor could we, and remain faithful to the principles of interstate federalism embodied in the Constitution.

Applying these principles to the case at hand, we find in the record before us a total absence of those affiliating circumstances that are a necessary predicate to any exercise of state-court jurisdiction. Petitioners carry on no activity whatsoever in Oklahoma. They close no sales and perform no services there. They avail themselves of none of the privileges and benefits of Oklahoma law. They solicit no business there either through salespersons or through advertising reasonably calculated to reach the State. Nor does the record show that they regularly sell cars at wholesale or retail to Oklahoma customers or residents or that they indirectly, through others, serve or seek to serve the Oklahoma market. In short, respondents seek to base jurisdiction on one, isolated occurrence and whatever inferences can be drawn therefrom: the fortuitous circumstance that a single Audi automobile, sold in New York to New York residents, happened to suffer an accident while passing through Oklahoma.

It is argued, however, that because an automobile is mobile by its very design and purpose it was "foreseeable" that the Robinsons' Audi would cause injury in Oklahoma. Yet "foreseeability" alone has never been a sufficient benchmark for personal jurisdiction under the Due Process Clause.

"IF FORESEEABILITY were the criterion, a local California tire retailer could be forced to defend in Pennsylvania when a blowout occurs there . . or a Florida soft-drink concessionaire could be summoned to Alaska to account for injuries happening there."

If foreseeability were the criterion, a local California tire retailer could be forced to defend in Pennsylvania when a blowout occurs there; a Wisconsin seller of a defective automobile jack could be haled before a distant court for damage caused in New Jersey; or a Florida soft-drink concessionaire could be summoned to Alaska to account for injuries happening there. Every seller of chattels would in effect appoint the chattel his agent for service of process. His amenability to suit would travel with the chattel. . . .

This is not to say, of course, that foreseeability is wholly irrelevant. **But the foreseeability that is critical to due process analysis is not the mere likelihood that a product will find its way into the forum State. Rather, it is that the defendant's conduct and connection with the forum State are such that he should reasonably anticipate being haled into court there. The Due Process Clause, by ensuring the "orderly administration of the laws," gives a degree of predictability to the legal system that allows potential defendants to structure their primary conduct with some minimum assurance as to where that conduct will and will not render them liable to suit.**

When a corporation "purposefully avails itself of the privilege of conducting activities within the forum State," it has clear notice that it is subject to suit there, and can act to alleviate the risk of burdensome litigation by procuring insurance, passing the expected costs on to customers, or, if the risks are too great, severing its connection with the State. Hence if the sale of a product of a manufacturer or distributor such as Audi or Volkswagen is not simply an isolated occurrence, but arises from the efforts of the manufacturer or distributor to serve directly or indirectly, the market for its product in other States, it is not unreasonable to subject it to suit in one of those States if its allegedly defective merchandise has there been the source of injury to its owner or to others. The forum State does not exceed its powers under the Due Process Clause if it asserts personal jurisdiction over a corporation that delivers its products into the stream of commerce with the expectation that they will be purchased by consumers in the forum State.

But there is no such or similar basis for Oklahoma jurisdiction over World-Wide or Seaway in this case. Seaway's sales are made in Massena, N. Y. World-Wide's market, although substantially larger, is limited to dealers in New York, New Jersey, and Connecticut. There is no evidence of record that any automobiles distributed by World-Wide are sold to retail customers outside this tristate area. It is foreseeable that the purchasers of automobiles sold by World-Wide and Seaway may take them to Oklahoma. But the mere "unilateral activity of those who claim some relationship with a nonresident defendant cannot satisfy the requirement of contact with the forum State."

In a variant on the previous argument, it is contended that jurisdiction can be supported by the fact that petitioners earn substantial revenue from goods used in Oklahoma . . This argument seems to make the point that the purchase of automobiles in New York, from which the petitioners earn substantial revenue, would not occur *but for* the fact that the automobiles are capable of use in distant States like Oklahoma . . In our view, whatever marginal revenues petitioners may receive by virtue of the fact that their products are capable of use in Oklahoma is far too attenuated a contact to justify that State's exercise of *in personam* jurisdiction over them.

Because we find that petitioners have no "contacts, ties, or relations" with the State of Oklahoma, the judgment of the Supreme Court of Oklahoma is *Reversed.*

Obtaining jurisdiction is not, as the VW case shows, a matter of foreseeability; it is instead a matter of whether there actually are contacts that subject a company or person to a state's legal authority.

C. JURISDICTION OVER THE PROPERTY

Other ways to obtain jurisdiction of the defendant are through the property owned by the defendant. In rem jurisdiction is when the court exercises its power to determine the status of property located within its territory and judgment is binding on all interest holders. *Quasi-in-rem* **jurisdiction** is an attempt to obtain personal jurisdiction through attachment of property found within the State, but here recovery is limited to the value of the property. In order to obtain *in rem* or *quasi-in-rem* jurisdiction, the property must (1) be found within the state, (2) property must be attached to the defendant at the outset of the proceeding, and (3) the property can be tangible or intangible (bank accounts, for example). Currently, the majority rule is that jurisdiction over attached property requires personal jurisdiction over the property owner.

D. SUBJECT MATTER JURISDICTION

Subject matter jurisdiction is the court's power to hear a case because of the nature of the dispute. It is determined in the state courts by the state constitution, state statutes, and judicial decisions. In the federal courts, it is determined by Article III of the Constitution, federal statutes, and judicial decisions. The aims of diversity jurisdiction in federal courts are to (1) prevent state-court prejudice against out-of-state actors, and (2) implement the constitutional guarantee that citizens of each state are entitled to all privileges of citizens of all states. Exclusive jurisdiction over certain matters is conferred to federal courts by Article III. The following cases cannot be heard in state court: Certain securities-law class actions; bankruptcy, patents and copyrights and actions against foreign consuls; actions to recover a fine, penalty or forfeiture under federal law; actions involving certain seizures.

II. Process of a Civil Trial

A. SERVICE

The Due Process Clause of the 14th Amendment requires that

- The defendant receive adequate notice of litigation
- Notice provides for service of process informing the defendant of the court proceedings
- Proceedings include a copy of the complaint against the defendant
- The summons commands the defendant to answer the plaintiff's complaint within a fixed period of time

One of the requirements of service of process is that it must be sufficient to allow any parties being sued to understand the nature of the suit and how they can present their objections. In *Mullane v. Central Hanover Bank & Trust Co.*, 339 U.S. 306, 314 (1950), the Supreme Court held that in a lawsuit for judicial settlement of accounts by a trustee of a common trust fund, notice published in a local New York newspaper was sufficient for some parties but not for others. While it may be surprising that such an impersonal method was deemed acceptable, courts continue to increase the standard of service.

Here are a few examples of what courts have and have not found to be proper service of process:

Service: Proper or Improper?

MCDONALD V. MABEE, 243 U.S. 90 (1917): The Supreme Court held that notice by publication in the last known state of residence was insufficient and required notice by mail to the defendant's last known address.

GREENE V. LINDSEY, 456 U.S. 444 (1982): The Supreme Court found that notice posted on door in a public housing project wasn't sufficient because kids could tear it down and the court required it to be supplemented by notice through mail.

DUSENBERRY V. UNITED STATES, 534 U.S. 161 (2002): The Supreme Court recently held that notice by certified mail to a prisoner was sufficient—even though the prison mail room signed for the letter, not the inmate, and no paper trail verifying the delivery could be found.

NATIONAL DEVELOPMENT CO. V. TRIAD HOLDING CORP, 930 F.2d 253 (1991): The court held service on the defendant's housekeeper at his New York City apartment was sufficient even though it was one of twelve homes owned by the defendant. The court said that the service was "reasonably calculated" to provide actual notice. It just so happened that the defendant was at the apartment that day.

FASHION PAGE, LTD. V. ZURICH INS. CO., 50 N.Y.2d 265 (1980): The court held that service on the defendant's secretary was sufficient because her testimony showed that she often received service in his absence. The court found this past conduct as evidence of implicit authorization to receive boss's service of process. However, the court noted that her simply saying she could accept, with no past conduct, would not be enough.

OMNI CAPITAL INTERNATIONAL V. RUDOLPH WOLFF, 484 U.S. 97 (1987): The Supreme Court held that foreign defendants conducting business in the U.S. were not amenable to service in any state and were therefore unaccountable to federal law. Congress enacted Rule 4(k)(2) as a response to the court decision Rule of Civil Procedure Rule 4(k)(2) states: For a claim that arises under federal law, serving a summons or filing a waiver of service establishes personal jurisdiction over a defendant if: (A) the defendant is not subject to jurisdiction in any state's courts of general jurisdiction; and (B) exercising jurisdiction is consistent with the United States Constitution and laws. The broad language in subsection (B) allows the government flexibility in obtaining jurisdiction over foreign defendants in the U.S.

B. CHOICE OF VENUE

In addition to personal jurisdiction and subject matter jurisdiction, venue must be proper. While state venue is determined by state law and federal venue is determined by federal law, these determinations of venue depend primarily on:

- Convenience to the parties
- Sensible relationship to the claim
- Consideration of judicial economy

These factors are considered by the courts in an effort to prevent "forum shopping," where one party attempts to bring a case in a court solely because the party believes that court will be favorable and has no other valid reason for bringing a case in a certain jurisdiction.

C. PLEADINGS

Once personal jurisdiction, subject matter jurisdiction and venue have been established, the plaintiff must plead his/her case. The function of modern pleading is to provide notice of the nature of a claim or defense. Other traditional functions include giving the court a chance to identify baseless claims in the interest of judicial economy, so the court does not waste any resources on a case that has no merits. The pleading also sets each party's view of the facts, and sets the issues for trial that will be decided by a judge and/or a jury.

The complaint, which includes date, place, injuries, and relief requested, can never be too specific. Attorneys tend to use over-pleading as a strategic move; they want to influence the judge before trial starts. The Federal Rules of Civil Procedure, Rule 8(a) require a pleading to state a claim for relief, and require that it contain:

- a short and plain statement of the grounds for the court's jurisdiction, unless the court already has jurisdiction and the claim needs no new jurisdictional support,
- a short and plain statement of the claim showing that the pleader is entitled to relief,
- a demand for relief sought, which may include relief in the alternative or different types of relief.

It is important to properly plead your case; otherwise, a judge may dismiss it for being too vague or baseless. You may not, however, state a claim of relief that contains legal conclusions.

Gillispie v. Goodyear Service Stores

258 N.C. 487, 128 S.E.2d 762 (1963)

Plaintiff alleges she and each of the four individual defendants are citizens and residents of Alamance County, North Carolina; that defendant Goodyear Tire & Rubber Company is a corporation doing business in North Carolina and having a place of business and store in Burlington, North Carolina; and that Goodyear Service Stores is a division of defendant Goodyear Tire & Rubber Company.

The remaining allegations of the complaint and the prayer for relief are as follows:

'4. On or about May 5, 1959, and May 6, 1959, the defendants, without cause or just excuse and maliciously came upon and trespassed upon the premises occupied by the plaintiff as a residence, and by the use of harsh and threatening language and physical force directed against the plaintiff assaulted the plaintiff and placed her in great fear, and humiliated and embarrassed her by subjecting her to public scorn and ridicule, and caused her to be seized and exhibited to the public as a prisoner, and to be confined in a public jail, all to her great humiliation, embarrassment and harm.

'5. By reason of the defendants' malicious and intentional assault against and humiliation of the plaintiff, the plaintiff was and has been damaged and injured in the amount of $25,000.00.

'6. The acts of the defendants as aforesaid were deliberate, malicious, and with the deliberate intention of harming the plaintiff, and the plaintiff is entitled to recover her actual damages as well as punitive damages from the defendants and each of them.

'THEREFORE, the plaintiff prays that she have and recover of the defendants the sum of $25,000.00 as damages and $10,000.00 in addition thereto as punitive damages, and that she have such other and further relief as may be just and proper.'

Separate demurrers were filed by: (1) defendants Goodyear Tire & Rubber Company, Goodyear Service Stores, a division of Goodyear Tire & Rubber Company, and O. J. Hartsell; (2) defendant Robert E. Harden; (3) defendant Melvin Wrenn; (4) defendant Arthur Jones. Although different in phraseology, each demurrer specifies two grounds of objection to the complaint, namely, (1) that the complaint does not state facts sufficient to constitute a cause of action, and (2) that there is a misjoinder of parties and causes of action.

The court entered a separate judgment with reference to each of said four demurrers. In each judgment, after a recital of the said grounds on which the demurrer was based and a recital that the court was of the opinion 'that said demurrer should be sustained,' it was 'ORDERED, ADJUDGED and DECREED that said demurrer be and the same is hereby sustained and the court, in its discretion, grants unto said plaintiff thirty (30) days within which to file amended complaint.'

Plaintiff excepted to each of said four judgments and appealed.

A complaint must contain '(a) plain and concise statement of the facts constituting a cause of action * * * .' 'The cardinal requirement of this statute * * * is that the facts constituting a cause of action, rather than the conclusions of the pleader, must be set out in the complaint, so as to disclose the issuable facts determinative of the plaintiff's right to relief." The cause of action consists of the facts alleged. The statutory requirement is that a complaint must allege the material, essential and ultimate facts upon which plaintiff's right of action is based. 'The law is presumed

to be known, but the facts to which the law is to be applied are not known until properly presented by the pleading and established by evidence.'

The facts alleged, but not the pleader's legal conclusions, are deemed admitted when the sufficiency of the complaint is tested by demurrer. 'Where the complaint merely alleges conclusions and not facts, it fails to state a cause of action and is demurrable. However, it is well settled that a complaint must be fatally defective before it will be rejected as insufficient, and 'if in any portion of it or to any extent it presents facts sufficient to constitute a cause of action the pleading will stand.'

When a complaint alleges defendant is indebted to plaintiff in a certain amount and such debt is due, but does not allege in what manner or for what cause defendant became indebted to plaintiff, it is demurrable for failure to state facts sufficient to constitute a cause of action.

'The liability for tort grows out of the violation of some legal duty by the defendant, not arising out of contract, and the complaint should state facts sufficient to show such legal duty and its violation, resulting in injury to the plaintiff. What these facts are must depend upon the elements which go to make up the particular tort complained of, under the substantive law.'

'In an action or defense based upon negligence, it is not sufficient to allege the mere happening of an event of an injurious nature and call it negligence on the part of the party sought to be charged. This is necessarily so because negligence is not a fact in itself, but is the legal result of certain facts. Therefore, the facts which constitute the negligence charged and also the facts which establish such negligence as the proximate cause, or as one of the proximate causes, of the injury must be alleged.'

In *Letterman v. Mica Co.*, a demurrer was sustained on the ground the facts alleged were insufficient to support the plaintiffs' allegation that the injury they sustained was proximately caused by wrongful conduct of the defendants.

As stated by BARNHILL, J. in *Parker v. White*: 'The competency of evidence, the form of the issues, and the charge of the court are all controlled in very large measure by the nature of the cause of action alleged by plaintiff. Hence, the trial judge, as well as the defendant, must know the exact right plaintiff seeks to assert or the legal wrong for which he seeks redress before there can be any intelligent trial under the rules of procedure which govern our system of jurisprudence.'

Plaintiff alleges, in a single sentence, that defendant, 'without cause or just excuse and maliciously, 'trespassed upon premises occupied by her as a residence, assaulted her and caused her to be seized and confined as a prisoner. The complaint states no facts upon which these legal conclusions may be predicated. Plaintiff's allegations do not disclose what occurred, when it occurred, where it occurred, who did what, the relationships between defendants and plaintiff or of defendants *inter se*, or any other factual data that might identify the occasion or describe the circumstances of the alleged wrongful conduct of defendants.

In *Stivers v. Baker*, it was held that a petition alleging the defendant unlawfully assaulted the plaintiff, thereby putting him in great fear, but not stating how the assault was made, stated a mere conclusion of law and was demurrable as not stating facts constituting a cause of action as required by the Kentucky statute. The court, in opinion by Holt, J., points out that a statement of the facts constituting a cause of action 'is not only necessary to enable the opposite party to form an issue, and to inform him of what his adversary intends to prove, but to enable the court to declare the law upon the facts stated. It cannot do so if a mere legal conclusion is stated. The term "assault" has a legal meaning; as much so as the word "trespass."

The judgments sustaining the demurrers are affirmed on the ground the complaint does not state facts sufficient to constitute any cause of action. It would seem appropriate that plaintiff, in accordance with leave granted in the judgments from which she appealed, now file an amended complaint and therein allege the facts upon which she bases her right to recover.

Affirmed.

The issue in the above case is, frankly, similar to a common flaw in students' explanation of a case. Students often conclude what the holding is for a case without explaining the reasons for the holding. It is tempting to write who won the case and who lost; that's an important aspect, but in order to see how the case might apply in the future, it is vital to flesh out the reasoning for the decision. If one simply focuses on who wins and who loses, one is engaged in conclusory writing.

Similarly, the court in the above case is saying that a complaint needs to explain why something happened and why there is a reason for a court case rather than just stating, or concluding, that such is the case.

After a plaintiff pleads the case, the defendant can file a motion to dismiss the claim. There are several reasons for dismissing a claim, and one of them is for failure to state a claim upon which relief can be granted. These motions to dismiss are not often granted, but they do allow the defendant to get out of the suit before incurring any expenses.

There are two tests for dismissing a claim:

- ***Legal Sufficiency:*** If the law does not recognize a claim given that all the factual allegations are accepted as true, a motion to dismiss is granted. As an example, suppose you very accurately reported that another person had said something insulting about your favorite sports team. Even if that is true, the law does not provide for damages simply because another person insults your favorite sports team. So, there is no legally recognizable claim you can make.

- ***Factual Allegations:*** If the facts are too vague or there are not enough facts alleged to show that the claim is plausible, the court will dismiss the claim.

It is important to note that when a plaintiff alleges that the defendant committed fraud, there is a heightened pleading requirement. **Fraud** itself is a false or misleading statement that induces someone to take action to their detriment. In alleging fraud or mistake, a party must state with particularity the circumstances constituting the fraud or mistake. Malice, intent, knowledge, and other conditions of a person's mind may be alleged generally. The courts have presented four policy reasons for heightened pleadings in fraud cases. These reasons are:

- Protection of reputation (allegations are a very serious matter)
- Deterrence of frivolous or strike suits
- Defense of completed transactions
- Provision of adequate notice

In *Denny v. Barber*, the U.S. Court of Appeals for the Second Circuit held that this heightened pleading requirement was not satisfied because of a lack of specific factual allegations against a bank in a securities fraud case. The court said that the plaintiffs were on "a fishing expedition" for evidence of fraud. Most courts demand that the plaintiff specify the "who, what, when, where and how" of a defendant's acts, and there has been a growing trend towards this requirement.

Even Congress has supported a higher pleading requirement for fraud cases. The Private Securities Litigation Reform Act (PSLRA) says, "[f]acts giving rise to a strong inference that the defendant acted with *scienter* must be stated with particularity." **Scienter** is the civil court's **mens rea**—a defendant's intention to deceive, manipulate, or defraud. The PSLRA was the brainchild of Congress and was created in response to the prevalence of fraud cases. It creates a higher burden of pleading for securities fraud in particular. There must be a "strong inference" of scienter requirement, meaning that the complaint must allege facts from which, if true, a reasonable person could infer that scienter is "cogent and at least as compelling as any opposing inference of non-fraudulent intent."

D. ANSWERING A COMPLAINT

After the plaintiff pleads his/her case against the defendant, the defendant must then respond to the complaint by filing an answer. **Answers** to a complaint generally contain denials, admissions, affirmative defenses, and counterclaims. A **denial** is when the defendant denies the truth of the complaints alleged against him/her. An admission is when the defendant admits to a fact alleged in the complaint. An **affirmative defense** is when the defendant admits to the action alleged, but claims it was caused by something else or that he has some recognized legal defense against liability. Lastly a **counterclaim** is the defendant's own claim against the plaintiff for damages. If the defendant files a counterclaim in the answer to the complaint, the plaintiff must then respond through a **reply**, which may contain similar elements to an answer to the complaint. Here is a sample answer to a complaint from the Supreme Court of New York:

Sample Complaint

COMPLAINT

Supreme Court of the State of New York
County of Broome

______________________________________ x

John Jones,
Plaintiff,

Answer

—vs— Index No.: 2004-0130

George Smith
Defendant.

______________________________________ x

As and for his Answer to the Complaint herein, the Defendant, George Smith, respectfully shows and alleges as follows:

1. Admits the truth of the allegations in paragraphs "1" and "2" of the Complaint.

2. Denies knowledge or information suffice to form a belief as to the truth of the allegations of paragraphs "3", "4", "5" and "6" of the Complaint.

3. Denies the allegations of paragraphs "7" and "8" of the Complaint.

4. Denies any and all allegations not heretofore previously admitted or denied.

As and For First Affirmative Defense

5. Defendant repeats and reiterates the allegations contained in paragraphs "1" through "4" as if fully set forth herein.

6. ____
____
____

As and for a second affirmative defense

7. Defendant repeats and reiterates the allegations contained in paragraphs "1" through "6" as is fully set forth herein

8. ____
____
____

Wherefore, Defendant prays that this Court dismiss the Complaint of the Plaintiff herein, with costs and disbursements to the Defendant, together with such other relief the Court finds to be just and proper.

Dated: (Date)

George Smith signature
George Smith, Defendant
125 Main Street
Binghamton, NY 13901
Phone #

TO: John Jones, Plaintiff
32 Adams Street
Vestal, NY 13850

—OR—

Plaintiff's Attorney
Address
City, State, ZIP

Verifications

George Smith, being duly sworn, deposes and says:

I am the Defendant in the above entitled action. I have read the foregoing Answer and know the contents thereof. The same are true to my knowledge, except as to matters therein stated to be alleged on information and belief as to those matters, I believe them to be true.

To the best of my knowledge, information and belief, formed after inquiry reasonable under the circumstances, the presentation of these papers or the contentions therein are not frivolous as defined in Subsection (c) of section 130-1.1 of the Rules of the Chief Administrative Judge (22 NYCRR).

George Smith signature
George Smith, Defendant

Sworn to me this (X) day of (month), (year).

William Brown signature
Notary Public

Form: http://www.nycourts.gov/courts/6jd/forms/SRForms/ans_examp.pdf

E. DISCOVERY

The discovery process is considered to be the most cumbersome part of civil cases in the United States. When preparing for trial or even before completion of the pleadings stages, both parties may obtain relevant evidence to build their case—in fact, they have a right to this evidence even if it is in the possession of the opposing side. This procedure is known as discovery.

The purpose of discovery is to preserve relevant information that might not be available at trial, to ascertain and isolate issues that actually are in controversy between the parties, and to find out what testimony and other evidence is available on each of the disputed factual issues. There are also several policy reasons for discovery in the U.S. courts. Discovery helps to promote transparency by making information about government and corporate practice available to a broader set of people than just the parties to a lawsuit. It also permits widespread discovery of the facts before trial, which eliminates an unfair "surprise" at trial. However, the scope of discovery in U.S. courts has become a cause of concern because abuse of the discovery procedure ends up being very pervasive and financially burdensome. Some refer to abuse of the discovery phase as a "fishing expedition."

Discovery can take place through several mechanisms. These include oral depositions, written depositions, interrogatories, document requests, and examinations (both physical and/or mental). Through these mechanisms, parties must present materials that are not legally privileged, that are relevant to any party's claim or defense, including financial information. It is obvious but worth noting that one thing a party is not obligated to disclose is the lawyer's legal strategy for trial.

When the evidence disclosed by the discovery phase makes the verdict clear, a party may move for summary judgment and a judge may make a final and binding determination on the merits. If the judge issues a summary judgment, the case does not need to go to trial.

F. THE TRIAL

If a case goes to trial, there are several stages of which all parties must be aware. First, there is the jury selection. Jury members are selected randomly from the territory of the jurisdiction. However, the parties have a right to conduct a voir dire of the selected jury members, which allows the parties a chance to eliminate jurors that are biased and cannot be fair or impartial. This does not mean that the courts allow for any type of discrimination by the attorneys themselves; there must be a valid reason for eliminating a juror, not based solely on race, gender, or religion.

Once the jury has been selected and both attorneys have conducted their *voir dires*, each side will give its **opening statements**. During the opening statements, attorneys will present the main factual and legal issues of their clients' cases, which serve as evidence in the trial. Generally, the plaintiff bears the burden of proof because he/she is the one who has instigated the lawsuit—therefore, the plaintiff must prove that the case is a valid one with sufficient evidence to support the alleged wrong. The defendant, on the other hand, will rebut the plaintiff's arguments and evidence, and seek to prove any affirmative defenses that were claimed during the answer to the complaint. If the defendant alleged any counter-claims, this is also the time to present evidence of the harms allegedly committed by the plaintiff. Both sides may present witnesses as part of their arguments.

After the opening statements and after both sides have presented their clients' cases, the plaintiff's attorney has one last chance to make his client's argument and disprove the defendant's case. This is called the **rebuttal**. At the end of the rebuttal, each side is allowed to make closing arguments.

Closing arguments are the parties' last chances to convince the jury to find in their favor. They will highlight the strengths in their cases while pointing to the weaknesses of the opposing side. Finally, the judge will instruct the jury members as to which laws they must apply when arriving at a verdict. This is called a **jury instruction**. Then, the jury will enter **judgment**. Usually this is the final say—the binding decision of the court. However, in some cases the verdict may be overturned by the judge if the judge finds bias or jury misconduct.

NOTES AND COMMENTS on the Legal Environment of Business

1. **CONFLICT OF LAWS,** the name of a law school course that looks to see what courts should hear cases when multiple courts could, in theory, do so, tends to be something of a sleepy subject (granting that there are those who do relish the topic), but it has tremendous importance in today's global economy. Not only may a case be heard in many different states, territories or districts of the United States, it might also be heard in different countries. Because of this, businesses have a significant incentive for determining what courts have jurisdictions over the persons and over the subject matter of a case. They often do this through "choice of law" provisions in contracts, where the agreement states that, in the event of a dispute, the parties agree that the case will be heard in a specific place. Before you click "yes" to the next software you download for Apple or Microsoft, take a look at the actual agreement and you will see this provision. Courts tend to look favorably on such agreements—though not always—as a way to de-clutter court calendars.

2. **A FEW DECADES AGO,** courts viewed alternate dispute resolution mechanisms suspiciously, as the province of the judicial system. But with full court calendars, judges increasingly found merit in contract provisions to arbitrate disputes or to agree to bring in non-binding mediation efforts. Even television shows like *Judge Judy, The People's Court or Judge Joe Brown* provide non-judicial ways to resolve disputes. Together with choice of law provisions, there are ways to decide cases while minimizing court time and legal costs.

NOTES AND COMMENTS on the Ethical Environment of Business

AS WE SAW in the previous chapter on the common law, predictable processes have their own ethical merit. Trials, after all, are the contemporary alternative to violence and so while they may seem expensive and onerous, they are an improvement over murderous feuds, vigilantism, and duels, and war. Knowing there is a process for settling disputes peacefully is itself an ethical value and it is worth stepping back and recognizing this development. Moreover, just as studies show that people can adapt to many different ethical styles and approaches, what seems to be most important is an evenly administered process, whatever the particulars of that process may be.

With that in mind, where do you think the current system, described in this chapter, can be improved? What are its weaknesses? How could it be fairer? What are its strengths? As a point of departure, what do you think of the jury system? Is this a part of the trial process that should be retained or jettisoned? What are its strengths and weaknesses? Would you prefer a jury trial if you were being charged with a crime? What if you were a business person in the high-tech field. Do you think a jury of your peers would produce a fairer result or would you rather have a judge decide your case?

One of the steps in the trial process is Discovery. As we have seen, this is the step in the trial process where the parties find out additional facts about the case. The notion is that the more facts are known, the easier it is for the parties to determine whether or not to proceed with trail or, instead, settle the case. The ethical corollary to this idea is that if one passes judgment on the basis of insufficient information, all you are doing is gossiping. So knowing more facts helps one make better judgments and decisions.

While good in theory, discovery has also been weaponized. That is, it becomes a tool to overwhelm the other side, especially when the parties have unequal financial conditions. A wealthy litigant can force a weaker party to spend more than they can afford with requests for documents, interrogatories, depositions and expert witnesses along the legal fees that go along with each one of those. In a case where both parties have deep pockets, such as two major corporations, a million pages of discovery can be produced.

How do assess the fairness of these consequences? If you were a wealthy business, would you use such tactics to force a weaker opponent to settle the case on terms advantageous to you? Would there be any limit on your use of such an advantage? Why or why not? Should a third party, such as the judicial system itself, step in to limit the amount of discovery that can be used and for certain purposes or is this potential inequity simply something that is part of the way business and the court system itself works?

Turning to jurisdiction, this is not as sleepy a subject as one might think. To be sure, looking at the cases like *Pennoyer or International Shoe* or *Volkswagen* may not seem to be especially exciting nor loaded with ethical issues. But step back for a moment. One would find a general agreement that different cultures do things differently. What is appropriate in one place of the world may not be acceptable in another, well, jurisdiction. That may even be true in the same state. Take a diverse state like Illinois, where the culture of metropolitan Chicago may be very different from the culture of rural Illinois. It might seem, then, that each community—or jurisdiction—should make decisions based on what the values are of that area.

Yet, modern society is defined by mobility. That is true of travel and it is true of the Internet. One can cross borders easily for commerce and for other things as well. In such cases, one is challenging notions of jurisdiction. Later, in the chapter on White Collar Crime, we will see a case where a person in California goes to jail in Tennessee simply because the material on their website could be purchased in Tennessee and that the website's material violated Tennessee law. The Californians never had stepped foot in Tennessee until they were prosecuted. Are results such as these fair? Should there simply be one standard of values for everyone since the Internet and international travel allows people to move so easily? How would that be done? Or should there be more restrictions on where a person could be sued? Would that, also, raise fairness questions?

CHAPTER

5

Administrative Aspects

The work of government, even in ancient times, has always been vast. In the Torah, Moses's father-in-law Jethro advises him to appoint judges who can decide disputes between members of the community in order to reduce the burden on Moses. In ancient Egypt, viziers were appointed by the Pharaoh to supervise specific areas of the government, such as the collection of taxes. Rulers during the Han dynasty in China delegated military power to regional potentates in order to control rebellions.[1]

The result is an administrative structure that requires some set of rules for establishing it, running it, and reviewing it. Of course, the ways governments do each of these three things differ. For instance, one will see a different set of review practices in a totalitarian structure than is seen in a democratic one. The basic questions of how one determines how and what to delegate, how these administrative organizations work, and how decisions they make get reviewed, though, are fundamental.

MOSES TAKES HIS LEAVE OF JETHRO, BY JAN VICTORS, C. 1635

In the United States, a first division occurs between the Federal and State governments. Each state can have its own unique set of administrative bodies overseeing issues that arise in the state. The state of Iowa will not have an administrative agency concerned with oceanic matters such as Florida or Hawaii might. But

1 Pines, Yuri. *The Everlasting Empire: The Political Culture of Ancient China and Its Imperial Legacy*. Princeton: Princeton University Press, 2012. 24. *Image courtesy of The Yorck Project and Wikimedia Commons.*

because of the 14th Amendment to the Constitution, the rules that apply to state administrative agencies tend to be very similar to those governing federal agencies. You will remember that the 14th Amendment extends issues of Equal Protection to the states. Federal courts have gradually added rights that are of specific Constitutional importance in reviewing state actions as well. Some of these issues will be covered in this chapter but primarily to illustrate concerns that apply to most administrative agencies in the country, regardless of the specific administrative source. The 1946 Administrative Procedure Act also sets out a standard way to address the procedures for federal agencies to follow.

I. Scope of Regulatory Agencies

ON THE FEDERAL LEVEL there are two types of agencies. One is comprised of fifteen agencies whose heads are part of the Executive Cabinet. In addition, there are a number of "independent" agencies established by Congress that are overseen by the executive branch: the Securities Exchange Commission, the National Labor Relations Board, the Federal Reserve Board and the Pension Benefit Guaranty Corporation, among others.

- Department of State
- Department of Treasury
- Department of Defense
- Department of Justice
- Department of the Interior
- Department of Agriculture
- Department of Commerce
- Department of Labor
- Department of Health and Human Services
- Department of Housing and Urban Development
- Department of Transportation
- Department of Energy
- Department of Education
- Department of Veterans Affairs
- Department of Homeland Security

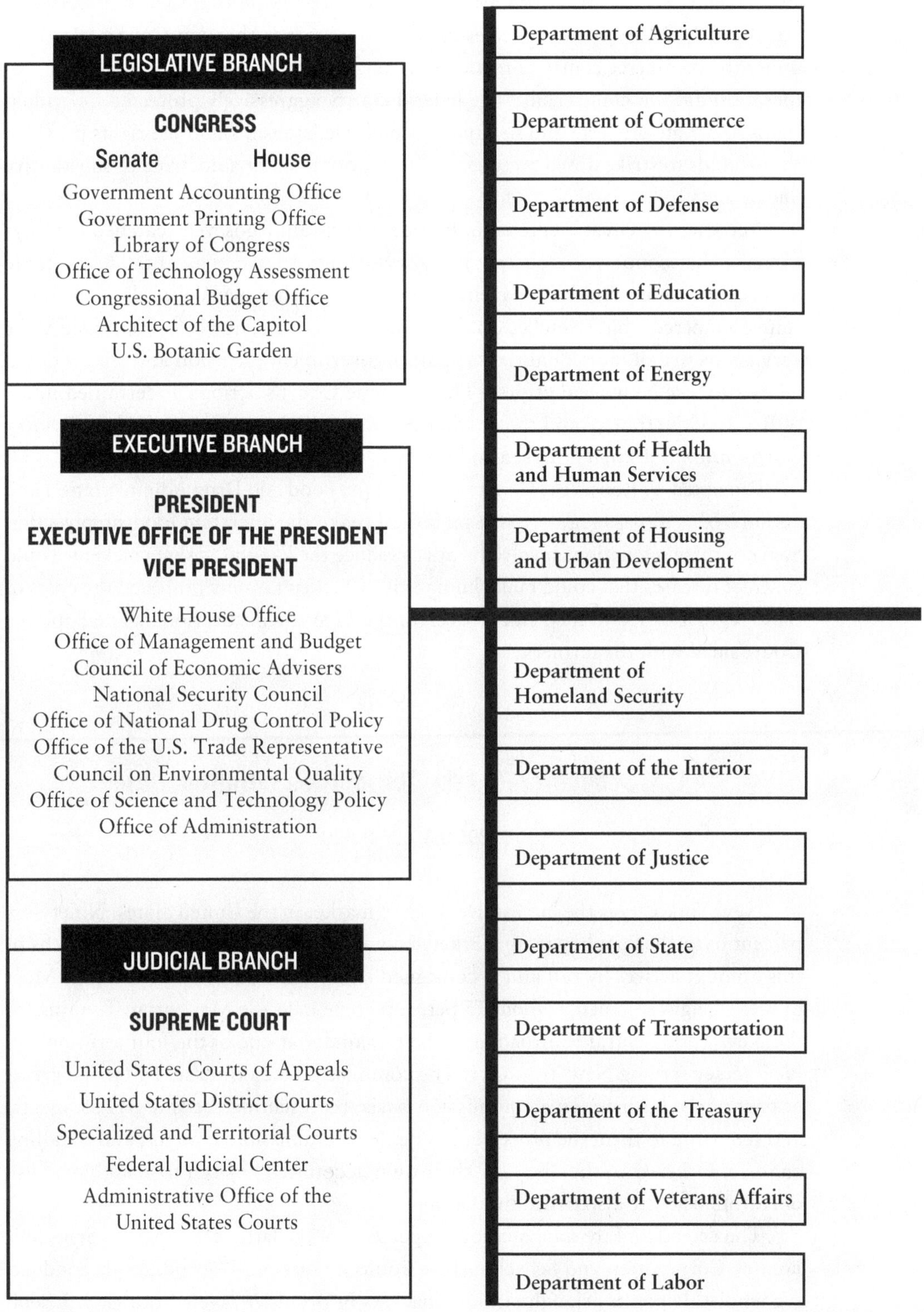
LEGISLATIVE BRANCH
CONGRESS
Senate
House
Government Accounting Office
Government Printing Office
Library of Congress
Office of Technology Assessment
Congressional Budget Office
Architect of the Capitol
U.S. Botanic Garden
EXECUTIVE BRANCH
PRESIDENT
EXECUTIVE OFFICE OF THE PRESIDENT
VICE PRESIDENT
White House Office
Office of Management and Budget
Council of Economic Advisers
National Security Council
Office of National Drug Control Policy
Office of the U.S. Trade Representative
Council on Environmental Quality
Office of Science and Technology Policy
Office of Administration
JUDICIAL BRANCH
SUPREME COURT
United States Courts of Appeals
United States District Courts
Specialized and Territorial Courts
Federal Judicial Center
Administrative Office of the United States Courts
Department of Agriculture
Department of Commerce
Department of Defense
Department of Education
Department of Energy
Department of Health and Human Services
Department of Housing and Urban Development
Department of Homeland Security
Department of the Interior
Department of Justice
Department of State
Department of Transportation
Department of the Treasury
Department of Veterans Affairs
Department of Labor

Even though there has been a long history of Cabinet-level administrative agencies in the U.S., it wasn't until after the Great Depression that their number grew significantly. Most of the agencies came into existence through Congress' power under the commerce clause to regulate matters of interstate commerce but this proliferation did not come easily. The federal courts aggressively protected individual rights to private property and state powers under federalism and those rights provided the grounds to strike down regulatory efforts, often under a doctrine of substantive due process.

Yet after the Great Depression, President Franklin Roosevelt searched for ways to make the economy less susceptible to major financial swings of the market. He also sought to use regulatory agencies to institute other oversight related to interstate commerce—but stretched its definition. The courts, however, continued to be very protective of individual rights against government intrusion and struck down many of these New Deal efforts. The Supreme Court's actions undermined much of Roosevelt's strategy and the conflict culminated with *A.L.A. Schechter Poultry Corporation v. United States*, also known as the "sick chicken" case.

Prompted by Roosevelt, Congress created the Food and Drug Administration and authorized it to pass regulations that would make the interstate food supply safer. Some of these regulations involved ways to reduce the likelihood that chickens would contract diseases that could make humans ill. Chicken farmers protested the costs of these regulations, and filed suit to declare the FDA unconstitutional. The Supreme Court sided with the farmers.

A.L.A. Schechter Poultry Corporation v. United States

295 U.S. 495 (1935)

New York City is the largest live poultry market in the United States. Ninety-six percent of the live poultry there marketed comes from other states. Three-fourths of this amount arrives by rail and is consigned to commission men or receivers. Most of these freight shipments (about 75 percent) come in at the Manhattan Terminal of the New York Central Railroad, and the remainder at one of the four terminals in New Jersey serving New York City. The commission men transact by far the greater part of the business on a commission basis, representing the shippers as agents, and remitting to them the proceeds of sale, less commissions, freight, and handling charges. Otherwise, they buy for their own account. They sell to slaughterhouse operators who are also called market men.

The defendants are slaughterhouse operators of the latter class. A.L.A. Schechter Poultry Corporation and Schechter Live Poultry Market are corporations conducting wholesale poultry slaughterhouse markets in Brooklyn, New York City. Joseph

Schechter operated the latter corporation and also guaranteed the credits of the former corporation, which was operated by Martin, Alex, and Aaron Schechter. Defendants ordinarily purchase their live poultry from commission men at the West Washington Market in New York City or at the railroad terminals serving the city, but occasionally they purchase from commission men in Philadelphia. They buy the poultry for slaughter and resale. After the poultry is trucked to their slaughterhouse markets in Brooklyn, it is there sold, usually within twenty-four hours, to retail poultry dealers and butchers who sell directly to consumers. The poultry purchased from defendants is immediately slaughtered, prior to delivery, by shochtim in defendants' employ. Defendants do not sell poultry in interstate commerce.

The 'Live Poultry Code' was promulgated under section 3 of the National Industrial Recovery Act. * * * [I]t was approved by the President on April 13, 1934. Its divisions indicate its nature and scope. The code has eight articles entitled (1) 'purposes,' (2) 'definitions,' (3) 'hours,' (4) 'wages,' (5) 'general labor provisions,' (6) 'administration,' (7) 'trade practice provisions,' and (8) 'general.'

The declared purpose is 'To effect the policies of title I of the National Industrial Recovery Act.' The code is established as 'a code for fair competition for the live poultry industry of the metropolitan area in and about the City of New York.' That area is described as embracing the five boroughs of New York City, the counties of Rockland, Westchester, Nassau, and Suffolk in the state of New York, the counties of Hudson and Bergen in the state of New Jersey, and the county of Fairfield in the state of Connecticut.

The 'industry' is defined as including 'every person engaged in the business of selling, purchasing of resale, transporting, or handling and/or slaughtering live poultry, from the time such poultry comes into the New York metropolitan area to the time it is first sold in slaughtered form,' and such 'related branches' as may from time to time be included by amendment. Employers are styled 'members of the industry,' and the term 'employee' is defined to embrace 'any and all persons engaged in the industry, however compensated,' except 'members.'

The code fixes the number of hours for workdays. It provides that no employee, with certain exceptions, shall be permitted to work in excess of forty hours in any one week, and that no employees, save as stated, 'shall be paid in any pay period less than at the rate of fifty (50) cents per hour.' The article containing 'general labor provisions' prohibits the employment of any person under 16 years of age, and declares that employees shall have the right of 'collective bargaining' and freedom of choice with respect to labor organizations, in the terms of section 7(a) of the act (15 USCA § 707(a)). The minimum number of employees, who shall be employed by slaughterhouse operators, is fixed; the number being graduated according to the average volume of weekly sales.

* * *

The President approved the code by an executive order (No. 6675–A) in which he found that the application for his approval had been duly made in accordance with the provisions of title 1 of the National Industrial Recover Act. * * *

MR. CHIEF JUSTICE HUGHES.

The question of chief importance relates to the provisions of the code as to the hours and wages of those employed in defendants' slaughterhouse markets. It is plain that these requirements are imposed in order to govern the details of defendants' management of their local business. The persons employed in slaughtering and selling in local trade are not employed in interstate commerce. Their hours and wages have no direct relation to interstate commerce. The question of how many hours these employees should work and what they should be paid differs in no essential respect from similar questions in other local businesses which handle commodities brought into a state and there dealt in as a part of its internal commerce. This appears from an examination of the considerations urged by the government with respect to conditions in the poultry trade. Thus, the government argues that hours and wages affect prices; that slaughterhouse men sell at a small margin above operating costs; that labor represents 50 to 60 percent. of these costs; that a slaughterhouse operator paying lower wages or reducing his cost by exacting long hours of work translates his saving into lower prices; that this results in demands for a cheaper grade of goods:

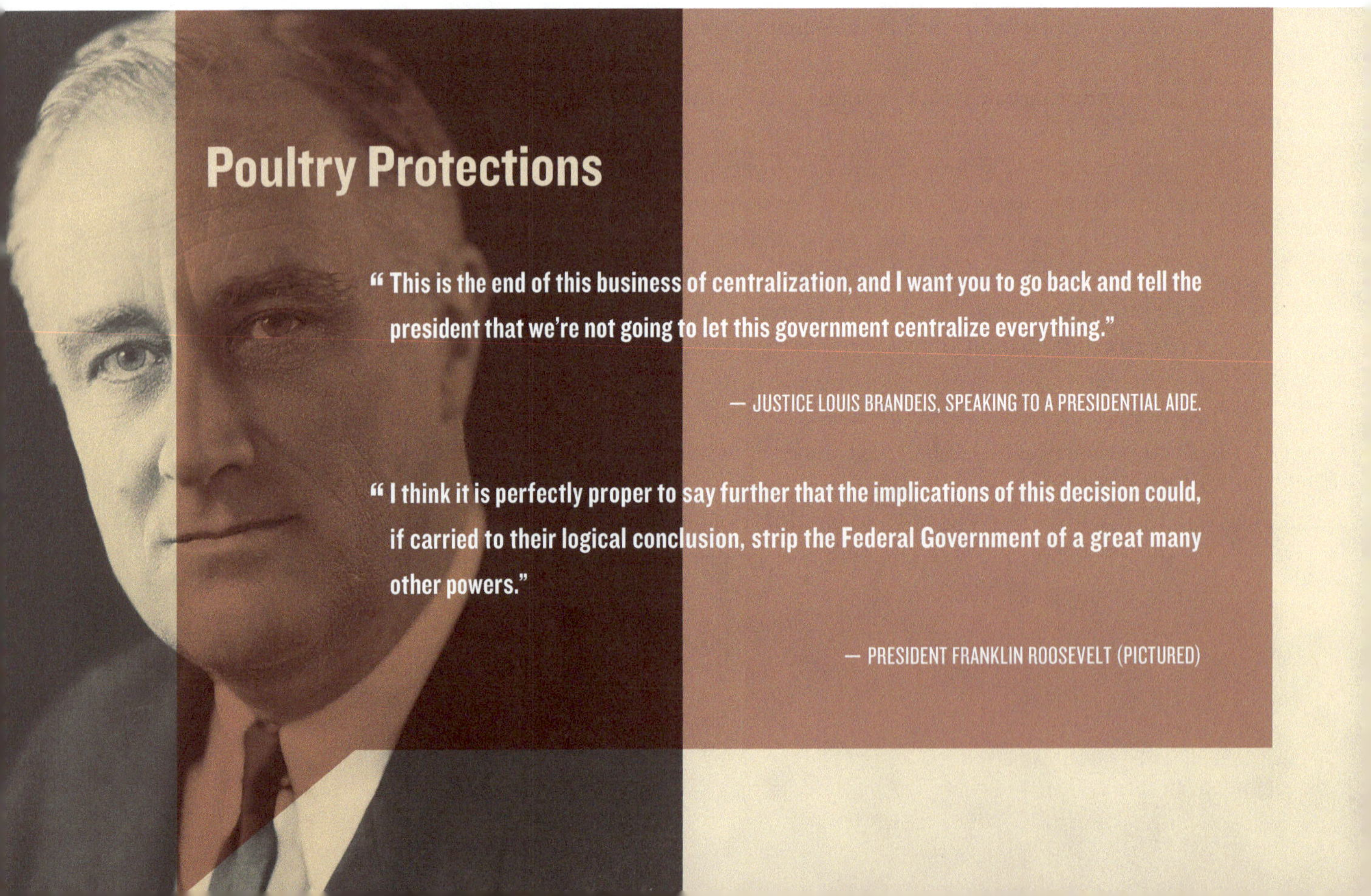

Poultry Protections

"This is the end of this business of centralization, and I want you to go back and tell the president that we're not going to let this government centralize everything."

— JUSTICE LOUIS BRANDEIS, SPEAKING TO A PRESIDENTIAL AIDE.

"I think it is perfectly proper to say further that the implications of this decision could, if carried to their logical conclusion, strip the Federal Government of a great many other powers."

— PRESIDENT FRANKLIN ROOSEVELT (PICTURED)

and that the cutting of prices brings about a demoralization of the price structure. Similar conditions may be adduced in relation to other businesses. The argument of the government proves too much. If the federal government may determine the wages and hours of employees in the internal commerce of a state, because of their relation to cost and prices and their indirect effect upon interstate commerce, it would seem that a similar control might be exerted over other elements of cost, also affecting prices, such as the number of employees, rents, advertising, methods of doing business, etc. All the processes of production and distribution that enter into cost could likewise be controlled. If the cost of doing an intrastate business is in itself the permitted object of federal control, the extent of the regulation of cost would be a question of discretion and not of power.

The government also makes the point that efforts to enact state legislation establishing high labor standards have been impeded by the belief that, unless similar action is taken generally, commerce will be diverted from the states adopting such standards, and that this fear of diversion has led to demands for federal legislation on the subject of wages and hours. The apparent implication is that the federal authority under the commerce clause should be deemed to extend to the establishment of rules to govern wages and hours in intrastate trade and industry generally throughout the country, thus overriding the authority of the states to deal with domestic problems arising from labor conditions in their internal commerce.

It is not the province of the Court to consider the economic advantages or disadvantages of such a centralized system. It is sufficient to say that the Federal Constitution does not provide for it. Our growth and development have called for wide use of the commerce power of the federal government in its control over the expanded activities of interstate commerce and in protecting that commerce from burdens, interferences, and conspiracies to restrain and monopolize it. But the authority of the federal government may not be pushed to such an extreme as to destroy the distinction, which the commerce clause itself establishes, between commerce 'among the several States' and the internal concerns of a state. The same answer must be made to the contention that is based upon the serious economic situation which led to the passage of the Recovery Act—the fall in prices, the decline in wages and employment, and the curtailment of the market for commodities. Stress is laid upon the great importance of maintaining wage distributions which would provide the necessary stimulus in starting 'the cumulative forces making for expanding commercial activity.' Without in any way disparaging this motive, it is enough to say that the recuperative efforts of the federal government must be made in a manner consistent with the authority granted by the Constitution.

We are of the opinion that the attempt through the provisions of the code to fix the hours and wages of employees of defendants in their intrastate business was not a valid exercise of federal power.

The other violations for which defendants were convicted related to the making of local sales. Ten counts, for violation of the provision as to 'straight killing,' were for permitting customers to make 'selections of individual chickens taken from particular coops and half coops.' Whether or not this practice is good or bad for the local trade, its effect, if any, upon interstate commerce was only indirect. The same may be said of violations of the code by intrastate transactions consisting of the sale 'of an unfit chicken' and of sales which were not in accord with the ordinances of the city of New York. The requirement of reports as to prices and volumes of defendants' sales was incident to the effort to control their intrastate business.

. . . On both the grounds we have discussed, the attempted delegation of legislative power and the attempted regulation of intrastate transactions which affect interstate commerce only indirectly, we hold the code provisions here in question to be invalid and that the judgment of conviction must be reversed.

This case may seem at odds with those covered in the Chapter on Constitutional Law, where it seemed that the Commerce Clause gave Congress almost unlimited latitude in regulating any kind of economic activity. There is a good reason for that. It is at odds with those cases in the chapter on Constitutional Law. The Courts did not always interpret the reach of the Commerce Clause as broadly as they do now. The turning point came when the government, especially during the FDR administration, empowered administrative agencies to regulate commerce.

JUSTICE OWEN ROBERTS

In fact, this case was the final straw for Roosevelt, who then proposed that for every justice over the age of seventy, another justice would be appointed. While the justices on the Court could not be removed other than for reasons of impeachment, there was (and remains) no set limit on the number of justices who comprise the Court. The over-seventy justices were those striking down New Deal legislation, but with a larger Court, Roosevelt believed the votes would tip to his side. Suddenly, or so it seemed, the Court became much more receptive to New Deal measures. In particular, Associate Justice Owen Roberts[2], considered a swing vote on many Supreme Court decisions, changed his views and began voting to uphold Roosevelt's new administrative agencies. FDR's plan never became law, but the threat it posed is credited with reorienting the Court's approach.

The following 1937 case, sometimes called "the switch in time that saved the Nine," overruled past decisions that restricted governments from interfering in the employment relationship, though as the case shows, the Court's emphasis on the frailties of women would certainly raise additional questions today.

2 "Owen J. Roberts" by Harris and Ewing. Image: U.S. Library of Congress Prints and Photographs Division

West Coast Hotel Co. v. Parrish

300 U.S. 379 (1937)

This case presents the question of the constitutional validity of the minimum wage law of the state of Washington. The act, entitled 'Minimum Wages for Women,' authorizes the fixing of minimum wages for women and minors. It provides:

> 'Section 1. The welfare of the State of Washington demands that women and minors be protected from conditions of labor which have a pernicious effect on their health and morals. The State of Washington, therefore, exercising herein its police and sovereign power declares that inadequate wages and unsanitary conditions of labor exert such pernicious effect.
>
> 'Sec. 2. It shall be unlawful to employ women or minors in any industry or occupation within the State of Washington under conditions of labor detrimental to their health or morals; and it shall be unlawful to employ women workers in any industry within the State of Washington at wages which are not adequate for their maintenance.
>
> 'Sec. 3. There is hereby created a commission to be known as the 'Industrial Welfare Commission' for the State of Washington, to establish such standards of wages and conditions of labor for women and minors employed within the State of Washington, as shall be held hereunder to be reasonable and not detrimental to health and morals, and which shall be sufficient for the decent maintenance of women.'

* * *

The appellant conducts a hotel. The appellee Elsie Parrish was employed as a chambermaid and (with her husband) brought this suit to recover the difference between the wages paid her and the minimum wage fixed pursuant to the state law. The minimum wage was $14.50 per week of 48 hours. The appellant challenged the act as repugnant to the due process clause of the Fourteenth Amendment of the Constitution of the United States. The Supreme Court of the state, reversing the trial court, sustained the statute and directed judgment for the plaintiffs. The case is here on appeal.

* * *

MR. CHIEF JUSTICE HUGHES.

* * *

The principle which must control our decision is not in doubt. The constitutional provision invoked is the due process clause of the Fourteenth Amendment governing the states, as the due process clause invoked in the Adkins Case governed Congress. In each case the violation alleged by those attacking minimum wage regulation for women is deprivation of freedom of contract. What is this freedom? The Constitution does not speak of freedom of contract. It speaks of liberty and prohibits the deprivation of liberty without due process of law. In prohibiting that deprivation, the Constitution does not recognize an absolute and uncontrollable liberty. Liberty in each of its phases has its history and connotation. But the liberty safeguarded is liberty in a social organization which requires the protection of law against the evils which menace the health, safety, morals, and welfare of the people. Liberty under the Constitution is thus necessarily subject to the restraints of due process, and regulation which is reasonable in relation to its subject and is adopted in the interests of the community is due process.

This essential limitation of liberty in general governs freedom of contract in particular. More than twenty-five years ago we set forth the applicable principle in these words, after referring to the cases where the liberty guaranteed by the Fourteenth Amendment had been broadly described.

> 'But it was recognized in the cases cited, as in many others, that freedom of contract is a qualified, and not an absolute, right. There is no absolute freedom to do as one wills or to contract as one chooses. The guaranty of liberty does not withdraw from legislative supervision that wide department of activity which consists of the making of contracts, or deny to government the power to provide restrictive safeguards. Liberty implies the absence of arbitrary restraint, not immunity from reasonable regulations and prohibitions imposed in the interests of the community.'
>
> This power under the Constitution to restrict freedom of contract has had many illustrations. That it may be exercised in the public interest with respect to contracts between employer and employee is undeniable . . .

"I AM SO GLAD, not only for myself, but for all the women of the state who have been working for just whatever they could get."

—Elsie Parrish, Plaintiff

It is manifest that this established principle is peculiarly applicable in relation to the employment of women in whose protection the state has a special interest. That phase of the subject received elaborate consideration in *Muller v. Oregon* (1908), where the constitutional authority of the state to limit the working hours of women was sustained. We emphasized the consideration that 'woman's physical structure and the performance of maternal functions place her at a disadvantage in the struggle for subsistence' and that her physical well being 'becomes an object of public interest and care in order to preserve the strength and vigor of the race.' We emphasized the need of protecting women against oppression despite her possession of contractual rights. We said that 'though limitations upon personal and contractual rights may be removed by legislation, there is that in her disposition and habits of life which will operate against a full assertion of those rights. She will still be where some legislation to protect her seems necessary to secure a real equality of right.' Hence she was 'properly placed in a class by herself, and legislation designed for her protection may be sustained, even when like legislation is not necessary for men, and could not be sustained.' We concluded that the limitations which the statute there in question 'places upon her contractual powers, upon her right to agree with her employer, as to the time she shall labor' were 'not imposed solely for her benefit, but also largely for the benefit of all.'

* * *

The minimum wage to be paid under the Washington statute is fixed after full consideration by representatives of employers, employees, and the public. It may be assumed that the minimum wage is fixed in consideration of the services that are performed in the particular occupations under normal conditions. Provision is made for special licenses at less wages in the case of women who are incapable of full service. The statement of Mr. Justice Holmes in the Adkins Case is pertinent: 'This statute does not compel anybody to pay anything. It simply forbids employment at rates below those fixed as the minimum requirement of health and right living. It is safe to assume that women will not be employed at even the lowest wages allowed unless they earn them, or unless the employer's business can sustain the burden. In short the law in its character and operation is like hundreds of so-called police laws that have been up-held.' And Chief Justice Taft forcibly pointed out the consideration which is basic in a statute of this character: 'Legislatures which adopt a requirement of maximum hours or minimum wages may be presumed to believe that when sweating employers are prevented from paying unduly low wages by positive law they will continue their business, abating that part of their profits, which were wrung from the necessities of their employees, and will concede the better terms required by the law, and that while in individual cases, hardship may result, the restriction will enure to the benefit of the general class of employees in whose interest the law is passed, and so to that of the community at large.'

We think that the views thus expressed are sound and that the decision in the *Adkins* Case was a departure from the true application of the principles governing the regulation by the state of the relation of employer and employed. Those principles have been reinforced by our subsequent decisions . . . With full recognition of the earnestness and vigor which characterize the prevailing opinion in the *Adkins* Case, we find it impossible to reconcile that ruling with these well-considered declarations . . . .

The Legislature was entitled to adopt measures to reduce the evils of the 'sweating system,' the exploiting of workers at wages so low as to be insufficient to meet the bare cost of living, thus making their very helplessness the occasion of a most injurious competition. The Legislature had the right to consider that its minimum wage requirements would be an important aid in carrying out its policy of protection. The adoption of similar requirements by many states evidences a deep-seated conviction both as to the presence of the evil and as to the means adapted to check it. Legislative response to that conviction cannot be regarded as arbitrary or capricious and that is all we have to decide. Even if the wisdom of the policy be regarded as debatable and its effects uncertain, still the Legislature is entitled to its judgment.

* * *

Our conclusion is that the case of *Adkins v. Children's Hospital*, *supra*, should be, and it is, overruled. The judgment of the Supreme Court of the state of Washington is affirmed.

With the New Deal in place, the alphabet soup of administrative agencies grew to the number and variety that one sees today. Less than ten years after the *West Coast Hotel* case, Congress passed the Administrative Procedure Act that sought to bring common standards to the work of these proliferating administrative agencies. The Act particularly involved agencies' rulemaking, interpretation, and enforcement, including judicial review of agency action.

II. Rulemaking, Lobbying and Capture

LEGISLATURES, whether at the national or state level, will often draft legislation to address a problem. Within the legislation, there will be a delegation of authority to an administrative agency to create more specific procedures to apply the law, to provide further guidance of how the law should be interpreted, and to set out examples to make the law more understandable.

Administrative agencies create thousands of pages of rules after a statute has been passed. When the administrative agencies create these rules, they must follow the procedures of the Administrative Procedure Act. The agency will solicit evidence and advice on how best to apply the statute from those who will be affected by the regulations. For example, if the Environmental Protection Agency is tasked with creating the rules to change the standards of air emissions, the EPA would draft a proposed set of rules.

Creating these rules requires expertise, which employees of agencies might have, but agencies will also look outside to university professors, companies and other interest groups with some experience and expertise in how new rules would impact the industry, especially if the rules involve laws on new subjects and technologies.

Members of the industry thus **lobby** or attempt to influence the EPA's decisions. On the one hand it appears as though lobbyists simply try to create rules that will most benefit their organization, but these lobbyists also have relevant data and experience. Some may have even started their own programs to limit air emissions and have a model to propose.

There is a difference between formal and informal rulemaking. With each, a notice of proposed rulemaking must be published in the *Federal Register*, the federal government's official journal, which contains government agency rules, proposed rules and public notices. Informal rulemaking only requires that the agency offer the for written comments to the proposed regulation, whereas in formal rulemaking, the agency must also conduct formal hearings in addition to allowing for written comments. Then, when the final rule is published in the *Federal Register*, the formal findings from the hearings must be published along with the rule, whereas in an informal process, only the rule must be published. Some **enabling legislation** requires that agencies utilize a formal rulemaking process, but informal rulemaking is quicker and more efficient. Most agencies utilize this process.

Procedural and **interpretative rules**, two other administrative actions that inform the public how an agency will proceed in various areas as well as the agency's view or interpretation of the legislation it must apply to cases, require little formality. Because these "rules" do not constitute actual rulemaking, *per se*, agencies do not have to follow the informal or formal procedures.

The rulemaking aspect of administrative agencies, as well as the issuance of interpretative and procedural rules, is a highly contested area of public policy from several points of view. First, if corporations have a great deal of technical information and lobbying expertise, there is the threat that an administrative agency can be **captured** by the industry. While administrative agencies do have government funding, they may not have sufficient funding to undertake all the scientific analysis that is necessary to make a well-researched rule. They will rely on corporations and organizations, who in turn also fund research (for example, in universities) to study the impact of actions in the area of consideration. While this can make for good policy because more information becomes available, it can also mean that the agency becomes increasingly dependent on those whom they regulate to design the very policies that affect them.

This idea of capture also can apply within an industry. It may be that a particular company has already designed an emissions process even though there are several other competing processes. If that company can persuade its regulating agency to adopt its process rather than a competitor's, the company will obtain a competitive edge over those who now must incur the costs of switching to a different process.

A final issue of the capture theory involves the strong interest corporations and other organizations have in hiring former employees of the agency. When a company hires a former agency employee, it captures the knowledge of the agency's inner workings—along with the employee's ties to former colleagues, which can be used to influence the rulemaking or interpretation of the rule. This jeopardizes the objectivity of the rulemaking process and opens the door for the administrative process to become simply another battleground for competition between actors in the industry.

The next article illustrates this conflict. It was first was posted to *The Huffington Post* in 2013 by Bruce Kushnick, Executive Director of the New Networks Institute. He argues strongly that regulatory protections have been weakened by corporate influences working from within the organization to benefit the telecommunications industry—at the expense of consumers.

ARTICLE: CAPTURE THEORY

Regulatory Capture of the FCC—Time to Clean House

–Bruce Kushnick, Executive Director of the New Networks Institute

AT&T, WITH THE HELP of Verizon and the cable companies have 'captured' the FCC—and have been able to get the federal agency to create and shape a working group designed specifically to remove all regulations and obligations, close down the Public Switched Telephone Networks (PSTN) and create new digital dead zones.

Think of this as: Imagine taking a company to court and you find out that the judge, most of the jury, and even your lawyer has a direct financial tie to the company you are suing. Think you'll win?

Moreover, AT&T's FCC play is part of a massive, well-choreographed, multi-year state and federal campaign being orchestrated with ALEC, the American Legislative Exchange Council, to remove all regulations and obligations and harm America's communications users—i.e., you, dear reader. . .

With the *Wall Street Journal* reporting a changing of the guard at the FCC, with FCC Chairman Julius Genachowski and the Republican Commissioner Robert McDowell leaving in the next few months, we need new people who are going to fix, expose and stand up to the corporations, not kowtow to them.

Regulatory Capture and Financial Conflicts of Interest vs. Open Government.

In August 2012, New Networks filed a petition with the FCC outlining how the Technical Advisory Council, (TAC) created a group to 'sunset the PSTN'—meaning shut down America's telecom networks of any regulations or obligations—and that the majority of the TAC members had major, financial conflicts of interest with AT&T and/or Verizon (and Centurylink, formerly Qwest)—the caretakers of America's networks. In fact, AT&T and Verizon are on this Council. Worse, the TAC is using manipulated data supplied by AT&T and the other telcos to bias anyone to their point of view.

. . .

"Regulatory Capture" is the takeover of a federal agency by the corporations it is regulating and it is not new to the FCC. At a conference in 2010 called Reforming the FCC, its website states that "Former Chair Reed Hundt, (1993-1997) for example, suggested that the acronym 'FCC' stands for 'Firmly Captured by Corporations' while former FCC Chief Economist Tom Hazlett counters that 'FCC' stands for 'Forever Captured by Corporations.'"

Regulatory capture is insidious as the agenda is set by the companies and then uses people and data to support the agenda—regardless of how it will harm those it claims to be helping.

And it is as much about things not discussed, not focused on, not investigated as it is about a proactive corporate position. For example, the TAC could have, as some have advocated, set up a group to create a transition path for moving to a 21st century utility that is open to all competitors, based on IP-enabled services and everyone is upgraded. Or the TAC could have given customers choices—like being able to at least pick a competitive broadband and Internet provider which offers services over the wires coming into the customer's home or office; The Telecom Act of 1996 stated this as a goal. Yet, through capture over the last decade, these same networks are now closed to competition. Instead, this group decided to run with AT&T's-ALEC's plan to close, 'sunset', the PSTN.

* * *

The Capture by AT&T et al of the FCC

The Technical Advisory Council is the epitome of a stacked jury where the verdict is already in—against you—before the trial even starts.

To start, AT&T and Verizon are on the Council—the two incumbents who control the majority of the U.S. telecommunications networks—wireline and wireless. In this way they don't have to go far to keep their eyes on the progress.

'Friends' of AT&T and Verizon

. . .The list of TAC members includes:

- Hardware and software vendors including Apple, Motorola, Intel, Cisco and Microsoft all of whom have multiple financial deals with AT&T and Verizon including wireless phones, tablets and technology.

- The cable companies, Comcast, Time Warner and Brighthouse not only sold spectrum to Verizon, but Verizon has a marketing deal with some of them to sell their cable products with Verizon's wireless services.

- Other hardware and consulting companies, from Accenture, Qualcomm, Alcatel-Lucent or Harris all have deals with either Verizon or AT&T or both.

In fact, the core 16 companies represent about $800 billion dollars in revenues in 2011. There are a number of other members with conflicts of interest:

- New Venture Partners is an investment firm which is part of the Verizon 4G investment forum.

- Silicon Flatirons is a "Center for law, technology, and entrepreneurship at the University of Colorado;" funders include AT&T, CenturyLink, and Verizon.

- There's also the Von Coalition, which has been lobbying for years to put through ALEC—state-based VOIP legislation. The VON Coalition originally started to when VOIP service was designed to bypass the phone companies, but it and the Coalition has been co-opted and is now funded by AT&T, Google and Microsoft among others. In fact, the Von Coalition has been in California, Colorado, New Hampshire, and Wyoming among other states to do on the state level what the TAC is doing on the Federal level.

Oh, but it gets worse. The head of the Council, Tom Wheeler, worked for the wireless and cable companies as former head of the cable association and the former head of the wireless association:

> "On the 20th anniversary of the cable television industry (1995), Tom was selected as one of the 20 most influential individuals in t444he industry's history and on the 25th anniversary of the cellular telecommunications industry (2008); he was named one of the top 10 innovators in the wireless industry. Tom was President of the National Cable Television Association (NCTA) from 1979 to 1984. After several years as CEO . . . he was asked to lead the Cellular Telecommunications & Internet Association (CTIA), where he was CEO until 2004."

TOM WHEELER

More recently, Wheeler works for Core Capital with his focus being wireless. He appears to not care about the telco wires, as told by his own writing. "The PSTN is a casualty of the digital world." His writings are called "Mobile Musings." And he is part of the Open Mobile Video Coalition which is working on "TV Everywhere," which was announced by Comcast and Time Warner. Wheeler is also currently being cited by some as a potential chairman of the FCC when the current chair leaves.

The Other Side? The Mathematics of Regulatory Capture Made Simple.

There is no serious 'other side.' We could identify only 5–7 companies and groups out of about 50, that are pro-wire' and pro PSTN. This includes wireline competitors XO, EarthLink and Level 3, but when added together their revenues are about 1 percent of the core group. This is important as they don't have the financial resources or skunkworks networks that the AT&T-ALEC cabal has.

Missing—Your voice or representation: Ironically, this is a 'technology' council yet the closing down of the networks and the creating of new digital dead zones is a political issue and a customer issue. Those who might actually discuss these points—such as advocates for consumers and customers were not invited to be part of this to give the council 'balance.'

Conclusion: Stop All Proceedings to Close Down the PSTN; Investigate Regulatory Capture and Clean House.

In short, it appears that the Council was set up by AT&T and the telephone and cable companies to close down regulations and obligations and they created a group that was pro wireless and pro VOIP—or more to the point anti-regulation and anti-PSTN.

The FCC will say that they are 'transparent,' data driven and all of those other terms that are political speak but meaningless. The FCC never explored other options like opening the networks or why the utility networks were never properly upgraded or anything that would show that they considered other alternatives to creating new digital dead zones.

Where is the FCC working group for 'structural separation'—i.e.; separating the companies' controls over the utility wires or opening the phone or cable companies' networks to competition? Or separating the wireline and wireless divisions so that they actually compete?

Personal Coda: In 2003, we were a member of the FCC Consumer Advisory Committee. We filed a complaint against the FCC and the Committee in 2005 as we found that the majority of members were either part of the industry—Verizon has been and continues to be on the Committee since its inception—or that the majority of consumer and astroturf groups were also funded by the industry. This is the reason why your phone bills are unreadable, prices continue to rise and many have few, if any, choices for fast broadband in America.

Maybe the new chairman and commissioner should be required to actually care about the public, economic growth and innovation—and clean house—instead of having sections of the FCC captured by the very industry they are supposed to be monitoring and regulating.

The movement between the private and public sector raises ethical questions in terms of conflicts of interest. As such, there has also been legislation that affects lobbying and impacts "the revolving door" between regulator and regulated.

III. Judicial Enforcement, Review and Suits

PEOPLE CHALLENGE ADMINISTRATIVE ACTIONS frequently; the judicial system provides an accessible opportunity to do so. An agency's action could be challenged because it violated proper procedures or because it has acted outside of its authority. The underlying law itself may be challenged as being unconstitutional, or because the agency's interpretation of the law is rejected by the courts, which have authority over the agency.

There are hurdles a litigant must pass in order for a court to hear a case to overturn an agency action. Three major issues arise in the enforcement actions of an administrative agency and their ensuing judicial review: due process, standing, and ripeness.

A. DUE PROCESS ISSUES GENERALLY

Like any other government action under the Constitution, when administrative agencies take action, they must provide basic due process rights. These include giving notice to a person if there is an enforcement action the agency is taking against them. If the IRS seeks to claim money from a taxpayer, it must first provide a notice of the proposed action and an opportunity to appeal the decision. The same is true for other administrative actions.

Due process issues have frequently found their way into the courts when an entitlement such as welfare benefits, social security or unemployment compensation is threatened. What makes these cases complicated is the fact that some government benefits, such as unemployment compensation, come from state funds as well as from the federal government. States may have what is called a durational residency requirement as part of eligibility standards. For example, if a state has no residency requirement, then unemployed individuals may come from all over the nation and immediately seek unemployment benefits, a situation which could cause major financial stress for the state government. Governments typically want to help their own citizens, but not to create a structure that encourages individuals from other states to take advantage of the resources of their home state.

The question arises, however, as to how long a person must reside in the state before qualifying for a benefit. Individuals have a right to travel and so if a state's restrictions are too harsh, then the durational residency requirement may violate the person's constitutional due process rights. The following case involves the request for an injunction against the state for denying a family's public assistance benefits, though the excerpt provided aims to demonstrate the larger issues of evaluating durational residency requirements.

Maldonado v. Houstoun

256 F.3d 181 (3d Cir. 2001)

Plaintiffs—Edwin and Maria Delores Maldonado, individually and next as friends of their children and on behalf of all others similarly situated, and a group of associations that represent their interests—have brought this action to challenge the constitutionality of the "multi-tier" durational residency requirement contained in Section 9(5)(ii) of Act 35 . . . . The defendants in this case are Feather O. Houstoun, the Secretary of the DPW, and Don Jose Stovall, the Executive Director of the Philadelphia County Board of Assistance . . . . Under the operation of this statute, families who have been residents of Pennsylvania for more than one year receive all of the benefits they would be eligible for under the state plan. Families who have resided in Pennsylvania for less than one year are limited to the amount of cash assistance that they would have received had they remained in their previous state of residence. . . [O]ther states have enacted similar provisions.

. . . In May 1997, the Maldonados moved to Pennsylvania from Guayama, Puerto Rico. The stated reason the family moved to Philadelphia was to receive medical care that would have not been available to them in Puerto Rico. Within seven days of arriving in Philadelphia, the Maldonados applied for welfare benefits. Because of the operation of Section 9(5)(ii), the Maldonados receive only $304 per month in Temporary Assistance to Needy Families (TANF) benefits rather than the $836 per month that similarly situated families who have lived in Pennsylvania for the past twelve months receive . . . . The Maldonados claim that the disparate treatment they receive by the operation of Section 9(5)(ii) is unconstitutional for three reasons. First, plaintiffs claim that the multi-tier durational residency requirement discriminates against new residents in violation of their fundamental right to travel . . . . Second, plaintiffs claim that Section 9(5)(ii) is unconstitutional because it violates the Equal Protection Clause. Plaintiffs argue that even under the rational review test, Section 9(5)(ii) must fail because no permissible rational purpose supports the distinctions created by the scheme between new residents and longer-term residents, or the distinctions among new residents who moved to Pennsylvania from different states with varied lower benefit levels . . . . Finally, plaintiffs contend that Section 9(5)(ii) violates the Privileges and Immunities Clauses of Article IV and the Fourteenth Amendment because it unjustifiably discriminates against new bona fide residents by treating them as Tennesseans or Kentuckians or other out-of-staters, rather than as citizens of Pennsylvania and the United States.

* * *

In a line of cases beginning with *Shapiro*, the Supreme Court has considered whether state durational residency requirements implicated the right to travel and interstate migration to such an extent so as to require the application of the compelling state interest test. In *Shapiro*, the Court found unconstitutional provisions denying welfare assistance to residents who had not resided for at least one year within the jurisdiction of the particular state in which the applicant had applied for benefits. The Court found that such provisions discriminate invidiously by "creat[ing] two classes of needy resident families indistinguishable from each other expect that one is composed of residents who have resided a year or more, and the second of residents who have resided less than a year, in the jurisdiction." The Court found that "any classification which serves to penalize the exercise of that right [to travel] unless shown to promote a compelling state interest, is unconstitutional." The Court could not find any compelling purposes behind the statutes in *Shapiro*.

* * *

The Supreme Court refined the *Shapiro* analysis in two subsequent decisions. In *Memorial Hospital v. Maricopa County*, (1974), the Supreme Court invalidated an Arizona provision requiring a year's residence in a county as a condition of receiving nonemergency medical care at county expense. The Court posed the issue as whether the state's classification "penalized" persons who had recently migrated to the state. If there were such a penalty the provision would be unconstitutional unless supported by a compelling state interest. The Court found that just as the denial of the necessities in life in *Shapiro* operated to penalize recent migrants so did the denial of nonemergency medical care. . . .Moreover, the Court, once again, rejected the argument that the state's interest in protecting its financial stability was of a sufficiently compelling nature. In *Dunn v. Blumstein*, (1972), the Court, relying on *Shapiro*, invalidated a durational residency provision requiring one-year's residence before a new resident could vote. * * *

[D]efendants candidly admit that Section 9(5)(ii) was enacted to prevent Pennsylvania from becoming a welfare magnet . . . . The Supreme Court has repeatedly stated that . . . "the purpose of inhibiting migration by needy persons into the State is constitutionally impermissible." . . . The Commonwealth simply cannot attempt to discourage poor persons from migrating to the Commonwealth in order to prevent the state from becoming a welfare magnet; the law is clear on this point . . . The saving of welfare costs cannot justify an otherwise invidious classification." Applying this precedent, it is obvious that Pennsylvania's purpose of preventing it from becoming a welfare magnet is constitutionally impermissible.

The second conclusion that this Court reaches, however, is that strict scrutiny should only be applied if the "primary objective" of Section 9(5)(ii) is to deter migration . . . . Defendants contend that the primary purpose behind the enactment of Section 9(5)(ii) is to encourage work and self-sufficiency: . . . "It is hereby declared to be the legislative intent to promote the self-sufficiency of all the people of the Commonwealth." It is rare that a Court is provided with such a clear statement of the legislative intent behind a statute.

After considering the purposes that Section 9(5)(ii) was enacted for, the Court concludes that plaintiffs cannot establish that the "primary objective" behind the enactment of Section 9(5)(ii) was to deter migration . . . . Thus, strict scrutiny will not be applied based on the "primary objective" of the statute.

Plaintiffs also fail to prove that Section 9(5)(ii) actually deters migration . . . . The plaintiffs here, just like the plaintiffs in *Shapiro*, simply offer no empirical evidence that Section 9(5)(ii) will discourage migration. . . . Indeed, plaintiffs' own witness, Professor Hartman, concluded that poor migrants do not move based on welfare benefits, *i.e.*, welfare benefits simply are not a consideration when poor migrants decide to move. Thus, the Court finds that plaintiffs cannot establish that Section 9(5)(ii) actually deters migration.

Finally, the Court finds that plaintiffs cannot demonstrate that Section 9(5)(ii)'s durational residency requirement results in a "penalty" on the right to interstate migration. . . . In this case, the newcomers to Pennsylvania are not being deprived of the things that are necessary for their very survival, since the plaintiffs and class members are eligible to receive TANF cash assistance benefits, albeit, at a reduced level, food stamps, clothing for job interviews, medical assistance, and job training and transportation, in addition to receiving assistance in finding employment, without regard to any durational residency requirement. In this case, the newcomers receive TANF cash assistance at the same level that they would have received in their state of prior residence. The plaintiffs also receive food stamps ($720 per month) and medical benefits ($1483.60 per month), and are eligible to receive the state's assistance in finding employment . . . . This conclusion is bolstered by the fact that the lower benefits provided do not make new residents any worse off because the new residents receive exactly what they were receiving or would have received in their state of prior residence. . . . Because the durational residency requirement of Section 9(5)(ii) dose not operate as a penalty on an individual's right to interstate migration, strict scrutiny is not appropriate. Thus, Section 9(5)(ii) need only be rationally related to a legitimate government purpose to survive the constitutional challenge mounted in the present case.

As stated above, the Commonwealth offers as its legitimate government objectives: (1) "discouraging persons from shopping around for the 'best benefit package of the year' " (2) an intent to encourage employment, self-respect and self-dependency among its welfare recipients, that is to encourage self-reliance over reliance on welfare. The first purpose, of course, is an unconstitutionally impermissible purpose . . . . The defendants admit that Section 9(5)(ii) was enacted in part to discourage welfare recipients from shopping around for benefits and to prevent an "influx of indigent people from other states." Because the first purpose is not valid, the Court must turn to the second purpose . . . The Supreme Court has stated that encouraging work is an "admittedly permissible state objective[ ]." Thus, the next question to be answered is whether Section 9(5)(ii) is rationally related to a legitimate government purpose.

Although the Supreme Court has stated that encouraging employment is a legitimate government purpose, the Court has also expressly held that a one-year waiting period that is justified as a means of encouraging new residents to seek and obtain employment sooner "provides no rational basis for imposing a one-year waiting period restriction on new residents only." . . . Indeed, Section (5)(ii) and its rules and regulations provide for multiple benefit levels for identically situated newcomers. For example, if you had two families, identically situated, arriving in Pennsylvania on the same day, establishing a residence in Pennsylvania and then applying for TANF benefits, but one of the families was from California and one was from Puerto Rico, the family from California would receive the same benefits that a long-term family would receive, and the family from Puerto Rico would receive the limited benefits. At the present time, approximately twenty states have welfare benefits higher then Pennsylvania's benefits; newcomers that come from any of these twenty states would automatically receive the full amount of Pennsylvania

TANF cash assistance. In addition, but more surprisingly, the residency requirement appears not to apply to poor migrants from other countries. Hence, new state residents from one of the United States that pays lower benefits will receive less cash assistance than new residents from foreign countries. From these observations, it is manifest that Section 9(5)(ii) is anything but rationally related to achieving its purpose of encouraging newcomers to work. Indeed, large groups of newcomers would automatically receive full benefits upon first arriving in Pennsylvania. This result underscores the irrationality of Section 9(5)(ii).

[The Court thereby granted the Maldonaldo's motion for a preliminary injunction and for a class certification of because there was no rational basis for the statutory provision.]

As explained in the chapter on Constitutional Law, due process considerations generally get matched with different standards of judicial tests, such as rational basis and strict scrutiny. The use of strict scrutiny, where the courts only sustain government action if there is a compelling state interest, makes it difficult for the government action to be upheld, but as the above case shows, even the rational basis test, which requires only that government offers a reasonable rationale for the law, can cause the courts to hold legislation unconstitutional.

B. STANDING AND RIPENESS

The proliferation of administrative agencies assures that governments reach into peoples' daily lives, regardless of how we may feel about it. Inevitably, if these agencies engage with citizens, there will be disputes, whether between a taxpayer and the IRS, a small business and the FDA, an entrepreneur hoping for an initial public offering and the SEC, or a larger employer with OSHA. As a practical matter, it is daunting for the average taxpayer to decide to challenge the IRS or for a tourist to challenge a national park. Administrative agencies remain large governmental organizations with plenty of resources and plenty of lawyers to do battle in the courtroom. Unless the party on the opposing side is a well-funded corporation or individual, the likely payoff of litigation is daunting.

At the same time, the United States, like many other well-established democratic countries, has a robust civil society, one of the things that makes a democracy work. In civil society there are thousands of organizations that obtain funding in a variety of different ways: donations from individuals, grants from corporations, foundations, and the government itself, even profit-seeking businesses embedded within the organization. These exist to champion the rights of individuals against government in general and against administrative agencies in particular. It is not that these organizations oppose governments *per se*, but that they seek to protect interests they fear will be excessively limited by governmental action.

So one finds organizations such as the American Civil Liberties Union, which will support individuals whose civil liberties have allegedly been violated so that the individual does not have to foot the bill, or the American Society for the Prevention of Cruelty to Animals, which will investigate and pursue reports of animal cruelty submitted by concerned citizens. The *Citizens United case* is a classic example of a non-profit organization, Citizen United, taking on an administrative agency.

Questions arise, however, as to whether these groups meet a judicial standard of standing to become involved in the case. To have standing, the person or organization bringing suit needs to show that they suffered an injury an actual injury rather than a philosophical or political difference of opinion. For example, a group opposing a new regulation that does not extend the federal government's duty to protect endangered wildlife outside of the U.S. may find moral issues with the regulation, but that does not provide an injury in fact that would allow them to step into the case. They would have to find an individual who has been injured by the regulation and take up the case on their behalf. If they are unable to find such an individual, the courts will find that they have no standing to bring the case before the courts. The following Supreme Court case illustrates this issue.

Lujan v. Defenders of Wildlife

504 U.S. 555 (1992)

This case involves a challenge to a rule promulgated by the Secretary of the Interior interpreting § 7 of the Endangered Species Act of 1973 (ESA), 16 U.S.C. § 1536, in such fashion as to render it applicable only to actions within the United States or on the high seas. The preliminary issue, and the only one we reach, is whether respondents here, plaintiffs below, have standing to seek judicial review of the rule.

The ESA seeks to protect species of animals against threats to their continuing existence caused by man. The ESA instructs the Secretary of the Interior to promulgate by regulation a list of those species which are either endangered or threatened under enumerated criteria, and to define the critical habitat of these species. * * *

> "Each Federal agency shall, in consultation with and with the assistance of the Secretary [of the Interior], insure that any action authorized, funded, or carried out by such agency . . . is not likely to jeopardize the continued existence of any endangered species or threatened species or result in the destruction or adverse modification of habitat of such species which is

> determined by the Secretary, after consultation as appropriate with affected States, to be critical."

In 1978, the Fish and Wildlife Service (FWS) and the National Marine Fisheries Service (NMFS), on behalf of the Secretary of the Interior and the Secretary of Commerce respectively, promulgated a joint regulation stating that the obligations imposed by § 7(a)(2) extend to actions taken in foreign nations. The next year, however, the Interior Department began to reexamine its position. A revised joint regulation, reinterpreting § 7(a)(2) to require consultation only for actions taken in the United States or on the high seas, was proposed in 1983 and promulgated in 1986.

Shortly thereafter, respondents, organizations dedicated to wildlife conservation and other environmental causes, filed this action against the Secretary of the Interior, seeking a declaratory judgment that the new regulation is in error as to the geographic scope of § 7(a)(2) and an injunction requiring the Secretary to promulgate a new regulation restoring the initial interpretation. The District Court granted the Secretary's motion to dismiss for lack of standing. The Court of Appeals for the Eighth Circuit reversed by a divided vote. On remand, the Secretary moved for summary judgment on the standing issue, and respondents moved for summary judgment on the merits. The District Court denied the Secretary's motion, on the ground that the Eighth Circuit had already determined the standing question in this case; it granted respondents' merits motion, and ordered the Secretary to publish a revised regulation. The Eighth Circuit affirmed. We granted certiorari.

Mr. Justice Scalia

Over the years, our cases have established that the irreducible constitutional minimum of standing contains three elements.

— First, the plaintiff must have suffered an "injury in fact"—an invasion of a legally protected interest which is (a) concrete and particularized and (b) "actual or imminent, not 'conjectural' or 'hypothetical.'

— Second, there must be a causal connection between the injury and the conduct complained of—the injury has to be "fairly . . . trace[able] to the challenged action of the defendant, and not . . . th[e] result [of] the independent action of some third party not before the court."

— Third, it must be "likely," as opposed to merely "speculative," that the injury will be "redressed by a favorable decision."

The party invoking federal jurisdiction bears the burden of establishing these elements . . . And at the final stage, those facts (if controverted) must be "supported adequately by the evidence adduced at trial."

When the suit is one challenging the legality of government action or inaction, the nature and extent of facts that must be averred (at the summary judgment stage) or proved (at the trial stage) in order to establish standing depends considerably upon

whether the plaintiff is himself an object of the action (or forgone action) at issue. If he is, there is ordinarily little question that the action or inaction has caused him injury, and that a judgment preventing or requiring the action will redress it. When, however, as in this case, a plaintiff's asserted injury arises from the government's allegedly unlawful regulation (or lack of regulation) of someone else, much more is needed. In that circumstance, causation and redressability ordinarily hinge on the response of the regulated (or regulable) third party to the government action or inaction—and perhaps on the response of others as well. * * * Thus, when the plaintiff is not himself the object of the government action or inaction he challenges, standing is not precluded, but it is ordinarily "substantially more difficult" to establish.

We think the Court of Appeals failed to apply the foregoing principles in denying the Secretary's motion for summary judgment. Respondents had not made the requisite demonstration of (at least) injury and redressability. * * * With respect to this aspect of the case, the Court of Appeals focused on the affidavits of two Defenders' members—Joyce Kelly and Amy Skilbred. Ms. Kelly stated that she traveled to Egypt in 1986 and "observed the traditional habitat of the endangered Nile crocodile there and intend[s] to do so again, and hope[s] to observe the crocodile directly," and that she "will suffer harm in fact as the result of [the] American . . . role . . . in overseeing the rehabilitation of the Aswan High Dam on the Nile . . . and [in] develop[ing] . . . Egypt's . . . Master Water Plan." Ms. Skilbred averred that she traveled to Sri Lanka in 1981 and "observed th[e] habitat" of "endangered species such as the Asian elephant and the leopard" at what is now the site of the Mahaweli project funded by the Agency for International Development (AID), although she "was unable to see any of the endangered species;" "this development project," she continued, "will seriously reduce endangered, threatened, and endemic species habitat including areas that I visited . . . [, which] may severely shorten the future of these species;" that threat, she concluded, harmed her because she "intend[s] to return to Sri Lanka in the future and hope[s] to be more fortunate in spotting at least the endangered elephant and leopard." When Ms. Skilbred was asked at a subsequent deposition if and when she had any plans to return to Sri Lanka, she reiterated that "I intend to go back to Sri Lanka," but confessed that she had no current plans: "I don't know [when]. There is a civil war going on right now. I don't know. Not next year, I will say. In the future."

We shall assume for the sake of argument that these affidavits contain facts showing that certain agency-funded projects threaten listed species—though that is questionable. They plainly contain no facts, however, showing how damage to the species will produce "imminent" injury to Mses. Kelly and Skilbred. That the women "had visited" the areas of the projects before the projects commenced proves nothing. As we have said in a related context, " 'Past exposure to illegal conduct does not in itself show a present case or controversy regarding injunctive relief . . . if unaccompanied by any continuing, present adverse effects.' " And the affiants' profession of an "inten[t]" to return to the places they had visited before—where they will presumably, this time, be deprived of the opportunity to observe animals of the endangered species—is simply not enough. Such "some day" intentions—without any description of concrete plans, or indeed even any specification of *when* the some day will be—do not support a finding of the "actual or imminent" injury that our cases require.

Besides relying upon the Kelly and Skilbred affidavits, respondents propose a series of novel standing theories. The first, inelegantly styled "ecosystem nexus," proposes that any person who uses *any part* of a "contiguous ecosystem" adversely affected by a funded activity has standing even if the activity is located a great distance away. This approach, as the Court of Appeals correctly observed, is inconsistent with our opinion in *National Wildlife Federation*, which held that a plaintiff claiming injury from environmental damage must use the area affected by the challenged activity and not an area roughly "in the vicinity" of it. * * *

Respondents' other theories are called, alas, the "animal nexus" approach, whereby anyone who has an interest in studying or seeing the endangered animals anywhere on the globe has standing; and the "vocational nexus" approach, under which anyone with a professional interest in such animals can sue. Under these theories, anyone who goes to see Asian elephants in the Bronx Zoo, and anyone who is a keeper of Asian elephants in the Bronx Zoo, has standing to sue because the Director of the Agency for International Development (AID) did not consult with the Secretary regarding the AID-funded project in Sri Lanka. This is beyond all reason. Standing is not "an ingenious academic exercise in the conceivable," but as we have said requires, at the summary judgment stage, a factual showing of perceptible harm.

. . .

The most obvious problem in the present case is redressability. Since the agencies funding the projects were not parties to the case, the District Court could accord relief only against the Secretary: He could be ordered to revise his regulation to require consultation for foreign projects. But this would not remedy respondents' alleged injury unless the funding agencies were bound by the Secretary's regulation, which is very much an open question. * * *

A further impediment to redressability is the fact that the agencies generally supply only a fraction of the funding for a foreign project. AID, for example, has provided less than 10% of the funding for the Mahaweli project. Respondents have produced nothing to indicate that the projects they have named will either be suspended, or do less harm to listed species, if that fraction is eliminated. As in Simon, it is entirely conjectural whether the nonagency activity that affects respondents will be altered or affected by the agency activity they seek to achieve. There is no standing.

. . .

We hold that respondents lack standing to bring this action and that the Court of Appeals erred in denying the summary judgment motion filed by the United States. The opinion of the Court of Appeals is hereby reversed, and the cause is remanded for proceedings consistent with this opinion.

The above case stands for the idea that a person has to have a tangible stake—i.e. experienced a personal impact—from a governmental action in order to have standing to sue. Simply being upset by a regulation will typically not be enough. This is one reason that one will find an advocacy organization—such as the ACLU—joining with a specific individual who was affected by a regulation. Without that individual, an organization such as the ACLU might also not have standing based on the principles by articulated in the above case.

Additional requirements to meet the standing test are that the administrative agency's action caused the injury in fact. This is a test akin to causation in a tort case, where the courts seek to determine that it was the actual administrative agency's action that caused the injury and not other extraneous factors.

A final element for judicial review is the concept of ripeness. This is a hard-to-define standard. It arises when courts see an issue brewing, but believe that it is more of a potential legal issue than a matter ready for legal consideration. The determination of whether a case is ripe or not is a judgment call by the courts, but three considerations are typically used:

1. Probability that the predicted harm will take place,
2. Hardship to the parties if immediate review is denied, and
3. Fitness of the record for resolving the legal issues presented.

C. EXACTLY WHO GETS SUED?

Under the doctrine of sovereign immunity, the government cannot be sued. On the one hand, this may seem strange. The basic principle of the legal system is that if someone has been harmed or wronged, they have a right to have their day in court. That's true if your car gets hit by another driver or if someone doesn't pay money they owe you. Yet when it comes to government, there are many times in which the government cannot be sued. In fact, the general rule is that the federal government cannot be sued unless they give permission to do so.

On the other hand, opening the government up to litigation poses significant risks. Think of the lawsuits in a time of war if injured parties could sue the government. There could be thousands, even millions of lawsuits from injured parties with very complicated sets of facts as to what occurred during the fog of war.

Given the impact of administrative actions and the political costs of claiming that the government is not accountable for its actions, which is what sovereign immunity provides, it is often waived by Congress so cases can be brought against agencies.

In nearly all such suits against the government, the suit is brought against the agency and not the individual. Even if a suit names the individual who runs the agency, such as the Attorney General, damages demanded in the suit would not be paid by the individual but instead by the government itself. The Supreme Court has established immunity from any tort suit for an administrative official who is acting within the scope of the official's duty for the agency. The following case illustrates just such a right.

Gonzalez v. Reno

325 F.3d 1228 (11th Cir. 2003)

On September 28, 2000, the Gonzalezes commenced this action under *Bivens v. Six Unknown Named Agents of Federal Bureau of Narcotics* (1971), by filing a complaint for damages against Attorney General Janet Reno, in her individual capacity; INS Commissioner Doris Meissner, in her individual capacity; Deputy Attorney General Eric Holder, in his individual capacity; INS agent Betty Mills; an unknown number of INS agents whose names are not known; an unknown number of U.S. Border Patrol agents whose names are not known; and an unknown number of U.S. Marshals whose names are not known. In their complaint, the Gonzalezes allege the following facts. On November 25, 1999, six-year-old Elian Gonzalez, a Cuban boy, was found floating on an inner tube off the coast of Fort Lauderdale, Florida. The Coast Guard brought Elian into the United States, and the INS paroled him into the country without inspection, then released him into the custody of his great-uncle, Lazaro Gonzalez ("Lazaro"). Lazaro filed a petition with the INS on behalf of Elian seeking political asylum for the child. Elian also filed a petition for asylum on his own behalf.

On January 5, 2000, INS Commissioner Meissner decided that the INS would not consider the requests for asylum because Elian's father, a Cuban citizen, had requested that Elian be returned to Cuba. On January 7, 2000, Lazaro filed a petition for temporary custody of Elian in the Family Division of the Circuit Court for Miami-Dade County, which was granted pending a full hearing on the matter.

On January 12, 2000, Attorney General Reno affirmed Meissner's decision not to consider the petitions for political asylum. Lazaro challenged Reno's ruling in the United States District Court for the Southern District of Florida, and the court upheld Reno's decision. Lazaro appealed to this court.

Photo: Alan Diaz, Reuters

"In the course of executing the warrants, the agents allegedly sprayed gas into the residence; broke down the front door with a battering ram and entered the residence without first announcing their presence; sprayed more gas; pointed guns at the occupants of the residence, threatening to shoot; shouted obscenities; and broke doors, furniture, and religious artifacts. As one federal agent pointed a weapon at one of the occupants and Elian, INS agent Betty Mills entered the room with a blanket and seized the child."

On April 6, 2000, while that appeal was pending, Elian's father arrived in the United States. On April 12, 2000, the INS instructed Lazaro to bring Elian to Opa Locka Airport, and advised Lazaro that the parole of Elian into his care was being transferred to Elian's father. On April 13, 2000, the circuit court dismissed Lazaro's petition for temporary custody and vacated its prior order granting temporary custody to Lazaro.

On April 19, 2000, a panel of this court entered an order enjoining Elian from departing, or attempting to depart, the United States; enjoining all persons acting on his behalf from aiding, or assisting or attempting to aid or assist, Elian's removal from the United States; and enjoining all officers, agents, and employees of the United States to take such reasonable and lawful measures as necessary to prevent the removal of Elian from the United States. On April 20, 2000, the Gonzalezes began negotiations with Reno, Meissner, and Holder toward the goal of transferring temporary custody of Elian.

Even though it was purporting to negotiate a peaceful transfer of the child, the INS issued an administrative warrant for Elian's arrest on April 21, 2000. The arrest warrant asserted that Elian was within the United States in violation of the immigration laws and could therefore be taken into custody. The INS then obtained a search warrant to enter the Gonzalezes' home and search for Elian.

At approximately 5:15 a.m. on April 22, 2000, armed federal agents arrived at the Gonzalezes' residence to execute the search and arrest warrants. In the course of executing the warrants, the agents allegedly sprayed gas into the residence; broke down the front door with a battering ram and entered the residence without first announcing their presence; sprayed more gas; pointed guns at the occupants of the residence, threatening to shoot; shouted obscenities; and broke doors, furniture, and religious artifacts. As one federal agent pointed a weapon at one of the occupants and Elian, INS agent Betty Mills entered the room with a blanket and seized the child.

[The Court then dismissed Counts related to First and Fifth Amendments and isolated only on claims pursuant to the Fourth Amendment]. With respect to the Gonzalezes' Fourth Amendment claims in Count II, the court held that the Gonzalezes lacked standing to challenge the validity of the administrative arrest warrant. The court dismissed the Gonzalezes' Fourth Amendment claims challenging the validity of the search warrant after concluding that the warrant was valid because the magistrate who issued it was presented with a facially valid arrest warrant and an affidavit establishing probable cause to believe that Elian was in the Gonzalezes' home. [The Court then dismissed claims against Betty Mills and the other federal agents.]

The court also denied the motion to dismiss with respect to the defense of qualified immunity. The court concluded that the complaint alleged the requisite "causal connection" between the supervisory actions of Reno, Meissner, and Holder and the alleged constitutional violation by the agents on the scene to hold them liable based on their supervisory status, notwithstanding their absence from the scene. The court based this finding on paragraphs 70 and 75 of the complaint, which alleged that Reno, Meissner, and Holder "personally directed and caused a paramilitary raid upon Plaintiffs' residence" and that the agents on the scene "acted under the personal direction of Defendants Janet Reno, Doris Meissner and Eric Holder."

> **"TO RECEIVE qualified immunity, the government official must first prove that he was acting within his discretionary authority. Here, it is clear—and undisputed—that defendants Reno, Meissner, and Holder acted within their discretionary authority."**

Reno, Meissner, and Holder now appeal, challenging the district court's rejection of their qualified immunity defense. * * *

The defense of **qualified immunity** completely protects government officials performing discretionary functions from suit in their individual capacities unless their conduct violates "clearly established statutory or constitutional rights of which a reasonable person would have known. The purpose of this immunity is to allow government officials to carry out their discretionary duties without the fear of personal liability or harassing litigation, protecting from suit all but the plainly incompetent or one who is knowingly violating the federal law." * * * To receive qualified immunity, the government official must first prove that he was acting within his discretionary authority. Here, it is clear—and undisputed—that defendants Reno, Meissner, and Holder acted within their discretionary authority.

Once the defendants have established that they were acting within their discretionary authority, the burden shifts to the plaintiffs to show that qualified immunity is not appropriate. The Supreme Court has set forth a two part analysis for determining whether qualified immunity is appropriate. The court must first ask "this threshold question: Taken in the light most favorable to the party asserting the injury, do the facts alleged show the officer's conduct violated a constitutional right?" "[I]f a violation could be made out on a favorable view of the parties' submissions, the next, sequential step is to ask whether the right was clearly established."

Our first step, then, is to determine whether the factual allegations in the complaint, if true, establish a constitutional violation by Reno, Meissner, and Holder. * * * "It is well established in this circuit that supervisory officials are not liable under [*Bivens*] for the unconstitutional acts of their subordinates 'on the basis of respondeat superior or vicarious liability.' " "The standard by which a supervisor is held liable in her individual capacity for the actions of a subordinate is extremely rigorous." Supervisors "can be held liable under [*Bivens*] when a reasonable person in the supervisor's position would have known that his conduct infringed the constitutional rights of the plaintiffs, and his conduct was causally related to the constitutional violation committed by his subordinate."

Supervisory liability occurs either when the supervisor personally participates in the alleged constitutional violation or when there is a causal connection between actions of the supervising official and the alleged constitutional violation." A causal connection can be established "when a history of widespread abuse puts the responsible supervisor on notice of the need to correct the alleged deprivation, and he fails to do so," or when the supervisor's improper "custom or policy . . . resulted in deliberate indifference to constitutional rights." A causal connection can also be established by facts which support an inference that the supervisor directed the subordinates to act unlawfully or knew that the subordinates would act unlawfully and failed to stop them from doing so.

* * * Plaintiffs allege that these defendants "personally directed and caused a paramilitary raid upon [their] residence, and had actual knowledge of, and agreed to, and approved of, and acquiesced in, the raid in violation of the Fourth Amendment rights of Plaintiffs herein." Plaintiffs also allege that the agents on the scene "acted under the personal direction of Defendants, Janet Reno, Doris Meissner and Eric Holder., and with the knowledge, agreement, approval, and acquiescence of Defendants, Janet Reno, Doris Meissner and Eric Holder." Finally, plaintiffs allege that these defendants "personally participated in the constitutional violations, and there was clearly a causal connection between their actions and the constitutional deprivation."

These vague and conclusory allegations do not establish supervisory liability. Plaintiffs make bold statements and legal conclusions without alleging any facts to support them. Plaintiffs appeal to the emotions by calling the events that transpired

a paramilitary raid, but they do not allege any facts to suggest that the defendants did anything more than personally direct and cause the execution of valid search and arrest warrants. Plaintiffs state that there is a causal connection between these defendants' acts and the excessive force used by the agents on the scene, but they do not allege any facts to support this causal connection. * * *

Because plaintiffs have failed to allege that the supervisory defendants' conduct constituted a constitutional violation, the supervisory defendants are entitled to qualified immunity under the first step in our qualified immunity analysis. The decision of the district court is therefore REVERSED.

If an official acts outside of his duties, perhaps by leaking to the press information about someone the agency is investigating—then a suit could be filed against that individual despite his/her protection as an agency official. In *Bivens v. Six Unknown Named Agents of Federal Bureau of Narcotics*, a 1971 Supreme Court case, the Court held that federal officials could be liable for constitutional torts and found six federal agents liable for damages when they acted under the "color of authority" conferred upon them by their administrative positions. In the case, the search and arrest of the plaintiff was extreme.

According to the Court, "the agents manacled petitioner in front of his wife and children, and threatened to arrest the entire family. They searched the apartment from stem to stern. Thereafter, petitioner was taken to the federal courthouse in Brooklyn where he was interrogated, booked, and subjected to a visual strip search." There was also a question of whether there even was a valid search warrant. In such cases, the Court did not foreclose the possibility that the petitioner could recover damages from the officers personally.

IV. Congressional Control of Administrative Agencies

AGENCIES COME INTO EXISTENCE through Congressional legislation, and Congress retains several ways to impact agencies' work, such as by changing the legislation that affects them. After the terrorist attacks of September 11th, 2001, for instance, the U.S. government undertook changes in its security gathering so that intelligence agencies were better able to communicate with each other. Some of this was achieved through executive orders, but some was also done through legislation.

Actually getting Congress to change legislation or to terminate an agency is very difficult. Once in existence, inertia and political pressures make it difficult to end or dramatically change an agency. Recognizing this, Congress will occasionally enact "sunset laws" that call for the automatic ending or review of an agency at a certain time. This is very rare at the federal level, however, because the agencies tend to develop close ties to Congressional constituents. It is much more likely to see agencies eliminated at the state level.

Congress can also control an agency by altering the flow of funds, or appropriations, the agency depends on to function. Finally, the most common and most informal method of Congressional impact on agency action is through direct contact. Elected leaders run for reelection, in part, to provide constituent services to their electorate. Thus, if a constituent has an issue with the FTC, the constituent may appeal to his or her Congress members for assistance. This kind of Congressional pressure occurs frequently, but there are risks for representatives who get too deeply involved in influencing administrative actions. That is particularly true when representatives act on behalf of an individual who is not simply a citizen in their district, but a campaign contributor as well.

V. Presidential Control of Administrative Agencies

PRESIDENTS IMPACT AGENCIES AS WELL. Perhaps the most common and direct influence is determining who runs the agency. The president appoints leaders and other high-level staff of administrative agencies, usually subject to the approval by Congress. In making such appointments, the president can exercise a great deal of influence on the direction of an agency. A president who campaigns on the promise of tougher enforcement of environmental regulations, for instance, will undoubtedly appoint a similarly motived leader to head the EPA, which will impact the entire organization. On the other hand, a president who believes that the EPA has been overzealous in its work will appoint a leader with those views in mind.

In addition to this power, presidents have required that executive agencies conduct cost-benefit analysis on all proposed regulations and show that the benefits outweigh the costs. Office of Management and Budget (OMB) also reviews regulatory actions planned for the upcoming year, thus providing another executive opportunity to influence changes. Under President Obama, the OMB issued the Open Government Initiative, which gives the OMB the authority to assist the President in overseeing and coordinating the Administration's legislative and regulatory policies.

VI. Other Controls

BEYOND GOVERNMENTAL CONTROL of administrative agencies, the democratic flow of information that allows debate can also play a significant role. A frustrated citizen may object to the conduct of an agency and use its actions as a basis of a campaign or referendum. The media frequently raises questions about the actions of administrative agencies and has the ability to obtain information about those actions through the usual tools of reviewing *The Federal Register*, reviewing comments and testimony at hearings, or interviewing individuals. The media (and citizens) also can obtain information about the actions of the agencies through the Freedom of Information Act (FOIA).

The FOIA requires that agencies provide documents to the public unless there is an exemption such as national security or issues pertaining to agency personnel and their privacy. The following provides a full list of these exemptions:

1. Documents classified as secret in the interest of national defense or foreign policy.
2. Documents related solely to internal personnel rules and practices.
3. Those specifically exempted by other statutes.
4. Trade secrets or privileged or confidential commercial or financial information obtained from a person.
5. Privileged inter-agency or intra-agency memorandum or letter.
6. Personnel, medical or similar file, the release of which would constitute a clearly unwarranted invasion of personal privacy.
7. Documents compiled for law enforcement purposes, the release of which:
    a. could reasonably be expected to interfere with law enforcement proceedings,
    b. would deprive a person of a right to a fair trial or an impartial adjudication,
    c. could reasonably be expected to constitute an unwarranted invasion of personal privacy,
    d. could reasonably be expected to disclose the identity of a confidential source,
    e. would disclose techniques, procedures or guidelines for investigations or prosecutions,
    f. could reasonably be expected to endanger an individual's life or physical safety.
8. Information contained in or related to examination, operating, or condition reports about financial institutions that the SEC regulates or supervises.
9. Documents containing exempt information about gas or oil wells.

Administrative Law is its own area of law. Yet because administrative agencies permeate so much of our life, administrative law also intersects with many other substantive areas of law such as Constitutional Law, Property Law, Intellectual Property, Corporate Law, Product Liability Law and many others. Thus, a Constitutional issue may very well be raised out of an administrative action. As a result, the procedures of this chapter make a difference both throughout the subject matter of this book and in daily life.

NOTES AND COMMENTS on the Legal Environment of Business

1. **A FREQUENT COMPLAINT IS** that individuals will work on Congressional staffs or in administrative agencies and then switch to the private sector, where their attractiveness to an employer includes knowing how to navigate the bureaucracy with friends and colleagues in the right places. Of course, citizens have a right to seek employment, and one's life and career experiences are obviously highly relevant to whether one gets a job or not. But there have been efforts to place restrictions on "the revolving door" between government and private industry. One summary of this can be found at *http://www.doi.gov/ethics/post_employment_activities.html.*

2. **WHAT IS YOUR VIEW** of doctrines such as standing and ripeness? Does it make sense to you that one has to have suffered some actual injury in order to sue an agency's action? Isn't being a citizen enough? Or does the doctrine preclude even more litigiousness than already exists in the country? Similarly, does ripeness inevitably create a situation in which an issue is ruled upon when it is too late, once harm is already done? Or, again, does such a doctrine efficiently preclude creatively speculative reasons for bringing one lawsuit after the other?

3. **IF YOU WERE TO WORK** for an administrative agency, which one would you choose? Which one would you least like to work for?

NOTES AND COMMENTS on the Ethical Environment of Business

1. **PERHAPS SURPRISINGLY, ADMINISTRATIVE LAW** is loaded with ethical issues. Should one be able to sue a government official, as was raised in the *Gonzales* case? Why should a person need to have "standing" in order to sue as was raised in the *Lujan* case?

2. **MORE RELATED TO THE ISSUES** of ethics in business, what do you make of the notion of regulatory capture? Is regulatory capture something that a business should do? In other words, if one of the duties of managers is to maximizing shareholder profitability, then shouldn't a company try to take control of a regulatory agency either by itself or perhaps with other like-minded companies? At the same time, would a stakeholder approach argue the same way or differently? How so?

3. **THEN, THERE IS THE ISSUE** of the movement between public and private sectors. This raises many ethical issues because the concern is that if a public official moves to the private sector, they may be able to exercise influence on their former government colleagues for the better of the company. Moreover, if a government employee knows that they will leave the public sector for a private sector job, might they not do their government work as effectively in order to ingratiate themselves with a potential, higher-paying private sector employer regulated by the agency the government employee works for? Building on the previous paragraph, should businesses encourage pubic sectors to leave to work for them? Is this enhancing the possibility of corruption or at least the perception of corruption? Or at least the appearance of some kind of impropriety?

4. **ON THE OTHER HAND**, there is also a belief that government works better if enriched by the insights of the private sector. Similarly, the private sector can function better if it is has a better sense of how government works. So with this in mind, how would you draw the line between when a government worker can move to work in a business that had been regulated by the same agency? What is the duty business has in such cases to its stakeholders and its shareholders? What would exemplary, virtuous conduct look like, in the cases covered in the chapter?

CHAPTER

6

Corporate Criminal Issues

In the wake of the turn-of-the-century corporate scandals, many called for increased emphasis on ethics instruction in business schools. One law professor argued that ethics wasn't really the problem; the outright flouting of the law was. Many corporate ethics issues are legal issues. Moreover, what is called "ethics" in the press, government and business are often laws involving issues such as conflicts of interest. The law is not the only issue involved in making ethical judgments, but law and ethics do interact in significant ways.

This chapter focuses on certain legal provisions that create unique criminal or civil liabilities. These provisions also provide a basis for a significant amount of corporate attention to ethics issues today. For example, prior to 1991, few companies had corporate mission statements, educational programs, ombudspersons or other forms of ethical guidance mechanisms. Since that year's amendments to the Federal Sentencing Guidelines, however, nearly every company has these things and because the 2004 amendments to the Guidelines call for corporations to build "organizational cultures" that attend to "ethics" as well as law, this procedural, criminal and regulatory mechanism has made it necessary for companies to adopt ethics and compliance programs. The lack of such a program has even been held as grounds for a shareholders' derivative lawsuit. Thus, law and ethics can blend in many ways, especially when criminal business issues arise.

I. General Notions of Corporate Liability

CRIMINAL PROSECUTIONS are brought by some government entity against a "person" (an actual or artificial one, such as a corporation) for violating a law enacted to protect the public. In a tort case, the "prosecutor" is an individual plaintiff who seeks monetary damages or other forms of equitable relief, such as an injunction in nuisance cases, for injuries caused by the defendant. In a criminal case, the prosecutor really *is* one: an attorney general, a states' attorney, a district attorney, etc. Because the prosecutor acts on behalf of the state, it is the state and the system of justice that is, in a sense, the plaintiff and victim in a criminal case. It is possible that a criminal defendant will also be subject to suit by the by victim through a related civil suit. One famous example of this is the O.J. Simpson civil and criminal trial, where he was acquitted for criminal charges but still found liable for civil damages. In this chapter, the focus will be on criminal law, though occasionally there will be reference to tort law.

Tort vs. Criminal Law

	Tort Law	Criminal Law
Definition	Civil law deals with the disputes between individuals, organizations, or between the two, in which compensation is awarded to the victim.	Criminal law is the body of law that deals with crime and the legal punishment of criminal offenses.
Burden of proof	"Preponderance of evidence" The burden of proof falls on the plaintiff.	"Beyond a reasonable doubt": Burden of proof is always on the state/government.
Examples	Landlord/tenant disputes, divorce proceedings, child custody proceedings, property disputes, personal injury, etc.	Theft, assault, robbery, trafficking in controlled substances, murder, etc.
Type of punishment	Civil litigation usually involves some type of compensation for injuries or damages as well as disposition of property and other disputes.	A guilty defendant is punished by incarceration and/or fines, or in exceptional cases, the death penalty. Crimes are divided into two broad classes: Felonies and Misdemeanors.
Case filed by	Private party	Government

A. BASIC COMPONENTS

A **subjective intent standard** requires the alleged criminal to either know what she is doing or be reckless in her actions. If the intent is purposeful (willful), knowing or reckless, then a higher level of punishment is warranted because the defendant's action were not accidental. Someone trying to blackmail (or extort) another person doesn't do so accidentally; the perpetrator purposefully devises a scheme to try to extort money from another person. Embezzlement is another example of a purposeful crime because it would be nearly impossible to achieve without the actual intent to embezzle.

An **objective intent standard** applies when the subjective intent of the defendant cannot be known, or at least not proven, yet the actions of the defendant indicate a disregard for others. This is a negligence standard and would apply to issues such as careless or drunken driving. Sometimes negligence may err into gross negligence and even recklessness. The defendant may not have set out to drive carelessly, but objectively speaking, he can be determined to have driven negligently by expressing a lack of regard for others through his choices. If so, he still may be guilty of a crime, though it may result in a lesser offense and involve a more lenient punishment because of the lack of provable, subjective intent.

ARTICLE: PURPOSEFUL CRIME

Embezzlement Versus Larceny: Ice Cream Truck?

http://www.forensicaccountingservices.com/2012/05/embezzlement-versus-larceny-ice-cream-truck/

Larceny is a legal term for theft or stealing, the taking of another's property for personal gain with no intent to return the property (permanently deprive rightful owner of their property).

- **Embezzlement** is a form of larceny, with some unique characteristics. Embezzlement involves an individual using (and exploiting) a position of trust and opportunity, committing theft acts over time, with or without intention of returning what was stolen, and the activity is concealed (covered up) so as to avoid detection, allowing the suspect to continue perpetrating future theft acts.
- **Stealing the end of day deposit** rather than taking it to the bank to be deposited into an organization's bank account would be larceny.
- **Stealing (skimming)** \$100 from each day's deposit, and altering the bank deposit slip to reflect the reduced amount to be deposited, would be along the lines of an embezzlement.

In a recent article, it appeared the driver of an ice cream truck stole the truck's contents. One event, discovered all at once, and not well concealed. Larceny, not embezzlement.

Had the driver skimmed cash or ice cream from the truck and deposits, and concealed the short (theft) by altering his records, that would have been an embezzlement.

There are some crimes that require no intent at all; these cases are known as **strict liability crimes** since merely committing the *actus reus* with no intent results in a violation. In these cases, the defendant may not have intended any criminal violation at all, but still ended up violating a statute. One example of strict liability that arises with relative frequency involves statutory rape crimes because the crime does not require that the defendant have any knowledge of the victim's age. Age restrictions on pornography and child pornography crimes are also strict liability. Each state has laws against pornography and the Supreme Court has given great deference to local communities' standards for what constitutes pornography. Yet the Internet crosses state lines by its very nature; what happens when someone under the age of eighteen accesses pornography?

The following case illustrates that issue and the issue of criminal violations with no intent. It deals with a unique kind of business—pornography—which often raises new legal and ethical issues as new technologies become available for its distribution. In the following case, what may be most interesting is the Court's determination of "community" and how new technology can create unforeseen liability because of the community one unexpectedly finds oneself in.

U.S. v. Thomas

74 F.3d 701 (6th Cir. 1996)

Edmunds, District Judge.

* * *

Robert Thomas and his wife Carleen Thomas began operating the Amateur Action Computer Bulletin Board System ("AABBS") from their home in Milpitas, California in February 1991. The AABBS was a computer bulletin board system that operated by using telephones, modems, and personal computers. Its features included e-mail, chat lines, public messages, and files that members could access, transfer, and download to their own computers and printers.

* * * After purchasing sexually-explicit magazines from public adult book stores in California, Defendant Robert Thomas used an electronic device called a scanner to convert pictures from the magazines into computer files called Graphic Interchange Format files or "GIF" files. The AABBS contained approximately 14,000 GIF files. Mr. Thomas also purchased, sold, and delivered sexually-explicit videotapes to AABBS members. Customers ordered the tapes by sending Robert Thomas an e-mail message, and Thomas typically delivered them by use of the United Parcel Service ("U.P.S.").

Persons calling the AABBS without a password could view the introductory screens of the system which contained brief, sexually-explicit descriptions of the GIF files and adult videotapes that were offered for sale. Access to the GIF files, however, was limited to members who were given a password after they paid a membership fee and submitted a signed application form that Defendant Robert Thomas reviewed. The application form requested the applicant's age, address, and telephone number and required a signature.

Members accessed the GIF files by using a telephone, modem and personal computer. A modem located in the Defendants' home answered the calls. After they established membership by typing in a password, members could then select, retrieve, and instantly transport GIF files to their own computer. A caller could then view the GIF file on his computer screen and print the image out using his printer. The GIF files contained the AABBS name and access telephone number; many also had "Distribute Freely" printed on the image itself.

In July 1993, a United States Postal Inspector, Agent David Dirmeyer ("Dirmeyer"), received a complaint regarding the AABBS from an individual who resided in the Western District of Tennessee. Dirmeyer dialed the AABBS' telephone number. As a non-member, he viewed a screen that read "Welcome to AABBS, the Nastiest Place On Earth," and was able to select various "menus" and read graphic descriptions of the GIF files and videotapes that were offered for sale.

Subsequently, Dirmeyer used an assumed name and sent in $55 along with an executed application form to the AABBS. Defendant Robert Thomas called Dirmeyer at his undercover telephone number in Memphis, Tennessee, acknowledged receipt of his application, and authorized him to log-on with his personal password. Thereafter, Dirmeyer dialed the AABBS's telephone number, logged-on and, using his computer/modem in Memphis, downloaded the GIF files listed in counts 2–7 of the Defendants' indictments. These GIF files depicted images of bestiality, oral sex, incest, sado-masochistic abuse, and sex scenes involving urination. Dirmeyer also ordered six sexually-explicit videotapes from the AABBS and received them via U.P.S. at a Memphis, Tennessee address. Dirmeyer also had several e-mail and chat-mode conversations with Defendant Robert Thomas.

On January 10, 1994, a search warrant was issued by a U.S. Magistrate Judge for the Northern District of California. The AABBS' location was subsequently searched, and the Defendants' computer system was seized.

On January 25, 1994, a federal grand jury for the Western District of Tennessee returned a twelve-count indictment charging Defendants Robert and Carleen Thomas with the following criminal violations: one count under 18 U.S.C. § 371 for conspiracy to violate federal obscenity laws—18 U.S.C. §§ 1462, 1465, six counts under 18 U.S.C. § 1465 for knowingly using and causing to be used a facility and means of interstate commerce—a combined computer/telephone system—for the purpose of transporting obscene, computer-generated materials (the GIF files) in interstate commerce, three counts under 18 U.S.C. § 1462 for shipping obscene videotapes via U.P.S., one count of causing the transportation of materials depicting minors engaged in sexually explicit conduct in violation of 18 U.S.C. § 2252(a)(1) as to Mr. Thomas only, and one count of forfeiture under 18 U.S.C. § 1467.

* * *

Defendants . . . argue that even if venue was proper under count 1 (conspiracy) and counts 8–10 (videotapes sent via U.P.S.), counts 2–7 (GIF files) should have been severed and transferred to California because Defendants did not cause the GIF files to be transmitted to the Western District of Tennessee. Rather, Defendants assert, it was Dirmeyer, a government agent, who, without their knowledge, accessed and downloaded the GIF files and caused them to enter Tennessee. We disagree. To establish a Section 1465 violation, the Government must prove that a defendant knowingly used a facility or means of interstate commerce for the purpose of distributing obscene materials. Contrary to Defendants' position, Section 1465 does not require the Government to prove that Defendants had specific knowledge of the destination of each transmittal at the time it occurred.

* * *

Section 1465 is an obscenity statute, and federal obscenity laws, by virtue of their inherent nexus to interstate and foreign commerce, generally involve acts in more than one jurisdiction or state. Furthermore, it is well-established that "there is no constitutional impediment to the government's power to prosecute pornography dealers in any district into which the material is sent."

* * *

In *Miller v. California* (1973), the Supreme Court set out a three-prong test for obscenity. It inquired whether (1) "'the average person applying contemporary community standards' would find that the work, taken as a whole appeals to the prurient interest;"(2) it "depicts or describes, in a patently offensive way, sexual conduct specifically defined by applicable state law;" and (3) "the work, taken as a whole, lacks serious literary, artistic, political, or scientific value."

Under the first prong of the *Miller* obscenity test, the jury is to apply "contemporary community standards." Defendants acknowledge the general principle that, in cases involving interstate transportation of obscene material, juries are properly instructed to apply the community standards of the geographic area where the materials are sent. Nonetheless, Defendants assert that this principle does not apply here for the same reasons they claim venue was improper. As demonstrated above, this argument cannot withstand scrutiny. The computer-generated images described in counts 2–7 were electronically transferred from Defendants' home in California to the Western District of Tennessee. Accordingly, the community standards of that judicial district were properly applied in this case.

* * *

Prosecutions may be brought either in the district of dispatch or the district of receipt, and obscenity is determined by the standards of the community where the trial takes place. Moreover, the federal courts have consistently recognized that it is not unconstitutional to subject interstate distributors of obscenity to varying community standards.

* * *

Defendants and *amicus curiae* appearing on their behalf argue that the computer technology used here requires a new definition of community, i.e., one that is based on the broad-ranging connections among people in cyberspace rather than the geographic locale of the federal judicial district of the criminal trial. Without a more flexible definition, they argue, there will be an impermissible chill on protected speech because BBS operators cannot select who gets the materials they make available on their bulletin boards. Therefore, they contend, BBS operators like Defendants will be forced to censor their materials so as not to run afoul of the standards of the community with the most restrictive standards.

Defendants' First Amendment issue, however, is not implicated by the facts of this case. This is not a situation where the bulletin board operator had no knowledge or control over the jurisdictions where materials were distributed for downloading or printing. Access to the Defendants' AABBS was limited. Membership was necessary and applications were submitted and screened before passwords were issued and materials were distributed. Thus, Defendants had in place methods to limit user access in jurisdictions where the risk of a finding of obscenity was greater than that in California. They knew they had a member in Memphis; the member's address and local phone number were provided on his application form. If Defendants did not wish to subject themselves to liability in jurisdictions with less tolerant standards for determining obscenity, they could have refused to give passwords to members in those districts, thus precluding the risk of liability.

This result is supported by the Supreme Court's decision in *Sable Communications of Cal., Inc. v. F.C.C.* where the Court rejected Sable's argument that it should not be compelled to tailor its dial-a-porn messages to the standards of the least tolerant community. The Court recognized that distributors of allegedly obscene materials may be subjected to the standards of the varying communities where they transmit their materials, citing *Hamling*, and further noted that Sable was "free to tailor its messages, on a selective basis, if it so chooses, to the communities it chooses to serve." The Court also found no constitutional impediment to forcing Sable to incur some costs in developing and implementing a method for screening a customer's location and "providing messages compatible with community standards."

* * *

For the foregoing reasons, this court *AFFIRMS* Robert and Carleen Thomas' convictions and sentences.

The *Thomas* case tends to surprise in at least two ways. One is with respect to free speech. Aren't individuals allowed to have whatever materials they wish in their own homes? While the Court confirmed this idea, once those materials are distributed, the distributors are liable under laws that exist wherever the materials are circulated. This means that California businesspeople have to concern themselves with the laws of Tennessee, or Turkey for that matter. Modern communications do change things and create blowback based on community norms.

The tug of war between home community and where business is done can play out in the opposite direction as well. Sometimes a country passes a law that requires "its" companies (a phrase itself pregnant with ambiguity) to follow certain laws no matter where they go. The U.S. Foreign Corrupt Practices Act provides an example of this.

II. Legislative and Regulatory Prohibitions

A. FOREIGN CORRUPT PRACTICES

One of the most controversial laws applicable to international business is the Foreign Corrupt Practices Act ("FCPA"). Passed into law in 1977 after the discovery that hundreds of U.S. companies were paying bribes, the FCPA makes it illegal for any U.S. company to offer to pay—or indeed to pay— a bribe to a foreign official in order to obtain or retain business. It also prohibits making a payment to a foreign political party or to a candidate for political office. The law also applies to foreign corporations that have securities listed on a U.S. securities exchange. The following case provides an example of the enforcement of the FCPA.

U.S. v. Kozeny

638 F.Supp.2d 348 (S.D.N.Y. 2009):

SHIRA A. SCHEINDLIN, DISTRICT JUDGE.

I. INTRODUCTION

Defendant Frederic Bourke moves pursuant to Federal Rule of Criminal Procedure 29 for an entry of a judgment of acquittal. For the reasons that follow, his motion is denied.

II. BACKGROUND

The Government's allegations in this case are complex, and it is unnecessary to recite them here. The relevant facts are as follows: SOCAR is the state-owned oil company of the Republic of Azerbaijan ("Azerbaijan"). In the mid-1990s, Azerbaijan began a program of privatization. The program gave the President of Azerbaijan, Heydar Aliyev, discretionary authority as to whether and when to privatize SOCAR. Bourke and others allegedly conspired to violate the FCPA by agreeing to make payments to Azeri officials to encourage the privatization of SOCAR and to permit them to participate in that privatization.

* * *

IV. DISCUSSION

A. *Count Two-Money Laundering Conspiracy*

Bourke argues that the Government has presented no evidence (1) "showing that [he] entered into any agreement with the specific intent of transporting money overseas for the purpose of promoting a violation of the FCPA;" and (2) "demonstrating that the scope of any such conspiracy extended into the statute of limitations period." I will address each of these arguments in turn.

1. **Lack of Intent**

Bourke contends that the Government has failed to prove that Bourke's intent in agreeing to transfer money overseas was to violate the FCPA rather than to purchase vouchers and options, which he notes is lawful.

As an initial matter, there is no dispute that Bourke invested in Oily Rock in March and July 1998. In order to sustain the money laundering conspiracy charge against Bourke, the Government must present evidence that Bourke had the "knowledge or awareness of the illegal nature of the charged activity and [that he intended] to advance the illegal objective." After a review of the evidence admitted at trial, I conclude that a reasonable jury could draw the inference that Bourke agreed with others that the intended use of his investment would be, in part, for the purpose of bribing Azeri officials.

Hans Bodmer, attorney to co-defendant Viktor Kozeny during the period of the privatization scheme, testified that he had a conversation with Bourke in early February 1998 regarding the bribery of Azeri officials. Bodmer testified that during one trip to Azerbaijan, Bourke asked him, "what is the arrangement, what are the Azeri interests." After obtaining Kozeny's approval to speak to Bourke about the specifics of the "arrangement," Bodmer then met with Bourke the following day. He testified that he then told Bourke that two-thirds of the vouchers had been issued to the Azeri officials under credit facility agreements at no risk to them. He also identified the Azeri officials who received these vouchers as Barat Nuriyev and his family and Nadir Nasibov and his family. It would certainly be reasonable for the jury to conclude that Bourke was aware of the bribery arrangements as early as February 1998.

In addition to Hans Bodmer, the Government also called Thomas Farrell, one of Kozeny's employees, as a witness. Farrell testified that some time after Bourke had invested in Oily Rock, Bourke requested that Farrell leave his office with him so that they might have a conversation. During that conversation, Bourke asked about the status of the privatization venture and whether President Aliyev or Barat Nuriyev had given any indications to Farrell about possible approval. Farrell testified that at one point in the conversation, Bourke had asked: "Has Viktor given them enough money?"

Farrell testified that Bourke raised the subject with him a second time during a trip to celebrate the opening of the Minaret offices in Baku, Azerbaijan in April 1998. Farrell testified that Bourke asked him about privatization and whether Farrell had heard anything from the officials in charge, such as Nuriyev. After Farrell gave Bourke a short status report, Bourke asked: "Well are—is Viktor giving enough to them?"

The testimony of Bodmer and Farrell, when considered in the light most favorable to the Government, is sufficient to prove beyond a reasonable doubt that Bourke agreed and intended that his investment not only be used for the purpose of purchasing vouchers and options, but also to ensure that the privatization of SOCAR occurred, by bribing the officials involved in the decision-making process. At oral argument, Bourke argued that proof that he knew that the investment money was being used partly to bribe officials is not enough; intent is required to sustain a conviction for conspiracy. However, even if *Bodmer's testimony shows only knowledge* of the bribery arrangements, a reasonable jury could infer from *Farrell's testimony* of Bourke's statements that Bourke *intended* that part of his July 1998 investment money be used to bribe officials.

* * *

B. *Count One-Conspiracy to Violate the FCPA and Travel Act*

Bourke next argues that he should be acquitted of Count One because "[n] o rational juror could find beyond a reasonable doubt that the post-July 22, 1998 payments (and other alleged overt acts) furthered the FCPA conspiracy, as opposed to the options fraud conspiracy." Bourke argues that by July 1998, the privatization venture was a "pipe dream," but that the options fraud conspiracy continued at "full speed." Bourke further notes that it would be "nothing but 'speculation and conjecture' to conclude that any such payments furthered the FCPA conspiracy-and that cannot be the basis for finding guilt beyond a reasonable doubt."

However, there is ample evidence to suggest that the purpose of many of the payments was to obtain assistance from the Azeri officials in the privatization venture. Farrell testified that bribes had been paid to the officials for the purpose of "help[ing] us purchase and obtain vouchers and options to [use in the] privatization auction." There is also testimony connecting specific bribes to the privatization venture. For instance, Farrell testified that at the meeting in which Kozeny agreed to give the officials a two-thirds share of the vouchers, he had also agreed to pay an "entry fee" of eight to twelve million dollars to President Aliyev in order to participate in the privatization of SOCAR, which was subsequently transferred in cash and by wire. A reasonable jury could properly conclude that any bribes made after July 22, 1998 were also made for the purpose of encouraging privatization rather than facilitating Kozeny's options fraud scheme.

Bourke's argument is also unpersuasive for another reason. As noted, there is sufficient evidence from which a reasonable jury could infer that Bourke knew of payments being made to Azeri officials by February 1998 and that he intended for similar payments to be made as of April 1998. In addition, there is evidence that he was involved in referring Nuriyev to a doctor in the United States and obtaining a visa for him to travel to the United States in August 1998. But there is also evidence that Bourke had no knowledge of the options fraud scheme until later-sometime around October 1998. It would therefore be plausible for a jury to infer that the purpose of the bribes—including some that were made after July 22, 1998—was to encourage the privatization of SOCAR, in which Bourke participated, rather than to facilitate the options fraud scheme, of which Bourke had no knowledge. Because this inference is supported by the evidence, it would not be the result of "speculation or conjecture." Bourke's motion with respect to Count One must therefore also be denied.

C. *Count Three-False Statements Charge*

* * *

Bourke's argument that he had not made a false statement because he "expressly stated his belief that Kozeny was 'paying off Azeri officials' (including Nuriyev) as

part of the options fraud scheme" is of no moment. As noted, a reasonable jury could find, based on the evidence offered at trial, that Bourke had no knowledge of the options fraud scheme until approximately October 1998. Therefore, Bourke's statement that Kozeny was bribing officials in furtherance of Kozeny's options fraud scheme would not explain Bourke's denial of knowledge of the bribery that had already occurred by April 1998. Bourke's motion with respect to Count Three is denied.

Bribery is not likely to occur by one person handing over a suitcase full of money to a foreign governmental official at lunch. Instead, it could happen by an agreement to hire a "local consultant to advise on local business matters." That "advice" is to convey money. The question then becomes whether the business person knew or reasonably should have expected that the consultant would use the money to pay a bribe. If it can be shown that the bribe-maker should reasonably know that money or other valuable resources will be conveyed to a governmental official in a way that is tantamount to paying a bribe, then it will be treated as such.

The FCPA does allow for what are known as "grease payments." which are payments made to a foreign official to expedite the performance of duties the person is already bound to perform. But the exact nature of what constitutes a grease payment that would fall outside of the scope of the FCPA seems to be in flux itself and, as the court said in *U.S. v. Kay* (2004), the scope of the FCPA can be quite large:

> "Congress meant to prohibit a range of payments wider than only those that directly influence the acquisition or retention of government contracts or similar commercial or industrial arrangements* * * The congressional target was bribery paid to engender assistance in improving the business opportunities of the payor or his beneficiary, irrespective of whether that assistance be direct or indirect, and irrespective of whether it be related to administering the law, awarding, extending, or renewing a contract, or executing or preserving an agreement.

The FCPA has been criticized by many businesses for creating a competitive disadvantage for American companies vis-à-vis foreign competitors who are legally able to pay bribes to secure business. On the other hand, some businesses claim that FCPA actually works to their benefit by removing ongoing demands for money from foreign governments. By removing bribes from the negotiating table, companies can more squarely focus on issues of price and quality.

B. OTHER EXAMPLES OF WHITE COLLAR CRIME

There are numerous examples of "white collar" crimes. The following is an illustrative, but certainly not exhaustive list:

- **Bank Fraud:** Engaging in an activity with the purpose of defrauding a bank.
- **Computer Fraud:** Hacking into databases holding information such as credit card numbers, social security numbers, or proprietary company information.
- **Credit Card Fraud:** Unauthorized use of a credit card, usually via theft.
- **Environmental Fraud:** Overbilling government contracts by claiming to do environmental work.
- **Health Care/Medicaid/Insurance Fraud:** Overbilling for health care treatment in excess of the treatments provided.
- **Insider Trading:** Use of securities information inaccessible to the public (inside information, advance notice of an announcement that will affect stock price) to inform trading decisions.
- **Money Laundering:** Hiding illegal commercial activities by making them appear to be part of a legitimate business enterprise.
- **Ponzi Scheme:** An investment scheme where the originator encourages investment with the promise of very high rates of return. The originator does not invest the money, but uses newly invested money to pay large returns to the earlier investors. Eventually, the scheme falls apart when a sufficient number of new investors can no longer be recruited to continue to pay the large returns.
- **Pyramid Scheme:** Similar to a Ponzi scheme except while Ponzi schemes are associated with investments, pyramid schemes generally are associated with businesses such as franchise arrangements.

CREDIT CARD THEFT COSTS BANKS $11 BILLION PER YEAR, AND CUSTOMERS LOSE ABOUT $4.8 BILLION.
Source: forbes.com

C. RICO

Sometimes white collar crimes can be compiled and prosecuted together, at least in the United States, under the Racketeer Influenced and Corrupt Organizations Act ("RICO"), which was designed as a tool to fight organized crime. Enacted in 1970, RICO imposes stiff civil and criminal penalties for organization it finds guilty.

There are nine categories of state crimes and additional federal criminal offenses under RICO. Consistent with the aim of fighting organized crime, these offenses include drug dealing, extortion, bribery, mail fraud, kidnapping, murder, and arson. If within a ten year window, an organization violates two of these criminal statutes (known as "predicate acts") then RICO can be triggered and criminal penalties of up to $25,000 and prison terms of up to twenty years per violation can be applied. Though designed for organized crime, regular businesses sometimes commit two predicate acts, so RICO has been applied to them as well.

D. ALIEN TORT STATUTE

Enacted in the 1700s, the Alien Tort Statute ("ATS") has become a major concern for multinational corporations. The ATS has been used by human rights groups to require corporations doing business overseas to adhere to certain U.S. and/or international laws. Companies respond that they have an obligation—a humbly respectful one, painted in the best light—to obey local laws and customs. Those using the ATS claim that companies use deference to local norms as an excuse to violate basic human rights standards. The ATS has been used in litigation against Chevron for abuses in complicity with the local government of Myanmar; Exxon too, has faced similar litigation, as have companies working in Iraq. Finally, Internet companies such as Yahoo and Google faced challenges from human rights groups for giving personal information of users to the government of China, which did not like postings that included words such as "democracy."

III. Reflexive Use of Criminal Law

IN 1984, Congress passed the Federal Sentencing Guidelines, which provide instructions to federal judges as to the severity of sentences that should be handed down to those convicted of federal crimes. When a famous or notorious criminal is about to be sentenced, commentators often anticipate the expected sentence, a prediction based on the Federal Sentencing Guidelines. They are the topic of the next section.

A. LEGAL INCENTIVES FOR ORGANIZATIONAL CULTURE AND ETHICS

Intuitively, one thinks of criminal law in terms of the government prosecuting wrongdoers. But increasingly, both Congress and the courts have sought to find ways to achieve compliance without creating more cases to be heard in court. They have done this by creating incentives for corporations to be actively involved in the administration of public policy as well as criminal issues. The Federal Sentencing Guidelines ("Guidelines") are not the only reflexive law to do this, but they are among the most important.

Congress established the Sentencing Commission, which who produced the Guidelines. It is important to note that these Guidelines are exactly that: guidelines. They are not meant to be followed meticulously.

In 1991, Congress amended the Guidelines to create provisions applicable to organizations. These provisions extend to a wide variety of organizations, including non-profit as well as for-profit corporations. They provide incentives for corporations to set up compliance programs that make it less likely for employees to violate the law, and include mission statements and codes of conduct. A high-level official in the organization oversees the program. There should be a forum—such as a hotline or an **ombudsperson**—where employees can safely report a violation without fear of reprisal. Corporations benefit from self-reporting violations rather than waiting for a violation to be discovered. There should also be training programs so that employees understand the specifics of the laws and the methods for compliance.

All of these things help comprise a compliance program. Corporations are eager to set up these programs because of the major monetary issues involved. If a company violates a criminal law, a judge uses the relevant base fine that applies based on the severity of the offense, as noted in the following chart (U.S. Sentencing Guidelines Manual § 8C2.4(d)):

Offense Level	Amount	Offense Level	Amount
6 or less	$5,000	7	$7,500
8	$10,000	9	$15,000
10	$20,000	11	$30,000
12	$40,000	13	$60,000
14	$85,000	15	$125,000
16	$175,000	17	$250,000
18	$350,000	19	$500,000

Offense Level	Amount	Offense Level	Amount
20	$650,000	21	$910,000
22	$1,200,000	23	$1,600,000
24	$2,100,000	25	$2,800,000
26	$3,700,000	27	$4,800,000
28	$6,300,000	29	$8,100,000
30	$10,500,000	31	$13,500,000
32	$17,500,000	33	$22,000,000
34	$28,500,000	35	$36,000,000
36	$45,500,000	37	$57,500,000
38 or more	$72,500,000.		

The amount of the fine will decrease if the judge sees that the corporation has made a good faith effort to implement the compliance program pursuant to the Guidelines. On the other hand, a fine could increase if there is no program or if there is no evidence that there has been a good faith effort to comply with the Guidelines. The Guidelines actually use a series of criteria to determine a culpability score, which is then added to the number of violations to determine the fine. (The actual language is set out in the Appendix)

These differences in monetary punishment can become significant and so, while not formally mandated as a law to follow, every major company has implemented a corporate compliance system. Indeed, in the *Caremark* case, 698 A.2d 959 (Del. Ch. 1996), the court held that it was a breach of fiduciary duty to shareholders to not have a compliance program in place. Under examination by the court as to whether the directors met their duties to monitor employee actions and comply with their fiduciary duties as well as the Sentencing Guidelines, the Directors came out rather well. But the important aspect of the case was not that the Directors breached their duty, but instead, that failure to institute a compliance program in accord with the Federal Sentencing Guidelines could be held to be a breach of their fiduciary obligations. That legal point provides a precedent for future shareholders to hold directors liable to the corporation itself. In *Caremark*, the Court said,

> "[I]t is important that the board exercise a good faith judgment that the corporation's information and reporting system is in concept and design

> adequate to assure the board that appropriate information will come to its attention in a timely manner as a matter of ordinary operations, so that it may satisfy its responsibility.
>
> Thus, I am of the view that a director's obligation includes a duty to attempt in good faith to assure that a corporate information and reporting system, which the board concludes is adequate, exists, and that failure to do so under some circumstances may, in theory at least, render a director liable for losses caused by non-compliance with applicable legal standards." * * *

Through a reflexive legal measure, governments can provide incentives for companies to comply with the law that are so significant for corporations that management really has little choice but to implement them. No company can refuse to implement a compliance program given the increase of fines. Empirical studies have also now been undertaken to determine what makes for effective compliance programs; two key factors are crucial to an effect compliance program.[1]

The first concerned whether a common set of standards was applied throughout the organization. If employees perceived that there was one set of standards for high-ranking officials in the organization and another set of standards for the rank-and-file, the compliance program was not as effective. This led to a second, related, finding that an effective compliance program mainly depended on whether the standards were enforced.

Effective compliance, then, is not simply drafting rules and making employees sign a statement that they have received and read the applicable rules, though that may be a step in the compliance process. Complicating things further were a set of amendments to the Guidelines in 2004 that mandated that compliance programs should create "organizational cultures" leading to "ethics" as well as legal compliance. In this way, companies were encouraged to go beyond legal minimums and consider how to create ethical corporate cultures that met applicable legal requirement of effective compliance programs.

If employees perceived that there were a set of standards for high-ranking officials in the organization and another set of standards for the rank-and-file, the compliance program was not as effective.

1 See, Cochran et al., *Corporate Ethics Programs As Control Systems* 42.1 Academy of Management J. 41 (Feb. 1999); Cochran et al., Integrated and Decoupled Corporate Social Performance 42.5 Academy of Management J 539 (Oct. 1999); Cochran et al., *Corporate Ethics Practices in the Mid-1990's: An Empirical Study of the Fortune 1000* 18.3 J. Business Ethics 283 (Feb. 1999).

Before discussing what ethical corporate culture may mean, it is worth noting that the Guidelines are not an aberration. A similar, reflexive model was implemented with respect to sexual harassment cases in a 1998 U.S. Supreme Court case, *Burlington Industries v. Ellerth* (1998). That case clarified the fact that employers could be vicariously liable for the actions of their employees. In a sexual harassment case, that means that a company could be liable for the sexually harassing actions of one of its employees. While the case confirmed that rule, it also provided a way—through compliance programs that included training programs, as well forums for resolving the issue—that employers could reduce the likelihood of facing sexual harassment cases and a long, expensive court process.

The pressure to improve corporate culture in order to head off legal and ethical indiscretions also requires a consideration of the relationship between ethics, law, and business that we sketch, more philosophically, in the opening and concluding chapters of the book.

NOTES AND COMMENTS on the Legal Environment of Business

1. **WITH CASES SUCH AS THOMAS** and regulations such as the Federal Sentencing Guidelines, one sees criminal enactments that draw upon ethical standards in order to determine whether an individual is in compliance with the law. With *Thomas,* the Court appealed to the relevant community standards on obscenity; with the FSG, courts look at "organizational culture" leading to "ethics and compliance." If you are a businessperson, how do you determine the ethical standards that help you comply with the law? What sources might you look to? Do you think it is fair to bring in ethical standards that are not defined *per se* by a legal authority that could have legal implications?

2. **ONE OF THE ARGUMENTS** for applying criminal sanctions for business misconduct is to get the attention of corporations with fines and bad publicity. Another reason is to make those who might hide under the guise of bureaucracy more accountable. Do either of these arguments persuade you? Is increasing criminalization of business misconduct a good idea or a bad idea?

3. **TAKE A LOOK** in a newspaper or magazine over the past year (or do an Internet search over that time frame) and see what kinds of criminal charges were brought by prosecutors against businesses. Do you see any trends or areas that seem to cause more problems than others?

4. **DO YOU THINK THE *THOMAS* CASE** was decided correctly? What implications does this have in terms of other businesses and the consequences of local laws and other norms on doing business?

5. **WHAT DO YOU THINK ABOUT THE EFFICACY** and fairness of the FCPA? Do you think that the U.S. forcing companies to abide by FCPA imperialistically forces business to change according to an "American way" of doing business? Research shows that every government in the world outlaws corruption and every major religion condemns it. Does FCPA only do what legal and moral consensus already demands?

NOTES AND COMMENTS on the Ethical Environment of Business

1. **WHITE COLLAR CRIME** issues continue the discussion we left with at the end of the chapter on the UCC. White collar crime, by definition, is the effort of the government to pass laws that criminalize certain kinds of (usually) economic misconduct. Hearkening back to the materials on jurisdiction, the notion that a government might identify activities that are such a threat to the public good that they need to be criminalized is not surprising. If the State of Illinois wants to punish corruption in Chicago, it is entitled to do so. What is surprising, however, is when governments punish things that range beyond their borders.

   The *Thomas* case is an example of this. Tennessee punishing a California resident can be explained because the Internet does reach across states. But should the U.S. punish the international soccer organization, FIFA?

2. **TURNING TO *ETHICS VIGNETTES*,** take a look at Chapter Two's case on the SEC charging HealthSouth's CEO with Fraud and the questions following that case. If the CEO could get away with the fraud, would it then be ethical? Why or why not? How would you determine whether it would be fraud? Of course, if the law specifies that it violates public standards, then one has a way to make a determination that the CEO's actions are problematic. But what if those laws don't exist? Do any of the frameworks described in Chapter 1 of *Ethics Vignettes* help? How do the CEO's actions impact the shareholders? The stakeholders? What virtues are violated by the CEO's actions?

3. **SIMILARLY, CHAPTER THREE** relates Johnson & Johnson having to pay more than $2.2 billion in fines. J&J, of course, had been one of the key exemplars of ethical corporate decision making as well as corporate culture for years. Yet, recently, cases like this have been the foundation for questions to arise about whether it has strayed from its ethical compass. In fact, some shareholders filed a derivative suit against management for failing to maintain the company's ethical culture. What caused the $2.2 billion fine? What causes this slide from exemplary to tainted company culture? What might be done to restore their values and culture?

CHAPTER

7

Property Law

The ancient law of property can seem to be a rather tame area. Yet private property ownership, one of the fundamental building blocks of free market economics, is essential to conceptions of American Democracy and has

tremendous vibrancy today in the form of Intellectual Property. Indeed, in emerging market countries or in those where Communist or Socialist regimes formerly governed, some of the first legal reforms generally addressed how to create an enforceable structure of private property rights. With secure property rights, one can own a home and amass wealth. Moreover, one might use real property for a business, perhaps to farm or extract minerals, or simply as a site for an office building or factory. Private property ownership provides the basis for a financial system that can lend money in the form of mortgages, which in turn can provide the liquid capital to build businesses. And property rights entail transfer rights, so that one can buy, sell and develop land to facilitate the transfer and exchange of wealth.

I. General Concepts and Classifications of Property Rights

OWNERSHIP OF PRIVATE PROPERTY stands as a counterweight against authoritarian and tyrannical government, which is a central reason why authoritarian governments typically refuse to allow citizens property rights. If individuals or corporations own property, there is a limit imposed on the powers government has over that property. This check on power becomes another fundamental basis for democracy. In Medieval England, the development of private property through the process of creating boundaries and the ensuing commercialization of property allowed wealthy landowners to check the power of King John, eventually forcing him to sign the *Magna Carta* in the 1200s.

In short, we owe many of our economic and political freedoms to the history of property law. In the near future, establishing property rights will also help navigate the process of globalization. To begin the study of this ancient concept of property (and, because it is ancient, the rather unusual terminology associated with it) it might be good to set out some different classifications of property.

A. TANGIBLE AND INTANGIBLE

Tangible property is something that one can physically hold, such as a house or car, cell phone, or book. **Intangible property** is property that you possess and have a right to, but cannot physically touch; others cannot take either away from you without punishment by law. You may well have a paper document that gives you evidence of it, but you are never going to have "it" in your hands. Today, a major example of this comes in the form of various kinds of intellectual property, such as a copyrights and trademarks, which are as protectable as the oil field you own and drill upon, but they are not something you can physically hold.

B. REAL AND PERSONAL

Real and **personal property** are both tangible, but the former is something you stand on and the latter is every other kind of tangible property. **Estate** is a common term in property terminology and a common reference point in this distinction. Real estate consists of land. You can walk and stand on it. Obviously, you can plow it, drill on it, build on it, or use it for any number of other purposes as well. Buildings—houses, condominiums, and office buildings—are real property as well. While hardly a legal definition *per se*, think of real property as what a real estate agent sells. They sell all of these things, but they don't sell watches, cars, or groceries. These items are personal property. You can put your hands on them—unlike a copyright—but they aren't the ground or a building on the ground.

C. DIVIDED AND UNDIVIDED

A person could have an undivided or divided interest in an item of property. In an **undivided interest**, you own and possess all there is to possess of the property. This idea can apply to personal property; for instance, you own a diamond ring without sharing that ownership with anyone else. That constitutes an undivided interest. The same applies to land; you may be the sole owner of a vacation home or an undeveloped piece of land.

On the other hand, you might share the ownership with someone else. The ways in which one can have shared ownership—a divided interest—are almost as many as the human imagination can conceive. You might co-own a bank account with your spouse. You may own an interest in an investment fund only after someone else dies. You may lease an apartment rather than owning a condominium. You may have a right to a seat in a stadium to watch a baseball game rather than owning the seat itself. Each of these stands as an example of a divided interest. Much of property law is about issues that arise with divided interests.

D. LIMITED OR UNLIMITED AS TO TIME

One kind of divided interest splits ownership according to when a person has certain kind of rights. Perhaps the easiest example of this is the life estate, a land ownership concept going back hundreds of years. Suppose a landowner wants to keep the property "in the family" but doesn't know if a child or grandchild will foolishly (at least in the property owner's mind) sell the land. The landowner could carve up ownership in the land according to time. He might give a "life estate" to his child, allowing the use—but not the sale—of the land during the child's life. At the same time, the grant of the land would preclude the child from deciding in her will to whom to leave the land after her death.

Instead, in accordance with the original landowner's will, the land might go to a grandchild for the grandchild's life. By doing this, the original landowner could extend his control over the disposition of the land for a hundred years. He can't stretch out the final disposition forever; there is a concept called "the rule against perpetuities" requiring that the land **vest** at some point, but that can be put off for quite a while. This is an example of having the use of land for a limited time. If the landowner's grandchild has a second life estate, she owns a property interest even before she gets to enjoy the actual use of the property. The interest is simply contingent on other things (such as the death of the person currently having use of the property). Whoever finally receives the property holds a **remainder interest** during all the time before they come into possession, even while others control the property during the life estates.

There could be many reasons for the landowner's decision to divide up property ownership like this. It could be that he is looking at some expensive tax considerations when the land finally is transferred and wants to delay that transfer with life estates, or he doesn't trust his children's judgment and doesn't want to give them the power (and temptation) to sell the property for money. So the landowner simply gives them the right to live in the family home without having the capacity to sell it. This lack of trust could pertain to the in-law who married the landowner's children, too. Perhaps he may trust his own children, but may not like the in-law and wants to make sure the in-law cannot get his hands on the family heritage. Life estates are one way to do this.

E. FIVE KINDS OF ESTATES—REAL PROPERTY

Recognizing that human imagination can think of many ways to divide up property, there are five key kinds of estates in real property.

- **The first is a Freehold Estate.** This is an outright ownership of the property which one typically can buy, sell, and develop without asking for permission from anyone else, except as limited by legal restrictions (such as zoning laws) on the use of the land.

- **The second is a Landlord-Tenant Relationship,** where a landowner rents out the property to a tenant. This could be in a residential situation (e.g. an apartment) or it could be for commercial property.

- **A third is a Co-Tenancy.** Here a person owns property together with another person. Most often this is an ownership with a family member; spouses own a house together or a joint bank account. Siblings own a farm together. A parent owns an investment fund to pay for college together with the children who will use the funds for their education.

- **A fourth pertains to Rights Above and Below the Ground.** Ownership of real estate provides some ownership of what is above the ground as well as what is below the surface. Thus a landowner may provide rights to a business constructing windmills that reach up from the ground, or to a mining company for minerals below that might be extracted.

- **Finally there are Incorporeal Interests,** which are not only interests such as copyrights and trademarks, but also certain rights with a land-based dimension such as easements, or rights connected to the land, but not rights in the real estate itself.

Ownership Variations (Concurrent Estates In Land)

Concurrent Estates in Land	Joint Tenancy	Tenancy in Common	Tenancy by Entirety
Ownership	Undivided Interest	Proportionate and undivided Interest	Undivided Interest
Right of Survivorship	Yes	No	Yes
Required Unity	• Unity of Time • Unity of Title • Unity of Possession • Unity of Interest	• Unity of possession	• Unity of Time • Unity of Title • Unity of Possession • Unity of Interest
Estate Language	"To X and Y as joint tenants with right of survivorship	"To X and Y" (as tenants in common)	"To Husband and Wife"
Methods of Termination	Unilaterally severed, then convertible as Tenancy in Common	Freely transferable	Mutually severed, death or divorce
passing of property	Upon death, property passes to the remaining joint tenants (operation of law)	Upon death, property passes to heirs	Upon death, property passes to heirs

Source: http://www.cpaexamacademy.com/lessons/regulation-reg/2-0-business-law/2-9-property/

II. Ownership Variations

A. FREEHOLD ESTATES

1. Fee Simple

The broadest ownership one can have is a **fee simple,** sometimes also called a **fee simple absolute.** Fee simple ownership means that one owns all the rights associated with the property. One can buy, gift, sell or develop it. One can subdivide it into successive interests. At death, one can direct the person who will have it next or if one does not have a will, the state will determine who should own it next. It is, in short, the cornerstone of all property rights.

2. Life Estates

Life estates are a straightforward way to divide up property ownership based on time. A person will have rights to the property during a period of time, usually a person's life, with the interest then passing to someone else. A life estate always needs to start with someone who has fee simple ownership. That person, the **Grantor**, determines how to divide up ownership of the property.

A conventional life estate would work like this. The Grantor is married with three children. He knows that his wife does not want to move from their home if he were to die. At the same time, for any number of reasons, he does not believe it is a good idea for his wife to have full, fee simple ownership of the property. So the Grantor executes a deed that states that the Grantor gives the property to his wife for her life and then, at her death, the remainder goes to their children.

This example is overly simplistic, in that surviving spouses have rights to property interests even if the other spouse tries to preclude them from getting them. The exact nature of those rights is complex, but the above example is helpful simply in setting out the ways in which a life estate can be created.

In this simple example, there is a Grantor. There is also a holder of the life estate, the spouse, and three people, the children, who have a remainder interest. The children are sometimes called **remaindermen**. Because there are multiple parties having interests in the same property, disputes are inevitable. In particular, the question arises as to the nature of rights and duties between the life estate holder and the remainderman.

There are variations of the simple example of a **Grantor → Life Estate Holder → Remaindermen**. When deeding the interests, the Grantor could reserve a life estate to himself first, so that the interests would run:

> **Grantor** (as fee simple owner) → **Grantor/Life Estate Holder** → **Spouse/Life Estate Holder** → **Children/Remaindermen**

Another variation would be that the Grantor creates a life estate for a term of years. He could establish a "life estate" not for "life," but for a period of, say, fifteen years, after which it then goes to another life estate holder or to a remaindermen.

Estates in Land	Fee Simple	Life Estate	Future Interest
Ownership Restricted	No	Yes	Yes
Duration of ownership	Indefinite	Limited to Life	Limited to Future

Source: http://www.cpaexamacademy.com/lessons/regulation-reg/2-0-business-law/2-9-property/

Yet another example is to create a life estate that is not based on the life of the life estate holder. Instead, the **measuring life** is someone else. Perhaps the Grantor's spouse has a significant disability. The Grantor does not want his spouse to face the trauma of having to move. At the same time, the spouse does not have the capacity to make decisions. There are several ways the family could protect the spouse: they could have the spouse sign a document called a **power of attorney**, which authorizes someone else to make decisions on her behalf. The family could go into court and have a judge declare that the person is unable to make decisions and have a guardian (usually a family member) appointed for her.

In addition to (or perhaps in lieu of) these steps, the Grantor could simply deed the property to one of his trusted children to use for the life of their mother. That one child would maintain the property as individuals looking out for another party—the mother—for the rest of her life. Then, at death, the actual ownership of the property would pass to all the children/remaindermen.

Today, many facing this situation might accomplish the same result through the creation of a trust, but the strategy above can still be used. A life estate holder's duties with respect to these kinds of property is as follows:

> "A life tenant is bound to keep the land and the structures comprising the estate 'in as good repair as they were when he took them, not excepting ordinary or natural wear and tear . . . . ' The obligation to make ordinary repairs is twofold. The tenant not only has the duty to make the ordinary repairs required to remedy a presently existing condition of substantial disrepair that may have injured the property substantially or permanently, but also has the duty to make any ordinary repairs necessary to prevent the property from progressively declining to the point where its deterioration, and the resultant injury to the inheritance, is substantial or permanent. In discharging the latter duty to make preventive ordinary repairs, for example, 'if a new roof is needed, [the tenant] is bound to put it on; if paint wears off, he is bound to repaint.' *Sauner v. Brewer* 220 Conn. 176 (1991).

The Grantor is not restricted to creating only one subsequent life estate at a time but may establish several. Rather than just creating two—one reserved for him and one for his wife—the Grantor could also create successive life estates for all of his children and then, only after all their deaths, provide for the property to pass to a remainderman. How long can this be stretched? Can a Grantor create such a succession of life estates that the property never "vests" or becomes a fee simple again?

The Rule Against Perpetuities was devised to deal with the problem of unvested or life-estates for children (**issue**) who had not yet come into being. While the rule seems relatively simple when stated—the estate must vest, if at all, within 21 years of the lives in being—the Rule is one of the most complex (and confusing) parts of property law for law students and even for lawyers.

These ongoing, successive interest issues may sound as if they are purely issues of personal estate planning but they frequently become deeply involved in business. Suppose, as is often the case with a person who owns a family business, a person's main asset is her business. At death, inheritance taxes may well be levied against the estate but there are innumerable ways to lessen or legally avoid the imposition of such taxes. One is to structure property ownership so that property does not "vest." Successive life estates help with this.

Another key tool in estate planning that pertains to keeping a business free of inheritance/estate taxes is the use of the **marital deduction**. In federal law, property passing to a surviving spouse is free from taxation. Of course, the surviving spouse will die sometime (thus triggering taxes), so a business person will want a mix of trying to pass property to the spouse and to others (such as children), with various rights for each. If one does not get the mix right, then taxes may be so significant that a business will need to be sold. In this way, issues of property ownership can end up making a very big difference in the long-term viability of a family business.

One of the most famous examples of the importance of aligning property rights with the tax law involved the necessary sale of the Chicago Cubs to the Tribune Company in order to pay the taxes on the estates of two members of the Wrigley family, famous for Wrigley's chewing gum. Even though the family employed some wealth-shifting techniques to reduce their estate tax liability, ultimately the heavy tax burden forced the Wrigley heir to sell the Cubs in 1981. Here is the account from the *Chicago Tribune*.*

Estate and Inheritance Taxes of $40 Million Led William Wrigley to Negotiate the Sale of the Chicago Cubs to Tribune Company

WILLIAM WRIGLEY'S estate tax problems resulted in large measure from the fact that his mother died so soon after his father in 1977, and from the fact that he did not want to dilute his controlling interest in either the Cubs or the Wm. Wrigley Jr. Co. These problems were compounded because the estate lacked enough cash or liquid assets to pay taxes.

Phillip Wrigley made a marital gift to his wife of one-half of his estate. That helped reduce the estate and inheritance tax owed on Phillip's estate. But the death of Helen meant that the entire estate was evaluated and taxed as a 'package.'

The Wrigley Estate did not qualify for substantial deferrals of estate taxes allowed to owners of closely-held businesses because neither the Cubs stock nor the Wrigley Co. stock comprised a sufficiently large portion of the total estate. The government allowed a four-year extension on the payment of the taxes. The maximum estate tax rate is 70 percent on estates of more than $5 million. Included in that 70 percent are credits for payment of state inheritance taxes.

* Limited factual excerpts from Bill Barnhart, "$40 Million Estate Tax Led Wrigley to Sell," *Chicago Tribune*, Jun. 17, 1981

B. CONCURRENT OWNERSHIP

Very often, people own property together with some else. Spouses frequently own their home, bank accounts, cars, and other property together. Parents sometimes share ownership with children. In a partnership, the same usually holds true. Thus, in addition to the possibility of dividing property according to time, property ownership can be divided between individuals as well. There are two key ways this can be done.

A very common form of joint ownership of property is **joint tenancy.** In a joint tenancy two or more parties share four unities in the property. First, they have **unity of possession** in that they both have an undivided interest in the property, which means each of them has a right to the entire property. If the property is a $100,000 bank account, they each have a right to the entire $100,000, not just "their half." Thus, if two people are pooling their resources in a joint bank account, they must realize that the other person could walk away with all the money.

A second concurrent "unity" is that the parties share title to the property through the same document. One could call this **unity of title.** Joint tenancy property needs to be created at one time in one document. In most states, there is a formulation that needs to be followed. The title of the document creating the joint tenancy must contain the phrase "as joint tenants and not as tenants in common", in part because other person could walk away with the money. There is risk associated with a joint tenancy, and courts want to be sure that a person entering into a joint tenancy knows what they are getting into.

Closely related to the second unity, the third unity is **unity of time.** The parties take the property at the same time, at the moment when the document is created. A joint tenancy arrangement is sometimes referred to as a "poor man's will" because the survivor automatically receives the entire interest of the property upon the other co-tenant's death. One does not have to go to Probate Court or have a will for this to happen; it does so automatically as a feature of the joint tenancy. Thus, a parent might take an already existing bank account and create a new account with one or more of her children's name on it as joint tenants. This creates a new property ownership to the property.

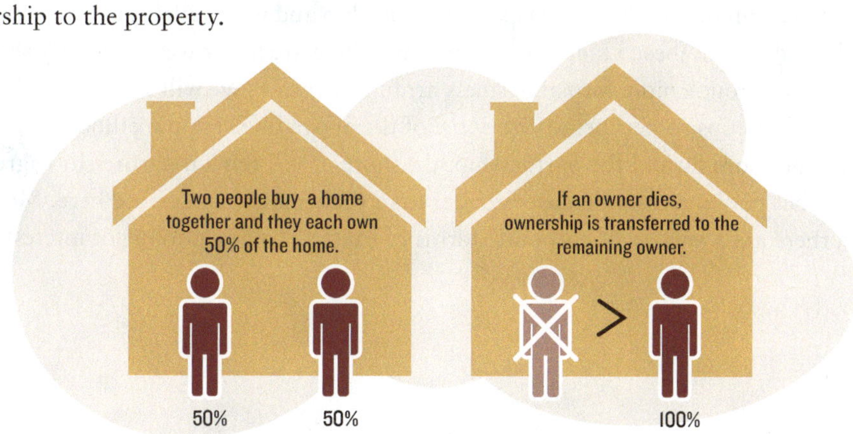

Source: http://hocmn.blogspot.com/2011_03_01_archive.html

The final unity is **unity of interest**, which means that the estate owned by each party is of the same type. For example, they each own an interest in a bank account or in real estate.

Creating a joint tenancy is not particularly difficult. The parties agree that they wish to own the property with the above characteristics and then must physically create a document that specifically identifies the joint tenancy. In other words, there must be written documentation of the joint tenancy, unlike a Tenancy in Common, exactly because it has the special features of allowing each tenant to fully take the property and because joint tenancies include a right of survivorship.

Death, of course, ends a joint tenancy and the survivor(s) takes the remaining interest. While this transfer avoids probate in most states, it does not avoid federal estate taxes. Other ways to sever a joint tenancy are by mutual agreement, by any transfer (potentially through a **straw man**), which is a person or entity that will never actually own the property, but who takes a momentary interest in the property so that it can be transferred back to the real parties in interest in the way they want the title to be held.

Another common form of joint ownership is a **tenancy in common**. Each tenant is entitled to equal use and possession of the property. The interests do not have to be of the same duration, nor do they need to be of equal amounts. One person could have a one-third share and the other a two-thirds share, rather than sharing the property 50-50.) . Unlike joint tenancies, a tenancy in common need not be in writing unless it pertains to real estate, in which case it must because of the Statute of Frauds. There is no right of survivorship, so if one joint tenant dies, his interest passes to his heirs rather than to the other joint tenant.

While joint tenancies and tenancies in common are the most prominent kinds of co-ownership, there are others. One example is something called **tenancy by the entirety**, which is limited to arrangements between spouses and cannot be severed either by the other co-tenant or by their creditors. They can only be terminated by mutual agreement, joint creditors, divorce, or death, when the property passes to the remaining tenant. Because of the strictness of tenancy by the entirety, they are not nearly as common as other forms of joint ownership and not available in every state.

In addition to these kinds of co-ownership, there are many ways to jointly share ownership through more formal business arrangements. As we will see in later chapters, partnerships sometimes utilize some of the above ownership methods, but the larger and more formal the partnership, the more it will rely on partnership agreements that pool interests that are broader than the tenancies described here. Moreover, there are a variety of corporate forms of that also allow pooling of interests.

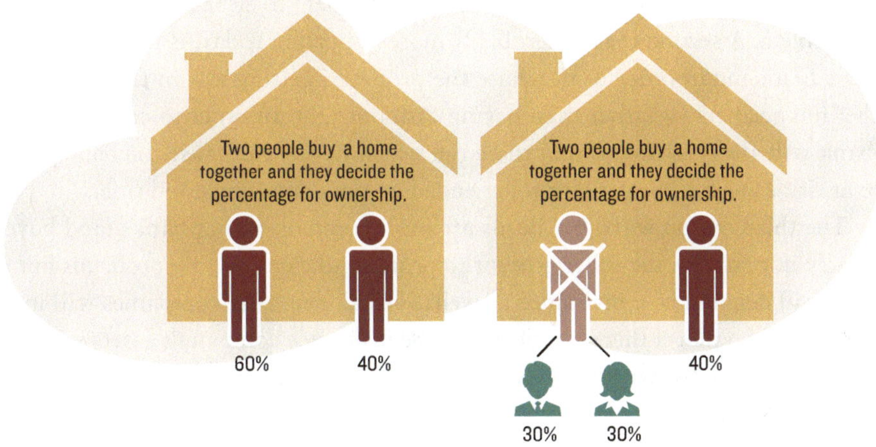

Source: http://superphotoscannerwallpaper.blogspot.com/2012/11/tenants-in-common.html

III. Transfer Issues of Real Estate

THE CHAPTER ON CONTRACTS, which will follow later in this book, will describe some of the issues pertaining to transfers of real estate, in particular the **Statute of Frauds.** This anciently rooted legal approach, still valid through the U.S. today, requires that transfers of real estate be in the form of a written **deed.** While some contracts can be enforceable if they are not in writing, the Statute of Frauds is much stricter. Title to the land will pass to another person if the deed is validly executed and delivered. There are several kinds of deeds. ,

The most common is called a **warranty deed.** As the name implies, these deeds warrant or guarantee that the owner does, in fact, own the property and will defend the authenticity of the title against competing claims or imperfections, even after transfer. A **quitclaim deed** is must less authoritative. With it, the grantor only transfers to another person *whatever interest* that grantor has. The interest may be the same as in a warranty deed, but it also could be nothing. The grantor is not assuring the buyer/grantee anything; she is just conveying whatever she has at the time. Another kind of deed is called a **special warranty deed.** This does assure some degree of ownership, but only insofar as the grantor ensures there were no liens placed on the property while the grantor owned the property. The grantor is not assuring the new buyer that there were no liens *before* the current/transferring owner took possession. With this overview, one can see how each kind of transfer might have its usefulness.

Warranty deeds tend to be the most common for three reasons. First, a new buyer wants to be sure that she is actually receiving property that no one else can claim. She is paying good money for the land or house and does not want to be surprised to learn that the grantor/seller did not own what he purported to own. With a warranty deed, the grantor/seller makes a commitment to clear up title in case there is a problem. A second reason, probably more important today, is that a buyer may utilize financing in order to purchase the property, getting a loan from a bank or other financial entity rather than paying cash outright. In order to cover their risk, a bank will always demand that there is a warranty deed because the bank's funds are at risk as well if the grantor/seller ended up not conveying good title.

The third reason warranty deeds are most common is that banks (and buyers) will rely not only on the seller/grantor to promise to clear up title problems but the banks will demand title insurance as well. Special insurance companies will insure the property so that if there is a problem, the insurance company's assets will cover any losses associated with a faulty title. Insurance companies, of course, are in the risk mitigation business, so they will not issue a title insurance policy—paid for by the buyer or seller—unless they are very sure there are no problems with the title to the property. The company will hire an attorney to do a **title opinion**, which will require the attorney to check all the court records to make sure the title is good and clear against other potential deed-holders and that there are no hidden liens or unreleased mortgages against the property. The attorney will charge a fee to the title company. Of course, then the lawyer also has some malpractice liability—also covered through insurance—assuring that the title opinion is accurate.

Thus, in most real estate transactions today, there are multiple layers of assurance (and insurance) that a conveyance is a good, lawful, free-of-defects transfer of real estate. At least this is true when banks are involved. When banks are not involved, one party can replicate all the above issues with respect to title insurance by directly dealing with the title insurance company. If one does not want to involve a title insurance company (and pay the premium for the policy), one could simply rely on an attorney's title opinion.

In some areas—especially rural ones—one will occasionally still find an older process called an **abstract of title**. In these cases, someone—usually a lawyer—will put together a history of documents that pertain to the property so that the property owner has all the documents regarding the property in one place. The idea is that everything that has ever been filed related to the property is in that one place, the abstract, so one can see, read, and review whether or not there are any glitches in the title.

Title insurance options are very difficult to obtain when one is dealing with a quitclaim deed. Quitclaim deeds are more typically executed when the property owner is simply getting out of a situation. In a divorce, one party may quitclaim his interest in the house to the other party. In some cases, someone may have acquired a small interest in an oil drilling operation a hundred years ago and, thereafter, paid little attention to it. The original owner of the fractional interest as well as her children and perhaps even her grandchildren may have died, thus creating a hundred individuals who have tiny fractional interests. Then, someone or some company may want to consolidate all the outstanding fractional interests for the company, which may include thousands of individual interests. None of these people has any idea whether they have good title to the land or not, so they will be unwilling to sign any kind of warranty deed. They may be willing to sign, however, a quitclaim deed to convey whatever interest they have. Thus, there are times and places where quitclaim deeds are more useful than others.

A modern example of a quitclaim deed is a **deed in lieu of foreclosure**, which might be used when a property owner is no longer able to pay the mortgage on the property. If the mortgagee is unable to make the mortgage, it's likely he is unable to pay other bills as well, and those creditors may have filed a separate lien against the property. Rather than face foreclosure, the property owner may simply deed the property to the bank; the property owner will not be in a position to guarantee good title, but he can quitclaim the interest he does have in the property. There may also be tax repercussions from the discharge of indebtedness, depending on the use of the property.

Other, less used forms of property transfer could include a **sheriff's deed**. If a person has gone through foreclosure, the bank may end up auctioning off its interest in a repossessed home or automobile. Because a foreclosure entails going through the court system, an officer of the government will conduct the auction and then convey the title to the person with the highest bid. That conveyance would be through a sheriff's deed, or some similarly named conveyance, depending on the particular state. A sheriff's deed will typically be another form of a quitclaim deed.

There are also a number of state-specific procedures regarding the registration of title, such as the indexing method for deeds and the state's approach to competing claims between bona fide purchasers. **Indexing methods** refer to the type of system the lawyer or landowner uses to search to see if they have a perfected title. There are two types of systems—**grantor-grantee indexes** and **tract indexes**. Grantor-grantee indexes trace the title through each disposition between persons, and the lawyer or landowner checks to see if the title is perfected by tracing the history of dispositions through each owner. Each piece of land has its own distinct history in the index. Related to this is the idea of notice to subsequent bona-fide purchasers. The case that follows involves adverse claims.

Bd. of Education of City of Minneapolis v. Hughes

118 Minn. 404, 136 N.W. 1095 (Minn.)

Bunn, J.

Action to determine adverse claims to a lot in Minneapolis. The complaint alleged that plaintiff owned the lot, and the answer denied this, and alleged title in defendant L. A. Hughes. The trial resulted in a decision in favor of plaintiff, and defendants appealed from an order denying a new trial.

The facts are not in controversy and are as follows: On May 16, 1906, Carrie B. Hoerger, a resident of Faribault, owned the lot in question, which was vacant and subject to unpaid delinquent taxes. Defendant L. A. Hughes offered to pay $25 for this lot. His offer was accepted, and he sent his check for the purchase price of this and two other lots bought at the same time to Ed. Hoerger, husband of the owner, together with a deed to be executed and returned. The name of the grantee in the deed was not inserted; the space for the same being left blank. It was executed and acknowledged by Carrie B. Hoerger and her husband on May 17, 1900, and delivered to defendant Hughes by mail. The check was retained and cashed. Hughes filled in the name of the grantee, but not until shortly prior to the date when the deed was recorded, which was December 11, 1910. On April 27, 1909, Duryea & Wilson, real estate dealers, paid Mrs. Hoerger $25 for a quitclaim deed to the lot, which was executed and delivered to them, but which was not recorded until December 21, 1910. On November 19, 1909, Duryea & Wilson executed and delivered to plaintiff a warranty deed to the lot, which deed was filed for record January 27, 1910. It thus appears that the deed to Hughes was recorded before the deed to Duryea & Wilson, though the deed from them to plaintiff was recorded before the deed to defendant.

The questions for our consideration may be thus stated: (1) Did the deed from Hoerger to Hughes ever become operative? (2) If so, is he a subsequent purchaser whose deed was first duly recorded, within the language of the recording act?

1. The decision of the first question involves a consideration of the effect of the delivery of a deed by the grantor to the grantee with the name of the latter omitted from the space provided for it, without express authority to the grantee to insert his own or another name in the blank space. It is settled that a deed that does not name a grantee is a nullity, and wholly inoperative as a conveyance, until the name of the grantee is legally inserted. It is clear, therefore, and this is conceded, that the deed to defendant Hughes was not operative as a conveyance until his name was inserted as grantee.

Defendant, however, contends that Hughes had implied authority from the grantor to fill the blank with his own name as grantee, and that when he did so the deed became operative. This contention must, we think, be sustained. Whatever the rule may have been in the past, or may be now in some jurisdictions, we are satisfied that at the present day, and in this state, a deed which is a nullity when delivered because the name of the grantee is omitted becomes operative without a new execution or acknowledgment if the grantee, with either express or implied authority from the grantor, inserts his name in the blank space left for the name of the grantee. * * *

Unquestionably the authorities are in conflict; but this court is committed to the rule that in case of the execution and delivery of a sealed instrument, complete in all respects save that the blank for the name of the grantee is not filled, the grantee may insert his name in the blank space, provided he has authority from the grantor to do so, and, further, that this authority may be in parol, and may be implied from circumstances. We consider this the better rule, and also that it should be and is the

law that when the grantor receives and retains the consideration, and delivers the deed in the condition described to the purchaser, authority to insert his name as grantee is presumed. Any other rule would be contrary to good sense and to equity. The same result could perhaps be reached by applying the doctrine of estoppel; but we prefer to base our decision on the ground of implied authority. Clearly the facts in the case at bar bring it within the principle announced, and we hold that Hughes, when he received the deed from Mrs. Hoerger, had implied authority to insert his name as grantee, in the absence of evidence showing the want of such authority. The delay in filling up the blank has no bearing on the question of the validity of the instrument when the blank was filled.

It is argued that holding that parol authority to fill the blank is sufficient violates the statute of frauds. This theory is the basis of many of the decisions that conflict with the views above expressed; but we do not think it sound. The cases in this state, and the Wisconsin, Iowa, and other decisions referred to, are abundant authority to the proposition that the authority of the grantee need not be in writing. Our conclusion is, therefore, that the deed to Hughes became operative as a conveyance when he inserted his name as grantee.

"THE DELAY in filling up the blank has no bearing on the question of the validity of the instrument when the blank was filled."

2. When the Hughes deed was recorded, there was of record a deed to the lot from Duryea & Wilson to plaintiff, but no record showing that Duryea & Wilson had any title to convey. The deed to them from the common grantor had not been recorded. We hold that this record of a deed from an apparent stranger to the title was not notice to Hughes of the prior unrecorded conveyance by his grantor. He was a subsequent purchaser in good faith for a valuable consideration, whose conveyance was first duly recorded; that is, Hughes' conveyance dates from the time when he filled the blank space, which was after the deed from his grantor to Duryea & Wilson. He was, therefore, a 'subsequent purchaser,' and is protected by the recording of his deed before the prior deed was recorded. The statute cannot be construed so as to give priority to a deed recorded before, which shows no conveyance from a record owner. It was necessary, not only that the deed to plaintiff should be recorded before the deed to Hughes, but also that the deed to plaintiff's grantor should be first recorded.

Our conclusion is that the learned trial court should have held on the evidence that defendant L. A. Hughes was the owner of the lot.

Order *reversed*, and new trial granted.

As we will see in Contract Law, courts are very particular about formalities when it comes to transfers of real property. This stems from centuries ago when real estate was the primary form of wealth a person might have. Assuring proper transfers was therefore very important and explains why courts look carefully at the authorization to convey property as well as the recording of deeds.

A. ADVERSE POSSESSION

Less common today than in the past, **adverse possession** remains a way to obtain ownership to property. Historically, it was more common when North America was being settled and there were large swaths of unoccupied land. At that time, there was a national interest in using property productively. If a landowner—even one who had full, good, exclusive title to property—was so careless about the land that he allowed another person to actively use it for twenty consecutive years, then that person could claim it under the concept of adverse possession.

Today, adverse possession has the same requirements and is far less common. The first requirements are that the person claiming ownership through adverse possession has actual and exclusive possession. This means that the person is really using it and living on it to the exclusion of others in the manner that an actual possessor would use the land. The second requirement is that the person's use is "open, visible, and notorious." This simply means it's being used in a way others are aware of, perhaps by building a house on it or farming it or clearly and publicly using the property as if it were his own. The third requirement is that the use is continuous and peaceable for twenty years. The fourth is that the use is hostile and adverse. Some states require additional elements, such as a claim of right (that the possessor act in good faith) or that the adverse possessor act under the color of title.

These requirements may seem to conflict with each other: How can ownership be both peaceable and hostile, innocent or acting in good faith but adverse? The idea is that while the person is making sure that others are not trespassing, no one else is really actively claiming that they, instead, own the land. Further, in calculating the twenty years, **tacking** is allowed as long as the interests of the parties are not adverse to one another. That means that if the person claiming adverse possession (for say eight years) conveys the property to someone else—for instance via intestacy to his child—then that child can count those eight years toward the twenty years necessary to satisfy the requirement.

Today, issues of adverse possession are likely to come up in boundary disputes. Fences are particularly good examples. Perhaps a neighbor in a subdivision or a farmer or a factory ends up putting a fence just across the boundary and instead builds the fence on the neighbor's land. The neighbor does not say anything for the twenty-year period. At the end of the twenty years, it is possible for the fence-owner to claim the land the fence is on via adverse possession. The following is an example of just such a case.

Helm v. Clark

244 P.3d 1052 (Wyoming 2010)

Kite, Chief Justice.

* * *

Mr. Clark and the Helms own adjoining agricultural properties in the NE ¼ of Section 12, Township 30 North, Range 119 West, 6th P.M., in Lincoln County, Wyoming. The properties have been in the Clark and Helm families since the 1920s. Mr. Clark's property is north of the Helms' and their respective deeds indicate that the sixteenth section line dividing the NE ¼ and the SE ¼ of the NE ¼ of Section 12 forms their property line, i.e., Mr. Clark owns the NE ¼ NE ¼ and the Helms own the SE ¼ NE ¼. A fence between the properties was built long ago and is south of the actual property line, meaning that part of the Helms' property is fenced in with Mr. Clark's property.

The Helms decided to move the fence to place it on the property line. Mr. Clark objected, and the Helms filed an ejectment action on October 25, 2007. Mr. Clark counterclaimed alleging that he had acquired title to the property north of the fence by adverse possession. The district court held a bench trial and ruled that Mr. Clark had proven the elements of adverse possession and the Helms had not provided a sufficient explanation to establish that Mr. Clark's use was permissive.

* * *

The district court ruled that Mr. Clark had established a *prima facie* case of adverse possession and shifted the burden to the Helms to explain the possession. On appeal, the Helms make a cursory attempt to show the district court incorrectly determined that Mr. Clark had established a *prima facie* case for adverse possession. They assert the district court failed to give proper weight to the facts that they paid taxes on the disputed property and Mr. Clark and his predecessors had executed title instruments affecting their deeded property but had not executed any such instruments affecting the disputed area. In certain cases, each of these factors may be important in determining whether possession is adverse. However, as the district court recognized, the fact that Mr. Clark had not paid taxes on the property is typical when a case involves use to a fence line. The claimant's failure to execute title instruments affecting the disputed property also is not unusual in fence line adverse possession cases. Although these facts weigh against a finding of adverse possession, they are not necessarily determinative.

* * *

After Mr. Clark presented his *prima facie* case for adverse possession, the burden shifted to the Helms to explain Mr. Clark's possession of the disputed area. They attempted to show that his use of the property was permissive because the fence was located off the property line as a matter of convenience. The placement, type and purpose of a fence are important factors in adverse possession cases. A fence that is intended to be the boundary between properties supports a claim for adverse possession. On the other hand, a fence that is placed in a certain location in order to separate pastures or irrigated meadows from grazing land or because the terrain makes it easier to build the fence in that location rather than on the property line is a fence of convenience. When a fence is located off the property line as a matter of convenience, use by the neighbor is considered permissive and will defeat a claim for adverse possession. The determination of whether a fence establishes a property boundary or is one of convenience is a question of fact.

"THE DETERMINATION of whether a fence establishes a property boundary or is one of convenience is a question of fact."

The district court rejected the Helms' argument that Mr. Clark's use was permissive and ruled the evidence supported a finding that the fence was a boundary fence rather than a fence of convenience:

> [T]he Clark–Helm fence . . . was [not] built as an interior fence. The land on either side of the fence is similar in nature requiring no separation due to the nature of the land. The fence runs from where it intersects with Section 7 [on the east] in a straight-line west over a ridge. Once it goes over the ridge it runs through mixed aspen and evergreen timber where its course meanders somewhat and trees are occasionally used as fence posts. But it is substantial in that it consists of five barbed wires. It runs through serviceberry bushes in places and the wire is off the posts in places in the spring. Trees have fallen over the fence in places. This is the normal condition of a longstanding fence enclosing pasturelands that are located in standing timber and subject to heavy snows. The fences needed to be repaired in the spring as Mr. Clark testified. This does not convert a boundary fence into a fence of convenience.
>
> [T]he Court finds that the Clark–Helm fence was constructed in the 1920's on a line that ran more or less straight consistent with the fence line located in the south boundary of [the adjacent property to the east in Section 7] . . . . The nature of this fence is consistent with a boundary fence. It is of the same type, if not better, . . . as that fence [on the west side of the Helms' property] and a better fence than the Helms' southern boundary fence. It was assumed to be on the surveyed line until about 1968. It is typical of the boundary fences that the Helms and Clarks had even though it may not have been built to modern standards. From 1968 onward the Plaintiffs Helms

were aware the Clarks were possessing their property on the other side of the fence yet they failed to take action to stop this possession.

The Helms challenge the district court's finding that the fence was a boundary fence, claiming that Mr. Clark and his predecessors admitted, in a related matter, that a different fence on the eastern boundary of the disputed area was one of convenience. During the trial, the Helms asked the district court to take judicial notice of the record in a case involving a property line dispute between Mr. Clark and his neighbors to the east in Section 7, Township 30 North, Range 118 West, 6th P.M., Lincoln County, Wyoming, Kenneth and Meleese Nebeker. Mr. Clark's father and uncle filed an affidavit in that case. They averred that the Clark/Nebeker fence was off the property line (it was located west of the actual property line so that part of Clark's property was fenced in with Nebekers' property); their father, Ernest L. Clark, had owned the lands on both sides of the fence in Sections 7 and 12; and the "fence was originally put in as a fence of convenience between farm land and hill pasture."

* * *

The Helms challenge the district court's rulings about the nature and location of the Clark/Helm fence. First, they assert the evidence did not establish that the fence was continuous from the eastern border to the western border of the Clark and Helm properties. The district court found that as the fence proceeds west from the eastern border, it generally runs in a straight line until it enters the timber, where "its course meanders somewhat," even using trees as fence posts at times. The trial evidence demonstrated that in some places along its course, the fence line proceeds through timber and dense undergrowth. David Helm testified that it was difficult to follow the fence line in spots because of the vegetation. However, the trial evidence also established that it is a substantial fence, including several barbed wires and gates, Mr. Clark maintained it each spring, and it effectively contained livestock. This evidence is sufficient to support the district court's findings that the Clark/Helm fence was continuous.

The Helms also contest the lack of evidence about the exact location of the fence and, accordingly, the disputed property. Although the record contains ample evidence that the parties and the district court understood the disputed area was that between the recorded property line and the fence, the evidence did not include a survey of the fence or a legal description of the disputed area. An advance plat, which stated that it was "subject to correction and approval" and apparently was not recorded, was admitted into evidence at the trial as Plaintiffs' Exhibit 2. The advance plat showed the recorded property line, the disputed area and the "approximate location of the existing fence line;" however, the fence line was not surveyed and was placed on the map for illustration purposes only. The parties stipulated that, at the eastern boundary, the Clark/Helm fence was approximately 294 feet south of the recorded property line. The record does not, however, contain evidence of the measurements of the disputed area as the fence continued to the west.

Despite the lack of evidence of the exact location and size of the disputed area, the district court concluded:

> The net result is that Defendant Ken Clark and his predecessors have adversely possessed land located north of the fence lines that are the focus of this dispute, the land being of a dimension 235 feet by 1320 feet titled in the Helms[.]

The trial evidence does not support the district court's conclusion because the parties stipulated that the fence was 294 feet off line at the eastern boundary, not 235 feet as the district court found, and there was no evidence as to the measurements of the disputed tract as it continued westward. Given the evidence that the fence meandered, the simple rectangular description given by the district court is not supported by the record.

An adequate legal description is required in adverse possession cases. As a practical matter, without a sufficient legal description, the county clerk will not be able to record the quiet title order and such order will not provide public notice of the ownership of the disputed parcel. Our statutes setting forth the requirements for conveyances of real property interests demonstrate the need for a proper legal description in matters of title to property.

The failure to provide a proper legal description does not, however, undermine the district court's ultimate finding that Mr. Clark proved he adversely possessed the property and was entitled to have title quieted in him. This is true because the parties and the court knew the general location of the property and "[o]nce all the elements of adverse possession are met, the possessor is vested with a fully new and distinct title. No judicial action is necessary." Thus, the proper remedy in this case is to remand for a determination by the district court of the actual legal description of the property adversely possessed by Mr. Clark.

Affirmed in part and *reversed* and *remanded* in part for proceedings consistent with this decision.

Adverse possession is a legal rule that rewards people for actually using property. If one uses property and pays taxes on it for a long time, the courts will allow ownership, even if the property was formally owned by someone else. This is one reason why, even if you don't mind your neighbor encroaching on your property line, it is worth not allowing it. With a subsequent purchase of the property, that new owner might claim actual ownership of some of your land.

B. EMINENT DOMAIN—GOVERNMENT CONDEMNATION FOR PUBLIC GOOD

There are times when the government can claim land from a private property owner under the Takings Clause through the government's power of **eminent domain.** Any exercise of eminent domain powers can create controversy as people generally dislike losing their house or property because of a government decision. But additional issues arise when the government exercise is not for a governmental (public) project, such as building a new road, but is used to enable another private property owner to own the property instead. This could happen, for instance, if the government tries to clear large swaths of land for the building of a sports stadium. The government believes that the building of the sports stadium would be in the public good, but it may be a private stadium owner who ends up profiting from the exercise of eminent domain. The following case provides an example of the use of eminent domain for public governmental purposes and also for private purposes that have been deemed by the government to be in the public interest.

Kelo v. City of New London, Connecticut

545 U.S. 469 (2005)

JUSTICE STEVENS delivered the opinion of the Court.

I

The city of New London (hereinafter City) sits at the junction of the Thames River and the Long Island Sound in southeastern Connecticut. Decades of economic decline led a state agency in 1990 to designate the City a "distressed municipality." In 1996, the Federal Government closed the Naval Undersea Warfare Center, which had been located in the Fort Trumbull area of the City and had employed over 1,500 people. In 1998, the City's unemployment rate was nearly double that of the State, and its population of just under 24,000 residents was at it's lowest since 1920.

These conditions prompted state and local officials to target New London, and particularly its Fort Trumbull area, for economic revitalization. To this end, respondent New London Development Corporation (NLDC), a private nonprofit entity established some years earlier to assist the City in planning economic development, was reactivated. In January 1998, the State authorized a $5.35 million bond issue to support the NLDC's planning activities and a $10 million bond issue toward the creation of a Fort Trumbull State Park. In February, the pharmaceutical company Pfizer Inc. announced that it would build a $300 million research facility on a site immediately adjacent to Fort Trumbull; local planners hoped that Pfizer would draw new business to the area, thereby serving as a catalyst to the area's rejuvenation. After receiving initial approval from the city council, the NLDC continued its planning activities and held a series of neighborhood meetings to educate the public about the process. In May, the city council authorized the NLDC to formally submit its plans to the relevant state agencies for review. Upon obtaining state-level approval, the NLDC finalized an integrated development plan focused on 90 acres of the Fort Trumbull area.

The NLDC intended the development plan to capitalize on the arrival of the Pfizer facility and the new commerce it was expected to attract. In addition to creating jobs, generating tax revenue, and helping to "build momentum for the revitalization of downtown New London," the plan was also designed to make the City more attractive and to create leisure and recreational opportunities on the waterfront and in the park.

The city council approved the plan in January 2000, and designated the NLDC as its development agent in charge of implementation. The city council also authorized the NLDC to purchase property or to acquire property by exercising eminent domain in the City's name. The NLDC successfully negotiated the purchase of most of the real estate in the 90–acre area, but its negotiations with petitioners failed. As a consequence, in November 2000, the NLDC initiated the condemnation proceedings that gave rise to this case.

Petitioner Susette Kelo has lived in the Fort Trumbull area since 1997. She has made extensive improvements to her house, which she prizes for its water view. Petitioner Wilhelmina Dery was born in her Fort Trumbull house in 1918 and has lived there her entire life. Her husband Charles (also a petitioner) has lived in the house since they married some 60 years ago. In all, the nine petitioners own 15 properties in Fort Trumbull—4 in parcel 3 of the development plan and 11 in parcel 4A. Ten of the parcels are occupied by the owner or a family member; the other five are held as investment properties. There is no allegation that any of these properties is blighted or otherwise in poor condition; rather, they were condemned only because they happen to be located in the development area.

In December 2000, petitioners brought this action in the New London Superior Court. They claimed, among other things, that the taking of their properties would violate the "public use" restriction in the Fifth Amendment. After a 7–day bench trial, the Superior Court granted a permanent restraining order prohibiting the taking of the properties located in parcel 4A (park or marina support). It, however, denied petitioners relief as to the properties located in parcel 3 (office space).

* * *

Two polar propositions are perfectly clear. On the one hand, it has long been accepted that the sovereign may not take the property of *A* for the sole purpose of transferring it to another private party *B*, even though *A* is paid just compensation.

On the other hand, it is equally clear that a State may transfer property from one private party to another if future "use by the public" is the purpose of the taking; the condemnation of land for a railroad with common-carrier duties is a familiar example. Neither of these propositions, however, determines the disposition of this case.

* * *

The disposition of this case therefore turns on the question whether the City's development plan serves a "public purpose." Without exception, our cases have defined that concept broadly, reflecting our longstanding policy of deference to legislative judgments in this field.

* * *

Viewed as a whole, our jurisprudence has recognized that the needs of society have varied between different parts of the Nation, just as they have evolved over time in response to changed circumstances. Our earliest cases in particular embodied a strong theme of federalism, emphasizing the "great respect" that we owe to state legislatures and state courts in discerning local public needs. For more than a century, our public use jurisprudence has wisely eschewed rigid formulas and intrusive scrutiny in favor of affording legislatures broad latitude in determining what public needs justify the use of the takings power.

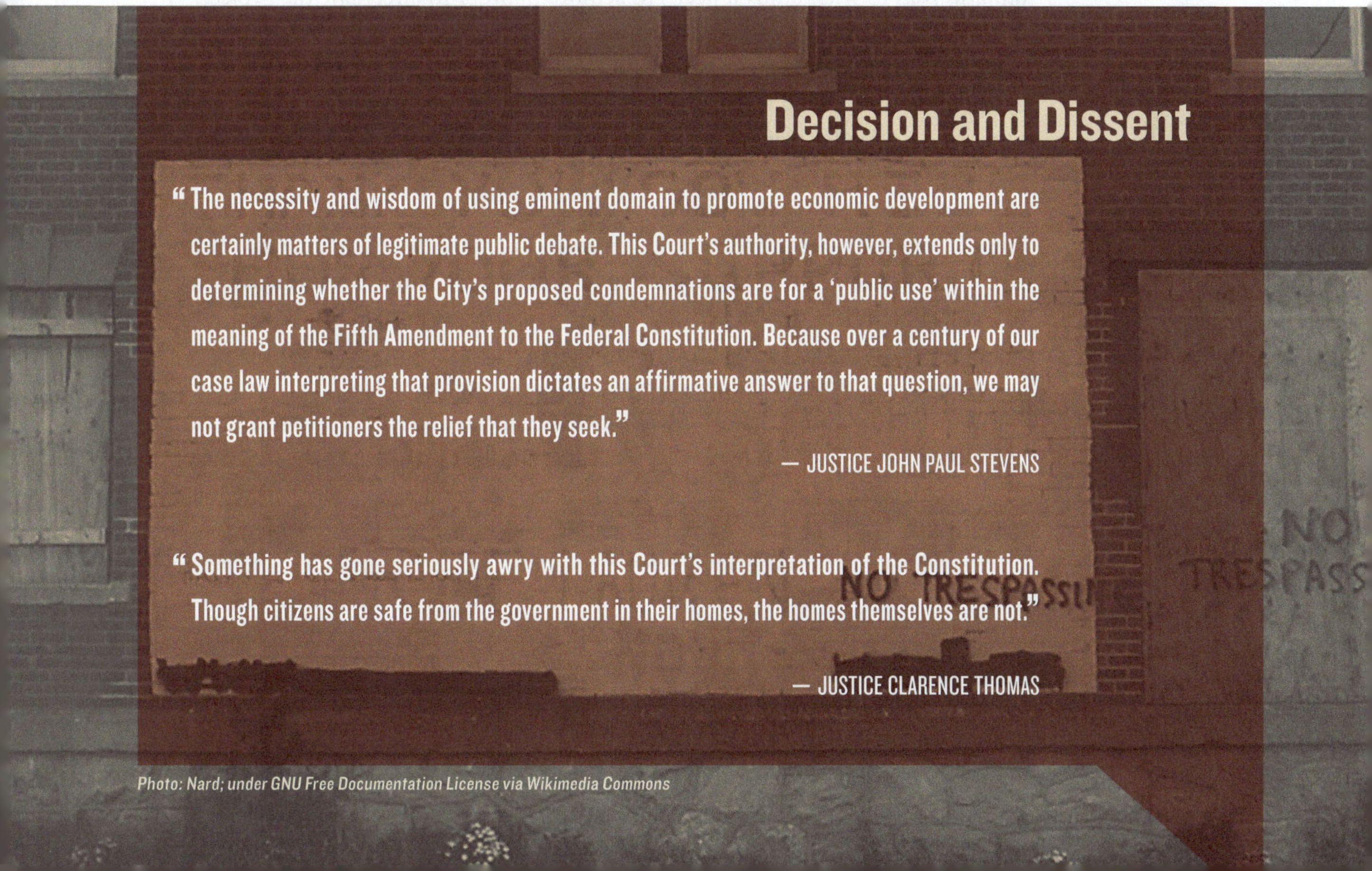

Decision and Dissent

"The necessity and wisdom of using eminent domain to promote economic development are certainly matters of legitimate public debate. This Court's authority, however, extends only to determining whether the City's proposed condemnations are for a 'public use' within the meaning of the Fifth Amendment to the Federal Constitution. Because over a century of our case law interpreting that provision dictates an affirmative answer to that question, we may not grant petitioners the relief that they seek."

— JUSTICE JOHN PAUL STEVENS

"Something has gone seriously awry with this Court's interpretation of the Constitution. Though citizens are safe from the government in their homes, the homes themselves are not."

— JUSTICE CLARENCE THOMAS

Photo: Nard; under GNU Free Documentation License via Wikimedia Commons

IV

Those who govern the City were not confronted with the need to remove blight in the Fort Trumbull area, but their determination that the area was sufficiently distressed to justify a program of economic rejuvenation is entitled to our deference. The City has carefully formulated an economic development plan that it believes will provide appreciable benefits to the community, including—but by no means limited to—new jobs and increased tax revenue. As with other exercises in urban planning and development, the City is endeavoring to coordinate a variety of commercial, residential, and recreational uses of land, with the hope that they will form a whole greater than the sum of its parts. To effectuate this plan, the City has invoked a state statute that specifically authorizes the use of eminent domain to promote economic development. Given the comprehensive character of the plan, the thorough deliberation that preceded its adoption, and the limited scope of our review, it is appropriate for us, as it was in *Berman,* to resolve the challenges of the individual owners, not on a piecemeal basis, but rather in light of the entire plan. Because that plan unquestionably serves a public purpose, the takings challenged here satisfy the public use requirement of the Fifth Amendment.

* * *

Just as we decline to second-guess the City's considered judgments about the efficacy of its development plan, we also decline to second-guess the City's determinations as to what lands it needs to acquire in order to effectuate the project. "It is not for the courts to oversee the choice of the boundary line nor to sit in review on the size of a particular project area. Once the question of the public purpose has been decided, the amount and character of land to be taken for the project and the need for a particular tract to complete the integrated plan rests in the discretion of the legislative branch."

In affirming the City's authority to take petitioners' properties, we do not minimize the hardship that condemnations may entail, notwithstanding the payment of just compensation. We emphasize that nothing in our opinion precludes any State from placing further restrictions on its exercise of the takings power. Indeed, many States already impose "public use" requirements that are stricter than the federal baseline. Some of these requirements have been established as a matter of state constitutional law, while others are expressed in state eminent domain statutes that carefully limit the grounds upon which takings may be exercised. As the submissions of the parties and their *amici* make clear, the necessity and wisdom of using eminent domain to promote economic development are certainly matters of legitimate public debate. This Court's authority, however, extends only to determining whether the City's proposed condemnations are for a "public use" within the meaning of the Fifth Amendment to the Federal Constitution. Because over a century of our case law interpreting that provision dictates an affirmative answer to that question, we may not grant petitioners the relief that they seek.

The judgment of the Supreme Court of Connecticut is *affirmed.*

With exceptions, property owners are often not very happy with the government condemning their property for a public use, such as a highway, or for a use by other property owners that the government views as beneficial to the public, for example, erecting a sports stadium. While courts do look at the justifications provided by government for the exercise of eminent domain as well as whether just compensation has been paid, courts also give a wide berth to such legislative determinations as exemplified in the above-excerpted case.

C. FORECLOSURES

Foreclosures have been around for a very long time, but they became more prominent in the wake of the financial crisis of 2008. A foreclosure can occur through the actions of any creditor. If creditors are owed money, they must find a way to recoup their losses, perhaps by locating an asset owned by the debtor. But they can't just seize the property; they must go through a court process that even a secured creditor must go through as well.

A **secured creditor** has collateral to secure the loan she provides; a bank providing a mortgage to a homeowner or an automobile finance company lending money to buy a car collateralized by the car are both examples of secured creditors. If the borrower falls behind on payments, the creditor typically has to provide notices and a chance for the borrower to repay the loan. Depending on the asset, the notices and workout requirements can be extensive, especially if the asset in question is the borrower's home.

The chart on the following page shows the process of home foreclosure from default to eviction.[1] If the borrower cannot repay the loan, she may decide to deed the collateral to the creditor through a deed in lieu of foreclosure. This transfers ownership of the property to the bank or some other creditor. It still may not satisfy the amount owed; whether the bank decides to find other property to seize to repay the debt is a judgment made by the creditor. Typically, there is some arrangement

---

1 For more information and state specific procedures, see, Federal Housing Finance Agency Office of Inspector General, "An Overview of the Home Foreclosure Process," *http://fhfaoig.gov/Content/Files/SAR Home Foreclosure Process_0.pdf.*

between borrower and creditor that, to avoid the expense of a foreclosure court case, the bank will accept the deed for the property and not continue to seek more money from the borrower. The same issues arise out of a **short sale**, which is a sale of the property for less than the debt that is secured by the property.

If neither of these occur, then the creditor must file a lawsuit against the borrower for repayment of the debt and to seize the asset. Again, the courts will provide safeguards to protect the debtor, especially with respect to a home, but if the foreclosure case goes to the end, the court will order that the land be sold to satisfy the judgment. The property then goes to a **judicial sale**, sometimes known as a **sheriff's sale**, where people can bid on the property. The creditor can bid the amount that is owed to them; that is often the highest bid. At that time, a sheriff's deed— or, depending on the state, some other kind of court-generated authority—conveys the property to the bank, which will then attempt to find a buyer for it.

IV. Incorporeal Interests: Non-possessory

INCORPOREAL INTERESTS are **non-possessory interests.** Most of the time in property law a person can physically possess—even physically hold—a watch or a car or their house. These are possessory interests. Sometimes, however, one can have an ownership interest in property where the property is possessed by someone else. These are non-possessory interests. A major example of these is easements, in which one party has the right to travel across another person's property for limited purpose. Utilities use easements all the time. With nearly any home, easements exist to the phone, cable, and electric companies.

The land over which the easement runs is called the **servient tenement** and the land served by the easement is called the **servient dominant**. There are three major types of easement. The most common are express easements, which are fairly straightforward with a clear, usually written agreement that an easement exists on the property. That is not to say that the parties negotiated the easement. More likely, when a person purchases property, the easement is already on the public records and the deed conveying the property will contain a clause that either specifies the easement or more generally notes that the property is subject to all publicly recorded easements.

An **easement by prescription** follows the same rules as adverse possession. If a person travels over a neighbor's property continuously for a period of twenty years, an easement is created. The following case looks at easement issues and, as the case shows, the claim that someone who does not even own an easement can still raise an easement ownership issue. For example, an argument about an easement could result from a dispute between two neighbors over who owns what property. It can also result from a landowner—or an easement holder—and a taxing authority that

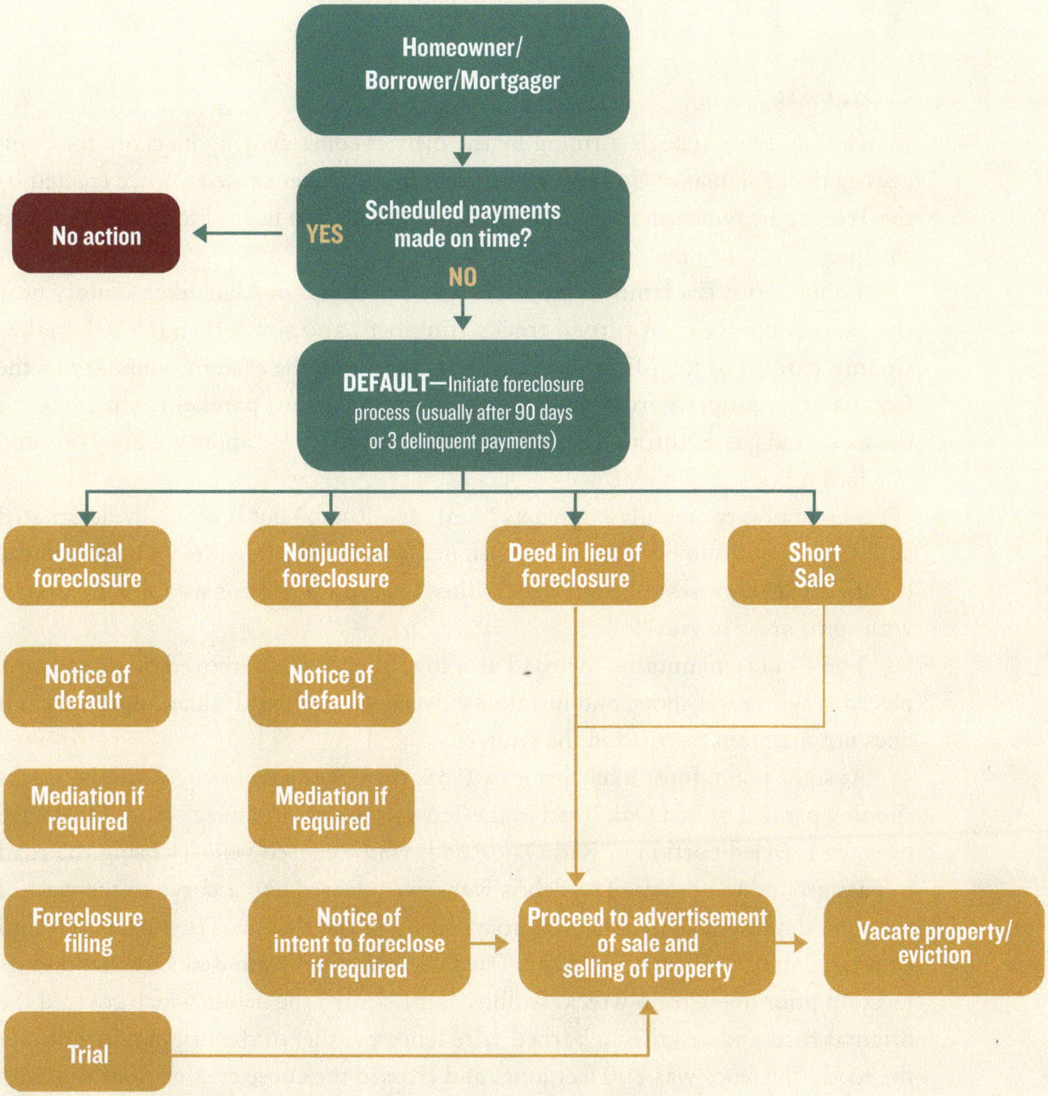

is trying to assess taxes on property. Landowners and a government authority that maintains an adjacent property such as a roadway may also encounter easement issues.

Collins Trust v. Allamakee County Bd. of Supervisors

599 N.W.2d 460 (Iowa 1999)

Cady, Justice.

Collins Trust appeals a ruling by the district court denying its claim for damages against Allamakee County after the county engineer caused a fence erected by the Trust to be removed as an immediate and dangerous hazard to persons using a roadway. We affirm the district court.

Collins Trust is a family trust which owns property in Allamakee County near the Mississippi River. Railroad tracks run north and south through Allamakee County parallel to the Mississippi River and separate the eastern boundary of the Collins Trust property from the river. A county road runs parallel to the tracks to the west, and passes through the Collins Trust property for approximately one and one-half miles.

The road is commonly known as "Red Oak Road," but is officially designated as County Road number 224. It was originally established in 1860. The portion of the road which passes through the Collins Trust property consists of a dirt base, with some areas of gravel.

The County maintains the road at a low level. It has removed downed trees, placed gravel in wet spots, and installed culverts to improve drainage in the area. It does not maintain the road in the winter.

At some point, most likely prior to 1955, there was a train wreck on the tracks running parallel to Red Oak Road in the Trust property. The wreck blocked passage over the traveled portion of Red Oak Road, which caused vehicles using the road to pass around the debris. The debris was never cleared and a curve to the west of the road developed. The curve encroached upon the Collins Trust property, and continued until 1991, when Collins Trust decided to relocate Red Oak Road to its location prior to the train wreck. Collins Trust cleared the debris which covered the original road and installed a barbed wire fence parallel to the original location of the road. The fence was 800 feet long, and crossed the curve created after the train wreck at the north and south ends. Collins Trust also planted walnut tree seedlings within the area enclosed by the newly erected fence.

The county engineer discovered the fence shortly after it was erected and, without providing notice to Collins Trust, directed County employees to remove it. The fencing materials were removed and piled on Collins Trust property. These materials eventually disappeared by theft. None of the walnut seedlings survived.

Collins Trust subsequently brought an action against the Allamakee County Board of Supervisors for damages resulting from the destruction of the fence and trees. Following a bench trial, the district court concluded the curve in the road resulting from the train wreck was acquired by the County by prescription, and the fence crossing the curve in the road was properly removed by the County as an immediate and dangerous hazard to persons or property using the highway.

On appeal Collins Trust claims the district court erred by finding the County acquired the curve in the road by prescriptive easement. It also claims the district court erred by finding the County properly removed the fence as an immediate and dangerous hazard to persons using the road.

* * *

One recognized method to establish an easement is by prescription. An easement by prescription is created under Iowa law when a person uses another's land under a claim of right or color of title, openly, notoriously, continuously, and hostilely for ten years or more. It is based on the principle of estoppel and is similar to the concept of adverse possession. In fact, we apply the principles of adverse possession to establish a prescriptive easement and use adverse possession to describe an easement by prescription. The fundamental distinction between the two doctrines is an easement by prescription concerns the use of property, while adverse possession deals with the acquisition of title to property by possession.

Collins Trust claims there was insufficient evidence to establish the requirements of an easement by prescription. It argues the use of the curve in the road by the public established neither hostile use of the property nor a claim of right. Additionally, the Trust claims it had no notice of any claim of right until the County removed the fence.

The hostility and claim of right requirements of a prescriptive easement are closely related. Hostility does not impute ill-will, but refers to declarations or acts revealing a claim of exclusive right to the land. Similarly, a claim of right requires evidence showing an easement is claimed as a right. Thus, mere use of land does not, by lapse of time, ripen into an easement. A party claiming an easement by prescription must prove, independent of use, the easement was claimed as a matter of right.

* * * The precise evidence to support the requirements of prescriptive easement can vary, and ultimately, each case rests on its own particular facts. However, under our standard of review, we find substantial evidence to support the district court finding that the curve in the road was used hostilely and by a claim of right.

The County not only annually maintained the road for several decades, but also installed and maintained a culvert in the curve of the road to promote drainage. This type of conduct was more than mere use, but was conduct which an owner of land would perform. It is sufficient to support a finding that the County claimed the curve in the road as a right. The fighting question turns to whether there is substantial evidence to support a finding that Collins Trust had express notice of the public's claim.

The open and notorious requirements of a prescriptive easement exist to help place the true owner of land on notice of the adverse use of the land by another. Under Iowa law the owner is required to have "express notice" of any claim of adverse possession. In *Larman*, we determined:

> These requirements ensure the landowner knows another's use of the property is claimed as a right hostile to the landowner's interest in the land. Otherwise, the landowner may incorrectly assume the other's use results merely from the landowner's willingness to accommodate the other's desire or need to use the land.

The notice requirement extends not only to the public use of the land, but also the public's claim to the land independent of use. The notice must either be actual or "from known facts of such nature as to impose a duty to make inquiry which would reveal the existence of an easement."

The record shows the Collins family was very familiar with the road running through its property and used it from time to time over the years. The family was also aware of the train wreck, and knew the road had moved into its property to curve around the wreckage. The family was aware the County maintained the road with its grader equipment and knew a culvert was installed in the curved portion of the road several decades ago. The family also knew the County installed the culvert. This evidence is sufficient to satisfy the "express notice" requirement, not only of the public use of the curve in the road for the last forty years or so, but the public's claim to the easement as well. The public expenditure of funds to maintain and repair the curve in the road over the years was known to Collins Trust and were acts of such a nature to support the public's claim of ownership. Consequently, we find the district court did not err by finding the County acquired the curve in the road by prescriptive easement.

A county is permitted to remove obstructions on highways located within its jurisdiction. Our legislature, however, requires the county to first give notice to the owner of the property causing the obstruction before it may be removed, unless the obstruction "constitutes an immediate and dangerous hazard" to persons or property lawfully using the right of way. If an "immediate and dangerous hazard" exists, the county is not required to give notice prior to removal and is not liable for any damages. Additionally, the costs of the removal become the responsibility of the owner of the obstruction.

Collins Trust claims the fence did not constitute an "immediate and dangerous hazard." It maintains travel was not hindered by the fence because the debris had been cleared from the original road and a path was available for motorists to use. Consequently, it asserts the County lost its statutory immunity from liability for damages by failing to provide notice.

What constitutes an "immediate and dangerous hazard" depends on the facts of each case and is generally a question for the finder of fact. The exception to the notice requirement exists to protect the public, and necessarily considers all the surrounding circumstances including the nature of the hazard and the likelihood of harm if not immediately removed. In this case, the fence was constructed of barbed wire and covered the entire width of the traveled portion of the road. The road was narrow and had no lights or signs to alert motorists of the obstruction or the change in the path of the road. Motorists had become accustomed to using the curve in the road over the years. Furthermore, the fence forced motorists to leave the established roadway and use an alternative, less stable, route created by the Trust. Under these facts, we find substantial evidence to support the determination by the trial court that the fence constituted an "immediate and dangerous hazard" to persons or property using the roadway.

We affirm the decision of the district court.

" IF AN 'IMMEDIATE and dangerous hazard' exists, the county is not required to give notice prior to removal and is not liable for any damages. Additionally, the costs of the removal become the responsibility of the owner of the obstruction."

Easements by prescriptions share some things in common with the notion of adverse possession presented earlier in this chapter. The extent of the right, however, is less. While an adverse possession can transfer entire ownership of property from one person to the other, a prescription easement more narrowly transfers the right to ingress and egress from one party the other.

A third kind of easement is one of **necessity.** Every property needs to have some kind of public access. Thus, even if no easement is specified, one will be created via the necessity doctrine. The question becomes where that access should be located. It is one thing to claim that one needs access; it is another to determine where that access should be located.

An owner of a landlocked piece of property owner has a right be able to get to it and from it. Sometimes, the landlocked owner is already using a route along someone else's property to access a way to service the property and in those cases, prescription by easement principles come into play. Yet whether or not such notorious use exists, there is a right to be able to make one's property accessible, as exemplified below.

Ashby v. Maechling

2010 MT 80, 356 Mont. 68, 229 P.3d 1210 (2010)

CHIEF JUSTICE MIKE MCGRATH delivered the Opinion of the Court.

* * *

The property at issue is west of U.S. Highway 93 in northern Ravalli County, Montana, and is bordered on the north by Missoula County. In 1932 Ravalli County acquired tax deed title to a large tract of land that included all of the property now owned by the parties. At that time the West County Line Road, which runs east-west along the Ravalli-Missoula County line, entered the east end of the large Ravalli County tract and provided access to it. In 1934 the County sold to George Jones the property now owned by Maechlings. The County retained the property now owned by Ashbys and sold it to Robert McKenzie in 1935. The Ashbys' tract is 120 acres and lies to the west of Maechlings' property. Maechling and Alcosser own and reside on 30 acres immediately east of Ashbys' land, and Dalton owns and resides on a tract immediately east of Maechling and Alcosser.

No established roads have ever entered the Ashbys' property and no permanent residence or agricultural use was ever established there. There is an irrigation ditch that crosses the parcel, but it has not been developed other than three episodes of logging, one in the 1800s, another in the 1970s and another conducted by Ashbys in 2007.

Ashbys bought their property in late 2004 along with a separate 150 acre parcel from the same seller. They knew at the time of purchase that there was no established access to the property and that their title insurance policy excepted access. Maechlings had for some time prior to 2004 maintained a locked gate on their property at the end of West County Line Road. The Road did not and apparently never has extended to the property now owned by Ashbys. In 2005 Ashbys wrote Maechling and Alcosser claiming an easement by necessity across their land for purposes of logging and offering not to sue them if Maechling and Alcosser sold Ashbys a perpetual non-exclusive easement for $10. Maechlings declined the offer, and this event precipitated Ashbys' claim for interference with the easement.

Ashbys sued in July 2005 seeking to establish that they had an easement by necessity across Maechlings' property to reach their 120-acre parcel, and for damages based upon Maechlings' alleged interference with the claimed easement.

* * *

We first consider the pivotal issue of whether the District Court properly held that an easement by necessity exists across Maechlings' land to access the Ashby land. Montana law has long recognized the existence of easements by necessity as a species of implied easements. At the same time, easements by necessity are "considered with *extreme* caution" because they deprive the servient tenement owner of property rights "through *mere* implication." Easements by necessity arise from a legal fiction that the owner of a tract of land would not isolate a portion of it without having intended to leave a way of access to the parcel over the lands being severed. Two essential elements of an easement by necessity are unity of ownership and strict necessity. The proponent of the easement by necessity must prove the necessary elements by clear and convincing evidence.

Unity of ownership exists where the owner of a tract of land severs part of the tract without providing an outlet to a public road. A single owner must at one time have owned both the tract to be benefited by the easement and the tract across which the easement would pass. Unity of ownership can originate decades before the judicial determination of whether there is an easement by necessity. The easement by necessity is created by operation of law at the time of severance of the parcels of land.

> **"EASEMENTS BY NECESSITY arise from a legal fiction that the owner of a tract of land would not isolate a portion of it without having intended to leave a way of access to the parcel over the lands being severed."**

In this case it is undisputed that in 1932 Ravalli County owned a tract of land referred to as the tax deed parcel that included the land now owned by all parties to this litigation. It is also undisputed that in 1934 the County severed parts of the larger tract to Maechlings' predecessors in interest and then to Ashbys' predecessors in interest. Therefore, the unity of ownership requirement was clearly met.

The element of strict necessity requires that there is no practical access to a public road from the landlocked parcel. Strict necessity must exist at the time the tracts are severed from the original ownership and at the time the easement is exercised. A developed way of access to the landlocked parcel need not actually exist at the time of severance, and an easement by necessity is "distinguished from other implied easements on the simple ground that [a developed way] need not be in existence at the time of conveyance . . . . "

In this case the District Court concluded upon a review of the evidence that there was no evidence of any practical road to connect Ashbys' parcel to a public road. Severance of the parcel now owned by Maechlings' landlocked the parcel now owned by Ashbys. No substantial evidence appears to contradict that conclusion.* * * Therefore, since there was clear and convincing evidence of both unity of ownership and strict necessity, the District Court properly concluded that an easement by necessity existed to provide access to the Ashby tract.

The second issue we consider is whether the District Court properly concluded that the West County Line Road is a public road. An easement by necessity exists, if at all, to connect the landlocked tract of land to a public road.

Maechlings contended that the West County Line Road is not a public road and therefore an easement by necessity could not be implied to provide access to it. * * * Here, the fact that the full length of the road was not opened in 1894 does not alter its status as a county road. Mere non-use, even for extended periods of time, is generally insufficient alone to indicate an intent to abandon a public way.

The record in this case, as explained in detail by the District Court's orders, sufficiently established that Ravalli County created and dedicated the West County Line Road as a public road. The District Court was correct in concluding that there were no material facts concerning whether the Road was created and that summary judgment on that issue was appropriate.

We next consider the issue of the scope of Ashbys' easement by necessity. * * * Ashbys have not specified any use they contemplate for their land, and in fact disclaim any plans for using it. They similarly did not specify the parameters of the easement by necessity, other than asserting that it must be sufficient to allow them to make any lawful use of the property. After conducting an evidentiary hearing and after extensive review of the facts and law, the District Court concluded that the scope of the Ashby easement

> is approximately 12–15 feet wide, as it currently exists, for one single-family residential, non-commercial use by owners of the Plaintiffs' Property, their lawful successors and assigns, including recreational access to wildlands on Plaintiffs' property and for irrigation system inspection, repair, maintenance and use, and use by Plaintiffs related to forest thinning and logging consistent with reasonable and responsible forest practices and for no other. All other uses or use by persons other than lawful owners, successors or assigns of Plaintiffs' property shall exceed the scope of this easement and is prohibited. This easement by necessity shall automatically terminate if and when other legal alternate easement access is obtained to Plaintiffs' Property.

Ashbys contend that the scope of their easement must be unlimited in order to serve any use they can lawfully make of the property. Maechlings contend that the easement as decreed is too broad in that it allows use for residential purposes and there has never been a residence on the Ashby property.

* * *

Here, there is no evidence of the actual contemplation of Ravalli County or its purchasers as to the present and future use of the property in 1934. The County acquired the land in a Depression-era tax foreclosure but was able to sell portions of it and return it to the tax rolls a few years later. There is no evidence that the County ever used the property and it is therefore likely that the County's interest and expectation at the time was to realize tax income from the tract. There is evidence that the Ashby land was at that time forested wildland with no established public vehicular access route. The evidence also shows that the Ashby land had been logged in the late 19th century but otherwise had been used, if at all, for wildland recreational purposes. Similarly, the evidence is that at the time of severance the area surrounding the County tax parcel was rural, forested, agricultural and the site of scattered rural residential dwellings.

Therefore, nothing in the history or condition of the property at the time of severance would support a finding that the extent of the implied easement by necessity across the land of the servient estates should be unlimited.

The District Court also properly considered that an easement by necessity, while not unlimited in scope, is not limited to the precise uses and prevailing technology at the time of severance. So, if the severance occurred at a time prior to the general use of motor vehicles and electric power, an easement by necessity may still allow for "reasonable technological developments" as long as the use does not cause unreasonable damage or interference with the rights of the servient estate owner. Thus, modern vehicle access and utility services may be allowed as part of an easement by necessity even though the easement arose as a legal matter before the general use of such improvements.

* * * Ashbys claim that they are entitled to damages of over $100,000 because Maechlings' rejection of the $10 perpetual easement in 2005 caused them to have to acquire a temporary easement from a third party to conduct the logging on the property in 2007. The District Court granted summary judgment against Ashbys on this claim. * * * While the essential acts that gave rise to the easement by necessity arose in the 1930s, Ashbys' right to the easement was not established until August 31, 2007. Prior to that time Maechlings could not have wrongfully interfered with Ashbys' easement. We therefore affirm the District Court's determination that Ashbys did not have a claim against Maechlings for interference with the easement by necessity.

The District Court's orders appealed from are affirmed.

Rents are another kind of property interest. There are two main types. One is when the grantor is entitled to a specific dollar amount. This is the most straightforward, with the grantor agreeing to rent a building, an apartment, or some land for a specific amount of money.

A second kind of rent comes from a portion of a product. For instance, many farm leases will provide for the tenant (the person farming the land) to split the profits from the crops grown with the landlord. In this case, the rent is a sharing of the sales of the product itself rather than a specific predetermined amount of money.

Whether recognized or not, a license is something that we use a great deal and can be defined as the right to use a particular thing for a set period. A good example is a ticket to a sporting or entertainment event. The ticketholder purchases the right to sit in Section 209, Row ZZ, Seats 3–4. That right exists only for that particular game. One has the right to exclude others from sitting in that seat by contacting the usher to remove a person sitting in the ticketholder's seat. The license for the seat is not assignable, which is one reason why scalping tickets is problematic. However, the ticket/license can also be revoked, especially when the ticketholder is behaving poorly. This combination of factors marks a license as a property right. You—and only you—have the right to occupy a particular piece of property (a stadium seat) and can exclude others from that piece of property. This is exactly the same situation as your house or a tract of farmland or a commercial property, but the duration is of a much more

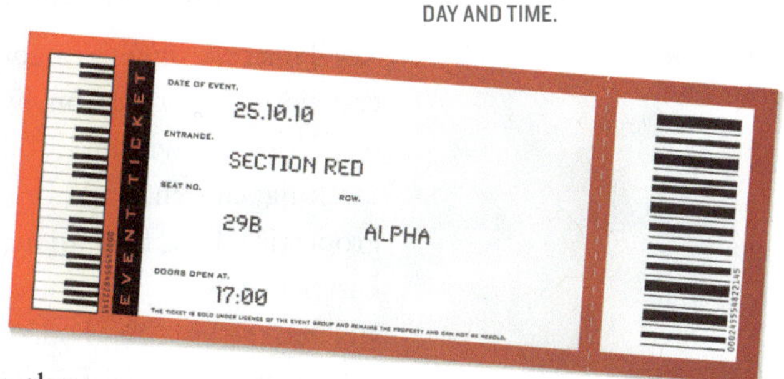

AN EXAMPLE OF A LICENSE IS A TICKET. A TICKETHOLDER ONLY PURCHASES THE RIGHT TO SIT IN A PARTICULAR SEAT, AND THAT RIGHT EXISTS ONLY FOR THAT EVENT ON THE ASSIGNED DAY AND TIME.

limited nature. Much stricter conditions can be placed on the use of the license than can be with many other forms of property.

V. Restrictive Covenants and Zoning

IN MANY SUBDIVISIONS, **restrictive covenants** limit what property owners can do with their homes. This applies primarily to issues such as providing common fencing, or whether the development allows any fencing at all. It might also apply to the construction of ancillary buildings such as decks or storage units or even mailboxes. The idea is that if one is going to live in a housing division, certain rules will follow, often justified as a way of ensuring property values are not diminished. Typically, these rules are recorded and made part of the public record so that when a person buys a home, the covenants automatically apply.

The following case addresses the issue of a restrictive covenant that is aimed at precluding the establishment of an adult movie theater. One might think that such cases are easily settled, yet the fact that this case goes all the way to the U.S. Supreme Court suggests that knotty issues can arise in these cases.

Renton v. Playtime Theatres, Inc.

475 U.S. 41 (1986)

JUSTICE REHNQUIST delivered the opinion of the Court.

This case involves a constitutional challenge to a zoning ordinance, enacted by appellant city of Renton, Washington, that prohibits adult motion picture theaters from locating within 1,000 feet of any residential zone, single- or multiple-family dwelling, church, park, or school. Appellees, Playtime Theatres, Inc., and Sea-First Properties, Inc., filed an action in the United States District Court for the Western District of Washington seeking a declaratory judgment that the Renton ordinance violated the First and Fourteenth Amendments and a permanent injunction against its enforcement. The District Court ruled in favor of Renton and denied the permanent injunction, but the Court of Appeals for the Ninth Circuit reversed and remanded for reconsideration. We noted probable jurisdiction and now reverse the judgment of the Ninth Circuit.

In May 1980, the Mayor of Renton, a city of approximately 32,000 people located just south of Seattle, suggested to the Renton City Council that it consider the advisability of enacting zoning legislation dealing with adult entertainment uses. No such uses existed in the city at that time. Upon the Mayor's suggestion, the City

Council referred the matter to the city's Planning and Development Committee. The Committee held public hearings, reviewed the experiences of Seattle and other cities, and received a report from the City Attorney's Office advising as to developments in other cities. The City Council, meanwhile, adopted Resolution No. 2368, which imposed a moratorium on the licensing of "any business . . . which . . . has as its primary purpose the selling, renting or showing of sexually explicit materials." The resolution contained a clause explaining that such businesses "would have a severe impact upon surrounding businesses and residences."

In April 1981, acting on the basis of the Planning and Development Committee's recommendation, the City Council enacted Ordinance No. 3526. The ordinance prohibited any "adult motion picture theater" from locating within 1,000 feet of any residential zone, single- or multiple-family dwelling, church, or park, and within one mile of any school. The term "adult motion picture theater" was defined as "[a] n enclosed building used for presenting motion picture films, video cassettes, cable television, or any other such visual media, distinguished or characteri[zed] by an emphasis on matter depicting, describing or relating to 'specified sexual activities' or 'specified anatomical areas' . . . for observation by patrons therein."

In early 1982, respondents acquired two existing theaters in downtown Renton, with the intention of using them to exhibit feature-length adult films. The theaters were located within the area proscribed by Ordinance No. 3526. At about the same time, respondents filed the previously mentioned lawsuit challenging the ordinance on First and Fourteenth Amendment grounds, and seeking declaratory and injunctive relief. While the federal action was pending, the City Council amended the ordinance in several respects, adding a statement of reasons for its enactment and reducing the minimum distance from any school to 1,000 feet.

* * *

In our view, the resolution of this case is largely dictated by our decision in *Young v. American Mini Theatres, Inc., supra*. There, although five Members of the Court did not agree on a single rationale for the decision, we held that the city of Detroit's zoning ordinance, which prohibited locating an adult theater within 1,000 feet of any two other "regulated uses" or within 500 feet of any residential zone, did not violate the First and Fourteenth Amendments. The Renton ordinance, like the one in *American Mini Theatres*, does not ban adult theaters altogether, but merely provides that such theaters may not be located within 1,000 feet of any residential zone, single- or multiple-family dwelling, church, park, or school. The ordinance is therefore properly analyzed as a form of time, place, and manner regulation.

Describing the ordinance as a time, place, and manner regulation is, of course, only the first step in our inquiry. This Court has long held that regulations enacted for the purpose of restraining speech on the basis of its content presumptively violate the First Amendment. On the other hand, so-called "content-neutral" time, place, and manner regulations are acceptable so long as they are designed to serve a substantial governmental interest and do not unreasonably limit alternative avenues of communication.

At first glance, the Renton ordinance, like the ordinance in *American Mini Theatres*, does not appear to fit neatly into either the "content-based" or the "content-neutral" category. To be sure, the ordinance treats theaters that specialize in adult films differently from other kinds of theaters. Nevertheless, as the District Court concluded, the Renton ordinance is aimed not at the *content* of the films shown at "adult motion picture theatres," but rather at the *secondary effects* of such theaters on the surrounding community. The District Court found that the City Council's "*predominate* concerns" were with the secondary effects of adult theaters, and not with the content of adult films themselves. But the Court of Appeals, relying on its decision in *Tovar v. Billmeyer*, held that this was not enough to sustain the ordinance. According to the Court of Appeals, if "*a motivating factor* " in enacting the ordinance was to restrict respondents' exercise of First Amendment rights the ordinance would be invalid, apparently no matter how small a part this motivating factor may have played in the City Council's decision. This view of the law was rejected in *United States v. O'Brien,* the very case that the Court of Appeals said it was applying:

> "It is a familiar principle of constitutional law that this Court will not strike down an otherwise constitutional statute on the basis of an alleged illicit legislative motive . . . .
>
> " . . . What motivates one legislator to make a speech about a statute is not necessarily what motivates scores of others to enact it, and the stakes are sufficiently high for us to eschew guesswork."

The District Court's finding as to "predominate" intent, left undisturbed by the Court of Appeals, is more than adequate to establish that the city's pursuit of its zoning interests here was unrelated to the suppression of free expression. The ordinance by its terms is designed to prevent crime, protect the city's retail trade, maintain property values, and generally "protec[t] and preserv[e] the quality of [the city's] neighborhoods, commercial districts, and the quality of urban life," not to suppress the expression of unpopular views. As Justice Powell observed in *American Mini Theatres,* "[i]f [the city] had been concerned with restricting the message purveyed by adult theaters, it would have tried to close them or restrict their number rather than circumscribe their choice as to location."

In short, the Renton ordinance is completely consistent with our definition of "content-neutral" speech regulations as those that "are *justified* without reference to the content of the regulated speech." The ordinance does not contravene the fundamental principle that underlies our concern about "content-based" speech regulations: that "government may not grant the use of a forum to people whose views it finds acceptable, but deny use to those wishing to express less favored or more controversial views."

It was with this understanding in mind that, in *American Mini Theatres*, a majority of this Court decided that, at least with respect to businesses that purvey sexually explicit materials, zoning ordinances designed to combat the undesirable secondary effects of such businesses are to be reviewed under the standards applicable to "content-neutral" time, place, and manner regulations. * * * The appropriate inquiry in this case, then, is whether the Renton ordinance is designed to serve a substantial governmental interest and allows for reasonable alternative avenues of communication. It is clear that the ordinance meets such a standard. As a majority of this Court recognized in *American Mini Theatres*, a city's "interest in attempting to preserve the quality of urban life is one that must be accorded high respect." Exactly the same vital governmental interests are at stake here.

* * *

In sum, we find that the Renton ordinance represents a valid governmental response to the "admittedly serious problems" created by adult theaters. Renton has not used "the power to zone as a pretext for suppressing expression," but rather has sought to make some areas available for adult theaters and their patrons, while at the same time preserving the quality of life in the community at large by preventing those theaters from locating in other areas. This, after all, is the essence of zoning. Here, as in *American Mini Theatres*, the city has enacted a zoning ordinance that meets these goals while also satisfying the dictates of the First Amendment. The judgment of the Court of Appeals is therefore

Reversed.

Zoning is crucially important for there to be a balance between economic development/activities and residential life. While small, in-home businesses such as coordinating a lawn-care company, preparing high school students to take the SAT, or providing violin lessons will likely cause no problems, no one wants their neighbor to be running an aluminum smelting factory next to their four bedroom house. So local governments extensively use zoning to carve out the places where activities can occur in an orderly time and place. Yet as soon as a zoning policy or ordinance is made, there will be requests for exceptions, such as requests for a variance from the zoning ordinance or a special use permit, which is the focus of the following case.

Willett v. Cerro Gordo County Bd. of Adjustment

490 N.W.2d 556 (Iowa 1992)

SNELL, JUSTICE.

Appellant, Thomas G. Willett, challenges a trial court's summary judgment ruling, which upheld the grant of a special use permit by the appellee, Cerro Gordo County Zoning Board of Adjustment. The board granted a special use permit to Tuttle Asphalt & Paving before Tuttle had received other necessary permits, a requirement under Cerro Gordo County, Iowa, Zoning Ordinance Article 20.2(JJ) and (KK). The trial court found that the requirement was merely a directory obligation, and failure to meet the requirement would not render the special use permit void. We affirm.

On February 25, 1991, Tuttle applied to the board for a special use permit to establish a rock extraction and processing project, a gravel extraction and processing project, and an asphalt plant on land located in Cerro Gordo County, Iowa. The board held a public hearing on the application on April 16, 1991. Following the hearing, the board adopted a resolution granting Tuttle a special use permit for the projects, subject to nine "conditions and/or requirements." Among these was the requirement that "all state and federal requirements must be adhered to."

* * *

County ordinances promulgated pursuant to authority delegated to a local governing body are extensions of state statutes and are to be construed as statutes. The Cerro Gordo County, Iowa, Zoning Ordinance was promulgated pursuant to Iowa Code chapter 358A (1991); the ordinance is an extension of that statute. The principles of statutory construction apply to the Cerro Gordo County, Iowa, Zoning Ordinance.

The parties argue over the import of "must" in the ordinance. The ordinance states that any permit required by any other governmental entity "must be obtained prior to applying for the special use permit." Willett argues that this language places an unavoidable duty on the applicant to obtain all other necessary permits first. Failure to do so would void any special use permit subsequently issued. The board argues that this language is obligatory, but the obligation may be waived by the board because it is merely "directory," not essential to the main objective of the ordinance.

The board's interpretation is derived from our construction of the word "shall" in other statutes. "Shall" and "must" are distinguished by our legislature in Iowa Code chapter 4 (1991), Construction of Statutes. "Shall" imposes a duty; "must" states a requirement. "Duty" and "requirement," however, are not defined in the Iowa Code. "Duty" is a "legal or moral obligation. Obligatory conduct or service. Mandatory obligation to perform." "To require" is to "direct, order, demand, instruct, command, claim, compel, request, need, exact." Both "duty" and "requirement" speak in terms of command and obligation, excluding the idea of discretion. Both direct some type of behavior that is obligatory in nature. As a matter of statutory construction, "shall" and "must" are often treated as synonyms. We find our rules of construction for "shall" to be instructive in our determination of the force of "must" in the Cerro Gordo County, Iowa, Zoning Ordinance.

The ordinance imposes a duty on the applicant to receive all other necessary permits before applying for the special use permit. A duty imposed by statute may be either "mandatory" or "directory." The dichotomy between a mandatory and a directory statute relates to whether a failure to perform the duty will have the effect of invalidating the governmental action that the requirement affects.

In determining whether a statute is mandatory or directory, we look to the nature of the duty in light of the purpose the statute was designed to serve. When the duty imposed by the provision is essential to effect the main purpose of the statute, the provision is mandatory, and failure to perform the duty will invalidate subsequent proceedings. When the duty imposed is not essential to the main statutory objective, however, the provision is directory, and failure to perform the duty will not affect the validity of subsequent proceedings unless prejudice is shown.

Zoning regulation is the local exercise of police power, to promote the "health, safety, morals, comfort, and general welfare [and] to conserve the values of property and encourage the most appropriate use of land . . . . " A special use permit allows property to be put to a purpose that the zoning ordinance conditionally allows. Article 20.1 of the Cerro Gordo County, Iowa, Zoning Ordinance, speaking of special uses, states, "It is recognized that certain uses possess characteristics of such unique and special form as to make impractical their being included automatically in any class of use . . . . [T]hese uses shall be subject to certain conditions and standards set forth in this Article." Cerro Gordo County, Iowa, Zoning Ordinance Article 20 is designed to promote public health and safety by regulation of special uses expressly permitted in the zone to ensure compatibility with other uses that exist in that zone. The purpose of the special use permit is to bring flexibility to the rigid restrictions of a zoning ordinance, while at the same time controlling troublesome or somewhat incompatible uses by establishing, in advance, standards that admit the use only under certain conditions and standards that must be met.

The requirement that an applicant receive all necessary permits from other governmental entities before applying for the special use permit is not essential to this purpose. First, the resolution adopted by the board conditioned issuance of the special use permit on receipt of all other requisite permits. Neighboring landowners were assured that operations would not begin until all state and federal requirements had been met. Tuttle cannot operate any of the facilities until he has received all necessary permits. To do so would be illegal and would subject Tuttle to injunction to cease operation.

Second, the mandate that the applicant receive the other permits first is a rule of convenience and timing. By enforcing this requirement, the board is assured that other agencies have examined and approved the activity in which the applicant seeks to engage on the site. If the duty is designed to assure "order and promptness" in the proceedings, the statute ordinarily is directory. The function of the Cerro Gordo County, Iowa, Zoning Ordinance requirement is to ensure "order and promptness" in obtaining other permits. We stated in *Taylor*:

> [S]tatutory provisions fixing the time, form and mode of proceedings of public functionaries are directory because they are not of the essence of the thing to be done but are designed to secure system, uniformity and dispatch in public business. Such statutes direct the thing to be done at a particular time but do not prohibit it from being done later when the rights of interested persons are not injuriously affected by the delay.

Third, the duty challenged was imposed on the applicant Tuttle, not the board. When the duty to be construed is not addressed to public officials and does not destroy a right or sacrifice a benefit to the public or individual, then the duty is generally directory. When the duty is directed toward the applicant, not the official, then the official may waive the duty. Willett did not lose any right or benefit by the board's waiver of the requirement. Tuttle was commanded to receive all necessary permits before operation commenced.

Having determined the requirement that an applicant for a special use permit under Cerro Gordo County, Iowa, Zoning Ordinance Article 20.2(JJ) and (KK) receive all other requisite permits before submitting the application is merely directory, the subsequent action of the board will not be void unless prejudice is shown. Willett has not alleged or shown that prejudice resulted from Tuttle's failure to present all other permits to the board with its application. Therefore, the special use permit is not invalid.

Accordingly, we affirm the ruling of the trial court dismissing Willett's petition and entering summary judgment in favor of the Cerro Gordo County Zoning Board of Adjustment.

AFFIRMED.

Just as they are often upset by eminent domain, property owners find themselves peeved by zoning laws. In both cases, the government is inserting itself into a property owner's use of the property. As the above two cases demonstrate, governments must justify the reasons for this interference. Both eminent domain and zoning stand as powerful tools for governments to shape the use of property.

NOTES AND COMMENTS on the Legal Environment of Business

1. **FROM A PHILOSOPHICAL STANDPOINT,** property concepts both underpin and extend beyond the law. Philosophers such as John Locke and, more recently, Thomas Donaldson and Patricia Werhane, have argued that one has a property right in one's labor. Under this formulation, not only do employees deserve humanitarian rights, but such rights also claim a kind of property law protection. What do you think? Do you think that one's labor is a kind of property, something that one owns? If not, why? If so, what implications do you think this has for various kinds of service and labor?

2. **THE RANGE OF PROPERTY LAW ISSUES,** as you have seen, is vast, from personal estate planning and boundary disputes with neighbors to commercial and industrial development via the powers of eminent domain. Do you think it is possible to live happily without private property? What would you lose without property law protections? Would you gain anything?

3. **HERE'S SOMETHING YOU WON'T EXPECT.** During the 1980s, one of the co-author's colleagues at Northwestern Law School—who also taught Property Law to the other co-author of this textbook—wrote poems to the property law themes. He also invited students to contribute their property poems, leading some students to write property law lyrics to songs. Why don't you take a stab at this yourselves?

NOTES AND COMMENTS on the Ethical Environment of Business

As noted in the Notes and Comments on the previous page, labor and property rights are not inimical. Locke and others have linked the two together. That's something to keep in mind when we get to the chapter on employment law, but for now, it is worth thinking about tangible property a bit more.

Run through the cases in this chapter again with the question of whether or not you think these cases are decided fairly? You can use the principles you rely on personally to determine whether or not something is fair or you may think of the principles underlying shareholder, stakeholder, and virtue theory.

Of particular interest may be the notion of usefulness. The easement and adverse possession cases rely heavily on the idea that the law tends to favor someone using property over someone simply having it in their possession. One could trace this back to the early days of this country and the enactment of legislation that provided free (or very cheap) land to settlers if they were to develop it. The same sense is true in adverse possession: even if it isn't your property, if you make use of it long enough, it might just become yours.

Is this a good idea? One might argue that in times past, it made some degree of nationalistic sense, but is there a benefit, too, to allow land to not be developed? Sustainability notions might suggest that we may overuse land. If that is true, then should the law change to not be so concerned about the use of the land and instead simply ask who has proper ownership of it?

One of the most important property interests ownership of shares of stock in a corporation. In the first chapter, we saw how the courts protected a shareholder's property interest in *Dodge v Ford*. Property ownership brings with it rights and that includes a return on investment or at least a distribution of accumulated assets on the basis of property ownership. In this chapter, we have seen that one cannot simply use property any way one chooses, but with an eye toward how that use impacts the public. Zoning is an effort to contain and regulate the uses of property.

With this in mind, do shareholders have a duty to consider a wider group of stakeholders? Notice that this is a little different than the typical debate of whether managers should act for the well-being of shareholders vs stakeholders. Those questions of questions ask what duties managers have. The question here is a little different: since property owners have some duties to others, should shareholders themselves have duties to stakeholders? If so, what would they be?

Earlier in Chapter 2, Professor Oswald made a strong argument that stakeholder theory (or the legal version of stakeholder theory called the corporate constituency statutes) represent a "takings" from the shareholders by permitting managers to consider non-shareholder constituents in making decisions. Does that change if the locus of the duty is not in managers, but in shareholders themselves?

Turning to *Ethics Vignettes*, read the article on the Tiger Woods scandal in the chapter on Marketing. If you were an executive for one of the companies for which Woods was a spokesman, would you keep him as your representative? What duties would you have to your shareholders? What duties would the shareholders have to Woods, if any How would you deal with Woods in the aftermath of scandal? What does the scandal itself say about the value of a person's reputation? Can you quantify it? Who "owns" reputation? It is something valued by Woods (and in other contexts, reputation is valued by companies themselves) but it is held by others, such as customers.

Also, take a look on the hydraulic fracking case in Chapter 7 of *Ethics Vignettes*. Here is a case where many people are raising questions about a property owner's use of real property and the impact in may have on others in several different ways. What are the lines you would draw for a property owner on how they use their property?

CHAPTER

8

Intellectual Property

In our increasingly technological and mediatized world, copyrights, trademarks and patents are valuable forms of property and sources of revenue. Companies invest significant capital to develop their brands and protect the symbols of their brands with **trademarks**, which include patterns and text as well as fixed images and moving images, all secured against copyright infringement. They obtain patents on everything from machinery to chemical formulas for pharmaceuticals. Entire courses and areas of the law are devoted to IP rights, but this book will only give the most cursory treatment of the legal issues involved.

I. General Principles

A. COPYRIGHTS

One of the most basic of intellectual properties is the copyright. Anytime a person creates anything that is in a **fixed media**, that person has a copyright in the property. That is true even of your class notes, and, yes, even your doodles in the margins. You have made an original creation of an idea, even by just writing your notes from a professor's lecture. You then have a copyright in those notes. As a practical matter, the copyrighted material may not be worth enough to sue over if someone, without your permission, were to photocopy them. However with valuable copyrights like songs, photographs, or movies, the stakes quickly grow.

Moreover, there is a question of proving whether materials that were used were subject to copyright in the first place. Indeed, many times, a central issue in copyright is proving who the original creator of the material was. One will often see the copyright symbol "©" on printed material indicating that the author claims a copyright on it. That provides some evidence that there is a copyright attached. A copyright registration proof from the U.S. Copyright Office is even better evidence in a copyright dispute. By filling out a form and attaching a copy of the material, the U.S. Copyright Office will issue a registration letter indicating that the author has claimed copyright on the material as of the date of the registration. Registration letters do not eliminate ownership disputes, but they do provide clear claims of copyright with a government-determined date and time noting when the claim was made.

The news occasionally mentions someone who claims they were the original composer of a song that has swept the world (and therefore made a lot of money). The alleged, original composer may then sue to obtain some of the money owed from the unauthorized use of her copyrighted material. More often, though, the controversy is not about the work's origin and the copyright holder, but whether the use is actually an **infringement**. The following case illustrates this kind of issue.

Bridgeport Music Inc., v. Dimension Films

410 F.3d 792 (6th Cir. 2005)

Ralph B. Guy, Jr., Circuit Judge.

Bridgeport and Westbound claim to own the musical composition and sound recording copyrights in "Get Off Your Ass and Jam" by George Clinton, Jr. and the Funkadelics. * * * There seems to be no dispute either that "Get Off" was digitally sampled or that the recording "100 Miles" was included on the sound track of *I Got the Hook Up*. Defendant No Limit Films, in conjunction with Priority Records, released the movie to theaters on May 27, 1998. The movie was apparently also released on VHS, DVD, and cable television. Fatal to Bridgeport's claims of infringement was the Release and Agreement it entered into with two of the original owners of the composition "100 Miles," Ruthless Attack Muzick (RAM) and Dollarz N Sense Music (DNSM), in December 1998, granting a sample use license to RAM, DNSM, and their licensees. Finding that No Limit Films had previously been granted an oral synchronization license to use the composition "100 Miles" in the sound track of *Hook Up*, the district court concluded Bridgeport's claims against No Limit Films were barred by the unambiguous terms of the Release and Agreement. Although Bridgeport does not appeal from this determination, it is relevant to the district court's later decision to award attorney fees to No Limit Films.

Westbound's claims are for infringement of the sound recording "Get Off." Because defendant does not deny it, we assume that the sound track of *Hook Up* used portions of "100 Miles" that included the allegedly infringing sample from "Get Off." The recording "Get Off" opens with a three-note combination solo guitar "riff" that lasts four seconds. According to one of plaintiffs' experts, Randy Kling, the recording "100 Miles" contains a sample from that guitar solo. Specifically, a two-second sample from the guitar solo was copied, the pitch was lowered, and the copied piece was "looped" and extended to 16 beats. Kling states that this sample appears in the sound recording "100 Miles" in five places; specifically, at 0:49, 1:52, 2:29, 3:20 and 3:46. By the district court's estimation, each looped segment lasted approximately 7 seconds.

* * *

Subject to sections 107 through 122, the owner of copyright under this title has the exclusive rights to do and to authorize any of the following:

1. To reproduce the copyrighted work in copies or phonorecords;
2. To prepare derivative works based upon the copyrighted work;
3. To distribute copies or phonorecords of the copyrighted work to the public by sale or other transfer of ownership, or by rental, lease, or lending;
4. In the case of literary, musical, dramatic, and choreographic works, pantomimes, and motion pictures and other audiovisual works to perform the copyrighted work publicly;
5. In the case of literary, musical, dramatic, and choreographic works, pantomimes, and pictorial, graphic, or sculptural works, including the individual images of a motion picture or other audiovisual work, to display the copyrighted work publicly; and
6. In the case of sound recordings, to perform the copyrighted work publicly by means of a digital audio transmission.

* * *

The copyright laws attempt to strike a balance between protecting original works and stifling further creativity. * * * Although musical compositions have always enjoyed copyright protection, it was not until 1971 that sound recordings were subject to a separate copyright. If one were to analogize to a book, it is not the book, i.e., the paper and binding, that is copyrightable, but its contents. There are probably any number of reasons why the decision was made by Congress to treat a sound recording differently from a book even though both are the medium in which an original work is fixed rather than the creation itself. None the least of them certainly were advances in technology which made the "pirating" of sound recordings an easy task. The balance that was struck was to give sound recording copyright holders the exclusive right "to duplicate the sound recording in the form of phonorecords or copies that directly or indirectly recapture the actual sounds fixed in the recording." This means that the world at large is free to imitate or simulate the creative work fixed in the recording so long as an actual copy of the sound recording itself is not made. That leads us directly to the issue in this case. If you cannot pirate the whole sound recording, can you "lift" or "sample" something less than the whole. Our answer to that question is in the negative.

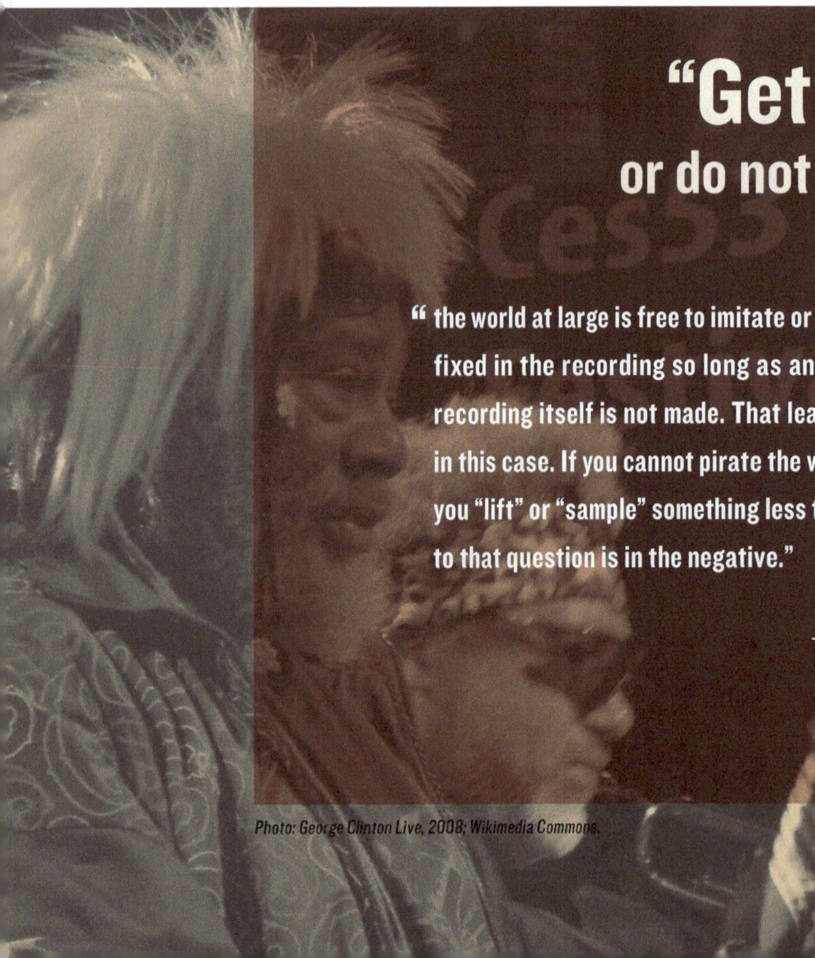

"Get a license or do not sample."

"the world at large is free to imitate or simulate the creative work fixed in the recording so long as an actual copy of the sound recording itself is not made. That leads us directly to the issue in this case. If you cannot pirate the whole sound recording, can you "lift" or "sample" something less than the whole. Our answer to that question is in the negative."

— CIRCUIT JUDGE RALPH B. GUY, JR.

Photo: George Clinton Live, 2008; Wikimedia Commons.

Section 114(b) provides that "[t]he exclusive right of the owner of copyright in a sound recording under clause (2) of section 106 is limited to the right to prepare a derivative work in which the actual sounds fixed in the sound recording are rearranged, remixed, or otherwise altered in sequence or quality." Further, the rights of sound recording copyright holders under clauses (1) and (2) of section 106 "do not extend to the making or duplication of another sound recording that consists *entirely* of an independent fixation of other sounds, even though such sounds imitate or simulate those in the copyrighted sound recording." The significance of this provision is amplified by the fact that the Copyright Act of 1976 added the word "entirely" to this language. In other words, a sound recording owner has the exclusive right to "sample" his own recording. We find much to recommend this interpretation.

To begin with, there is ease of enforcement. Get a license or do not sample. We do not see this as stifling creativity in any significant way. It must be remembered that if an artist wants to incorporate a "riff" from another work in his or her recording, he is free to duplicate the sound of that "riff" in the studio. Second, the market will control the license price and keep it within bounds. The sound recording copyright holder cannot exact a license fee greater than what it would cost the person seeking the license to just duplicate the sample in the course of making the new recording. Third, sampling is never accidental. It is not like the case of a composer who has a melody in his head, perhaps not even realizing that the reason he hears this melody is that it is the work of another which he had heard before. When you sample a sound recording you know you are taking another's work product.

This analysis admittedly raises the question of why one should, without infringing, be able to take three notes from a musical composition, for example, but not three notes by way of sampling from a sound recording. Why is there no *de minimis* taking or why should substantial similarity not enter the equation. Our first answer to this question is what we have earlier indicated. We think this result is dictated by the applicable statute. Second, even when a small part of a sound recording is sampled, the part taken is something of value. No further proof of that is necessary than the fact that the producer of the record or the artist on the record intentionally sampled because it would (1) save costs, or (2) add something to the new recording, or (3) both. For the sound recording copyright holder, it is not the "song" but the sounds that are fixed in the medium of his choice. When those sounds are sampled they are taken directly from that fixed medium. It is a physical taking rather than an intellectual one.

* * * Since our holding arguably sets forth a new rule, several other observations are in order. First, although there were no existing sound recording judicial precedents to follow, we did not pull this interpretation out of thin air. Several law review and text writers, some of whom have been referenced in this opinion, have suggested that this is the proper interpretation of the copyright statute as it pertains to sound recordings. Since digital sampling has become so commonplace and rap music has become such a significant part of the record industry, it is not surprising that there

are probably a hundred articles dealing with sampling and its ramifications. It is also not surprising that the viewpoint expressed in a number of these articles appears driven by whose ox is being gored. As is so often the case, where one stands depends on where one sits. For example, the sound recording copyright holders favor this interpretation as do the studio musicians and their labor organization. On the other hand, many of the hip hop artists may view this rule as stifling creativity. The record companies and performing artists are not all of one mind, however, since in many instances, today's sampler is tomorrow's samplee. The incidence of "live and let live" has been relatively high, which explains why so many instances of sampling go unprotested and why so many sampling controversies have been settled.

Second, to pursue further the subject of stifling creativity, many artists and record companies have sought licenses as a matter of course. Since there is no record of those instances of sampling that either go unnoticed or are ignored, one cannot come up with precise figures, but it is clear that a significant number of persons and companies have elected to go the licensing route. Also there is a large body of pre-1972 sound recordings that is not subject to federal copyright protection. Additionally, just as many artists and companies choose to sample and take their chances, it is likely that will continue to be the case.

"The legislative history is of little help because digital sampling wasn't being done in 1971. If this is not what Congress intended or is not what they would intend now, it is easy enough for the record industry, as they have done in the past, to go back to Congress for a clarification or change in the law."

Third, the record industry, including the recording artists, has the ability and know-how to work out guidelines, including a fixed schedule of license fees, if they so choose.

Fourth, we realize we are announcing a new rule and because it is new, it should not play any role in the assessment of concepts such as "willful" or "intentional" in cases that are currently before the courts or had their genesis before this decision was announced.

Finally, and unfortunately, there is no Rosetta stone for the interpretation of the copyright statute. We have taken a "literal reading" approach. The legislative history is of little help because digital sampling wasn't being done in 1971. If this is not what Congress intended or is not what they would intend now, it is easy enough for the record industry, as they have done in the past, to go back to Congress for a clarification or change in the law. This is the best place for the change to be made, rather than in the courts, because as this case demonstrates, the court is never aware of much more than the tip of the iceberg. To properly sort out this type of problem with its complex technical and business overtones, one needs the type of investigative resources as well as the ability to hold hearings that is possessed by Congress.

These conclusions require us to reverse the entry of summary judgment entered in favor of No Limit Films on Westbound's claims of copyright infringement. Since the district judge found no infringement, there was no necessity to consider the affirmative defense of "fair use." On remand, the trial judge is free to consider this defense and we express no opinion on its applicability to these facts.

AFFIRMED in part, *REVERSED* in part, and *REMANDED* for further proceedings consistent with this opinion.

The United States Patent and Trademark Office provides this summary definition of copyrights:

> **COPYRIGHTS** protect works of authorship, such as writings, music, and works of art that have been tangibly expressed. The Library of Congress registers copyrights which last the life of the author plus 50 years. *Gone With The Wind* (the book and the film), Beatles recordings and video games are all works that are copyrighted.

Fair use is an affirmative defense to copyright infringement and one of the major questions litigated in copyright cases, including the use of materials for classroom and educational purposes. Can't teachers just make a copy of an article they think is interesting and distribute it to a class? Don't the benefits flowing from education allow for such a use? Yet because someone took the time to create that educational material or to write the article, copying is a form of theft. Or, more philosophically, as copyright's cousin—patents—are justified in the Constitution, there is a belief that society as a whole will be better off if creators have the financial incentive to create. If the creator's work will simply be copied for free, then the incentive to create dramatically drops. What about uses that are creative and innovative beyond the sphere of education? Answering these questions is not always easy and because of the fine lines that result from the facts in a particular case, fair use dilemmas can arise.

According to the copyright law, courts are to use four factors in determining whether a use (a copy) is fair use or whether it is an infringement on the author's copyright.

- The purpose and character of the use, including whether such use is of commercial nature or is for nonprofit educational purposes
- The nature of the copyrighted work
- The amount and substantiality of the portion used in relation to the copyrighted work as a whole
- The effect of the use upon the potential market for, or value of, the copyrighted work

The following two cases set out examples of the parameters of fair use, first in the educational context and the second, in copyrighted, musical **sampling**.

Marcus v. Rowley

695 F.2d 1171 (9th Cir. 1983)

PFAELZER, DISTRICT JUDGE:

From September 1972 to June 1974, plaintiff, Eloise Toby Marcus was employed by the defendant, San Diego Unified School District ("District") as a teacher of home economics. Plaintiff resigned from the District's employ in 1974 and taught adult education classes intermittently from 1975 to 1980. Shortly after leaving her teaching position with the District, she wrote a booklet entitled "Cake Decorating Made Easy." Plaintiff's booklet consisted of thirty-five pages of which twenty-nine were her original creation. The remaining six pages consisted of material incorporated with the permission of the authors of the materials for which the authors were given appropriate credit.

Plaintiff properly registered the copyright for "Cake Decorating Made Easy" with the Register of Copyrights, and one hundred and twenty-five copies of the booklet were published in the spring of 1975. All of the copies of plaintiff's booklet contained a designation of copyright as evidenced by an encircled "c" followed by "1975 Eloise Marcus." This designation appeared on the table of contents page, the first page, and the page following the cover-title sheet.

Plaintiff sold all but six of the copies of her booklet for $2.00 each to the students in the adult education cake decorating classes which she taught. Plaintiff's profit was $1.00 on the sale of each booklet. Copies of plaintiff's booklet were never distributed to or sold by a bookstore or other outlet. Plaintiff never authorized anyone to copy or reproduce her booklet or any part of it.

Defendant, Shirley Rowley ("Rowley"), teaches food service career classes in the District. In the spring of 1975, she enrolled in one of plaintiff's cake decorating classes and purchased a copy of plaintiff's book. During the following summer, Rowley prepared a booklet entitled "Cake Decorating Learning Activity Package" ("LAP") for use in her food service career classes. The LAP consisted of twenty-four pages and was designed to be used by students who wished to study an optional section of her course devoted to cake decorating. Defendant had fifteen copies of the LAP made and put them in a file so that they would be available to her students. She used the LAP during the 1975, 1976 and 1977 school years. The trial court found that sixty of Rowley's two hundred twenty-five students elected to study cake decorating. The trial court further found that neither Rowley nor the District derived any profit from the LAP.

Rowley admits copying eleven of the twenty-four pages in her LAP from plaintiff's booklet. The eleven pages copied consisted of the supply list, icing recipes, three sheets dealing with color flow and mixing colors, four pages showing how to make and use a decorating bag, and two pages explaining how to make flowers and sugar molds. Four additional pages in defendant's LAP also appear in plaintiff's booklet, but these pages primarily contain information collected by and used with the permission of the Consumer Service Department of the American Institute of Baking.[1] * * * Rowley did not give plaintiff credit for the eleven pages she copied, nor did she acknowledge plaintiff as the owner of a copyright with respect to those pages.

Plaintiff learned of Rowley's LAP * * * when a student in plaintiff's adult education class refused to purchase plaintiff's book. The student's son had obtained a copy of the LAP from Rowley's class. After examining Rowley's booklet, the student accused plaintiff of plagiarizing Rowley's work. Following these events, plaintiff made a claim of infringement against Rowley and the District. Both denied infringement and the plaintiff filed suit.

* * *

The first factor to be considered in determining the applicability of the doctrine of fair use is the purpose and character of the use, and specifically whether the use is of a commercial nature or is for a nonprofit educational purpose. It is uncontroverted that Rowley's use of the LAP was for a nonprofit educational purpose and that the LAP was distributed to students at no charge. These facts necessarily weigh in Rowley's favor. Nevertheless, a finding of a nonprofit educational purpose does not automatically compel a finding of fair use.

This court has often articulated the principle that a finding that the alleged infringers copied the material to use it for the same intrinsic purpose for which the copyright owner intended it to be used is strong indicia of no fair use. * * * In this case, both plaintiff's and defendant's booklets were prepared for the purpose of teaching cake decorating, a fact which weighs against a finding of fair use. * * *

Here, there was no attempt by defendant to secure plaintiff's permission to copy the contents of her booklet or to credit plaintiff for the use of her material even though Rowley's copying was for the most part verbatim. Rowley's conduct in this respect weighs against a finding of fair use.

The second factor to be weighed is the nature of the copyrighted work. * * * Here, plaintiff's booklet involved both informational and creative aspects. Some pages in her booklet undoubtedly contained information available in other cake decorating books or in recipe books. Other parts of her booklet contained creative hints she derived from her own experiences or ideas; certainly the manner in which plaintiff assembled her book represented a creative expression. Thus, on balance, it does not appear that analysis of this factor is of any real assistance in reaching a conclusion as to applicability of fair use.

---

1 The other nine pages of defendant's booklet consisted of the cover, the introduction, and seven pages of lesson plans.

The third factor to be considered is **the amount and substantiality of the portion used in relation to the copyrighted work as a whole.** * * * In this case, almost 50% of defendant's LAP was a verbatim copy of plaintiff's booklet and that 50% contained virtually all of the substance of defendant's book. Defendant copied the explanations of how to make the decorating bag, how to mix colors, and how to make various decorations as well as the icing recipes. In fact, the only substantive pages of plaintiff's booklet which defendant did not put into her booklet were hints on how to ice a cake and an explanation of how to make leaves. * * * Defendant's LAP could have been a photocopy of plaintiff's booklet but for the fact that defendant retyped plaintiff's material. This case presents a clear example of both substantial quantitative and qualitative copying.

The final factor to be considered with respect to the fair use defense is the effect which the allegedly infringing use had on the potential market for or value of the copyrighted work. The 1967 House Report * * * explains that "a use which supplants any part of the normal market for a copyrighted work would ordinarily be considered an infringement." Here, despite the fact that at least one of plaintiff's students refused to purchase her booklet as a result of defendant's copying, the trial court found that it was unable to conclude that the defendant's copying had any effect on the market for the plaintiff's booklet. * * * The mere absence of measurable pecuniary damage does not require a finding of fair use. Fair use is to be determined by a consideration of all of the evidence in the case. Thus, despite the trial court's finding, we conclude that the factors analyzed weigh decisively in favor of the conclusion of no fair use. This conclusion is in harmony with the Congressional guidelines which, as a final point, also merit consideration with respect to the issue of fair use in an educational context.

THE CONGRESSIONAL GUIDELINES

* * * The guidelines relating to multiple copies for classroom use indicate that such copying is permissible if three tests are met. First, the copying must meet the test of "brevity" and "spontaneity." "**Brevity**" is defined, for prose, as "[e]ither a complete article, story or essay of less than 2,500 words, or an excerpt from any prose work of not more than 1,000 words or . . . 10% of the work, whichever is less . . . . " Rowley's copying would not be permissible under either of these tests.

The guidelines also provide a separate definition of "brevity" for "special works." "**Special works**" are works "which often combine language with illustrations and which are intended sometimes for children and at other times for a more general audience." Plaintiff's booklet arguably would fall into this category. The guidelines provide that, notwithstanding the guidelines for prose, " 'special works' may not be reproduced in their entirety; however, an excerpt comprising not more than two of the published pages of such special work and containing not more than 10% of the words found in the text thereof, may be reproduced." Rowley's copying would not be permissible under this test.

Under the guidelines, "**spontaneity**" requires that "[t]he copying is at the instance and inspiration of the individual teacher, and . . . [t]he inspiration and decision to use the work and the moment of its use for maximum teaching effectiveness are so close in time that it would be unreasonable to expect a timely reply to a request for permission." Defendant compiled her LAP during the summer of 1975 and first used it in her classes during the 1975–76 school year. She also used the LAP for the following two school years. Rowley's copying would not meet this requirement either.

The second test under the guidelines is that of "**cumulative effect.**" This test requires that the copied material be for only one course in the school. This aspect of the test would probably be met on these facts. The test also limits the number of pieces which may be copied from the same author and the number of times a teacher may make multiple copies for one course during one term. These latter two tests also appear to be met. The facts indicate that defendant copied only one piece of plaintiff's work. Defendant's conduct, therefore, would satisfy the second test under the guidelines.

The third test requires that each copy include a **notice of copyright.** As stated, defendant's LAP did not acknowledge plaintiff's authorship or copyright and therefore would not meet this test.

In conclusion, it appears that Rowley's copying would not qualify as fair use under the guidelines. * * *

The direct infringement by one person on another person's copyright, as seen in the above case, constitutes one kind of intellectual property issue. Balancing tests try to protect the copyright holder as well as to further social benefits related to creativity (for example, in sampling) and for educational purposes (for example, fair use). Yet there are other issues associated with copyright, such as in the maintenance of a forum or a website, where others may infringe on copyrights. In other words, it is not the company hosting the website that copies protected material, but those using the website who do. Does the website or forum owner have liability for the infringements perpetrated by the users of the website? The following well-known case sets out the issues and tests with respect to this issue.

A&M Records, Inc. v. Napster

239 F.3d 1004 (9th Cir. 2001)

Beezer, Circuit Judge:

I

* * * Through a process commonly called "peer-to-peer" file sharing, Napster allows its users to: (1) make MP3 music files stored on individual computer hard drives available for copying by other Napster users; (2) search for MP3 music files stored on other users' computers; and (3) transfer exact copies of the contents of other users' MP3 files from one computer to another via the Internet. These functions are made possible by Napster's MusicShare software, available free of charge from Napster's Internet site, and Napster's network servers and server-side software. Napster provides technical support for the indexing and searching of MP3 files, as well as for its other functions, including a "chat room," where users can meet to discuss music, and a directory where participating artists can provide information about their music.

In order to copy MP3 files through the Napster system, a user must first access Napster's Internet site and download[2] the MusicShare software to his individual computer. Once the software is installed, the user can access the Napster system. A first-time user is required to register with the Napster system by creating a "user name" and password.

If a registered user wants to list available files stored in his computer's hard drive on Napster for others to access, he must first create a "user library" directory on his computer's hard drive. The user then saves his MP3 files in the library directory, using self-designated file names. He next must log into the Napster system using his user name and password. His MusicShare software then searches his user library and verifies that the available files are properly formatted. If in the correct MP3 format, the names of the MP3 files will be uploaded from the user's computer to the Napster servers. The content of the MP3 files remains stored in the user's computer.

Once uploaded to the Napster servers, the user's MP3 file names are stored in a server-side "library" under the user's name and become part of a "collective directory" of files available for transfer during the time the user is logged onto the Napster system. The collective directory is fluid; it tracks users who are connected in real time, displaying only file names that are immediately accessible.

Napster allows a user to locate other users' MP3 files in two ways: through Napster's search function and through its "hotlist" function.

---

2 "To download means to receive information, typically a file, from another computer to yours via your modem . . . . The opposite term is upload, which means to send a file to another computer." *United States v. Mohrbacher*, 182 F.3d 1041, 1048 (9th Cir. 1999) (quoting Robin Williams, Jargon, *An Informal Dictionary of Computer Terms* 170-71 (1993)).

Software located on the Napster servers maintains a "search index" of Napster's collective directory. To search the files available from Napster users currently connected to the network servers, the individual user accesses a form in the MusicShare software stored in his computer and enters either the name of a song or an artist as the object of the search. The form is then transmitted to a Napster server and automatically compared to the MP3 file names listed in the server's search index. Napster's server compiles a list of all MP3 file names pulled from the search index which include the same search terms entered on the search form and transmits the list to the searching user. The Napster server does not search the contents of any MP3 file; rather, the search is limited to "a text search of the file names indexed in a particular cluster. * * *

To use the "hotlist" function, the Napster user creates a list of other users' names from whom he has obtained MP3 files in the past. When logged onto Napster's servers, the system alerts the user if any user on his list (a "hotlisted user") is also logged onto the system. If so, the user can access an index of all MP3 file names in a particular hotlisted user's library and request a file in the library by selecting the file name. The contents of the hotlisted user's MP3 file are not stored on the Napster system.

To transfer a copy of the contents of a requested MP3 file, the Napster server software obtains the Internet address of the requesting user and the Internet address of the "host user" (the user with the available files). The Napster servers then communicate the host user's Internet address to the requesting user. The requesting user's computer uses this information to establish a connection with the host user and downloads a copy of the contents of the MP3 file from one computer to the other over the Internet, "peer-to-peer." A downloaded MP3 file can be played directly from the user's hard drive using Napster's MusicShare program or other software. The file may also be transferred back onto an audio CD if the user has access to equipment designed for that purpose. In both cases, the quality of the original sound recording is slightly diminished by transfer to the MP3 format.

* * *

We first address plaintiffs' claim that Napster is liable for contributory copyright infringement. * * * It is apparent from the record that Napster has knowledge, both actual and constructive, of direct infringement. Napster claims that it is nevertheless protected from contributory liability by the teaching of *Sony Corp. v. Universal City Studios, Inc.* We disagree. We observe that Napster's actual, specific knowledge of direct infringement renders Sony's holding of limited assistance to Napster. * * *

The *Sony* Court refused to hold the manufacturer and retailers of video tape recorders liable for contributory infringement despite evidence that such machines could be and were used to infringe plaintiffs' copyrighted television shows. *Sony* stated that if liability "is to be imposed on petitioners in this case, it must rest on the fact that *they have sold equipment with constructive knowledge of the fact that their customers may use that equipment to make unauthorized copies* of copyrighted material." The *Sony* Court declined to impute the requisite level of knowledge where the defendants made and sold equipment capable of both infringing and "substantial noninfringing uses."

* * *

We agree that if a computer system operator learns of specific infringing material available on his system and fails to purge such material from the system, the operator knows of and contributes to direct infringement. Conversely, absent any specific information which identifies infringing activity, a computer system operator cannot be liable for contributory infringement merely because the structure of the system allows for the exchange of copyrighted material. To enjoin simply because a computer network allows for infringing use would, in our opinion, violate *Sony* and potentially restrict activity unrelated to infringing use.

We nevertheless conclude that sufficient knowledge exists to impose contributory liability when linked to demonstrated infringing use of the Napster system. The record supports the district court's finding that Napster has *actual* knowledge that *specific* infringing material is available using its system, that it could block access to the system by suppliers of the infringing material, and that it failed to remove the material.

* * *

We turn to the question whether Napster engages in vicarious copyright infringement. Vicarious copyright liability is an "outgrowth" of *respondeat superior*. In the context of copyright law, vicarious liability extends beyond an employer/employee relationship to cases in which a defendant "has the right and ability to supervise the infringing activity and also has a direct financial interest in such activities."

* * * Financial benefit exists where the availability of infringing material "acts as a 'draw' for customers. Ample evidence supports the district court's finding that Napster's future revenue is directly dependent upon "increases in userbase." More users register with the Napster system as the "quality and quantity of available music increases."

* * * The ability to block infringers' access to a particular environment for any reason whatsoever is evidence of the right and ability to supervise. * * * Napster has an express reservation of rights policy, stating on its website that it expressly reserves the "right to refuse service and terminate accounts in [its] discretion, including, but not limited to, if Napster believes that user conduct violates applicable law . . . or for any reason in Napster's sole discretion, with or without cause."

* * * **Napster * * * has the ability to locate infringing material listed on its search indices, and the right to terminate users' access to the system. The file name**

indices, therefore, are within the "premises" that Napster has the ability to police. We recognize that the files are user-named and may not match copyrighted material exactly (for example, the artist or song could be spelled wrong). For Napster to function effectively, however, file names must reasonably or roughly correspond to the material contained in the files, otherwise no user could ever locate any desired music. * * * Napster's failure to police the system's "premises," combined with a showing that Napster financially benefits from the continuing availability of infringing files on its system, leads to the imposition of vicarious liability.

* * *

Too often, people think that if it is on the Internet, it's legal to copy it. Some of that thinking appears in the *Napster* case; the result of that case significantly changed the music-sharing industry. Yet, the same argument can apply to a great number of other examples as well. The takeaway is simply that just because material is on the Internet does not mean it is not protected from some kind of intellectual property law.

B. TRADEMARKS AND PATENTS

Patents are specifically protected by Article One, Section 8(8) of the Constitution:

> The Congress shall have power. . . . To promote the progress of science and useful arts, by securing for limited times to authors and inventors the exclusive right to their respective writings and discoveries.

Patents can be broken into three categories: utility patents, design patents, and plant patents. As you will see, many of the cases resolve the question of when a **preliminary injunction**—an order that prohibits a company from producing the allegedly infringing product—is an appropriate remedy. The general rule is that the harm must be likely, irreparable and that monetary damages must be unable to remedy the injury.

Utility patents pertain to the way in which manufactured products are uniquely made. These are inventions of new materials for which creators seek patents and can apply to a wide variety of processes and materials. As the Trademark and Patent Office identifies, they could include fiber optics, computer hardware or medications. If a company creates these new inventions or formulations, it will seek patent protection to prevent competitors from using the patent. Pharmaceutical companies regularly engage in patent disputes with other companies in the industry, specifically around generic versions of their drugs. Computer companies also compete with each other and in doing so, often mimic successful designs. The line between normal competition and patent infringement can be a thin one. The following case is reproduced at length because of its in-depth treatment of this issue and its readily apparent impact on any reader.

Apple, Inc. v. Samsung Electronics Co., Inc.

678 F.3d 1314 (Fed Cir. 2012)

Bryson, Circuit Judge.

A

Apple, Inc., is the owner of several design and utility patents pertaining to smartphones and tablet computers. U.S. Design Patent Nos. D593,087 ("the D'087 patent") and D618,677 ("the D'677 patent") are directed to designs that Apple contends are generally embodied in the iPhone, Apple's popular smartphone. * * * Representative depictions of the designs claimed in the D'087 and D'677 patents are reproduced below:

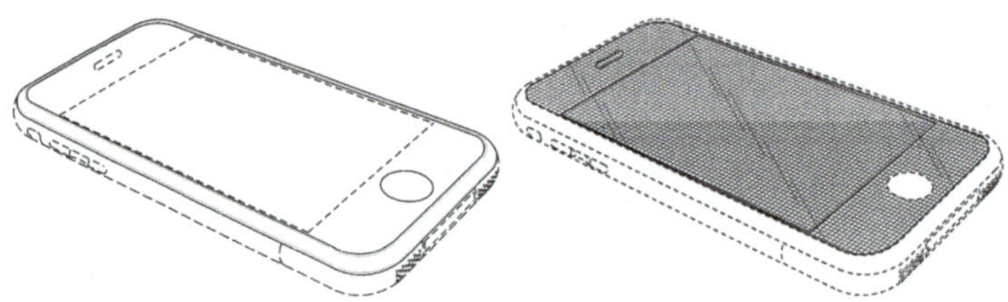

(D'677 Patent, Fig. 1)

Apple also owns U.S. Design Patent No. D504,889 ("the D'889 patent"), which is directed to the design of a tablet computer. * * * Apple claims that its iPad tablet computer embodies the design of the D'889 patent. A figure representing the claimed design shows the following:

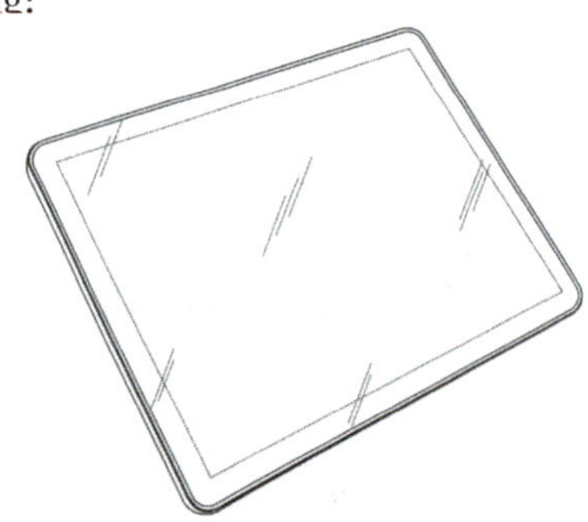

(D'889 Patent, Fig.2)

Apple has also asserted U.S. Patent No. 7,469,381 ("the '381 patent"), a utility patent that claims a software feature known as the "bounce-back" feature, which is found on Apple's smartphones and tablets, such as the iPhone and the iPad. The bounce-back feature is activated when the user is scrolling through a document displayed on the device. If the user attempts to scroll past the end of the document, an area beyond the edge of the document is displayed to indicate that the user has reached the document's end. Once the user input ceases (i.e., when the user lifts up the finger that is used for scrolling), the previously visible part of the document "bounces back" into view. * * *

B

Apple filed suit against Samsung on April 15, 2011, alleging, *inter alia*, infringement of the D'677 and '381 patents. Two months later, Apple amended its complaint and asserted that Samsung was also infringing the D'087 and D' 889 patents. Specifically, Apple claimed that two of Samsung's smartphones, the Galaxy S 4G and the Infuse 4G, which were released on February 23, 2011, and May 15, 2011, respectively, infringed the D'087 and the D'677 patents. Apple also alleged that Samsung's Galaxy Tab 10.1 tablet, which was released in June 2011, infringed the D'889 patent, and that all three devices infringed the '381 patent. On July 1, 2011, Apple moved for a preliminary injunction to block the importation into and sale within the United States of the accused Samsung devices.

* * *

II

"A plaintiff seeking a preliminary injunction must establish that he is likely to succeed on the merits, that he is likely to suffer irreparable harm in the absence of preliminary relief, that the balance of equities tips in his favor, and that an injunction is in the public interest." The decision to grant or deny a preliminary injunction lies within the sound discretion of the district court, and we will not reverse its judgment absent an abuse of that discretion.

In its comprehensive opinion, the district court addressed a large number of legal and factual issues; we have no reason to disagree with the district court on many of those issues, on which the court applied the law correctly or made findings that are not subject to serious challenge, particularly in light of the exacting standard of review that applies to this appeal. We focus our discussion on those aspects of the district court's decision that present close questions or as to which the court committed error that could affect the outcome of this appeal.

The D'677 Patent

The district court held that the design claimed in the D'677 patent was not anticipated or rendered obvious by the prior art. On appeal, Samsung has not made a persuasive case that the district court's conclusion was incorrect. With respect to irreparable harm, however, the district court found that Apple had not shown that it was likely to suffer irreparable injury in the absence of an injunction. The court based its ruling mainly on Apple's failure to show that there was a nexus between the likely infringement of the patented design and Apple's claims of lost market share and brand dilution. On appeal, Apple challenges that ruling on two grounds. First, it contends that it need not show a nexus in order to establish irreparable injury. Second, it contends that even if consumer motives are relevant to the irreparable harm inquiry, the evidence shows that there was a nexus between the asserted infringement and the market injury to Apple.

We hold that the district court was correct to require a showing of some causal nexus between Samsung's infringement and the alleged harm to Apple as part of the showing of irreparable harm. To show irreparable harm, it is necessary to show that the infringement caused harm in the first place. Sales lost to an infringing product cannot irreparably harm a patentee if consumers buy that product for reasons other than the patented feature. If the patented feature does not drive the demand for the product, sales would be lost even if the offending feature were absent from the accused product. Thus, a likelihood of irreparable harm cannot be shown if sales would be lost regardless of the infringing conduct.

* * *

A mere showing that Apple might lose some insubstantial market share as a result of Samsung's infringement is not enough. As the Supreme Court has pointed out, a party seeking injunctive relief must make "a clear showing" that it is at risk of irreparable harm, which entails showing "a likelihood of substantial and immediate irreparable injury." Given our deferential standard of review, we are not prepared to overturn the district court's finding that Apple failed to satisfy its burden of establishing the likelihood of irreparable harm.

Apple argues that the district court erroneously ruled that erosion of a distinctive design could never serve as the basis for a finding of irreparable harm. The district court remarked that "if the introduction of a design-patent-infringing product were sufficient to establish the erosion of design 'distinctiveness,' and therefore irreparable harm, an injunction would presumably issue in every case in which a defendant introduced an infringing product into the market." Contrary to Apple's contention, however, that observation does not reflect a wholesale rejection of design dilution as a theory of irreparable harm, which we agree would have been improper. Instead, the district court went on to note that "Apple has not articulated a theory as to how erosion of 'design distinctiveness' leads to irreparable harm in this case," and that

Apple had offered only "conclusory statements and theoretical arguments" in support of its theory. Without "concrete evidence to support its argument," the district court ruled, "Apple has not yet established that this harm to its reputation for innovation is likely to occur." As to Apple's "brand dilution" argument, the district court found that, even assuming "brand dilution" could arise from design patent infringement, "Apple has not demonstrated that brand dilution is likely to occur." The district court's opinion thus makes clear that it did not categorically reject Apple's "design erosion" and "brand dilution" theories, but instead rejected those theories for lack of evidence at this stage of the proceedings.

The district court based its finding as to irreparable harm in part on Apple's delay in seeking preliminary injunctive relief against Samsung's smartphones. Apple objects—and we agree—that the district court should not have faulted Apple for not filing suit as early as 2007, since Apple's design patents had not issued as of that date. Nonetheless, it was reasonable for the district court to consider the issue of delay and to find that Apple had not proceeded as quickly as it could have in seeking preliminary injunctive relief. The district court correctly noted that delay in bringing an infringement action and seeking a preliminary injunction are factors that could suggest that the patentee is not irreparably harmed by the infringement. While the district court rejected the "extreme" position that Apple's failure to seek a preliminary injunction against Samsung's first generation of infringing products precludes it from ever seeking preliminary injunctive relief, the court looked to Apple's "overall diligence in seeking a preliminary injunction," and concluded that, on balance, Apple's "delay in diligently pursuing its infringement claim against Samsung tips in Samsung's favor." We decline Apple's invitation to reject the district court's "delay" analysis altogether, and based on the district court's conclusions as to the nexus and delay factors, we uphold the court's finding that Apple failed to show that it was likely to suffer irreparable harm in the absence of a preliminary injunction.

The D'087 Patent

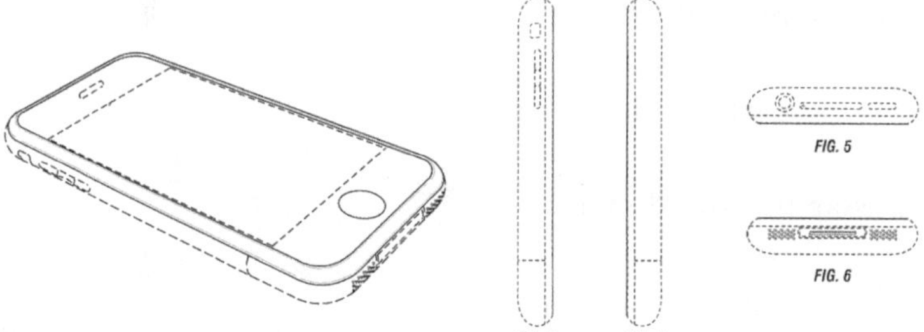

The district court concluded that the D'087 patent was likely anticipated by the Japanese '638 patent and that Apple had therefore failed to establish a likelihood of success on the merits. The court based its ruling on its conclusion that "the front view of the D'087 patent appears to be substantially similar to the front view of the '638 reference." The court refused to consider any other views of the '638 reference because it found that Apple "never claimed all views of the D'087 patent." That finding was erroneous.

The D'087 patent claims a partial view of the side of the smartphone. The bezel encircling the front face of the patented design extends from the front of the phone to its sides. It is also prominently displayed with solid lines in each figure of the D'087 patent that shows the profile of the device:

In that respect, the D'087 patent differs from the D'677 patent, which did not claim a bezel and did not claim any elements of the side view other than the flat front surface (i.e., the side view in the D'677 patent consisted entirely of broken lines). Therefore, the district court erred when it refused to consider the partial side view of the D'087 patent and the resultant flat contour of the front face that the patent disclosed.

Based only on the front view of the patented design, the district court found that the '638 reference raised substantial questions regarding the validity of the D'087 patent. Given our holding that the court misconstrued the full scope of the D'087 patent, that finding cannot stand. Samsung's assertion—that even if the patent claims a portion of the side view, the district court "properly found no material differences between the designs"—finds no support in the record, as the court expressly refused to compare anything more than the front views of the patent in question and the prior art reference. When the claimed portion of the side view is taken into account, the differences between the arched, convex front of the '638 reference distinguish it from the perfectly flat front face of the D'087 patent.

D'087 Patent JP '638 Patent

We therefore reject the district court's ruling that the D'087 patent is likely anticipated by the '638 reference.

Notwithstanding our disagreement with the district court on the issue of validity, we uphold the court's order denying relief on the D'087 patent. Because the irreparable harm analysis is identical for both smartphone design patents, and because we have affirmed the district court's finding of no irreparable harm with respect to the D'677

patent, we cannot say that the court abused its discretion when it refused to enjoin Samsung smartphones for infringing the D'087 patent. Consequently, we affirm the court's denial of a preliminary injunction based on the D'087 patent.

The '381 Patent

We also affirm the district court's denial of an injunction based on the '381 patent. The court denied the injunction on the ground that Apple failed to show that it would likely be irreparably harmed by the infringement because it failed to demonstrate that consumer purchasing decisions were based on the presence of the bounce-back feature. Apple again challenges this "consumer motive" requirement. As explained above, we conclude that the district court was correct to require a nexus between infringement of the patent and some market-based injury, be it as a result of consumer preference or some other kind of causal link. Absent such a showing, Apple cannot establish a likelihood of irreparable harm necessary for a preliminary injunction.

Apple relies on evidence that Samsung employees themselves believed that Samsung needed the bounce-back feature to compete with Apple. According to Apple, that internal Samsung evidence is sufficient to establish the requisite nexus. While the evidence that Samsung's employees believed it to be important to incorporate the patented feature into Samsung's products is certainly relevant to the issue of nexus between the patent and market harm, it is not dispositive. That is because the relevant inquiry focuses on the objective reasons as to why the patentee lost sales, not on the infringer's subjective beliefs as to why it gained them (or would be likely to gain them). In light of the deference to which its decision is entitled, we cannot say that the district court erred in refusing to enjoin Samsung's infringement of the '381 patent.

The D'889 Patent

In addressing the D'889 patent, the tablet computer design patent, the district court concluded that Apple had shown that it was likely to suffer irreparable harm from Samsung's alleged infringement. However, the court denied injunctive relief because it found that Apple had failed to establish a likelihood of success on the merits. In particular, it found that Samsung had raised a substantial question as to the validity of the D'889 patent. We sustain the court's finding of a likelihood of irreparable harm, but we hold that the court erred in its analysis of the validity issue.

With respect to irreparable harm, the district court considered the relevant factors, properly weighed them, and concluded that Apple had shown that it was likely to suffer irreparable harm from the sales of Samsung's infringing tablets. The factors included the relative market share of Apple and Samsung and the absence of other competitors in the relevant market. The court also determined, based on evidence submitted by the parties, that design mattered more to customers in making tablet purchases, which helped Apple establish the requisite nexus. The fact that Apple had claimed all views of the patented device and the fact that it was prompt in asserting its patent rights were also properly accorded weight by the court. Given our deferential standard of review, we cannot say that the court abused its discretion when it found that Apple demonstrated a likelihood of irreparable harm.

We disagree with the district court, however, in its conclusion that Apple had failed to show that it was likely to succeed on the merits. The district court concluded that the validity of the D'889 patent was subject to a substantial challenge based on two prior art references: the 1994 Fidler reference and the TC1000 tablet.

1994 Fidler Tablet

Hewlett–Packard Compaq Tablet TC1000

In addressing a claim of obviousness in a design patent, "the ultimate inquiry . . . is whether the claimed design would have been obvious to a designer of ordinary skill who designs articles of the type involved." To determine whether "one of ordinary skill would have combined teachings of the prior art to create the same overall visual appearance as the claimed design," the finder of fact must employ a two-step process. First, "one must find a single reference, 'a something in existence, the design characteristics of which are basically the same as the claimed design.' " Second, "other references may be used to modify [the primary reference] to create a design that has the same overall visual appearance as the claimed design." However, the "secondary references may only be used to modify the primary reference if they are 'so related to the primary reference that the appearance of certain ornamental features in one would suggest the application of those features to the other.' "

The district court began its obviousness analysis by finding that the Fidler reference "creates basically the same visual impression as the D'889 patent" because both are rectangular tablets with four evenly rounded corners and a flat reflective surface for the front screen surrounded by a rim on all four sides. The court characterized the back of the Fidler reference as being "essentially flat." It then concluded that although the Fidler reference did not have a flat glass surface, that did not prevent it from creating the same overall visual impression as the D'889 design. The court looked to the TC1000 tablet to supply the missing flat glass screen and the thin rim that surrounds the front face of the device. The court also relied on the testimony of Samsung's expert, who concluded that "a designer of ordinary skill . . . would have found it obvious to create the D'889 tablet consisting of a rectangular design with four evenly rounded corners, a relatively thin depth, a smooth back that curves up . . . and a flat, clear front surface that extended beyond the edges of the display."

We hold that the district court erred in finding that the Fidler tablet created the same visual impression as the D'889 patent. A side-by-side comparison of the two designs shows substantial differences in the overall visual appearance between the patented design and the Fidler reference:

D504,889

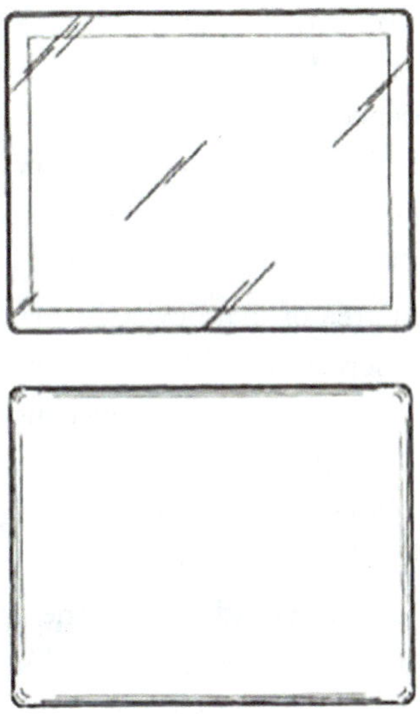

1994 Fidler

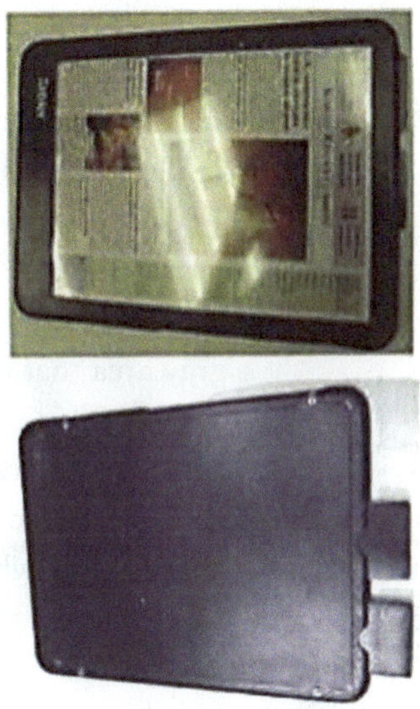

First, the Fidler tablet is not symmetrical: The bottom edge is noticeably wider than the others. More importantly, the frame of the Fidler tablet creates a very different impression from the "unframed" D'889 design. In the Fidler tablet, the frame surrounding the screen contrasts sharply with the screen itself. The Fidler screen appears to sink into the frame, creating a "picture frame" effect and breaking the continuity between the frame and the screen embedded within it. The transparent glass-like front surface of the D'889 patent, however, covers essentially the entire front face of the patented design without any breaks or interruptions. As a result, the D'889 design creates the visual impression of an unbroken slab of glass extending from edge to edge on the front side of the tablet. The Fidler reference does not create such an impression.

There are other noticeable differences between the Fidler tablet and the D'889 patent that contribute to the distinct visual appearance of the two designs. Unlike the D'889 patent, the Fidler reference contains no thin bezel surrounding the edge of the front side. Additionally, one corner of the frame in the Fidler reference contains multiple perforations. Also in contrast to the D'889 patent, the sides of the Fidler reference are neither smooth nor symmetrical; it has two card-like projections extending out from its top edge and an indentation in one of its sides. And the back of the Fidler reference also conveys a visual impression different from that of the D'889 design.

In design patent obviousness analysis, a primary reference must be "something in existence, the design characteristics of which are basically the same as the claimed design in order to support a holding of obviousness." Based on the differences between the Fidler tablet and the D'889 design, we hold that the Fidler tablet does not give the same visual impression as the D'889 patent, and therefore the district court erred in looking to Fidler as the primary reference against the D'889 patent.

"IN ADDRESSING A CLAIM of obviousness in a design patent, 'the ultimate inquiry . . . is whether the claimed design would have been obvious to a designer of ordinary skill who designs articles of the type involved.' "

'Even assuming that Fidler qualified as a primary reference, the TC1000 secondary reference could not bridge the gap between Fidler and the D'889 design. First, while the TC1000 has a flat glass front, the screen area of that device is surrounded by a gray area that frames the screen. In addition, the perimeter of the TC1000 is encircled by a wide rounded-over metallic rim. And the screen area contains indicator lights in several places, unlike the minimalist design claimed in the D'889 patent. "[T]he teachings of prior art designs may be combined only when the designs are 'so related that the appearance of certain ornamental features in one [design] would suggest the application of those features to the other.' " The TC1000 is so different in visual appearance from the Fidler reference that it does not qualify as a comparison reference under that standard.

Samsung contends that the district court properly focused on overall visual appearance rather than on the "design concepts" highlighted by Apple. In our assessment, however, the district court's error was to view the various designs from too high a level of abstraction. Fidler does not qualify as a primary reference simply by disclosing a rectangular tablet with four evenly rounded corners and a flat back. Rather than looking to the "general concept" of a tablet, the district court should have focused on the distinctive "visual appearances" of the reference and the claimed design. When those visual impressions are compared, it becomes apparent that the Fidler reference, with or without the TC1000, cannot serve to render the D'889 patent invalid for obviousness.

In the alternative, Samsung urges us to consider several other tablet and tablet-like designs as suitable primary references. All of those references consist of rectangular designs with rounded corners dominated by a display area. But those designs all suffer from the same problems as the Fidler reference, because all of them show either a thick surrounding frame in which a display is embedded or contain extensive ornamentation on the front of the tablet. The offered designs do not create the same visual impression as Apple's claimed design and thus do not qualify as primary references. In the absence of a qualifying primary reference, we hold that the district court erred in concluding that there is likely to be a substantial question as to the validity of the D'889 patent.

Because the district court found that there is a substantial question as to the validity of the D'889 patent, it did not make any findings with regard to the remaining two questions bearing on whether to issue a preliminary injunction—the balance of hardships and the public interest. The court conducted a detailed assessment of the balance of hardships with respect to the D'677 and '381 patents after finding that they were likely to survive a validity challenge. With respect to the D'889 patent, however, the district court has not determined the extent to which Samsung would be harmed if the sales of Galaxy Tab 10.1 were enjoined, and how the potential harm to Samsung resulting from entering an injunction compares to the potential harm to Apple should the district court deny interim relief. Nor has the district court evaluated the public interest at stake with respect to the sales of Samsung's Galaxy Tab 10.1. Because the district court has not yet weighed the balance of hardships to the parties and the public interest factors, we do not have a sufficient basis for concluding that the failure to enter an injunction was an abuse of discretion. It is normally not appropriate for this court to make such highly factual inquiries for the first time on appeal. That is particularly true for an order granting preliminary relief, as a district court order denying relief can be upheld based on negative findings on fewer than all of the four factors.

* * *

In sum, we affirm the denial of a preliminary injunction with respect to the D'087, D'677, and '381 patents. We vacate the order denying an injunction with respect to the D'889 patent and remand the case to the district court for further proceedings on that portion of Apple's motion for preliminary relief.

Each party shall bear its own costs for this appeal.

AFFIRMED IN PART, VACATED IN PART, and REMANDED

While most of the cases in this book are aimed a short and succinct takeaways of legal principles, this case demonstrates another aspect of law cases: their complexity and expected costliness. Intellectual property law cases—and others as well—often cost millions of dollars for each side because of these complexities.

A second kind of patent is a **design patent**, which pertains to the appearance of a product that sets it apart, uniquely, from other products. The Patent and Trademark office identifies Star Wars characters, the look of an athletic shoe, or a bicycle helmet as examples. The following case looks at shoes and the extent to which one company can "knockoff" the design and feel of another company's product.

L.A. Gear v. Thom McAn Shoe Co.

988 F.2d 1117 (Fed. Cir. 1993)

Pauline Newman, Circuit Judge.

In 1987 L.A. Gear designed a line of women's and girls' athletic shoes identified as the L.A. Gear's "Hot Shots" shoes. United States Design Patent No. 299,081 was granted on December 27, 1988 ("the '081 patent"). Figure 4 of the patent is shown:

Although color is not part of the patented design, the colors used on these shoes and their placement are part of the trade dress for which L.A. Gear claims protection from unfair competition.

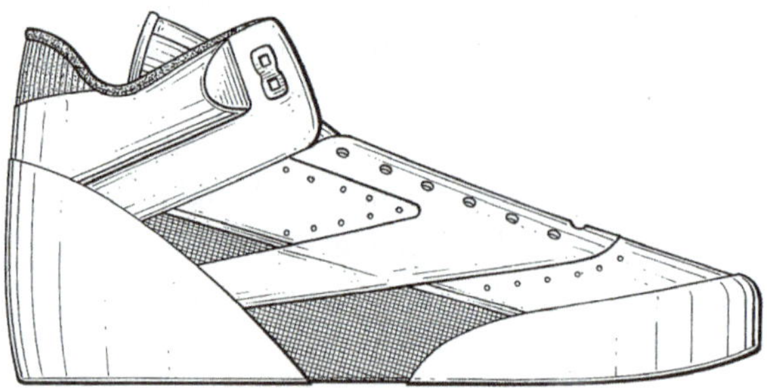

In the summer and fall of 1987 L.A. Gear exhibited the Hot Shots line of shoes to retailers at trade shows, and announced that these shoes had been selected as L.A. Gear's "hero" or featured shoe line, on which major promotion and advertising would be focused for the ensuing year. There was evidence at trial that L.A. Gear concentrated over seventy percent of its advertising expenditures on these shoes, including television commercials, billboards, and advertisements in magazines and newspapers, at a cost of over five million dollars in 1988. The district court found that the advertising was in color and prominently featured the design of the shoe.

A L.A. Gear Hot Shots shoe is pictured:

This line of shoes was a commercial success, with four million pairs sold by February, 1989. The sales volume was significantly higher than for any of L.A. Gear's other styles. The shoes were sold primarily in department stores, sporting goods stores, and athletic shoe stores, at a retail price ranging from $35 to $60. L.A. Gear testified that it had a policy against sale of its shoes in discount stores.

Melville Corporation sells shoes in discount stores, through its divisions Thom McAn and Meldisco. Thom McAn sells shoes in its own stores, and Meldisco sells shoes in K Mart stores. The Pagoda Trading Company arranges for the manufacture of shoes in the Far East and their importation into the United States.

* * *

35 U.S.C. § 171 provides that a patent may be obtained for the ornamental design of an article of manufacture.

> Whoever invents any new, original and ornamental design for an article of manufacture may obtain a patent therefor, subject to the conditions and requirements of this title . . . .

* * *

Melville asserted at trial, and argues on appeal, that the design of the '081 patent is "functional" and that the patent is therefore invalid. Invalidity due to functionality is an affirmative defense to a claim of infringement of a design patent, and must be proved by the party asserting the defense. Applying the presumption of validity, invalidity of a design patent must be established by clear and convincing evidence.

A design patent is directed to the appearance of an article of manufacture. An article of manufacture necessarily serves a utilitarian purpose, and the design of a useful article is deemed to be functional when the appearance of the claimed design is "dictated by" the use or purpose of the article. If the particular design is essential to the use of the article, it can not be the subject of a design patent.

* * * That elements of the '081 design, such as the delta wing or the side mesh, also provide support for the foot does not mean that the specific design of each element, and the combination of these elements into the patented design, is dictated by primarily functional considerations. The elements of the design may indeed serve a utilitarian purpose, but it is the ornamental aspect that is the basis of the design patent. * * * In today's marketplace, the primacy of appearance in the design of shoes can not be ignored when analyzing functionality.

The district court found that the '081 design was primarily ornamental, and that the patent was not invalid on the ground of functionality. Clear error has not been shown in this ruling, which is affirmed.

[The Court then considered the issues of the obviousness of the patent design, which is omitted here.]

In 35 U.S.C. § 289 infringement is defined as unauthorized manufacture or sale of "the patented design, or any colorable imitation thereof." Design patent infringement is a question of fact, to be proven by a preponderance of the evidence.

Design patent infringement requires a showing that the accused design is substantially the same as the claimed design. The criterion is deception of the ordinary observer, such that one design would be confused with the other:

> We hold, therefore, that if, in the eye of an ordinary observer, giving such attention as a purchaser usually gives, two designs are substantially the same, if the resemblance is such as to deceive such an observer, inducing him to purchase one supposing it to be the other, the first one patented is infringed by the other.

* * * Substantial similarity is not disputed; indeed, copying is admitted. However, Melville complains that the district court's treatment of the issue of patent infringement was "cursory," in that the court referred, in the part of its opinion relating to patent infringement, to its findings on likelihood of confusion relative to the trade dress issue.

In discussing trade dress, the district court had found that the L.A. Gear shoes and the accused shoes were substantially similar in design, such that the ordinary observer would confuse one with the other. Although design patent analysis requires comparison of the claimed design with the accused articles, Melville has not argued that the patent drawing differs from the embodiment in the L.A. Gear shoe, and has offered no reason why the finding of substantial similarity between the actual shoes was not applicable to the infringement analysis. When the patented design and the design of the article sold by the patentee are substantially the same, it is not error to compare the patentee's and the accused articles directly; indeed, such comparison may facilitate application of the Gorham criterion of whether an ordinary purchaser would be deceived into thinking that one were the other. It was in this context that the district court analyzed likelihood of confusion. No methodological error has been shown in this analysis.

Design patent infringement relates solely to the patented design, and does not require proof of unfair competition in the marketplace or allow of avoidance of infringement by labeling. The district court did not confuse the criteria relevant to these causes of action. Although Melville argues specific differences in features of the four models that were found to infringe the '081 patent, the district court found that "the placement of all the major design elements is the same, creating the same distinctive overall look," and recognized that the novelty resided in the overall appearance of the combination. The court found, in the terms of *Gorham v. White*, that the four infringing models were confusingly similar to the patented design, as viewed by an ordinary observer.

Reversible error has not been shown. The district court's holding of design patent infringement is affirmed.

Willfulness of Infringement

The district court concluded that Melville's patent infringement was not willful, and denied L.A. Gear's request for enhanced damages and attorney fees. Willfulness of infringement is a question of fact, and the district court's finding thereon shall be sustained unless it is clearly in error.

Melville relied on its counsel's obligations under Rule 11 to support its assertion that it had a good faith belief in the invalidity and unenforceability of the '081 patent. L.A. Gear points out, correctly, that a defensive pleading of invalidity or unenforceability may pass muster under Rule 11, yet not provide adequate defense to the charge of willful infringement. Indeed, in this case the pled defense of unenforceability was not pursued at trial; and the only ground asserted for patent invalidity (*i.e.*, functionality) did not present a close question of fact or law.

Melville introduced no evidence of whether it obtained an opinion of counsel that the '081 patent was not valid or not infringed, or any other support for a good faith belief that it was entitled to perform the infringing acts. Although a party to litigation may indeed withhold disclosure of the advice given by its counsel, as a privileged communication, it will not be presumed that such withheld advice was favorable to the party's position. We have held that the assertion of privilege with respect to infringement and validity opinions of counsel may support the drawing of adverse inferences.

* * * Melville admitted copying, offering as its only justification the proposition that copying is prevalent in the fashion industry, an issue not relevant to patent infringement. The '081 patent issued several months after the complaint for unfair competition under § 43(a) was filed by L.A. Gear. L.A. Gear warned Melville of the impending issuance of the patent. * * *

The district court's ruling that Melville's infringement was not willful is reversed.

* * *

Important to this and other patent cases is the distinction between **functionality** and **obviousness**. What is creative—and protected by intellectual property laws—is what is not (at least initially) obvious. Thus, as well as the clear copying of the design—using the dubious and rejected justification that others are also copying the design—the importance of the above case lies in its zeroing in on the importance of a patentable invention that is not obvious. In other words, what patent law tries to do is to protect and incentivize creativity, the very essence of which is that the invention was not obvious but instead is something new and original.

The final area of patent pertains specifically to plants, which has become a significant area given agricultural issues and other food-related engineering. Farmers and agricultural companies have been creating hybrid plants for centuries. The framers of the Constitution were aware of this and specifically identified plant breeding, including flowers, as a patentable process. Some of the bigger issues today arise from genetically modified foods, which expands plant breeding even further. In 2013, the Supreme Court, ruled on this issue in the context of plant patents and the doctrine of **patent exhaustion**.

Bowman v. Monsanto Co.

133 S.Ct. 1761 (2013)

Justice Kagan delivered the opinion of the Court.

Under the doctrine of patent exhaustion, the authorized sale of a patented article gives the purchaser, or any subsequent owner, a right to use or resell that article. Such a sale, however, does not allow the purchaser to make new copies of the patented invention. The question in this case is whether a farmer who buys patented seeds may reproduce them through planting and harvesting without the patent holder's permission. We hold that he may not.

I

Respondent Monsanto invented a genetic modification that enables soybean plants to survive exposure to glyphosate, the active ingredient in many herbicides (including Monsanto's own Roundup). Monsanto markets soybean seed containing this altered genetic material as Roundup Ready seed. Farmers planting that seed can use a glyphosate-based herbicide to kill weeds without damaging their crops. Two patents issued to Monsanto cover various aspects of its Roundup Ready technology, including a seed incorporating the genetic alteration.

Monsanto sells, and allows other companies to sell, Roundup Ready soybean seeds to growers who assent to a special licensing agreement. That agreement permits a grower to plant the purchased seeds in one (and only one) season. He can then consume the resulting crop or sell it as a commodity, usually to a grain elevator or agricultural processor. But under the agreement, the farmer may not save any of the harvested soybeans for replanting, nor may he supply them to anyone else for that purpose. These restrictions reflect the ease of producing new generations of Roundup Ready seed. Because glyphosate resistance comes from the seed's genetic material, that trait is passed on from the planted seed to the harvested soybeans: Indeed, a single Roundup Ready seed can grow a plant containing dozens of genetically identical beans, each of which, if replanted, can grow another such plant—and so on and so on. The agreement's terms prevent the farmer from co-opting that process to produce his own Roundup Ready seeds, forcing him instead to buy from Monsanto each season.

Petitioner Vernon Bowman is a farmer in Indiana who, it is fair to say, appreciates Roundup Ready soybean seed. He purchased Roundup Ready each year, from a company affiliated with Monsanto, for his first crop of the season. In accord with the agreement just described, he used all of that seed for planting, and sold his entire crop to a grain elevator (which typically would resell it to an agricultural processor for human or animal consumption).

Bowman, however, devised a less orthodox approach for his second crop of each season. Because he thought such late-season planting "risky," he did not want to pay the premium price that Monsanto charges for Roundup Ready seed. He therefore went to a grain elevator; purchased "commodity soybeans" intended for human or animal consumption; and planted them in his fields. Those soybeans came from prior harvests of other local farmers. And because most of those farmers also used Roundup Ready seed, Bowman could anticipate that many of the purchased soybeans would contain Monsanto's patented technology. When he applied a glyphosate-based herbicide to his fields, he confirmed that this was so; a significant proportion of the new plants survived the treatment, and produced in their turn a new crop of soybeans with the Roundup Ready trait. Bowman saved seed from that crop to use in his late-season planting the next year—and then the next, and the next, until he had harvested eight crops in that way. Each year, that is, he planted saved seed from the year before (sometimes adding more soybeans bought from the grain elevator), sprayed his fields with glyphosate to kill weeds (and any non-resistant plants), and produced a new crop of glyphosate-resistant—*i.e.*, Roundup Ready—soybeans.

After discovering this practice, Monsanto sued Bowman for infringing its patents on Roundup Ready seed. Bowman raised patent exhaustion as a defense, arguing that Monsanto could not control his use of the soybeans because they were the subject of a prior authorized sale (from local farmers to the grain elevator). The District Court rejected that argument, and awarded damages to Monsanto of $84,456. The Federal Circuit affirmed. It reasoned that patent exhaustion did not protect Bowman because he had "created a newly infringing article." The "right to use" a patented article following an authorized sale, the court explained, "does not include the right to construct an essentially new article on the template of the original, for the right to make the article remains with the patentee." Accordingly, Bowman could not " 'replicate' Monsanto's patented technology by planting it in the ground to create newly infringing genetic material, seeds, and plants."

We granted certiorari to consider the important question of patent law raised in this case and now affirm.

II

The doctrine of patent exhaustion limits a patentee's right to control what others can do with an article embodying or containing an invention. Under the doctrine, "the initial authorized sale of a patented item terminates all patent rights to that item. And by "exhaust[ing] the [patentee's] monopoly" in that item, the sale confers on the purchaser, or any subsequent owner, "the right to use [or] sell" the thing as he sees fit. We have explained the basis for the doctrine as follows: "[T]he purpose of the patent law is fulfilled with respect to any particular article when the patentee has received his reward . . . by the sale of the article;" once that "purpose is realized the patent law affords no basis for restraining the use and enjoyment of the thing sold."

Consistent with that rationale, the doctrine restricts a patentee's rights only as to the "particular article" sold; it leaves untouched the patentee's ability to prevent a buyer from making new copies of the patented item. "[T]he purchaser of the [patented] machine . . . does not acquire any right to construct another machine either for his own use or to be vended to another." Rather, "a second creation" of the patented item "call[s] the monopoly, conferred by the patent grant, into play for a second time." That is because the patent holder has "received his reward" only for the actual article sold, and not for subsequent recreations of it. If the purchaser of that article could make and sell endless copies, the patent would effectively protect the invention for just a single sale. Bowman himself disputes none of this analysis as a general matter: He forthrightly acknowledges the "well settled" principle "that the exhaustion doctrine does not extend to the right to 'make' a new product."

Unfortunately for Bowman, that principle decides this case against him. Under the patent exhaustion doctrine, Bowman could resell the patented soybeans he purchased from the grain elevator; so too he could consume the beans himself or feed them to his animals. Monsanto, although the patent holder, would have no business interfering in those uses of Roundup Ready beans. But the exhaustion doctrine does not enable Bowman to make additional patented soybeans without Monsanto's permission (either express or implied). And that is precisely what Bowman did. He took the soybeans he purchased home; planted them in his fields at the time he thought best; applied glyphosate to kill weeds (as well as any soy plants lacking the Roundup Ready trait); and finally harvested more (many more) beans than he started with. That is how "to 'make' a new product," to use Bowman's words, when the original

product is a seed. Because Bowman thus reproduced Monsanto's patented invention, the exhaustion doctrine does not protect him.

* * *

Bowman has another seeds-are-special argument: that soybeans naturally "self-replicate or 'sprout' unless stored in a controlled manner," and thus "it was the planted soybean, not Bowman" himself, that made replicas of Monsanto's patented invention. But we think that blame-the-bean defense tough to credit. Bowman was not a passive observer of his soybeans' multiplication; or put another way, the seeds he purchased (miraculous though they might be in other respects) did not spontaneously create eight successive soybean crops. As we have explained, Bowman devised and executed a novel way to harvest crops from Roundup Ready seeds without paying the usual premium. * * * In all this, the bean surely figured. But it was Bowman, and not the bean, who controlled the reproduction (unto the eighth generation) of Monsanto's patented invention.

* * * We accordingly *affirm* the judgment of the Court of Appeals for the Federal Circuit.

Trademarks are another kind of intellectual property. Trademark protection applies to unique, identifying attributes of products that set them apart in the market. These would include words, names, symbols, sounds and colors and the roar of the MGM lion, the pink color of Owens-Corning insulation and the shape of the Coca-Cola bottle. Trademark protection can be ongoing; they can be renewed as long as the mark is being used in business. The following case explores trademark and its increasing importance and expansion.

Rescuecom Corp. v. Google, Inc.

562 F.3d 123 (2d Cir. 2009)

LEVAL, CIRCUIT JUDGE:

As this appeal follows the grant of a motion to dismiss, we must take as true the facts alleged in the Complaint and draw all reasonable inferences in favor of Rescuecom. Rescuecom is a national computer service franchising company that offers on-site computer services and sales. Rescuecom conducts a substantial amount of business over the Internet and receives between 17,000 to 30,000 visitors to its website each month. It also advertises over the Internet, using many web-based services, including those offered by Google. Since 1998, "Rescuecom" has been a registered federal trademark, and there is no dispute as to its validity.

Google operates a popular Internet search engine, which users access by visiting *www.google.com*. Using Google's website, a person searching for the website of a particular entity in trade (or simply for information about it) can enter that entity's name or trademark into Google's search engine and launch a search. Google's proprietary system responds to such a search request in two ways. First, Google provides a list of links to websites, ordered in what Google deems to be of descending relevance to the user's search terms based on its proprietary algorithms. * * *

The second way Google responds to a search request is by showing context-based advertising. When a searcher uses Google's search engine by submitting a search term, Google may place advertisements on the user's screen. Google will do so if an advertiser, having determined that its ad is likely to be of interest to a searcher who enters the particular term, has purchased from Google the placement of its ad on the screen of the searcher who entered that search term. What Google places on the searcher's screen is more than simply an advertisement. It is also a link to the advertiser's website, so that in response to such an ad, if the searcher clicks on the link, he will open the advertiser's website, which offers not only additional information about the advertiser, but also perhaps the option to purchase the goods and services of the advertiser over the Internet. Google uses at least two programs to offer such context-based links: AdWords and Keyword Suggestion Tool.

* * * Google's objective in its AdWords and Keyword Suggestion Tool programs is to sell keywords to advertisers. Rescuecom alleges that Google makes 97% of its revenue from selling advertisements through its AdWords program. Google therefore has an economic incentive to increase the number of advertisements and links that appear for every term entered into its search engine.

Many of Rescuecom's competitors advertise on the Internet. Through its Keyword Suggestion Tool, Google has recommended the Rescuecom trademark to Rescuecom's competitors as a search term to be purchased. Rescuecom's competitors, some responding to Google's recommendation, have purchased Rescuecom's trademark as a keyword in Google's AdWords program, so that whenever a user launches a search for the term "Rescuecom," seeking to be connected to Rescuecom's website, the competitors' advertisement and link will appear on the searcher's screen. This practice allegedly allows Rescuecom's competitors to deceive and divert users searching for Rescuecom's website. According to Rescuecom's allegations, when a Google user launches a search for the term "Rescuecom" because the searcher wishes to purchase Rescuecom's services, links to websites of its competitors will appear on the searcher's screen in a manner likely to cause the searcher to believe mistakenly that a competitor's advertisement (and website link) is sponsored by, endorsed by, approved by, or affiliated with Rescuecom.

The District Court granted Google's 12(b)(6) motion and dismissed Rescuecom's claims. The court believed that our *1–800* decision compels the conclusion that Google's allegedly infringing activity does not involve use of Rescuecom's mark in commerce, which is an essential element of an action under the Lanham Act. The district court explained its decision saying that even if Google employed Rescuecom's mark in a manner likely to cause confusion or deceive searchers into believing that competitors are affiliated with Rescuecom and its mark, so that they believe the services of Rescuecom's competitors are those of Rescuecom, Google's actions are not a "use in commerce" under the Lanham Act because the competitor's advertisements triggered by Google's programs did not exhibit Rescuecom's trademark.

* * *

Our court ruled in *1–800* that a complaint fails to state a claim under the Lanham Act unless it alleges that the defendant has made "use in commerce" of the plaintiff's trademark as the term "use in commerce" is defined in 15 U.S.C. § 1127. The district court believed that this case was on all fours with *1–800*, and that its dismissal was required for the same reasons as given in *1–800*. We believe the cases are materially different. The allegations of Rescuecom's complaint adequately plead a use in commerce.

In *1–800*, the plaintiff alleged that the defendant infringed the plaintiff's trademark through its proprietary software, which the defendant freely distributed to computer users who would download and install the program on their computer. The program provided contextually relevant advertising to the user by generating pop-up advertisements to the user depending on the website or search term the user entered in his browser. For example, if a user typed "eye care" into his browser, the defendant's program would randomly display a pop-up advertisement of a company engaged in the field of eye care. Similarly, if the searcher launched a search for a particular company engaged in eye care, the defendant's program would display the pop-up ad of a company associated with eye care. The pop-up ad appeared in a separate browser window from the website the user accessed, and the defendant's brand was displayed in the window frame surrounding the ad, so that there was no confusion as to the nature of the pop-up as an advertisement, nor as to the fact that the defendant, not the trademark owner, was responsible for displaying the ad, in response to the particular term searched.

* * * At the outset, we note two significant aspects of our holding in *1–800*, which distinguish it from the present case. A key element of our court's decision in *1–800* was that under the plaintiff's allegations, the defendant did not use, reproduce, or display the plaintiff's mark *at all*. The search term that was alleged to trigger the pop-up ad was the plaintiff's *website address*. *1–800* noted, notwithstanding the similarities between the website address and the mark, that the website address was not used or claimed by the plaintiff as a trademark. Thus, the transactions alleged to be infringing were not transactions involving use of the plaintiff's trademark. *1–800* suggested in dictum that is highly relevant to our case that had the defendant used the plaintiff's *trademark* as the trigger to pop-up an advertisement, such conduct might, depending on other elements, have been actionable.

Second, [e]ven if an advertiser wanted to display its advertisement to a searcher using the plaintiff's trademark as a search term, the defendant's program did not offer this possibility. * * * The display of a particular advertisement was controlled by the category associated with the website or keyword, rather than the website or keyword itself. The defendant's program relied upon categorical associations such as "eye care" to select a pop-up ad randomly from a predefined list of ads appropriate to that category. To the extent that an advertisement for a competitor of the plaintiff was displayed when a user opened the plaintiff's website, the trigger to display the ad was not based on the defendant's sale or recommendation of a particular trademark.

The present case contrasts starkly with those important aspects of the *1–800* decision. First, in contrast to *1–800*, where we emphasized that the defendant made no use whatsoever of the plaintiff's trademark, here what Google is recommending and selling to its advertisers is Rescuecom's trademark. Second, in contrast with the facts of *1–800* where the defendant did not "use or display," much less sell, trademarks as search terms to its advertisers, here Google displays, offers, and sells Rescuecom's mark to Google's advertising customers when selling its advertising services. In addition, Google encourages the purchase of Rescuecom's mark through its Keyword Suggestion Tool. Google's utilization of Rescuecom's mark fits literally within the terms specified by 15 U.S.C. § 1127. According to the Complaint, Google uses and sells Rescuecom's mark "in the sale . . . of [Google's advertising] services . . . rendered in commerce."

* * * **Unlike the practices discussed in 1–800, the practices here attributed to Google by Rescuecom's complaint are that Google has made use in commerce of Rescuecom's mark.** * * * **What Rescuecom alleges is that by the manner of Google's display of sponsored links of competing brands in response to a search for Rescuecom's brand name (which fails adequately to identify the sponsored link as an advertisement, rather than a relevant search result), Google creates a likelihood of consumer confusion as to trademarks. If the searcher sees a different brand name as the top entry in response to the search for "Rescuecom," the searcher is likely to believe mistakenly that the different name which appears is affiliated with the brand name sought in the search and will not suspect, because the fact is not adequately signaled by Google's presentation, that this is not the most relevant response to the search.**

We conclude that the district court was mistaken in believing that our precedent in 1–800 requires dismissal.

The judgment of the district court is vacated and the case is remanded for further proceedings.

This brief tour of Intellectual Property only touches the surface of the issues currently in play in business and the courts. IP is an exploding area of the law and business pertaining to online navigating tools, search engines, links, frames, and crawlers. Posting and using material online raises issues beyond those raised in the *Napster* case. How do we protect key elements of websites such as online trademarks, domain names and the other online content? Other issues arise from conducting business online. How do we protect trade secrets? How do courts obtain personal jurisdiction over individuals who violate intellectual property, but who may live in far-away countries? It is hard to imagine a more vibrant area of the law today.

NOTES AND COMMENTS on the Legal Environment of Business

1. **THE LAW HAS ALWAYS STRUGGLED TO KEEP** up with technological developments, especially as they pertain to commerce. As noted in the chapter on common law, the English kings established new court venues to both enhance commercial development and to acquire more power. Intellectual Property is the current incarnation of a technological explosion with business applications; it is worth keeping abreast of how the law is changing and what forms of dispute resolution arise. A web source such as *http://www.ip-watch.org* will help you stay current with intellectual property developments from around the globe. Because IP law is "hot," one can also find a good deal of information on the websites of law firms.

2. **SECURING INTELLECTUAL PROPERTY** protection certainly is valuable, but ownership of intellectual property also carries with it responsibilities to protect it. This is not a general statement about ethical duties, but one of protecting one's own legal assets. Especially with respect to trademark and patent protection, the IP owner must be on the lookout for potential infringements that undermine the value of the intellectual property; not protecting against infringements can result in the loss of the trademark status itself. The principles of adverse possession from the previous chapter do not apply directly to IP issues, but they do caution an IP owner that the use of property makes a difference to the courts in determining who has superior rights.

3. **SOME BELIEVE THAT IP PROTECTION** has gone too far. Some businesses patent processes that in the past would not have been viewed as having anything particularly unique to them. But because they are modulated through a computer interface, they gain patent law protection. The publisher of this textbook, for example, holds a patent on a business process that ranks attorneys through a specified process manipulated by computer software. As a result, West Academic Publishing has a protectable patent. Do you think this is a good thing for the law and for business or do you think examples like this pose problems?

NOTES AND COMMENTS on the Ethical Environment of Business

1. **WHEREAS THEFT OR** misuses of tangible property can be readily observed, it is sometimes much hard to do so with respect to intellectual property. What reader has never downloaded or shared an image from the Internet or ripped a song from an album? In some instances, these are perfectly legal and, indeed, without any significant ethical qualms. Yet, as the cases in this chapter show, there are legal issues inherent in such things as well. So as these ethical environment sections typically advise, let's again run through the cases in this book to question whether they were fairly decided? Should a person be able to copy a segment of a song or a cookbook in making their own version of another song or cookbook? What about sharing a song, Napster-like, on the web? And not only sharing with others, but maintaining a site like Napster did? Do you agree that a company like Napster should also be found to have infringed on a copyright? What about copying designs as in the *Apple/Samsung* case or the *Tom McAn* case? At what point is copying honoring another person and at one point is it theft? What if one's culture believes it is the former and another believes it is the latter? Which moral values should prevail?

2. **INTELLECTUAL PROPERTY DOES** not have to be high-tech or hardware oriented. Yet it often is. With this in mind, another set of ethical questions can arise as to what those who made money in technology-related industries do with that money. Read, for example in *Ethics Vignettes*, the article on Bill Gates in Chapter 4 and the questions that follow that article? How do you ethically assess the activities that led to the profit as opposed to what one does with accumulated wealth after one has made the money? In other words, would you say that as long as you give some money away, you can use any tactics to make the money itself? Or, with respect to philanthropy, is it always a good thing or can it sometimes be harmful? How can you know in advance which it is likely to be?

3. **ANOTHER ASPECT OF ETHICS** as related to technology (which again does not exhaust the examples of intellectual property but is an important dimension), is purchasing the technology in the first place. We all love our computers and cell phones, but we often do not consider where the components for these items come from and the working conditions that may produce the product or its components. Do you think you can buy the latest, coolest, and most convenient technology if

you are aware that people who make the components are abused? Why or why not? What alternatives do you have to try to address such issues? One might, for example, do without the technology, but are there any other steps one can take to buy with a clean conscience?

CHAPTER

9

Contracts: Common Law Fundamentals and Concepts

Exchange is fundamental to human society and even life itself. The tiniest of plants and animals exchange air, minerals, and water. It should not be surprising then that human beings extend this naturalistic trait and extend it socially by exchanging goods and services to meet their wants and needs. Contracts become essential for such social exchanges. For capitalistic societies, the freedom of people to create agreements to reliably facilitate exchange has given rise to a rich, complex body of contract law. In this chapter, you will be introduced to general concepts and classifications as well as four core elements of contracts and also examine special topics, such as issues concerning written agreements and remedies.

MARRIAGE À-LA-MODE: THE MARRIAGE CONTRACT,
William Hogarth (1697–1764)
Photo: Stephen McCaffrey

I. General Concepts and Classifications of Contracts

THERE ARE SEVERAL WAYS to isolate the steps necessary to create a valid **contract.** For purposes of this book, we look at four:

1. Two parties must have capacity
2. There must be a meeting of the minds
3. Each party must provide legal consideration
4. Agreements formed must not violate law or public policy

As with most areas of the law, there are variations and exceptions to each of these categories. There are also additional provisions that appear. For example, one may have a valid contract—that is, an agreement that meets all four of the above requirements—but the agreement may not be enforceable. That may be because of the **Statute of Frauds**, which requires that some contracts must be in writing in order for them to be enforceable. Sometimes the level of contingency will also be an element: is there a condition precedent necessary to trigger an obligation to perform, a condition subsequent, or simultaneously occurring conditions?

Both the Statute of Frauds and contract contingencies will be discussed in this chapter, but the above four categories adequately handle most contractual situations and provide a straightforward analytical template by which one can determine whether or not a valid, binding contract exists.

Another way to group contracts is as **executed** vs. **executory**, with the latter being a contract containing promises to do something in the future, while the former describes contracts that have already been performed.

Contracts may also be analyzed on the basis of sales contracts, which apply to commercial transactions. Business people need to be aware of both because some common law contracts also apply to commercial transactions. This chapter will look at the foundational common law principles and the following chapter will look at the Uniform Commercial Code, which covers sales contracts in more detail.

It is worth noting that treatises on contracts, particularly the **Second Restatement of Contracts**, are often invoked by courts to explain or add support to their legal reasoning. The Restatement, as it is informally referred to, appears throughout contract law, and we will refer to the relevant provisions when discussing various aspects of contract formation and breach. It is important to keep in mind that the last entire Restatement, published in 1981, is supplemented by other materials that deal with areas related to the types of contracts we will discuss, such as software contracts and employment law. Finally, the Restatement is what it purports to be, a restatement of contract law, meaning it is not binding upon the courts.[1]

A. PARTIES TO THE CONTRACT MUST HAVE CAPACITY

In many ways, the idea that there can be only one party to a contract defies logic. Unless one is utilizing some psychological issues and making contracts with oneself—a New Year's Resolution perhaps—there will always be two or more parties to a contract in some shape or form. The bigger question is whether each party has the **capacity** to enter into a contract. Because the ability to contract is a linchpin of free market economics, ascertaining capacity is crucial. One of the moral justifications for the free market is that it allows people to freely pursue their interests, including in business. The requirements of a valid, enforceable contract intend that the institution of contracts has enough independent fairness to let people contract freely for the kinds of business transactions they wish to carry out free from government intervention. If one of the elements of contracts is violated, governmental dispute resolution (i.e. the courts) is available to enforce a contract or to provide remedies, but otherwise, contract is about two or more parties willingly doing business with each other.

PUBLICITY PHOTO FROM THE 1930S OF CHILD ACTRESS SHIRLEY TEMPLE SIGNING A HOLLYWOOD FILM CONTRACT.
Image: Corbis

Essential to independent, procedural fairness of contracts is making sure that each party understands what he is doing. Does he understand the contract and its terms? Can he determine the risk he is undertaking? If he doesn't, then there is concern that the person will be taken advantage of and the contract will be unfair.

Courts have created categories to determine the whether there are internal or external impediments to capacity.

I. Internal Impediments to Capacity

An internal impediment to capacity refers to something within the make-up of the individual that prevents her from being able to understand the contracts she might otherwise be able to enter into. There are three major examples. The first is related to a person's age, the second concerns whether they have a mental disability, and the third relates to a temporary impairment, such as being under the influence of alcohol.

1 All references to the Restatement come from Steven Burton and Melvin Eisenberg, eds., *Contract Law: Selected Source Materials Annotated* (2011) 149–299.

a. Internal Impediment to Capacity Due to Age

In most instances, an individual must be 18 years of age to have the capacity to enter into contracts. If a person is under the age of 18 and does enter into a contract, the contract is voidable. This means that the "child" (actually, the parents or guardians of the child) may cancel the contract.

Three issues arise in these cases: first, who is responsible for determining if the "child" is 18 years of age or not; second, how does a voiding of the contract actually happen; and third, if the minor has accepted some benefits from the contract, how are they handled when the contract is voided?

The following two cases illustrate these points.

Wadge v. Kittleson

12 N.D. 452, 97 N.W. 856 (1903)

YOUNG, C. J.

Plaintiff sues upon a promissory note for $225 executed and delivered by the defendant on April 13, 1901, and by its terms due on October 1st thereafter. The defendant, in his answer, admitted the execution of the note, but denied that he is indebted thereon, and alleged as a defense that on the date of the execution of the note he was a minor; that he did not reach his majority until May 12, 1901; that the note was given for a team of horses purchased by him from the plaintiff, and for no other consideration; that on the 4th day of February, 1902, and within one year after reaching his majority, he restored the team to the plaintiff, and rescinded the purchase, and demanded a return of his note. The case was tried to a jury, and a verdict was returned for the plaintiff for the full amount of the note, with interest. Defendant moved for a new trial [. . .]. This appeal is from the order denying the motion for new trial.

* * *

It is entirely clear, under section 2703, that the contract of a minor who is over 18 years of age is not void, but merely voidable—that is, it is enforceable unless disaffirmed within the period and in the manner provided by the statute; and, further, that his liability rests upon his contract, and not upon a *quantum meruit*. The action was properly brought upon the note.

The evidence wholly fails to show a disaffirmance of the contract. On the contrary, it shows a complete ratification by the defendant after attaining his majority. It appears that when the defendant purchased the team he lacked but 29 days of his majority; that he was the owner of 160 acres of land, which he was then farming, and that he also farmed 480 acres of other land, which he had rented; that after the purchase of the team he used it in plowing his land, harvesting and threshing his crop, and marketing his grain, and for general farming purposes. On two different occasions he promised the plaintiff to pay the note—once in August, and again in November. On February 4th, thereafter he delivered the team at a livery barn, and served notice on plaintiff that he had disaffirmed the contract upon the ground that he was a minor when he made the purchase. There is no complaint that the team was not in good condition when purchased, or that the sale was in any respect unfair. When the defendant attempted to disaffirm his contract and return the team, one of the horses was practically worthless, and the other was worth not to exceed $30. He retained possession of the team and used it for almost nine months after reaching his majority. The worthless condition of the team was due to his use of the same, and to his abuse and neglect. Upon this state of facts, we are of opinion that the defendant's attempted disaffirmance was without legal effect. The first reason for this conclusion is that after reaching his majority he unequivocally ratified the contract. When he purchased the team he was over 18 years of age. His contract, therefore, under the statute, was not void, but, as we have seen, was voidable at his option—that is, it was enforceable until avoided by a disaffirmance; and it could be disaffirmed only in the manner provided by the statute. He had the right of election for one year after reaching his majority to affirm or disaffirm. He elected to affirm. This is evidenced by nine months' continuous use of the property, and by his promises to pay the note. By affirming the contract after reaching his majority, he lost the right to thereafter disaffirm it. A minor, after reaching his majority, has full capacity to choose for himself, and may, within the statutory period, make his election; but he cannot affirm and thereafter disaffirm his voidable contracts. He is bound by his ratification. Ratification, when once made, creates no new contract, but merely removes the objection to the voidable contract.

"A MINOR, after reaching his majority, has full capacity to choose for himself, and may, within the statutory period, make his election; but he cannot affirm and thereafter disaffirm his voidable contracts."

* * *

In this case the retention of the property and its use by the defendant, including his promises to pay the note, all occurring after he reached his majority, constituted a complete ratification of the contract.

* * *

Finding no error in the record, the order appealed from will be *affirmed*. All concur.

Halbman v. Lemke

99 Wis.2d 241, 298 N.W.2d 562 (1980)

Callow, Justice.

On this review we must decide whether a minor who disaffirms a contract for the purchase of a vehicle which is not a necessity must make restitution to the vendor for damage sustained by the vehicle prior to the time the contract was disaffirmed. The court of appeals affirmed the judgment in part, reversed in part, and remanded the cause to the circuit court [. . .].

This matter was before the trial court upon stipulated facts. On or about July 13, 1973, James Halbman, Jr. (Halbman), a minor, entered into an agreement with Michael Lemke (Lemke) whereby Lemke agreed to sell Halbman a 1968 Oldsmobile for the sum of $1,250. Lemke was the manager of L & M Standard Station in Greenfield, Wisconsin, and Halbman was an employee at L & M. At the time the agreement was made Halbman paid Lemke $1,000 cash and took possession of the car. Arrangements were made for Halbman to pay $25 per week until the balance was paid, at which time title would be transferred. About five weeks after the purchase agreement, and after Halbman had paid a total of $1,100 of the purchase price, a connecting rod on the vehicle's engine broke. Lemke, while denying any obligation, offered to assist Halbman in installing a used engine in the vehicle if Halbman, at his expense, could secure one. Halbman declined the offer and in September took the vehicle to a garage where it was repaired at a cost of $637.40. Halbman did not pay the repair bill.

In October of 1973 Lemke endorsed the vehicle's title over to Halbman, although the full purchase price had not been paid by Halbman, in an effort to avoid any liability for the operation, maintenance, or use of the vehicle. On October 15, 1973, Halbman returned the title to Lemke by letter which disaffirmed the purchase contract and demanded the return of all money theretofore paid by Halbman. Lemke did not return the money paid by Halbman.

The repair bill remained unpaid, and the vehicle remained in the garage where the repairs had been made. In the spring of 1974, in satisfaction of a garageman's lien for the outstanding amount, the garage elected to remove the vehicle's engine and transmission and then towed the vehicle to the residence of James Halbman, Sr., the father of the plaintiff minor. Lemke was asked several times to remove the vehicle from the senior Halbman's home, but he declined to do so, claiming he was under no legal obligation to remove it. During the period when the vehicle was at the garage and then subsequently at the home of the plaintiff's father, it was subjected to vandalism, making it unsalvageable.

Halbman initiated this action seeking the return of the $1,100 he had paid toward the purchase of the vehicle, and Lemke counterclaimed for $150, the amount still owing on the contract. Based upon the uncontroverted facts, the trial court granted judgment in favor of Halbman, concluding that when a minor disaffirms a contract for the purchase of an item, he need only offer to return the property remaining in his hands without making restitution for any use or depreciation. In the order granting judgment, the trial court also allowed interest to the plaintiff dating from the disaffirmance of the contract. On post-judgment motions, the court amended its order for judgment to allow interest to the plaintiff from the date of the original order for judgment, July 26, 1978.

. . .

The sole issue before us is whether a minor, having disaffirmed a contract for the purchase of an item which is not a necessity and having tendered the property back to the vendor, must make restitution to the vendor for damage to the property prior to the disaffirmance. Lemke argues that he should be entitled to recover for the damage to the vehicle up to the time of disaffirmance, which he claims equals the amount of the repair bill.

"ALTHOUGH THE ORIGINS of the doctrine are somewhat obscure, it is generally recognized that its purpose is the protection of minors from foolishly squandering their wealth through improvident contracts with crafty adults who would take advantage of them in the marketplace."

Neither party challenges the absolute right of a minor to disaffirm a contract for the purchase of items which are not necessities. That right, variously known as the *doctrine of incapacity* or the "*infancy doctrine*," is one of the oldest and most venerable of our common law traditions. Although the origins of the doctrine are somewhat obscure, it is generally recognized that its purpose is the protection of minors from foolishly squandering their wealth through improvident contracts with crafty adults who would take advantage of them in the marketplace. Thus it is settled law in this state that a contract of a minor for items which are not necessities is void or voidable at the minor's option.

Once there has been a disaffirmance, however, as in this case between a minor vendee and an adult vendor, unresolved problems arise regarding the rights and responsibilities of the parties relative to the disposition of the consideration exchanged on the contract. As a general rule a minor who disaffirms a contract is entitled to recover all consideration he has conferred incident to the transaction. In return the minor is expected to restore as much of the consideration as, at the time of disaffirmance, remains in the minor's possession. The minor's right to disaffirm is not contingent upon the return of the property, however, as disaffirmance is permitted even where such return cannot be made.

The return of property remaining in the hands of the minor is not the issue presented here. In this case we have a situation where the property cannot be returned to the vendor in its entirety because it has been damaged and therefore diminished in value, and the vendor seeks to recover the depreciation. Although this court has been cognizant of this issue on previous occasions, we have not heretofore resolved it.

* * *

Here Lemke seeks restitution of the value of the depreciation by virtue of the damage to the vehicle prior to disaffirmance. Such a recovery would require Halbman to return more than that remaining in his possession. It seeks compensatory value for that which he cannot return. Where there is misrepresentation by a minor or willful destruction of property, the vendor may be able to recover damages in tort. But absent these factors, as in the present case, we believe that to require a disaffirming minor to make restitution for diminished value is, in effect, to bind the minor to a part of the obligation which by law he is privileged to avoid.

* * *

Recently the Illinois Court of Appeals came to the same conclusion. In *Weisbrook v. Clyde C. Netzley, Inc.* (1978), a minor sought to disaffirm a contract for the purchase of a vehicle which developed engine trouble after its purchase. In the minor's action the dealer counterclaimed for restitution for use and depreciation. The court affirmed judgment for the minor and, with respect to the dealer's claim for restitution, stated:

> "In the present case, of course, the minor plaintiff never misrepresented his age and, in fact, informed defendant that he was 17 years old. Nor did plaintiff represent to defendant that his father was to be the owner or have any interest in the automobile. There is no evidence in the present case that plaintiff at the time of entering the contract with defendant intended anything more than to enjoy his new automobile. He borrowed the total purchase price and paid it to defendant carrying out the transaction fully at the time of taking delivery of the vehicle. Plaintiff sought to disaffirm the contract and the return of the purchase price only when defendant declined to make repairs to it. In these circumstances we believe the weight of authority would permit the minor plaintiff to disaffirm the voidable contract and that defendant-vendor would not be entitled to recoup any damages which he believes he suffered as a result thereof."

We believe this result is consistent with the purpose of the infancy doctrine. The decision of the court of appeals is *affirmed.*

Who has the capacity to contract? According to the Restatement, if a person is:

a. Under guardianship, or

b. An infant (someone under the age of 18), or

c. Mentally ill, or

d. Intoxicated

Then a contracted attempted to be made by them is voidable.

Legislatures' abilities to circumvent the incapacity requirement are especially useful in professions that often involve minors, such as film and television acting. California and New York have both passed laws that make entertainment contracts enforceable if a minor appears before a judge and the judge determines that the minor is capable of understanding and fulfilling his obligations. Upon breach, then, the minor is liable under the contract and cannot attempt to void the agreement by pleading incapacity.[2]

b. Internal Impediment to Capacity Due to Mental Disability

A second kind of internal impediment is due to a mental disability. Depending on whether or not a court has adjudicated a person to have a mental disability that impairs her decision making, a contract may be either void or voidable.

If a Court has adjudicated a person as not having the capacity to handle her own contracts, then any contract the person enters into is void. Instead, her court-appointed guardian or someone who has an approved power of attorney should handle contracts for the person with the impairment. While this rule makes sense insofar as it protects the person with the disability, it also places a high duty on anyone the person interacts with to take steps to assure that any dealing is with the person's guardian.

Some individuals have a degree of incapacity, but not so much so that they require a court proceeding to be declared incapacitated due to mental disease or defect. This could happen in several different ways. Perhaps the most common is when the

---

2 Ethan Bordman, "Lights, Camera, Contract!" 91-Sep. Mich. B.J. 27 (2012). See also, *In Re Applications of Atlantic Recording Corp.*, 192 Misc.2d 622 (2002) (Court, applying the Arts and Cultural Affairs Law § 35.03 2.e., prohibited members of the band Dream Street from voiding a judicially-approved contract in an attempt to keep and perform together under the group's name.).

person and/or family members realize that there is a disability and so simply act for the person either informally (i.e. making sure someone is with the person with the disability at any time when the person is making any kind of serious contract) or formally if the person executes a **power of attorney**.

Powers of attorney authorize and empower another individual to make decisions on behalf of someone else. One does not have to have a disability to have a power of attorney. Married couples often have the power to act on the other's behalf. **Advance directives** for health care purposes, which authorize another person to make medical decisions for someone else, are also examples of a power of attorney.

A common use of a power of attorney that touches upon potential disability issues is when an elderly person executes one to authorize an adult child to act on the elderly person's behalf. That elderly person may know that, as they age, there may come a time when she is no longer able to make decisions for herself and so, while she retains capacity to make contracts (such as a power of attorney itself), she authorizes in advance someone who can act for her.

The Restatement defines a mental illness or defect, with respect to capacity, as follows:

§ 15: Mental Illness or Defect

1. A person incurs only voidable contractual duties by entering into a transaction if by reason of a mental illness or defect

    a. He is unable to understand in a reasonable manner the nature and consequences of the transaction, or

    b. He is unable to act in a reasonable manner in relation to the transaction and the other party has reason to know of his condition.

2. Where the contract is made on fair terms and the other party is without knowledge of the mental illness or defect, the power of avoidance [in other words, a voidable duty] under Subsection 1. terminates to the extent that the contract has been so performed in whole or in part or the circumstances have so changed that avoidance would be unjust. In such a case a court may grant relief as justice requires.

In cases where a person has not been adjudicated insane, the rules of capacity revert to those applying to age; that is, they are **voidable** rather than **void**.

This difference between which contracts are void and which are voidable is important. Voidable contracts are those that can be canceled by the person with the disability, whereas void contracts have no effect at all. That is, neither party can enforce them. With respect to mental disability, a person who has been adjudged by a court not to have the mental capacity to carry out their own affairs has no capacity and any attempts to contract with that person are void. One could enter into contract with the guardian of that person, but not with the person herself. However, if a person has not been adjudicated incompetent (sometimes referred to as "insane" in older court opinions), but does have a degree of mental incapacity, then contracts with that person are voidable by that person with the disability, not by the person contracting with the person who has the disability.

Most of the time, contractual incapacity questions deal with issues of voidability, including questions related to age, whether the person has been induced to fraudulently enter into a contract, or if the person is under duress—all concepts covered later in this chapter. There are times, however, when void contracts come into play. In the following case, these questions of void and voidable contracts on the basis of a mental disability are addressed by the court.

Lloyd v. Jordan

544 So.2d 957 (Ala. 1989)

ADAMS, JUSTICE.

Olivia Lloyd, the widow of George Loring Lloyd, appeals from the probate court's judgment establishing Betty Lou Jordan and Marion F. Pitts as the co- beneficiaries of an annuity purchased by George Loring Lloyd, who allegedly executed a change of beneficiary form before his death naming Olivia Lloyd, not Jordan and Pitts, as the beneficiary of the annuity.

The record reflects that George Lloyd purchased the annuity from the Executive Life Insurance Company of Beverly Hills, California, in September 1983 and named his daughters by a previous marriage, Jordan and Pitts, as co-beneficiaries. George Lloyd also executed a will in June 1985 that devised all of his property to Jordan and Pitts and made no provision for Olivia Lloyd. It appears that although they had divorced after the execution of the will, George Lloyd and Olivia Lloyd remarried in August 1987. Testimony from George Lloyd's physician, however, indicated that Lloyd was showing signs of mental instability and chronic dementia related to hypoxemia in April 1987, and, in fact, he was declared *non compos mentis* in September 1987.

In August 1987, Olivia Lloyd obtained a change of beneficiary form from Executive Life, and George Lloyd allegedly executed the form to change the beneficiary of the annuity to Olivia Lloyd. We note that this change of beneficiary form does not appear in the record. After George Lloyd's death, Jordan and Pitts petitioned the probate court to enter an order designating them as the proper beneficiaries of the annuity on grounds that Lloyd was mentally incompetent and lacked capacity to execute the change of beneficiary form. The issue for our review is whether the probate court erred in its order that Jordan and Pitts be designated beneficiaries of the annuity. The court heard *ore tenus* testimony and, therefore, its judgment will not be disturbed unless it is unsupported by the evidence; this Court "will indulge all favorable presumptions to sustain that court's conclusion, and it will be disturbed on appeal only if shown to be plainly erroneous or manifestly unjust."

Contracts of insane persons are absolutely void and a contract executed before the maker's adjudication of insanity or appointment of a guardian is suspect when it appears that apparent consent to the contract may have been unreal because of mental incapacity:

> "It is essential to the validity of a contract that the parties thereto possess not only the legal status affording capacity to contract, . . . but also the mental competence affording capacity to consent. The rule which has been said to be well stated in *Corpus Juris Secundum* is that to make a valid contract, each party must be of sufficient mental capacity to appreciate the effect of what he is doing, and must also be able to exercise his will with reference thereto. A court of equity guards with jealous care all contracts with persons of unsound mind. In this connection, it has been said that 'insanity' and 'incompetence' are words of vague and varying import.
>
> "There is no contract where one of the parties was, by reason of physical debility, age, mental aberration, or otherwise, incapable of understanding and appreciating the nature, force, and effect of the agreement he is alleged to have made, as where he was unable to do so because insane, or mentally infirm, or because of incapacity resulting from lunacy, idiocy, senile dementia or imbecility, or any other defect or disease of the mind, whatever the cause, or because suffering from a degree of intoxication precluding rational thought . . . . However, mere mental weakness falling short of incapacity to appreciate the business in hand will not invalidate a contract, nor will mere mental weakness or unsoundness to some degree, in the absence of fraud or undue influence.
>
> "Physical condition not adversely affecting mental competence is immaterial; and neither age, sickness, extreme distress, nor debility of body will affect the capacity to make a contract if sufficient intelligence remains to understand the transaction." 17 C.J.S. *Contracts* § 1331., at 855–57 (1963).

We recognize, however, that a person's contract will not necessarily be invalidated because he was aged, mentally weak, and feeble in mind; or suffered from loss of memory, senile dementia, fatigue, or ill health.

> "Where, however, mental weakness or incapacity is accompanied by other inequitable incidents, it may afford ground for invalidation of the contract, as where, in addition to mental weakness or incapacity, it further appears that there was inadequacy of consideration or a confidential relationship, or fraud, duress, undue influence, imposition, concealment, misrepresentation, overreaching, overexercise of authority, ignorance and want of advice, or even unfairness; mental weakness may render a person more susceptible to these factors." 17 C.J.S. *Contracts* § 1331., at 858–59 (1963).

Consequently, a contract cannot be avoided on ground of mental incapacity or weakness unless it is shown that the incapacity was of such a character that, at the time of execution, "the person had no reasonable perception or understanding of the nature and terms of the contract" or the incapacity was accompanied by, *inter alia*, undue influence.

Testimony at the trial from George Lloyd's physician indicated that in April 1987, before executing the change of beneficiary form, he was suffering from mental instability and the onset of chronic dementia (mental deterioration or senility). Olivia Lloyd and George Lloyd remarried in August 1987, and, shortly thereafter, Olivia Lloyd obtained the change of beneficiary form for George Lloyd to sign. We note that Olivia Lloyd testified that she "couldn't say" that George Lloyd "knew what he was doing" on the day he signed the form; and George Lloyd's mental condition was apparently deteriorating to the extent that a guardian was appointed at the time he was declared non compos mentis one month after the execution of the form.

Therefore, we believe that sufficient evidence existed to support the trial court's finding that George Lloyd was incapable of understanding and appreciating the nature and effect of the change of beneficiary form that he signed. Thus, its order that Jordan and Pitts be renamed as beneficiaries of the annuity is not plainly erroneous or manifestly unjust, and it is due to be affirmed.

AFFIRMED.

---

c. Hybrid: Altered Capacity to Contract

A third kind of impediment to capacity stands between internal and external impediments. What if a person under the influence of a prescribed drug makes a contract? The person may be someone who has full capacity to make decisions, but under the influence of given medications for an injury, condition, or surgery, the person no longer retains that capacity. The impediment is partly external—the medication—and partly internal. The following case illustrates this point.

Sparrow v. Demonico

461 Mass. 322, 960 N.E.2d 296 (2012)

DUFFLY, J.

A family dispute over ownership of what had been the family home in Woburn prompted Frances M. Sparrow to file a complaint in the Superior Court against her sister, Susan A. Demonico, and Susan's husband, David D. Demonico. Prior to trial, the parties resolved their differences by a settlement agreement reached during voluntary mediation.

* * *

We conclude that our evolving standard of contractual incapacity does not in all cases require proof that a party's claimed mental illness or defect was of some significant duration or that it is permanent, progressive, or degenerative; but, without medical evidence or expert testimony that the mental condition interfered with the party's understanding of the transaction, or her ability to act reasonably in relation to it, the evidence will not be sufficient to support a conclusion of incapacity. Because the evidence was insufficient to support a determination of incapacity in this case, we vacate the motion judge's order and remand for entry of an order enforcing the settlement agreement.

Sparrow's complaint, filed initially in July, 2003, and later amended, alleged that Sparrow was entitled to a one-half interest in the Woburn property, consistent with the wishes of her (and Susan's) now-deceased mother, under theories of constructive and resulting trusts. Susan, who resided in the Woburn property at the time of the mediation, and David, who had been separated from Susan for several years and was no longer residing with her, asserted that they were the sole owners of the property, as reflected in a deed, and denied that Sparrow had any interest in it.

* * *

On the date of the scheduled mediation, Susan drove from her home to David's residence. From there, David drove them to the location of the mediation session because, in David's view, Susan was not capable of driving to the mediation. The mediation began at approximately 9 A.M. and ended at 3 P.M. The judge, crediting David's testimony, found:

> "Susan was having a breakdown that day, according to David, and was slurring her words, although she had not had any alcoholic beverages on that day. She became less coherent throughout the day, was crying and out

of control . . . . They left the mediation before it was over as Susan could not handle it."

The judge noted Susan's testimony that she had been taking a medication, Zoloft, prior to the mediation, but that she had stopped taking the medication at some point before the mediation, and that she cried much of the day; he specifically credited Susan's testimony that she "was out of control emotionally during the mediation" and found also that "she was not thinking rationally" on that day.

As noted, both sides were represented by counsel throughout the mediation. At some point before they departed from the mediation session, the Demonicos authorized their attorney to execute a settlement agreement on their behalf. According to the terms of a written agreement titled, "Memorandum of Settlement," which was signed by Sparrow, her attorney, and the Demonicos's attorney, and witnessed by the mediator, the Demonicos agreed to pay Sparrow "the settlement amount of $100,000" from the proceeds of the sale of the property, which would occur "as soon as practicable," and in any event within a specified timeframe. The agreement also set forth other affirmative requirements regarding the marketing and sale of the property.

A settlement agreement is a contract and its enforceability is determined by applying general contract law. It has been long established that a contract is voidable by a person who, due to mental illness or defect, lacked the capacity to contract at the time of entering into the agreement. The burden is on the party seeking to void the contract to establish that the person was incapacitated at the time of the transaction.

"IT HAS BEEN LONG established that a contract is voidable by a person who, due to mental illness or defect, lacked the capacity to contract at the time of entering into the agreement.

As Justice Holmes observed, it is a question of fact whether a person was competent to enter into a transaction—that is, whether the person suffered from "insanity" or "was of unsound mind, and incapable of understanding and deciding upon the terms of the contract." In *Reed v. Mattapan Deposit & Trust Co.*, 198 Mass. 306, 314 (1908), we described this inquiry as the "true test" of mental incapacity:

> "But while great mental weakness of the individual may exist without being accompanied by an entire loss of reason, and mental incapacity in one case is not necessarily so in another, in such an inquiry the true test is, was the party whose contract it is sought to avoid in such a state of insanity at the time as to render him incapable of transacting the business. When this fact is established the contract is voidable by the lunatic or his representatives, and it is no defense under our decisions that the other party acted fairly and without knowledge of his unsoundness or of any circumstances which ought to have put him upon inquiry."

We applied this test, also known as the "cognitive test," without significant modification for fifty years thereafter.

Over time, however, the traditional test for contractual incapacity, both in Massachusetts, and in other jurisdictions evolved to incorporate an increased understanding of the nature of mental illness in its various forms. Based on this understanding, we adopted a second, alternative test for incapacity.

In *Krasner v. Berk*, we recognized that there may be circumstances when, although a party claiming incapacity has some, or sufficient, understanding of the nature and consequences of the transaction, the contract would still be voidable where, "by reason of mental illness or defect, [the person] is unable to act in a reasonable manner in relation to the transaction and the other party has reason to know of his condition." This modern test—also described as an "affective" or "volitional" test—recognizes that competence can be lost, not only through cognitive disorders, but through affective disorders that encompass motivation or exercise of will.

Under this modern, affective test, "[w]here a person has some understanding of a particular transaction which is affected by mental illness or defect, the controlling consideration is whether the transaction in its result is one which a reasonably competent person might have made." Also relevant to the inquiry in these circumstances is whether the party claiming mental incapacity was represented by independent, competent counsel.

* * *

The Demonicos . . . [that] Susan's incapacity without showing a permanent, degenerative, progressive, or long-standing mental illness. They point to evidence that Susan's asserted mental impairment arose and was limited to the period of the mediation session, and argue that this evidence was sufficient to support a conclusion of incapacity, despite the lack of medical evidence or expert testimony as to the nature of Susan's mental impairment and its effect on her decision-making ability.

We have not previously addressed whether medical evidence is required to establish an incapacity to contract, and the Demonicos have not directed our attention to case law in other jurisdictions that would support their contention. In our prior decisions concerning the issue of incapacity to contract, however, evidence of mental illness or defect has been presented consistently through medical evidence, including the testimony of physicians and mental health providers or experts, in addition to lay testimony. Moreover, in other contexts, we have held that a lay witness is not competent to give an opinion as to mental condition. Expanding on this analysis, we conclude that medical evidence is necessary to establish that a person lacked the capacity to contract due to the existence of a mental condition.

* * *

Here, there was lay evidence, credited by the judge, that Susan's speech was "slurr[ed]," that she was in a state of uncontrollable crying, and that she had experienced an inability to focus or "think rationally" throughout the day of the mediation. Susan testified also that she had recently discontinued taking the prescribed medication Zoloft. However, she presented no medical evidence regarding a diagnosis that would have required her to take the medication, or the effect, if any, that ceasing to take the medication would have had on her medical or mental condition. There was also no evidence that Susan's condition at the mediation was related to or caused by her discontinuing the medication.

* * *

The evidence did not support a conclusion that, under the traditional test for incapacity, Susan was incapable of understanding the nature and quality of the transaction, or of grasping its significance. Indeed, based on Susan's testimony, she understood at the time that she was participating in a mediation to discuss settlement of the lawsuit; she was aware that the subject of the mediation was to resolve the dispute regarding the family home in Woburn; she participated in the mediation and listened to the arguments of counsel; and she "couldn't believe how things [were] turning out."

It is apparent from Susan's testimony that, even if she suffered from a transient mental defect, or "breakdown" as the judge concluded, she had at least some understanding of the nature of the transaction and was aware of its consequences. Under the modern test to establish Susan's incapacity, the evidence was similarly insufficient. There was no evidence that the settlement agreement was unreasonable, or that a reasonably competent person would not have entered into it.

Because the evidence does not support a conclusion that Susan lacked the mental capacity to authorize settlement on the day of the mediation, it was error to deny Sparrow's motion to enforce the agreement. The order denying the motion to enforce the mediated settlement agreement is vacated. The case is remanded to the Superior Court for entry of an order that the settlement agreement be enforced.

So ordered.

Now, let us take this point one step further and see what happens when the diminution of capacity occurs through the legal consumption of alcohol or a prescription medication. There are competing legal interests in such cases. On the one hand, the courts want to protect against someone taking advantage of a person who does not have the capacity to know what they are getting into, the same concerns that exist with any kind of capacity questions. On the other hand, a person can choose whether to get drunk or to abuse prescription medication and the courts do not want the "hey, I was drunk" excuse to be too easily invoked to get out of contractual responsibilities. The following case illustrates this.

Williamson v. Matthews

379 So.2d 1245 (Ala. 1980)

PER CURIAM.

This is an appeal from an order denying appellant Williamson injunctive relief seeking to cancel a deed and to set aside a sale of property from Williamson to the Matthews. We reverse and remand.

The Matthews learned from members of their family that Williamson wanted to sell her home. Her mortgage was in default, and the mortgagee was threatening foreclosure. There was some evidence to the effect that Williamson wanted to get enough equity to help her finance a mobile home. When they went to Williamson's house to inquire about it, Williamson showed the Matthews through the house. Bobby Matthews asked Williamson how much she wanted for it. Williamson told the Matthews to come back the next day. It is at this point that the parties are in disagreement. The Matthews contend that Williamson offered to sell her equity for \$1,700, and Williamson contends that she offered to sell her equity for \$17,000, and that the Matthews agreed to pay off the mortgage. It is undisputed that on September 27, 1978, the parties went to attorney Arthur J. Cook's office to execute a contract for the sale of the property. The contract of sale stated the purchase price to be \$1,800 (\$100 increase reflecting an agreement between the parties concerning some of the furniture in the home) plus the unpaid balance of the mortgage. Attorney Cook testified that he read the terms of the sale to both parties.

The parties then met on October 10, 1978, at attorney Larry Keener's office to sign the deed and to close a loan from appellee Family Savings Federal Credit Union to the Matthews so that the Matthews could buy the property from Williamson. Appellee The Brooklyn Savings Bank was about to foreclose the mortgage on Williamson's property. Keener disbursed part of the loan proceeds to Williamson. Williamson signed the deed to the property.

This Court was advised at oral argument that further disbursement of funds has been held up pending final disposition of this appeal.

Immediately after the sale, Williamson became concerned that she had not received her full consideration and consulted an attorney. Two days later, on October 12, 1978, Williamson filed a petition for injunctive relief alleging inadequate consideration and mental weakness. The trial court granted Williamson a temporary restraining order preventing the sale from being completed, but at a full hearing on the petition for injunctive relief, the court denied Williamson the relief she requested. Williamson moved for and was granted a rehearing and further testimony was taken on the issue of Williamson's alleged mental weakness. Following the rehearing, the court issued a final order, again denying Williamson injunctive relief. This appeal followed.

. . .

Although in the case at bar there is no proof of suppression of fact, presentation of falsehood, abuse of confidence, fiduciary relationship between the parties, overreaching, or undue influence, the Court in Judge did not limit "this something else" besides mere inadequacy of consideration to these factors alone.

Williamson contends that the "something else" in the case at bar is mental weakness, either due to some form of permanent mental incapacity or due to intoxication. Of course, the contracts of an insane person are absolutely void. Williamson, however, is not contending that she was insane at the time of the contract, but rather is contending that she had a mental incapacity, which coupled with inadequacy of consideration requires the setting aside of the transaction.

Our rule in such a case is that a party cannot avoid, free from fraud or undue influence, a contract on the ground of mental incapacity, unless it be shown that the incapacity was of such a character that, at the time of execution, the person had no reasonable perception or understanding of the nature and terms of the contract.

Our rule regarding incapacity due to intoxication is much the same. The drunkenness of a party at the time of making a contract may render the contract voidable, but it does not render it void; and to render the contract voidable, it must be made to appear that the party was intoxicated to such a degree that he was, at the time of the contracting, incapable of exercising judgment, understanding the proposed engagement, and of knowing what he was about when he entered into the contract sought to be avoided. Proof merely that the party was drunk on the day the sale was executed does not per se, show that he was without contractual capacity; there must be some evidence of a resultant condition indicative of that extreme impairment of the faculties which amounts to contractual incapacity.

The burden was therefore cast on Williamson to show, by clear and convincing evidence, that she was incapable, at the time of execution, of executing the contract for sale and of executing the deed.

We hold that Williamson met this burden. The testimony elicited at trial by Williamson's attorney charted a history of aberrative behavior. A Mrs. Logan, Williamson's mother, provided lengthy testimony about her daughter's past aberrations. Additionally, Dr. Fredric Feist provided expert testimony regarding Williamson at the rehearing. He stated that she showed signs of an early organic brain syndrome due to her excessive drinking, that she had emotional problems, that he thought that some of her brain cells were destroyed, and that her ability to transact business had been impaired.

Indulging the usual presumption due the trial court, we nevertheless hold that, under the facts of this case, it appears to us that Williamson was not, at the time of execution, capable of fully and completely understanding the nature and terms of the contract and of the deed. Williamson's contention that she was intoxicated supports this holding. Testimony was admitted from various witnesses to the effect that

Williamson had a history of drinking, that she still had the problem at the time she executed the contract, and that she had in fact taken a couple of drinks before leaving for the meeting in attorney Arthur Cook's office. We do not hold that Williamson was so intoxicated as to render her incapable of contracting. However, numerous factors combine to warrant the conclusion that she was operating under diminished capacity. Testimony showed that Williamson's capacity to transact business was impaired, that she had a history of drinking, that she had been drinking the day she conducted negotiations, and that she had an apparent weakened will because she was pressured by the possibility of an impending foreclosure. Moreover, Williamson made complaint to an attorney only hours after the transaction. These factors are combined with a gross inadequacy of consideration.

No mitigating factors exist to the contrary. No right of any intervening third party is involved. Further disbursement of the loan proceeds has been frozen until final disposition of this appeal. No hardship is worked upon any party.

Although the evidence was presented before the trial court *ore tenus*, and in such a case where there is evidence to support the trial court's judgment, this Court will not ordinarily reverse that judgment unless there is a showing of plain and palpable error or manifest injustice. We consider that the record supports a finding in this case of such manifest injustice as to require a reversal of the judgment.

We recognize that two able and conscientious attorneys handled parts of the transaction. They are in no wise responsible for, nor were they aware of, the factors which prompt us to require a reversal of this case.

Reversed and remanded.

TORBERT, C. J., and BLOODWORTH, FAULKNER, ALMON and EMBRY, JJ., concur.

The Restatement is not very kind to those whose incapacity results from alcohol consumption. Section 16 provides,

> **§ 16 Intoxicated Persons**
>
> A person incurs only voidable contractual duties by entering into a transaction if the other party has reason to know that by reason of intoxication.
>
> a. He is unable to understand in a reasonable manner the nature and consequences of the transaction, or
>
> b. He is unable to act in a reasonable manner in relation to the transaction.

2. External Impediments to Capacity

There are times when a person's capacity is removed because of an outside force.

a. Duress

With duress, there is some kind of outside pressure placed on the person that makes independent judgment impossible. Think of someone holding a gun to another person's head, demanding that he sign a document that will benefit the gun-holder. The person told to sign the contract is under duress. He no longer has the capacity to independently determine whether the contract he is told to sign is in his best interests or not.

Two kinds of duress trigger different legal rules with respect to whether the contract is void or voidable. If the threat made to the person is sufficient to cause a reasonable person to believe that her physical well being (or that of loved one or friend) is jeopardized, then the "contract' signed is void. In the example above, as long as the gun and the person holding it are reasonably perceived to be a real threat, then the contract is void even if it turns out later that the gun was fake or unloaded and that the individual had no intention of perpetrating any harm. What matters is the reasonable belief of the person under duress.

One can vary the example, though, so that there is a threat, but not one that creates a void contract. What if there is a threat, but the exact nature of potential harm is not as great or is questionable? What if a petite gymnast from the women's Olympic team threatens to beat up an All-Pro, NFL linebacker? Unless there is some evidence that the gymnast is also holding a weapon or is a highly skilled martial arts devotee, the threat to the linebacker may create a voidable contract, but certainly not one that is, per se, void. For that matter, as per the example, it may not qualify for any special treatment.

The point is that for any kind of duress, the test goes to the reasonable belief in the threat by the person allegedly under duress. Depending on the exact threat, the external impediment to the person's capacity may lead to a void or voidable contract, or may have no impact on capacity at all. In any negotiation, one party might caution, or even warn the other side that there would be consequences if a contract is not signed or not signed on a particular set of terms. "No one else will offer you as good a deal" or "you'll go out of business if you insist on these terms" would be cautions or threats that are part of haggling. Yet there are times when threats become improper. The Restatement defines an improper threat as follows:

§ 176: When a Threat Is Improper

1. A threat is improper if

   a. What is threatened is a crime or a tort, or the threat itself would be a crime or a tort if it resulted in obtaining property,

   b. What is threatened is a criminal persecution,

   c. What is threatened is the use of civil process and the threat is made in bad faith, or

   d. The threat is a breach of the duty of good faith and fear dealing under a contract with the recipient

2. A threat is improper if the resulting exchange is not on fair terms, and

   a. The threatened act would harm the recipient and would not significantly benefit the parry making the threat,

   b. The effectiveness of the threat inducing the manifestation of assent is significantly increased by prior unfair dealing by the party making the threat, or

   c. What is threatened is otherwise a use of power for illegitimate ends.

The following case illustrates what can happen when duress reaches the point where a contract can be voidable.

Eckstein v. Eckstein

38 Md.App. 506, 379 A.2d 757 (1978)

LISS, JUDGE.

Judith Eckstein, appellant (hereinafter "wife"), and Donald Eckstein, appellee (hereinafter "husband"), were married in Maryland on May 25, 1968. The wife had one daughter from a previous marriage, Kimberly, who was adopted by the husband after their marriage; and a second daughter, Donna, was born to the Ecksteins. At the time of the separation between the parties the children were eight and six years old respectively. The wife had a history of mental disturbances, and in September of

1973, she sought professional help from a psychiatrist, Dr. Gultken Ovacik. During the course of her sessions with Dr. Ovacik, in January of 1974, the wife was committed to the Prince George's Hospital Psychiatric Ward for treatment, where she remained confined for a period of 46 days. Dr. Ovacik, who continued to see her at the hospital, testified that her last visit with him during that period was April 3, 1974, at which time she advised him that she was not going to see him again because her husband objected to her seeing a psychiatrist. She did not see him again until July 21, 1975. The doctor testified that he found the wife to be suffering from a reactive depression when he saw her in April of 1974 and that the condition had not changed when he saw her in July of 1975. Her history indicated that she had attempted suicide four or five times and that she was hospitalized on at least three occasions as a result of these attempts. Dr. Ovacik indicated that in his opinion she was suffering from the reactive depression well before he first saw her in September of 1973.

The marriage was hardly an idyll of matrimonial bliss, and the parties separated temporarily on a number of occasions. During one of these separations in 1971, the husband had his lawyer, a Mr. Leitch, prepare a separation and property settlement agreement; and on April 13, 1971, the husband took the wife who had no counsel and was not given an opportunity to consult counsel to his lawyer's office. The wife signed the agreement, and later that afternoon, she took an overdose of prescribed drugs and was hospitalized. The husband communicated with her by phone while she was in the hospital, and a reconciliation ensued. Several other separations had occurred between the parties and during one such period (in November of 1970), the wife employed an attorney who prepared a separation agreement more favorable to her than the one she ultimately signed but which her husband refused to sign.

On the evening of February 1, 1975, the wife left the marital abode in the parties' jointly owned 1973 Volkswagen van with only the clothes on her back. She had no funds and the husband promptly closed the couple's joint bank account. The wife consulted Legal Aid but was advised that she did not qualify for their assistance. Shortly after the wife left her husband, he discovered her whereabouts and the location of the van and with the assistance of the wife's stepfather seized and secreted the van. The husband refused the wife's request to visit or communicate with her children and refused to give her her clothing. He told her that she could see her children and take her clothes only if she signed a separation agreement prepared by Mr. Leitch, his attorney. Subsequent events disclosed that the agreement was almost an exact duplicate of the one she signed in 1971 after which she attempted suicide.

On February 10, 1975, she was directed by her husband to go to Mr. Leitch's office; she had no money to employ counsel. At Mr. Leitch's office she was advised that her husband was in the suite but would not talk to her in person. A copy of the separation agreement was given to her to read. She asked several questions of Mr. Leitch who testified that he did not recollect what the questions were but that he refused to give her any advice because he was representing her husband. He asked her if she wanted to talk to her husband and put him on an inter-office phone to discuss the matter with her. The husband also admitted that the wife asked several questions about the agreement but stated that he could not remember what the inquiries were and he did not answer them. The wife testified that her husband told her that if she did not sign the agreement he would get her for desertion, that she would never see her children again, and that she would get nothing neither her clothes nor the van unless she signed the agreement as written. No changes were made in the document, and the wife signed the agreement in Mr. Leitch's office. Immediately after signing, her clothes were surrendered to her and she was given the keys to the Volkswagen van.

The separation agreement provided that the wife give custody of the children to her husband. She agreed to deed to her husband her interest in the jointly owned home of the parties. She agreed to assign to her husband her interest in a jointly owned new 1975 Chevrolet van; she received the Volkswagen. She waived alimony, support, maintenance, court costs, attorney's fees, and any right of inheritance in her husband's estate. She was to receive one-half of the income tax refunds due the parties, of which her share would be approximately $1,000. She was paid $1100 at the time of the execution of the agreement. The husband agreed to retain the wife on his health insurance policy until they were divorced. The wife was to receive any of their furniture which she desired.

On February 10, 1976, the husband filed a bill of complaint in the Circuit Court for Prince George's County in which he prayed the court to grant him a divorce a *vinculo matrimonii* on the ground of voluntary separation and to require specific performance of the third and fourth paragraphs of the property settlement agreement executed by the parties on February 10, 1975. These paragraphs concerned the exchange of the titles to the two vans owned by the parties.

The wife filed an answer in which she prayed that the court grant the divorce but alleged lack of mental capacity on her part and coercion, duress, fraud, breach of contract, lack of consideration and gross overreaching on the part of the husband in securing the execution of the agreement, and requested that the court set aside the property settlement between the parties. She also sought custody of the minor children and counsel fees. The trial court, with the approval of both parties, treated the answer filed by the wife as a cross-bill of complaint seeking affirmative relief. At the conclusion of two days of testimony, the trial court granted the husband's prayer for a divorce a vinculo; granted him custody of the minor children, with visitation rights to the wife; and upheld the validity of the separation and property agreement. All the prayers for relief of the wife were denied, and her cross-bill of complaint was dismissed.

* * *

A separation agreement, being a contract between the parties, is subject to the same general rules governing other contracts. * * * Any agreement, contract, or deed obtained by oppressing a person by threats regarding the safety or liberty of himself, or his property, or a member of his family so as to deprive him of the free exercise of his will and prevent the mutuality of assent required for a valid contract may be avoided on the ground of duress.

* * *

The circumstances surrounding the signing of the agreement were bizarre, to say the least. * * * When she told her husband that she would not sign the agreement, which was identical with the one she repudiated in 1971, he repeated his threats that she would get nothing neither her van, nor her clothes, nor the right to see or communicate with her children. No changes at all were made in the agreement as prepared by Mr. Leitch.

It is significant, we believe, that when under the circumstances she capitulated and signed the agreement, Mr. Leitch immediately delivered to her, in cash, the $1100 she was to receive for her interest in the property, and her clothes and the van were surrendered to her. These facts indicate to us a strong determination by the husband and his lawyer to pressure the wife into then and there executing the agreement.

* * *

We conclude that it was irregular for the husband and his counsel to prepare a complicated legal document and deeds conveying to the husband her interest in jointly held property without at least offering her an opportunity to have her questions answered by her own legal advisor. It was, we believe, improper to submit the documents to her on a take it or leave it basis and to coerce her signature by withholding her property and threatening to prevent her from seeing or communicating with her children. We might well have reached that conclusion even if the evidence was clear that the wife was a competent, stable, knowledgeable woman; but when, as here, it is obvious that the husband and his lawyer were dealing with an emotionally and mentally unstable individual, we think that the conclusion that the execution of the agreement was obtained by duress is inescapable. With no funds, no lawyer, no clothes, no transportation, and no viable alternative, it is not surprising that the wife capitulated and signed the agreement. We cannot accept that action, under all the circumstances, as one taken by her of her own free will.

---

b. Undue Influence

Undue influence tends to be more subtle than situations of physical duress. In these kinds of cases, one individual places so much confidence in another person that they essentially give away their capacity to contract. Suppose, for example, that a parent has three children. Two of the children live far away, while one lives close by the parent and does an enormous amount of work for the parent, especially as the parent ages. More and more, the parent looks to the nearby child to make decisions on the parent's behalf. Increasingly, the parent begins to defer to the children's discretion. The parent still has the capacity to make decisions, but increasingly rely on this trusted child.

At some point, the child may start to recommend the parent enter into contracts that are in the best interest of the child rather than the parent. At this point, the trusted relationship turns into one where there is undue influence. Under §177 of the Restatement, undue influence occurs when:

1. Undue influence is unfair persuasion of a party who is under the domination of the person exercising the persuasion or who by virtue of the relation between them is justified in assuming that the person will not act in a manner inconsistent with his welfare.

2. If a party's manifestation of assent is induced by undue influence by the other party, the contract is voidable by the victim.

3. If a party's manifestation of assent is induced by one who is not a party to the transaction, the contract is voidable by the victim unless the other party to the transaction in good faith and without reason to know of the undue influence either gives value or relies materially on the transaction.

B. MEETING OF THE MINDS

1. Explicit Contracts

Explicit contracts are easy to see and to analyze because, as the category indicates, their explicitness makes them visible with ascertainable promises. With explicit contracts, terms are clearly negotiated with each party promising to do something.

An explicit contract does not have to be in writing. A simple exchange of promises between two people can form a contract without anything in writing. While some contracts are only enforceable if they are in writing, such as contracts for real estate, written contracts provide evidence. What, exactly, did the parties promise to do? If the contract is merely verbal or implied through actions, there is a chance for ambiguity and potential conflict as each party remembers their promises a bit differently. A writing helps to make clear what both parties promised in the event they have to go to a third party—such as a judge—to enforce the contract.

2. Implied Contracts

Implied contracts can be harder to analyze. They typically involve a set of promises, requests, or statements by one party and then some kind of action by another. A key question, then, becomes whether there was an actual agreement or not between the two parties. Another issue arises when one person undertakes an action to benefit the other party and whether the benefitted party will obtain some kind of "unjust enrichment" by not providing some kind of compensation to the other party.

The Restatement actually understands the meeting of the minds as implicit in the concept of mutual assent, discussed below.

a. By Conduct

If Jennifer were to say to Richard, "I will give you $100 to paint my house," there is no contract. This would be construed as an offer. Richard has some options at this point. One of them is to paint the house within a reasonable time. Let's say he does this right away. If he does, he provides a benefit to Jennifer and performs the actions for which she has indicated she is willing to pay $100. Richard's actions constitute an implied acceptance; his actions manifest his assent. Section 19 of the Restatement states that "the conduct of a party is not effective as a manifestation of his assent unless he intends to engage in the conduct and knows or has reason to know that the other party may infer from his conduct that he assents."

b. Quasi-Contract and Unilateral Contracts

All contracts require an offer and acceptance for the formation of a contract. However, in the case of unilateral contracts, the party accepts the offer by performing. Unilateral contracts arise in a myriad of situations, such as in the area of prizes and contests, where contestants attempt to claim prizes based upon a company's advertised offer. In these cases, the person performing—i.e. the person accepting the offer—is not compelled to act, but will receive compensation for completing the task before any revocation by the offeror.

Another area where implied contracts arise frequently is in employment law. Courts have been divided about whether an employee handbook constitutes an offer to contract on those terms with an employee and whether an employee can accept by beginning to perform. That particular issue will be covered in a later chapter on Employment Law, but as the next section shows, materials in a brochure can constitute terms of a contract.

3. Mutual Assent

Contracts are about two parties (or more) entering into an agreement that they believe to be in their best interest. They're also about freedom of choice and mutual benefit in creating relationship with reciprocal rights and duties. The heart of contracts is that the parties agree on those rights and duties. They understand that one party will pay money, and the other party will paint the fence. What is crucial is their **mutual assent** to the arrangement. As we will see in the following chapter on the Uniform Commercial Code, there can be some kinds of sales issues where there does not have to be a perfect meeting of the minds. But whether there is a pure meeting of the minds or not, there does need to be a valid offer and a valid acceptance in order for there to be a valid contract under common law. The meeting of the minds requirement, however, is not required in sales contracts, which are governed by the Uniform Commercial Code, covered in the next chapter.

The following two sections deal with mutual assent through offer and acceptance. In sections 17 through 70 of the Restatement, the drafters cover manifestations of assent in general, the making of offers, the duration of the offeree's power to accept, and the acceptance of offers. These provisions are too numerous to reprint here, but if you have questions about the concepts explored below, the rules of the Restatement and their comments may provide helpful guidance.

a. Offer

The first step in analyzing any contract is determining whether an offeror (the person making the offer) is actually making an offer or not. To make a valid offer, the offeror must create a reasonable expectation in the mind of an offeree that an offer is being made on the basis of sufficiently concrete terms. Central to an offer, then, is a communication between the parties. The most straightforward form of such a communication is if the offeror simply states, verbally or in writing, that they wish to enter into a contract. And so if one person says to another, I will give you $100 to paint my house if you do it this afternoon, that person has created a reasonable expectation in the mind of the offeree than an offer is being extended to her on the basis of the offered terms. The result would be the same if the offeree put the statement in writing. In at least two ways, however, things can get more complicated.

One way is when there is a statement of interest in entering into a contract that is not conveyed to the offeree. So if the offeror above said to a third party, Jill, "I would love for Bill to paint my house and I would give him $100 if he did it today," a reasonable expectation would not be created in Bill's mind that an offer had been made to him to paint the house unless Jill happens to be his agent. Similarly, if the offeror made a general statement that "it would be worth $100 to have my house painted today," there again would not be a reasonable expectation created in the mind of the offeree that an actual offer is being extended unless there is some additional action accompanying the words; say, for example, the offeror waving $100 in Bill's face when making the general statement.

In addition to making the statement to an intended party, the second key issue is whether the terms of the offer are sufficiently firm to form the basis of a contract. If a retailer posts an advertisement claiming "we'll give you the best deal in town," that will not be sufficiently certain for a customer to bind the business to a specific price for a specific item. Advertisements in a periodical such as a newspaper for the sale of a product or to solicit an application have frequently been the cause of litigation in offer cases, as the following cases demonstrate.

Lefkowitz v. Great Minneapolis Surplus Store

251 Minn. 188, 86 N.W.2d 689 (1957)

Murphy, Justice.

This is an appeal from an order of the Municipal Court of Minneapolis denying the motion of the defendant for amended findings of fact, or, in the alternative, for a new trial. The order for judgment awarded the plaintiff the sum of $138.50 as damages for breach of contract.

This case grows out of the alleged refusal of the defendant to sell to the plaintiff a certain fur piece which it had offered for sale in a newspaper advertisement. It appears from the record that on April 6, 1956, the defendant published the following advertisement in a Minneapolis newspaper:

'Saturday 9 A.M. Sharp 3 Brand New Fur Coats Worth to $100.00

First Come First Served $1 Each'

On April 13, the defendant again published an advertisement in the same newspaper as follows:

'Saturday 9 A.M. 2 Brand New Pastel Mink 3-Skin Scarfs Selling for.$89.50

Out they go Saturday. Each . . . $1.00

1 Black Lapin Stole Beautiful, worth $139.50 . . . $1.00

First Come First Served'

The record supports the findings of the court that on each of the Saturdays following the publication of the above-described ads the plaintiff was the first to present himself at the appropriate counter in the defendant's store and on each occasion demanded the coat and the stole so advertised and indicated his readiness to pay the sale price of $1. On both occasions, the defendant refused to sell the merchandise to the plaintiff, stating on the first occasion that by a 'house rule' the offer was intended for women only and sales would not be made to men, and on the second visit that plaintiff knew defendant's house rules.

The trial court properly disallowed plaintiff's claim for the value of the fur coats since the value of these articles was speculative and uncertain. The only evidence of value was the advertisement itself to the effect that the coats were 'Worth to $100.00,' how much less being speculative especially in view of the price for which they were offered for sale. With reference to the offer of the defendant on April 13, 1956, to sell the '1 Black Lapin Stole * * * worth $139.50 * * * ' the trial court held that the value of this article was established and granted judgment in favor of the plaintiff for that amount less the $1 quoted purchase price.

■ DETAIL FROM A PERIOD NEWSPAPER ADVERTISEMENT FOR THE GREAT MINNEAPOLIS SURPLUS STORE.

* * *

There are numerous authorities which hold that a particular advertisement in a newspaper or circular letter relating to a sale of articles may be construed by the court as constituting an offer, acceptance of which would complete a contract.

The test of whether a binding obligation may originate in advertisements addressed to the general public is 'whether the facts show that some performance was promised in positive terms in return for something requested.'

The authorities above cited emphasize that, where the offer is clear, definite, and explicit, and leaves nothing open for negotiation, it constitutes an offer, acceptance of which will complete the contract. The most recent case on the subject is *Johnson v. Capital City Ford Co.*, in which the court pointed out that a newspaper advertisement relating to the purchase and sale of automobiles may constitute an offer, acceptance of which will consummate a contract and create an obligation in the offeror to perform according to the terms of the published offer.

Whether in any individual instance a newspaper advertisement is an offer rather than an invitation to make an offer depends on the legal intention of the parties and the surrounding circumstances. We are of the view on the facts before us that the offer by the defendant of the sale of the Lapin fur was clear, definite, and explicit, and left nothing open for negotiation. The plaintiff having successful managed to be the first one to appear at the seller's place of business to be served, as requested by the advertisement, and having offered the stated purchase price of the article, he was entitled to performance on the part of the defendant. We think the trial court was correct in holding that there was in the conduct of the parties a sufficient mutuality of obligation to constitute a contract of sale.

2. The defendant contends that the offer was modified by a 'house rule' to the effect that only women were qualified to receive the bargains advertised. The advertisement contained no such restriction. This objection may be disposed of briefly by stating that, while an advertiser has the right at any time before acceptance to modify his offer, he does not have the right, after acceptance, to impose new or arbitrary conditions not contained in the published offer.

Affirmed.

It is important to remember that simply because there is an advertisement in a newspaper or other media, it does not mean there is an offer. There have to be definite enough terms to form a reasonable expectation in the mind of the offeree that the offeror is actually presenting contractual terms. An ad that makes it look like one will be surrounded by cool, beautiful people if only one opens the right can of beer, does not meet that test. Such an advertisement is trying to create a perception of the attractiveness of the product; no reasonable person would expect that by opening the right can of beer, one will find oneself in such a position. *Lefkowitz* is interesting because the company was explicit in how and when they would sell the furs. The following case makes a similar point with respect to an application to medical school.

Steinberg v. Chicago Medical School

69 Ill.2d 320, 371 N.E.2d 634 (1977)

DOOLEY, JUSTICE:

Robert Steinberg received a catalog, applied for admission to defendant, Chicago Medical School, for the academic year 1974-75, and paid a $15 fee. He was rejected. Steinberg filed a class action against the school claiming it had failed to evaluate his application and those of other applicants according to the academic criteria in the school's bulletin. According to the complaint, defendant used nonacademic criteria, primarily the ability of the applicant or his family to pledge or make payment of large sums of money to the school.

The 1974-75 bulletin distributed to prospective students contained this statement of standards by which applicants were to be evaluated:

> "Students are selected on the basis of scholarship, character, and motivation without regard to race, creed, or sex. The student's potential for the study and practice of medicine will be evaluated on the basis of academic achievement, Medical College Admission Test results, personal appraisals

by a pre-professional advisory committee or individual instructors, and the personal interview, if requested by the Committee on Admissions."

* * *

Steinberg alleges that he and others similarly situated received a brochure describing the criteria that defendant would employ in evaluating applications. He urges that such constituted an invitation for an offer to apply, that the filing of the applications constituted an offer to have their credentials appraised under the terms described by defendant, and that defendant's voluntary reception of the application and fee constituted an acceptance, the final act necessary for the creation of a binding contract.

This situation is similar to that wherein a merchant advertises goods for sale at a fixed price. While the advertisement itself is not an offer to contract, it constitutes an invitation to deal on the terms described in the advertisement. Although in some cases the advertisement itself may be an offer (see *Lefkowitz v. Great Minneapolis Surplus Store, Inc.*, (1957), usually it constitutes only an invitation to deal on the advertised terms. Only when the merchant takes the money is there an acceptance of the offer to purchase.

Here the description in the brochure containing the terms under which an application will be appraised constituted an invitation for an offer. The tender of the application, as well as the payment of the fee pursuant to the terms of the brochure, was an offer to apply. Acceptance of the application and fee constituted acceptance of an offer to apply under the criteria defendant had established.

* * *

Here our scope of review is exceedingly narrow. Does the complaint set forth facts which could mean that defendant contracted, under the circumstances, to appraise applicants and their applications according to the criteria it described? This is the sole inquiry on this motion to dismiss. We believe the allegations suffice and affirm the appellate court in holding count I stated a cause of action.

Count III alleges that, with intent to deceive and defraud plaintiffs, defendant stated in its catalogs it would use certain criteria to evaluate applications; that these representations were false in that applicants were selected primarily for monetary considerations; that plaintiffs relied on said representations and were each thereby induced to submit their applications and pay $15 to their damage.

These allegations support a cause of action for fraud. Misrepresentation of an existing material fact coupled with scienter, deception, and injury are more than adequate. *Roth v. Roth*, (1970), succinctly stated when a misrepresentation may constitute fraud:

"A misrepresentation in order to constitute a fraud must consist of a statement of material fact, false and known to be so by the party making it, made to induce the other party to act, and, in acting, the other party must rely on the truth of the statement. (*Roda v. Berko.*)"

* * *

Here an action for fraud is consistent with the recognition of a contract action. The law creates obligations "on the ground that they are dictated by reason and justice." The right to recover on a "constructive contract," although phrased in contract terminology, is not based on an agreement between parties but is an obligation created by law. "Such contracts are contracts merely in the sense that (they) * * * are created and governed by the principles of equity." So here the facts of this situation mandate that equity imply an obligation by the defendant. We note this since the circumstances before us justify a contract action, as well as a fraud action, or, in the event no contract in fact can be proven, an action on an implied-in-law obligation of the defendant.

---

b. Acceptance

Because contracts require a mirror image—another expression to acknowledge that the parties have had a meeting of the minds—in order to be valid, the offeree (the person accepting the offer) has three choices when an offer is extended to him.

1. Accept the offer, which creates a contract,
2. reject the offer,
3. reject the offer and make a counteroffer instead.

The first two choices are straightforward. Either a contract is formed on the basis of the offered terms (to which the offeree agrees) or the contract is rejected and nothing happens. A counteroffer, however, reverses the relationship between the parties. Now the original offeree becomes the offeror because the counteroffer is exactly that: another offer. Acceptance can occur either by performance or by the acceptance of the promise. Both require notification to the offeror.

Given the speed of communication today, the so-called **mailbox rule** has lost some of its relevance. But it can still rear its head and its logic lies behind subsequent policy. Put simply, for the most part, communications of components of an offer and acceptance become effective when they are received by the other party. An offer is effective when the offeree receives it (so that a reasonable expectation is raised in the mind of the offeree that an offer is being made that the offeree can accept). The same rule is true for a rejection (made by the offeree) or a revocation (made by the offeror). Because a counteroffer is a combination of a rejection (by the offeree) with a new offer, the rule still holds that the counteroffer becomes effective when received by the offeree.

The wrinkle comes with an acceptance. An acceptance is deemed effective when the offeree says "yes" and does something to send that acceptance to the offeror, such as placing a letter indicating the acceptance in the mail (with proper postage, etc.). She mails an acceptance (immediately effective) and then calls up the offeror and, changing her mind, rejects the offer before the acceptance reaches the offeror. Which is effective? In such cases, courts generally revert to the rule of whichever is received first. Bear in mind that this simplifies the mailbox rule quite a bit and many nuances await. At the same time, with the rise of electronic communications and their speed, the instances of the mailbox rule increasingly diminish.[3]

C. CONSIDERATION

The third requirement for a valid contract is consideration. Consideration is a legal term of art. It does not mean that the parties treat each other with respect and courtesy as the commonly used definition of consideration would suggest. Instead, consideration, for legal purposes, means that each party has given up something of value in order to bind each other to the contract. Consideration does not attempt to evaluate whether a bargain was fair or not, or that each party gave up roughly equally valuable items or performed equally valuable services, but it does ask if both parties gave up something of **legal value.**

Like the sections on offer and acceptance, the Restatement covers a much broader range of concepts than we will in this text. Sections 71 through 109 set forth the requirements that there be consideration, contracts under seal. To begin, though, let us look at § 71:

§ 71: Requirement of Exchange: Types of Exchange:

1. To constitute consideration, a performance or a return promise must be bargained for.

3 If you are interested in the law governing electronic transmissions, consult the Uniform Electronic Transactions Act (UETA) promulgated by the National Conference of Commissioners on Uniform State Laws (NCCUSL), now the Uniform Law Commission. Forty-seven states, the District of Columbia, and the Virgin Islands have enacted the code, and New York, Washington and Illinois have similar state laws.

2. A performance or return promise is bargained for if it is sought by the promisor in exchange for his promise and is given by the promisee in exchange for that promise.

3. The performance may consist of

   a. an act other than a promise, or

   b. a forbearance, or

   c. the creation, modification, or destruction of a legal relation.

4. The performance or return promise may be given to the promisor or to some other person. It may be given by the promisee or by some other person.

I. General Framework

The general test for whether the consideration test has been met is whether consideration is mutual—that both parties have given up something—and that what they have given up is determined to be of adequate, legal value. The ideas that both parties have given up something and that what they have given up is of adequate, legal value tend to merge because what typically happens is if one party did not, in fact, provide something of adequate legal value, there is no mutuality of exchange.

Let's assume that Mike is teaching a business law class and says he will give $100,000 to anyone who gets up and walks around the room. Several students take him up on the offer and then demand the $100,000. There are two parties, both of them presumably have capacity, and there is a meeting of the minds as to the identity of the parties and the terms of the agreement. But would courts enforce a contract for $100,000 for walking around a (presumably small) room? More likely, the Court would say that the contract lacks consideration. There is not adequate legal value given by simply getting up and walking around the room.

On the other hand, let's say Mike promised that he would give $1,000 if any member of the class ran a marathon. Several students do just that, and then demand payment. Courts may well hold this to be consideration on the part of both parties. Certainly offering $1,000 rather than $100,000 makes it more likely to agree this is a real offer as opposed to some kind of playful joke, but more importantly, the effort of running a marathon is far greater than that required to walk around the room.

A business person may already have a duty to perform some action. This raises the question of whether the person can demand additional consideration for something that he is already obligated to do. The following case assesses whether an automobile insurer can require additional consideration from an insured in order for the insurer to fully process a claim or whether the insurer has a pre-existing duty to process the claim based on the contract that is already in place.

Yerkovich v. AAA

461 Mich. 732, 610 N.W.2d 542 (2000)

Michael F. Cavanagh, J.

* * *

Plaintiff's minor daughter was injured in an automobile accident when the driver of the vehicle in which she was riding negligently collided with another vehicle. At the time of the accident, plaintiff was a participant in the Michigan United Food and Commercial Workers Unions and Food Employers Health and Welfare Fund. The fund is a self-funded employee welfare benefit plan created and administered pursuant to the Employee Retirement Income Security Act (ERISA) [. . .]. Plaintiff also had a no-fault policy issued by defendant AAA.

Plaintiff filed this action on behalf of her daughter against both defendants, seeking payment of medical expenses. The fund had initially denied coverage, claiming plaintiff had failed to execute a subrogation agreement. The fund claimed this was required by the plan's subrogation clause. Plaintiff eventually signed the "Subrogation Agreement and Assignment" form, and the fund paid $6,832 in medical expense benefits. The AAA also denied coverage, claiming that plaintiff's policy contained a coordination of benefits clause that made the fund primarily responsible for medical expenses from the accident. Plaintiff also filed a negligence claim seeking noneconomic damages against the driver of the vehicle in which her daughter was riding. That case was settled for $20,000.

* * *

At issue in this case is the interpretation of the plan agreement between the fund and plaintiff. Specifically, we must answer whether the fund was entitled to a refund from plaintiff for medical expenses. The fund provided plaintiff with a plan booklet that laid out the rights, benefits, and duties of the parties. Under the "General Provisions" section, the plan provided a subsection entitled "Third Party Subrogation." The fund argues that, under this section, plaintiff was required to sign further documents ensuring its rights to subrogation, reimbursement, repayment, and assignment.

* * *

> [Y]ou or your dependants will have certain responsibilities to the Plan. When you or your eligible dependent submit a claim to this Plan for injuries, the Fund Office will have you complete a form requesting information as to how the injuries occurred and the identity of any potentially responsible third parties. At the request of the Fund Office, *you must also sign any other documents* and do whatever else is reasonably necessary *to secure this Plan's right of subrogation.* You must not do anything to impair or negate this Plan's right of subrogation; *if* any of your acts or omissions to act compromise this Plan's right of subrogation, this Plan will seek *reimbursement* of all appropriate benefits paid directly to you . . . .
>
> If you recover lost wage benefits from another source, e.g. from an individual who caused the injury which resulted in your receiving Time Loss Weekly Benefits, the Plan has the *right to seek repayment from you* [. . . .] [Court's note: Emphasis added.]

Under this plan, the fund declared "subrogation" rights in order to recover from a third party medical expense benefits it paid. In contrast, it declared the right to "repayment" from plaintiff for lost wage benefits it paid in the event that plaintiff recovered the lost wages "from any other source."

* * *

Although the agreement provides that the fund may "recover *from the person who caused the injury*," the fund seeks to recover instead from plaintiff. It has done so by arguing that the second agreement signed by plaintiff required plaintiff to repay, reimburse, subrogate, and assign sums and rights to the fund. It is agreed that plaintiff signed the second agreement-that greatly expanded her duties under the plan agreement-only after the fund conditioned the payment of medical expenses on her signing the second agreement.

Under the plan agreement, the fund was entitled to seek recovery from the negligent driver for the medical expenses it paid. Plaintiff, in return, was required to sign documents necessary to secure the fund's right of subrogation. Plaintiff was also required to provide any information requested regarding the injuries and the identity of the tortfeasor. *If* plaintiff impaired that right of "subrogation," the fund could *then* seek reimbursement. Plaintiff has done nothing to hinder or obstruct the fund's rights of subrogation. Plaintiff did not sue the tortfeasor for medical expenses or any economic damages. Instead, plaintiff recovered from the tortfeasor purely noneconomic damages for pain and suffering. The fund does not claim that it has paid noneconomic damages. It does not claim that it had a right of subrogation for noneconomic damages, only for benefits it paid. It paid only medical expense benefits. Nor does the plan agreement provide that it may seek reimbursement from plaintiff for medical expenses from plaintiff's noneconomic damage recovery. Under the language of the plan agreement, the fund's right of reimbursement is triggered only if the plaintiff impairs or negates the fund's right of subrogation. This was not triggered. In fact, the fund may step into plaintiff's shoes and sue the negligent driver for medical expenses incurred, because plaintiff has yet to seek them.

Moreover, the fund might have, but did not, place language in the plan agreement requiring reimbursement of medical expenses from plaintiff. Instead, it sought only subrogation as defined in the second paragraph. Therefore, it has no right to reimbursement from plaintiff for medical expenses. This view is strengthened by examining the final paragraph quoted from the plan agreement where the fund demanded "repayment" from the *plaintiff* for lost wage benefits, in contrast to the "subrogation" clause, which allows recovery from the *person who caused the injury* for medical expense benefits.

The fund argues that subrogation *and* reimbursement rights are triggered whenever a plan participant recovers monies for the same injury or accident from a third party. It also urges that we should apply an "arbitrary and capricious" standard of review to the fund's interpretation of the plan agreement, citing *Firestone Tire & Rubber Co. v. Bruch*, 489 U.S. 101(1989). Even under such a standard, we cannot read into the plan agreement that which does not exist. The fund had the opportunity to write into its agreement repayment or reimbursement rights. It did not.

"AN ESSENTIAL element of a contract is legal consideration. Under the preexisting duty rule, it is well settled that doing what one is legally bound to do is not consideration for a new promise."

Whether the second agreement entitled the fund to reimbursement is irrelevant to our analysis because the fund was under a preexisting duty to pay plaintiff's medical expenses and could not require her to take on additional duties absent additional consideration.

An essential element of a contract is legal consideration. Under the preexisting duty rule, it is well settled that doing what one is legally bound to do is not consideration for a new promise. This rule bars the modification of an existing contractual relationship when the purported consideration for the modification consists of the performance or promise to perform that which one party was already required to do under the terms of the existing agreement.

In this case, the plan agreement provided that the fund had a preexisting duty to pay plaintiff's medical expenses. This promise was conditioned upon the fund's right of subrogation being protected. As stated, these rights were protected.

Although the parties focus on the second agreement, we find it is void for lack of consideration. Plaintiff was required only to sign documents ensuring the fund's right of subrogation as defined by the fund. The second agreement instead attempted to add to plaintiff's duties and burdens. The second agreement added an obligation to "repay" sums paid by the fund out of "any judgment or settlement" she received.

The next paragraph required her to "reimburse" the fund out of any recovery she received. Although the third paragraph included subrogation rights, we will not interpret the language to allow greater rights or duties than those in the original plan agreement. The final paragraphs added assignments of plaintiff's claims and rights to the fund. The result is that plaintiff took on additional obligations, without consideration, in order to be paid that which she was already owed. All such additional obligations are unenforceable.

CONCLUSION

The original plan agreement between plaintiff and the fund required the fund to pay plaintiff's medical expenses as long as its right of subrogation was protected. Absent a breach by plaintiff, the fund had no rights of reimbursement for medical expense benefits from plaintiff. We hold that the preexisting duty rule barred the fund from requiring plaintiff to take on additional burdens, without consideration, in order to get paid that which she was owed. Because the second contract was invalid for lack of consideration, we hold that the fund was not entitled to a reimbursement from plaintiff. We, therefore, reverse the Court of Appeals affirmance of the trial court's grant of summary disposition and order defendant fund to repay to the plaintiff any sums plaintiff paid to reimburse the fund.

The preexisting duty rule can be confusing. One might think of it like this: Assume a lifeguard already has a duty to save someone from drowning. One day, the lifeguard sees someone actually in trouble and says, "I'll save you if you promise to give me $100." The desperate person agrees but then refuses to give the lifeguard the $100 afterwards. Since the lifeguard had a preexisting duty, the second agreement for $100 would not be enforceable.

2. Detrimental Reliance

Borrowing from a Uniform Commercial Code concept, courts also use a test of whether one party detrimentally relied on another person's promises as consideration to bind a contract. Suppose a university asked a professor to teach an additional class. The professor had planned to continue work as a consultant with a client but would not have time to both teach the class and continue the consulting assignment. The university offered extra compensation for teaching the class and so the professor declined to continue the consulting assignment. Then the university decided not to offer the class. In such a case, the professor had detrimentally relied on the promises of the university and could enforce the terms of the contract because of that detrimental reliance.

In the Restatement, § 90 defines a "Promise Reasonably Inducing Action or Forbearance" as,

1. A promise which the promisor should reasonably expect to induce action or forbearance on the part of the promisee or a third person and which does induce such action or forbearance is binding if injustice can be avoided only by enforcement of the promise. The remedy granted for breach may be limited as justice requires.

2. A charitable subscription or a marriage settlement is binding under Subsection 1. without proof that the promise induced action or forbearance.

The second subdivision states that a gift to charity or a marriage settlement does not have to produce action in order to bind the parties based on reliance.[4]

3. Statutory Exceptions

There are some statutory exceptions to the requirement of consideration. The more common examples today are covered in the following chapter on the Uniform Commercial Code and pertain to business-related sales contracts where the consideration will be inferred. The rationale for such cases draws heavily on the notions of detrimental reliance just described.[5]

D. LEGAL PURPOSE AND PUBLIC POLICY CONSTRAINTS

Even if the parties agree to a contract, it does not mean the contract is valid. To be a valid contract, it must also not be for a purpose that violates the law or public policy. At the extreme, this makes complete sense: we would not want the court system to enforce a "contract" for murder or a conspiracy to commit theft. But beyond those self-evident kinds of prohibited contracts, there are others that are more nuanced. The basic provision of The Restatement that holds contracts unenforceable on the grounds of public policy states that "A promise or other term of an agreement is unenforceable on grounds of public policy if legislation provides that it is unenforceable or the interest in its enforcement is clearly outweighed in the circumstances by a public policy against the enforcement of such terms."[6] There are several examples below of how a contract could violate public policy or the law itself.

---

4 For an example of a charitable subscription case, see Justice Cardozo, writing in *Allegheny College v. National Chautauqua County Bank*, 247 N.Y. 369 (1927), which first announced the rule now codified in subsection two.

5 There are also some older rules concerning "seals" and "waivers" where if a party is deemed to have provided consideration by undertaking a unique act, which while interesting, take us a bit too far afield from a more focused treatment of consideration.

6 The Restatement also provides:

I. Prohibition Against Illegal Contracts

While the contract to murder raises no questions about validity—clearly, it is invalid—the more likely cases to arise are those in which a contract violates a requirement of a license or regulation. This might include building or continuing to run a casino after a legislature has revoked a license to operate or allowed a license to expire. Without an authorization, casino gambling would be illegal, and so contracts to continue the business would be unenforceable. Another example would be a contract to build a building or to expand a building without having received permission from a zoning authority. The following case exemplifies these kinds of unenforceability of contract based on conflict with an existing law or regulation.

Jimerson v. Tetlin Native Corp.

144 P.3d 470 (Alaska 2006)

MATTHEWS, JUSTICE.

The Tetlin Native Corporation (TNC) is a village corporation formed pursuant to ANCSA and organized as an Alaska business corporation. On July 17, 1996, TNC transferred approximately 643,174 acres of its land to the Tetlin Tribal Council. This left TNC with 100,000 acres of land.

Subsequently, the appellants, Shirley Jimerson and Ramona David, conducted a campaign to recall TNC's board of directors. The campaign was successful, and on January 12, 1999, Jimerson and David were elected to the board.

On March 15, 1999, TNC and Jimerson and David, as directors and individual shareholders (collectively Jimerson), filed a complaint in Alaska Superior Court in Fairbanks against certain shareholders and directors of TNC. The complaint alleged breach of fiduciary duties and wrongful transfer of TNC land, and requested $257,200,000 in damages and declaratory and injunctive relief. On April 20, 1999, the case was removed to the United States District Court for the District of Alaska.

On August 6, 1999, the Jimerson board was recalled. The new board passed a resolution that TNC dismiss all law suits brought by the Jimerson board. On October 6, 1999, TNC moved to dismiss without prejudice all claims it had against the

§ 179: Bases of Public Policies Against Enforcement

A public policy against the enforcement of promises or other terms may be derived by the court from

a. legislation relevant to such a policy, or
b. the need to protect some aspect of the public welfare, as is the case for the judicial policies against, for example,
   i. restraint of trade (§§ 186–188),
   ii. impairment of family relations (§§ 189–191), and
   iii. interference with other protected interests (§§ 192–196, 356).

shareholders and former and current directors of TNC. The district court denied TNC's motion to dismiss and urged the parties to reach a settlement.

The court's advice bore fruit, and the parties reached a settlement agreement. In August 2001 the district court approved the agreement and entered judgment on it. The settlement agreement acknowledged that TNC shareholders may not have been fully informed regarding dissenters' rights in the 1996 land transfer and provided for

> [a] transfer of a portion of Tetlin Native Corporation's remaining lands . . . to a new corporation to be formed by dissenting shareholders . . . who elect to transfer their shares of Tetlin Native Corporation ANCSA stock back to the corporation in exchange for shares in the new corporation.

In May 2003 Jimerson filed a motion in district court to enforce the settlement agreement. TNC opposed the motion and moved for relief from the judgment, contending that the district court lacked subject-matter jurisdiction. The district court concluded that the case presented no substantial federal question and declared the judgment based on the settlement agreement void for lack of jurisdiction. The case was then remanded to the superior court.

On February 23, 2004, Jimerson filed a motion in the superior court to enforce the settlement agreement. TNC opposed the motion, arguing that the settlement agreement was unenforceable as against public policy for three reasons: 1. the agreement provided for an exchange of shares in violation of ANCSA's prohibition on alienation, 2. the agreement violated the Alaska Corporations Code, and 3. the attorney for plaintiffs had a conflict of interest.

On June 18, 2004, the superior court denied Jimerson's motion to enforce the settlement agreement on the grounds that the agreement was unenforceable because it violated ANCSA's prohibition on alienation.

Jimerson appeals this denial.

III. DISCUSSION

We have adopted the Restatement principle that "[a] promise or other term of an agreement is unenforceable on grounds of public policy if legislation provides that it is unenforceable . . . . " This court has "no power, either in law or in equity, to enforce an agreement which directly contravenes a legislative enactment."

The issue before this court is whether the transaction contemplated by the settlement agreement is prohibited by ANCSA. The settlement agreement transferred a portion of TNC's remaining land to a new corporation and then allowed "dissenting shareholders" to "transfer their shares of Tetlin Native Corporation ANCSA stock back to the corporation in exchange for shares in the new corporation."

When Congress enumerates exceptions to a rule, we can infer that no other exceptions apply. Section 7(h)1.c. lists three exceptions that allow stock to be transferred to a Native or a descendent of a Native: 1. pursuant to a court decree

of separation, divorce, or child support, 2. if the stock limits the holder's ability to practice his or her profession, or 3. as an inter vivos gift to certain relatives. Section 7(h)2. permits shares to escheat to the corporation if the holder has no heirs, and permits a corporation to repurchase shares transferred by the laws of intestate succession to a person who is not a Native or descendant of a Native. The transaction contemplated by the settlement agreement does not fall within any of these exceptions. We therefore infer that no exception applies for transfer of ANCSA stock back to a Native corporation in exchange for stock in a newly created corporation.

* * *

We AFFIRM the superior court's denial of Jimerson's motion for enforcement of the settlement agreement.

Think of a violation of law or public policy in terms of a gambling casino. Special laws need to be passed in order to authorize the existence of a casino, so if one enters into a contract to build a casino in a jurisdiction where casinos are illegal, the contract is likely unenforceable.

2. Public Policy Issues

Contracts that violate public policy present the same issues as those that violate the law and are unenforceable for the same reason. The challenging part about the violation of public policy standard is knowing when such violations will arise. Like many common law instances, there may not be a preexisting law that a contract would clearly violate. Instead, the "agreement" between the parties raises questions that make courts uncomfortable and therefore unwilling to enforce for "public policy" reasons. Because court decisions become law, when a court finds that a contract violates public policy, that violation becomes a violation of the law itself and the decision becomes precedent for subsequent cases. Three examples of attempted contracts that may violate public policy are **unconscionable contracts, covenants not to compete, and waivers of liability.**

a. Unconscionability

Beginning in the 1960s and marked by the adoption of adhesion analysis in *Steven v. Fidelity & Casualty Co.*, 58 Cal.2d 862 (1962), courts faced litigation where a company (for example, Sears) was attempting to enforce a contract. The contract in this benchmark case was between the company and an individual who was buying a home appliance, such as a washer or dryer. Many of the customers purchasing the appliance were poorly educated immigrants who were often illiterate and unable to speak or write English. They also bought the appliance on an installment basis, so that they paid a set amount each month. The contracts provided that if the customer missed a payment, the interest rate on the outstanding balance would rise significantly. As a result, the customer was often unable to continue to pay the loan and the appliance was eventually seized by the company.

In reaction, courts developed the idea of "unconscionability." In other words, the terms of the contract so shocked the conscience as to make them unenforceable. More specifically, the standards developed by the court were that if there were grossly unequal bargaining positions and the terms of the contract were so one-sided and unfair as to shock the conscience, the court may view the objectionable terms of the contract as unenforceable. Restatement § 208 allows courts to refuse to enforce unconscionable contracts in part or in whole.

It is worth noting that it is very unlikely that someone reading this book would be in a position to claim that they have been so unfairly treated by a company that they can trigger the unconscionability doctrine. One reason is that students in a college or graduate school are not poor and illiterate consumers unable to read the terms. While it is true that a student (or a professor!) has limited bargaining potential compared to Microsoft, they can still read the contract, find a lawyer or walk away from unfair terms.

b. Covenants Not to Compete

Courts take a balancing approach to covenants not to compete, also known as **non-compete clauses**. The idea behind a covenant not to compete is that a company spends time and money training employees or, in a takeover case, may be spending money to buy out another company. The employers do not want an employee to take the knowledge and training they have gained, move to a competitor, and compete. Thus, companies will include a provision in the employee's contract that says the employee is precluded from taking another job with a competing firm for a period of time. The most attractive new employer for an employee, of course, is one that values exactly the experience and knowledge learned by being in the same or similar industry, and so these covenants can unexpectedly inhibit mobility.

Courts recognize the property interest companies have in investing in their employees and willenforce these covenants. They also recognize the importance of freedom of contract, including the freedom to work with whomever one wants to work. So courts will evaluate these covenants on the basis of geographical and time restrictions that prevent an employee from working elsewhere. These considerations had one set of applications prior to the Internet and its undermining of geographic significance; today, there is another set of considerations that reflect the realities of an Internet-influenced world. The following case looks at this balance between freedom of employees to move to new positions and the property rights of companies to protect their investments and secrets.

Market*Access Int'l, Inc. et al., v. KMD Media, LLC

72 Va.Cir. 355 (2006)

JONATHAN C. THACHER, CIRCUIT COURT JUDGE.

* * *

Plaintiff Market Access is an Arlington-based company that provides marketing, trade association conference planning, and training seminars for government and private industry personnel in the field of homeland security. Plaintiff Homeland Defense Journal, Inc. (HDJI) produces and distributes trade publications relating to homeland security and information technology security.

Market Access contracted with Defendant Pro-Media to sell advertising space in its publications. Under this agreement, Pro-Media agreed not to compete with the Plaintiff by selling or promoting publications that competed with Market Access' publications. The agreement also included a non-disclosure provision preventing Pro-Media from disclosing Market Access' proprietary client database.

Plaintiffs allege that Defendant Silverberg, who was hired to be the managing editor of Homeland Defense Journal, conspired with Market Access consultant Wandres, Pro-Media, and others to create a competing publication to Market Access' planned homeland security newsletter, alternatively called *Homeland Security Today* or *HSToday*. As part of the alleged conspiracy, Plaintiffs contend that the Defendants organized Defendant KMD as a means of publishing a print magazine called *HSToday* and a web site bearing the same name.

Count II of Plaintiff's Second Amended Motion for Judgment alleges Breach of Contract. Plaintiffs allege that Defendant Pro-Media breached its duties under the non-competition portion of its agreement with Market Access. The relevant non-compete language contained in the parties agreement is as follows:

> "Under this agreement, Sales Representative shall not compete with Company, directly or indirectly in the sale or promotion of products that directly compete with Company's existing publication, *Homeland Defense Journal*, for one year following the termination of this agreement . . . . Company acknowledges that the primary business area of Sales Representative is the representation of several military publications (both in the U.S. and abroad),

> and that Sales Representative will continue to represent publications of this nature during the scope of this agreement. . . ."

Defendant Pro-Media demurrers on the grounds that the non-compete agreement is unenforceable as a matter of law.

* * *

In considering whether non-competition agreements are enforceable as a matter of law the Virginia Supreme Court has ruled that such an agreement may be enforced if the agreement is 1. narrowly drawn to protect an employer's business interest, is 2. not unduly burdensome on an employee's ability to earn a living, and 3. is not against public policy. In Virginia, non-competition agreements are viewed as disfavored restraints on trade and thus the burden of proof that the agreement is reasonable and any ambiguities in the agreement are construed against the party seeking to enforce the agreement. Central to the analysis considering the reasonableness of these agreements is whether there are reasonable limits on duration, geographic area and whether the scope of the restrictions is narrowly tailored to protect the employer's interest. Any non-competition agreement that is overbroad is unenforceable as a matter of law.

* * *

Virginia courts are hesitant to enforce non-competition agreements that essentially prohibit a person from seeking employment in his or her chosen field. For that reason, many non-competition agreements contain geographical provisions limiting the area where the employee is not permitted to seek competing work to the area the business can expect to "reach." Where a business is regional in scope this is relatively easy, but with the advent of the Internet and the nationalization of everything from products to ideas, this has become substantially more difficult. *Homeland Defense Journal* holds itself out as a national publication, and indeed homeland security itself is an issue that often lends itself to discussion on the national level.

Pro-Media argues that the lack of any geographic limitation renders the non-competition agreement unenforceable as a matter of law because it essentially infers a worldwide restriction. The analysis conducted by the Virginia Supreme Court in the *Omniplex, Motion Control, and Simmons* cases does not support this contention. While in each of these cases the lack of geographic limitations was a part of the analysis, it was by no means solely determinative of the issue of whether the agreements were enforceable as a matter of law.

The Virginia Supreme Court has upheld non-competition agreements that are narrowly-drawn even when they encompass a larger geographic area. In *Blue Ridge Anesthesia & Critical Care, Inc. v. Gidick*, 239 Va. 369 (1990), a non- competition agreement that spanned four states—Virginia, North Carolina, West Virginia, and Maryland, as well as the District of Columbia—was not considered overbroad. The plaintiff company sold and serviced critical care and anesthesia equipment in that region and the Court noted that the agreement did not prohibit former employees from selling similar equipment outside the designated territory, nor did it prohibit the former employees from selling different medical equipment within the company's territory.

In *Roanoke Engineering Sales Co. v. Rosenbaum*, 223 Va. 548 (1982), the Virginia Supreme Court held that a three-year, multi-state non-competition agreement was not overbroad because the former employee had knowledge of the employer's business interests in all its branches. The Court said the agreement was "coterminous" with the territory in which the firm did business and was therefore not overbroad.

What can be garnered from the analysis of each of these cases is that when the competition at issue is direct and the agreements are narrowly drawn to prohibit such direct competition the non-competition agreements are more likely to be enforceable.

While the language of the non-competition agreement at issue clearly does not contain language limiting the geographic scope of the agreement, the language of the agreement does limit the duration of the non-compete agreement to one year and limits the prohibited activities to those in direct competition with *Homeland Defense Journal.*

"WHEN THE COMPETITION at issue is direct and the agreements are narrowly drawn to prohibit such direct competition the non-competition agreements are more likely to be enforceable."

The mere fact that there is no geographic limitation is not fatal to the enforceability of the non-compete agreement between Market Access and Pro-Media. The language of the agreement contemplates Pro-Media's continued relationships with other military publications and only specifically Pro-Media's activities to those that would directly compete with Market Access' *Homeland Defense Journal* publication. Thus it does not prohibit Pro-Media from continuing to work in its field in a manner the Virginia Supreme Court found objectionable in *Omniplex* or *Motion Control*. Nor does the one year limitation on direct competition with *Homeland Defense Journal* appear unreasonable considering the Court's analysis in *Rosenbaum*. The terms of the non-competition agreement at issue appear to be narrowly tailored to protect Market Access' legitimate business interests while not prohibiting Pro-Media from competing in its chosen field. The non-compete agreement at issue also appears to be narrowly tailored so that it does not offend public policy.

CONCLUSION

The Court disagrees with the contention that the non-competition agreement between Market Access and Pro-Media is unenforceable as a matter of law. Therefore Pro-Media's Demurrer to Count II alleging Breach of Contract [non-compete agreements] by Pro-Media is overruled. Attached to this opinion is an order reflecting the Court's ruling.

E. OTHER ISSUES

Even if a contract is valid—that is, it complies with all the above steps—its enforceability may still be in question. Some agreements must be in writing because of the Statute of Frauds. Even if a contract does not have to be in writing, issues can arise when a contract is, in fact, put into writing and the parties indicate that it is meant to be a final agreement. This prohibition on looking to evidence outside of the written document is known as the **parol evidence rule**.

I. Statute of Frauds

The rationale behind the Statute of Frauds was that the subject matter of some contracts was so important—and so important to protect from fraudulent activities—so as to require these contracts to be in writing. The Statute of Frauds served two related functions: an evidentiary and a commemorative role. Requiring writings for certain transactions, like those for the sale of land, gave the court and the parties the ability to prove the existence of a contract without resorting to implied or oral contracts. Related is the notion that some transactions are so important, or may become effective at such a distant time, that courts have decided they must specifically impress the importance of obligations on the parties by requiring a writing.[7]

---

7 Chapter 5, Sections 100 through 124, cover the Statute of Frauds; § 100 defines the scope of the statute:

1. The following classes of contracts are subject to a statute, commonly called the Statute of Frauds, forbidding enforcement unless there is a written memorandum or an applicable exception:
    a. a contract of an executor or administrator to answer for a duty of his decedent (the executor-administrator provision);
    b. a contract to answer for the duty of another (the suretyship provision);
    c. a contract made upon consideration of marriage (the marriage provision);
    d. a contract for the sale of an interest in land (the land contract provision);
    e. a contract that is not to be performed within one year from the making thereof (the one-year provision).
2. The following classes of contracts, which were traditionally subject to the Statute of Frauds, are now governed by Statute of Frauds provisions of the Uniform Commercial Code:
    a. a contract for the sale of goods for the price of $500 or more (Uniform Commercial Code § 2–201);
    b. a contract for the sale of securities (Uniform Commercial Code § 8–319);
    c. a contract for the sale of personal property not otherwise covered, to the extent of enforcement by way of action or defense beyond $5,000 in amount or value of remedy (Uniform Commercial Code § 1–206).
3. In addition the Uniform Commercial Code requires a writing signed by the debtor for an agreement which creates or provides for a security interest in personal property or fixtures not in the possession of the secured party.
4. Statutes in most states provide that no acknowledgment or promise is sufficient evidence of a new or continuing contract to take a case out of the operation of a statute of limitations unless made in some writing

a. Real Estate Related

Real estate is the main focus of the application of the Statute of Frauds. Any transfer of real estate requires that the contract be in writing. This applies, of course, to a conveyance of ownership from one person to the other, which is called a **transfer of fee simple ownership.** It is nearly impossible to sell or buy real estate outright without recording the transaction in writing. If one has a mortgage on the property, any lender will insist that the mortgagor's right to the property be in writing; otherwise the mortgagee's security interest is in jeopardy. One cannot record any ownership of the real estate without a writing; indeed, a **deed** is a writing necessary in order for land ownership to be recorded in a government office. Without such a recording, one's ownership interest would be in jeopardy. **Leases** are more ambiguous in nature and subject to the Statute of Frauds, but many leases are informal, oral agreements that are never reduced to writing. The following is a contemporary, but typical, Statute of Frauds and real estate analysis.

Ayalla v. Southridge Presbyterian Church

37 Kan.App.2d 312, 152 P.3d 670 (2007)

Green, P.J.

* * *

Ayalla sued Southridge Presbyterian for breach of contract. Ayalla set forth the following allegations in support of her claim.

Southridge Presbyterian, owner of a residential home, offered to sell it for the amount of $134,500. On April 25, 2005, Ayalla viewed the home. Ayalla made a written offer to purchase the home for $130,000 on April 26, 2005. The written offer was made on a residential real estate sale contract form furnished by Southridge Presbyterian's real estate agent, Jim Henderson. Ayalla gave Henderson a check for $1,000 as an earnest money deposit. Henderson later negotiated the closing costs with Mike Pyper, Ayalla's mortgage broker.

On April 28, 2005, Henderson orally notified Pyper that Southridge Presbyterian had accepted Ayalla's offer. Pyper left a message with Ayalla's nephew regarding Southridge Presbyterian's acceptance. The following day, Henderson orally told

signed by the party to be charged, but that the statute does not alter the effect of any payment of principal or interest.

5. In many states other classes of contracts are subject to a requirement of a writing.

Ayalla personally of Southridge Presbyterian's acceptance. Henderson and Ayalla agreed to meet on May 1, 2005, to complete the paperwork, and Ayalla made plans to take that day off work. Based on Southridge Presbyterian's oral acceptance, Ayalla scheduled a home inspection to take place on May 2 or 3.

Ayalla and her friends and family gathered together on May 1 to celebrate. Before her scheduled meeting with Henderson, however, he called and told Ayalla that Southridge Presbyterian had accepted a higher offer of $142,500 from the Hamiltons.

Ayalla alleged that this event caused anguish and monetary damages in the amount of $12,900. Ayalla's damages calculation consisted of $12,500 for the loss of the benefit of her bargain, $200 for her lost wages on May 1, and $200 for her legal expenses. In her petition, Ayalla requested a preliminary injunction, specific performance of the contract, restitution based on Southridge Presbyterian's unjust enrichment, monetary damages in the amount of $12,900, and other such relief the court deemed appropriate.

Following the filing of Ayalla's petition, Southridge Presbyterian moved to dismiss Ayalla's action based on the statute of frauds. Ayalla alleged in her answer to Southridge Presbyterian's motion to dismiss that the sale contract, which was prepared and signed by Henderson on behalf of Southridge Presbyterian, was a sufficient memorandum to satisfy the statute of frauds. Ayalla further alleged that Southridge Presbyterian engaged in fraud when it failed to disclose Ayalla's accepted offer to the Hamiltons. The trial court denied the motion due to the existence of outstanding discovery.

* * *

STATUTE OF FRAUDS

Ayalla asserts two main theories in support of her argument regarding the statute of frauds: 1. that an enforceable agreement existed between herself and Southridge Presbyterian based on Henderson's oral acceptance of her written offer; and 2. that the sale contract, which was signed by Henderson, was sufficient to satisfy the statute of frauds.

Southridge Presbyterian contends that no written agreement existed between itself and Ayalla for the sale of the real estate; therefore, the statute of frauds precludes relief.

Enacted to prevent fraud and injustice, the statute of frauds requires that an enforceable contract for the sale of real estate be in writing and signed by the party against whom enforcement is sought.

* * *

Based on the statute of frauds, the trial court determined that no enforceable agreement existed between the parties. The court stated the following:

> "[T]here is no evidence of any contract ever signed by anyone on behalf of Southridge Presbyterian Church to sell [Ayalla] that property . . . . [Henderson's] signature did not say that Southridge Presbyterian was making any specific offer to [Ayalla] to sell the property. All it did was say that this form contract which is a pre-printed form is a form approved by the Kansas City Regional Association of Realtors and that Remax Realty who had printed up this document had not changed it from the form contract that had been approved."

The trial court continued, "[t]he form [contract] was never signed by anyone representing Southridge Presbyterian. Accordingly[,] it has not been signed by the party against whom it is to be charged."

* * *

Because Southridge Presbyterian has asserted the defense of the statute of frauds, the only material fact is whether the parties' alleged agreement was evidenced by a writing signed by Southridge Presbyterian. Ayalla admitted that Henderson's signature on the sale contract did not evidence Southridge Presbyterian's agreement to sell her the house. Moreover, Ayalla failed to show that Henderson was properly authorized by Southridge Presbyterian to act in the capacity of the seller. Further, Ayalla conceded that she did not receive a signed contract from Southridge Presbyterian. As a result, the only material fact is not in dispute.

Next, we turn to the question of whether Southridge Presbyterian was entitled to judgment as a matter of law. Because the issue of whether an alleged contract satisfies the statute of frauds involves the interpretation of a statute, this court's review is unlimited.

Citing *Van Dyke v. Glover* (1996), Ayalla first asserts that the oral acceptance of a written offer satisfies the statute of frauds. In *Van Dyke*, however, the written offer was made and signed by the party to be charged. Here, the written offer was made by Ayalla and was never signed by Southridge Presbyterian. The essential point in the trial court's ruling was the absence of a memorandum signed by Southridge Presbyterian as the party against whom Ayalla was seeking enforcement of the alleged oral agreement. As a result, *Van Dyke* does not support Ayalla's position.

Ayalla also argues that parties may bind themselves to an enforceable contract even though they contemplate the future execution of a formal instrument as evidence of their agreement. * * *

These cases do not aid Ayalla because they do not negate the requirement that an agreement for the sale of real estate must be evidenced by a writing signed by the party to be charged. Rather, the principle and cases simply indicate that under some circumstances, parties may bind themselves to an enforceable contract before they reduce their agreement to a formal instrument. In two of the cases cited by Ayalla, this principle was applicable when the parties had created a signed memorandum of the agreement but contemplated the future creation of a more formal instrument. In the third case cited by Ayalla, the statute of frauds was not applicable to the transaction. In the last case cited, the court held that the oral contract was *not* enforceable because it had not been reduced to a signed writing.

Ayalla next argues that the sale contract, signed by Henderson, was sufficient to satisfy the statute of frauds. According to Ayalla, the sale contract satisfies the writing requirement, and Henderson's signature satisfies the requirement that the writing be signed by the party to be charged.

The trial court correctly explained to Ayalla that Henderson's signature on the sale contract did not satisfy the signature requirement of the statute of frauds. As the trial court noted, Henderson signed the sale contract in a box that was designed to certify the form as containing, without addition or deletion, the language approved by the Kansas City Regional Association of Realtors. Notably, Henderson signed the sale contract before he had even informed Southridge Presbyterian of Ayalla's offer. Henderson's signature was not meant to be an acceptance of Ayalla's offer but simply a certification that the form was an approved real estate contract form.

Ayalla also argues in her brief that her actions indicate a contract was formed and cites *Reznik v. McKee, Trustee*, (1975), for the principle that a court may determine the existence and terms of a contract based on a combination of written instruments and the parties' actions in connection with the writings. The trial court ruled that no enforceable agreement existed between Ayalla and Southridge Presbyterian because the signature requirement of the statute of frauds had not been satisfied. This argument by Ayalla, therefore, does not advance her position because it does not negate the absence of a writing signed by Southridge Presbyterian.

It is important to remember that contracts may not be enforced because they do not comply with the Statute of Fraud. Yet many contracts are successfully completed even though they violate the formal provisions of the Statute of Frauds. Why is this case? This is a question that pertains to many issues in this chapter. Many contracts are successfully completed even though they violate contract rules. Contracts are made with minors and people with disabilities all the time, but if everyone is happy with the contract—or if no one raises a complaint if they are unhappy—then the violation of the contract never comes before a court to address. Thus, while a person may raise the Statute of Frauds as a violation that might void a contract, or make it unenforceable, if no one objects to the violation, then, to use a basketball term, no harm no foul.

To give another example, some realtors are very meticulous in making sure that all of their contracts dot every "i" and cross every "t". Yet different areas of the country may be quite lax about the formalities. As long as the parties perform the contracts and/or successfully work out disagreements, then the Statute of Frauds does not come into play. But if there is an argument that cannot be resolved, then the State of Frauds can stand as a significant legal issue the parties must confront.

b. Employment Contracts

The Statute of Frauds also applies to two other kinds of cases. The first are employment contracts that cannot be performed in less than a year. The application of this rule can be counterintuitive. The Statute of Frauds requirement does not apply to a contract "for life" because it is possible for the contract to be performed within one year (because the employee could die within a year). A contract for a day less than a year also does not apply because the time period specified is, by definition, less than a year. However, a contract for two years would be subject to the Statute of Frauds. Thus, if a contract for services is to extend for more than one year, it needs to be in writing to be enforceable.

For example, a business may contract with an accounting firm to do the business's audit for three years. Assuming there are multiple accountants in the accounting firm (and the likelihood of all of them dying within a year remote), then the service contract is for more than one year and needs to be in writing. However if the business asks the same firm to do its taxes, which would be performed within one year because returns needs to be filed annually, then the contract does not have to be in writing. Or if the business contracted with a single accountant to do its taxes (even with the anticipation that this arrangement may extend over decades) it also would not have to be in writing because that (single) accountant could die within the year. In this case, the contract would not have to be in writing to be enforceable.

The following cases look at Statute of Frauds issues and this idea of specifying the length of duration for a services contract.

Parker v. Crider Poultry Inc.

275 Ga. 361, 565 S.E.2d 797 (2002)

Benham, Justice.

Appellant Jeffrey Parker formerly served as president and chief executive officer of appellees Crider, Inc., and Crider Poultry. In May 1998, while serving in those positions, Parker sent a letter resigning his positions effective August 1998. The Crider corporations filed suit against him seeking repayment of a bonus advanced to Parker and damages for an alleged breach of fiduciary duty. Parker filed a counterclaim in which he claimed appellees had breached his employment agreement by refusing to honor the three-month notice period set out in the parties' agreement by either permitting him to work for the three months between the date of his notice and the effective date of his resignation, or by paying him his salary for the three-month period. The trial court granted partial summary judgment to appellees on the counterclaim and the Court of Appeals affirmed the trial court's action. We granted Parker's petition for a writ of certiorari to the Court of Appeals, asking whether the Court of Appeals erred when it held that Parker could not recover on his claim for breach of the notice provision.

1. Both the trial court and the Court of Appeals based their judgments on the interplay between the Statute of Frauds[8] and a letter drafted and signed by W.A. Crider, Jr., on behalf of the Crider corporations, and counter-signed by appellant Parker. The letter set forth the base salary to be paid Parker, the formula for computing an incentive bonus, appellant's title and starting date, other benefits, and provided "Three months notice for either party." Citing *Gatins v. NCR Corp.*, 180 Ga.App. 595 (1986), the trial court determined that appellant's claim failed because the letter agreement did not comply with the Statute of Frauds since "a writing with an indefinite term does not comply with the statute." The Court of Appeals affirmed the trial court's judgment on the ground that the letter agreement was a contract that the Statute of Frauds required to be in writing because "the performance of [Parker's] employment agreement was not to be completed within one year" since he had submitted his letter of resignation more than two years after he had started working for Crider. Our review of the law leads us to conclude that both courts erred in their determination that the employment agreement between Parker and the Crider corporations fell within the Statute of Frauds.

The letter agreement did not state the duration of the term of employment. An employment contract containing no definite term of employment is terminable at the will of either party. A contract of employment of indefinite duration does not fall within the Statute of Frauds. This is so because, at its inception, a contract of employment for an indefinite duration is an agreement capable of being performed within one year, and the possibility of performance of the contract within one year is sufficient to remove it from the Statute of Frauds. The number of years the parties operate under an employment contract of indefinite duration does not affect the applicability of the Statute of Frauds. Thus, the Court of Appeals erred when it determined that the employment agreement relied upon by Parker was within the Statute of Frauds because Parker had completed over a year of employment under the contract before the dispute arose. The trial court misplaced its reliance when it cited Gatins because that case is distinguishable in that the contracts sought to be enforced therein were not to be performed within one year of their making and

---

8 The Statute of Frauds is codified at OCGA § 13-5-30 and provides that certain types of obligations must be in writing and signed by the party to be charged in order for the obligation to be binding on the promisor. The obligation pertinent to the case at bar is found in subsection (5) of the statute: "Any agreement that is not to be performed within one year from the making thereof" must be in writing and signed by the party to be charged in order to be binding on the promisor.

therefore had to be in writing under the Statute of Frauds. When a contract is required to be in writing, the writings relied upon must contain the entire agreement.

2. Because of their separate determinations that the Statute of Frauds was applicable to Parker's employment agreement, neither the trial court nor the Court of Appeals addressed the merits of Parker's assertion that the Crider corporations breached the employment agreement when they did not adhere to the three-months' notice provision. While an employee with an employment agreement of indefinite duration may not successfully pursue a wrongful termination claim upon termination of employment, the employee has a claim for breach of contract if the employer had agreed to give notice of termination but did not. In the case at bar, Parker sent a letter to W.A. Crider, Jr., on May 7, 1998, informing Crider that

> This serves as my written notice of my intention to exercise, under our agreement, my option to resign my position by providing three months notice to you. Therefore, I resign as President/CEO of Crider, Inc. and Crider Poultry, Inc. ninety days from this date or on Wednesday, August 5, 1998.

In his deposition, Parker testified that he recognized Crider had the authority to determine whether Parker worked during the three-month period between notice and resignation, that Crider accepted the resignation immediately on May 7, and that Parker did not return to work at Crider during the three-month period. It is unclear whether Parker's failure to work at Crider during the notice period was due to the fact that Crider accepted the notice of resignation and made it effective on the day of receipt, thereby effectively terminating Parker's employment without giving the required three months' notice, or whether Parker made the decision not to report to work for the three-month period, thereby effectively terminating his employment without giving the required three-months' notice. In light of the unresolved factual issue, summary judgment was inappropriate, making erroneous both the trial court's grant of summary judgment to appellees on Parker's counterclaim, and the Court of Appeals' affirmance of that judgment.

Judgment reversed.

All the Justices concur, except FLETCHER, C.J., who concurs in the judgment only in Division 2.

---

c. Suretyship

The other, additional kind of case is **suretyship**. Today, this might be more commonly known as co-signing a loan for another person. Anytime a person is obligating himself to pay the debt of another, it must be in writing in order to be enforceable. Promises to repay a debt of another person also need to be in writing because courts want there to be strong evidence of a person undertaking that kind of obligation. The following case looks at interplay between suretyship and the Statute of Frauds.

Webb Manufacturing Co. v. Sinoff

449 Pa.Super. 534, 674 A.2d 723 (1996)

HUDOCK, JUDGE:

* * *

This case commenced on September 30, 1994 when Webb Manufacturing Company (Webb) filed a complaint alleging that Brad Sinoff and Larry Sinoff (Sinoffs), on behalf of Apple Marketing, entered a contract to purchase goods and services. Webb averred that Sinoffs "in their capacity as principles [sic] of Apple Marketing" guaranteed to pay for the goods and services supplied by Webb in the event that Apple Marketing could not pay for them. Webb further averred that Sinoffs guaranteed the payment for the goods and services to induce Webb to enter such contract. Webb claimed that without Sinoffs' personal guarantee, it would not have agreed to ship the goods to Apple Marketing.

On April 7, 1995, Sinoffs filed preliminary objections in the nature of a demurrer claiming that Webb's claim was barred by the Statute of Frauds. Sinoffs also claimed that Webb could not recover against them individually since they conspicuously entered the contract in their capacity as agents of Apple Marketing.

* * *

The trial court concluded that Webb could not recover from Sinoffs in their personal capacity because it "failed to produce any written promise by [Sinoffs] to pay the debt of Apple Marketing[ ]" and thus failed to meet the requirements of the Statute of Frauds. Without evidence that Sinoffs executed a written agreement to personally answer for the debt of Apple Marketing, the trial court concluded that Webb's breach of contract claim was unenforceable under the Statute of Frauds.

The pertinent provision of the Pennsylvania Statute of Frauds is found at 33 P.S. section 3, which provides in pertinent part:

> No action shall be brought . . . whereby to charge the defendant, upon any special promise, to answer for the debt or default of another, unless the agreement upon which such action shall be brought, or some memorandum

> or note thereof, shall be in writing, and signed by the party to be charged therewith, or some other person by him authorized.

We have previously explained the purpose of this rule:

> Promises to pay the debt of another must be in writing for at least two reasons. The first is *evidentiary*. The second, *cautionary*.
>
> Like other provisions of the statute [of frauds], the suretyship provision serves an evidentiary function. Indeed, Williston suggested that the circumstance that 'the promisor has received no benefit from the transaction ... may make perjury more likely, because while in the case of one who has received something the circumstances themselves which are capable of proof show probable liability, in the case of a guaranty nothing but the promise is of evidentiary value.' Furthermore, though in many instances the surety is paid by the principal for his undertaking, in others the surety's motivation is purely gratuitous and, 'as the lack of any benefit received by the guarantor increases the hardship of his being called upon to pay, it also increases the importance of being very sure that he is justly charged.'
>
> In addition to its evidentiary role, the provision serves a cautionary function. By bringing home to the prospective surety the significance of his act, it guards against ill-considered action. Otherwise, he might lightly undertake the engagement, unwisely assuming that there is only a remote possibility that the principal will not perform his duty ....
>
> * * *

In cases where the promisor is a shareholder or officer of a corporation whose debt he has personally guaranteed, courts consider the percentage of the shareholder/guarantor's corporate ownership as a significant, although not sole criteria. For example, in *Acme Equipment Company Inc. v. Allegheny Steel Corporation*, 207 Pa.Super. 436 (1966), Rudy Valentino, the President and owner of 25% of Allegheny Steel Corporation, orally guaranteed to Acme Equipment Company that he would pay the debt incurred by Allegheny. When Acme attempted to enforce the oral guarantee, the trial court entered a compulsory nonsuit in favor of Valentino since the promise fell within the Statute of Frauds. On appeal, this Court examined whether Valentino made the promise for his own pecuniary interest. We explained:

> Although the [Statute of Frauds] does not apply if the main object of the promisor is to serve his own pecuniary or business purpose, ... the statute is not rendered inapplicable merely because a stockholder may indirectly

> receive some gain when he promises to pay the debt of a corporation. In *Bayard v. Pennsylvania Knitting Mills Corp.*, 290 Pa. 79, 84 (1927), the Supreme Court stated: "Ordinarily, the interest which a stockholder has is not individual, for he cannot be held for the corporate debts, and, if a promise to indemnify its creditor is made, the statute of frauds applies. * * * The mere fact that such person is concerned in promoting the financial success of the company is not sufficient to justify the treating of the promise of guaranty as an original undertaking. * * * "

* * *

In the present case the trial court did not consider whether the Sinoffs made the alleged oral guarantee for their own pecuniary or business ends. The court concluded that Webb admitted in paragraph 8 of its complaint that it contracted with Apple Marketing and not Sinoffs in their individual capacity. Paragraph 8 of Webb's complaint read:

> 8. [Appellees] Larry Sinoff and Brad Sinoff, in their capacity as principles [sic] of Apple Marketing, guaranteed the above-referenced bill in the event that Apple Marketing did not pay for said goods and/or services as was agreed. [Court's emphasis]

The trial court concluded that the "leading object" exception did not apply as a matter of law since Webb averred in paragraph eight that Sinoffs acted in their capacity as principals of Apple Marketing.

* * *

After examining the complaint in its entirety, we find Webb pled sufficient facts to raise the "leading object" exception to the Statute of Frauds, thus preventing the entry of a demurrer. Webb averred that Sinoffs made the guarantee "in the event that Apple Marketing did not pay for said goods and/or services as was agreed." Webb further averred that: "[Sinoffs] guaranteed the above-referenced bill in order to induce [Appellant] Webb Manufacturing to sell said goods and/or services to Apple Marketing." Cognizant of the standard that a demurrer may only be sustained when it is clear and free from doubt that the law will not permit recovery by the plaintiff upon the facts averred in the complaint, and that all doubts must be resolved against granting the demurrer, we find that the trial court erred in granting Sinoffs' demurrer. Accepting as true Webb's averment that it would not have sold Apple Marketing goods and services without Sinoffs' personal guarantee, Webb asserted sufficient facts to raise the "leading object" exception to the Statute of Frauds. If further facts are adduced when the parties replead or during discovery or at trial which prove that

Sinoffs guaranteed Apple Marketing's debts for their personal benefit, Webb may prevent the lack of a written agreement and the Statute of Frauds from barring its ability to enforce the oral agreement. We find the facts of *Grant R. Wright, Inc. v. Haworth Energy Resources, Inc.*, (1984), analogous.

* * *

Order *reversed*. Case remanded for further proceedings consistent with this opinion. Jurisdiction is relinquished.

[JAMIESON, JUDGE, concurring omitted.]

---

2. Parol Evidence Rule

In most contracts, the parties negotiate before reaching a final agreement. If a dispute arises, there can sometimes be ambiguity about what was actually agreed upon and what may have been discussed. Not all of those negotiations may be reflected in the final agreement, but if the agreement is in writing and states that all of the terms of the contract are limited to what is stated in the final agreement, then the parol evidence rule is triggered. This Rule says that only the terms in writing control the agreement between the parties and outside evidence cannot be introduced to indicate any additional terms negotiated between the parties.

Here is how the Restatement (§ 213) describes the rule:

§ 213: Effect of Integrated Agreement on Prior Agreements (Parol Evidence Rule)

1. A binding integrated agreement discharges prior agreements to the extent that it is inconsistent with them.

2. A binding completely integrated agreement discharges prior agreements to the extent that they are within its scope.

3. An integrated agreement that is not binding or that is voidable and avoided does not discharge a prior agreement. But an integrated agreement, even though not binding, may be effective to render inoperative a term which would have been part of the agreement if it had not been integrated.

For example, suppose you are buying a car. After haggling with the dealer, you are ready to sign the agreement to buy the car. That written contract contains a statement that the agreement constitutes the entire meeting of the minds between the parties. But you can't resist trying to add in one more item to "seal the deal." So you get the salesperson to agree to add in free car servicing for a period of three years. A few months later, you take your car to the dealer's service wing to ask for a free oil change and they refuse because it was not part of the agreement. The salesperson feigns ignorance. The argument escalates and you end up in court. Who will win?

According to the parol evidence rule, the dealer probably wins because you are trying to enforce a term that, pursuant to the contract you signed, is not in a contract that constitutes the entire agreement between the parties. Thus, the parol evidence rule has real consequences in contract disputes.

The next case combines a discussion of parol evidence with the role of clarifying testimony that might shed light on what the parties really did agree to. At common law, it was extremely difficult to introduce parol evidence when the contract lacked ambiguous language. As the following case shows, courts have progressively treated this presumption more leniently.

Lapierre v. Cabral

122 N.H. 301, 444 A.2d 522 (1982)

King, Chief Justice.

The issues presented in this case are whether the trial court erred in concluding that the contract between the plaintiff and a third party was assignable to the defendant and in refusing to admit parol evidence regarding possible financing conditions applicable to the plaintiff's and the defendant's contract of assignment. While we rule that the court should have admitted parol evidence, we find that the defendant did not sustain his burden of proof, and therefore, we affirm.

The plaintiff, Roland Lapierre, is a real estate developer in Nashua, New Hampshire, and the defendant, Richard Cabral, was also extensively engaged in the real estate business for many years.

On November 10, 1977, Lapierre and Guerrette Real Estate, Inc. of Nashua (Guerrette) entered into a written agreement in which Guerrette gave Lapierre an option to purchase land and buildings located on Main Street in Nashua for $200,000, with a schedule of installment payments to be secured by a first mortgage on the Main Street property. The contract was subject to an existing lease with Cabral which was to expire on July 8, 1979. As lessee, Cabral had expended about $15,000 on leasehold improvements that could not be taken to any other location.

Simultaneously with the execution of the option to purchase, Guerrette and Lapierre entered into a purchase-and-sale agreement for the same property. On July 17, 1978, the parties amended the option agreement, extending the period for payments and providing for the subordination of the mortgage to a purchase money or development mortgage which Lapierre placed on the property.

By instrument dated October 16, 1978, Lapierre assigned his option to purchase the Main Street property as well as two deposits totaling $15,000 he had already paid to Guerrette to Cabral. The assignment of the option contract provided that the closing was to take place on or before October 16, 1978. Cabral would then have the obligation to pay Lapierre the sum of $25,000. Under the agreement, Cabral would have no right to assign the option without the written consent of Lapierre. Additionally, the writing included a clause stating that the instrument represented all agreements between the parties.

On April 9, 1979, Guerrette and Lapierre executed a further amendment to the purchase-and-sale agreement which increased the payment at closing from $100,000 to $150,000, extended the term to pay off the mortgage and increased the amount of the interest.

Lapierre made demands upon Cabral in April 1979, for the $25,000, but no payment was made, and at the expiration of the option on July 8, 1979, the $15,000 paid by Lapierre to Guerrette was forfeited. Both Lapierre and Cabral were aware that the option to purchase the real estate had to be exercised by June 8, 1979. Cabral never exercised the option, and Lapierre said he found out that Cabral was not going through with the deal when Cabral leased space elsewhere. Consequently, Lapierre brought an action against Cabral for breach of their assignment contract. The Master (*Margaret Q. Flynn*, Esq.) found for the plaintiff, and her finding was approved by the Superior Court (*Bean*, J.).

At trial, the defendant alleged that because the plaintiff had arranged all the financing terms for the purchase of the property with Guerrette, that Guerrette had relied on the plaintiff's credit, thereby making the option personal to the plaintiff and not assignable to the defendant. The master found that the option was assignable, and we agree.

The option contract between the plaintiff and Guerrette contained words of assignability, and that language constitutes some evidence that the contract was assignable. The existence of financing terms in the plaintiff's option contract with Guerrette does not necessarily indicate that Guerrette relied on the plaintiff's personal credit. The words of assignability must control, absent any evidence that the parties intended the contract to be unassignable. The master, therefore, properly concluded that the option was validly assigned to the defendant.

The defendant also claims that the assignment contract between the defendant and the plaintiff did not satisfy the Statute of Frauds because no closing date was expressed in the writing. Even assuming that the payment date stated in the writing was not intended as a closing date, the writing still satisfies the Statute of Frauds.

The Statute of Frauds requires that contracts for the purchase of real estate be in writing, RSA 506:1, and that the writing express the essential terms of the contract. Because the purchase price, the identity of the parties, and a description of the real estate were expressed in writing, the parties' contract does not violate the Statute of Frauds. Time for performance is not an essential term under the Statute of Frauds.

The defendant finally alleges that the master erred by excluding evidence attempting to prove that the parties' option contract was conditioned on the defendant's ability to obtain 100% financing for the purchase of the property. The master heard the defendant's evidence on this issue, but then concluded that the evidence was inadmissible. Although we disagree with the master's decision that the parol evidence rule precluded the admission of this evidence, we agree with the master's decision that the defendant failed to meet his burden of proof as to the existence of a financing condition.

"THE FIRST STEP in determining whether parol evidence is admissible is to consider whether the writing is a total integration and completely expresses the agreement of the parties."

We agree with the trial court that no ambiguity existed in the writing sufficient to justify admission of parol evidence. In the absence of an ambiguity, the plain meaning rule prohibits the admission of parol evidence "that would contradict the plain meaning of the terms of the contract." Although this court has liberally defined "ambiguity" to include an ambiguity not apparent on the face of the instrument or an ambiguity not capable of resolution by mere examination of the instrument, this case does not involve an assertion of ambiguity.

The trial court failed to consider other aspects of the parol evidence rule. Even absent an ambiguity, parol evidence can be admitted in certain instances to prove the existence of terms or conditions not expressed in the writing.

The first step in determining whether parol evidence is admissible is to consider whether the writing is a total integration and completely expresses the agreement of the parties. Even when an integration clause is included in the writing, as in this case, this court will allow the admission of parol evidence to prove that the writing was not a total integration. In *Steinfield [v. Monadnock Mills]*, 81 N.H. at 153, this court held that the parties' intent to create a total integration can be proved by the circumstances surrounding the writing; "[t]he document alone will not suffice." The integration clause, however, is some evidence that the parties intended the writing to be a total integration. Ultimately, the issue of whether the writing is a total integration is an issue of fact determined by the trier of fact.

If a party proves the absence of a total integration, parol evidence is admissible to prove a term not inconsistent with the writing.

In the instant case, the parol evidence concerning the financing condition should have been admitted, notwithstanding the possibility that the contract might have been a total integration or that the additional term might have been interpreted as inconsistent with the writing. Exceptions to the parol evidence rule allow the admission of parol evidence even in instances where there is a total integration and a lack of an ambiguity. For that reason, the defendant's evidence concerning the possibility that the parties' assignment contract was conditioned on his ability to

obtain satisfactory financing for the eventual purchase of the property should have been admitted.

After hearing the evidence, the master stated that even if the parol evidence were admissible, the defendant would fail to meet his burden of proof. The burden of persuasion depends on the weight and credibility of the evidence and therefore is an issue for the trier of fact. Although the defendant produced some evidence that his purchase of the property would not take place unless he obtained 100% financing, the defendant did not prove that his obligation to make payment under the assignment contract was likewise conditioned. We cannot find, therefore, that the master committed reversible error by finding that the parties had not intended their assignment contract to be conditioned on the defendant's ability to obtain financing.

Affirmed.

All concurred.

There are exceptions to the parol evidence rule. One exception is to prove fraud. Perhaps the contract says that the written document contains the entire meeting of the minds of the parties, but one party claims the other mislead them into signing the agreement. The written agreement would never be able to settle such a charge of misrepresentation so the courts would allow outside testimony related to demonstrating whether or not there was fraud.

A second common exception is to resolve an ambiguity. Sometimes contracts have conflicting terms. The contract might say, in one paragraph, that the delivery of the proverbial "widgets" would occur in one place (or on one date) but a different place and time is specified in another part of the document. The only way to determine which places and times are correct would be to introduce evidence outside the agreement.

F. REMEDIES

Having a court determine that the other party improperly breached a contract is of limited value unless you can obtain some kind of remedy to alleviate your damages and to justify bringing suit in event of a breach. Three types of damages are available in contract cases—**expectancy, reliance**, and **restitution damages.** Each compensates the non-breaching party with respect to the damages they suffered. Expectancy means that the court puts the party in the same place they would have been had the breach not occurred. Reliance compensates the party to the extent that they spent money in reliance on the contract. Restitution (alternatively referred to as *quantum meruit*) compensates the non-breaching party by depriving the breaching party of their advantage in order to avoid unjust enrichment. While occasionally the non-breaching party's expenditures will equal the breaching parties' enrichment, it is important to remember that restitution and reliance focus on different parties and the results of the frustrated transaction.

I. Legal Remedies

Legal damages are money damages. The aim of the court is to ascertain what amount of money should be paid by the breaching party. For instance, a contractor who agrees to build a house for a client who later attempts to repudiate the contract could potentially recover the profit he would have earned if the house was never completed, the amount he spent in constructing the house, or the value of the house if it was completed and the buyers attempted to occupy the property. Different damage values may also determine the type of legal strategy a client may employ as they attempt to maximize their recovery. Sections 344 and 345 of the Restatement provide a brief overview (for the rest, see §§ 344–385):

> **§ 344: Purposes of Remedies**
>
> Judicial remedies under the rules stated in this Restatement serve to protect one or more of the following interests of a promisee:
>
> a. his "expectation interest," which is his interest in having the benefit of his bargain by being put in as good a position as he would have been in had the contract been performed,
>
> b. his "reliance interest," which is his interest in being reimbursed for loss caused by reliance on the contract by being put in as good a position as he would have been in had the contract not been made, or
>
> c. his "restitution interest," which is his interest in having restored to him any benefit that he has conferred on the other party.
>
> **§ 345: Judicial Remedies Available**
>
> The judicial remedies available for the protection of the interests stated in § 344 include a judgment or order
>
> a. awarding a sum of money due under the contract or as damages,
>
> b. requiring specific performance of a contract or enjoining its non-performance,

c. requiring restoration of a specific thing to prevent unjust enrichment,

d. awarding a sum of money to prevent unjust enrichment,

e. declaring the rights of the parties, and

f. enforcing an arbitration award.

The following case is an example of a court awarding restitution-based damages. Remember, restitution is determined by the undue benefit to the defendant and not by the plaintiff's expense. As the case will also make clear, there is some confusion in the case law about the relation of unjust enrichment and *quantum meruit*.

Certified Fire Protection, Inc. v. Precision Construction, Inc.

283 P.3d 250 (Nev. 2012)

BY THE COURT, PICKERING, J.:

* * *

Respondent/cross-appellant Precision Construction, Inc., a general contractor pursuing a contract for a warehouse construction project in 2005, solicited bids from subcontractors for the design and installation of an early suppression, fast response sprinkler system. Certified picked up a set of plans detailing the sprinkler system's requirements and, in mid-November, submitted a bid of $480,000. Precision notified Certified that it had won the bid, and Precision entered into a contract with the owner to complete the project.

On December 5, Certified obtained a copy of the subcontract along with a set of construction plans and sprinkler system specifications. The subcontract's provisions required Certified to complete the preliminary design drawings of the sprinkler system within two weeks and to obtain a certificate naming Precision as an additional insured. Over the next few weeks, Precision asked Certified several times to sign the subcontract and provide the additional-insured certificate.

Certified objected to the subcontract as imposing terms that differed from the bid specifications. It complained that the unanticipated terms changed the scope of work—including the size of pipes to be used, the placement of the fire riser, and the two-week time frame for producing drawings—and that it would have to amend its bid accordingly. Certified also took exception to some of the generic contractual provisions, including the additional-insured requirement.

On December 20, Precision notified all subcontractors, including Certified, that construction was under way. Certified hired Ron Dusky to draft the sprinkler system designs and, sometime in mid-January 2006, Dusky began drafting the designs. On January 19, with the subcontract still unsigned, Certified submitted a $33,575 progress bill to Precision, representing that it had completed seven percent of its work. But the design drawings apparently were still unfinished (or at least undelivered) because six days later, Precision wrote Doug Sartain, Certified's owner, requesting the sprinkler plans "ASAP" and advising that Precision would not process the progress payment without a signed subcontract. The next day, January 26, Precision again contacted Sartain, asking whether Certified planned to continue with the project and notifying him that its delay in submitting the plans was delaying the whole project.

On January 27, Certified reiterated its objections to the subcontract but assured Precision that it had begun the fire protection drawings. Certified completed the design work and submitted the sprinkler system drawings on February 1. Precision and Certified communicated several more times about getting the subcontract signed, and, on February 8, Precision learned that the drawings contained errors that needed correcting. It again asked Certified about the unsigned subcontract.

On February 16, Precision terminated its relationship with Certified for refusing to sign the subcontract, for not providing the additional-insured endorsement, and for incorrect designs. At Precision's request, Certified submitted an itemized billing for the work it had performed; its bill reported costs of $25,185.04, which included design work and permit fees for the project. Precision deemed the costs too high and never paid. Certified placed a mechanic's lien on the property and sued to recover for its design-related work. Certified's complaint sought to foreclose the mechanic's lien and damages for unjust enrichment, *quantum meruit*, and breach of contract.

* * *

Certified argues that the progress bill it sent to Precision established the price term and Precision's urging that Certified get started on the designs established the scope of work for the express design-work-only contract it claims. But the record does not establish that Precision agreed to pay a sum certain for the design—related work. Certified's $33,575 progress bill—which represented seven percent of the whole subcontract—went unpaid, and Precision told Certified it would not make a progress payment until the whole subcontract had been executed. Beyond this, witness testimony established that a party in Precision's position would not execute a contract for only design drawings; such drawings are specifically tailored for the company rendering them and not useful to another installer. Thus, Certified's argument that Precision was parceling out the work—with Certified doing the designs only—makes no sense.

Not only were price and scope of work terms missing from the claimed design-work contract, the parties never agreed to a time for performance. Certified objected to Precision's proposed two-week timeline for producing the design drawings as "not realistic," and the parties never agreed to another time frame. That the time-for-performance term mattered is demonstrated by Precision's repeated prompting of Certified to complete the designs and Certified's refusal to bind itself to Precision's desired two-week turnaround. "When essential terms such as these have yet to be agreed upon by the parties, a contract cannot be formed."

And while the district court's judgment on partial findings does not reference a design-only contract, the record substantially supports its conclusion that no enforceable contract existed.

B.

Next, Certified argues that absent an express contract, it should be able to recover under a theory of implied contract, either by *quantum meruit* or unjust enrichment.

Certified confessedly is confused by *quantum meruit* and unjust enrichment, noting that "the distinction between the two theories in Nevada is unclear." "One source of confusion is that *quantum meruit* is a cause of action in two fields: restitution and contract."

Quantum meruit historically was one of the common counts—a subspecies of the writ of *indebitatus* or general *assumpsit*—available as a remedy at law to enforce implied promises or contracts. A party who pleaded *quantum meruit* sought recovery of the reasonable value, or "as much as he has deserved" for services rendered.

Thus, *quantum meruit*'s first application is in actions based upon contracts implied-in-fact. A contract implied-in-fact must be "manifested by conduct"; it "is a true contract that arises from the tacit agreement of the parties." To find a contract implied-in-fact, the fact-finder must conclude that the parties intended to contract and promises were exchanged, the general obligations for which must be sufficiently clear. It is at that point that a party may invoke *quantum meruit* as a gap-filler to supply the absent term. Where such a contract exists, then, *quantum meruit* ensures the laborer receives the reasonable value, usually market price, for his services.

Certified maintains that it had an implied contract with Precision for the design-related work. As discussed above, however, substantial evidence supports the district court's finding that there was no contract, express or implied, for the design work standing alone. There are simply too many gaps to fill in the asserted contract for *quantum meruit* to take hold. Precision never agreed to a contract for only design-related work, the parties never agreed to a price for that work, and they disputed the time of performance. When Precision selected Certified, it did so on the basis that Certified would design *and install* the fire suppression system, not that it would draft the designs and leave installation to someone else. The evidence established that design drawings are installer-specific and so not useful to a replacement subcontractor. Accordingly, the district court properly denied recovery in *quantum meruit* for an implied-in-fact contract.

Quantum meruit's other role is in providing restitution for unjust enrichment: "Liability in restitution for the market value of goods or services is the remedy traditionally known as *quantum meruit*." "'Where unjust enrichment is found, the law implies a quasi-contract which requires the defendant to pay to plaintiff the value of the benefit conferred. In other words, the defendant makes restitution to the plaintiff in *quantum meruit*.'"

When a plaintiff seeks "as much as he ... deserve[s]" based on a theory of restitution (as opposed to implied-in-fact contract), he must establish each element of unjust enrichment. *Quantum meruit*, then, is "the usual measurement of enrichment in cases where nonreturnable benefits have been furnished at the defendant's request, but where the parties made no enforceable agreement as to price."

"PLEADING OF *quantum meruit* for unjust enrichment does not discharge the plaintiffs obligation to demonstrate that the defendant received a benefit from services provided."

Unjust enrichment exists when the plaintiff confers a benefit on the defendant, the defendant appreciates such benefit, and there is " 'acceptance and retention by the defendant of such benefit under circumstances such that it would be inequitable for him to retain the benefit without payment of the value thereof.' Thus—contrary to Certified's argument—a pleading of *quantum meruit* for unjust enrichment does not discharge the plaintiffs obligation to demonstrate that the defendant received a benefit from services provided.

"[B]enefit" in the unjust enrichment context can include "services beneficial to or at the request of the other," "denotes any form of advantage," and is not confined to retention of money or property. But while "[r]estitution may strip a wrongdoer of all profits gained in a transaction with [a] claimant ... principles of unjust enrichment will not support the imposition of a liability that leaves an innocent recipient worse off ... than if the transaction with the claimant had never taken place."

That is the state of our law, too. * * * Here, the district court found that Precision had not "unjustly retain [ed] any money or property because no work performed could be utilized by the replacement fire sprinkler subcontractor," and that included the sprinkler designs. Every one of Certified's witnesses admitted as much on cross-examination. Thus, Certified's owner, Doug Sartain, testified that Certified installed nothing at the job site and its preparatory work could not be utilized by the replacement subcontractor. Gary Wooldridge, Certified's project manager, confirmed Sartain's statements that the design work and permitting performed by Certified could not be used by their replacement subcontractor (though he did say the water flow test could have been utilized). Finally, Ron Dusky, the man who drafted the plans, stated in his deposition (which was read into the record) that the designs Certified submitted contained mistakes that would have required one to two weeks to remedy. This was never done. Certified submitted no evidence of an ascertainable advantage Precision drew from the work it performed. It was incomplete, incorrect,

and late. Therefore, we agree with the district court that Certified cannot recover in *quantum meruit* or unjust enrichment.

Accordingly, we affirm.

A second kind of legal remedy is **reliance.** When focusing on reliance interests, the court attempts to isolate the particular expense the party that began performance expended in reliance on the contract. Courts pay particular attention to fixed costs and if the party incurred losses based in particular reliance on the contract. The reliance on the contract must also be reasonable in order to induce reliance.

Finally, expectancy damages try to provide parties with what they would have received had the contract been completed, or literally "the benefit of the bargain." The following case involves a lengthy comparison of expectancy, reliance, and restitution interests and the social and public policy reasons that argue towards and against these forms of recovery. The case draws on what is known, informally, as the "Hairy Hand" case, a classic contract case, and it talks about both reliance and expectancy theories.

Sullivan v. O'Connor

363 Mass. 579, 296 N.E.2d 183 (1973)

KAPLAN, JUSTICE.

The plaintiff patient secured a jury verdict of $13,500 against the defendant surgeon for breach of contract in respect to an operation upon the plaintiff's nose. * * * The plaintiff was a professional entertainer, and this was known to the defendant. The agreement was as alleged in the declaration. More particularly, judging from exhibits, the plaintiff's nose had been straight, but long and prominent; the defendant undertook by two operations to reduce its prominence and somewhat to shorten it, thus making it more pleasing in relation to the plaintiff's other features. Actually[,] the plaintiff was obliged to undergo three operations, and her appearance was worsened. Her nose now had a concave line to about the midpoint, at which it became bulbous; viewed frontally, the nose from bridge to midpoint was flattened and broadened, and the two sides of the tip had lost symmetry. This configuration evidently could not be improved by further surgery. The plaintiff did not demonstrate, however, that her change of appearance had resulted in loss of employment.

* * *

If an action on the basis of contract is allowed, we have next the question of the measure of damages to be applied where liability is found. Some cases have taken the simple view that the promise by the physician is to be treated like an ordinary commercial promise, and accordingly that the successful plaintiff is entitled to a standard measure of recovery for breach of contract-'compensatory' ('expectancy') damages, an amount intended to put the plaintiff in the position he would be in if the contract had been performed, or, presumably, at the plaintiff's election, 'restitution' damages, an amount corresponding to any benefit conferred by the plaintiff upon the defendant in the performance of the contract disrupted by the defendant's breach. Thus in *Hawkins v. McGee*, [the infamous "Hairy Hand" case made even more famous by the classic law school movie *The Paperchase* (1973)], the defendant doctor was taken to have promised the plaintiff to convert his damaged hand by means of an operation into a good or perfect hand, but the doctor so operated as to damage the hand still further. The court, following the usual expectancy formula, would have asked the jury to estimate and award to the plaintiff the difference between the value of a good or perfect hand, as promised, and the value of the hand after the operation. (The same formula would apply, although the dollar result would be less, if the operation had neither worsened nor improved the condition of the hand.) If the plaintiff had not yet paid the doctor his fee, that amount would be deducted from the recovery. There could be no recovery for the pain and suffering of the operation, since that detriment would have been incurred even if the operation had been successful; one can say that this detriment was not 'caused' by the breach. But where the plaintiff by reason of the operation was put to more pain that he would have had to endure, had the doctor performed as promised, he should be compensated for that difference as a proper part of his expectancy recovery. It may be noted that on an alternative count for malpractice the plaintiff in the Hawkins case had been nonsuited; but on ordinary principles this could not affect the contract claim, for it is hardly a defence to a breach of contract that the promisor acted innocently and without negligence. The New Hampshire court further refined the *Hawkins* analysis in McQuaid v. Michou, all in the direction of treating the patient-physician cases on the ordinary footing of expectancy.

* * *

For breach of the patient-physician agreements under consideration, a recovery limited to restitution seems plainly too meager, if the agreements are to be enforced at all. On the other hand, an expectancy recovery may well be excessive. The factors, already mentioned, which have made the cause of action somewhat suspect, also suggest moderation as to the breadth of the recovery that should be permitted. Where, as in the case at bar and in a number of the reported cases, the doctor has been absolved of negligence by the trier, an expectancy measure may be thought harsh. We should recall here that the fee paid by the patient to the doctor for the

alleged promise would usually be quite disproportionate to the putative expectancy recovery. To attempt, moreover, to put a value on the condition that would or might have resulted, had the treatment succeeded as promised, may sometimes put an exceptional strain on the imagination of the fact finder. As a general consideration, Fuller and Perdue argue that the reasons for granting damages for broken promises to the extent of the expectancy are at their strongest when the promises are made in a business context, when they have to do with the production or distribution of goods or the allocation of functions in the market place; they become weaker as the context shifts from a commercial to a noncommercial field.

* * *

The question of recovery on a reliance basis for pain and suffering or mental distress requires further attention. We find expressions in the decisions that pain and suffering (or the like) are simply not compensable in actions for breach of contract. The defendant seemingly espouses this proposition in the present case. True, if the buyer under a contract for the purchase of a lot of merchandise, in suing for the seller's breach, should claim damages for mental anguish caused by his disappointment in the transaction, he would not succeed; he would be told, perhaps, that the asserted psychological injury was not fairly foreseeable by the defendant as a probable consequence of the breach of such a business contract. But there is no general rule barring such items of damage in actions for breach of contract. It is all a question of the subject matter and background of the contract, and when the contract calls for an operation on the person of the plaintiff, psychological as well as physical injury may be expected to figure somewhere in the recovery, depending on the particular circumstances. The point is explained in *Stewart v. Rudner.* Again, it is said in a few of the New York cases, concerned with the classification of actions for statute of limitations purposes, that the absence of allegations demanding recovery for pain and suffering is characteristic of a contract claim by a patient against a physician, that such allegations rather belong in a claim for malpractice. These remarks seem unduly sweeping. Suffering or distress resulting from the breach going beyond that which was envisaged by the treatment as agreed, should be compensable on the same ground as the worsening of the patient's condition because of the breach. Indeed it can be argued that the very suffering or distress 'contracted for'-that which would have been incurred if the treatment achieved the promised result-should also be compensable on the theory underlying the New York cases. For that suffering is 'wasted' if the treatment fails. Otherwise stated, compensation for this waste is arguably required in order to complete the restoration of the status quo ante.

In the light of the foregoing discussion, all the defendant's exceptions fail: the plaintiff was not confined to the recovery of her out-of-pocket expenditures; she was entitled to recover also for the worsening of her condition, and for the pain and suffering and mental distress involved in the third operation. These items were compensable on either an expectancy or a reliance view. We might have been required to elect between the two views if the pain and suffering connected with the first two operations contemplated by the agreement, or the whole difference in value between the present and the promised conditions, were being claimed as elements of damage. But the plaintiff waives her possible claim to the former element, and to so much of the latter as represents the difference in value between the promised condition and the condition before the operations.

Plaintiff's exceptions waived.

Defendant's exceptions *overruled*.

---

2. Equitable Remedies

In addition to legal damages, courts can craft equitable solutions. These damages, as we have already seen, go beyond financial compensation. In these cases, the courts recognize that money will not make the parties whole. There is a specific thing to be had or an event to be avoided that is the essence of the contract.

a. Specific Performance

PRESIDENT JOHN F. KENNEDY IN THE FAMOUS OVAL OFFICE ROCKING CHAIR. *Image: Abbie Rowe. White House Photographs. John F. Kennedy Presidential Library and Museum, Boston.*

Sometimes, the contract the parties make concerns something unique. Perhaps one party bid on the rocking chair used by President Kennedy. If the other party does not deliver the contract, money damages will only go so far to remedy the situation. The party who bid on the rocking chair wants THAT rocking chair, not money to buy another rocking chair, not even another rocking chair, but the rocking chair that President Kennedy used. This would be a case made for specific performance because the party bidding for the rocking chair would petition to the court to require that the breaching party deliver THAT rocking chair.

These examples also occur with real estate and with performances for special talents. When shopping for houses to live in and raise a family, people are not simply looking for a collection of rooms underneath a roof but rather a house that will be a home. There may be something unique and appealing about the particular unit so that if the seller breaches and does not perform the **contracted conveyance**, the suit would likely ask not just for money damages, but for the conveyance of THAT home.

To use one final example, suppose the contract is for a particularly talented individual to sing a concert. Perhaps one of the authors of this text was born on the same day and year as the late Michael Jackson. The author also happens to be a singer. However, if when Mr. Jackson was alive he was contracted to sing a concert and came down with a cold and refused to perform, it would not do for him to suggest that this book's author replace him even if Mr. Jackson also said that he would throw in some money to cover any difference in quality of performance. A fan who purchased a ticket to hear Mr. Jackson perform would not be satisfied; the fan wanted to hear Michael Jackson, not someone else.

One area where specific performance arises frequently is within the context of land conveyances, particularly because land is not fungible and may have unique properties that cannot be compensated by monetary damages. The following case discusses the doctrine of **privity**, which allows third-party beneficiaries to sue on the contract if the transaction was made for their benefit despite the fact that they were not parties to the original transaction. Privity claims most often arise in situations involving wills and loans, where parties believe that a contract intended to benefit them should entitle them to sue for **specific performance**. As the next case illustrates, though, specific performance is subject to the usual requirements of contract formation.

b. Injunction

Another common equitable remedy is an **injunction**, which is a court action that stops any further action from occurring. The following case shows how injunctions are used to prevent an irreparable injury from occurring. In such cases, money damages do not remedy the aggrieved party; stopping the problematic action is necessary because the prospective damage might be irreparable. However, courts are reluctant to compel performance of an action even in cases where they will prohibit another type of action. The following case explores the connection between injunctive relief and specific performance.

Florida Panthers Hockey Club, Ltd. v. Miami Sports and Exhibition Authority

939 F.Supp 855 (S.D. Fla. 1996)

K. MICHAEL MOORE, DISTRICT JUDGE.

* * * On August 7, 1996, Plaintiff The Florida Panthers Hockey Club, Ltd. (the "Panthers") commenced this action against Defendants Miami Sports and Exhibition Authority ("MSEA") and the City of Miami (the "City"). Count I of the Panthers' complaint seeks a declaration of its rights under a license agreement between the Panthers and non-party Leisure Management International. Counts II through IV

seek injunctive relief and damages arising out of alleged violations of Section 2 of the Sherman Act.

The Panthers is a franchise of the National Hockey League ("NHL"). MSEA is an independent and autonomous authority of the City. MSEA owns the Miami Arena, and the City owns the land upon which the Miami Arena is situated.

On October 10, 1986, MSEA, Decoma Miami Associates, Ltd. ("DMAL") and the City entered into a Land Lease Agreement for the construction of the Miami Arena. On October 19, 1986, MSEA and DMAL executed a contract entitled "Miami Arena Contract" which set forth the rights and obligations of the parties in connection with the operation of the Miami Arena. On December 13, 1990, MSEA and DMAL entered into the First Amendment to the Miami Arena Contract. The Miami Arena Contract and the First Amendment will be referred to collectively as "the Miami Arena Contract." On October 19, 1986, DMAL hired Leisure Management International ("LMI") as an independent contractor to discharge some of DMAL's responsibilities, including the responsibility for entering into agreements for the use of the Miami Arena.

On April 2, 1993, LMI, on DMAL's behalf, entered into a license agreement with the South Florida Hockey Club, Ltd., the predecessor to the Panthers. On June 21, 1993, LMI and the Panthers entered into a First Amendment to the Panthers License. The Panthers License and the First Amendment will be referred to collectively as "the Panthers License." The Panthers License provided for an initial term of two hockey seasons but gave the Panthers, at its sole discretion, four one-year options to extend the Panthers License.

Under the Panthers License, the Panthers had to exercise its option to renew for the 1996–1997 hockey season on or before August 1, 1995. The Panthers elected not to exercise its option for the 1996–1997 season and advised MSEA to that effect by letter dated May 31, 1995. In that letter, the Panthers advised MSEA, "This is to advise you that because of the extremely unfavorable economic terms of the License Agreement, we don't wish to exercise the second one-year option (for the 1996–1997 season). However, if the economic terms of a new License Agreement for the Miami Arena could be obtained which were comparable to those economic terms presently granted to the Miami Heat basketball team, we would seriously consider remaining in the Miami Arena for that subsequent season."

John Blaisdell, president of LMI, testified that LMI, on DMAL's behalf, and the Panthers began negotiating a new license agreement. On May 30, 1996, LMI and DMAL entered into an agreement entitled "Second Amendment to License Agreement" (the "Panthers License Amendment"). Blaisdell testified that the terms of the Panthers License Amendment continued to favor MSEA tremendously. Blaisdell further testified that the Panthers License Amendment did not include any material changes from the Panthers License; rather, the terms and conditions of the Panthers License Amendment substantially conformed to the Panthers License. No evidence was offered to the contrary.

By letter dated June 7, 1996, MSEA rejected the Second Amendment to the License Agreement. In that letter, MSEA indicated that " . . . we do not believe that the proposed amendments are in the best economic interests of MSEA nor [sic] consistent with the accomplishment of our public purpose. In addition, it is our conclusion that the proposed terms are not reasonably necessary to the operation of the Miami Arena. Instead, we believe that MSEA will be better served by a license[,] which commences on August 1, 1996, and expires on July 31, 2006. We reject paragraphs 3, 4, 5 and 6 of the proposed amendments." By letter dated July 9, 1996, MSEA directed the Panthers to vacate the Miami Arena by July 15, 1996.

* * *

The question of whether the Plaintiff has a substantial likelihood of success on the merits for the contract claim focuses on whether MSEA has an obligation not to unreasonably withhold consent of the Panthers License Amendment. The Court finds that MSEA does have such an obligation.

The Plaintiff contends that the Panthers License Amendment contains substantially similar terms and conditions as the Panthers License and continues to be a boon for MSEA. The Plaintiff argues that MSEA, therefore, cannot unreasonably withhold consent of the Panthers License Amendment and that a preliminary injunction is required to compel approval.

MSEA counters that the Panthers License Amendment is a "personal services" contract and, thus, is not subject to a suit for specific performance. While a personal services contract cannot be enforced by injunction or specific performance, the Panthers License Amendment is not such a contract. The Panthers License Amendment is a lease agreement and such an agreement may be subject to specific performance. The Court, therefore, finds that the remedy of specific performance is available. Certainly, specific performance is only available if it appears from the agreement that the rights and obligations of the parties with respect to the terms and conditions of the contract and the actions to be taken by the parties are clear, definite and certain.

MSEA also counters that, since the Panthers failed to exercise its option to renew the Panthers License, the agreement was effectively cancelled. Further, MSEA argues that cancellation of the Panthers License meant that the Panthers could not enter into a new license agreement. The Court finds MSEA's argument misleading insofar as MSEA delegated to DMAL the "full and exclusive" power and authority to "negotiate, execute, and perform" contracts including licenses. Therefore, even if the Panthers License was cancelled upon the Plaintiff's failure to exercise its option, DMAL/LMI could enter into a new agreement with the Panthers or any other party who desired to use the Miami Arena.

DMAL's power and authority to enter into contracts for the use of the Miami Arena is limited if the contract involves an Owner Affiliate or "schedule[s] events or performances in the Arena for more than 20 days during any one Operating Year." In those instances, MSEA's approval of the contract is required. However, the standard for MSEA approval is clearly defined in and limited under the Miami Arena Contract. Section 7.4 of the Miami Arena Contract provides, in pertinent part:

> Such Owner approval shall
>
> i. be given by the Chairman of Owner or his designees,
>
> ii. not be unreasonably withheld and
>
> iii. be subject to the standards for Owner review and approval * * *

MSEA argues that provision D.6.4 is inapplicable to the situation and that MSEA had an unfettered right to disapprove the Panthers License Amendment. The Court rejects this argument. Provision D.7.4 incorporates the standard set forth in D.6.4 for Owner approval, and D.6.4 clearly places limits on an Owner's right to disapprove a contract. MSEA, therefore, may not unconditionally choose not to follow these standards.

* * * The Court, however, disagrees with MSEA that the irreparable harm is merely economic in nature and that money damages can adequately compensate the Panthers should it ultimately succeed on the merits. The overwhelming evidence presented establishes that the Panthers' existence and success rests, in large part, on the interest and loyalty of the fans. As William Torrey and Brian Burke testified, the potential harm to the Panthers is incalculable and extends beyond the financial injury. If the Panthers cannot play in the Miami Arena, it may lose home game advantage and may lose goodwill among its fans. Further, the Panthers' relationship with the NHL may be adversely affected.

The inquiry under the third prong of a preliminary injunction motion requires the Court to determine whether the threatened injury to the movant outweighs the harm that an injunction may cause to the non-movant. The Court is satisfied that the Plaintiff has demonstrated its potential injury outweighs any harm the injunction may cause to MSEA. * * *

The Court finds that an injunction would not disserve the public. Indeed, professional sports serves the public interest and, in this particular instance, the Panthers Lease Amendment provides economic benefits to the public.

---

c. Rewriting the Contract

A final example of an equitable remedy is when the court steps in or refuses to re-write a contract that the party claims is unfair. Courts tend to favor and protect the autonomy of parties to contract freely. However, sometimes the court concludes that equity necessitates revisions—these revisions are known as "the blue pencil rule." Restatement § 155 allows parties to reform the written expression of a contract when there is mistake by both parties; other sections also implicitly endorse the ability of the court to rewrite a contract, including allowing the court to strike some or all of an unconscionable contract (§ 208). The following case presents a dialogue between the majority and dissent about the propriety of revising the language of a contract. As you read this case, also think about all the principles we have covered in this chapter and consider whether you find the arguments about the autonomy of parties or the equitable powers of the courts to enforce fair bargains more persuasive. Because this case serves as a review for these principles, it runs longer than the usual cases in this chapter.

Wilkie v. Auto-Owners Ins. Co.

469 Mich. 41, 664 N.W.2d 776 (2003)

TAYLOR, J.

This case involves a dispute between Auto-Owners Insurance Company and its insureds, Janna L. Frank and the decedent, Paul K. Wilkie, regarding underinsured-motorist coverage. Defendant Auto-Owners argues that plaintiffs Frank and Wilkie's recoveries from Auto-Owners are limited under the terms of the policy to $50,000 each. Frank and Wilkie argue that they are each owed $75,000. The trial court and Court of Appeals agreed with Frank and Wilkie. We reverse.

I. Facts

On April 17, 1996, Janna Frank was driving east on Maple Rapids Road in Clinton County, with Paul Wilkie as a passenger. At the same time, Stephen Ward was driving west on Maple Rapids Road. Witnesses described his driving as erratic shortly before his vehicle crossed the center line and collided with Frank's car, injuring her and causing the deaths of Ward and Wilkie.

Ward's vehicle was insured under a Citizens Insurance Company no-fault automobile-insurance policy having limits of $50,000. Wilkie's estate and Frank shared this sum, with each receiving $25,000. Wilkie's vehicle was insured under an Auto-Owners no-fault automobile-insurance policy that provided, in addition to the mandatory coverages required under Michigan's no-fault automobile-insurance statute an optional coverage described as underinsured-motorist coverage. Speaking generally, this coverage was intended to supplement insurance proceeds received by the insured from the tortfeasor had the tortfeasor not been underinsured. This added coverage had limits of $100,000 for each person to a total of $300,000 for each occurrence, and also provided that Auto-Owners' liability was limited to the amount by which these limits exceeded the underinsured motorist's own insurance coverage. The policy clearly stated that the Auto-Owners' limits of liability were not to be increased because of the number of persons injured, claims made, or automobiles involved in the accident.

Auto-Owners did not contest that the accident was Ward's fault and agreed that both Wilkie's and Frank's damages were at least $100,000. Disputed, however, was the total amount due from Auto-Owners to Wilkie and Frank. Auto-Owners asserted that it only owed Wilkie and Frank $50,000 each. As it understood the contract terms, the $100,000 policy limit would be reduced by the $50,000 coverage of the Ward policy. Wilkie and Frank, for their part, claimed that Auto-Owners owed each of them $75,000. They reasoned that, having equally split the Ward policy limits of $50,000, only the $25,000 they received should have been subtracted from the $100,000 policy limit to determine the amount each was due.

Unable to reach a resolution of this dispute, Wilkie and Frank sought declaratory relief against Auto-Owners in the Clinton Circuit Court. The plaintiffs moved for summary disposition predicated on their understanding of the contract's requirements. The trial court granted their motion and ruled that only the amount actually received by each of them, $25,000, and not the entire amount of Ward's policy limits, $50,000, should be set off against the amount available to them, $100,000, under the underinsured-motorist provision. Thus, according to the trial court, Wilkie and Frank were each entitled to $75,000 from Auto-Owners.

* * *

Under the language of the underinsurance policy at issue here, the insurer agreed to pay $100,000 for each person to a total of $300,000 for each occurrence for bodily or compensatory damages to individuals covered by the policy if each person would have been entitled to recover all those sums from the other driver, but was precluded from doing so because the other driver was underinsured. The insurer's liability was then limited by a provision that states that the amount by which the $100,000 for each person to a total of $300,000 for each occurrence exceeds the total limits available to the owner or operator of the underinsured vehicle will determine the amount to be paid. Further clarity is given to this clause by the next provisions, which say that the amounts available are not increased because of the claims made or persons injured.

The Court of Appeals, as urged by the plaintiffs, approached this language by holding that ¶ 4a.1 of the contract was ambiguous because it could be "reasonably understood in differing ways." That is, ¶ 4a.1 of the contract could be interpreted to direct that the $100,000 from the Auto-Owners policy be reduced by either $50,000 or $25,000, depending on how one chose to read it. That being the case, the Court construed the contract against its drafter, Auto-Owners. The Court's ambiguity analysis of the language of ¶ 4a.1 is, at best, questionable because the language appears clearer than the Court found it to be. Paragraph 4a.1 states that the limit of liability for underinsured-motorist coverage shall not exceed "the amount by which the Underinsured Motorist Coverage limits stated in the Declarations exceeds the *total limits* of all bodily injury liability bonds and policies *available to the owner* or operator of the underinsured automobile . . . . " (Emphasis added.) In this case, the underinsured-motorist coverage limit stated in Auto Owner's declaration is $100,000. The *total limit* of all bodily-injury liability policies *available to the owner* of the underinsured automobile, i.e., Ward, is $50,000. Therefore, the amount by which the underinsured-motorist-coverage limits stated in the declarations exceeds the total limits of all bodily-injury policies available to the owner of the underinsured automobile is clearly $50,000, not $75,000. Contrary to the contention of Court of Appeals, this provision cannot be "reasonably understood" to be referring to the amount actually received by the claimant because the provision specifically refers to the *total* available to the *owner.* Yet, whatever the merits of the Court of Appeals analysis, the panel's conclusion is fatally undermined when ¶ 4a.1 is read, as it must be, with ¶¶ 4b.2 and 3. These later paragraphs settle any perceived ambiguity in ¶ 4a.1 by stating that the amounts to be paid will not be increased because of claims made, suits brought, or persons injured. Interpreting this provision to mean that each plaintiff is entitled to $75,000 would increase the limit of liability "because of" the number of claims brought or persons injured, which is clearly contrary to the plain language of ¶¶ 4b.2 and 3.

Quite simply, if ¶ 4a.1 appears ambiguous by itself, when read with ¶¶ 4b.2 and 3 the ambiguity is eliminated. That being the case, the insurance contract at issue is unambiguous and should be enforced as its terms dictate. Thus, no consideration of the doctrine of construing the contract against the drafter is appropriate.

B

The Court of Appeals, in declining to give the contract the construction ¶¶ 4b.2 and 3 compel, also relied on the argument that to allow such a construction would defy the insured's reasonable expectations, which, as the Court characterized them, would be that no change in the amount due would be occasioned by the vicissitudes of such things as claims made or persons injured.

This approach, where judges divine the parties' reasonable expectations and then rewrite the contract accordingly, is contrary to the bedrock principle of American contract law that parties are free to contract as they see fit, and the courts are to enforce the agreement as written absent some highly unusual circumstance, such as a contract in violation of law or public policy. This Court has recently discussed, and reinforced, its fidelity to this understanding of contract law in *Terrien v. Zwit*, 467 Mich. 56 (2002). The notion, that free men and women may reach agreements regarding their affairs without government interference and that courts will enforce those agreements, is ancient and irrefutable. It draws strength from common-law roots and can be seen in our fundamental charter, the United States Constitution, where government is forbidden from impairing the contracts of citizens, art. I, § 10, cl. 1. Our own state constitutions over the years of statehood have similarly echoed this limitation on government power. It is, in short, an unmistakable and ineradicable part of the legal fabric of our society. Few have expressed the force of this venerable axiom better than the late Professor Arthur Corbin, of Yale Law School, who wrote on this topic in his definitive study of contract law, *Corbin on Contracts*, as follows:

"THE NOTION, that free men and women may reach agreements regarding their affairs without government interference and that courts will enforce those agreements, is ancient and irrefutable."

> One does not have "liberty of contract" unless organized society both forbears and enforces, forbears to penalize him for making his bargain and enforces it for him after it is made. [15 Corbin, Contracts (Interim ed.), ch. 79, § 1376, p. 17.]

> In contrast to this legal pedigree extending over the centuries, the rule of reasonable expectations is of recent origin. Moreover, it is antagonistic to this understanding of the rule of law, and is, accordingly, in our view, invalid as an approach to contract interpretation.

The rule of reasonable expectations had innocent origins in 1970. Professor Robert E. Keeton of Harvard Law School wrote an article entitled *Insurance law rights at variance with policy provisions*, [. . .] in which he examined and attempted to rationalize a number of cases in which the results appeared to defy the principle that contracts will be construed according to their unambiguous terms. To explain this phenomenon, as best he could, he concluded that certain courts would evidently not enforce clear contract language in the face of one of the parties' "reasonable expectations" of coverage. As Professor Keeton described it:

> The objectively reasonable expectations of the applicants and intended beneficiaries regarding the terms of insurance contracts will be honored even though painstaking study of the policy provision would have negated those expectations.

Whether Professor Keeton intended this analysis to spawn a frontal assault on the ability of our citizens to manage, by contract, their own affairs, it had that effect because numerous courts, to one degree or another, adopted some form of the rule.

* * *

The rule of reasonable expectations clearly has no application to unambiguous contracts. That is, one's alleged "reasonable expectations" cannot supersede the clear language of a contract. Therefore, if this rule has any meaning, it can only be that, if there is more than one way to reasonably interpret a contract, i.e., the contract is ambiguous, and one of these interpretations is in accord with the reasonable expectations of the insured, this interpretation should prevail. However, this is saying no more than that, if a contract is ambiguous and the parties' intent cannot be discerned from extrinsic evidence, the contract should be interpreted against the insurer. In other words, when its application is limited to ambiguous contracts, the rule of reasonable expectations is just a surrogate for the rule of construing against the drafter. As the Court of Appeals has recently explained:

> Well-settled principles of contract interpretation require one to first look to a contract's plain language. If the plain language is clear, there can be only one reasonable interpretation of its meaning and, therefore, only one meaning the parties could reasonable expect to apply. If the language is ambiguous, longstanding principles of contract law require that the ambiguous provision be construed against the drafter. Applied in an insurance context, the drafter is always the insurer. Thus, it appears that the "rule of reasonable expectations" is nothing more than a unique title given to traditional contract principles applied to insurance contracts . . . .

* * *

The rights and duties of parties to a contract are derived from the terms of the agreement. As this Court has previously stated, "The general rule [of contracts] is that competent persons shall have the utmost liberty of contracting and that their agreements voluntarily and fairly made shall be held valid and enforced in the courts." Under this legal principle, the parties are generally free to agree to whatever they like, and, in most circumstances, it is beyond the authority of the courts to interfere with the parties' agreement. Respect for the freedom to contract entails that we enforce only those obligations actually assented to by the parties. We believe that the rule of reasonable expectations markedly fails in this respect. The words of Justice Kavanagh bear repeating:

> [T]he expectation that a contract will be enforceable other than according to its terms surely may not be said to be reasonable. If a person signs a contract without reading all of it or without understanding it, under some circumstances that person can avoid its obligations on the theory that there was no contract at all for there was no meeting of the minds.

> But to allow such a person to bind another to an obligation not covered by the contract as written because the first person thought the other was bound to such an obligation is neither reasonable nor just.

Accordingly, we hold that the rule of reasonable expectations has no application in Michigan, and those cases that recognized this doctrine are to that extent overruled.

IV. Conclusion

We reverse the judgment of the Court of Appeals and find the insurance contract between Auto-Owners and Wilkie unambiguously limited Auto-Owners' liability to $50,000 each for Wilkie and Frank.

Even though this chapter is the longest in the book, what has been presented is an overview of an obviously complicated area of law. Contracts are the lifeblood of business too. Exchange relationships—buying and selling items, agreeing to work for someone—are all examples of contracts. Agency law is a form of contract law and itself forms the basis of business organizations such as partnerships and corporations. Employment law is also a kind of both agency law and contract law. Products liability has aspects of both torts and contracts. The following chapter on the Uniform Commercial Code is contract law as applied to the sale of goods. Thus, the principles covered in this chapter have their own independent importance and serve as a foundation for most of the subsequent chapters of this book.

NOTES AND COMMENTS on the Legal Environment of Business

1. **THE NOTION OF CONTRACTS** has had great impact on a variety of fields beyond the law. Economics and finance scholars often focus statistics models on contracting parties and seek to determine the most efficient and optimal outcomes and terms. The same holds true with ethics scholarship, which draws upon social contract principles to determine what individuals (and society) believe to be fair and just. Thus, in addition to mastering the elements of contracts from this chapter, you should bear in mind that the concepts and principles have analogues that apply in a wider variety of areas.

2. **ONE OF THE CHALLENGES OF CONTRACTS** is the balance between what two parties agree to and what society allows. Or, to put this into economic terms, how does a contract handle externalities? To put into ethical terms, what is the social contract within which negotiated contracts become permissible? How much outside monitoring do you think should apply to the agreements made between individual parties? As long as the two parties agree, should the law, society, and others leave the agreement alone or not? At what level should we consider social norms that govern contracts: locally, nationally or globally?

3. **SOME OF THE ANSWERS** to these questions are addressed in the following chapter where an effort has been made to create a uniform set of rules for contracts involving sales that also leaves open considerable room for individual contractors to flexibly do business. Keep the above thoughts in mind when looking at the next chapter on the Uniform Commercial Code.

NOTES AND COMMENTS on the Ethical Environment of Business

1. **AT THEIR CORE,** contracts are about trust. One party promises the other something and both parties promise that the other will deliver on their promise. Most of the time, exactly that happens. The court system would never be able to enforce all the agreements people and companies make with one another. Obviously, the presence of law cases in this chapter shows that things do go wrong, but that is not what motivates people to enter into a contract. They desire to exchange something and the most efficient way for that to take place is for each side to do what they promised. There is clear ethical content in this as there is in making honest transactions and in providing quality goods and services.

   Contracts also rely on notions of freedom and autonomy. The notions of capacity lie in each person being able to understand what is in their best interests. Within certain limits, individuals are free to contract with others to fulfill their own interests. Here again, there are strong ethical precepts within contracts.

   This is a key reason why philosophers rely on contracts to think of what a fair society would look like. In a social contract experiment, such as John Rawls' famous example, individuals would agree as to what society would be fair. In their "original position" when they are "behind a veil of ignorance," they do not know whether they will be rich or poor, tall or short, wealth or poor of any of the other features that define our lives. Not knowing who will be, what kind of contract would people negotiate? Using models of psychological models of risk assessment, Rawls answered that people would want to be sure that, if they were vulnerable, the vulnerable would not be made worse off. Thus, he derived principles of distributive justice on the background of individuals with autonomy and freedom agreeing on what would be fair.

   Business ethicists Tom Donaldson and Tom Dunfee adapted these ideas into what they call Integrative Social Contracts. They posit an overarching social contract along the lines proposed by Rawls (as well as by many Kantian philosophers) but also recognize that there are extant social contracts. These extant contracts are what communities already use as principles of justice. Donaldson and Dunfee argue that there should be moral free space for these extant norms to develop and as long as people have the choice as to whether to belong to that community, the norms of that extant community are authentic. Then they take a step further to argue that there are also cross-cultural, universal hypernorms and if extant norms are in accordance with these hypernorms, then the norms are also legitimate.

   The point is that these contemporary business ethics positions—and Integrative Social Contracts Theory is a major theory today—the same principles underlying the contracts you have studied in this chapter also provide guidance for making ethical decisions in business.

2. **MOVING TO THE** more practical, as is the custom of this section, take a look at the cases in this chapter and ask whether or not you believe they are decided fairly or not. What are the principles that you would apply in order to determine whether or not these cases where decided fairly?

   More specially, think of the cases that are concerned with fraud. This may seem like a simple question, but what is the problem with fraud? Why is it a problem legally and why is it a problem ethically?

3. **AT WHAT POINT** does negotiating turn from bargaining to fraud? For example, do you have to tell the whole truth about how much you would pay for your house? Is it fraud to say you'll only pay $500,000 if you would be delighted to buy the house for $600,000? At what point does good hard negotiating cross the line?

4. **WITH RESPECT TO *ETHICS VIGNETTES*,** take a look at the *Barlow Clowes International* case in Chapter 2. Is this an example of fraud? Do off-shore financial accounts, by their very nature, constitute a fraud, an appearance of an impropriety, or at least merit a presumption of suspicion? Or are they simply savvy business practices? What about the nature of the transactions themselves in the *Barlow Clowes* case? The judge indicates that they would be dishonest from the normal use of the term? What does that mean? How would you characterize them? Do you think the judge should use the same standards?

5. **ARE FRAUDS PERPETRATED** by charities even worse than common, ordinary business frauds or is there no difference at all? What do you think should be done when charities appear to commit fraud?

CHAPTER

10

Contracts: The Uniform Commercial Code

In the late 1930s, there was an increasing awareness of the need for a more uniform set of laws governing exchanges. Prior to the twentieth century, individual state contract law, which of course can vary from state to state, controlled exchanges. But with an increasingly interdependent country and commerce flowing regularly across state borders, there was a need to provide more predictable laws so that businesspersons could effectively plan their affairs. The UCC was first passed into law in 1952. Since then, every state (except Louisiana) has enacted it, as has the District of Columbia and the Virgin Islands. There have been several subsequent amendments as well, such as those in 1987 to address the rising importance of leases and in 2003 to address electronic commerce.

The Code is an effort of the National Conference of Commissioners on Uniform State Laws and the American Law Institute. Gathering some of the nation's top scholars, these organizations propose a uniform set of laws; that do not become law until adopted. It is up to the states to decide whether or not to enact them.

The Code has the following Articles:

1. General Provisions and Definitions
2. Sales (Article 2) and Leases (Article 2A)
3. Negotiable Instruments
4. Bank Deposits and Collections (Article 4) and Funds Transfers (Article 4A)
5. Letters of Credit
6. Bulk Transfers
7. Warehouse Receipts, Bills of Lading and Other Documents of Title
8. Investment Securities
9. Secured Transactions
10. Effective Date and Repealer
11. Effective Date and Transitions

From the above list one can tell that the scope of the UCC is vast. Negotiable Instruments and Secured Transactions each merit a separate course in law schools. Because this textbook does not aim to cover all the legal issues that can pertain to business, but instead the most common ones, we limit our coverage to Article 2 on Sales. This is the UCC version of contract law. Much of it mirrors what we have already seen concerning contracts, but there are some important variations.

The UCC's aim is to make the laws governing sales contracts clearer and simpler. The UCC achieves this aim by having a common statute governing sales applicable to nearly all of the states. If the UCC did only that, it would make the law more predictable for businesses. But the UCC does more than this. It takes notice of a well-developed market that provides a great deal of information to businesspeople and judges alike. With a goal of facilitating business transactions, the UCC pragmatically provides multiple procedures for filling in gaps in a contract. Is the price missing on a contract? The court could read it in by resorting to information from market prices. Do standardized contract forms conflict with each other? The court, within some limits as pertaining to **material terms** can read them in a way to form the contract. Does the contract need to be modified? New consideration is not a requirement.

The basic provisions of contract law already covered in this book still apply to the UCC. This chapter will identify some key provisions and variations from the common law of contracts. The following chart provides a way to start on that analysis.

TOPIC	CHARACTERISTICS	COMPARED TO COMMON LAW
MERCHANTS EXCEPTION	Particular rules when both parties are merchants	Does not exist in Common Law
CONTRACT TERMS	Open Price, Delivery, Price, BOTF; Firm Offers	Much reliance on business customs for merchants to fill in the blanks; More liberal as well for non-merchants, but generally return to a meeting of minds
WRITINGS	Statute of frauds: For merchants: 10-day confirming, special manufacturing rule; For non-merchants: $500 rule enforceable if admitted in court or pleadings, partial performance Parol Evidence Rule: course of dealing, trade usage, course of performance	Common Law has much stricter application on both Statute of Frauds and Parol Evidence Rule
CONSIDERATION	Similar except with respect to modification of contract	Pre-existing duty rule stricter and Firm Offer harder to establish
REMEDIES	Expectation damages and equitable damages	More targeted

I. Merchants Rules

ARTICLE 2 OF THE UCC applies to the sale of goods, as opposed to real estate or services (though there can be times when there is a mix of real estate or services with goods). Thus, it has a wide application. However it also has specific provisions that apply when both the parties are merchants. What is a merchant? Section 2-104 defines a merchant in one of three ways: (1) if the person deals in the kind of goods involved in the contract (such as wholesaler, retailer, or manufacturer, (2) If the person holds himself out has having unique skills and knowledge relevant to the transaction, and (3) if the person employs someone as an intermediary (such as an agent or broker). It is important to note that the determination of a whether or not a person is a merchant depends on the transaction, not the person himself. For example, a retailer of bicycles may be a merchant when he is buying bikes, helmets, and other related items from a supplier, but not a merchant at all when buying a business suit. Special rules for merchants apply throughout the UCC. Major ones will be covered in the appropriate section.

The following case discusses issues related to defining a merchant—in this case a farmer—as well as several other provisions of the UCC, which will be discussed later in this chapter.

Brooks Cotton Company, Inc. v. Williams

381 S.W.3d 414, 77 UCC Rep.Serv.2d 493 (2012)

J. Steven Stafford, J.

Defendant/Appellant Bradley F. Williams is a cotton and soybean farmer with a high school education. According to Plaintiff/Appellee Brooks Cotton Company, Inc. ("Brooks Cotton"), on or about August 5, 2010, Mr. Williams entered into a oral contract to sell his 2010 cotton production to Brooks Cotton. The alleged contract was recorded in the Brooks Cotton purchase book on August 6, 2010 and provided that Mr. Williams would sell his entire 1000 acre cotton production to Brooks Cotton. The price allegedly agreed upon was $0.20 per pound over the guaranteed government loan amount of $0.542 per pound, totaling $0.742 per pound of cotton. At the time of the alleged agreement, Mr. Williams had not yet harvested his cotton. According to the record, Mr. Williams ultimately produced approximately 1206 bales of cotton in 2010. If the contract had been performed as allegedly agreed, the total contract price for Mr. Williams' cotton would have been approximately $446,000.00. Brooks Cotton sent written confirmation of the alleged agreement to Mr. Williams on or about September 4, 2010, nearly thirty days after the contract was allegedly agreed to on the phone. Mr. Williams asserts that he never entered into an oral contract with Brooks Cotton, although he did not call or write Brooks Cotton to object to the written terms sent to him.

Mr. Williams did not deliver all of his 2010 cotton production to Brooks Cotton. On October 30, 2010, Mr. Williams partially performed on the alleged oral contract, delivering 307 bales of the estimated 1206 bales of cotton produced by his farm in 2010. Mr. Williams refused to deliver the remaining cotton, asserting that there was not a valid contract between Mr. Williams and Brooks Cotton.

On or about November 18, 2010, Brooks Cotton filed a Complaint for Specific Performance, Injunctive Relief, and Damages against Mr. Williams. An injunction hearing was held on November 30, 2010. Mr. Williams testified at the hearing regarding his experience and skills in marketing cotton, stating that he had been a cotton farmer for approximately twenty-five years. Mr. Williams testified that, in the majority of the years prior to 2010, he had entered into a contract with Brooks Cotton to sell his cotton crop. In most of those years, however, Mr. Williams agreed to the contract in person at Brooks Cotton's office after the cotton had been harvested, rather than over the telephone prior to the harvest. Mr. Williams did

testify that he was familiar with the practice of "booking" cotton over the phone, as he had previously "booked" his cotton with Brooks Cotton in 2003. Mr. Williams testified, however, that he did not "book" his cotton with Brooks Cotton in August 2010, but that he merely called to discuss cotton prices. In addition, Mr. Williams explained his process for determining the price at which he will sell his cotton, wherein he reviews the selling price of his cotton crop in the previous three years. Although Mr. Williams testified that he receives daily texts regarding the price of cotton, he explained that he was not familiar with the common practice of "hedging" engaged in by many cotton merchants. David Brooks of Brooks Cotton explained that hedging is a common practice in the cotton trade. In addition, Mr. Williams testified that he never uses his potential cotton crop as collateral on loans to finance the cotton crop, instead relying on various equipment and land. Mr. Williams went on to testify that he owed approximately $400,000.00 to the bank in loans, but that he had approximately $40,000.00 in bank accounts due to his off-season construction work. Based on the testimony, the court issued a preliminary injunction on the sale of Mr. Williams' 2010 production of cotton.

* * *

The central issue presented in this interlocutory appeal is whether a farmer, such as Mr. Williams, may be considered a merchant under the UCC In this case, Mr. Williams' designation as a merchant is critical to the outcome of the lawsuit. If Mr. Williams is considered a merchant, then the merchant exception to the Statute of Frauds applies and the case can proceed; if Mr. Williams cannot be considered a merchant, regardless of whether he entered into an oral contract with Brooks Cotton, an oral contract will not be sufficient to bind him.

"THE CENTRAL ISSUE presented in this interlocutory appeal is whether a farmer, such as Mr. Williams, may be considered a merchant under the UCC."

Generally contracts need not be in writing to be enforceable, unless they are of the kind that the Statute of Frauds or other law requires to be written. One type of contract that must be in writing is a contract for the sale of goods priced over $500.00 * * * It is undisputed that the alleged contract for the sale of Mr. Williams' 2010 cotton production far exceeded $500.00. Accordingly, unless an exception applies, the Statute of Frauds requires that the contract be in writing to be enforceable. However, the UCC provides an exception to this rule in situations where both parties are merchants:

> Between merchants if within a reasonable time a writing or record in confirmation of the contract and sufficient against the sender is received and the party receiving it has reason to know its contents, it satisfies the

> requirements of subsection (1) against such party unless written notice of objection to its contents is given within ten (10) days after it is received.
>
> * * *

[W]e adopt the rule that a farmer may be considered a merchant for the purposes of the merchant exception to the Statute of Frauds, when the farmer possesses sufficient expertise in not only the cultivation, but also the sale of crops. However, the determination of whether a particular farmer is a merchant is a mixed question of fact and law, which must be determined on a case-by-case basis, taking into account "the individual experience and activities of the person involved." Accordingly, we reverse the trial court's determination that "Tennessee's farmer[s]," as a whole, are considered merchants for purposes of the Statute of Frauds. Instead, trial courts should consider the following, nonexhaustive, criteria in determining whether a particular farmer is a merchant for purposes of the Statute of Frauds:

> (1) the length of time the farmer has been engaged in the practice of selling his product to the marketers of his product; (2) the degree of business acumen shown by the farmer in his dealings with other parties; (3) the farmer's awareness of the operation and existence of farm markets; and (4) the farmer's past experience with or knowledge of the customs and practices which are unique to the particular marketing of the product which he sells.

Applying the above factors to Mr. Williams, we note that several factors weigh in favor of a determination that Mr. Williams was a merchant for purposes of the Statute of Frauds. First, Mr. Williams testified that he had been a cotton farmer for approximately twenty-five years and that throughout the years, he sold both his and his landlord's cotton production. Next, Mr. Williams testified that he had previously engaged in oral crop "booking," a practice that other farmers testified was common in the cotton trade. Mr. Williams also testified that he determined when to sell his cotton, and at what price, by using a three-year history of his cotton sales, as well as daily notifications about the price of cotton on the cotton market. Mr. Williams also testified that he receives periodicals about cotton farming, such as *Cotton Grower.*

However, some factors weigh against a determination that Mr. Williams is a merchant for purposes of the Statute of Frauds. First, Mr. Williams testified that he does not engage in the practice of hedging; indeed, Mr. Williams testified that he was unaware of what the term "hedging" meant. However, the testimony of Mr. Brooks, as well as the depositions of several other area farmers, established that hedging is a practice that is unique and integral to the marketing of cotton. In addition, though Mr. Williams testified that he had previously orally booked his cotton with Brooks Cotton, his testimony shows that he had only engaged in this practice once over the last several years. Further, the record is unclear whether the periodicals Mr. Williams receives deal with the cotton trade, or solely with cotton farming.

* * *

The judgment of the Chancery Court of Crockett County is affirmed in part, reversed in part, and remanded for further proceedings in accordance with this opinion. Costs are taxed equally to Appellant Bradley F. Williams, and his surety, and to Appellee Brooks Cotton Company, Inc., for all of which execution may issue if necessary.

Regardless of whether or not you intend to become a farmer, the case above is important because it defines the set of criteria used to determine what constitutes a "merchant". It is hard to imagine a time and place when a corporation's sales would not make them a merchant. But even that statement might be too broad. If Williams had been an incorporated farmer, would that have made a difference? It might because it shows more business acumen, but it doesn't necessarily prove that he is aware of hedging practices, something important to the case. Thus, the determination of whether someone is merchant or not is not always straightforward and depends a great deal on the facts of the case and their application to criteria, as set out above.

II. Contract Terms

IN COMMON LAW, a contract required a meeting of the minds. The offer and acceptance of the contract needed to be, if not the mirror-image of each other, very close to that. The UCC relaxes this requirement. As noted above, provided there is a manifestation of intent that the parties desired to enter into a contract with each other, Section 2-204(3) (and 2A-204(3) for leases) permits a court to read terms into the contract in order to put the contract into effect. Thus if a contract calls for the sale and conveyance of 1,000 widgets, but fails to state the sales price, the court can consult the market in order to determine the typical price for widgets of similar quality.

The same holds true for delivery. Perhaps the parties entered into an agreement, but failed to designate the time and place of delivery. By consulting normal trade usage and custom, the court could read into a contract where and when a delivery of a product would take place. Bear in mind, of course, that most transactions already do this as the parties work through missing elements themselves. But there are times and places where the ambiguity gives rise to a lawsuit in which the court is called upon to interpret the contract.

In the following case, the court looks extensively at trade usage, here with respect to collective card games, as a way to determine whether or not the contract had been breached and whether certain acts constituted an acceptance of the goods in question.

Cartamundi USA, Inc. v. Bunky's Enterprises, Inc.

2012 WL 3933056 (Conn. Super. Ct. 2012)

Linda K. Lager, Judge.

In January 2008, Gress obtained a license on behalf of Bunky's to use the "Terminator™" name as well as images for the purpose of a collectible card game he created known as "Terminator 2–Judgment Day." Gress negotiated with Cartamundi's employee Rosemary Mills (Mills), an account manager and sales executive, over a period of months regarding the manufacture of the game which he had designed. On June 9, 2008 she sent him proposal #70095 (the June 9th proposal) which contained information pertaining to the collation of the product, the quantity, packaging, assembly and pricing (exhibit 1). The collation, packaging, assembly, delivery, quantity and payment terms were set forth on page 2 of the June 9th proposal. The proposal also included eighteen numbered paragraphs under the title "Printing Trade Customs" as well as a section entitled "Additional Terms and Conditions."

On June 16, 2008, Mills e-mailed to Gress what she described as "a corrected formal" containing a revised second page for proposal #70095 (exhibit 6) (corrected formal). The correction pertained to the collation of "rare" and "ultra rare" cards. Collation refers to the assembly of the cards into final packaging. Initially, the cards are printed in large sheets, referred to as forms, and then cut into single cards. According to the proposal, there were going to be two forms of common cards and one form of rare and ultra rare cards (exhibits 1, 6). Cartamundi then would assemble the cards according to the collation terms agreed to by the parties. Those terms are set forth in the section of the proposal titled "PACKAGING/DELIVERY" on the second page.

The June 9th proposal stated that each "case" would contain two packs with a rare card and one pack with a ultra rare card inserted in lieu of a common card while the "corrected formal" stated that each "POP" would contain two packs with a rare card and one pack with a ultra rare card inserted in lieu of a common card. A "POP" is a display box. Each POP was to contain 30 packs of five cards each or 150 cards. A case would consist of ten to twelve POPs or 1500 to 1800 cards. The second page of the corrected formal specified that the order quantity was 100,000 booster packs and 1,000 starter boxes. The second page also contained a production schedule and the payment terms.

On June 19, 2008, Gress authorized Cartamundi in writing to proceed with the production as specified in the corrected formal. Gress also paid the required 50% down in advance of production by way of a check drawn on Bunky's account in the amount of $17,110.00 dated June 25, 2008 (exhibit D). Production then commenced. A master set of pre-press proofs was sent to Gress who returned it to Cartamundi without any markings. Cartamundi manufactured the game in conformance with the terms of the corrected formal. On or about August 15, 2008, Cartamundi shipped a few cases of the finished product to Gress who was attending a convention. At that time Gress opened up a number of packs in order to create a card catalogue but was unable to put together a full set of cards from the packs that he opened. As a result, he believed certain cards were missing. He never complained to Cartamundi in writing about missing cards although he did complain, in an undated letter, about the ratio of rare and ultra rare cards per display box (exhibit 7).

The completed order remains in Cartamundi's warehouse. An invoice that was sent to the defendant for the balance due of $17,110.00 (exhibit 2) has not been paid. Additional pertinent facts will be set forth below.

II.

* * *

The June 16, 2008 e-mail from Mills, including her cover letter and the attached first two pages of proposal #70095 as corrected, followed by the submission of Gress's signature on proposal #70095 on June 19, 2008 and Bunky's issuance of a check in the requisite amount on June 25, 2008, provides ample documentary evidence of the existence and essential terms of the contract. The fact that Cartamundi manufactured and packaged the game in conformance with the terms of the corrected formal is also evidence of the terms of the agreement.

* * *

The only difference between the June 9th proposal and the "corrected formal" concerns the packaging of the rare and ultra rare cards. Under the collation terms of the corrected formal, more of the rare and ultra rare cards would be packaged than under the collation terms of the June 9th proposal. Thus the different collation terms were beneficial, not harmful, to Bunky's and did not materially alter the contract. UCC § 2-207(2)(b). See 2 Anderson, Uniform Commercial Code (3d ed.1997) § 2-207:81. Furthermore, the UCC presumes that different or additional terms will be included in the contract. Assuming, without deciding, that Bunky's did not assent to the change in the collation terms, Bunky's has failed to establish "that, under the circumstances, it cannot be presumed that a reasonable merchant would have consented to the additional term." A "profession of surprise" is not enough.

Under Texas law, the elements of a breach of contract claim are: (1) the existence of a valid contract between plaintiff and defendant; (2) the plaintiff's performance or tender of performance; (3) the defendant's breach of the contract; and (4) the plaintiff's damage as a result of the breach. Connecticut law is similar. The court has determined that there was a valid contract between Cartamundi and Bunky's. The evidence establishes that Cartamundi performed the contract by producing and assembling the card packages in conformance with the terms of the corrected formal and by sending a partial shipment to Gress on or about August 15, 2008. Whether Bunky's breached the contract and the measure of damages is governed by the UCC and not the common law.

* * *

The evidence is insufficient to establish both the existence and scope of trade usage. The express contract terms regarding the collation of the POPs are clear. There is no credible evidence of implied terms that are inconsistent with the contract's express terms. The evidence establishes that Cartamundi tendered the goods in conformance with the terms of the contract, exhibits 5, 8, at the time and place Bunky's had specified. The court concludes as a matter of fact that the goods were conforming within the meaning of UCC § 2-106.

* * *

Cartamundi maintains that Bunky's waived any right to reject the goods because it did not provide any notice within fifteen days of the partial delivery made on or about August 15, 2008 as required by paragraph 16 of the "Printing Trade Customs" that were part of the contract. It is not necessary to address this issue because the evidence fails to establish that Bunky's, acting in good faith, clearly and unambiguously rejected the goods which, in all respects, conformed to the contract. Although Gress testified that he did not receive the run of cards that he had expected because he was unable to fully catalogue the cards based on the partial delivery to the convention, his undated written notification to Cartamundi concerning a "bad run" only referenced the ratio of rare and ultra rare cards to common cards (exhibit 7). Cartamundi reviewed those complaints and followed up on the issue of card ratios in e-mails dated September 3 and 5, 2008 explaining that the collation conformed to the contract. There is no documentary evidence of any follow-up to this exchange.

Bunky's did not return the cards that were delivered to Gress at the convention. Gress not only opened the packs to put together a card catalogue but he also gave packs of cards to potential customers at the convention. Gress and his wife opened additional packs following the convention in an effort to catalogue the cards. These were reasonable uses consistent with ownership.

Based on the credible evidence, the court concludes that Bunky's accepted the goods within the meaning of UCC § 2-606 and never made an effective rejection within the meaning of UCC § 2-602. "Once acceptance of goods occurs, [t]he buyer must pay at the contract rate for any goods accepted.

V.

Since Bunky's accepted conforming goods, it was obligated to pay the contract price to Cartamundi. Bunky's did not pay the balance of the invoice (exhibit 2).

Cartamundi is entitled to damages for the contract price, along with incidental damages. UCC § 2–708(1) damages are inadequate in this case because Cartamundi has produced a specialty item, a collectible card game, that cannot be resold to another buyer.

* * *

Based on the foregoing, judgment shall enter in favor of the plaintiff Cartamundi USA, Inc. and against the defendant Bunky's Enterprises, Inc., on the complaint and in favor of the counterclaim defendant Cartamundi USA, Inc. and against the counterclaim plaintiff Bunky's Enterprises, Inc. on the counterclaim. * * *

The above case invokes Section 2-207 of the Uniform Commercial Code. That section is often used by courts to find a way to construe a contract between the parties. The following materials continue the exploration of that section.

Courts do not tend to read a **quantity term** into a contract. Many sources exist to determine the price of an item. Trade usage and custom help a great deal to determine delivery points. But quantity is something determined more between the specific buyer and seller than by the market. Even so, Section 2-306(1) will allow courts to read quantity terms for certain kinds of **output contracts**, or contracts in which a buyer agrees to buy all the seller's production (or output) of a product or when a seller agrees to satisfy all of the buyer's need for a product, say for a component part the buyer needs for subsequent manufacture of a finished product. In such cases, the court can find evidence of what the quantity term would be.

Section 2-207 has caused more than a few headaches for law students, business law students, and even lawyers and businesspeople. It is sometimes called "The Battle of the Forms." The reality is that in today's business environment, contracts are created by the exchange of forms prepared by each party's lawyer. The **offeror** sends over a form and rather than the buyer simply accepting the offeror's form, the buyer instead sends back his own form to accept. Of course, the buyer's form does not have identical terms to that of the seller's. This would not create a contract at common law because there would be no mirror image; common law requires that all parties agree on exactly the same terms. However, the UCC provides a (complicated) procedure for putting these forms—as inconsistent as they may be—together to form a contract. The basic rules are as follows:

First, if the **offeree** sends an acceptance within a reasonable time, then a contract is formed even if it contains terms different from those set out by the offeror. An exception is if the offeree explicitly says that there is no contract unless the offeror accepts those differing terms. If that requirement is included, then there is no contract. But if the offeree does not require that the offeror specifically accept those terms, then those terms, again even if they differ from those of the offeror, become part of the contract.

How does one navigate the fact that terms in the contract conflict with each other? The UCC says that the additional terms are proposals to be added to the contract unless they **materially alter** the contract or if **seasonable notice** has already been given objecting to the terms.

Finally, the court will look at the conduct of the parties. If the parties are acting as if they have a contract, the court will find that they do have a contract on the basis of the terms in which they do agree, plus any other terms that can be ascertained from other sections of the UCC.

It does not take long for the number of disputes that can arise out of Section 2-207 to multiply. On exactly which terms are the parties agreeing by their conduct? What is a seasonable notice of objection? What constitutes a material alteration?

In working through the battle of the forms, as well as other sections of the UCC, it is important for businesspeople (and their lawyer) to bear in mind problems that can be arise from too much rule-making and too onerous a set of contractual requirements. The businessperson who brags that his lawyer is so tough that no one will sign the contract she drafts does not have a tough lawyer; that's a dumb lawyer. Businesspeople won't make any money if no one will sign a contract with them.

III. Writings

THE UCC has several important provisions pertaining to writing. Section 2-205 (and 2A-205 for leases) provides for a **firm offer**, which is a kind of option contract where the offeror keeps the offer open for a specific period of time, but not more than three months. If an offeror makes a firm offer, he is not able to revoke it as he normally would prior to acceptance. This can be enforced even without consideration for leaving the offer open. The key is that the offeror indicates that it is a firm offer.

The Statute of Frauds, you'll remember, applies at common law to contracts for real estate, suretyship, and services lasting more than one year. The UCC adds provisions that contracts for more than five hundred dollars ($500) are not enforceable unless they are in writing or some other record establishes the specifics of the contract. The $500 requirement can make for some tricky questions. If a contract was subject to the Statute of Frauds (i.e. it was for more than $500) but the modification reduces it below $500, the modification does not need to be in writing.

Consistent with its effort to support contracts, the writing requirement need not be instantaneous. It can be met with a written confirmation within a reasonable time. If the seller is making "specially manufactured" goods for the buyer, an oral agreement can be enforced unless the goods can be easily sold elsewhere.

The Uniform Electronic Transactions Act and the Electronic Signatures in Global and National Commerce Act both make clear that email and other electronic signatures can meet the requirements of the Statute of Frauds.

At common law, the parol evidence rule would not allow for provisions that are not reduced to writings within the contract itself unless there is some ambiguity or to prove fraud or a defense. Under the UCC, trade usage would be allowed beyond the terms of the contract, as would other contemporaneous terms unless it is clear that no additional terms could, indeed, be added.

We have already seen that a firm offer does not require consideration to make it binding. The UCC follows this rule with one exception: the UCC also provides that modifications of contracts need not have additional consideration provided that it is done in good faith. That would not be true at common law, but the UCC is, as we have seen throughout the chapter, more adaptable in finding the existence of a contract.

IV. Remedies

THE UCC'S APPROACH to damages is to put the parties into the position they would have been had the contract been performed. This expectation model includes **compensatory damages**, but does not trigger **punitive damages.**

The goal of putting the parties into the position they would have been had the contract been performed does not require just one approach. For example, if a buyer is insolvent, the seller can stop delivery or reclaim goods; if a buyer is solvent, the seller can sue for the price of goods or resell the goods and get **cover damages,** which looks like this:

market price at the time of performance	
-	paid contract price
+	incidental damages
-	expenses saved because of the breach
= cover damages	

The following case demonstrates how this works.

Kabbalah Jeans, Inc. v. Cn USA International Corp.

26 Misc.3d 1241(A), 907 N.Y.S.2d 438 (2010)

CAROLYN E. DEMAREST, J.

* * * Plaintiff, a distributor of clothing, claims that it had a meeting in February 2008 with defendant, a manufacturer, wherein the parties agreed that plaintiff would purchase certain custom made clothing items from defendant to be manufactured by defendant for plaintiff at its overseas factory. The first purchase order generated by defendant was dated March 12, 2008, and reflected that defendant was to manufacture and deliver to plaintiff by April 2, 2008 and April 8, 2008 certain custom clothing items for $39,772.80. The purchase order explicitly stated, in language immediately to the left of the total price for the goods ordered, that defendant was "not responsible for delays in delivery." Although these goods arrived late, plaintiff paid defendant the full price for these goods.

On April 24, 2008, a second purchase order was generated by defendant, reflecting an agreement by defendant to manufacture at its overseas factory certain custom clothing items, which consisted of men's button-down fashion shirts, for an agreed upon total price of $60,480. The quantities, descriptions, and prices of the goods ordered were listed in this purchase order. However, there was no expected date of delivery listed in this purchase order. As with the earlier purchase order, this purchase order explicitly stated, in language immediately to the left of the total price for the goods ordered, that defendant was "not responsible for delays in delivery."

A third purchase order dated May 2, 2008, which was generated by defendant, reflected that plaintiff ordered additional custom clothing items to be manufactured by defendant at its overseas factory for the total price of $101,606.40. This purchase order listed the quantities, descriptions, and prices for these items, but did not list any delivery date. As with the two earlier purchase orders, this purchase order explicitly stated, in language immediately to the left of the total price for the goods ordered, that defendant was "not responsible for delays in delivery."

On May 2, 2008, plaintiff paid a deposit in the amount of $26,606 .40 (consisting of a payment of $11,088 and a credit from a prior transaction in the sum of $15,518.40) toward the amounts due and owing under the April 24, 2008 and May 2, 2008 purchase orders. Despite the absence of a delivery date in the April 24, 2008 and May 2, 2008 purchase orders, plaintiff claims that there was a conversation between it and defendant, in which defendant represented that the merchandise would be available for pick up by plaintiff at defendant's warehouse facility on or before Father's Day of 2008 (i.e., June 15, 2008).

Defendant manufactured the custom clothing items listed on the two purchase orders for plaintiff and tendered delivery of these goods to plaintiff. Defendant asserts that this tender of delivery of the goods to plaintiff occurred on June 26,

2008. Plaintiff refused to accept the goods or to pay defendant the $135,480 balance due for the goods based upon the ground that the goods had not been delivered by Father's Day.

Since defendant refused to return plaintiff's deposit and demanded that plaintiff pay the balance of the purchase price, plaintiff, on July 29, 2008, filed this action against defendant. Plaintiff's complaint alleges that defendant breached the agreement with it by failing to timely deliver the goods by Father's Day 2008. Plaintiff's first cause of action seeks the return of plaintiff's deposit in the sum of $26,606.40. Plaintiff's second cause of action seeks to recover lost profits in the amount of $100,000 based upon defendant's breach of the agreement. Defendant has interposed an answer, which asserts three counterclaims, seeking the $135,480 balance due and owing from plaintiff under the purchase orders for the goods. Defendant's first counterclaim alleges a breach of contract by plaintiff, defendant's second counterclaim alleges a repudiation by plaintiff, and defendant's third counterclaim seeks recovery of the price from plaintiff.

Defendant, in support of its motion, asserts that it manufactured and delivered the goods in accordance with the terms of the contract, as set forth in the purchase orders, and that plaintiff has breached the contract by failing to accept the goods and tender payment of the balance of the purchase price. In opposition to defendant's motion, plaintiff has submitted the affidavit of its vice president, Jacobov, who asserts that clothing is seasonal, and that plaintiff had ordered the merchandise from defendant for the summer season. Plaintiff claims that defendant orally represented that the goods would be delivered by Father's Day 2008, and that the delivery was late because it was delivered approximately two to three weeks into the summer season. Plaintiff asserts that due to this delay, most of its customers had cancelled their orders, and that since the merchandise was of a seasonal nature, it would not be saleable at a profit to it due to defendant's late delivery.

Since the parties are merchants as that term is defined in Uniform Commercial Code (UCC) 2–104(1), and the transactions at issue are for the sale of goods as defined in UCC 2–105(1), the transactions are covered by UCC article 2 which governs the sale of goods. UCC 2–201(2) provides:

> "Between merchants if within a reasonable time a writing in confirmation of the contract and sufficient against the sender is received and the party receiving it has reason to know its contents, it satisfies the requirements of [the Statute of Frauds for the sale of goods for the price of $500 or more] against such party unless written notice of objection to its contents is given within ten days after it is received."

* * *

It is undisputed that plaintiff received the purchase orders and that plaintiff did not object to their contents within 10 days of such receipt. In addition, plaintiff admits, in its complaint and deposition testimony, that a contract for sale was made Plaintiff acknowledges that these purchase orders reflect the terms of the contract. * * * Pursuant to UCC 2-601(a), a buyer may reject goods if the goods or the tender of delivery fail in any respect to conform to the contract. Here, however, there was no term in the contract, as evidenced by the written purchase orders, requiring the delivery to take place by a certain date.

Pursuant to UCC 2–309(1), where the time for delivery is not agreed upon, it shall be a reasonable time. As discussed above, however, plaintiff alleges that a date no later than Father's Day 2008 was orally agreed upon, and that defendant did not deliver the goods until June 26, 2008, approximately one week after Father's Day (or, as alleged in plaintiff's complaint, until July 2, 2008, approximately two weeks after Father's Day). Even assuming that this delivery term was orally agreed upon, the unambiguous terms of the purchase orders stated that defendant was not responsible for any delays in delivery. Shlomi Skaf (Skaf), plaintiff's principal owner, at his deposition, confirmed that this disclaimer language was present on the purchase orders. Jacobov (who, as noted above, is plaintiff's vice president) testified, at his deposition, that he understood this phrase in the purchase orders to mean that defendant was "not responsible for delays." Skaf further testified, at his deposition, that he "saw [this language] but . . . didn't pay attention to it" Thus, pursuant to the written contractual terms, as memorialized in the purchase orders, the mere one or two-week delay in defendant's delivery of the goods would not entitle plaintiff to reject the goods.

Plaintiff contends that this notation in the purchase orders regarding a delay in delivery should not be considered a contract term because the purchase orders were delivered after the oral agreement to buy the goods was made, and because the purchase orders were never signed by it. As set forth above, however, UCC 2–201 does not require that the written memorialization occur at the same time as the alleged oral agreement or that the buyer sign the purchase order where it otherwise complies with that section and where no objection to the purchase order is made within 10 days.

Plaintiff further argues that the delay disclaimer language in the purchase orders nevertheless should not be found to be a contract term based upon its allegation that the oral agreement mandated delivery on or before Father's Day 2008. This argument must be rejected. * * * While plaintiff claims that it is the custom and usage of the industry that if merchandise is not received by a deadline date, the sale is deemed to be cancelled, it has submitted no evidentiary proof of any such custom and usage. Indeed, the agreement as to the delivery date alleged by plaintiff cannot be established by course of dealing or performance or usage of trade since the prior March 12, 2008 purchase order was delivered late and accepted by plaintiff.

* * *

By establishing that the parties had a contract and that plaintiff owed money on the contract, defendant has made out a *prima facie* case that it was not liable for breach of contract, but, rather, that plaintiff had breached its contract with it by refusing to accept the goods. It was, therefore, incumbent upon plaintiff to proffer evidentiary proof, in admissible form, sufficient to raise a triable issue of fact, which it has failed to do. Consequently, inasmuch as defendant has demonstrated that it did not breach the terms of the contract, as memorialized by the purchase orders, and that plaintiff has breached the contract by wrongfully refusing to accept the goods tendered by it, plaintiff is not entitled to a return of its $26,606.40 deposit nor lost profits. Thus, summary judgment dismissing plaintiff's first and second causes of action must be granted.

Defendant, in support of its counterclaims, asserts that plaintiff wrongfully rejected the goods and breached the contract between them. * * * Here, defendant has not resold the goods under UCC 2–706 nor does it seek the difference between the market price at the time and place for tender and the unpaid contract price under UCC 2–708. Rather, defendant seeks to recover the balance of the contract price of $135,480. Pursuant to UCC 2–709(1)(b), when the buyer fails to pay the price, the seller may recover the price "of goods identified to the contract if the seller is unable after reasonable effort to resell them at a reasonable price or the circumstances reasonably indicate that such effort will be unavailing." * * *

Thus, defendant is entitled to recover the contract balance of $135,480 from plaintiff in accordance with UCC 2–709. Although defendant's third counterclaim alleges storage costs, defendant has not provided any evidence of specific incidental damages incurred by it nor does it request incidental damages in its motion. Since the court finds that defendant is entitled to summary judgment in its favor in the amount of $135,480 on its third counterclaim for price, defendant's motion, insofar as it also seeks summary judgment in its favor in the amount of $135,480 based upon its first counterclaim for breach of contract and its second counterclaim for repudiation, is duplicative and rendered moot.

Accordingly, defendant's motion for summary judgment dismissing plaintiff's first and second causes of action, and for summary judgment in its favor on its third counterclaim for price in the amount of $135,480, is granted.

This constitutes the decision, order, and judgment of the court.

The buyer's remedies in the case of a breach are to reject any non-conforming goods or to accept non-conforming goods and sue for the difference in value between the two. The buyer can also sue for specific performance. The following cases demonstrate these options. As with other UCC cases, notice how fact-specific these cases can be and the freedom the courts feel they have to attempt to fashion a remedy that might blend money damages together with specific performance, two remedies that are generally thought to be mutually exclusive.

King Aircraft Sales, Inc., v. Lane

68 Wash.App. 706, 846 P.2d 550 (1993)

PEKELIS, ACTING CHIEF JUDGE.

Joe Lane, Jr., d/b/a The Lane Company, and Lane Aviation, Inc. (Lane) appeal the judgment of the trial court awarding King Aircraft Sales, Inc., d/b/a King Aviation Services (King) $338,280.60 in damages, prejudgment interest, attorney fees, and statutory costs for its breach of a contract to sell two airplanes to King. The principal issue presented in this appeal, one of first impression in Washington, is whether the trial court may award money damages as a remedy in a claim for specific performance under the Uniform Commercial Code * * *

The trial court found that in October 1988, King made a written offer to purchase two "quality, no damage" aircraft from Lane for $870,000. The offer was accompanied by a $10,000 deposit. Lane accepted the King offer both in writing and by depositing the $10,000 deposit. The acceptance created a contract of sale between the parties. King was to perform certain requirements but prior to the expiration of the time to perform, Lane advised King it was backing out of the agreement and that it had reached agreement with another party, Western Aircraft (Western), for the sale of the planes. Because at the time Lane backed out of the contract the time for King's performance had not yet expired, the trial court concluded that Lane's action was a breach of the contract.

King made it clear to both Lane and Western that it intended to enforce its contract with Lane and filed suit in Texas state court, seeking a temporary restraining order (TRO) to prohibit the sale of the aircraft to anyone other than King. The Texas state court issued the TRO. However, the case was later removed to a federal court in Texas, which denied King's motion to extend the TRO.

Lane then rescinded the Western contract and returned Western's deposit. Although Lane refused to honor the original contract with King, in settlement attempts pending litigation, it offered to sell the planes to King for the same price, but "as is", rather than "quality, no damage" airplanes as required in the original contract. King refused to purchase the planes under the terms of Lane's proposal and insisted on compliance with the original contract. At this time King had tentatively arranged to resell the planes for a profit of approximately $165,000.

* * *

In January of 1989, long before trial, Lane sold both planes "as is" to Priester Aviation (Priester) for $870,000. Priester put the planes on the market and resold them separately in a series of transactions.

After the Washington TRO was quashed, King moved for leave to reinstate and amend its complaint in Texas federal court to add a claim for legal remedies and once again add Lane as a defendant. The federal court granted the motion and an amended complaint was filed. However, Lane moved to dismiss the federal action for lack of personal jurisdiction. Lane's motion was granted and the action was dismissed without prejudice.

* * *

King's claim for specific performance and "other appropriate relief" was tried before the court without a jury. After trial, the court in its oral opinion ruled that Lane had breached the contract between the parties and that King should recover the "value" of the planes, as measured by the profit made by Priester, on its resale of the planes. Neither party had introduced evidence on this point, so the court ordered the parties to conduct post-trial discovery on the sale of the planes by Priester. Both parties objected to reopening the case for additional discovery.

* * *

The trial court concluded that under the total surrounding circumstances this case appropriately fell within the "other proper circumstances" clause of the specific performance statute of RCW 62A.2–716(1) and therefore King was entitled to specific performance. * * * The trial court concluded this value could be measured either by the blue book value, including increased price adjustments for the prime condition of the planes, or by King's expectation of profit. The trial court chose the latter and awarded judgment to King as set forth above.

Lane's principal claim on appeal is that because this was solely an action for specific performance under the UCC, and because the goods had been sold and thus inaccessible, no remedy was available to King. Lane contends the trial court had no authority to make a dollar value award. Its argument is as follows: Because King failed to plead a claim for monetary damages in its original complaint and had twice been denied permission by the court to add such a claim, no right to a damages remedy existed. However, because an adequate remedy at law existed, albeit not one available to King, specific performance was not proper here either.

We disagree and find that the remedy fashioned by the trial court was proper under the UCC and Washington common law.

* * *

The UCC, like its predecessor, the Uniform Sales Act, does not expressly require that the remedy at law be inadequate in order to invoke specific performance. However, the stated intent of the drafters of the UCC was to continue "in general prior policy as to specific performance and injunction against breach", and also "to further a more liberal attitude than some courts have shown" toward specific performance.

Nevertheless, there is a split of authority among those jurisdictions which have considered whether a buyer's remedy at law must be inadequate before specific performance can be granted.

* * * The general term "in other proper circumstances" expresses the drafters' intent to "further a more liberal attitude than some courts have shown in connection with the specific performance of contracts of sale." This Comment was not directed to the courts of this state, for long before the Code, we, in Missouri, took a practical approach in determining whether specific performance would lie for the breach of contract for the sale of goods and did not limit this relief only to the sale of "unique" goods.

We * * * find the liberal interpretation urged by the UCC drafters to be entirely consistent with the common law of our state. * * *

Lane claims that King has not met the requirements of § 2–716 because it has not shown an inability to cover. Lane contends that King could have covered by accepting Lane's "as is" proposal of November 4. King's failure to do so, argues Lane, was "commercially unreasonable." * * *

Here, the trial court held in conclusion 4 that King was under no obligation to purchase the planes on terms other than as contained in the contract. Specifically, the trial court found that King was under no obligation to accept the new November 4 proposal, which the trial court deemed to be considerably different from the original contract agreement. Lane neither assigns error to this conclusion nor to finding 29 which supports it. Lane has also failed to assign error to that part of conclusion 5 stating that plaintiff was unable to "cover" with alternate aircraft, but has only assigned error to the apparent contradiction between finding 39 (airplanes not unique) and conclusion 5 (both aircraft are unique). An unchallenged conclusion of law becomes the law of the case. Therefore, the findings and conclusions listed above will not be disturbed on appeal.

We conclude the trial court properly determined that specific performance was an appropriate remedy here. At the time King commenced its action for specific performance Lane was still in possession of the planes; thus, the court properly acquired equity jurisdiction. The airplanes, although not necessarily "unique", were rare enough so as to make the ability to cover virtually impossible. Furthermore, Lane, by its own act of selling the planes, incapacitated itself from performance. Under these circumstances, the court of equity did not err in finding that "other proper circumstances" were present for issuance of relief under a claim of specific performance under the UCC. The trial court had the discretion to award the legal remedy of damages or other relief deemed just by the trial court. For the reasons above, we conclude that under RCW 62A.2–716 and Washington common law the trial court's determination that "other proper circumstances" existed is correct and permitted it to fashion the relief it did.

* * *

The requirement that damages be liquidated or determinable limits awards of prejudgment interest to situations where no discretion on the part of the trier of fact is required to determine the reasonable amount of damages.

Here, the trial court findings indicated alternative grounds for "damages." Besides making a discretionary decision as to which ground to award as the "value," i.e., the lost profit mode, the court considered factors such as the costs of sale, corrosion proofing the engine, and arguably speculation at the "potential" sales prices King would have received. We conclude that with the exception of the $10,000 good faith deposit held by Lane, the damages were neither liquidated nor determinable and therefore prejudgment interest does not lie.

As such, we reverse and remand this issue to the trial court for recalculation of prejudgment interest based only on the $10,000 good faith deposit.

The decision of the trial court is affirmed in part and reversed in part and remanded to the trial court for proceedings consistent with this opinion.

The Uniform Commercial Code is important to business but it can be a complicated statute. The nuances of any specific provision of the UCC are probably best left to a businessperson's attorney. Yet there are some basic principles that will help a businessperson even before calling a lawyer. First, if one is a merchant, as we have seen, special rules apply. Second, those rules encourage both caution and flexibility. The UCC takes the words of businesspeople seriously, so what a businessperson writes and says are important. At the same time, sometimes businesspersons simply act and leave the verbiage for later or don't worry about the language at all and simply put agreements into effect. In those cases, courts are willing to fill in the blanks in order to find contracts as long as it seems like the parties are trying to conduct a commercial relationship.

The UCC is not unique. It is the product of academics, legislators and judges trying to fashion a uniform law that could be adopted by the different states. Its uniformity allows for businesses to plan based on the predictability of finding comparable laws from one jurisdiction to another. Other efforts, often noted throughout the text in their forms of Restatements, try to do something similar with respect to Products Liability, Agency and other areas of the law. These efforts sometimes result in model laws enacted by the states, which is happened with the UCC. Yet the desire to codify and unify cuts in different directions; it provides uniformity and predictability, but it also homogenizes. We will see examples of this push and pull between uniformity and diversity later in the book.

NOTES AND COMMENTS on the Legal Environment of Business

1. **ARTICLE 2 OF THE UCC** applies to the sale of goods. Should the scope of the UCC be extended to all contracts, such as for services?

2. **ONE OF THE MAIN ARGUMENTS** for the UCC, and other similar uniform statutes, is that they provide more systemic reliability for businesses to rely upon. Do you agree? Would businesses be better off if each state and territory had its own set of laws? Does the same analogy apply globally as well? What would be the pros and cons of a uniform contracts system worldwide?

3. **WHILE THE UCC** aims to make uniform, systematize and use market information sources to "fill in the blanks" and find the existence of business contracts, all so that commerce can operate more predictably and efficiently, it remains a complex document. Determining who is a merchant or how to calculate remedies often gets into rarefied legal air. Should the UCC be made even more straightforward so that it is more accessible to business people? How would you go about doing this?

NOTES AND COMMENTS on the Ethical Environment of Business

1. **REVIEW THE CASES FROM THIS CHAPTER.** Do you believe they were decided fairly? Why or why not? Do you think the effort of the UCC to find contracts between business people, even if they have not fully come to a meeting of the minds is a good one? Or does it assume too much and that instead, we should take a more common law approach that makes sure that both parties agree on exactly the same thing? What are the tradeoffs between the approaches? Which you do prefer?

2. **WHY SHOULDN'T WE** extend the UCC to sales of services or property? Why should they be different from the sale of goods? What does that difference say about the nature of the transactions concerning services and property, including the moral value of them? Do you think they should be treated differently, as they are now, or should they be treated the same? Explain why or why not?

3. **ONE OF THE ADVANTAGES** of a code, here of a commercial code, is that the requirements are set out explicitly, more so than when one has to figure out the law by looking only at custom and precedent. Yet, as the cases in this chapter show, one still has to do that, otherwise, there wouldn't be cases! If a code is fully able to account for all the things that can go wrong or if it can provide complete guidance, then one would not have to appeal to the court system to resolve disagreements. With that in mind, do commercial codes help or not?

4. **ASSUMING THERE IS SOME BENEFIT** to codes, the next question becomes whether codes of conduct are helpful with respect to ethics as well. Many companies have codes of conduct. Industries do too. Yet, do these simply become another set of laws? Do they inspire any one? What benefits do they provide?

5. **DO YOU THINK** that more laws and regulation are the way to improve ethical conduct? How do they help? Certainly, telling a person that if they violate a provision of a law, they will go to jail is a way to get someone's attention and provide a strong deterrent. If you were working for a company, what would be the most effective for you to conduct yourself more ethically?

CHAPTER

11

Torts

Imagine that, after college, you continued to law school. You are now practicing law in a small town, living in a house across from a local college. Your alma mater did not have fraternities and sororities, but they play a major role in the college you now live next to. Your small house is on the intersection of a major street, Euclid Avenue, and Eighth Street, a very small road that dead-ends at a swampy area about two hundred yards away. Beyond the swampy area is the town's wastewater treatment plant.

Directly across Euclid Avenue, near your house, is the college's football field and track. Less than a hundred yards up the street and a small hill is the college fraternity complex. Your house is at the bottom of this hill.

Apparently, when one of the fraternity brothers becomes "lavaliered, pinned or engaged," his brothers consume large quantities of alcohol, strip the romantically-committed fellow to his underwear and carry him down the Euclid Avenue hill. Aiming to take him onto Eighth Street, they aren't usually in a condition to navigate very carefully, so they always end up crossing over onto your hilly yard. They then continue to stagger down Eighth Street with the elevated brother's girlfriend following along, carrying his clothes.

When they reach their destination, they toss the guy into the smelly swamp, cheer, and sing some kind of traditional song. The stinking brother emerges from the swamp and embraces his girlfriend.

You, having no experience with fraternities and sororities, are at a complete loss as to this ritual, but it happens with regularity. What also occurs regularly is the entourage stumbling when crossing—i.e. trespassing—over your property.

What if they fall? What if they drop the guy over their heads and seriously injure him? Could any of the injured parties sue you? All you have done is watch, bewildered, as they performed this odd ritual, but are your finances, home and even your pet dog subject to being seized and sold because of the recklessness of the fraternity guys?

You might be at risk. This chapter will help you understand why.

I. Negligence

A. THE PRIMA FACIE CASE

Business people and business students tend to become frustrated about tort cases. **Torts**, which are injuries to a person or property, rather than a sweet dessert, are litigated in lawsuits where one can see million dollar judgments to compensate a victim—and even larger punitive damages that provide money to the victim beyond what damages the victim actually incurred.

Tort cases are comprised of a **prima facie** case. In other words, the case at hand must pass initial tests to be able to get into a court of law but even then, the plaintiff may not win. It simply means that there is a good enough case to file the case in court and start the trial process.

There are times when a plaintiff files a frivolous case, ones that have so little—if any—merit, that courts believe there is no reason to continue. In some situations, frivolous cases are filed primarily to harass the defendant and be enough of a nuisance to get some settlement from the defendant, who would rather not spend the time and expense of going through the court process.

Examples of frivolous cases include meritless complaints, unnecessarily stalling litigation, deliberate disobedience of court orders and the failure to produce evidence during the discovery process. Courts have several tools at their disposal to address these issues, including very straightforward ones such as directly challenging lawyers to move the trial process along or threatening lawyers (or litigants) with contempt of court sanctions, which can result in jail. In addition, courts can consider making one of the parties pay for all the costs of the case, sometimes including the other side's attorney's fees.

In narrowly defined circumstances, federal courts have inherent power to assess attorneys' fees against parties who have acted in bad faith, resulting in a frivolous suit. The general rule is that a litigant cannot recover his counsel fees, but that rule does not apply when the opposing party has acted in bad faith, including bad faith in the conduct of the litigation. In view of a court's power over members of its bar, if it may tax counsel fees against a party who has litigated in bad faith, it certainly may assess those expenses against counsel who willfully abuse judicial processes.

Assessing costs against the party frivolously filing the case or obstructing the hearing of the case is but one option. In the following case, the court throws out the case itself.

Link v. Wabash Railroad Co.

370 U.S. 626 (1962)

The action, growing out of a collision between petitioner's automobile and one of respondent's trains, was commenced on August 24, 1954. Some six years later, and more than three years after petitioner had finally prevailed on respondent's motion for judgment on the pleadings (during which time two fixed trial dates had been postponed), the District Court, on September 29, 1960, duly notified counsel for each side of the scheduling of a pretrial conference to be held at the courthouse in Hammond, Indiana, on October 12, 1960, at 1 p.m. During the preceding morning, October 11, petitioner's counsel telephoned respondent's lawyer from Indianapolis, stating that 'he was doing some work on some papers,' that he expected to be at the pretrial conference, but that he might not attend the taking of a deposition of the plaintiff scheduled for the same day. At about 10:45 on the morning of October 12 petitioner's counsel telephoned the Hammond courthouse from Indianapolis (about 160 miles away), and after asking for the judge, who then was on the bench, requested the judge's secretary to convey to him this message: 'that he (counsel) was busy preparing papers to file with the (Indiana) Supreme Court,' that 'he couldn't be here by 1:00 o'clock, but he would be here either Thursday afternoon (October 13) or any time Friday (October 14) if it (the pretrial conference) could be reset.'

When petitioner's counsel did not appear at the pretrial conference the District Court, after reviewing the history of the case and finding that counsel had failed 'to indicate . . . a reasonable reason' for his nonappearance, dismissed the action 'for failure of the plaintiff's counsel to appear at the pretrial, for failure to prosecute this action.' The court, acting two hours after the appointed hour for the conference, stated that the dismissal was in the 'exercise (of) its inherent power.' The Court of Appeals affirmed by a divided vote. The Supreme Court granted certiorari.

MR. JUSTICE HARLAN delivered the opinion of the Court.

The authority of a federal trial court to dismiss a plaintiff's action with prejudice because of his failure to prosecute cannot seriously be doubted. The power to invoke this sanction is necessary in order to prevent undue delays in the disposition of pending cases and to avoid congestion in the calendars of the District Courts. The power is of ancient origin, having its roots in judgments of nonsuit and *non prosequitur* entered at common law, e.g., 3 Blackstone, *Commentaries* (1768), 295–296, and dismissals for want of prosecution of bills in equity, *e.g., id.*, at 451. It has been expressly recognized in Federal Rule of Civil Procedure 41(b), which provides, in pertinent part:

> **Involuntary Dismissal: Effect Thereof.** For failure of the plaintiff to prosecute or to comply with these rules or any order of court, a defendant may move for dismissal of an action or of any claim against him. * * * Unless the court in its order for dismissal otherwise specifies, a dismissal under this subdivision and any dismissal not provided for in this rule, other than a dismissal for lack of jurisdiction or for improper venue, operates as an adjudication upon the merits.'

Petitioner contends that the language of this Rule, by negative implication, prohibits involuntary dismissals for failure of the plaintiff to prosecute except upon motion by the defendant. In the present case there was no such motion.

We do not read Rule 41(b) as implying any such restriction. Neither the permissive language of the Rule—which merely authorizes a motion by the defendant—nor its policy requires us to conclude that it was the purpose of the Rule to abrogate the power of courts, acting on their own initiative, to clear their calendars of cases that have remained dormant because of the inaction or dilatoriness of the parties seeking relief.

Nor does the absence of notice as to the possibility of dismissal or the failure to hold an adversary hearing necessarily render such a dismissal void. It is true, of course, that 'the fundamental requirement of due process is an opportunity to be heard upon such notice and proceedings as are adequate to safeguard the right for which the constitutional protection is invoked.' But this does not mean that every order entered without notice and a preliminary adversary hearing offends due process.

On this record we are unable to say that the District Court's dismissal of this action for failure to prosecute, as evidenced only partly by the failure of petitioner's counsel to appear at a duly scheduled pretrial conference, amounted to an abuse of discretion. It was certainly within the bounds of permissible discretion for the court to conclude that the telephone excuse offered by petitioner's counsel was inadequate to explain his failure to attend. And it could reasonably be inferred from his absence, as well as from the drawn-out history of the litigation, that petitioner had been deliberately proceeding in dilatory fashion.

There is certainly no merit to the contention that dismissal of petitioner's claim because of his counsel's unexcused conduct imposes an unjust penalty on the client. Petitioner voluntarily chose this attorney as his representative in the action, and he cannot now avoid the consequences of the acts or omissions of this freely selected agent. Any other notion would be wholly inconsistent with our system of representative litigation, in which each party is deemed bound by the acts of his lawyer-agent and is considered to have 'notice of all facts, notice of which can be charged upon the attorney.'

Though Justice Harlan referred to the need to prevent frivolous cases in order to avoid "congestion in the calendars," that congestion is not simply one of time management and delay. As Justice Powell has indicated, such delay would create disrespect for the law and the legal system itself.

Assuming that the plaintiff has not filed a frivolous case, there are four key elements of a negligence case:

DUTY: Did the defendant have a duty to conform his conduct to a specific **standard of care**?	**BREACH:** Did the defendant's conduct fall below the applicable standard of care?
CAUSATION: Did the defendant's failure to meet the applicable standard of care cause the plaintiff's harm, either directly or proximately?	**DAMAGE:** Did the plaintiff suffer harm that can be compensated monetarily?

I. Duty

For a judge to hold that the plaintiff is entitled to damages for a negligence case, the defendant must have breached a duty. How do you know if you have a duty or not? How do you know if you have breached a duty? Three sources of duty exist. One source, found in statutes, ordinances and other legislation, sets out clear standards of duty, though you actually have to read the law to know it. A second source can be found in common law precedents that help identify the duty. Here too, unless one has read legal cases, one may not know that one has a duty. A third set is more based on common sense, though some people may argue about just how common and how sensible some of the duties may be.

In common law, the duties of landowners differ depending on whether the plaintiff is a **licensee**, an **invitee**, or a trespasser. A landowner owes a licensee—a social guest who enters the premises with permission—the duty to warn of discovered hidden dangers (not overt and not natural conditions). To an invitee, a person who is on the premises by invitation (public area or business), a landowner owes the duty to warn of dangers and to take reasonable measures to make the premises safe. Generally, there are no duties owed to trespassers, with the exception of **attractive nuisances** and

A landowner owes a licensee—a social guest who enters the premises with permission—the duty to warn of discovered hidden dangers (not overt and not natural conditions). To an invitee, a person who is on the premises by invitation (public area or business), a landowner owes the duty to warn of dangers and to take reasonable measures to make the premises safe.

anticipated or discovered trespassers. In those special circumstances, there is only a duty to exercise reasonable care for artificial conditions likely to cause death or serious bodily injury.

Tort law is specific to each state and changes over time. In *Heins v. Webster County*, for instance, the Supreme Court of Nebraska wrestled with state court precedents that mandated different duties to those coming to visit a hospital. If one was visiting socially, one set of laws applied that provided minimal duties from the hospital to the visitor. If one was visiting as a volunteer—for instance, as Santa Claus at a holiday event—another, stricter set of duties applied. The court discusses the different duties owed and comes to the decision to get rid of the distinctions between duties owed to invitees and those owed to licensees with a more general balancing test, illustrating that even in 1996, tort law doctrine continues to evolve.

Imposing duties on landowners for people using the property, whether licensee or invitee, is one thing. It does seem to be common sense to impose duties to keep such visitors reasonably safe. But cases have not stopped at the issue of guests. In some cases, courts have found that the duty owed by businesses includes the duty to take reasonable protective measures against foreseeable criminal acts of third parties.

Claxton v. Atlantic Richfield Co.

108 Cal. App. 4th 327, 133 Cal. Rptr. 2d 425 (2003)

A gas station customer who was subjected to a racially motivated assault on the gas station premises brought an action against the owners and operators of the station, alleging that defendants failed to take reasonable steps to secure their premises against foreseeable criminal acts of third parties. The trial court granted defendants' nonsuit motion on the ground that the prior incidents on the premises, which were not racially motivated, were insufficiently similar to the attack on plaintiff to give rise to a duty to prevent the type of attack that occurred.

Under the circumstances, the appropriate test in determining foreseeability was prior similar incidents, not prior identical incidents. The station's manager had earlier been robbed at knifepoint by the same party who attacked plaintiff, and this had been reported both to defendant oil company and to the manager's supervisor. Additionally, there had been other robberies and assaults, an altercation between gangs of different races, and numerous crimes in the adjacent park. These incidents amounted to substantial evidence of a reasonably foreseeable risk of violent criminal assaults at the station.

The determination of duty in a given situation "involves the balancing of a number of considerations; the major ones are the foreseeability of harm to the plaintiff, the degree of certainty that the plaintiff suffered injury, the closeness of the connection between the defendant's conduct and the injury suffered, the moral blame attached to the defendant's conduct, the policy of preventing future harm, the extent of the burden to the defendant and consequences to the community of imposing a duty to exercise care with resulting liability for breach, and the availability, cost, and prevalence of insurance for the risk involved."

With respect to the question of the scope of a landowner's duty to provide protection from foreseeable third party crime, "the scope of the duty is determined in part by balancing the foreseeability of the harm against the burden of the duty to be imposed." [I]n cases where the burden of preventing future harm is great, a high degree of foreseeability may be required. On the other hand, in cases where there are strong policy reasons for preventing the harm, or the harm can be prevented by simple means, a lesser degree of foreseeability may be required . . . [D]uty in such circumstances is determined by a balancing of 'foreseeability' of the criminal acts against the 'burdensomeness, vagueness, and efficacy' of the proposed security measures."

A high degree of foreseeability is required in order to find that the scope of a landowner's duty of care includes the hiring of security guards, and the requisite degree of foreseeability rarely, if ever, can be proven in the absence of prior similar incidents of violent crime on the landowner's premises. The trial court's ruling that in the absence of any previous racially-motivated robberies or assaults, there were no prior similar incidents is without legal support. As set forth in *Ann M. and Sharon P.*, the test is prior "similar" incidents, not prior *identical* incidents. Therefore, it is immaterial whether any prior robberies or assaults at the station were motivated by racial animus, or were merely garden-variety antisocial behavior. Claxton presented substantial evidence of prior robberies and assaults, as well as other indications of a reasonably foreseeable risk of violent criminal assaults at the station. Therefore, the nonsuit motion should have been summarily denied.

The Court of Appeal reversed, holding that the trial court erred in granting nonsuit for defendants.

---

a. Statutory Duty

The most straightforward duties are those where a legislature, city council, county board, or some other body with law-making powers has enacted a law that specifies a person's duty. For example, in the United States, all 50 states have enacted laws of the road that specify that we drive on the right side of a divided highway. This duty goes back to 1792, when Pennsylvania passed the first law requiring all traffic to keep right. Since then, each state has passed a similar law. If you drive on the left side of a divided highway, except of course to pass a car in a permitted passing zone, you are driving the car negligently. This is also sometimes known as **negligence per se.**

In *Jones v. Inmont Corporation*, the Federal District for the Southern District of Ohio held that an agent of the company was dumping waste in an open pit or ditch in Kentucky that had no license to receive such waste. We know that the company violated a duty because of several statutes, such as the Comprehensive Environmental Response Compensation and Liability Act of 1980, 42 U.S.C. § 9601 (CERCLA) and the Resource Conservation and Recovery Act of 1976, 42 U.S.C. § 6901 (RCRA). The court, therefore, did not have to look at common law precedent or custom to determine duty; the legislature preemptively prescribed it.

Legislators actively enact provisions such as these on a regular basis. Here are some examples of such laws:

- Product liability laws
- Joint and several liability
- Respondeat superior laws
- Strict liability for ultra-hazardous activities
- Landlord-tenant laws
- The Consumer Protection Act
- Fair Labor Standards Act
- Title VII of the Civil Rights Act
- The Equal Pay Act
- Comprehensive Environmental Response, Clean Up and Liability Act
- Occupational Safety and Health Act
- Family and Medical Leave Act
- Employee Retirement Income Security Act
- Immigration and Nationality Act
- Contract Work Hours and Safety Standards Act, and Migrant and Seasonal Worker Protection Act

These are simply a few examples; the list could be extended much further. For someone going into business, it would make very good sense to ask an attorney or to research the specific, applicable law to make sure one knows what legislation already pertains to the business.

b. Duty Via Precedent

As we have already seen, once a court has determined a case, it has also created a precedent that other courts can cite to resolve their own cases, either by holding that the case is similar to the earlier precedent or can be somehow distinguished. One of the more famous cases—a products liability case—is when an elderly woman spilled hot coffee on her lap at a drive-through McDonalds' window.[1] The damages were later reduced, but the principle of the case provides precedent for the **duty sellers** of hot coffee have so that it protects the **reasonably foreseeable plaintiff.**

Indeed, once one is outside statutory-duty cases, the test for whether a person (including a company) has a duty is whether the defendant acted in a way to protect the reasonably foreseeable plaintiff. All of us have duties, whether we know about them or acknowledge them. We are to act in a way that does not endanger other people. Moreover, the definition of a person's duty also depends on the kind of person the (potential) defendant may be.

For example, suppose you are a blind person who, in order to navigate the street, uses a walking stick. When walking down the street, your walking stick accidentally strikes another person on the ankle. It is not likely that this will constitute a breach of duty. You are acting as a prudent person with the disability of being blind. At least as described—a blind person walking down the street at a reasonable pace and using a walking stick as one would typically do as a blind person—you have not breached any kind of duty.

However, what if you are instead swinging the walking stick above your head like a cowboy would twirl a lasso and, in doing so, hit the same person on the street in the head? Could that person have just cause to sue you? The answer is yes, because now you are not acting as a reasonably prudent blind person who is conducting themselves in a way to protect a reasonably foreseeable plaintiff. Thus, what constitutes duty can vary.

i. Duty Dependent Upon Age

There are some differentiations of duties based on age. A five year old must behave as a reasonably prudent five year old, a being that of course may not exist. The more interesting cases are those where the person is closer to being an adult.

1 *Liebeck vs. McDonalds Restaurants, P.T.S., Inc.* District Court of New Mexico, 1994 CV-93-02419.

A fifteen year old must behave as a reasonably prudent fifteen year old and if she doesn't, then the fifteen year old, and perhaps her parents, may have to pay damages. The following case sets out the duties (or lack thereof) of young children.

Howland v. Sears, Roebuck & Co.

438 F.2d 725 (6th Cir. 1971)

A mother took her two sons, Timothy (eight years old) and Thomas (nine years old) to a local Sears, Roebuck and Company retail store. Thomas was looking at bicycles when he noticed a shelf across from the bicycle rack that stored small arms ammunition.

Thomas testified that he noticed an open drawer in the base table and he took out a box of bullets which had written upon it ".22 long, keep out of reach of children." Thomas put the box of bullets in his pocket. He testified he did not attempt to pay for the box of bullets he had taken from the store and did not tell his mother that he had taken the bullets. However, he did show the bullets to Timothy.

When the boys were at home, they began playing with the bullets and at one point put the bullets on concrete and started hitting the bullets with hammers. Mr. Howland testified that he had told both Thomas and Timothy not to play with bullets because they were dangerous. Timothy testified his father had told him on an occasion previous to the day in question that he could be blinded playing with bullets. Mr. Howland was unaware his children were playing with bullets and did not specifically warn them on the evening of the injury. At about 6:00, Thomas and Timothy went outside to play and Timothy immediately began exploding bullets. The second bullet which Timothy exploded sent a piece of metal into his left eye. He was rushed to a hospital. But after initial surgery, it was determined necessary to remove his left eye. Timothy's left eye was replaced with a permanent artificial eye.

The family sued Sears, Roebuck & Co. for negligence in leaving the ammunition drawer open so that his minor brother could remove ammunition and Timothy, a minor, could subsequently explode a bullet and blind himself. On **Contributory Negligence**, the District Court did not permit Timothy a rebuttable presumption that he was incapable of committing negligence or contributory negligence because he was between the ages of 7 and 14. A jury verdict rendered judgment for Sears, Roebuck & Co. and Timothy appealed.

On appeal, the primary question is whether the District Court properly charged the jury on the jury questions of negligence, contributory negligence, assumption of the risk and proximate cause. On the issue of contributory negligence . . . Federal jurisdiction is premised on diversity of the parties. Hence the issue of Appellant's contributory negligence is controlled by Ohio law. As a general rule, the defense of contributory negligence of the complaining party may be raised even when the complaining party is a minor. This is so because, except where a child is incapable of understanding and appreciating the perils threatening him, a minor is required to exercise ordinary care for his own safety and protection. In that minors, however, have less capacity for self care and judgment than an adult, children are generally accorded a special status in applying the rules of contributory negligence.

The State of Ohio has had great difficulty in fashioning a judicial standard to make the delicate judgment of when a minor has the capacity for self care in the conduct of his activities. At very early ages, of course, this determination is not difficult. Just as a child of very tender years may not be held criminally responsible at the common law . . . he also does not have the capacity to form sufficiently intelligent judgments from his observations so that one may equitably hold him responsible for the protection of his own safekeeping. In *Holbrock v. Hamilton* Distributing, Inc. the Supreme Court of Ohio held 'as a matter of law that a child under seven years of age is incapable of contributory negligence, (and that) the submission of that issue to the jury constituted error.' In creating a conclusive presumption of 'general incapacity * * * (where a child is) under seven years of age,' the Ohio Supreme Court provided in their own words, 'a clear and simple rule which we believe will reach just and accurate results while also achieving a desirable judicial economy.'

In the instant case we are concerned with the capacity and judgment of a child who was two weeks less than nine years old, but who had repeated a year of school . . .

In *Lake Erie & W. Railroad Co. v. Mackey*, (a case which involved the alleged negligence and contributory negligence of a nine year old child) the rule . . . was modified for infants between seven and fourteen years of age. The *Mackey* court . . . held that a child is presumed to possess only such discretion as is common to children, and is, therefore, held only to the exercise of such care as is reasonably expected from children of his own age and capacity. But the *Mackey* court observed that by analogy to the principles of capacity in criminal law, there is a rebuttable legal presumption that a child of nine years of age is incapable of being contributorily negligent. This presumption may be rebutted by a factual showing that the child is of sufficient maturity and capacity to avoid danger and make intelligent judgments with regard to the particular activities in which he had engaged.

We determine it is Ohio law that minors are generally chargeable with the capacity for committing contributory negligence, except where they are under seven years of age. And further we determine that where a minor is between seven and fourteen years of age a rebuttable presumption arises that the minor involved is 'incapable' of forming the necessary judgments for self care. The charge by the District Court to the jury did not give the Appellant the benefit of the rebuttable presumption that a child of his age and maturity was entitled to under the law of the State of Ohio. We find such error prejudicial. The judgment of the District Court is reversed and the cause is remanded for a new trial.

According to state laws, the ages at which minors are exempt from arguments of negligence or contributory negligence will differ. If a child is exempt from the defenses of negligence or contributory negligence, he cannot be found at fault for his injury, despite his behavior leading up to the injury. This protection afforded to minors leaves open the possibility that businesses such as Sears, Roebuck & Co. could be found wholly responsible for a child's injury. As a general rule, however, the responsible child standard seen in *Howland v. Sears, Roebuck & Co.* is not applied when a child is engaged in adult activity. Then, the standard of care increases even though the person is under eighteen years of age. Here is a case where the court held a minor to an adult standard of care.

Robinson v. Lindsay

92 Wash.2d 410, 598 P.2d 392 (1979)

Kelly Robinson, the plaintiff, lost full use of a thumb in a snowmobile accident when she was 11 years of age. The defendant, Billy Anderson, 13 years of age at the time of the accident, was the driver of the snowmobile. After a jury verdict in favor of Anderson, the trial court ordered a new trial. The defendant appealed.

The single issue on appeal is whether a minor operating a snowmobile is to be held to an adult standard of care. The trial court failed to instruct the jury as to that standard and ordered a new trial because it believed the jury should have been so instructed. We agree and affirm the order granting a new trial.

The trial court instructed the jury to use the following standard of care of negligence in reaching its decision:

> In considering the claimed negligence of a child, you are instructed that it is the duty of a child to exercise the same care that a reasonably careful child of the same age, intelligence, maturity, training and experience would exercise under the same or similar circumstances.

Respondent properly excepted to the giving of this instruction and to the court's failure to give an adult standard of care.

Traditionally, a flexible standard of care has been used to determine if children's actions were negligent. Under some circumstances, however, courts have developed a rationale for applying an adult standard. In the courts' search for a uniform standard of behavior to use in determining whether or not a person's conduct has fallen below minimal acceptable standards, the law has developed a fictitious person, the "reasonable man of ordinary prudence."

In the past we have always compared a child's conduct to that expected of a reasonably careful child of the same age, intelligence, maturity, training and experience. This case is the first to consider the question of a child's liability for injuries sustained as a result of his or her operation of a motorized vehicle or participation in an inherently dangerous activity.

Such a rule protects the need of children to be children but at the same time discourages immature individuals from engaging in inherently dangerous activities. Children will still be free to enjoy traditional childhood activities without being held to an adult standard of care. Although accidents sometimes occur as the result of such activities, they are not activities generally considered capable of resulting in "grave danger to others and to the minor himself if the care used in the course of the activity drops below that care which the reasonable and prudent adult would use . . ."

Other courts adopting the adult standard of care for children engaged in adult activities have emphasized the hazards to the public if the rule is otherwise. The operation of a snowmobile likewise requires adult care and competence. Currently 2.2 million snowmobiles are in operation in the United States. Studies show that collisions and other snowmobile accidents claim hundreds of casualties each year and that the incidence of accidents is particularly high among inexperienced operators.

At the time of the accident, the 13-year-old petitioner had operated snowmobiles for about 2 years. When the injury occurred, petitioner was operating a 30-horsepower snowmobile at speeds of 10–20 miles per hour. The record indicates that the machine itself was capable of 65 miles per hour. Because petitioner was operating a powerful motorized vehicle, he should be held to the standard of care and conduct expected of an adult.

The order granting a new trial is affirmed.

---

ii. Duty Dependent Upon Nature of Disability

As indicated earlier, people are held to a standard of reasonableness. The same standards of reasonableness apply to people with disabilities. **Ordinary care** is such that an ordinarily prudent person with a like infirmity would have exercised the same precautions under similar circumstances. For example, a blind person must behave as a reasonably prudent blind person. If a blind person, using a walking stick, touched another person, the blind person would not have violated his duty of care as long as he was using the walking stick in a reasonable manner. However, if the blind person was wildly swinging the walking stick above his head and struck a passerby, then the blind person would have violated his duty to protect against reasonably foreseeable plaintiffs.

iii. Common Carriers

Commercial aviation as well as trains, buses, and other forms of transportation open to the general public carry very high duties of care. Common carriers are responsible for even the slightest negligence and are required to do all that human care, vigilance, and foresight could reasonably do under all circumstances. Furthermore, common carriers may even be held liable for intentional infliction of emotional distress if an insult causes a patron to suffer mental distress. The traditional requirements for the insult to be extreme or outrageous and for the distress to be extreme are not applied.

Andrews v. United Airlines, Inc.

24 F.3d 39 (9th Cir.1994)

During the mad scramble that usually follows hard upon an airplane's arrival at the gate, a briefcase fell from an overhead compartment and seriously injured plaintiff Billie Jean Andrews. No one knows who opened the compartment or what caused the briefcase to fall, and Andrews doesn't claim that airline personnel were involved in stowing the object or opening the bin. Her claim, rather, is that the injury was foreseeable and the airline didn't prevent it. The district court dismissed the suit on summary judgment, and we review *de novo*. This is a diversity action brought in California, whose tort law applies.

We are called upon to determine whether United Airlines took adequate measures to deal with that elementary notion of physics—what goes up, must come down. For, while the skies are friendly enough, the ground can be a mighty dangerous place when heavy objects tumble from overhead compartments. The parties agree that United Airlines is a common carrier and as such "owe[s] both a duty of utmost care and the vigilance of a very cautious person towards [its] passengers." Though United is "responsible for any, even the slightest, negligence and [is] required to do all that human care, vigilance, and foresight reasonably can do under all the circumstances," "[T]he degree of care and diligence which [it] must exercise is only such as can reasonably be exercised consistent with the character and mode of conveyance adopted and the practical operation of [its] business. . . ."

To show that United did not satisfy its duty of care toward its passengers, Ms. Andrews presented the testimony of two witnesses. The first was Janice Northcott, United's Manager of Inflight Safety, who disclosed that in 1987 the airline had received 135 reports of items falling from overhead bins. As a result of these incidents, Ms. Northcott testified, United decided to add a warning to its arrival announcements, to wit, that items stored overhead might have shifted during flight and passengers should use caution in opening the bins. This announcement later became the industry standard.

Ms. Andrews's second witness was safety and human factors expert Dr. David Thompson, who testified that United's announcement was ineffective because passengers opening overhead bins couldn't see objects poised to fall until the bins were opened, by which time it was too late. Dr. Thompson also testified that United could have taken additional steps to prevent the hazard, such as retrofitting its overhead bins with baggage nets, as some airlines had already done, or by requiring passengers to store only lightweight items overhead.

United argues that Andrews presented too little proof to satisfy her burden under One hundred thirty-five reported incidents, United points out, are trivial when spread over the millions of passengers travelling on its 175,000 flights every year. Even that number overstates the problem, according to United, because it includes events where passengers merely observed items falling from overhead bins but no one was struck or injured. Indeed, United sees the low incidence of injuries as incontrovertible proof that the safety measures suggested by plaintiff's expert would not merit the additional cost and inconvenience to airline passengers.

It is a close question, but we conclude that plaintiff has made a sufficient case to overcome summary judgment. United is hard-pressed to dispute that its passengers are subject to a hazard from objects falling out of overhead bins, considering the warning its flight crews give hundreds of times each day. The case then turns on whether the hazard is serious enough to warrant more than a warning. Given the heightened duty of a common carrier, even a small risk of serious injury to passengers may form the basis of liability if that risk could be eliminated "consistent with the character and mode of [airline travel] and the practical operation of [that] business . . . ." United has demonstrated neither that retrofitting overhead bins with netting (or other means) would be prohibitively expensive, nor that such steps would grossly interfere with the convenience of its passengers. Thus, a jury could find United has failed to do "all that human care, vigilance, and foresight reasonably can do under all the circumstances."

Reversed and remanded.

Because of the heightened duty of a common carrier, even a small risk of injury to passengers may form the basis of liability. However, the courts will also consider the costs and convenience of preventing the injury.

---

iv. Superior Skills

Doctors, lawyers, accountants, and other professionals can be sued under a negligence theory for malpractice. Specialists can be found guilty of malpractice if they have not exercised the proper degree of care. In exercising this heightened degree of care and skill, specialists have an additional duty of disclosure and can be sued for not disclosing material risks before acting.

Anytime one faces a medical procedure, there is risk. A patient must determine whether it is worth facing those risks and to make that decision, they must depend on disclosures provided by the doctor or hospital. The following case examines some of the issues pertaining to the adequacy of disclosures.

Canterbury v. Spence

464 F.2d 772 (D.C. Cir. 1972)

At the time of the events which gave rise to this litigation, appellant was nineteen years of age, a clerk-typist employed by the Federal Bureau of Investigation. In December, 1958, he began to experience severe pain between his shoulder blades. He consulted two general practitioners, but the medications they prescribed failed to eliminate the pain. Thereafter, appellant secured an appointment with Dr. Spence, who is a neurosurgeon. Dr. Spence examined appellant in his office at some length but found nothing amiss. On Dr. Spence's advice appellant was x-rayed, but the films did not identify any abnormality. Dr. Spence then recommended that appellant undergo a myelogram—a procedure in which dye is injected into the spinal column and traced to find evidence of disease or other disorder—at the Washington Hospital Center.

Appellant explained to Dr. Spence that his mother was a widow of slender financial means living in Cyclone, West Virginia, and that she could be reached through a neighbor's telephone. Appellant called his mother the day after the myelogram was performed and, failing to contact her, left Dr. Spence's telephone number with the neighbor. When Mrs. Canterbury returned the call, Dr. Spence told her that the surgery was occasioned by a suspected ruptured disc. Mrs. Canterbury then asked if the recommended operation was serious and Dr. Spence replied "not anymore than any other operation." He added that he knew Mrs. Canterbury was not well off and that her presence in Washington would not be necessary. The testimony is contradictory as to whether during the course of the conversation Mrs. Canterbury expressed her consent to the operation. Appellant himself apparently did not converse again with Dr. Spence prior to the operation.

Dr. Spence performed the laminectomy on February 11 at the Washington Hospital Center. Mrs. Canterbury traveled to Washington, arriving on that date but after the operation was over, and signed a consent form at the hospital. Neither the appellant or his mother were told of the one percent possibility of paralysis resulting from laminectomy.

A day after the operation he fell from his hospital bed after having been left without assistance while voiding. A few hours after the fall, the lower half of his body was paralyzed, and he had to be operated on again. Despite extensive medical care, he has never been what he was before. The patient brought action against the surgeon and the hospital. At the end of the patient's case in chief, the United States District Court for the District of Columbia directed verdicts for the surgeon and hospital, and the patient appealed.

The Court of Appeals held that evidence presented a jury issue as to sufficiency of the surgeon's disclosure, i.e., whether a one percent possibility of paralysis resulting from laminectomy was peril of sufficient magnitude to bring a disclosure duty into play; evidence also presented an issue as to whether the operation was negligently performed. The Court also held that evidence including evidence that the patient progressed after the operation until he fell while unattended but, a few hours thereafter, his condition had deteriorated and testimony that there were complaints of paralysis and respiratory difficulty and medical testimony that paralysis can be brought on by trauma or shock presented an issue whether there was dereliction of the hospital's duty to exercise reasonable care for the safety and well-being of the patient, and an issue of causality.

Once the circumstances give rise to a duty on the physician's part to inform his patient, the next inquiry is the scope of the disclosure the physician is legally obliged to make. The courts have frequently confronted this problem but no uniform standard defining the adequacy of the divulgence emerges from the decisions. Some have said "full" disclosure, a norm we are unwilling to adopt literally. It seems obviously prohibitive and unrealistic to expect physicians to discuss with their patients every risk of proposed treatment—no matter how small or remote—and generally unnecessary from the patient's viewpoint as well. Indeed, the cases speaking in terms of "full" disclosure appear to envision something less than total disclosure, leaving unanswered the question of just how much.

In our view, the patient's right of self-decision shapes the boundaries of the duty to reveal. That right can be effectively exercised only if the patient possesses enough information to enable an intelligent choice. The scope of the physician's communications to the patient, then, must be measured by the patient's need, and that need is the information material to the decision. Thus the test for determining whether a particular peril must be divulged is its materiality to the patient's decision: all risks potentially affecting the decision must be unmasked. And to safeguard the patient's interest in achieving his own determination on treatment, the law must itself set the standard for adequate disclosure.

Of necessity, the content of the disclosure rests in the first instance with the physician. Ordinarily it is only he who is in position to identify particular dangers; always he must make a judgment, in terms of materiality, as to whether and to what extent revelation to the patient is called for. He cannot know with complete exactitude what the patient would consider important to his decision, but on the basis of his medical training and experience he can sense how the average, reasonable patient expectably would react. Indeed, with knowledge of, or ability to learn, his patient's background and current condition, he is in a position superior to that of most others—attorneys, for example—who are called upon to make judgments on pain of liability in damages for unreasonable miscalculation . . . .

The scope of the standard is not subjective as to either the physician or the patient; it remains objective with due regard for the patient's informational needs and with suitable leeway for the physician's situation. In broad outline, we agree that "[a] risk is thus material when a reasonable person, in what the physician knows or should know to be the patient's position, would be likely to attach significance to the risk or cluster of risks in deciding whether or not to forgo the proposed therapy."

---

v. Other Examples of Duty: "Common Sense" Duties, Reasonability, and "Taking the Plaintiff as You Find Him."

The above examples do not exhaust the possible definitions of duty. Remember, the idea of negligence law is for an individual to act as a reasonably prudent person who will protect against a reasonably foreseeable plaintiff. This test can be applied to other negligence cases quite easily. Thus, even if a person memorized all the statutes pertaining to negligence and read all the court cases on negligence, one would not have exhausted the possible range of negligence cases.

The linchpin of these cases is the "reasonability" standard. How does a "reasonable" person act? What constitutes a "reasonably foreseeable plaintiff?" The reasonability test is meant to be objective. Subjectively speaking, we can all think of something another person did that made us angry. We may even think that they should be sued for it. But the test of reasonableness is meant for us to take a step back and look at the action a bit more objectively. That is what courts will do. Some may object that reasonability is simply the subjective view of a given judge. There is some truth to this, since two judges may see something differently, but bear in mind that a trial judge is not the final word on the determination of a case for several reasons.

The linchpin of these cases is the "reasonability" standard. How does a "reasonable" person act? What constitutes a "reasonably foreseeable plaintiff?" The reasonability test is meant to be objective.

One reason is that there are two sides to a case and so a judge, regardless of what she first might think about a case, will end up having to hear from both sides and that tends to make judgments less subjective. Second, if there is a statute or precedent, then the judge, whatever he personally thinks, still has to follow the law and precedent or to find a way to argue that previous law is not controlling. Third, regardless of what a trial judge (or jury) holds, the case can be appealed. Thus, while some decisions may seem absurd to an outsider, there are several checks within the system to assure that an objective standard, flexible as it is, does still apply.

A further complication is the adage of "taking the plaintiff as you find him." The defendant may not know the vulnerabilities of the plaintiff in advance but be held liable for them. A further elucidation of this point will be made in the section on causation below and the issues that arise with an "eggshell plaintiff."

2. Breach of Duty

Once one has determined the existence of a duty relevant to the situation, the next step of breach of duty is very straightforward: did they adhere to the duty? If the alleged defendant adhered to the duty, then there is no case. The plaintiff would need to find some other theory to hold the defendant liable.

3. Causation

There are two types of causation in a tort case: **actual** and **proximate**. While lawyers and law students love to analyze the difference between the two, the cause that really matters is proximate cause. The difference between the two mainly provides an analytical category for those things that lead up to an injury while keeping them separate from the particular aspect that caused the plaintiff's injury. An actual cause is something that leads to the occurrence of the injury, but the proximate cause is the specific thing that causes the injury. Whatever is the proximate cause will also be an actual cause, but there are some actual causes that are not proximate causes.

For example, suppose you are standing on an urban street corner and a bus comes thundering toward you and edges toward the curb to make a scheduled stop, rolls over your foot, which is on the sidewalk. The proximate cause—the thing that caused your smashed foot—is the bus driver's negligent driving of the bus. But there are many actual causes. "But for" (a way lawyers sometimes characterize the actual cause test) the fact that you were on the corner at that moment rather than five minutes earlier (because the line at Starbucks was longer than you expected), you would not have been hurt. So does that mean that you can sue Starbucks or the people lined up in front of you for having caused your injury? Of course not, but they are in the chain of events that led up to the injury.

Here are two cases that set out the differences between actual and proximate cause.

Stubbs v. City of Rochester

226 N.Y. 516 (1919)

During the year 1910 and for many years prior thereto the defendant under legislative authority was engaged in the business of selling water to its inhabitants. A duty was imposed on the commissioner of public works to provide an abundant supply of wholesome water for public and private use, to devise plans and sources of water supply, to plan and supervise the distribution of water through the city and to protect it against contamination. The city has two systems of water supply. One for potable water brought by it from Hemlock Lake some distance south of the city to reservoirs near the city and thence distributed by gravity to consumers. That system is known as the Hemlock system.

The plaintiff, a resident of the city of Rochester and a machinist, was employed by a firm whose place of business was at the corner of Allen and Platt streets, about one block from the Brown street bridge. The factory was supplied with Hemlock Lake water for drinking purposes. Plaintiff drank the water from time to time, using his individual drinking glass. He was taken ill September 6, 1910, with typhoid fever and was sick in bed for six weeks and unable to work for some twelve weeks. Asserting that his illness was caused by reason of drinking contaminated water supplied by the city, the plaintiff sought to recover damages by reason thereof. This case is on appeal from a judgment entered September 13, 1916, upon an order of the Appellate Division of the Supreme Court in the fourth judicial department, overruling plaintiffs' exceptions, ordered to be heard in the first instance by the Appellate Division, denying a motion for a new trial and directing judgment in favor of defendant upon the nonsuit granted at the Trial Term.

The evidence disclosed upon the trial clearly established that the water furnished by the defendant for potable purposes in the locality of the Brown street bridge was contaminated. The important question in this case is—did the plaintiff produce evidence from which inference might reasonably be drawn that the cause of his illness was due to the use of contaminated water furnished by defendant. Counsel for respondent argues that even assuming that the city may be held liable to plaintiff for damages caused by its negligence in furnishing contaminated water for drinking purposes, (a) that the evidence adduced by plaintiff fails to disclose that he contracted typhoid fever by drinking contaminated water; (b) that it was incumbent upon the plaintiff to establish that his illness was not due to any other cause to which typhoid fever may be attributed for which defendant is not liable. The evidence does disclose several causes of typhoid fever which is a germ disease, the germ being known as the typhoid bacillus, which causes may be classified as follows:

First. Drinking of polluted water. *Second.* Raw fruits and vegetables in certain named localities where human excrement is used to fertilize the soil are sometimes sources of typhoid infection. *Third.* The consumption of shell fish, though not a frequent cause. *Fourth.* The consumption of infected milk and vegetables. *Fifth.* The house fly in certain localities. *Sixth.* Personal contact with an infected person by one who has a predilection for typhoid infection and is not objectively sick with the disease. *Seventh.* Ice if affected with typhoid bacilli. *Eighth.* Fruits, vegetables, etc., washed in infected water. *Ninth.* The medical authorities recognize that there are still other causes and means unknown. This fact was developed on cross-examination of physicians called by plaintiff.

Counsel for respondent asserts that there was a failure of proof on the part of plaintiff in that he did not establish that he contracted disease by drinking contaminated water and in support of his argument cites a rule of law, that when there are several possible causes of injury for one or more of which a defendant is not responsible, plaintiff cannot recover without proving that the injury was sustained wholly or in part by a cause for which defendant was responsible. He submits that it was essential for plaintiff to eliminate all other of seven causes from which the disease might have been contracted. If the argument should prevail and the rule of law stated is not subject to any limitation the present case illustrates the impossibility of a recovery in any case based upon like facts.

The plaintiff was employed in the immediate locality where the water was contaminated. He drank the water daily. The consumption of contaminated water is a very frequent cause of typhoid fever. In the locality there were a large number of cases of typhoid fever and near to sixty individuals who drank the water and had suffered from typhoid fever in that neighborhood appeared as witnesses on behalf of plaintiff. The plaintiff gave evidence of his habits, his home surroundings and his method of living, and the medical testimony indicated that his illness was caused by drinking contaminated water. Without reiteration of the facts disclosed on the trial I do not believe that the case on the part of plaintiff was so lacking in proof as matter of law that his complaint should be dismissed. On the contrary the most favorable inferences deducible from the plaintiff were such as would justify a submission of the facts to a jury as to the reasonable inferences to be drawn therefrom, and a verdict rendered thereon for either party would rest not in conjecture but upon reasonable possibilities.

The judgment should be reversed and a new trial granted, costs to abide the event.

★ EGGSHELL SKULL DOCTRINE STATES THAT IF A PERSON HAD A SKULL AS FRAGILE AS AN EGG SHELL, AND A DEFENDANT'S ACTIONS CAUSED A SKULL FRACTURE, THE DEFENDANT WOULD STILL BE HELD LIABLE FOR ALL THE DAMAGES, EVEN IF THERE WAS NO INTENT TO CAUSE SEVERE INJURY.

In a claim of actual cause, a plaintiff must show that the defendant's negligence actually caused the injury. However, the possibility that there may be other causes for the injury does not compel the plaintiff to prove that none of the other possible factors was actually the cause. The plaintiff only has to prove that under a reasonable inference, the defendant's negligence caused the injury. In some cases, it is only necessary to prove that the defendant's negligence increased the chances of injury. In the following case, this idea is explored with respect what is known as an **eggshell plaintiff**, also known as the **thin skull doctrine**.

Consider, for example, your professor walks by you in the classroom and lightly places her hand on your shoulder to tell you that you did a good job on a paper. Unknown to the professor, you have extremely fragile bones and the lightest touch causes them to shatter. This is what is known as an eggshell plaintiff and the sensitivity and fragility of some plaintiffs raises questions about what causes an injury.

Benn v. Thomas

512 N.W.2d 537 (Iowa 1994)

On February 15, 1989, on an icy road in Missouri, a semi-tractor and trailer rear-ended a van in which Loras J. Benn was a passenger. In the accident, Loras suffered a bruised chest and a fractured ankle. Six days later he died of a heart attack.

Subsequently, Carol A. Benn, as executor of Loras's estate, filed suit against defendants Leland R. Thomas, the driver of the semi-tractor, K-G Ltd., the owner of the semi-tractor and trailer, and Heartland Express, the permanent lessee of the semi-tractor and trailer. The plaintiff estate sought damages for Loras's injuries and death. At trial, the estate's medical expert, Dr. James E. Davia, testified that Loras had a history of coronary disease and insulin-dependent diabetes. Loras had a heart attack in 1985 and was at risk of having another. Dr. Davia testified that he viewed "the accident that [Loras] was in and the attendant problems that it cause[d] in the body as the straw that broke the camel's back" and the cause of Loras's death. Other medical evidence indicated the accident did not cause his death. Based on Dr. Davis's testimony, the estate requested an instruction to the jury based on the "e The district court denied this request. The jury returned a verdict for the estate in the amount of $17,000 for Loras's injuries but nothing for his death. In the special verdict, the jury determined the defendant's negligence in connection with the accident did not proximately cause Loras's death.

The main question here is whether the trial court erred in refusing to instruct the jury on the "eggshell plaintiff" rule in view of the fact that plaintiff's decedent, who had a history of coronary disease, died of a heart attack six days after suffering a bruised chest and fractured ankle in a motor vehicle accident caused by defendant's negligence. The court of appeals concluded that the trial court's refusal constituted reversible error. We agree with the court of appeals and reverse the judgment of the trial court and remand for a new trial.

The estate claims that the court erred in failing to include, in addition to its proximate cause instruction to the jury, a requested instruction on the eggshell plaintiff rule. Such an instruction would advise the jury that it could find that the accident aggravated Loras's heart condition and caused his fatal heart attack.

A tortfeasor whose act, superimposed upon a prior latent condition, results in an injury may be liable in damages for the full disability. This rule deems the injury, and not the dormant condition, the proximate cause of the plaintiff's harm. *Id.* This precept is often referred to as the "eggshell plaintiff" rule, which has its roots in cases such as where the court observed:

> If a man is negligently run over or otherwise negligently injured in his body, it is no answer to the sufferer's claim for damages that he would have suffered less injury, or no injury at all, if he had not had an unusually thin skull or an unusually weak heart.

The proximate cause instruction in this case provided:

> The conduct of a party is a proximate cause of damage when it is a substantial factor in producing damage and when the damage would not have happened except for the conduct.

"Substantial" means the party's conduct has such an effect in producing damage as to lead a reasonable person to regard it as a cause . . . The eggshell plaintiff rule rejects the limit of foreseeability that courts ordinarily require in the determination of proximate cause. Once the plaintiff establishes that the defendant caused some injury to the plaintiff, the rule imposes liability for the full extent of those injuries, not merely those that were foreseeable to the defendant. Defendant nevertheless maintains that an eggshell plaintiff instruction would draw undue emphasis and attention to Loras's prior infirm condition. We have, however, explicitly approved such an instruction in two prior cases.

Moreover, the other jurisdictions that have addressed the issue have concluded that a court's refusal to instruct on the eggshell plaintiff rule constitutes a failure to convey the applicable law. To deprive the plaintiff estate of the requested instruction under this record would fail to convey to the jury a central principle of tort liability.

The record in this case warranted an instruction on the eggshell plaintiff rule. We therefore affirm the decision of the court of appeals. We reverse the judgment of the district court and remand the cause to the district court for a new trial consistent with this opinion.

The Eggshell/Thin Skull doctrine leads courts to "take their plaintiffs as they find them." In other words, one can't depend on another person being of "ordinary," for lack of a better word, condition. A victim who is fragile can still recover from a defendant even if the tort in question would not ordinarily cause an injury. There are exceptions to this rule, but it is important to remember that this eggshell plaintiff rule is the general rule of law. If the plaintiff suffers a foreseeable injury (given his existing condition) resulting from the defendant's conduct, the defendant's actions are the proximate cause. Once proximate cause is shown, the defendant may be liable to the full extent of the injury.

4. Damages

While negligence and other tort cases can cause controversy, especially among businesspeople, damages, we might say, are the "proximate cause" of the anger. When a person goes to court, she has to ask the judge or jury to do something. Occasionally, all a plaintiff wants is a public determination of poor behavior on the part of the defendant. Some people actually only want an apology. But the vast majority of people initiate tort suits to ask for monetary damages and, in a tort case, that is what a court can order. There are two categories of damages: compensatory and punitive.

a. Compensatory

Compensatory damages attempt to make an injured plaintiff whole, or put another way, to make up for what the plaintiff lost as a result of being hurt. Examples include lost wages or income from having to take time off work because of the injury or expenses for medical care. This is worth thinking about. When a person signs up for health insurance coverage, they **subrogate** their rights to the insurance company for recovering health care costs in case of an injury. Thus, even if you have no interest in suing someone who injured you because your expenses were covered by insurance, your health insurance company would be able to do so in order to get the money it paid for your medical care back from the defendant. The following case illustrates subrogation rights as well as the idea that compensatory damages are designed to do just that: compensate, not overcompensate.

Allstate Insurance Co. v. Mazzola

175 F.3d 255 (2d Cir. 1999)

The automobile insurer, as subrogee of insured, sued the driver and owner of an automobile involved in an accident, to recover first-party medical benefits paid for insured's injuries. The United States District Court for the Southern District of New York granted summary judgment for defendants based on release they obtained from insured. Insurer appealed.

The Court of Appeals held that the insurer could maintain equitable subrogation claim. "Subrogation is the right one party has against a third party following payment, in whole or in part, of a legal obligation that ought to have been met by the third party." The doctrine of equitable subrogation allows insurers to "stand in the shoes" of their insured to seek **indemnification** by pursuing any claims that the insured may have had against third parties legally responsible for the loss. In short, one party known as the subrogee is substituted for and succeeds to the rights of another party, known as the subrogor. The doctrine of subrogation, which is based upon principles of equity has a dual objective as stated by New York courts:

THE DOCTRINE OF EQUITABLE SUBROGATION allows insurers to "stand in the shoes" of their insured to seek indemnification.

> It seeks, first, to prevent the insured from recovering twice for one harm, as it might if it could recover from both the insurer and from a third person who caused the harm, and second, to require the party who has caused the damage to reimburse the insurer for the payment the insurer has made.

The first issue concerns whether Allstate's inability to recover under New York Insurance Law §§ 5104(b) and 5105(a)3 bars a remedy under the doctrine of equitable subrogation as applied by New York courts. Allstate does not quarrel with the district court's ruling in so far as it held that the company may not recover no-fault medical benefits paid on behalf of Kevin Hall from the defendants under these statutes.[2] (In addition, the plaintiff acknowledges that sections 5104(b) and 5105(a) provide the exclusive remedy for insurers seeking to bring an action to recoup "first party benefits" or the first $50,000 of no-fault benefits paid to their insured. However, Allstate contends that sections 5104(b) and 5105(a) do not bar an equitable subrogation claim to recover the remaining amount of $83,637.22 in excess of the nonrecoverable $50,000. We agree.

As a creature of equity, the right of subrogation does not arise from, nor is it dependent upon, statute or the terms of a contract of insurance." One court stated this axiom in the following manner:

> **"If the insured were permitted to keep the payment from [the insurer] under his additional endorsement and recover from [the tortfeasor] for extended economic loss, he would sustain a double recovery. Such result is clearly not contemplated under the no-fault statutory scheme. Subrogation is the principle which exists to prevent double recovery by the insured and to force the wrongdoer to bear the ultimate costs. The purpose of the statutory scheme is to make whole an injured party, not to provide him with a**

2 The district court concluded that Allstate could not recover pursuant to section 5104(b) because the statute provides relief only in actions brought against a "noncovered person." Since Mazzola was insured by Royal at a level above that required by New York law, he constituted a covered person, rather than a non-covered person as required by section 5104(b). The district court also found that the requirements of section 5105(a) were not satisfied because the vehicles involved in the accident each weighed less than six thousand five hundred pounds unloaded and were not used principally for the transportation of persons or property for hire.

windfall. * * * As a corollary, the doctrine of equitable subrogation must be liberally applied for the protection of insurers, its intended beneficiaries.

Another kind of compensatory damages, standing in between medical damages and the following category of pain and suffering, is a price placed on loss of a physical capability. If a person has been in an accident that left them paralyzed, the courts, after hearing evidence, will place a price on the loss of the ability to walk or the loss of a limb. In a wrongful death case, Courts have placed a value on "loss of consortium" which means the loss of having sex with one's spouse. Thus, the notion of compensatory damages is broad. If one has been injured, more than a bone might broken; a career or a physical capability might be severely diminished or ended. A person might also experience pain and suffering from the injury, either from actual physical discomfort or from embarrassment created by their situation. The following case looks at that kind of issue.

Seffert v. Los Angeles Transit Lines

56 Cal. 2d 498, 15 Cal. Rptr. 161, 364 P.2d 337 (1961)

Defendants appeal from a judgment for plaintiff for $187,903.75 entered on a jury verdict. Their motion for a new trial for errors of law and excessiveness of damages was denied.

At the trial plaintiff contended that she was properly entering defendants' bus when the doors closed suddenly catching her right hand and left foot. The bus started, dragged her some distance, and then threw her to the pavement. Defendants contended that the injury resulted from plaintiff's own negligence, that she was late for work and either ran into the side of the bus after the doors had closed or ran after the bus and attempted to enter after the doors had nearly closed.

The evidence supports plaintiff's version of the facts. Several eyewitnesses testified that plaintiff started to board the bus while it was standing with the doors wide open. Defendants do not challenge the sufficiency of the evidence. They do contend, however, that prejudicial errors were committed during the trial and that the verdict is excessive. * * *

The evidence most favorable to the plaintiff shows that prior to the accident plaintiff was in good health, and had suffered no prior serious injuries. She was single, and had been self-supporting for 20 of her 42 years. The accident happened on October 11, 1957. The trial took place in July and August of 1959.

As already pointed out, the injury occurred when plaintiff was caught in the doors of defendants' bus when it started up before she had gained full entry. As a result she was dragged for some distance. The record is uncontradicted that her injuries were serious, painful, disabling and permanent.

Since the accident, and because of it, plaintiff has undergone nine operations and has spent eight months in various hospitals and rehabilitation centers. These operations involved painful skin grafting and other painful procedures. Although plaintiff has gone back to work, she testified that she has difficulty standing, walking or even sitting, and must lie down frequently; that the leg is still very painful; that she can, even on her best days, walk not over three blocks and that very slowly; that her back hurts from walking; that she is tired and weak; that her sleep is disturbed; that she has frequent spasms in which the leg shakes uncontrollably; that she feels depressed and unhappy, and suffers humiliation and embarrassment.

Plaintiff claims that there is evidence that her total pecuniary loss, past and future, amounts to $53,903.75. This was the figure used by plaintiff's counsel in his argument to the jury, in which he also claimed $134,000 for pain and suffering, past and future. Since the verdict was exactly the total of these two estimates, it is reasonable to assume that the jury accepted the amount proposed by counsel for each item.

The summary of plaintiff as to pecuniary loss, past and future, is as follows:

Past Medical Expenses:

Doctor and Hospital Bills	$10,330.50
Drugs and other medical expenses stipulated to in the amount of	2,273.25
	5,500.00
	$18,103.75
Future Medical Expenses:	
$2,000 per year for next 10 years	20,000.00
$200 per year for the 24 years thereafter	4,800.00
Drugs for 34 years	1,000.00
SUBTOTAL	25,800.00
TOTAL	43,903.75
Possible future loss of earnings	10,000.00
Total Pecuniary Loss	**$53,903.75**

There is substantial evidence to support these estimates. The amounts for past doctor and hospital bills, for the cost of drugs, and for a past loss of earnings, were either stipulated to, evidence was offered on, or is a simple matter of calculation. These items totaled $18,103.75. While the amount of $25,800 estimated as the cost of future medical expense, for loss of future earnings and for the future cost of drugs, may seem high, there was substantial evidence that future medical expense is certain to be high. There is also substantial evidence that plaintiff's future earning capacity may be substantially impaired by reason of the injury. The amounts estimated for those various items are not out of line, and find support in the evidence.

This leaves the amount of $134,000 presumably allowed for the nonpecuniary items of damage, including pain and suffering, past and future. It is this allowance that defendants seriously attack as being excessive as a matter of law.

While the appellate court should consider the amounts awarded in prior cases for similar injuries, obviously, each case must be decided on its own facts and circumstances. Such examination demonstrates that such awards vary greatly. Injuries are seldom identical and the amount of pain and suffering involved in similar physical injuries varies widely. These factors must be considered. (*Leming v. Oilfields Trucking Co.*; *Crane v. Smith.*) Basically, the question that should be decided by the appellate courts is whether or not the verdict is so out of line with reason that it shocks the conscience and necessarily implies that the verdict must have been the result of passion and prejudice.

In the instant case, the nonpecuniary items of damage include allowances for pain and suffering, past and future, humiliation as a result of being disfigured and being permanently crippled, and constant anxiety and fear that the leg will have to be amputated. While the amount of the award is high, and may be more than we would have awarded were we the trier of the facts, considering the nature of the injury, the great pain and suffering, past and future, and the other items of damage, we cannot say, as a matter of law, that it is so high that it shocks the conscience and gives rise to the presumption that it was the result of passion or prejudice on the part of the jurors.

With pain and suffering, the courts try to determine the price of a plaintiff's pain. The court would likely hear evidence of how much pain and suffering the plaintiff is in. The plaintiff's lawyer might ask the jury: "Wouldn't it be worth $5 an hour not to be in this kind of pain? Or $10 an hour?" The lawyer might try to read body language and jurors' minds to see how much further to push the question. But if the lawyer thinks that $10 has stuck, approvingly, in the jurors' mind, then one can do the math from there: that means $240 a day or $87,600 a year. Say the person has a remaining life expectancy of 50 years, and a pain and suffering amount of $4,380,000. That would have to be discounted back to the **net present value of the total** in order to make a current damage award, but one can see how breaking pain and suffering into small, discrete amounts that seem very reasonable to a juror's mind can add up into large damage awards for pain and suffering. Courts will also consider damages for loss of enjoyment of life as part of pain and suffering.

b. Punitive

In some cases, a plaintiff may not only get compensatory damages, but punitive damages as well. Punitive damages, as the name suggests, are meant not to compensate a victim-plaintiff but instead to punish the **tortfeasor** (defendant). These damages are also known as **exemplary damages** because they are meant to make an example of the defendant who has engaged in problematic behavior. The idea is to make the punishment for the wrongdoing so significant that the defendant will have the incentive to change his behavior or production process or whatever was the proximate cause that triggered the injury.

In *Taylor v. Superior Court*, the Court held an alcoholic, who was aware of the seriousness of his problem and the danger driving while intoxicated posed, was forced to pay punitive damages even though the theory against the defendant was based in negligence rather than intentional torts. In this and in many other instances, courts have found various ways to impose punitive damages on defendants.

B. TWO LATIN WRINKLES

1. Res Ispa Loquitor

Res ipsa loquitor is a term applied to negligence cases where it is very difficult for the plaintiff to determine how and what exactly caused the injury. It means "the thing speaks for itself." *Res ipsa loquitor* is not a separate theory of liability; instead it is simply a shifting of the normal burden of proof from the plaintiff (who normally has to prove the case with a preponderance of the evidence) to the defendant, who must prove that they were not negligent.

Imagine a person is walking by another's barn and a bale of hay comes flying out of the barn, landing on the person's head. Bales of hay do not typically come flying out of barns and hitting bystanders without some degree of negligence (unless the bystander happens to be climbing into a horse's or cow's eating area). How is that bystander able to prove negligence? In these kinds of cases where *res ipsa loquitor* was first used, the thing—bales of flying haying hitting people—speaks for itself. In such situations, the burden of proof of establishing the duty and the breach of duty shifts from the plaintiff to the defendant.

> ***Res Ispa Loquitor:***
> **"The thing speaks for itself"**
>
> ***Respondeat Superior:***
> **"Let the master answer."**

The tests for applying *res ipsa loquitor* are:

- Does the action typically happen only with a party's negligence?
- Was the item causing the damage solely within the defendant's control when the damages occurred; and

- Was the plaintiff innocent of any contributing negligence?

Today, *res ipsa* cases primarily apply to products liability cases, which will be covered later. For now, it is well to situate it within its origins in negligence.

2. Respondeat Superior

Sometimes a third party is liable for the negligent actions of another person, such as when one person (an agent) is working for another person (a principal), especially when that agent is a regular employee of the principal/employer. If the agent injures someone while on the job and working for the employer, then the employer as well as the employee could be held liable for damages caused by the employee's negligence. A later chapter on agency law will cover this issue in more detail.

C. DEFENSES

Historically, contributory negligence significantly limited the likelihood that a plaintiff would recover damages from the defendant. **Contributory negligence** held that any negligence of the plaintiff would bar recovery, no matter how negligent the defendant's conduct was. For example, suppose the plaintiff and the defendant were driving their respective cars on a two-lane highway. The speed limit stands at 55 miles per hour. The plaintiff is travelling at 57 miles per hour and the defendant, driving drunk, is travelling 110. The defendant drifts over the center lane and hits the plaintiff's car, which is still squarely in its own lane. Fault here seems straightforward, but because the plaintiff is driving above the speed limit, he is negligent too. At least in theory, this could be used historically to bar recovery.

Courts modified the harshness of this approach with theories such as "last clear chance." This theory asks, even if the plaintiff was negligent, did the defendant have the last chance to avoid the injury (for instance, by not drifting over the center line)? Courts may also look to see if a defendant has voluntarily assumed the risk. Both of these mitigating theories, especially assumption of risk, still can be utilized in a case, but the modern rule tends to look at comparative rather than contributory negligence.

With **comparative negligence**, the Court looks to see how much each party is negligent. In the above scenario, the plaintiff driving 57 mph might be two percent negligent for driving over the speed limit, but the defendant driving 110 miles per hour, while drunk and drifting over the center line would likely be 98 percent negligent. With a 98–2 negligence factor, the plaintiff's recover would be reduced by his

2 percent of negligence. The comparative negligence rule thus simplifies analysis of fault and recovery.

Assumption of risk remains an important defense. If a fan goes to a major league baseball game and sits in the lower seats down the third base/left field line, gets hit by a line drive, and then sues the baseball team for negligence, the baseball team has a strong case to argue that the fan assumed the risk of being hit at a game, especially given the choice of seats that might be available. If a fan wanted to have more protection, she could sit behind home plate (where in all major league stadiums, there is netting to prevent being hit by a foul ball) or in more remote seats less likely to have a blistering line drive hit toward them. Of course, the hard issues come when one tries to determine whether a fan fully knew of the risk she was incurring.

"...THE PLAINTIFF driving 57 miles per hour might be two percent negligent for driving over the speed limit, but the defendant driving 110 miles per hour, while drunk and drifting over the center line would likely be 98 percent negligent."

II. Strict Liability

A. HISTORICAL ANTECEDENTS

Strict liability is sometimes also referred to as **absolute duty**. The concept behind strict liability is simple: some activities are so dangerous that the person who introduces them to the public is absolutely liable if something goes wrong. One cannot be careful. One cannot exercise such prudence so as to avoid a charge of negligence. Simply by introducing the activity or product, the opportunity for reasonable care has been lost. One is strictly liable for anything that goes wrong.

■ UNDER STRICT LIABILITY THE IDEA IS THAT THERE IS NO WAY TO INTRODUCE A MOUNTAIN LION INTO A COMMUNITY SAFELY.

For example, suppose a person kept a mountain lion cub as a pet. When the owner first got the cub, the neighborhood was a small, sparsely populated neighborhood. But with population growth, that neighborhood became well within a heavily congested urban area. The lion grew and although it was de-fanged and de-clawed, it was still a 350 pound animal. One day, the lion got out and jumped on an elderly neighbor. De-fanged or not, it still bruised the neighbor.

If negligence was the only theory of liability, then the owner might claim that he had been reasonably prudent in keeping the lion in an enclosure and de-fanging and de-clawing him. It doesn't matter with strict liability. Under strict liability the idea is that there is no way to introduce a mountain lion into a community safely.

The following case illustrates this example.

Collins v. Otto

149 Colo. 489, 369 P.2d 564 (1962)

The plaintiff was a four year old child who alleged defendants owned and wrongfully harbored a coyote, a wild animal of vicious propensities. On May 22, 1960, the child was attacked and bitten by the coyote and seriously injured. The Ottos admitted ownership of the animal for a period of about two years. They had fitted it with a collar and kept it on a chain about 15 ft. long. At the time of the attack on plaintiff, the coyote had recently been delivered of a litter and some of her puppies were still with her. Mr. Otto admitted that he gave one of the puppies to David to pet in the presence of the coyote.

Although the Ottos denied that they knew the coyote was vicious, they both testified that it was their custom not to let children approach it to pet it unless in their presence. Mrs. Otto testified that all of the neighborhood children had been warned not to go close to the coyote unless she or her husband were present. Mrs. Otto further testified that she worried about it and kept a very strong chain on the animal, and she did not tell the children that the coyote might hurt them but just warned the children to stay away unless she or her husband were present.

That the coyote attacked the boy is not disputed. An eye witness testified as to the viciousness of the attack, and the medical testimony established that lacerations of the forehead, eyelid, face, ears, and back of head were the result of the bites of the coyote. The injuries were quite extensive, leaving scars requiring at least two operations by a plastic surgeon.

The Ottos defended on the theory of the contributory negligence of this four year old child and on the basis that they had no prior knowledge of the viciousness of the animal.

The law is virtually universal that one who harbors a wild animal, which by its very nature is vicious and unpredictable, does so at his peril, and liability for injuries inflicted by such animal is absolute. * * *

As a universal rule of torts, those who harbor wild animals, which by their nature are vicious and unpredictable, are strictly liable for the any injuries caused by those animals. While other tort liability requires previous knowledge, it is not a defense to claim that one had no knowledge of the vicious nature of a wild animal. However, the strict liability rule for owning wild animals is not absolute. In cases where the injured party assumed a "primary assumption of risk," the owners may not be strictly liable.

B. CONTEMPORARY EXAMPLES

1. "One Free Bite"

If the owner of a mountain lion is strictly liable for any damages caused by the lion, what about the owner of a domesticated animal? The answer is, as is usually the case in law, that it depends. It depends on the history of the animal and also on the breed of the animal. A dog owner will be aware that a pit bull has a greater dangerous propensity, on the whole, than a Basset Hound. For the most part, a commonly domesticated dog or cat will not be considered to be unreasonably dangerous. As a result, the liability theory that attaches to domesticated animals is one of negligence rather than strict liability.

WHIMSICALLY PUT, your dog gets one free bite. After that—once you are aware of the pet's dangerous propensity—strict liability applies.

That changes, however, if an owner becomes aware of the dangerous propensity of the pet. Whimsically put, your dog gets one free bite. After that—once you are aware of the pet's dangerous propensity—strict liability applies.

Rules are also a bit different with respect to animals that trespass. The courts hold that owners of animals that trespass are strictly liable for the damages inflicted by the trespass. Furthermore, depending on state law, owners may be held strictly liable for damages incurred on public property. The following case is set as a Constitutional Equal Protecton case, but note that the underlying claim is whether it is fair to impose different standards of liability on trespassing animals depending on whether they are trespassing on other people's land or whether they are trespassing on public property (such as a highway).

Vanderwater v. Hatch

835 F.2d 239 (10th Cir. 1987)

Plaintiff, Dee Dee Vanderwater, brought this diversity action seeking damages for injuries she suffered in a collision between a motorcycle on which she was a passenger and a yearling cow owned by defendant, Roger Hatch. The collision occurred at approximately 10:00 p.m. on a stretch of rural highway in northern Utah, adjacent to a fenced pasture owned by Hatch in which he was then keeping approximately twenty-five yearling cattle. Beginning one-half to three-fourths of a mile west of the accident scene, the highway crosses a five-mile stretch of open range in which cattle are permitted to wander without restriction. *See* Utah Code Ann. § 41-6-38. Hatch kept about 120 cows on this open range, where there were also 400 to 500 cows belonging to other area ranchers. Hatch testified that most of his range cattle were cows with calves, but that he also kept a few yearlings on open range. Two witnesses travelling the opposite direction from plaintiff reported passing through a group of dark-colored cattle on the road seconds before the collision. One, Arthur DeSorcy, remembered seeing five or six cattle standing in the road. The other witness, Rennie DeSorcy, remembered seeing "ten to as many as 15" cattle, which he described as "half way between a calf and an adult cow as far as the size of them." The yearling cow involved in the accident was killed; there was no clear testimony concerning where the other cattle went or were taken following the accident.

Plaintiff argues that Utah Code Ann. § 41-6-38 violates the Equal Protection Clause of the Fourteenth Amendment to the United States Constitution because it imposes a greater burden of proof on her than Utah Code Ann. § 4-25-8 imposes on other plaintiffs similarly situated. Section 4-25-8 generally imposes strict liability on the owner of any livestock "that trespasses upon the premises of another person . . . to the owner or occupant of such premises for any damage inflicted by the trespass." *Id.; see Nelson v. Tanner*, (1948) (interpreting former code section). Vanderwater construes such damage to include personal injuries. *See* Restatement (Second) of Torts § 504(2) (1977) (possessor of trespassing livestock is strictly liable for harm "to the land or to its possessor or a member of his household"). We conclude that plaintiff's equal protection challenge is without merit. Because the statutes in issue do not employ suspect classifications or implicate fundamental rights, they "must be upheld against equal protection attack [if] the legislative means are rationally related to a legitimate governmental purpose. Moreover, such legislation carries with it a presumption of rationality that can only be overcome by a clear showing of arbitrariness and irrationality." *Hodel v. Indiana* (1981). **We cannot find it irrational for the Utah legislature to treat persons injured on public highways differently from those injured on their own lands. The legislature reasonably could have concluded that people's interest in the crops, fences, and even personal security on their own land is both greater and different in kind than travelers' interest in safety on the highway.** We need not agree with the different burden of proof imposed by the statute in order to uphold its constitutionality; nor need we inquire further into the actual, subjective motivation of the Utah legislature. *See United States Railroad Retirement Board v. Fritz* (1980). The interests involved are sufficiently dissimilar to reasonably warrant the different degrees of protection provided by §§ 4-25-8 and 41-6-38.

What is important in this case is that legislature can impose strict liability on trespassing animals and are relatively free to determine which kinds of trespassing merits strict liability or some lesser standard. If your domesticated animal trespasses, know that there could be strict liability imposed against you for any damages the animal causes, such as biting someone or harming property.

2. Abnormally Dangerous Activities

Unless you take your dog to the office, have an office at home, or are in the pet business, pets may not be a major concern in the workplace. The theories of liability established with wild, domesticated and dangerous animals, however, apply to commercial issues. Why? Because the underlying theory is that if one is introducing a dangerous thing to society, then that person should bear significant liability for anything that goes wrong. This is true of dangerous animals and it is true of dangerous commercial activities. The application of these strict liability theories commercially tends to appear in products liability cases, where the absolute standard applies. More about this application will be reviewed in the chapter on product liability. But strict liability isn't mainly about pets.

Strict liability took a step into the business world when commerce introduced new ways of doing business that were determined to be ultra-hazardous. Two examples of this were dynamite blasting (for instance, to clear areas for new roads) or crop-dusting farmland. The courts determined that these were such dangerous activities that strict liability was the appropriate standard to be applied. In a case involving an accident that occurred during the transportation of toxic chemicals, *Indiana Harbor Belt Railroad Co. v. American Cyanamid Co.*, 916 F.2d 1174 (7th Cir. 1990), Judge Posner laid out six factors that should be considered in determining whether an activity is ultra-hazardous:

Factors in Ultra-Hazardous Activities	
1. How great the risk of harm was.	4. Whether the activity is commonly engaged in.
2. The seriousness of the harm that could result.	5. Whether the activity is appropriate for the location.
3. Whether the risk could be prevented with the exercise of due care.	6. Whether the social value of the activity outweighs the risks.

C. DEFENSES

When applied to product liability cases, there are some defenses a defendant can raise. It is, however, very difficult for the defendant to raise effective defenses in a strict liability case because the nature of the liability is that the defendant has introduced something to society that is unreasonably dangerous and, thus, is liable for any damages that result from that animal, practice, or thing. To return to the dangerous animal example, it would be foolish to taunt a mountain lion and, all other things being equal, one would likely conclude that such taunting would be negligent conduct. Yet if your urban neighbor actually attempts to keep a 350 pound mountain lion as a pet, the neighbor would still be liable because the introduction of a mountain lion into an urban area triggers strict liability.

III. Intentional Torts

NEGLIGENCE AND STRICT LIABILITY proceed on the basis that the tortfeasor— the person causing the injury—did not mean to injure the plaintiff, but either because the defendant was not careful (did not act as a reasonably prudent person) or because she introduced an unreasonable danger into society. Intentional torts are much more straightforward and can also trigger criminal charges.

With **intentional torts**, the defendant "meant" or intended to do a prohibited act. The duty and its breach are not analytically quite the same as they are in a negligence case. Causation and damages are the same, with punitive damages more likely in an intentional tort case.

In an intentional tort case, the first step is to define whether there is a prohibited act (analogous to the duty step in a negligence case) and then whether the defendant performed the prohibited act. Here are some examples of prohibited acts:

- Unauthorized touching
- Reasonable apprehension that a battery is about to occur
- Interfering with another person's property
- Making false statements that damage another person in their work
- Harassing or otherwise verbally abusing another person
- Battery
- Assault
- Trespass
- Defamation
- Intentional infliction of emotional harm

The level of intention is crucial. Accidents do happen; mistakes get made. Those can be handled by negligence theories. The following case looks at whether an alleged battery actually possessed the requisite level of intention.

Wishnatsky v. Huey

584 N.W.2d 859 (N.D. App. 1998)

On January 10, 1996, Huey, an assistant attorney general, was engaged in a conversation with attorney Peter B. Crary in Crary's office. Without knocking or announcing his entry, Wishnatsky, who performs paralegal work for Crary, attempted to enter the office. Huey pushed the door closed, thereby pushing Wishnatsky back into the hall. Wishnatsky reentered the office and Huey left.

Wishnatsky brought an action against Huey, seeking damages for battery. Huey moved for summary judgment of dismissal. The trial court granted Huey's motion and a judgment of dismissal was entered. Wishnatsky moved to alter the judgment. The trial court denied Wishnatsky's motion.

Wishnatsky appealed, contending the evidence he submitted in response to Huey's motion for summary judgment satisfies the elements of a battery claim and the trial court erred in granting Huey's motion. Wishnatsky also contends Huey is not entitled to prosecutorial or statutory immunity.

"In its original conception [battery] meant the infliction of physical injury." VIII Sir William Holdsworth, *A History of English Law* 422 (2d Impression 1973). By the Eighteenth Century, the requirement of an actual physical injury had been eliminated:

> At Nisi Prius, upon evidence in trespass for assault and battery, Holt, C.J. declared, 1. That the least touching of another in anger is a battery. 2. If two or more meet in a narrow passage, and without any violence or design of harm, the one touches the other gently, it is no battery. 3. If any of them use violence against the other, to force his way in a rude inordinate manner, it is a battery; or any struggle about the passage, to that degree as may do hurt, is a battery. * * *

We certainly agree with the Supreme Court's determination that when Wishnatsky attempted to enter the room in which Huey was conversing with Crary, "Huey apparently reacted in a rude and abrupt manner in attempting to exclude Wishnatsky from that conversation." As a matter of law, however, Huey's "rude and abrupt" conduct did not rise to the level of battery.

To find battery, the plaintiff must prove that the act (1) was intentional, (2) caused contact with the plaintiff and (3) was harmful or offensive. Showing harm

requires physical impairment, pain or illness. For an act to be offensive, the act would have to offend a reasonable sense of personal dignity.

A. ASSAULT

An **assault** can be thought of as an action that puts another person into reasonable apprehension that a **battery** is about to be perpetrated against the person. Assaults quite often go along with batteries, but they are separate torts and, on occasion, one can occur without the other. The following case looks at the separateness of these torts as well as how they often do go together.

Picard v. Barry Pontiac-Buick, Inc.

654 A.2d 690 (R.I. 1995)

The plaintiff, Victorie A. Picard, brought her mother's car to Barry Pontiac-Buick, Inc. (Barry Pontiac), where the car had been purchased, to have the light repaired. The car failed an annual inspection because, according to a Barry Pontiac representative, the brakes needed to be replaced. The plaintiff brought the car to Kent's Alignment Service (Kent's Alignment), where the car passed inspection. The plaintiff then contacted a local television news "troubleshooter" reporter, presumably to report her experience at the two inspection sites.

The plaintiff returned to Barry Pontiac for a reinspection, bringing a camera with her. The plaintiff began to take a picture of the defendant while he was inspecting the breaks. After the camera snapped, the events that gave rise to this case occurred.

The plaintiff testified that defendant "lunged" at her and "grabbed [her] around around [sic] the shoulders," although plaintiff did not experience any pain. The plaintiff then testified on cross-examination that after defendant grabbed her by both her shoulders, she and defendant "spun around wrestling." According to plaintiff, defendant released her after someone said, "let her go." The plaintiff then left the garage with her goddaughter. The plaintiff brought action against the automobile mechanic for assault and battery. The Superior Court, Newport County, entered judgment for plaintiff, and the defendant appealed.

The Supreme Court held that: (1) customer established reasonable apprehension of injury necessary for prima facie case of assault; (2) mechanic's contact with customer's camera was sufficient to constitute battery.

Assault and battery are separate acts, usually arising from the same transaction, each having independent significance. "An assault is a physical act of a threatening nature or an offer of corporal injury which puts an individual in reasonable fear of imminent bodily harm." It is a plaintiff's apprehension of injury which renders a defendant's act compensable.

> "[t]he damages recoverable for [assault] are those for the plaintiff's mental disturbance, including fright, humiliation and the like, as well as any physical illness which may result from them"). This apprehension must be the type of fear normally aroused in the mind of a reasonable person.

The plaintiff testified that she was frightened by defendant's actions. A review of the attendant circumstances attests that such a reaction was reasonable. The defendant admitted approaching plaintiff, and the photograph taken that day clearly showed defendant pointing his finger at plaintiff as defendant approached her. Because plaintiff's apprehension of imminent bodily harm was reasonable at that point, plaintiff has established a *prima facie* case of assault.

Often people mix up assault and battery. A battery, in short form, is an unauthorized touching whereas an assault is when a person is put into reasonable apprehension that a battery is about to be perpetrated against them. To put it another way, if Jim slugs Pete from behind, Jim would be guilty of a battery (an unauthorized touching) but not an assault because Pete didn't see the punch coming and therefore was not put into apprehension that the battery was about to occur.

B. TRESPASS

A defendant may be found guilty of **trespass** to land if they intentionally enter or remain (if entry was legal) or place an object or refuse to remove an object on the plaintiff's land without permission. That is fairly straight forward. If I walk onto your land or jump on top of your car, it is clearly a trespass. Similarly, if my pet crosses over onto your land, it is a trespass. But what if I release a substance into your property? Is that a trespass? The following case looks at that issue.

Martin v. Reynolds Metals Co.

297 F.2d 49, 5 Fed. R. Serv. 2d 467 (9th Cir. 1961)

The plaintiffs allege that during the period from August 22, 1951 to January 1, 1956 the defendant, in the operation of its aluminum reduction plant near Troutdale, Oregon caused certain fluoride compounds in the form of gases and particulates to become airborne and settle upon the plaintiffs' land rendering it unfit for raising livestock during that period. Plaintiffs allege that their cattle were poisoned by ingesting the fluorides which contaminate the forage and water on their land. They sought damages in the amount of $450,000 for the loss of use of their land for grazing purposes and for the deterioration of the land through the growth of brush, trees and weeds resulting from the lack of use of the premises for grazing purposes. The plaintiffs also sought punitive damages in the amount of $30,000.

The plaintiffs and the defendant each moved for a directed verdict, whereupon the trial court found that the plaintiffs had suffered damage in the amount of $71,500 in the loss of use of their land and $20,000 for the deterioration of their land and entered judgment accordingly. The trial court rejected the plaintiffs' claim for punitive damages.

In the course of the pleadings the defendant raised the issue as to whether the complaint alleged a cause of action in trespass. The defendant contended that at most a cause of action in nuisance was stated.

We must determine . . . whether all or only a part of this damage may be shown; all, if the invasion constitutes a trespass, a part only (*i.e.*, the damage which resulted within the two-year period of the statute of limitations) if the invasion was a nuisance and not a trespass.

The gist of the defendant's argument is as follows: a trespass arises only when there has been a 'breaking and entering upon real property,' constituting a direct, as distinguished from a consequential, invasion of the possessor's interest in land; and the settling upon the land of fluoride compounds consisting of gases, fumes and particulates is not sufficient to satisfy these requirements.

Before appraising the argument we shall first describe more particularly the physical and chemical nature of the substance which was deposited upon plaintiffs' land. In reducing alumina (the oxide of aluminum) to aluminum the alumina is subjected to an electrolytic process which causes the emanation of fluoridic compounds consisting principally of hydrogen fluoride, calcium fluoride, iron fluoride and silicon tetrafluoride. The individual particulates which form these chemical compounds are not visible to the naked eye. A part of them were captured by a fume collection system which was installed in November, 1950; the remainder became airborne and a part of the uncaptured particles eventually were deposited upon plaintiffs' land.

Trespass and private nuisance are separate fields of tort liability relating to actionable interference with the possession of land. They may be distinguished by comparing the interest invaded; an actionable invasion of a possessor's interest in the exclusive possession of land is a trespass; an actionable invasion of a possessor's interest in the use and enjoyment of his land is a nuisance. 4 Restatement, Torts 224, Intro. Note Chapter 40.

However, there are cases which have held that the defendant's interference with plaintiff's possession resulting from the settling upon his land of effluents emanating from defendant's operations is exclusively nontrespassory . . . Although in such cases the separate particles which collectively cause the invasion are minute, the deposit of each of the particles constitutes a physical intrusion and, but for the size of the particle, would clearly give rise to an action of trespass. The defendant asks us to take account of the difference in size of the physical agency through which the intrusion occurs and relegate entirely to the field of nuisance law certain invasions which do not meet the dimensional test, whatever that is. In pressing this argument upon us the defendant must admit that there are cases which have held that a trespass results from the movement or deposit of rather small objects over or upon the surface of the possessor's land.

The view recognizing a trespassory invasion where there is no 'thing' which can be seen with the naked eye undoubtedly runs counter to the definition of trespass expressed in some quarters. 1 Restatement, Torts § 158, Comment h (1934); Prosser, *Torts* § 13 (2d Ed.1955). It is quite possible that in an earlier day when science had not yet peered into the molecular and atomic world of small particles, the courts could not fit an invasion through unseen physical instrumentalities into the requirement that a trespass can result only from a direct invasion. But in this atomic age even the uneducated know the great and awful force contained in the atom and what it can do to a man's property if it is released. In fact, the now famous equation E=mc2 has taught us that mass and energy are equivalents and that our concept of 'things' must be reframed. If these observations on science in relation to the law of trespass should appear theoretical and unreal in the abstract, they become very practical and real to the possessor of land when the unseen force cracks the foundation of his house. The force is just as real if it is chemical in nature and must be awakened by the intervention of another agency before it does harm.

If, then, we must look to the character of the instrumentality which is used in making an intrusion upon another's land we prefer to emphasize the object's energy or force rather than its size. Viewed in this way we may define trespass as any intrusion which invades the possessor's protected interest in exclusive possession, whether that intrusion is by visible or invisible pieces of matter or by energy which can be measured only by the mathematical language of the physicist.

We are of the opinion, therefore, that the intrusion of the fluoride particulates in the present case constituted a trespass.

C. DEFAMATION

The law defines **defamation** as a published communication that tends to harm the reputation of another as to lower him in the estimation of the community or to deter third persons from associating or dealing with him. The standards for defamation differ for certain groups. For example, there is a general rule that you cannot defame the deceased. Public officials and celebrities have a very high standard to meet in order to prove defamation: they must show that there was actual knowledge of falsehood or a reckless disregard for falsehood. Lastly, large groups generally cannot be defamed, while it is possible for small groups to be defamed. Here are some examples to demonstrate how the rules of defamation differ.

Milkovich v. Lorain Journal Co.

497 U.S I (1990)

Respondent J. Theodore Diadiun authored an article in an Ohio newspaper implying that petitioner Michael Milkovich, a local high school wrestling coach, lied under oath in a judicial proceeding about an incident involving petitioner and his team which occurred at a wrestling match. Petitioner sued Diadiun and the newspaper for libel, and the Ohio Court of Appeals affirmed a lower court entry of summary judgment against petitioner. This judgment was based in part on the grounds that the article constituted an "opinion" protected from the reach of state defamation law by the First Amendment to the United States Constitution. The case was appealed to the Supreme Court.

Chief Justice Rehnquist, held that: (1) separate constitutional privilege for "opinion" was not required in addition to established safeguards regarding defamation to ensure freedom of expression guaranteed by First Amendment, and (2) reasonable fact finder could conclude that statements in reporter's column implied assertion that high school coach perjured himself in judicial proceeding, and implication that coach committed perjury was sufficiently factual to be susceptible of being proved true or false and might permit defamation recovery.

Defamation law developed not only as a means of allowing an individual to vindicate his good name, but also for the purpose of obtaining redress for harm caused by such statements. As the common law developed in this country, apart from the issue of damages, one usually needed only allege an unprivileged publication of false and defamatory matter to state a cause of action for defamation. The common law generally did not place any additional restrictions on the type of statement that could be actionable. Indeed, defamatory communications were deemed actionable regardless of whether they were deemed to be statements of fact or opinion. See, *e.g.*,

Restatement of Torts, *supra*, §§ 565-567. As noted in the 1977 Restatement (Second) of Torts § 566, Comment a:

> "Under the law of defamation, an expression of opinion could be defamatory if the expression was sufficiently derogatory of another as to cause harm to his reputation, so as to lower him in the estimation of the community or to deter third persons from associating or dealing with him . . . . The expression of opinion was also actionable in a suit for defamation, despite the normal requirement that the communication be false as well as defamatory . . . . This position was maintained even though the truth or falsity of an opinion—as distinguished from a statement of fact—is not a matter that can be objectively determined and truth is a complete defense to a suit for defamation."

However, due to concerns that unduly burdensome defamation laws could stifle valuable public debate, the privilege of "fair comment" was incorporated into the common law as an affirmative defense to an action for defamation. "The principle of 'fair comment' afford[ed] legal immunity for the honest expression of opinion on matters of legitimate public interest when based upon a true or privileged statement of fact." 1 F. Harper & F. James, *Law of Torts* § 5.28, p. 456 (1956) (footnote omitted). As this statement implies, comment was generally privileged when it concerned a matter of public concern, was based upon true or privileged facts, represented the actual opinion of the speaker, and was not made solely for the purpose of causing harm. See R*estatement of Torts, supra,* § 606. "According to the majority rule, the privilege of fair comment applied only to an expression of opinion and not to a false statement of fact, whether it was expressly stated or implied from an expression of opinion." Restatement (Second) of Torts, *supra,* § 566, Comment a. Thus under the common law, the privilege of "fair comment" was the device employed to strike the appropriate balance between the need for vigorous public discourse and the need to redress injury to citizens wrought by invidious or irresponsible speech.

> **"COMMENT WAS GENERALLY privileged when it concerned a matter of public concern, was based upon true or privileged facts, represented the actual opinion of the speaker, and was not made solely for the purpose of causing harm."**

. . . The next step in this constitutional evolution was the Court's consideration of a private individual's defamation actions involving statements of public concern. Although the issue was initially in doubt, see *Rosenbloom v. Metromedia, Inc.*, 403 U.S. 29, 91 S.Ct. 1811, 29 L.Ed.2d 296 (1971), the Court ultimately concluded that *The New York Times* malice standard was inappropriate for a private person attempting to prove he was defamed on matters of public interest. *Gertz v. Robert Welch, Inc., supra.* As we explained:

> "Public officials and public figures usually enjoy significantly greater access to the channels of effective communication and hence have a more realistic opportunity to counteract false statements than private individuals normally enjoy. . . . . ."[More important,] public officials and public figures have voluntarily exposed themselves to increased risk of injury from defamatory falsehood concerning them. No such assumption is justified with respect to a private individual." *Id.* 418 U.S., at 344–345, 94 S.Ct., at 3009 . . .

Next, the *Bresler Letter Carriers-Falwell* line of cases provides protection for statements that cannot "reasonably [be] interpreted as stating actual facts" about an individual. *Falwell*, 485 U.S., at 50, 108 S.Ct., at 879. This provides assurance that public debate will not suffer for lack of "imaginative expression" or the "rhetorical hyperbole" which has traditionally added much to the discourse of our Nation. *See id.*, at 53–55, 108 S.Ct., at 880–882.

We are not persuaded that, in addition to these protections, an additional separate constitutional privilege for "opinion" is required to ensure the freedom of expression guaranteed by the First Amendment. The dispositive question in the present case then becomes whether a reasonable factfinder could conclude that the statements in the Diadiun column imply an assertion that petitioner Milkovich perjured himself in a judicial proceeding. We think this question must be answered in the affirmative. As the Ohio Supreme Court itself observed: "[T]he clear impact in some nine sentences and a caption is that [Milkovich] 'lied at the hearing after . . . having given his solemn oath to tell the truth.' " ***Scott*****, 25 Ohio St.3d, at 251, 496 N.E.2d, at 707. This is not the sort of loose, figurative, or hyperbolic language which would negate the impression that the writer was seriously maintaining that petitioner committed the crime of perjury. Nor does the general tenor of the article negate this impression.**

D. INTENTIONAL INFLICTION OF EMOTIONAL DISTRESS (IIED)

IIED occurs when one intentionally or recklessly causes severe emotional damage to another through extreme and outrageous conduct. The standards for IIED are extremely difficult to meet and must be outrageous and extreme in order to qualify as an IIED.

As with all torts (including products liability, which is a combination of torts and contracts), there may be multiple charges for a particular incident. For example, suppose two drivers got into a road rage altercation, which resulted in one of them crashing his car into the other's. Then the two drivers got out, exchanged words and started to fight. There could be trespass, battery, assault, and perhaps even emotional harm charges from this one incident. Running a car into someone else intentionally is not only an intentional tort; it is also negligent operation of an automobile. In an actual lawsuit, the injured party (and that could be both parties in the scenario above), would sue the other side on alleged multiple theories or reasons why the other party should be held liable. Thus, one does not have to choose theories; one can take a shotgun approach; that is, to sue on the basis of as many possible theories one can reasonably fashion and hope that one strikes. In the following chapter on products liability, we will also see another use of the shotgun approach in suing as many different people as possible.

E. DEFENSES

Defenses to intentional torts typically revolve around some notion of consent or self-defense. If the plaintiff consented to the intentional tort, either expressly or through her actions, then the defendant may raise that consent as a defense to a suit by the plaintiff against the defendant. To take an obvious example, if the plaintiff and defendant engage in a sport with physical contact involved—football, boxing, wrestling, etc.—then one of them cannot claim that the other committed a battery. It is part of the sport to touch the other party. However there are limits. A hockey player clubbing another player with his stick might very well be a battery even

ARTICLE: IIED

Man Claims Emotional Distress Due to Bird Insults

www.loweringthebar.net; January 16, 2011

THE AFP REPORTS that a Taiwanese man has sued his neighbors claiming that they trained their mynah bird to swear at him and that the bird's relentless taunting caused him serious emotional distress.

Few details were available, but it appeared that Wang Han-chin had previously complained to police that his neighbors were too loud, and he alleged that in revenge they had trained their bird to call him a "clueless big-mouthed idiot" when he left for work in the morning. Wang claimed that the bird's insults caused him serious distress, and had affected his concentration at work to the point that he had somehow burned himself. Prosecutors apparently declined to charge the neighbors with anything "due to insufficient evidence linking the bird to his injuries," and that seems to have led to a civil lawsuit.

In a similar case in 2006, which also shows that my database of "similar cases" is getting pretty comprehensive, a 78-year-old Pennsylvania woman charged one of her neighbors with repeatedly meowing at her in retaliation for complaining to police about their cat's infiltration of her flower garden. Alexandra Carasia also claimed the conduct had caused her emotional harm, and even used the word "torture" to describe her experience, completing the final degradation of that word from something that once meant "heinous war crime" into a term that can also encompass repeated meowing.

That case was also similar in that the charges were quickly dismissed.

though hockey is a violent sport. In a football game, touching would be, in a sense, authorized. Or imagine a possibility in which prior to a karate match, one of the soon-to-be participants hit the other. That could be a battery even though, a few minutes later, it might be consented to within the context of the actual match. The timing of the consent becomes important.

More serious cases concern issues of sexual assault. What may begin as a consensual act could turn into a non-consensual one; at the point it becomes non-consensual, the act could then become a battery.

Self-defense constitutes another defense. A person has a right to defend themselves against another's attack. One's right to self-defense consists of using the amount of force necessary to repel the attack, thus significantly limiting a right to increase the amount of force. For example, if someone were to attack you with their fists, that is not likely to justify you pulling out a shotgun and shooting them. You could use your own fists and, if the other person was bigger or a more skilled fighter, you might be able to add a baseball bat to fend off the attack. But the more one adds weapons with fatal potential, the more risk one undertakes of losing the justification of self-defense.

The same rules apply to a third party who is under attack. As long as that person has a right to his own self-defense, an intervening third party can use the same reasonable measure on behalf of that person to repel the attack.

It is worth noting, in these rules, that the use of a watchdog or a spring-loaded gun bring significant risk to the person under attack. This becomes an even bigger issue in terms of defending one's property. The law nearly always sides with protection of the person or the protection of property, and so the range of defense one uses to protect property is much narrower.

As this chapter has shown, torts covers a vast area from malpractice to fender benders to sexual harassment and quite a bit more. Torts plays on moral notions with its concepts of duty. To the extent those duties are specified by legislatures or courts, one has a place to look for knowing what one's duties are. Even then, though, the range is enormous. Yet because torts create liabilities for not acting to protect a reasonable foreseeable plaintiff, impose duties for activities that might be threats to society, and further inquiries about intention, there are many avenues one can travel to find liability of a defendant.

Torts are also foundational. Along with Contracts, Torts form the basis of the following chapter so we will again see many of the concepts covered in this chapter.

NOTES AND COMMENTS on the Legal Environment of Business

1. **TORT LAW ALWAYS** raises questions about responsibility. Going back to the opening of this chapter, why does a landowner have any liability for a group of drunken students crossing his land? What about their responsibility? Often a property owner or a business has a capacity to prevent harm. Whether that is considered fair by all parties or not, it is the way the law works in the United States and so businesses must manage their affairs with the specter of liability in mind.

   In this chapter, the plight of the "eggshell plaintiff" was noted. A person committing a tort does not need to desire for his actions—say an unauthorized touching (a batter) as gentle as touching a shoulder—to cause tremendous damage to a victim. But if the victim is fragile, the tortfeasor does "take the plaintiff as he finds him." Is this a reasonable state of affairs? Is there a better rule of law to handle such cases? If so, what would it look like?

2. **SHOULD A PERSON** be able to use deadly force to protect property? What would be the pros and cons of that proposition?

NOTES AND COMMENTS on the Ethical Environment of Business

1. **THE SHAREHOLDER AND STAKEHOLDER** frameworks are known as deontological approaches to ethics. That means that the question each framework begin with is the determination of what a manager's duty is. Under shareholder theory, the duty to carry out the lawful directives of shareholders, which will always include some significant—over the only—consideration of making money for the shareholders. Under stakeholder theory, the duty is to run the firm for the benefit of all who are affected and this includes considering respect for stakeholder rights and justice as well as creating the greatest good for the greatest number. Because duty is central to these ethical frameworks, it is not surprising that there is a good deal of overlap between ethics and torts. Torts deal with duty. In a negligence case, the first step is to determine what duty existed. With strict liability, the duty becomes absolute. Thus, as we do with each Ethical Environment of Business section, it is worth revisiting each of the cases in the chapter, but rather than looking at each case with the question of whether it was decided fairly, we can look at the cases in this chapter on torts with the question of what the duty was (for negligence and strict liability cases) and how the courts figured out the source for that duty. You'll find

that consideration of rights, fairness, utilitarianism, and complying with the law all rise to the forefront just as they would in an ethics analysis.

That leaves intentional torts, but here again, it begins with a core ethical principle: intent. Immanuel Kant said that a good intent—or good will—is the only thing that can be good without qualification. The utilitarians, who emphasize consequences of actions, would object that we can only evaluate actions according to intent, but there really is no strong objection to the position that people's intentions matter a great deal in conducting an ethical analysis. Sure, people make mistakes and misguided and so bad things may still happen as a result of a person's good intent, but we are very likely to soften any judgment on that person if they were sincerely trying to do a good thing.

Of course, another issue with measuring intent is that the motives for any decision are frequently mixed. Does a sole proprietor give money to charity because she sincerely believes in the charity, because she knows her reputation will be enhanced in the community (and therefore her business prospects) by appearing to be philanthropic, or is it a combination of both?

While acknowledging some of the difficulties of measuring intent, the fact remains that intention is an important category in ethical analysis. Of course, by its very name, intentional torts, trades heavily on the importance of intent. So, when you go back through the intentional tort cases, ask how is intent determined and measured? Do courts do a good job with this? What would you do?

2. **APART FROM THESE FIRST STEPS**—duty and intent—in each one of the approaches to torts (negligence, strict liability, and intentional), there is room for ample discussion on how to determine what caused an injury. The questions of damages is a hotly disputed legal question today. Should we allow for punitive damages? Are they fair? Should there be limits? If we don't have punitive damages, then what incentives are there for an injured party to go through the complicated and expensive legal system to find compensation? What about contingent fee arrangements? Are they fair? If not, what person without means will ever find a way to recover damages from an injury? At the same time, are these out of hand? The same questions can be posed to the compensatory damage component of pain and suffering.

    Thus, torts is an area of law teeming with ethical issues and by going through these cases with some of the questions posed above, one can have an engaging discussion about ethics and business.

3. **TAKE A LOOK** at Chapter 5's article on the cost of safety with it comes to airlines. We've seen in this chapter that common carriers have almost unlimited duties to protect their passengers from harm. This chapter looks at the costs of doing so. What do you think is the fair law in balancing safety and cost? How would you establish duty in these kinds of cases? What factors would you consider? Would it make a difference if you were the CEO of an airline as opposed to a CEO of a non-airline company who had to fly a great deal for business?

CHAPTER

12

Products Liability

Products liability is a relatively modern invention. A legal commentator has contrasted the historic adage, *caveat emptor* (buyer beware), with one more aligned with a commercial age governed in part by products liability laws:

caveat venditor (seller beware). Historically, the buyer was to be aware; today the seller needs to be. To be sure, products caused harm in the past, but the explosion of products liability cases arose from the Industrial Revolution and the resulting increase in the variety and number of products, often from mass production, that were sold to the public. Whether cars, augurs, toasters, or hair driers, products sometimes don't work the way they are supposed to. Occasionally, their malfunctions injure people and lawsuits get filed to obtain damages for those injuries. What kinds of cases are these? Through the ingenuity of litigating attorneys and the flexibility of the common law court system, these cases draw from both tort and contract theories of liability.

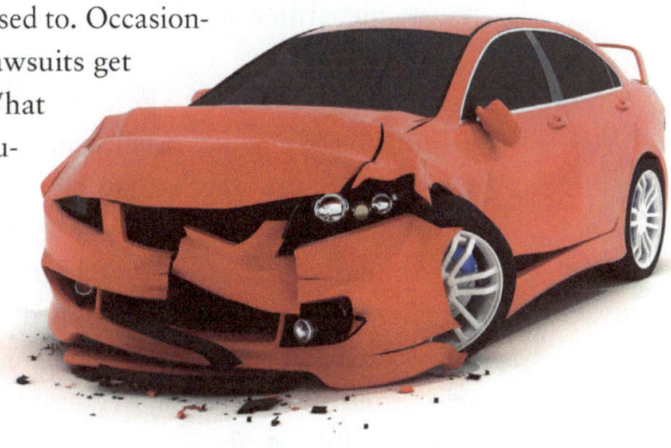

I. General Concepts and Classifications of Products Liability

PERHAPS THE KEY STEP in unleashing these kinds of cases was through the minimization of the obstacle called **privity of contract**. That legal rule allowed an injured plaintiff to sue a seller who had sold a defective product to him through tort or contract, but not other suppliers and manufacturers who had supplied component parts of manufactured items that the seller relied on to place the product into the market. Prior to the Industrial Revolution and the mass production of products, privity of contract made sense because transactions were far more one-to-one exchanges. Sellers were much more likely to also be the manufacturer. But the complexity of contemporary manufacturing turns sellers into mere retailers who take a product made by someone else and then sell it to the customer. While the retailer is the seller, it is the parties making the product who construct it in ways that could be defective.

Cases chipped away at the privity doctrine, culminating in the 1916 landmark case, *MacPherson v. Buick Motor Co.* In that case, one of the wheels of the vehicle was made of defective wood and while Mr. MacPhearson was operating the vehicle, one of the spokes crumbled, resulting in an accident. Before he became a Justice of the U.S. Supreme Court, the eminent Benjamin Cardozo wrote:

> If the nature of a thing is such that it is reasonably certain to place life and limb in peril when negligently made, it is then a thing of danger. Its nature gives warning of the consequences to be expected. If to the element of danger there is added knowledge that the thing will be used by persons other than the purchaser and used with now tests, then, irrespective of contra, the manufacturer of this thing of danger is under a duty to make it carefully.

Indeed, one thing to keep in mind is that there may be four or five theories of liability that a plaintiff may use in a lawsuit, drawn from both torts and contracts,. The plaintiff does not have to pick just one theory; he can allege multiple reasons for liability.

Similarly, because manufacturing often entails a variety of companies, from suppliers to designers to component manufacturers to final manufacturers to retailers, there could be multiple potential defendants in the chain of production and sale. Often all are sued, so in case one escapes liability, several remain who can still be successfully sued.

It is even possible that if it's unclear who caused an injury, they can be sued anyway. For instance, if a person takes a drug and dies or is harmed by the drug, it may be medically ascertained that a certain combination of chemicals caused the harm, but it may not be possible to prove which company produced the specific product that the consumer/plaintiff ingested. In such cases, a concept called **enterprise liability theory** could be used to sue all the manufacturers of the competing products, with damage awards divided according the market share in the geographical area at the time the product was used.

For these reasons, as well as due to fear that both punitive and compensatory damages might be awarded after a long, expensive trial, potential defendants are often motivated to settle cases. In some ways, this further incentivizes lawsuits, because individuals with marginal cases may sue simply in hopes of getting significant settlements without having to go through the process of a trial.

Two other concepts also make products liability controversial generally and unpopular with businesspeople. One of those concerns the economics of lawsuits. Most product liability (and tort) litigation is driven with very little or no cost, except for the time invested, to the plaintiff. Lawyers accept these kinds of cases on a **contingent fee arrangement.** These call for the plaintiff/victim to forward no money to the lawyer, nor to pay the lawyer anything unless the lawyer obtains a settlement or trial verdict from the defendant. Lawyers may have a base contingent fee of 33.3% if they settle the case prior to trial. The fee may increase depending on whether the case goes to trial or to appeal, or it may be higher simply because of the complexity of the case. It is common for the contingent fee to go up to 40-45% for complex cases, such as products liability cases. To determine the enforceability of contingency fees set by lawyers, the American Bar Association set out its Model Rules of Professional Conduct, which exempt contingent fees for domestic dispute cases whose outcome is dependent upon securing a divorce, alimony, or support settlement and for criminal defense cases.

Furthermore, applicable contingent fees must be considered reasonable. In *Venegas v. Mitchell*, a U.S. Supreme Court case decided in 1990, an attorney representing the plaintiff in a civil rights case sued his client for recovery of contingent fees.[1] In civil rights cases, the losing party is statutorily obligated to pay for the other side's attorney's costs and in this case, the court-calculated attorneys' costs amounted to $75,000. In the suit, the attorney claimed his client owed him an additional amount due to the agreed upon 40% contingent fee. The Supreme Court held that a statutory award of attorney's fees did not release a client from paying his attorney an additional contingent fee and that the 40% fee was reasonable. The attorney was eventually rewarded $406,000.

Another concern businesspeople (and others) have about damage awards relates to their size. There has been ongoing political debate calling for caps on damage awards, some of which have been adopted. In 2005, President George W. Bush proposed a nationwide cap of $250,000 on damage awards for medical malpractice

---

1 *Venegas v. Mitchell*, 495 U.S. 82 (1990).

suits. Since then, over half of the states have passed legislation limiting damages for malpractice suits, with caps ranging from $250,000 to $650,000. Some states have also passed legislation limiting compensatory damages for products liability cases. In Michigan, for example, the compensatory damages for products liability cases cannot exceed $500,000. In other states, such as California, proposed legislation to cap compensatory damages has been struck down.

Figure 2. Tort costs relative to GDP
(in billions)

Year	U.S. tort costs	U.S. GDP	Tort costs as % of GDP
1950	$ 1.8	$ 294	0.62%
1960	5.4	526	1.03
1970	13.9	1,038	1.34
1980	42.7	2,788	1.53
1990	130.2	5,801	2.24
2000	179.1	9,952	1.80
2003	245.7	11,142	2.21
2004	260.3	11,853	2.20
2005	261.4	12,623	2.07
2006	246.9	13,377	1.85
2007	252.0	14,029	1.80
2008	254.9	14,292	1.78
2009	251.8	13,939	1.81
2010	264.6	14,527	1.82

*Throughout this report, unadjusted, or nominal, GDP is used.
Most news releases on GDP rely on inflation-adjusted, or real, GDP.

As we saw in the chapter on torts, compensation for pain and suffering can add up to large damage awards. In North Carolina, the Kanahwa County jury awarded $11.5 million in compensatory damages to a family for the death of their mother, who was found severely dehydrated as the result of the negligence of a nursing home.

The even bigger clamor about damage awards relates to punitive damages. The case of the woman who (initially with success) sued McDonalds for over $1 million because coffee burned her legs after she placed the cup there after going through the restaurant's drive-through has become popular culture folklore. The fact that damages were later reduced has been buried in the news. Instead, what remains is the (not necessarily misleading) perception that companies can be hit with huge punitive damage awards that appear to exceed the gravity of the injury in question.

A FINE LIMITED to compensatory damages could well be swallowed as a cost of doing business by a huge multinational company. But the punitive damage weapon creates a different risk calculation. Punitive damages can change the ways companies manufacture and sell products.

Why is this? The philosophy underlying punitive damages contends that there needs to be a punishment significant enough so that the tortfeasor/defendant will change their ways. A fine limited to compensatory damages could well be swallowed by a huge multinational company as the cost of doing business. But the punitive damage weapon creates a different risk calculation. Punitive damages can change the ways companies manufacture and sell products. Thus, from a public policy standpoint, one rationale for punitive damages is that it provides incentives for the manufacture and sale of safer products.

The question of who should receive punitive damages is also part of the debate over the product liability system. In most states, the current structure of the damage award system calls for the plaintiff to receive damage awards. Unless there is controversy over the amount of pain and suffering awards, this principle tends to be accepted by all parties to the debate. Once the party has been compensated for damages suffered, however, the debate kicks in as to whether the victim should also receive punitive damages. After all, punitive damages do not compensate the victim; they are awarded to punish the defendant for egregious conduct and to make an example of the defendant so others do not behave similarly. So why would the victim receive punitive damages? Why wouldn't the punitive portion of the damages go elsewhere?

This is where the debate really becomes contentious and unsettled. According to the laws of some states, the state itself is entitled to a certain percentage ranging from 20% to 100% of the punitive damages awarded.[2] Illinois has taken another approach and gives the court discretion to allocate punitive awards to either the prevailing party, the plaintiff's attorney, or the state. The development of these laws is based upon the idea that punitive damages reflect an interest of the state to deter future misconduct rather than an interest in compensating the victim—that's what compensatory damages are for. Plaintiff attorneys, a strong lobbying force whose fees are contingent on the overall size of the awards, contend that they need incentives to make plaintiffs willing to move forward on cases.

The other side, comprised of business lobbyists and defense attorneys, raise constitutional issues and claim that punitive damages are often so large and arbitrary they violate the Due Process clause of the Fourteenth Amendment; that is, taking away property without adequate notice of the amount in question violates Constitutional rights. They also argue that the current system amounts to a lottery and that the punitive damages component adds a significant cost to business expenses for the companies, which in turn will either reduce shareholder profit or raise consumer prices as their costs are passed along into the marketplace. If products need to be made safer, the regulatory process rather than the less predictable current system should be responsible.

Laws passed in over half the states now limit punitive damages. Some states tie compensatory damages to punitive damages so that punitive damages cannot

2 Such states include Colorado, Florida, Alaska, Oregon, Indiana, New York, Utah, Iowa, Georgia and Missouri. (http://www.atra.org/issues/punitive-damages-reform).

exceed a certain ratio to the compensatory element.[3] Another strategy is to have separate trials on damages so that the sympathies engendered by the determination of liability do not spill over into the computations of punitive damage awards. On a federal level, some defense attorneys employ Federal Rule of Civil Procedure 42(b) to split punitive damages while some states have made this option available through state law. In Texas, a defendant may move to have punitive damages determined in a separate trial from compensatory damages. However, in the interest of judicial efficiency, the court retains the discretion to determine whether a bifurcated trial is warranted. In Missouri, on the other hand, the right to a bifurcated trial concerning punitive damages is guaranteed by state law if requested by one of the parties. Other ways to limit punitive damages have included mandating a higher burden of proof from the plaintiff in justifying the amount of the punitive damage award. A claim for punitive damages in a products liability case in Ohio requires an elevated standard of "clear and convincing evidence," which is not required by common law.

As you can see, products liability raises many questions that are debated in public policy circles today. Each of the above arguments are also frequently presented in ethical terms centering around personal responsibility issues. What responsibilities do plaintiffs have for their own safety? A classic example comes from the manufacture and sale of ladders. Because plaintiffs frequently misuse ladders by standing too far up on a ladder or reaching beyond where one can safely reach, ladder manufacturers attempt to make the product safer by placing warning labels on the product. If you purchase a ladder at a hardware store, you will see multiple warning labels because companies fear being sued by a careless plaintiff.

While courts do allow for the consideration of many kinds of lawsuits, there are times when the personal responsibility of the victim is so obvious that courts will throw out the case. The following example demonstrates this point.

3 For example, in Wisconsin, punitive damages cannot exceed twice the amount of compensatory damages or $200,000.00, whichever is greater. In New Jersey, punitive damages are capped at five times the compensatory damages or $350,000, whichever is greater.

Wyda v. Makita Elec. Works, Ltd.

232 A.D.2d 407 (1996)

A worker who was injured while using a saw brought action to recover for personal injuries based on negligence and strict products liability against the saw manufacturer. It is undisputed that when the accident occurred the plaintiff's employer, the third-party defendant, had wedged the saw's moveable blade guard open by placing a piece of wood between the guard and the body of the saw, removing the safety feature on the saw blade. The safety feature was designed to be a permanent fixture on the saw and was not designed to be removed. The Supreme Court, Westchester County, denied manufacturer's motion for summary judgment. Manufacturer appealed.

The Supreme Court, Appellate Division, held that removal of safety feature on saw blade by the worker's employer was substantial material alteration to saw, such that the worker could not maintain action against manufacturer. A manufacturer may not be cast in damages, either on a strict products liability or negligence cause of action, where, after the product leaves the possession and control of the manufacturer, there is a subsequent modification which "substantially alters the product and is the proximate cause of the plaintiff's injuries" Material alterations at the hand of a third party which work a substantial change in the condition in which the product was sold "by destroying the functional utility of a key safety feature, however foreseeable that modification may have been, are not within the ambit of a manufacturer's responsibility."

Another dimension of personal responsibility involves filing frivolous lawsuits, as we saw in the chapter on torts. Legislatures and courts have created penalties for plaintiffs who have no legitimate case, but file suit either to harass another party or to get an easy settlement.

In addition to the personal responsibility of plaintiffs, their attorneys, especially the so-called "ambulance chasers." also face ethical arguments.. Do plaintiffs want to sue, or do their lawyers convince them to sue? It is probably a bit of both, but there is little doubt that a sizeable group of attorneys base their careers on this kind of litigation. Without nefarious motives, lawyers educate their clients on their legal options, and the lawsuits described in this chapter are, indeed, legal options. Thus, the ethical issue can be joined according to how different parties "see" what happens between lawyer and client: unethical manipulation or client education.

The responsibility of manufacturers is also very much in play. The claim of all product liability cases is that the company not only caused damages, but did something wrong; they were negligent. They are strictly liable because they introduced something unreasonably dangerous into society and breached a contractual promise.

There is always a dimension of wrongdoing alleged and, if true, then the wrongdoer should be liable.

Without exhausting the possible ethical issues, a final analytical assessment is based on utilitarianism. What legal system of product liability creates the greatest good for the greatest number? All sides to this debate argue that their approach meets this standard.

II. Contractual Theories of Product Liability

IN TORT LAW, there often is no preexisting relationship between the plaintiff and the defendant. The plaintiff drives a car and is hit by the car driven by the defendant. The defendant's dog bites the plaintiff. A trespassing child drowns while swimming in the pool of someone in the child's subdivision who has never met the child's family. In all these cases, there was no contract between the parties. But in products liability cases, there is. The nature of that contractual relationship is important because, as noted in the beginning of this chapter, liability is clearer if there is privity of contract. That is, the two parties directly contracting with each other—a retailer and consumer—generate clearer liability than do the parties who made the product the retailer sold. But even when there is no direct relationship between seller and buyer, courts may find enough contractual relationship between the parties for warranty theories to create liability.

The common usage of warranty, promise to repair or replace a defective product, can be a remedy used in the application of the warranties covered in this chapter. Yet the warranties provided under the UCC go beyond this common usage and provide potential, additional liability. In proving that a warranty theory applies, the plaintiff needs to:

- Prove that a warranty existed
- Show that the warranty was breached
- Demonstrate that the breach was the proximate cause of the plaintiff's injury
- Prove that notice of the breach was given to the seller

In some cases, the seller/manufacturer must also give notice of a breach of the warranty to buyer(s), as in the case of a product recall or another announcement or warning of a potential product defect.

A. EXPRESS WARRANTY

Express warranties result when there is a statement or portrayal of a particular capability of the product. It could be in the form of an affirmation of a fact or promise or a description of the goods: "this drilling rig will pump up to one million barrels of oil a day," or "this copying machine will make thirty copies a minute." With statements like these, a warranty attaches in accordance with the Uniform Commercial Code, Section 2-313.

★ A WARRANTY NEEDS TO BE A BASIS OF THE BARGAIN BETWEEN THE BUYER AND THE SELLER.

As the cases following show, the UCC provision indicates that the expression need not be in words, but can be in other forms, such as a portrayal or by providing a sample. If a product is graphically portrayed to perform a task—even as simple as brewing a hot cup of coffee—the expression is deemed to be an indication of what the product will do for the purchaser. The warranty needs to be a basis of the bargain between the buyer and the seller. The following case demonstrates the application of this kind of express warranty.

Bayliner Marine Corp. v. Crow

257 Va. 121, 509 S.E. 2d 499 (1999)

In the summer of 1989, John R. Crow was invited by John Atherton, then a sales representative for Tidewater Yacht Agency, Inc. (Tidewater), to ride on a new model sport fishing boat known as a 3486 Trophy Convertible, manufactured by Bayliner Marine Corporation (Bayliner). During an excursion lasting about 20 minutes, Crow piloted the boat for a short period of time but was not able to determine its speed because there was no equipment on board for such testing.

When Crow asked Atherton about the maximum speed of the boat, Atherton explained that he had no personal experience with the boat or information from other customers concerning the boat's performance. Therefore, Atherton consulted two documents described as "prop matrixes," which were included by Bayliner in its dealer's manual. Atherton gave Crow copies of the "prop matrixes," which listed the boat models offered by Bayliner and stated the recommended propeller sizes, gear ratios, and engine sizes for each model. The "prop matrixes" also listed the maximum speed for each model. The 3486 Trophy Convertible was listed as having a maximum speed of 30 miles per hour when equipped with a size "20x20" or "2019" propeller. The boat Crow purchased did not have either size propeller but, instead, had a size "20x17" propeller.

At the bottom of one of the "prop matrixes" was the following disclaimer: "This data is intended for comparative purposes only, and is available without reference to weather conditions or other variables. All testing was done at or near sea level, with full fuel and water tanks, and approximately 600 lb. passenger and gear weight." Atherton also showed Crow a Bayliner brochure describing the 1989 boat models, including the 3486 Trophy Convertible. The brochure included a picture of that model fully rigged for offshore fishing, accompanied by the statement that this model "delivers the kind of performance you need to get to the prime offshore fishing grounds." In August 1989, Crow entered into a written contract for the purchase of the 3486 Trophy Convertible in which he had ridden. The purchase price was $120,000, exclusive of taxes. Crow did not test drive the boat after the additional equipment was installed or at any other time prior to taking delivery.

When Crow took delivery of the boat in September 1989, he piloted it onto the Elizabeth River. He noticed that the boat's speed measuring equipment, which was installed in accordance with the contract terms, indicated that the boat's maximum speed was 13 miles per hour. Crow immediately returned to Tidewater and reported the problem.

During the next 12 to 14 months, while Crow retained ownership and possession of the boat, Tidewater made numerous repairs and adjustments to the boat in an attempt to increase its speed capability. Despite these efforts, the boat consistently achieved a maximum speed of only 17 miles per hour. . . In July 1990, a representative from Bayliner wrote Crow a letter stating that the performance representations made at the time of purchase were incorrect, and that 23 to 25 miles per hour was the maximum speed the boat could achieve.

In 1992, Crow filed a motion for judgment against Tidewater, Bayliner, and Brunswick Corporation, the manufacturer of the boat's diesel engines. Crow alleged, among other things, that Bayliner breached express warranties, and implied warranties of merchantability and fitness for a particular purpose.

At a bench trial in 1994, Crow, Atherton, and Gordon W. Shelton, III, Tidewater's owner, testified that speed is a critical quality in boats used for offshore sport fishing in the Tidewater area of Virginia because of the distance between the coast and the offshore fishing grounds. According to these witnesses, a typical offshore fishing site in that area is 90 miles from the coast. Therefore, the speed at which the boat can travel to and from fishing sites has a major impact on the amount of time left in a day for fishing. Crow testified that because of the boat's slow speed, he could not use the boat for offshore fishing, that he had no other use for it, and that he would not have purchased the boat if he had known that its maximum speed was 23 to 25 miles per hour.

The trial court entered judgment in favor of Crow against Bayliner on the counts of breach of express warranty and breach of implied warranties of merchantability and fitness for a particular purpose. The court awarded Crow damages of $135,000, plus prejudgment interest from June 1993. The court explained that the

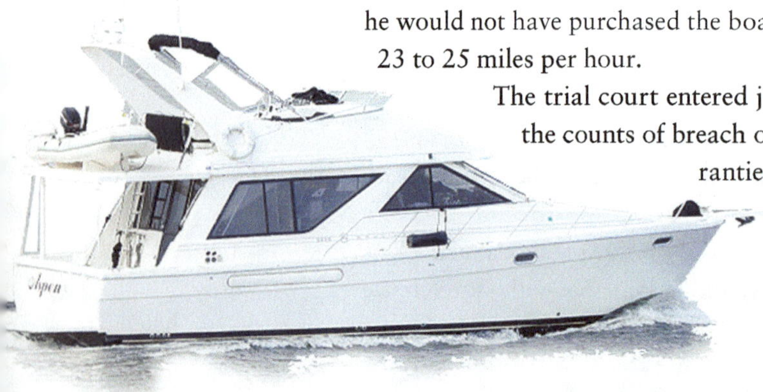

$135,000 award represented the purchase price of the boat, and about $15,000 in "damages" for a portion of the expenses Crow claimed in storing, maintaining, insuring, and financing the boat.

On appeal, we review the evidence in the light most favorable to Crow, the prevailing party at trial. We will uphold the trial court's judgment unless it is plainly wrong or without evidence to support it.

Crow argues that the "prop matrixes" he received created an express warranty by Bayliner that the boat he purchased was capable of a maximum speed of 30 miles per hour. We disagree.

Code § 8.2-313 provides, in relevant part: Express warranties by the seller are created as follows:

a. Any affirmation of fact or promise made by the seller to the buyer which relates to the goods and becomes part of the basis of the bargain creates an express warranty that the goods shall conform to the affirmation or promise.

b. Any description of the goods which is made a part of the basis of the bargain creates an express warranty that the goods shall conform to the description.

The issue whether a particular affirmation of fact made by the seller constitutes an express warranty is generally a question of fact. In *Daughtrey*, we examined whether a jeweler's statement on an appraisal form constituted an express warranty. We held that the jeweler's description of the particular diamonds being purchased as "v.v.s. quality" constituted an express warranty that the diamonds were, in fact, of that grade.

Unlike the representation in *Daughtrey*, however, the statements in the "prop matrixes" provided by Bayliner did not relate to the particular boat purchased by Crow, or to one having substantially similar characteristics. By their plain terms, the figures stated in the "prop matrixes" referred to a boat with different sized propellers that carried equipment weighing substantially less than the equipment on Crow's boat. Therefore, we conclude that the statements contained in the "prop matrixes" did not constitute an express warranty by Bayliner about the performance capabilities of the particular boat purchased by Crow. Crow also contends that Bayliner made an express warranty regarding the boat's maximum speed in the statement in Bayliner's sales brochure that this model boat "delivers the kind of performance you need to get to the prime offshore fishing grounds." While the general rule is that a description of the goods that forms a basis of the bargain constitutes an express warranty, Code § 8.2-313(2) directs that "a statement purporting to be merely the seller's opinion or commendation of the goods does not create a warranty."

The statement made by Bayliner in its sales brochure is merely a commendation of the boat's performance and does not describe a specific characteristic or feature of the boat. The statement simply expressed the manufacturer's opinion concerning the quality of the boat's performance and did not create an express warranty that the boat was capable of attaining a speed of 30 miles per hour. Therefore, we conclude that the evidence does not support the trial court's finding that Bayliner breached an express warranty made to Crow . . .

. . . For these reasons, we will reverse the trial court's judgment and enter final judgment in favor of Bayliner.

It is virtually impossible to disclaim express warranties. After all, the idea of an express warranty is that the seller is trying to convince a buyer to purchase the product on the basis of the expression of the product's capability. One cannot promise that a product does something and then disclaim any responsibility if it doesn't deliver on what was promised.

From a business standpoint, express warranties can be a point of tension between the marketing department and the legal office. Marketers have a strong interest in advertising the product as attractively as possible, whereas the legal office is interested in limiting potential risk.

Express warranties are different from what is known as **puffing**, which is an expression of opinion rather than fact and is not legally binding. Companies are understood to be exaggerating when they say their products are the greatest things in the world or run advertisements suggesting that if customers use their products, amazing and wonderful things will happen. In the 1980s and 1990s, advertisements showed a guy drinking a can of Coors beer when suddenly the Coors Bikini Team would appear. Does this become an express warranty? Are there grounds for a lawsuit if a beer drinker opens a can of Coors and the Bikini Team does not materialize? Obviously not; this advertisement is mere puffing.

Not all cases are quite so extreme. Sometimes the issues for whether there is an express warranty lie more in whether the *description* of the product creates an express warranty or not. The following case provides a more serious discussion of the parameters of express warranties.

Royal Indemnity Co. v. Tyco Fire Products, LP

281 Va. 157, 704 S.E.2d 91 (2011)

This case arose out of a fire that started on the exterior balcony of an apartment building on February 8, 2003. Two exterior sidewall sprinkler heads installed on two separate balconies where the fire originated failed to activate, which allowed the fire to spread to other parts of the building and adjoining buildings causing substantial damage.

Royal Indemnity Company and American Empire Surplus Lines Insurance Company (together, Royal) filed an amended motion for judgment in the amount of $10,317,083.78 against Tyco Fire Products (Tyco) and SimplexGrinnell, LP (Simplex) alleging that the sprinkler heads, which were manufactured by Tyco and installed by Simplex prior to June 1997, failed to properly activate causing substantial damage to the apartment complex. Royal asserted various negligence-based causes of action against both Tyco and Simplex, including negligent design and manufacture of the sprinkler heads, and post-sale duty to warn. Royal also asserted warranty claims against both defendants, claiming that the defendants breached an alleged warranty of future performance.

In its complaint, Royal alleged that the sprinkler heads failed to operate properly. Specifically, Royal asserted that "[s]cientific inspection of the pressure tested sprinkler heads . . . determined that corrosion existed at the interface between the brass plug and O-ring assembly and inlet which . . . prevented the inlet plugs from disengaging and operating as intended upon the breaking of the frangible bulbs."

Tyco and Simplex filed pleas in bar asserting that the negligence-based causes of action were barred by the statute of repose, Code § 8.01–250. After an *ore tenus* hearing and receipt of stipulated evidence, the circuit court granted the defendants' pleas in bar ruling that the sprinkler heads were ordinary building materials under the statute of repose.

The defendants also filed pleas in bar arguing that Royal's warranty claims were barred by the statute of limitations. After a hearing, the circuit court sustained the pleas in bar ruling the warranty claims were barred by the applicable statutes of limitations. We awarded Royal this appeal.

In this product liability case, we address issues concerning the statute of repose and breach of warranty. We conclude that exterior sidewall sprinkler heads are "equipment" under Code § 8.01–250 and reverse the judgment of the circuit court that the sprinkler heads are ordinary building materials. We also hold that a manufacturer's description of how a sprinkler head functions does not constitute an express warranty of future performance . . .

Regarding Tyco's plea in bar, the circuit court ruled that the breach of warranty claims concerning the sprinkler heads were barred by the four-year statute of limitations per Code § 8.2–725, which applies to contracts for the sale of goods. In making this ruling, the circuit court rejected Royal's contention that the "technical data sheet," which is the accompanying literature to the sprinkler heads, contained an express warranty of future performance. Royal argues that the circuit court erred in ruling that the "technical data sheet" did not contain an express warranty of future performance. We disagree with Royal.

Code § 8.2–725(1) provides that a breach of a contract for sale must be commenced within four years after the cause of action accrues. A cause of action for breach of a contract for the sale of goods accrues when the breach occurs. Code § 8.2–725(2). In a contract for the sale of goods, the breach of warranty occurs when tender of delivery is made, except that where a warranty explicitly extends to future performance of the goods and discovery of the breach must await the time of such performance the cause of action accrues when the breach is or should have been discovered.

It is undisputed that Royal's breach of warranty claim was filed more than four years after delivery of the sprinkler heads. Thus, the issue is whether there was an express warranty of future performance. Code § 8.2–313, titled "Express warranties by affirmation, promise, description, sample [,]" provides:

1. Express warranties by the seller are created as follows:
    a. Any affirmation of fact or promise made by the seller to the buyer which relates to the goods and becomes part of the basis of the bargain creates an express warranty that the goods shall conform to the affirmation or promise.
    b. Any description of the goods which is made part of the basis of the bargain creates an express warranty that the goods shall conform to the description.
    c. Any sample or model which is made part of the basis of the bargain creates an express warranty that the whole of the goods shall conform to the sample or model.
2. It is not necessary to the creation of an express warranty that the seller use formal words such as "warrant" or "guarantee" or that he have a specific intention to make a warranty, but an affirmation merely of the value of the goods or a statement purporting to be merely the seller's opinion or commendation of the goods does not create a warranty.

The "technical data sheet" contains a description of how the sprinkler heads work. The description, which Royal asserts is a warranty of future performance, states:

> When the F960/Q-46 is in service, water is prevented from entering the assembly by the Plug and O–Ring Seal in the Inlet of the Sprinkler. Upon exposure to a temperature sufficient to operate the Bulb, the Bulb shatters and the Bulb Seat is released. The compressed Spring is then able to expand and push the Water Tube as well as the Guide Tube outward. This action simultaneously pulls outward on the Yoke, withdrawing the Plug and O-Ring Seal from the Inlet and initiating water flow.

There is no evidence in the record showing that this language became "part of the basis of the bargain" such that it may be an express warranty of future

performance. Indeed, the language amounts to nothing more than a simple description of how the sprinkler heads operate. Nowhere in the description of how the sprinkler heads work does Tyco promise that the sprinkler heads will operate correctly for a particular period of time. Manufacturers of products often provide such information, especially when the products are mechanical devices. To hold that such language amounts to an express warranty of future performance would result in Tyco insuring its sprinkler heads indefinitely. It would be an absurd result to conclude that a description given by a manufacturer as to how a device operates amounts to an express warranty of future performance for an unlimited duration.

> **"IT WOULD BE an absurd result to conclude that a description given by a manufacturer as to how a device operates amounts to an express warranty of future performance for an unlimited duration."**

Additionally, the "technical data sheet" explicitly provided a one-year warranty that the sprinkler head shall be "free from defects in material and workmanship." The warranty language is under the heading "WARRANTY" in the "technical data sheet." If Tyco wished to provide any further warranty, surely it would have put additional language under this section. Considering the explicit one-year warranty contained in the "technical data sheet," the product description cannot be said to constitute an express warranty of future performance for an indefinite period of time. For these reasons, we hold that the circuit court did not err in sustaining Tyco's plea in bar.

Regarding the circuit court's ruling on Simplex' plea in bar, Royal argues that the court erred by dismissing the "warranty cause of action on the grounds that the statements concerning [the sprinkler heads'] future performance under the Virginia Uniform Commercial Code did not constitute a warranty of future performance." We cannot address this assignment of error because Royal alleges that the circuit court erred in making a ruling that it did not make. The circuit court did not sustain Simplex' plea in bar on the ground that there was no warranty of future performance. In fact, the circuit court ruled that the Uniform Commercial Code did not apply to Royal's warranty claim against Simplex because the underlying contract, which was "for the 'design and installation of a fire protection system,' " was not a contract "predominately [for] the sale of goods." Accordingly, we cannot address Royal's argument that the circuit court erred in sustaining Simplex' plea in bar. Rule 5:25.

In the appeal against Tyco, for the reasons stated, we will reverse in part, affirm in part, and remand this case to the circuit court. On remand, the circuit court shall address Royal's negligence-based causes of action against Tyco.

In the appeal against Simplex, for the reasons stated, we will affirm the judgment of the circuit court.

Express warranties are fairly straightforward. The key is to determine exactly what was expressed or guaranteed. If that determination can be made, then it is not difficult to conclude that the product should fulfill that purpose. Implied warranties, however, are harder to specify.

B. IMPLIED WARRANTY OF MERCHANTABILITY

Perhaps the most commonly used warranty theory is the **Implied Warranty of Merchantability.** The following language from the Uniform Commercial Code sets out the provisions in Section 2-314:

1. Unless excluded or modified (Section 2-316), a warranty that the goods shall be merchantable is implied in a contract for their sale if the seller is a merchant with respect to goods of that kind. Under this section the serving for value of food or drink to be consumed either on the premises or elsewhere is a sale.

2. Goods to be merchantable must be at least such as

   a. pass without objection in the trade under the contract description; and

   b. in the case of fungible goods, are of fair average quality within the description; and

   c. are fit for the ordinary purposes for which such goods are used; and

   d. run, within the variations permitted by the agreement, of even kind, quality and quantity within each unit and among all units involved; and

   e. are adequately contained, packaged, and labeled as the agreement may require; and

   f. conform to the promises or affirmations of fact made on the container or label if any.

3. Unless excluded or modified (Section 2-316) other implied warranties may arise from course of dealing or usage of trade.

The idea behind this warranty is that new products are supposed to work for their normal, ordinary purposes. If you buy a dishwasher, it is supposed to wash dishes. If you buy a coffee pot, it is supposed to brew coffee. There is an automatic, implied warranty without any particular expression of capability. The following case looks at implied warranties when a car does not work the way it is supposed to. An important aspect of this case, as it is for most implied warranty cases, is the time one has to identify and report a defect in the product. If one waits too long, then questions arise as to whether the defect was in the product or caused by the use of the product by the consumer.

Crowe v. CarMax Auto Superstores, Inc.

272 Ga. App. 249, 612 S.E.2d 90 (2005)

Tina and Thad Crowe appeal from the trial court's order granting summary judgment to defendant CarMax Auto Superstores, Inc. . . . The Crowes purchased a 1999 Dodge Durango automobile from CarMax on October 5, 2002. They received a 30-day/1,000 mile express warranty from CarMax, and they purchased an 18-month/18,000 mile "Mechanical Repair Agreement" (MRA). The obligor on this extended warranty was Consumer Program Administrators, Inc., not CarMax. Over the course of the next year, the Crowes brought the vehicle to CarMax and other repair facilities numerous times for a variety of repairs. All repairs made within the original and extended warranty periods were made without cost to the Crowes, except for deductibles, although those were sometimes waived. Nevertheless, the Crowes contend they lost confidence in the vehicle, and on May 30, 2003, the Crowes filed a complaint against CarMax, asserting claims for breach of implied and express warranties under the Magnuson-Moss Warranty Act and Georgia law. The trial court granted summary judgment to CarMax on both the express and implied warranty claims, and the Crowes do not challenge that ruling insofar as it pertains to their express warranty claims. However, the Crowes challenge the grant of summary judgment on their implied warranty claim, contending that they have established a viable claim under the Magnuson-Moss Warranty Act.

The Magnuson-Moss Warranty Act allows "a consumer who is damaged by the failure of a supplier, warrantor, or service contractor to comply with any obligation under . . . (an) implied warranty . . . (to) bring suit for damages and other legal and equitable relief." The Act defines "implied warranty" as "an implied warranty arising under State law . . . in connection with the sale by a supplier of a consumer product." [To recover, therefore, [the Crowes] must show that [CarMax] breached the implied warranty of merchantability arising under Georgia law.

Under OCGA § 11-2-314(1), "a warranty that the goods shall be merchantable is implied in a contract for their sale if the seller is a merchant with respect to goods of that kind." "This warranty protects consumers from defects or conditions existing at the time of sale." In *Jones v. Marcus*, this court held that "it is obvious that the alleged defect or condition must have existed at the time of the sale." This is logical, because it is clear that "the implied warranties warrant against defects or conditions existing at the time of sale, but [they] do not provide a warranty of continuing serviceability." It follows that proof that the vehicle was defective *when it was sold* is an essential element of the Crowes' claim for breach of the implied warranty of merchantability.

The Crowes contend the trial court erred by finding that they did not meet their burden of showing that a jury question exists concerning whether the vehicle was defective at the time of sale. We find no error. Although the vehicle was first returned to CarMax just five days after it was sold, the record shows that those repairs were primarily to remedy cosmetic defects that CarMax agreed to fix at the time of sale. The Crowes returned the car again on October 22, after what they contend was 11 days of actual use. The problems noted on that visit were that the vehicle was consuming massive amounts of oil, that the instrument panel lights were flickering, and that the four-wheel-drive illumination light was not working. Tina Crowe testified that the problems were fixed on that visit.

The vehicle was returned to CarMax on November 13, 2002, because the check engine light was on. The repair ticket indicated that "false codes" were detected and removed. However, the problem with the check engine light reappeared in January 2003, and the vehicle was returned to CarMax. At this time a broken ground wire was found, and Tina Crowe testified the problem was fixed to her satisfaction, as was a problem with the rear windshield wiper, which was remedied by replacing the wiper motor.

★ THE MAGNUSON-MOSS WARRANTY ACT ALLOWS A CONSUMER WHO IS DAMAGED BY THE FAILURE OF A SUPPLIER, WARRANTOR, OR SERVICE CONTRACTOR TO BRING SUIT FOR DAMAGES AND EQUITABLE RELIEF.

On the January visit, it was also noted that the vehicle was jerking and the engine was revving up to 6,000 rpm when driving. Tina Crowe testified that the problem with the engine revving persisted for several months and that she returned the car for repairs several times before the control module was replaced and the problem fixed in April 2003. The record shows that during this same period the engine was running rough, but that problem was attributed to carbon build-up in the cylinders and was also remedied. Tina Crowe testified she did not take the vehicle back to CarMax after the MRA expired, but instead took it to another facility for repair when it began stalling out in June 2003. At that time a fuel system tune-up was performed. A low out speed sensor was replaced in August, and a ball bearing was replaced on the front of the car in October 2003. At that time the Crowes had owned the vehicle a little over a year, and the odometer reading was at 65,621 miles, indicating the car had been driven over 25,000 miles during that time. Tina Crowe testified that at the time of her deposition in December 2003 there were no current problems with the car.

Based on this evidence, the trial court found that the Crowes failed to establish that the vehicle was defective when sold. We agree that this evidence does not present

a jury question on this essential element of their claim. Although the vehicle was repaired on numerous occasions over the course of the first year of ownership, as the trial court noted, for the most part these repairs were for different items or concerns on each occasion, and the problems were all remedied at the time the car was first brought in or on a subsequent visit. And although the Crowes argue strenuously that at least some evidence of a defect at the time of sale is shown by the fact that the car had to be returned for repairs after it was driven for just 11 days, the record shows that the primary complaint at that time was that the vehicle was consuming massive amounts of oil and that problem was remedied on that repair visit and did not recur. Moreover, although the vehicle had only been owned for a short period, it had already been driven in excess of 1,100 miles. The recurring problem with the engine revving was not detected until about three months later, and at that time the car had been driven almost 5,000 more miles. Although it took several attempts, that problem was also fixed. We note also that by the time the bearings had to be replaced in October 2003, the car had been driven over 25,000 miles since it was purchased about 13 months previously. Moreover, at the time of Tina Crowe's deposition in December 2003, there were no current problems with the car. Under these facts, we agree that no defect has been shown to exist at the time of purchase, and to find otherwise would require the jury to rely on speculation or conjecture, improper bases for imposing liability. The trial court did not err in granting summary judgment on the implied warranty claim.

Judgment affirmed.

Given the fact that implied warranties give consumers a great deal of power over the sellers, companies would often like to lessen their responsibility to the consumer by disclaiming any warranties associated with the product. Thus, a key question that arises with implied warranties of merchantability is whether the seller can disclaim the warranty that goes with the product. This is very hard to do with new products. After all, a new product should perform what it's designed to do; that is why the company sold the product in the first place. So it would be strange for a company to say that it is selling a good product and then claim they are not responsible for whether it works or not.

Sellers have an easier time disclaiming a warranty with respect to used products, which are commonly understood to have potential wear and tear that could cause problems. Provided the consumer knows the product is used, it is more likely the seller could disclaim an implied warranty and/or indicate that the buyer is taking the product "as is."

While it is much harder to disclaim an implied warranty for a new product, the procedures to do so are the same as for a used product. In order to effectively disclaim the implied warranty of merchantability from a new product, the seller must mention the word "merchantability" in the disclaimer in a conspicuous way. The test for whether a seller effectively does this is based on whether a reasonable person who is buying the product, and thus to whom the seller is directing the disclaimer, would have noticed it. This would require that the disclaimer be in capital letters that are as large or larger than the text surrounding the disclaimer and/or that it appears in a font color and size intended to catch the buyer's attention. Placing the words "AS IS" in the same, stand-out font size or color is important too. These requirements suggest that disclaiming an implied warranty of merchantability is no easy task. The following case shows just how difficult it can be.

Woodruff v. Clark County Farm Bureau Co-op. Ass'n

153 Ind.App. 31, 286 N.E.2d 188 (1972)

From 1945 until 1960 Woodruff was engaged in the business of raising broiler chickens near Remington, Indiana. In 1960 he phased out his broiler business and began raising chickens for the production of eggs . . . In July of 1964, Ken Bowlin (Bowlin), a Farm Bureau representative, discovered that Woodruff intended to replace his flock of chickens. Farm Bureau did not have any chickens in Woodruff's area, but Bowlin contacted Woodruff in an attempt to persuade him to try Farm Bureau chickens.

As a consequence of this initial conversation, Woodruff met with Searcy and other Farm Bureau representatives at Indianapolis and travelled to the Clark County Farm Bureau to observe its flock of chickens. While at the Clark County Farm, Woodruff observed that the chickens were out of feed and that they were 'congested' . . . After viewing these conditions Woodruff testified that he was assured by Farm Bureau that he would get only the good chickens and that 'they would do a good job in my chicken-house.'

Woodruff further noted that he did not raise any questions at the Clark County farm regarding vaccination or mortality rates because he had confidence in Farm Bureau and that it was customary for chicken farmers to vaccinate against coccidiosis at an early stage. He presumed that 'they had been in it for a long time and they certainly had brains enough to know what to do, and it was not for me to ask about it.'

Following the examination of the Clark County chickens, Woodruff and the Farm Bureau representatives travelled to Jackson County, where they viewed another flock of chickens. Woodruff again observed that the chicken feeders were empty, the chickens were badly stunted and their feathers were ruffled. While he generally condemned the Jackson County operation, the response to his comments at Jackson County was much the same as at the Clark County farm—that he would get only the good chickens, 'that the chickens would be culled' and he 'would get only good birds.'

After observing the Jackson County birds, Woodruff and the Farm Bureau representatives drove back to Indianapolis. At some time during the return trip to Indianapolis, Farm Bureau and Woodruff entered into an oral agreement whereby Woodruff agreed to purchase chickens from Farm Bureau for $1.55 per chicken.

On July 23, 1964 the chickens were delivered to Woodruff with Mr. Wayne Isaacs, of the Farm Bureau, present. Woodruff himself culled approximately 1,400 chickens out of the total delivered . . . Woodruff did understand that he could return any of them that appeared to be unacceptable. At the time of delivery Woodruff was advised that the chickens would develop in the proper manner i.e. that they would 'bloom out or straighten up and fly right.'

As the chickens progressed in age many of them were dying, so in the early part of August 1964, Woodruff contacted Bowlin concerning the mortality rate. At Bowlin's insistence, Woodruff called the Indianapolis Farm Bureau office and requested that someone examine the chickens. Subsequently, Searcy and two other Farm Bureau representatives visited Woodruff and concluded that the chickens were in no great danger. Nevertheless, the high mortality rate continued, so Woodruff again contacted Farm Bureau representatives, who returned a second time to examine the chickens. At the second meeting, Woodruff was asked if he was using anything in his feed for coccidiosis. Woodruff replied:

> 'I've got nothing in my feed for coccidiosis; when chickens get this age you are not supposed to have anything in your feed for coccidiosis. Any normal chicken from any reputable company will have their immunity by the time they are twenty weeks old.'

The Farm Bureau representatives then departed without giving Woodruff any indication as to the condition of the birds.

Woodruff began feeding the birds a special feed, but the mortality rate continued at the same pace. The condition did not improve and eventually Woodruff's poultry business was destroyed. Woodruff testified that he lost approximately $45,000.00 of gross income because the chickens never exceeded sixty percent of production capabilities. Woodruff also testified that ultimately approximately 2500 chickens died and probably 1600 more were condemned because of their condition.

In August 1966, Woodruff filed a Complaint against Farm Bureau for damages for breach of warranty, misrepresentation and fraud.

In the sale of the chickens by Farm Bureau to Woodruff, implied warranties of merchantability and fitness for a particular purpose arose as a matter of law. In 1963 Indiana adopted the Uniform Commercial Code (UCC) as part of its statutory law on commercial transactions.

Where the seller at the time of contracting has reason to know any particular purpose for which the goods are required and that the buyer is relying on the seller's skill or judgment to select or furnish suitable goods, there is unless excluded or modified under the next section an implied warranty that the goods shall be fit for such purpose.

The facts before us indicate no dispute that Farm Bureau is a merchant with respect to the chickens it sold Woodruff—it is in the business of selling chickens, among other things, for the purpose for which Woodruff purchased them. Consequently, an implied warranty of merchantability did arise by operation of law from the sole fact that Farm Bureau was a regular merchant with respect to the sale of chickens. Moreover, Farm Bureau knew the particular purpose for which Woodruff intended to use these chickens, i.e., production of eggs. This knowledge is indicated by the fact that Farm Bureau initially contacted Woodruff hoping to persuade him to purchase Farm Bureau chickens for the production of eggs.

While Woodruff had raised broiler chickens for some fifteen years he was relatively new to the egg production business. His deposition indicates that he had confidence in the people he was dealing with and that he relied on their skill and judgment to select and furnish suitable chickens for the production of eggs. Thus, a material issue of fact existed as to whether the implied warranties of merchant- ability and fitness for a particular purpose were violated. Unless otherwise excluded or modified, they remained in full force at the time of the sale and delivery of the chickens by Farm Bureau to Woodruff. The effect of the disclaimers then becomes paramount.

It is our opinion that the disclaiming language in the Receipts is insufficient as a matter of law to negate the implied warranties of merchantability and fitness for a particular purpose.

* * *

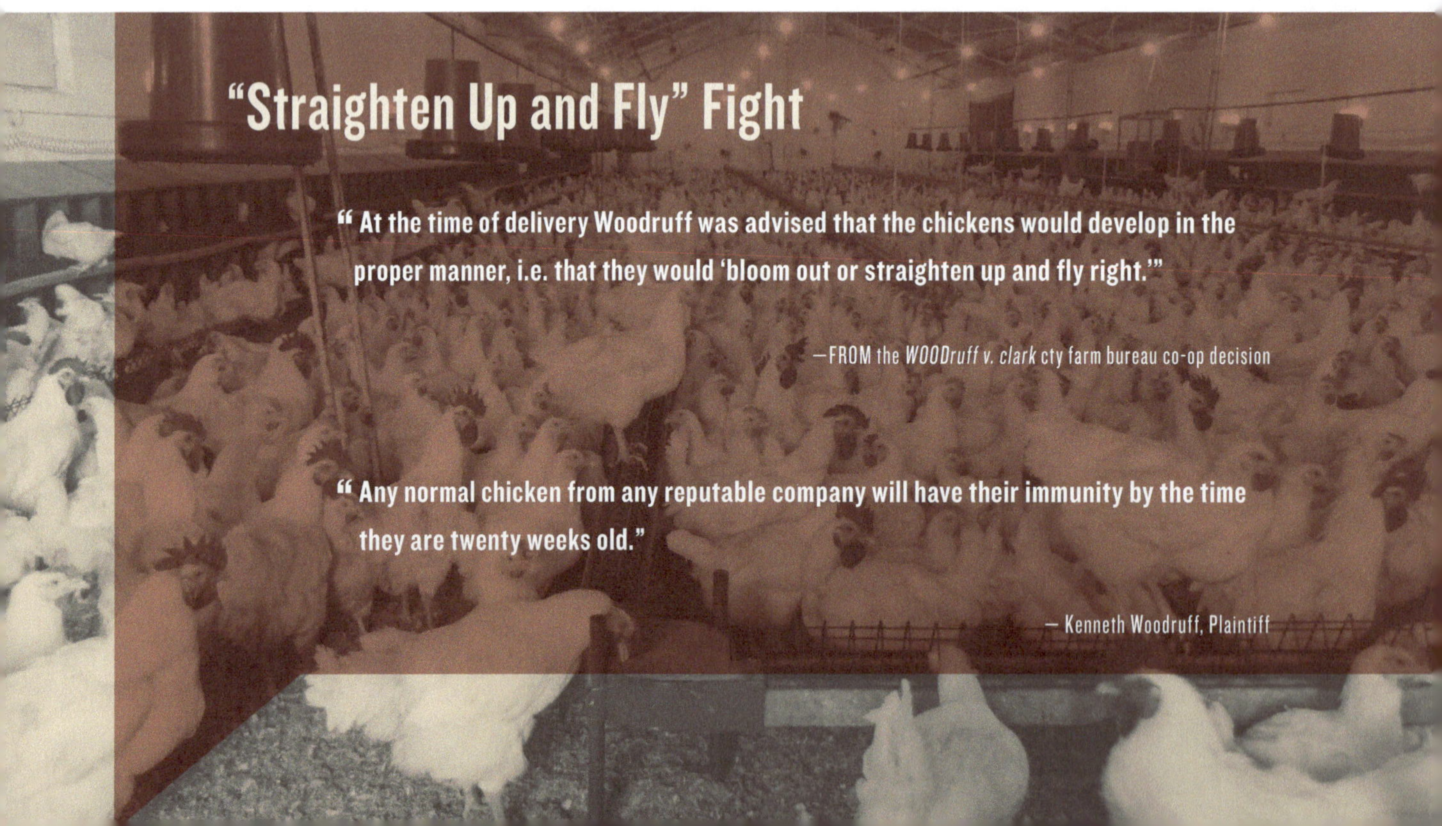

Disclaimers of implied warranties . . . are not favored and are strictly construed against the sellers for reasons of public policy. In order to exclude or modify an implied warranty of merchantability under § 19-2-316(2), (herein referred to as Number 2), the disclaimer 'must mention merchantability' and the written exclusionary language 'must be conspicuous.' The disclaiming language in the Receipts omits any such reference, and further none of the language of the disclaimer is in any way made 'conspicuous.'

* * *

Bringing the buyer's attention to exclusion of implied warranties is frequently emphasized by the cases in interpreting the UCC . . . Since the exclusionary language contained in the 'Delivery Receipts' in the case before us was not drawn to the attention of Woodruff at the time of delivery, and since there was nothing contained within the body of the purported disclaimers drawing Woodruff's attention to the exclusionary language or making that language conspicuous in and of itself, these 'Delivery Receipts' were insufficient as a matter of law to negate any implied warranties.

C. IMPLIED WARRANTY FOR PARTICULAR PURPOSE

An Implied Warranty for a Particular Purpose, UCC Section 2-315, has elements of both express warranty and implied warranty of merchantability. In an actual case, it would not be surprising for a plaintiff suing primarily on the basis of an implied warranty for a particular purpose to not also be suing under the theories of express warranty and implied warranty of merchantability theories. With an implied warranty for a particular purpose, the seller knows of the particular need or purpose of the buyer and designs a product that will satisfy that need. Indeed, the tests for this kind of warranty are that:

1. The seller has reason to know of the particular purpose of the buyer; and

2. The seller knows that the buyer is relying on the seller's skill and judgment.

Implied with the contract will be a warranty that with that amount of customization, the product will actually do what the buyer asked for. Further, if a product is being designed for the particular purpose of the buyer, it would be very likely that the seller states that the product will satisfy the buyer's needs, thus making it an express warranty. Following is the relevant excerpt from the Uniform Commercial Code:

> Where the seller at the time of contracting has reason to know any particular purpose for which the goods are required and that the buyer is relying on the seller's skill or judgment to select or furnish suitable goods, there is unless excluded or modified under the next section an implied warranty that the goods shall be fit for such purpose. (UCC § 2-315)

The following case applies this implied warranty for a particular purpose standard, but there is a wrinkle; the buyer is not just an ordinary buyer with little knowledge of the product the seller is providing. He has expertise. Notice the impact the buyer's expertise has on the application of this theory.

Matter of Clements and Van Wagnen Const. Co.

23 B.R. 617 (Bankr.E.D.Mich.1982)

Plaintiff filed its complaint on June 11, 1981, praying for damages resulting from defective cement supplied by defendant. Defendant filed this motion for summary judgment on March 24, 1982. Pursuant to a contract between the parties defendant delivered cement to plaintiff to be used in the construction of sidewalks on a project being carried out by plaintiff. According to the express terms of the contract it was specified that the cement delivered to plaintiff was to have an air-void content between three and six percent of the concrete volume. The parties agree that the air-void content of the cement delivered pursuant to their contract was 4.2% of the concrete volume. 4.2% air-void content is within the specification set forth in the contract. Despite the contractually proper air-void content, the sidewalks constructed with defendant's cement became cracked. Plaintiff has presented no evidence, nor alleged, that the air-void specifications set forth in the contract were those of the defendant.

The existence of an implied warranty of fitness for a particular purpose is contingent on two general facts. First, the seller must be aware at the time of contracting of a particular purpose for which the buyer intends to use the goods. Second, the buyer must rely on the seller's skill or judgment to select or furnish goods suitable for that particular purpose.

No warranty of fitness for a particular purpose can be implied unless the buyer is relying on the seller's skill and judgment to select or manufacture suitable goods for a particular purpose for which the seller knows the goods are required.

In the case of *Price Brothers Co. v. Philadelphia Gear Co.* the court had occasion to rule on the very issue before this court today. Price Brothers submitted a purchase order to Philadelphia Gear specifying certain performance characteristics of the components ordered, apparently arrived at with Philadelphia Gear's assistance. The components were produced in conformance with the specifications of the buyer set forth in its purchase order. Price Brothers later experienced difficulties with a machine built with components produced by seller, attributing the problems to an alleged failure of the Philadelphia Gear components to perform as warranted.

The 6th Circuit reversed the trial court on the following basis: The trial court's conclusion that Philadelphia Gear breached an implied warranty of fitness for a particular purpose must be reversed because of the degree of specificity of Price Brothers' purchase order and Price Brothers' own undisputed high degree of knowledge regarding the mechanical requirements of its own pipe wrapping machine make any finding that Price Brothers relied on Philadelphia Gear's selection clearly erroneous.

In the present case Price Brothers ordered components from Philadelphia Gear by use of a purchase order specifying performance criteria. It is of no avail to Price Brothers that Philadelphia Gear may have assisted Price Brothers in arriving at these specifications. The fact that the specifications were jointly arrived at by Price Brothers engineers and Philadelphia Gear representatives only emphasizes the fact that Price Brothers exercised its own judgment in selecting the components ordered and did not rely on Philadelphia Gear to supply components.

It is the view of this court that the specification of air-void parameters by plaintiff in this matter is sufficient, standing alone, to warrant summary judgment on the issue of an implied warranty of fitness in favor of the defendant. Plaintiff has made no showing, nor advanced any facts which would indicate a positive reliance on defendant's expertise on the part of plaintiff. Indeed, plaintiff is a construction contractor, not without some expertise in such matters.

The overriding fact, however, is that in spite of any expertise defendant had, plaintiff simply did not rely on that expertise. The fact that defendant was in the business of producing concrete, and knew of the particular manner in which its concrete was to be employed, does not give rise to a finding of reliance. The specification of allowable air-void percentages in the contract indicates a lack of reliance on the part of the plaintiff.

There is, as a matter of law, no implied warranty of fitness for a particular purpose when goods are manufactured in accordance with specifications provided by the buyer. Where no evidence has been advanced by plaintiff that the specifications of air-void content were those of the defendant, no question of fact exists as to reliance.

It is therefore ordered that summary judgment is granted in favor of the movant-defendant, and plaintiff's cause of action based upon breach of an implied warranty of fitness for a particular purpose is hereby dismissed.

This case may well have come out differently had the plaintiff not had expertise on the matter. If the buyer had no such expertise, there may well have been total reliance on the defendant to provide the materials and construction desired for the project and the tests for an implied warranty of merchantability would have been met. The reliance on another party's expertise is crucial to this warranty.

D. WARRANTY OF TITLE

The three warranties discussed above comprise the vast majorities of product liability usages. But a fourth can play a role on occasion. This is the **warranty of title,** in which the seller guarantees that she has good and rightful title (or ownership) of a product and that no creditor has an interest in the product, such as a security agreement which counts the product as collateral for a loan. Next up is a case in which a buyer alleges that the seller breached an implied warranty of title.

Lawson v. Turner

404 So. 2d 424 (Fla. 1st DCA 1981)

In 1973, Cox purchased a 1970 GMC dump truck from a Mr. Tyson. Turner was guarantor on Cox's note at the bank for the purchase price. Turner, in fact, handled most of the negotiations of the purchase for Cox. Cox drove the truck for several months but was unable to earn enough money driving the truck to pay the note at the bank. Cox returned the truck to Turner's place of business and explained the situation to Willis, his stepfather, and Turner.

Willis then took over the truck and began driving it, hoping to earn enough money to pay the note. After several months Willis decided to sell the truck to Lawson for $7,500.00. In September 1973, Lawson, Willis, and Turner met at the bank to take care of the paper work for the transfer of the truck to Lawson. Lawson paid Willis for the equity in the truck and assumed payments. Turner remained guarantor on the bank note for Lawson also. Title to the truck was not transferred at that time, but Turner told Lawson that as soon as the title arrived from Tyson, he would guarantee delivery of it to Lawson.

Subsequently, the truck was discovered to be stolen and Lawson surrendered it to its rightful owner. Lawson brought suit for damages. At trial, the parties stipulated: (1) the truck was stolen; (2) none of the parties knew the truck was stolen; (3) Cox was a seller of the truck; and (4) the truck was surrendered to its rightful owner when it was discovered to be stolen. At trial, Willis also testified he was seller of the truck. Turner denied being a seller, arguing he was merely the guarantor of the bank note for Cox and Lawson. Lawson brought suit against Turner, Cox, and Willis seeking damages for breach of implied warranty of title resulting from his purchase of a used dump truck which was subsequently discovered to be a stolen vehicle. Lawson appeals the trial court's denial of his motion for a directed verdict.

Section 672.312, Florida Statutes (1973) states: (1) Subject to subsection (2) there is in a contract for sale a warranty by the seller that: (a) The title conveyed shall be good, and its transfer rightful; and (b) The goods shall be delivered free from any security interest or other lien or encumbrance of which the buyer at the time of contracting has no knowledge. (2) A warranty under subsection (1) will be excluded or modified only by specific language or by circumstances which give the buyer reason to know that the person selling does not claim title in himself or that he is purporting to sell only such right or title as he or a third person may have.

Accordingly, under the statute there was an implied warranty of title by the sellers **of the truck to Lawson. In the absence of a specific exclusion, a third party defendant who sold a semi-trailer to the defendant and the defendant who sold it to the plaintiff both impliedly warranted good title. Although a defendant had no knowledge that an automobile which he purchased from a third party and ultimately sold to the plaintiff was stolen, he was nevertheless liable to the plaintiff for breach**

of the warranty of title. The damages for breach of the implied warranty of title are set forth in Section 672.714(2) and (3), Florida Statutes (1973). Therefore, in the absence of an exclusion of the implied warranty, the sellers are liable to Lawson for breach of the implied warranty of title.

In order to exclude the implied warranty of title, the seller must do so in very precise and unambiguous language. In *Sunseri v. RKO-Stanley Warner Theaters, Inc.*, the following language in a bill of sale for recreational equipment was held insufficiently specific to exclude the implied warranty of title:

It is expressly understood and agreed that seller shall in nowise be deemed or held to be obligated, liable, or accountable upon or under guaranties (sic.) or warranties, in any manner or form including, but not limited to, the implied warranties of title, merchantability, . . .

> The evidence in the case below in no way approached the attempted disclaimer in Sunseri. The only language which could be construed as an attempted disclaimer is Turner's statement to Lawson that he did not have the title, but he would guarantee Lawson would get it as soon as he received it from Tyson. We hold, therefore, as a matter of law, this language is insufficient to exclude the implied warranty of title in the transaction below.

The evidence adduced at trial was insufficient to prove that Turner was a seller of the truck, but based upon the parties' stipulations and Willis' admissions, we find that Cox and Willis were sellers. They, therefore, breached the implied warranty of title when they sold the stolen truck to Lawson. The trial judge should have granted Lawson's motion for directed verdict as to Cox and Willis.

Accordingly, the judgment is affirmed as to Turner and is reversed as to Cox and Willis. This cause is remanded with instructions that the trial court enter a directed verdict in favor of Lawson against Cox and Willis.

III. Tort Theories of Product Liability

A. NEGLIGENCE

Nearly every products liability case will contain a charge of negligence, the most basic of tort liability theories,. If the defendant had been more careful, the injury would not have occurred. But that simple version of negligence underplays the scope of negligence theories available in a products liability case. One might be negligent in terms of product design, the selection of component parts, the manufacturing process, the quality review process, or many other facets. At any step of the manufacture and sale of the product, there could be a negligence issue, so in a products liability case, there may be a half dozen or more negligence charges.

In just about every one of these negligence charges, the plaintiff will also seek to utilize *res ipsa loquitor* so that he does not have to prove negligence. Instead, the defendant will have to prove that he was not negligent. Courts believe this makes sense because pursuant to the tests for *res ipsa loquitor*, each step (of design, selection of component parts, manufacturing, quality review, etc.) is in the control of the defendant with no input from the plaintiff and it would be very difficult for the plaintiff to obtain the records from the defendant necessary to establish negligence.

Thus, a products liability case will trigger significant costs for the defendant even if the defendant ends up prevailing in the case itself. So there is incentive for a company to settle the case rather than prove they were not negligent in each of these steps. Further, because court cases are generally of public record, companies may not want a great deal of inside information to be made available. Unless a trade secret is involved that would allow for consideration of evidence only among the litigants and decision makers of the case, anyone—including competitors or other parties interested in finding grounds to file suit—could obtain confidential company information.

The following cases demonstrate how negligence operates in product liability suits. The first is one of the more famous cases in legal history and addresses the question of whether a manufacturer only owes a duty to the person who purchases the car—which would be consistent with a contractual theory of liability—or whether liability extends to others as well. Moreover, there is the question of whether the manufacturer of the vehicle is liable for the car's defects when a component is made by another party. In this case, another manufacturer supplied the wheels to Buick, which then added them to the vehicle. Is Buick still liable when the wheels sold with the car it brings to market fail, even though it did not manufacture them?

MacPherson v. Buick Motor Co.

217 N.Y. 382, 111 N.E. 1050 (1916)

The defendant is a manufacturer of automobiles. It sold an automobile to a retail dealer. The retail dealer resold to the plaintiff. While the plaintiff was in the car, it suddenly collapsed. He was thrown out and injured. One of the wheels was made of defective wood, and its spokes crumbled into fragments. The wheel was not made by the defendant; it was bought from another manufacturer. There is evidence, however, that its defects could have been discovered by reasonable inspection, and that inspection was omitted. There is no claim that the defendant knew of the defect and willfully concealed it. The charge is one, not of fraud, but of negligence.

The question to be determined is whether the defendant owed a duty of care and vigilance to any one but the immediate purchaser. The foundations of this branch of the law, at least in this state, were laid in *Thomas v. Winchester.* A poison was falsely labeled. The sale was made to a druggist, who in turn sold to a customer. The customer recovered damages from the seller who affixed the label. 'The defendant's negligence,' it was said, 'put human life in imminent danger.' A poison falsely labeled is likely to injure any one who gets it. Because the danger is to be foreseen, there is a duty to avoid the injury. Cases were cited by way of illustration in which manufacturers were not subject to any duty irrespective of contract. The distinction was said to be that their conduct, though negligent, was not likely to result in injury to any one except the purchaser. We are not required to say whether the chance of injury was always as remote as the distinction assumes. Some of the illustrations might be rejected to-day. The *principle* of the distinction is for present purposes the important thing.

Thomas v. Winchester became quickly a landmark of the law . . . . There has never in this state been doubt or disavowal of the principle itself. The chief cases are well known, yet to recall some of them will be helpful. *Loop v. Litchfield* (42 N.Y. 351) is the earliest. It was the case of a defect in a small balance wheel used on a circular saw. The manufacturer pointed out the defect to the buyer, who wished a cheap article and was ready to assume the risk. The risk can hardly have been an imminent one, for the wheel lasted five years before it broke. In the meanwhile the buyer had made a lease of the machinery. It was held that the manufacturer was not answerable to the lessee. *Loop v. Litchfield* was followed in *Losee v. Clute*, the case of the explosion of a steam boiler. That decision has been criticized . . . but it must be confined to its special facts. It was put upon the ground that the risk of injury was too remote. The buyer in that case had not only accepted the boiler, but had tested it. The manufacturer knew that his own test was not the final one. The finality of the test has a bearing on the measure of diligence owing to persons other than the purchaser . . .

These early cases suggest a narrow construction of the rule. Later cases, however, evince a more liberal spirit. First in importance is *Devlin v. Smith.* The defendant, a contractor, built a scaffold for a painter. The painter's servants were injured. The contractor was held liable. He knew that the scaffold, if improperly constructed, was a most dangerous trap. He knew that it was to be used by the workmen. He was building it for that very purpose. Building it for their use, he owed them a duty, irrespective of his contract with their master, to build it with care.

From *Devlin v. Smith* we pass over intermediate cases and turn to the latest case in this court in which *Thomas v. Winchester* was followed. That case is *Statler v. Ray Mfg. Co.* The defendant manufactured a large coffee urn. It was installed in a restaurant. When heated, the urn exploded and injured the plaintiff. We held that the manufacturer was liable. We said that the urn 'was of such a character inherently that, when applied to the purposes for which it was designed, it was liable to become a source of great danger to many people if not carefully and properly constructed.' It may be that *Devlin v. Smith and Statler v. Ray Mfg. Co.* have extended the rule of *Thomas v. Winchester.* If so, this court is committed to the extension. The defendant argues that things imminently dangerous to life are poisons, explosives, deadly weapons—things whose normal function it is to injure or destroy. But whatever the rule in *Thomas v. Winchester* may once have been, it has no longer that restricted meaning. A scaffold (*Devlin v. Smith, supra*) is not inherently a destructive instrument. It becomes destructive only if imperfectly constructed. A large coffee urn (*Statler v. Ray Mfg. Co., supra*) may have within itself, if negligently made, the potency of danger, yet no one thinks of it as an implement whose normal function is destruction. What is true of the coffee urn is equally true of bottles of aerated water . . .

"BEYOND ALL QUESTION, the nature of an automobile gives warning of probable danger if its construction is defective. This automobile was designed to go fifty miles an hour. Unless its wheels were sound and strong, injury was almost certain."

The rule has received a like extension in our courts of intermediate appeal. In *Burke v. Ireland* it was applied to a builder who constructed a defective building; in *Kahner v. Otis Elevator Co.* to the manufacturer of an elevator; in *Davies v. Pelham Hod Elevating Co.* to a contractor who furnished a defective rope with knowledge of the purpose for which the rope was to be used. We are not required at this time either to approve or to disapprove the application of the rule that was made in these cases. It is enough that they help to characterize the trend of judicial thought.

We hold, then, that the principle of *Thomas v. Winchester* is not limited to poisons, explosives, and things of like nature, to things which in their normal operation are implements of destruction. If the nature of a thing is such that it is reasonably certain to place life and limb in peril when negligently made, it is then a thing of danger. Its nature gives warning of the consequences to be expected. If to the element of danger there is added knowledge that the thing will be used by persons other than the purchaser, and used without new tests, then, irrespective of contract, the manufacturer of this thing of danger is under a duty to make it carefully. That is as far as we are required to go for the decision of this case. There must be knowledge of a danger, not merely possible, but probable. It is *possible* to use almost anything in a way that will make it dangerous if defective. That is not enough to charge the manufacturer with a duty independent of his contract. Whether a given thing is dangerous may be sometimes a question for the court and sometimes a question for the jury.

There must also be knowledge that in the usual course of events the danger will be shared by others than the buyer. Such knowledge may often be inferred from the nature of the transaction. But it is possible that even knowledge of the danger and of the use will not always be enough. The proximity or remoteness of the relation is a factor to be considered. We are dealing now with the liability of the manufacturer of the finished product, who puts it on the market to be used without inspection by his customers. If he is negligent, where danger is to be foreseen, a liability will follow. We are not required at this time to say that it is legitimate to go back of the manufacturer of the finished product and hold the manufacturers of the component parts. To make their negligence a cause of imminent danger, an independent cause must often intervene; the manufacturer of the finished product must also fail in *his* duty of inspection. It may be that in those circumstances the negligence of the earlier members of the series is too remote to constitute, as to the ultimate user, an actionable wrong. We leave that question open. We shall have to deal with it when it arises. The difficulty which it suggests is not present in this case. There is here no break in the chain of cause and effect. In such circumstances, the presence of a known danger, attendant upon a known use, makes vigilance a duty. We have put aside the notion that the duty to safeguard life and limb, when the consequences of negligence may be foreseen, grows out of contract and nothing else. We have put the source of the obligation where it ought to be. We have put its source in the law.

From this survey of the decisions, there thus emerges a definition of the duty of a manufacturer which enables us to measure this defendant's liability. Beyond all question, the nature of an automobile gives warning of probable danger if its construction is defective. This automobile was designed to go fifty miles an hour. Unless its wheels were sound and strong, injury was almost certain. It was as much a thing of danger as a defective engine for a railroad. The defendant knew the danger. It knew also that the car would be used by persons other than the buyer. This was apparent from its size; there were seats for three persons. It was apparent also from the fact that the buyer was a dealer in cars, who bought to resell. The maker of this car supplied it for the use of purchasers from the dealer just as plainly as the contractor in *Devlin v. Smith* supplied the scaffold for use by the servants of the owner. The dealer was indeed the one person of whom it might be said with some approach to certainty that by him the car would not be used. Yet the defendant would have us say that he was the one person whom it was under a legal duty to protect. The law does not lead us to so inconsequent a conclusion. Precedents drawn from the days of travel by stage coach do not fit the conditions of travel to-day. The principle that the danger must be imminent does not change, but the things subject to the principle do change. They are whatever the needs of life in a developing civilization require them to be.

We think the defendant was not absolved from a duty of inspection because it bought the wheels from a reputable manufacturer. It was not merely a dealer in automobiles. It was a manufacturer of automobiles. It was responsible for the finished product. It was not at liberty to put the finished product on the market without subjecting the component parts to ordinary and simple tests. Under the charge of the trial judge nothing more was required of it. The obligation to inspect must vary with the nature of the thing to be inspected. The more probable the danger, the greater the need of caution . . . Both by its relation to the work and by the nature of its business, it is charged with a stricter duty.

The judgment should be affirmed with costs.

If the nature of a finished product placed on the market by a manufacturer to be used without inspection by his customers is such that it is reasonably certain to place life and limb in peril if the product is negligently made, it is then a thing of danger. Its nature gives warning of the consequences to be expected, or to draw upon the ideas of the Torts chapter, it is an unreasonable dangerous product (like the pet mountain lion). If, in addition to the element of danger, there is added knowledge that the thing will be used by persons other than the purchaser and used without new tests, then, irrespective of contract, the manufacturer of this thing of danger is under a duty to make it carefully. This principle is not limited to poisons, explosives and things of like nature, which in their normal operation are implements of destruction.

Res ispa loquitor, which shifts the burden of proof from the plaintiff to the defendant, plays a large role in products liability cases. Usually, the plaintiff has to show that the defendant was negligent. But in some cases, the plaintiff can shift the burden and force the defendant to prove the negative: that they were *not* negligent. The following case is an example of the application of *res ipsa loquitur.*

Escola v. Coca Cola Bottling Co. of Fresno

24 Cal.2d 453, 150 P.2d 436 (1944)

Plaintiff, a waitress in a restaurant, was injured when a bottle of Coca Cola broke in her hand. She alleged that defendant company, which had bottled and delivered the alleged defective bottle to her employer, was negligent in selling "bottles containing said beverage which on account of excessive pressure of gas or by reason of some defect in the bottle was dangerous . . . and likely to explode." This appeal is from a judgment upon a jury verdict in favor of plaintiff.

Defendant's driver delivered several cases of Coca Cola to the restaurant, placing them on the floor, one on top of the other, under and behind the counter, where they remained at least thirty-six hours. Immediately before the accident, plaintiff picked up the top case and set it upon a near-by ice cream cabinet in front of and about three feet from the refrigerator. She then proceeded to take the bottles from the case with her right hand, one at a time, and put them into the refrigerator. Plaintiff testified that after she had placed three bottles in the refrigerator and had moved the fourth bottle about eighteen inches from the case "it exploded in my hand." The bottle broke into two jagged pieces and inflicted a deep five-inch cut, severing blood vessels, nerves and muscles of the thumb and palm of the hand. . . .

One of defendant's drivers, called as a witness by plaintiff, testified that he had seen other bottles of Coca Cola in the past explode and had found broken bottles in the warehouse when he took the cases out, but that he did not know what made them blow up. Plaintiff then rested her case, having announced to the court that being unable to show any specific acts of negligence she relied completely on the doctrine of *res ipsa loquitur.* Defendant contends that the doctrine of *res ipsa loquitur* does not apply in this case, and that the evidence is insufficient to support the judgment.

Res ipsa loquitur does not apply unless (1) defendant had exclusive control of the thing causing the injury and (2) the accident is of such a nature that it ordinarily would not occur in the absence of negligence by the defendant.

"RES IPSA LOQUITUR does not apply unless (1) defendant had exclusive control of the thing causing the injury and (2) the accident is of such a nature that it ordinarily would not occur in the absence of negligence by the defendant."

Many authorities state that the happening of the accident does not speak for itself where it took place some time after defendant had relinquished control of the instrumentality causing the injury. Under the more logical view, however, the doctrine may be applied upon the theory that defendant had control at the time of the alleged negligent act, although not at the time of the accident, *provided* plaintiff first proves that the condition of the instrumentality had not been changed after it left the defendant's possession.

As said in *Dunn v. Hoffman Beverage Co.*, "defendant is not charged with the duty of showing affirmatively that something happened to the bottle after it left its control or management; . . . to get to the jury the plaintiff must show that there was due care during that period." Plaintiff must also prove that she handled the bottle carefully. The reason for this prerequisite is set forth in *Prosser on Torts*, where the author states: "Allied to the condition of exclusive control in the defendant is that of absence of any action on the part of the plaintiff contributing to the accident. Its purpose, of course, is to eliminate the possibility that it was the plaintiff who was responsible. If the boiler of a locomotive explodes while the plaintiff engineer is operating it, the inference of his own negligence is at least as great as that of the defendant, and *res ipsa loquitur* will not apply until he has accounted for his own conduct."

It is not necessary, of course, that plaintiff eliminate every remote possibility of injury to the bottle after defendant lost control, and the requirement is satisfied if there is evidence permitting a reasonable inference that it was not accessible to extraneous harmful forces and that it was carefully handled by plaintiff or any third person who may have moved or touched it. If such evidence is presented, the question becomes one for the trier of fact and, accordingly, the issue should be submitted to the jury under proper instructions.

In the present case no instructions were requested or given on this phase of the case, although general instructions upon *res ipsa loquitur* were given. Defendant, however, has made no claim of error with reference thereto on this appeal. Upon an examination of the record, the evidence appears sufficient to support a reasonable inference that the bottle here involved was not damaged by any extraneous force after delivery to the restaurant by defendant. It follows, therefore, that the bottle was in some manner defective at the time defendant relinquished control, because sound and properly prepared bottles of carbonated liquids do not ordinarily explode when carefully handled.

The next question, then, is whether plaintiff may rely upon the doctrine of *res ipsa loquitur* to supply an inference that defendant's negligence was responsible for the defective condition of the bottle at the time it was delivered to the restaurant. Under the general rules pertaining to the doctrine, as set forth above, it must appear that bottles of carbonated liquid are not ordinarily defective without negligence by the bottling company. In *1 Shearman and Redfield on Negligence*, it is stated that: "The doctrine . . . requires evidence which shows at least the probability that a particular accident could not have occurred without legal wrong by the defendant."

An explosion such as took place here might have been caused by an excessive internal pressure in a sound bottle, by a defect in the glass of a bottle containing a safe pressure, or by a combination of these two possible causes. The question is whether under the evidence there was a probability that defendant was negligent in any of these respects. If so, the doctrine of *res ipsa loquitur* applies.

The bottle was admittedly charged with gas under pressure, and the charging of the bottle was within the exclusive control of defendant. As it is a matter of common knowledge that an overcharge would not ordinarily result without negligence, it follows under the doctrine of *res ipsa loquitur* that if the bottle was in fact excessively charged an inference of defendant's negligence would arise. If the explosion resulted from a defective bottle containing a safe pressure, the defendant would be liable if it negligently failed to discover such flaw. If the defect were visible, an inference of negligence would arise from the failure of defendant to discover it. Where defects are discoverable, it may be assumed that they will not ordinarily escape detection if a reasonable inspection is made, and if such a defect is overlooked an inference arises that a proper inspection was not made. A difficult problem is presented where the defect is unknown and consequently might have been one not discoverable by a reasonable, practicable inspection. In the Honea case we refused to take judicial notice of the technical practices and information available to the bottling industry for finding defects which cannot be seen. In the present case, however, we are supplied with evidence of the standard methods used for testing bottles.

A chemical engineer for the Owens-Illinois Glass Company and its Pacific Coast subsidiary, maker of Coca Cola bottles, explained how glass is manufactured and the methods used in testing and inspecting bottles. He testified that his company is the largest manufacturer of glass containers in the United States, and that it uses the standard methods for testing bottles recommended by the glass containers association. A pressure test is made by taking a sample from each mold every three hours-approximately one out of every 600 bottles-and subjecting the sample to an internal pressure of 450 pounds per square inch, which is sustained for one minute.

(The normal pressure in Coca Cola bottles is less than 50 pounds per square inch.) The sample bottles are also subjected to the standard thermal shock test. The witness stated that these tests are "pretty near" infallible.

It thus appears that there is available to the industry a commonly-used method of testing bottles for defects not apparent to the eye, which is almost infallible. Since Coca Cola bottles are subjected to these tests by the manufacturer, it is not likely that they contain defects when delivered to the bottler which are not discoverable by visual inspection. Both new and used bottles are filled and distributed by defendant. The used bottles are not again subjected to the tests referred to above, and it may be inferred that defects not discoverable by visual inspection do not develop in bottles after they are manufactured. Obviously, if such defects do occur in used bottles there is a duty upon the bottler to make appropriate tests before they are refilled, and if such tests are not commercially practicable the bottles should not be re-used. This would seem to be particularly true where a charged liquid is placed in the bottle. It follows that a defect which would make the bottle unsound could be discovered by reasonable and practicable tests.

Although it is not clear in this case whether the explosion was caused by an excessive charge or a defect in the glass, there is a sufficient showing that neither cause would ordinarily have been present if due care had been used. Further, defendant had exclusive control over both the charging and inspection of the bottles. Accordingly, all the requirements necessary to entitle plaintiff to rely on the doctrine of *res ipsa loquitur* to supply an inference of negligence are present.

It is true that defendant presented evidence tending to show that it exercised considerable precaution by carefully regulating and checking the pressure in the bottles and by making visual inspections for defects in the glass at several stages during the bottling process. It is well settled, however, that when a defendant produces evidence to rebut the inference of negligence which arises upon application of the doctrine of *res ipsa loquitur,* it is ordinarily a question of fact for the jury to determine whether the inference has been dispelled.

The judgment is affirmed.

The doctrine of *res ipsa loquitur* is very helpful for plaintiffs in product liability cases, where it is not uncommon for the plaintiffs to be unfamiliar with how products are manufactured. That knowledge would, however, be in the hands of the defendant. If a product would not be harmful if manufactured properly, then courts will resort to *res ipsa* to require the defendants to demonstrate that there was no negligence. *Res ipsa* is not another theory of liability; it is merely a shifting of the burden of proof, and it is a shifting that provides significant leverage for a plaintiff.

B. STRICT LIABILITY

Strict liability is awkwardly named for a product liability case because in some respects, any manufactured product could be unreasonably dangerous. In other words, strict liability in products liability has a tautological aspect to it: if a product harms someone, it must be dangerous and if it is dangerous, then strict liability applies. Following the logic of strict liability, any damages caused by the product would make the company liable if any one of its products caused harm. This seems both extreme and too neat. Couldn't there be times when a product caused harm not because of strict liability, but rather simply because the company was negligent?

In reality, even when there is "strict liability" there are also negligence tests used to determine company liability. The courts use balancing tests to determine whether it would be cost effective to make the product safer and still available to the market. As a result, the doctrine of strict liability often masks some of the negligence-type language that is inherent in the construction of a strict liability case.

While this balancing of negligence-type tests is worth keeping in mind, there are relatively straightforward cases in which engaging in ultrahazardous activities does trigger a high standard of liability for the company introducing the activity to the public. The following case demonstrates the application of the ultrahazardous dimension of strict (product) liability.

Brewer v. Oriard Powder Co.

401 P.2d 844, 66 Wash.2d 187 (1965)

This is an action to recover damages for personal injuries suffered by plaintiffs while employed by Murphy Brothers, who had contracted for construction work on a United States missile site. The injuries, which were very serious, were caused by a premature explosion of dynamite which had been issued to them by their employer to be used in blasting holes for the construction. The plaintiffs' employer had purchased the dynamite from Oriard Powder Company. The dynamite had been manufactured by Atlas Chemical Industries. The dynamite and essential detonating components were sold and delivered by Atlas to Oriard and, in turn, to Murphy Brothers in the original containers.

The plaintiffs alleged that Atlas had manufactured and sold dangerous, unfit and defective dynamite explosives, primers, blasting caps, related components and accessories which were unfit and dangerous for normal use. They further alleged that Atlas had failed to adequately test or inspect these explosives prior to sale and had knowledge that they were defective and dangerous. The plaintiffs' complaint stated that Oriard was engaged in the sale of these unfit, defective and dangerous products and that it 'had notice of circumstances of the dangers relating to said products and their use by the public and was negligent in failing to test and experiment with said explosives before its products were sold to the public.'

Their third cause of action was that the defendants breached their express and implied warranties of fitness in the manufacture, distribution and sale of the products involved. In a fourth cause of action, the plaintiffs alleged that defendants are absolutely liable to plaintiffs for the injuries and damages sustained. The defendants' answers to this complaint contain general denials and allegations of contributory negligence and assumption of risk. The defendant Oriard asks in the event the plaintiffs recover judgment against Oriard that it, in turn, be awarded judgment against Atlas.

The trial court declined to grant Oriard's motion for summary judgment but dismissed plaintiffs' complaint with prejudice and awarded judgment in favor of the defendants at the conclusion of the opening statement of counsel for the plaintiffs. This is an appeal from the judgment of dismissal.

The question to be resolved by us in this case is: Is the theory of breach of implied warranty of fitness applicable under the facts and circumstances of this case?

The right of an injured person to recover from a manufacturer or retailer for breach of implied warranty in the absence of privity of contract presents what might well be described as the Sargasso Sea of the law. It is filled with entangling theories, rules and doctrines from which courts throughout the United States and England have been attempting to extricate themselves for decades. . . . There is a certain and steady trend in the direction of fixing greater responsibility in manufacturers and sellers.

This court was in the vanguard of the movement to solve these vexing problems when we decided the case of *Mazetti v. Armour & Co.* In that case, it was held that a manufacturer may be liable for damages, irrespective of privity of contract, in the manufacture and sale of food products. The Mazetti case extended that liability to a restaurateur who had purchased from a retail grocer contaminated and impure canned meat manufactured by the defendant. This court discussed the various theories upon which other courts had reached similar conclusions and stated as a basis of the decision: 'Our holding is that, in the absence of an express warranty of quality, a manufacturer of food products under modern conditions impliedly warrants his goods when dispensed in original packages, and that such warranty is available to all who may be damaged by reason of their use in the legitimate channels of trade.' It has been well established by this court that privity of contract is not required in order that there be an implied warranty of fitness where the article involved is food, clothing, drugs, or cosmetics. The reason for these exceptions would appear to be that these items are manufactured and sold with knowledge that they will come into direct contact with the human body either externally or internally.

We held in *LaHue v. Coca Cola Bottling, Inc.*, that, in an action by a remote vendee against the manufacturer of bottled beverages, privity of contract was not an essential element and this was an exception to the general rule of nonliability.

Although that suit was based upon the theory of breach of implied warranty, the court pointed out that the liability rests more upon a theory of violation of duty to members of the general public to protect them from injuries due to the wrongful manufacture or distribution of food products or beverages.

"IF IMPURE FOOD, flammable clothing, and toxic cosmetics are so inherently dangerous to the consumer or ultimate user that we waive the requisite of privity of contract, the exception certainly must be extended to dynamite or explosives."

In *Esborg v. Bailey Drug Co., supra*, we extended the doctrine of implied warranty without privity of contract to a cosmetic intended for application to the hair, scalp or skin. In the carefully considered opinion in *Freeman v. Navarre*, this court recognized the changes which have appeared in the law relative to the privity rule. We stated: 'The exception to the privity of contract doctrine has been extended in our state to so-called inherently dangerous instrumentalities.'

This court emphasized the continuing trend away from the privity rule in warranty cases . . . 'The seller's warranty is a curious hybrid of tort and contract. It has not lost its original tort character. Of course, if breach of actual representations can be proved and there is privity of parties, the action may be in contract; but primarily, a manufacturer's liability for having furnished an inherently dangerous product to the public sounds in tort. That the action is a product of the common-law decisions has been recognized in a variety of situations.'

The *Greenman* case, cited in Dipangrazio, undoubtedly goes beyond anything necessary for disposition of the case now before the court, since it is based upon strict liability without negligence or privity. . . . It seems that a searching judicial review of the privity rule is in order, but that such is not necessary for the disposition of the appeal in the case at bar. If impure food, flammable clothing, and toxic cosmetics are so inherently dangerous to the consumer or ultimate user that we waive the requisite of privity of contract, the exception certainly must be extended to dynamite or explosives. The manufacturer knows that dynamite and its components and accessories will finally be touched, handled and used by employees of the retail purchaser and, being aware of this, must be held to impliedly warrant the fitness of his product. Few commodities are more dangerous than dynamite and it can be far more lethal than canned food, housedresses, toothpaste, or lipstick.

Consequently, we now hold that a manufacturer of dynamite is liable to the ultimate user for breach of implied warranty of fitness without regard to privity of contract. The appellants alleged in their complaint that Oriard had notice of the circumstances of the dangers relating to these explosives and their use by the public and was negligent in failing to test them before they were sold. The appellants further mentioned in their opening statement that they had never been warned of the possibility of premature explosion. Under these circumstances, we do not feel that Oriard is entitled to dismissal of the complaint against it and award of summary judgment at this time.

The judgment of the trial court dismissing appellants' claim with prejudice is reversed and the cause remanded for trial.

Like negligence, strict liability can apply to a number of different parts of the manufacturing process. For example, a manufacturer can be found subject to strict liability for defects present in the actual manufacturing process, or for defects in the design of the product. A defect in the manufacturing process is proven by showing that the product did not meet the manufacturer's own specifications. A design is considered defective if it makes the product unreasonably dangerous—the argument is that there was a reasonable, alternative design that would have made the product safer. The courts consider different factors on a case-by-case basis to determine what is "reasonable" or "unreasonable." The following case demonstrates how the courts apply strict liability to manufacturing defects and design defects.

Transue v. Aesthetech Corp.

341 F.3d 911 (9th Cir. 2003)I

In 1985, Transue received silicone-gel filled breast implants manufactured by Medical Engineering Corporation, Inc., a wholly-owned subsidiary of Bristol-Myers Squibb Company (collectively, "BMS"). The implantation was performed by Dr. Hobart J. White of Tacoma, Washington. Transue alleges that the implants ruptured inside of her body, causing tissue death, scarring, pain, and permanent silicone contamination of her body. BMS claims that a 1993 mammogram, a 1994 ultrasound, the opinion of the only plastic surgeon who testified at trial, Dr. Stevens, and a 1995 xerogram all indicate that the implants did not rupture while inside Transue's body. In 1995, Transue underwent explant surgery to remove the implants and replaced them with saline implants, which she currently uses. Transue alleges that her injuries are permanent and that she will have to undergo periodic implant and explant surgery for her lifetime.

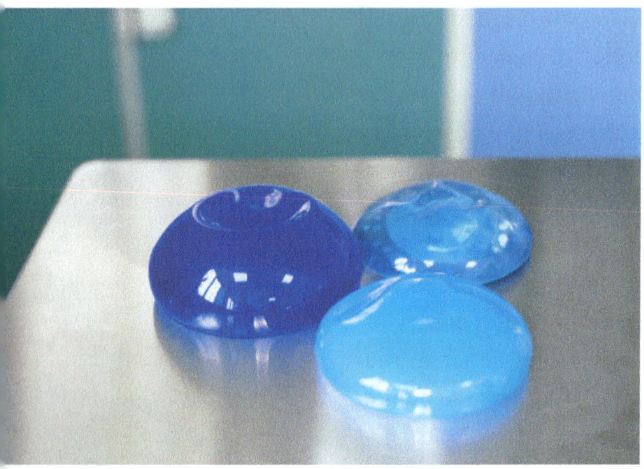

★ SILICONE BREAST IMPLANTS. *Image: Thinkstock*

* * *

Despite Transue's argument to the contrary, "[t]here is no debate" that Washington courts have expressly adopted the Comment K exception to strict liability in the case of unavoidably unsafe products. Moreover, as discussed below, the Washington Supreme Court has indicated that Comment K provides an exemption for medical products generally.

The Washington Supreme Court treated the issue in three cases leading up to its recent opinion in *Ruiz-Guzman*. First, in *Terhune v. A.H. Robins Co.*, the court found that the Dalkon Shield implanted contraceptive device qualified for Comment K exemption because of its availability only through a physician. Second, in *Rogers v. Miles Laboratories, Inc.*, the court held that blood and blood products qualify for Comment K exemption. Third, a plurality of the court in *Young v. Key Pharmaceuticals, Inc.*, held that "a separate determination of whether a product is unavoidably unsafe need not be made on a case-by-case basis if that product is a prescription drug." Finally, in its recent opinion in *Ruiz-Guzman*, the court held that "[b]y its own terms, Comment K is especially applicable to medical products. The exceptions for medical products recognize the unique protection provided to the consumers of such products by the prescribing physician (and/ or pharmacist) intermediary." The court held that a "product-by-product" determination is to be made with regard to whether pesticides are governed by Comment K, "as opposed to a *blanket exemption* like that for medical products." While this statement in *Ruiz-Guzman* appears to be dicta, the Washington Supreme Court expressed its belief that all medical products receive blanket Comment K exemption.

It appears that the issue of whether a breast implant, specifically, is a "medical device or product" that is unavoidably unsafe and therefore receives Comment K exemption has not been directly addressed by Washington courts. However, breast implants fall within the rationale of *Ruiz-Guzman* for providing Comment K immunity for medical devices and products. This rationale emphasizes the presence of physicians as intermediaries between manufacturers and consumers, and recognizes that "[a] physician possesses the medical training to assess adverse health effects of a medical product and to tailor that assessment to a particular patient."

* * *

Despite the conclusion above that Comment K applies to breast implants, Comment K should not be construed to provide protection for manufacturing defect claims based on unavoidably unsafe products. For the purposes of manufacturing defects, the relevant portion of Comment K states: "Such a product, *properly prepared*, and accompanied by proper directions and warning, is not defective, nor is it unreasonably dangerous. . . . The seller of such products, again with the qualification that they are *properly prepared* and marketed, and proper warning is given, where the situation calls for it, is not to be held to strict liability. . . ."

At trial, Transue argued that the proper standard for a manufacturing defect, even under Comment K, is strict liability. The district court, however, read the word "properly," italicized above, to indicate that a negligence standard is appropriate . . . Indeed, a number of authorities from other jurisdictions persuasively indicate that such a jump is not warranted and that, in fact, Comment K is not intended to apply a negligence standard to manufacturing defect claims in the context of unavoidably unsafe products. As the Idaho Supreme Court wrote:

> By its terms, Comment K excepts unavoidably unsafe products from strict liability only where the plaintiff alleges a design defect, and not where the plaintiff alleges a manufacturing flaw or an inadequate warning. Comment K intends to shield from strict liability products which cannot be designed more safely; however, if such products are mismanufactured or unaccompanied by adequate warnings, then the seller may be liable even if the plaintiff cannot establish the seller's negligence. Courts and commentators universally agree to this limitation on Comment K's grant of immunity from strict liability.

The point was reiterated recently by a California court in the context of a breast implant case. The *Artiglio* court explained *Brown* as holding that:

> Liability for defective design [of prescription drugs] could not be premised on strict liability, but would require proof of negligence. Strict liability would continue applicable for manufacturing defects; and liability for failure to warn of known or reasonably knowable risks in the use of the product remains viable "under general principles of negligence."

This understanding of Comment K is further supported by commentary in the Restatement (Third) of Torts: Product Liability, discussing a section analogous to § 402A of the Restatement (Second) of Torts. "Limitations on the liability for prescription drug and medical-device designs do not support treating drug and medical-device manufacturers differently from commercial sellers of other products with respect to manufacturing defects. Courts have traditionally subjected manufacturers of prescription products to liability for harm caused by manufacturing defects." Rest. (3d) Torts: Prod. Liab.§ 6 (1998) Comment C.

Therefore, the district court erred in denying Transue's request that a strict liability jury instruction be given with respect to her claim alleging a manufacturing defect.

BMS argues that, even if Washington law recognizes strict liability for manufacturing defects where Comment K **applies, the plaintiff did not present sufficient evidence to entitle her to a manufacturing defect instruction. The district court issued jury instructions covering Transue's manufacturing defect claim. While the district court noted that BMS was challenging the appellant's contention that a manufacturing defect existed and the appellant's theory of causation, there was no indication by the district court that there was insufficient evidence to support a jury instruction on the alleged manufacturing defect. . . . Instead, the district court**

indicated that the manufacturing defect instruction was simply to employ the same standard as the design defect instruction. The district court gave these manufacturing defect instructions: Jury Instruction No. 11: "Plaintiff claims that defendants were negligent . . . by failing to use ordinary care in the manufacturing of plaintiff's implants. . . . "; Jury Instruction No. 14: "With regard to plaintiff's claim that the manufacturer was negligent in designing and/or manufacturing her breast implants, the plaintiff has the burden of proving each of the following propositions. . . ." Because circumstantial evidence may be a sufficient basis for instructing a jury, we are satisfied that BMS has failed to demonstrate that the error relating to the manufacturing defect instruction was more probably than not harmless.

Based on the erroneous jury instructions given by the district court, the case is reversed and remanded.

Unavoidably unsafe products, as in Comment K, are excluded from strict liability only when the plaintiff alleges a design defect and not when the plaintiff alleges a manufacturing flaw or an inadequate warning.

As seen in the case above, Section 402A of the Restatement (Second) of Torts, Comment K, provides a blanket exception for unavoidably unsafe products in strict liability product defect claims. Comment K states:

> There are some products which, in the present state of human knowledge, are quite incapable of being made safe for their intended and ordinary use. These are especially common in the field of drugs. An outstanding example is the vaccine for the Pasteur treatment of rabies, which not uncommonly leads to very serious and damaging consequences when it is injected. Since the disease itself invariably leads to a dreadful death, both the marketing and the use of the vaccine are fully justified, notwithstanding the unavoidable high degree of risk which they involve. Such a product, properly prepared, and accompanied by proper directions and warning, is not defective, nor is it unreasonably dangerous. The same is true of many other drugs, vaccines, and the like, many of which for this very reason cannot legally be sold except to physicians, or under the prescription of a physician. It is also true in particular of many new or experimental drugs as to which, because of lack of time and opportunity for sufficient medical experience, there can be no assurance of safety, or perhaps even of purity of ingredients, but such experience as there is justifies the marketing and use of the drug notwithstanding a medically recognizable risk. The seller of such products, again with the qualification that they are properly prepared and marketed, and proper warning is given, where the situation calls for it, is not to be held to strict liability for unfortunate consequences attending their use, merely because he

> has undertaken to supply the public with an apparently useful and desirable product, attended with a known but apparently reasonable risk.

The conventional application of strict liability tends to differ from that of products liability cases, where the courts allow some negligence-like testing of manufacturing processes to determine liability. As you remember, anyone who keeps a pet mountain lion is liable for the damages caused by the mountain lion no matter how "careful" or "prudent" the lion owner has been. A lion is simply too dangerous. There is no testing as to whether one has exercised proper prudence.

Yet in products liability cases, courts do allow companies to demonstrate that the costs associated in making a product safer would be so expensive that the product would be unable to compete in the market. Thus, there are balancing tests within the strict liability framework that do look much like a negligence case as seen in the following case.

Barker v. Lull Engineering Co.

573 P.2d 443 (Cal. 1978)

In August 1970, plaintiff Ray Barker was injured at a construction site at the University of California at Santa Cruz while operating a high-lift loader manufactured by defendant Lull Engineering Co. and leased to plaintiff's employer by defendant George M. Philpott Co., Inc. Claiming that his injuries were proximately caused, *inter alia*, by the alleged defective design of the loader, Barker instituted the present tort action seeking to recover damages for his injuries. The jury returned a verdict in favor of defendants, and plaintiff appeals from the judgment entered upon that verdict, contending primarily that . . . the trial court erred in instructing the jury "that strict liability for a defect in design of a product is based on a finding that the product was unreasonably dangerous for its intended use . . . ."

As numerous recent judicial decisions and academic commentaries have recognized, the formulation of a satisfactory definition of "design defect" has proven a formidable task; trial judges have repeatedly confronted difficulties in attempting to devise accurate and helpful instructions in design defect cases. Aware of these problems, we have undertaken a review of the past California decisions which have grappled with the design defect issue, and have measured their conclusions against the fundamental policies which underlie the entire strict product liability doctrine.

As we explain in more detail below, we have concluded from this review that a product is defective in design either (1) if the product has failed to perform as safely as an ordinary consumer would expect when used in an intended or reasonably foreseeable manner, or (2) if, in light of the relevant factors discussed below, the benefits of the challenged design do not outweigh the risk of danger inherent in such design. In addition, we explain how the burden of proof with respect to the latter "risk-benefit" standard should be allocated.

This dual standard for design defect assures an injured plaintiff protection from products that either fall below ordinary consumer expectations as to safety, or that, on balance, are not as safely designed as they should be. At the same time, the standard permits a manufacturer who has marketed a product which satisfies ordinary consumer expectations to demonstrate the relative complexity of design decisions and the trade-offs that are frequently required in the adoption of alternative designs. Finally, this test reflects our continued adherence to the principle that, in a product liability action, the trier of fact must focus on the product, not on the manufacturer's conduct, and that the plaintiff need not prove that the manufacturer acted unreasonably or negligently in order to prevail in such an action.

Plaintiff's principal expert witness initially testified that by reason of its relatively narrow base the loader was unstable and had a tendency to roll over when lifting loads to considerable heights . . . Evidence at trial revealed that cranes and some high lift loader models are either regularly equipped with outriggers or offer outriggers as optional equipment. Plaintiff's expert testified that the availability of outriggers would probably have averted the present accident. The expert additionally testified that the loader was defective in that it was not equipped with a roll bar or seat belts. He stated that such safety devices were essential to protect the operator in the event that the machine rolled over. Plaintiff theorized that the lack of such safety equipment was a proximate cause of his injuries because in the absence of such devices he had no reasonable choice but to leap from the loader as it began to tip. If a seat belt and roll bar had been provided, plaintiff argued, he could have remained in the loader and would not have been struck by the falling lumber. Finally, plaintiff's experts testified that the absence of a "park" position on the loader's transmission, that could have been utilized to avoid the possibility of the loader's movement during a lift, constituted a further defect in design which may have caused the accident.

Defendants explain that in a manufacturing defect case, a jury may find a product defective because it deviates from the manufacturer's intended result, but may still decline to impose liability under the Restatement test on the ground that such defect did not render the product unreasonably dangerous. In a design defect case, by contrast, defendants assert that a defect is defined by reference to the "unreasonably dangerous" standard . . . In essence, defendants argue that under the instruction which the trial court gave in the instant case, plaintiff was not required to prove both that the loader was defective and that such defect made the loader unreasonably dangerous, but only that the loader was defectively designed by virtue of its unreasonable dangerousness.

First, our cases establish that a product may be found defective in design if the plaintiff demonstrates that the product failed to perform as safely as an ordinary consumer would expect when used in an intended or reasonably foreseeable manner.

When a product fails to satisfy such ordinary consumer expectations as to safety in its intended or reasonably foreseeable operation, a manufacturer is strictly liable for resulting injuries . . .

The expectations of the ordinary consumer cannot be viewed as the exclusive yardstick for evaluating design defectiveness because "(i)n many situations . . . the consumer would not know what to expect, because he would have no idea how safe the product could be made." Numerous California decisions have implicitly recognized this fact and have made clear, through varying linguistic formulations, that a product may be found defective in design, even if it satisfies ordinary consumer expectations, if through hindsight the jury determines that the product's design embodies "excessive preventable danger," or, in other words, if the jury finds that the risk of danger inherent in the challenged design outweighs the benefits of such design.

"When a product fails to satisfy such ordinary consumer expectations as to safety in its intended or reasonably foreseeable operation, a manufacturer is strictly liable for resulting injuries. . ."

A review of past cases indicates that in evaluating the adequacy of a product's design pursuant to this latter standard, a jury may consider, among other relevant factors, the gravity of the danger posed by the challenged design, the likelihood that such danger would occur, the mechanical feasibility of a safer alternative design, the financial cost of an improved design, and the adverse consequences to the product and to the consumer that would result from an alternative design.

If a jury in determining liability for a defect in design is instructed only that it should decide whether or not there is "a defective design," it may reach to the extreme conclusion that the plaintiff, having suffered injury, should without further showing, recover; on the other hand, it may go to the opposite extreme and conclude that because the product matches the intended design the plaintiff, under no conceivable circumstance, could recover. The submitted definition eschews both extremes and attempts a balanced approach.

We hold that a trial judge may properly instruct the jury that a product is defective in design (1) if the plaintiff demonstrates that the product failed to perform as safely as an ordinary consumer would expect when used in an intended or reasonably foreseeable manner, or (2) if the plaintiff proves that the product's design proximately caused his injury and the defendant fails to prove, in light of the relevant factors discussed above, that on balance the benefits of the challenged design outweigh the risk of danger inherent in such design.

Because the jury may have interpreted the erroneous instruction given in the instant case as requiring plaintiff to prove that the high-lift loader was ultrahazardous or more dangerous than the average consumer contemplated, and because the instruction additionally misinformed the jury that the defectiveness of the product must be evaluated in light of the product's "intended use" rather than its "reasonably foreseeable use," we cannot find that the error was harmless on the facts of this case.

The judgment in favor of defendants is reversed.

To determine if a product is "unreasonably dangerous" for purposes of a strict liability claim, the courts should consider a number of factors, including whether the product's design represents a fair balance between the cost of designing a safer product, the risk of injury, and whether the product satisfies consumer expectations. For example, a manufacturer could make a totally safe product, but to do so would make it so expensive that no one would every buy it. Because the courts do weigh such considerations, the courts' standards sound very much like a negligence test: whether the manufacturer is exercising due care and acting reasonably. This all occurs within the scope of "strict liability."

IV. Special Issues of Damages

AS INDICATED AT THE BEGINNING of this chapter, damages can be large in product liability cases. Some part of this stems from the belief that, as with punitive damages, the award needs to be high enough to get the attention of a large, wealthy company. If the award is small, it may be ignored and simply be viewed as a cost of doing business. No changes will be made. Punitive damages provide an opportunity to make products safer, which is part of the logic behind any kind of punitive damage award, at least one against a large company. However, as seen in the case below, the Supreme Court has attempted to mitigate the trend towards grossly excessive punitive damages, which it considers unconstitutional.

BMW of North America, Inc. v. Gore

517 U.S. 559 (1996)

After Dr. Gore purchased a new BMW automobile from an authorized Alabama dealer, he discovered that the car had been repainted. He brought this suit for compensatory and punitive damages against petitioner, the American distributor of BMW's, alleging, *inter alia*, that the failure to disclose the repainting constituted fraud under Alabama law. At trial, BMW acknowledged that it followed a nationwide policy of not advising its dealers, and hence their customers, of pre-delivery damage to new cars when the cost of repair did not exceed 3 percent of the car's suggested retail price. Gore's vehicle fell into that category. The jury returned a verdict finding BMW liable for compensatory damages of $4,000, and assessing $4 million in punitive damages.

The Due Process Clause of the Fourteenth Amendment prohibits a State from imposing a "grossly excessive" punishment on a tortfeasor. The wrongdoing involved in this case was the decision by a national distributor of automobiles not to advise its dealers, and hence their customers, of pre-delivery damage to new cars when the cost of repair amounted to less than 3 percent of the car's suggested retail price. The question presented is whether a $2 million punitive damages award to the purchaser of one of these cars exceeds the constitutional limit.

Punitive damages may properly be imposed to further a State's legitimate interests in punishing unlawful conduct and deterring its repetition. In our federal system, States necessarily have considerable flexibility in determining the level of punitive damages that they will allow in different classes of cases and in any particular case. Most States that authorize exemplary damages afford the jury similar latitude, requiring only that the damages awarded be reasonably necessary to vindicate the State's legitimate interests in punishment and deterrence. Only when an award can fairly be categorized as "grossly excessive" in relation to these interests does it enter the zone of arbitrariness that violates the Due Process Clause of the Fourteenth Amendment. For that reason, the federal excessiveness inquiry appropriately begins with an identification of the state interests that a punitive award is designed to serve. We therefore focus our attention first on the scope of Alabama's legitimate interests in punishing BMW and deterring it from future misconduct.

No one doubts that a State may protect its citizens by prohibiting deceptive trade practices and by requiring automobile distributors to disclose presale repairs that affect the value of a new car. But the States need not, and in fact do not, provide such protection in a uniform manner. Some States rely on the judicial process to formulate and enforce an appropriate disclosure requirement by applying principles of contract and tort law. Other States have enacted various forms of legislation that define the disclosure obligations of automobile manufacturers, distributors, and dealers. The result is a patchwork of rules representing the diverse policy judgments of lawmakers in 50 States.

We may assume, *arguendo*, that it would be wise for every State to adopt Dr. Gore's preferred rule, requiring full disclosure of every presale repair to a car, no matter how trivial and regardless of its actual impact on the value of the car. But while we do not doubt that Congress has ample authority to enact such a policy for the entire Nation, it is clear that no single State could do so, or even impose its own policy choice on neighboring States. Similarly, one State's power to impose burdens on the interstate market for automobiles is not only subordinate to the federal power over interstate commerce . . . We think it follows from these principles of state sovereignty and comity that a State may not impose economic sanctions on violators of its laws with the intent of changing the tortfeasors' lawful conduct in other States. Before this Court Dr. Gore argued that the large punitive damages award was necessary to induce BMW to change the nationwide policy that it adopted in 1983. But by attempting to alter BMW's nationwide policy, Alabama would be infringing on the policy choices of other States. To avoid such encroachment, the economic penalties that a State such as Alabama inflicts on those who transgress its laws, whether the penalties take the form of legislatively authorized fines or judicially imposed punitive damages, must be supported by the State's interest in protecting its own consumers and its own economy. Alabama may insist that BMW adhere to a particular disclosure policy in that State. Alabama does not have the power, however, to punish BMW for conduct that was lawful where it occurred and that had no impact on Alabama or its residents. Nor may Alabama impose sanctions on BMW in order to deter conduct that is lawful in other jurisdictions.

In this case, we accept the Alabama Supreme Court's interpretation of the jury verdict as reflecting a computation of the amount of punitive damages "based in large part on conduct that happened in other jurisdictions." As the Alabama Supreme Court noted, neither the jury nor the trial court was presented with evidence that any of BMW's out-of-state conduct was unlawful. "The only testimony touching the issue showed that approximately 60% of the vehicles that were refinished were sold in states where failure to disclose the repair was not an unfair trade practice." The Alabama Supreme Court therefore properly eschewed reliance on BMW's out-of-state conduct and based its remitted award solely on conduct that occurred within Alabama. The award must be analyzed in the light of the same conduct, with consideration given only to the interests of Alabama consumers, rather than those of the entire Nation. When the scope of the interest in punishment and deterrence that an Alabama court may appropriately consider is properly limited, it is apparent—for reasons that we shall now address—that this award is grossly excessive.

Elementary notions of fairness enshrined in our constitutional jurisprudence dictate that a person receive fair notice not only of the conduct that will subject him to punishment, but also of the severity of the penalty that a State may impose. Three guideposts, each of which indicates that BMW did not receive adequate notice of the magnitude of the sanction that Alabama might impose for adhering to the nondisclosure policy adopted in 1983, lead us to the conclusion that the $2 million award against BMW is grossly excessive: the degree of reprehensibility of the nondisclosure; the disparity between the harm or potential harm suffered by Dr. Gore and his punitive damages award; and the difference between this remedy and the civil penalties authorized or imposed in comparable cases.

The sanction imposed in this case cannot be justified on the ground that it was necessary to deter future misconduct without considering whether less drastic remedies could be expected to achieve that goal. The fact that a multimillion dollar penalty prompted a change in policy sheds no light on the question whether a lesser deterrent would have adequately protected the interests of Alabama consumers. The fact that BMW is a large corporation rather than an impecunious individual does not diminish its entitlement to fair notice of the demands that the several States impose on the conduct of its business. Indeed, its status as an active participant in the national economy implicates the federal interest in preventing individual States

from imposing undue burdens on interstate commerce. While each State has ample power to protect its own consumers, none may use the punitive damages deterrent as a means of imposing its regulatory policies on the entire Nation.

The judgment is reversed, and the case is remanded for further proceedings not inconsistent with this opinion.

A second reason for large damage awards can be attributed to the ways trials proceed. There is an old trial law adage called "waving the bloody foot." This means that the more a plaintiff has been injured, the more the lawyer wants that injured plaintiff in plain view, even right in front of a jury. By "waving the bloody foot," the plaintiff's lawyer will generate sympathy for the client. Jury members, the tactic assumes, will then be more sympathetic to the injured plaintiff and be more prone to making an award. That is particularly true if in the contrast to the defendant is a wealthy, anonymous corporation that has deep pockets and probably a lot of insurance as well. While some of these attributes are, in theory, inadmissible as evidence, lawyers find ways of making this contrast clear in the courtroom. As a result, compensatory damages may be higher as well.

The following case demonstrates the high cost that can come with compensatory damage awards.

Harley-Davidson Motor Co., Inc. v. Wisniewski

50 Md.App. 339 437 A.2d 700 (1981)

Michael S. Wisniewski, plaintiff below and appellee herein, purchased a new Harley-Davidson motorcycle from Garrett's Harley-Davidson in April of 1978. On September 16, 1978, appellee was riding his motorcycle at approximately 25 m.p.h. on an "S" shaped curve along Key Highway in South Baltimore when the throttle slipped off the handlebar. He lost control of the bike, crossed into the lanes of on-coming traffic and collided with a car traveling in the opposite lane at approximately the same speed.

The throttle control mechanism of the motorcycle was the type which operates the throttle by rotating the right handgrip on the handlebar. The alleged defect in this case was stated as an improper assembly of the throttle control clamp causing a clamp screw to suddenly fracture. This, it is contended, permitted the throttle control mechanism to come off the handlebar while the appellee was operating his motorcycle.

Appellee's principal injuries consisted of leg fractures of the right tibia and left femur. He required hospitalization for slightly less than two months and his total expenses for medical care and hospitalization were $14,786.20. In addition, he lost $11,152 in income. Repairs to his motorcycle cost $2,964.09. The stipulated total of medical bills, lost income and property damage was $28,902.29.

The Superior Court granted seller partial summary judgment as to punitive damages, but denied manufacturer's motions for summary judgment on punitive damages, and, after trial, entered judgment on jury verdict awarding rider $544,604 for compensatory damages and $1,900,000 punitive damages against manufacturer. After judgment was entered in favor of seller against manufacturer for indemnity for full amount of seller's liability to rider, both seller and manufacturer appealed.

Harley-Davidson raises the following two issues to be determined by this Court:

> I. Whether the trial court erred in denying appellant's motion for a directed verdict on the issue of punitive damages?
>
> II. Whether the trial court should have granted a new trial on the issue of compensatory damages because of the claimed prejudice by the allegedly erroneous submission of the punitive damage issue to the jury?

In our consideration of the issues raised by the appellants in this case, we note initially that appellants do not challenge the jury's specific finding of negligence on the part of the appellants. The question then remains whether there was sufficient evidence to require the trial judge to submit to the jury the question of the assessment of punitive damages against the appellant. Maryland has adhered to the principle that a manufacturer is required to compensate a consumer for all injuries proximately caused by products either defectively designed or manufactured.

We have carefully considered the voluminous record extract filed in this case and we find no evidence that Harley-Davidson was aware of the cross-threaded throttle clamps. Nor does the evidence reveal the existence of a design defect which would inherently present the probability of recurrence of the danger to the consumer. There was more than sufficient evidence to establish negligence on the part of Harley- Davidson. It was obvious from the testimony that the appellant had used less than an ideal assembly process which involved the complete tightening of each of the throttle screws separately, rather than alternating each to the desired level of torque. There was, however, no evidence to establish the manufacturer's substantial knowledge of the existence of the danger to the plaintiff.

> **"IN ORDER to find 'recklessness' in such circumstances there must be a readily perceptible danger and a conscious choice by the manufacturer to market the product despite the risk."**

In order to find "recklessness" in such circumstances there must be a readily perceptible danger and a conscious choice by the manufacturer to market the product despite the risk. We find nothing in the record to substantiate knowledge of the existence of the danger by the manufacturer or gross indifference to its existence. Under all the circumstances, we conclude that the trial court erred when it denied Harley-Davidson's motions for directed verdict on the issue of punitive damages.

Appellant finally urges that it is entitled to a new trial on the issue of compensatory damages because it was substantially prejudiced by the trial court's erroneous submission of the punitive damage issue to the jury. It points out that Maryland has never had occasion to evaluate the prejudicial impact on compensatory damages of an erroneous denial of a motion for directed verdict on a claim for punitive damages. This Court, however, has held that evidence of a defendant's wealth is probative and admissible only where a *prima facie* case for punitive damages has been established. Appellant suggests that the evidence of wealth of the defendant and the impassioned plea by plaintiff's counsel for punishment of Harley-Davidson created an obvious potential for prejudice and resulted in an improper verdict for compensatory damages. It suggests the only cure for this prejudicial potential is, in effect, the adoption of a per se rule that where such error occurs, a new trial as to compensatory damages must be allowed. We do not agree that such a rigid rule is mandated. We prefer to examine the evidence, on a case-by-case basis, and to determine whether a new trial on the issue of compensatory damages is required where a case has been erroneously submitted to the jury on the issue of punitive damages.

Our examination of the evidence in this case convinces us that there is no proof that the verdict for compensatory damages in this case was based on prejudice or bias. The appellee, a comparatively young man, sustained serious injuries to both legs which resulted in the permanent shortening of one of his limbs. The plaintiff, without objection, submitted to the jury a per diem calculation of what plaintiff considered an appropriate award for pain and suffering of $465,702. The plaintiff requested $615,000 as compensatory damages. The trial judge specifically instructed the jury not to consider the defendant's financial circumstances in reaching its decision of an appropriate award for compensatory damages. The only response of Harley-Davidson to plaintiff's request for assessment of compensatory damages was an assertion that the jury did not necessarily have to accept the figures of the plaintiff but could put in their own, and a disclosure to the jury that the plaintiff's top pretrial demand was for the sum of $250,000. In the light of all these circumstances we do not find that the jury's award of compensatory damages in the amount of $544,604 was influenced by a desire to punish the appellant, particularly since the jury returned a verdict against the defendant in the amount of $1,900,000 as punitive damages.

Judgment for punitive damages vacated, judgment for compensatory damages affirmed.

V. Defenses

THERE ARE FEW MORE POTENT DISCUSSIONS in the law pertaining to ethical issues today than the question of whether plaintiffs bringing suit should have a greater sense of personal responsibility. After all, shouldn't plaintiffs realize some of the dangers they are getting themselves into? Another approach is to note that life is not without risk, so why place manufacturers in the position of insuring against times when things go awry?

Courts do take these kinds of arguments into account when they consider possible defenses. There are reasons why we should not hold a manufacturer/seller liable for the damages their product caused. Courts are more willing to cut off liability if the plaintiff is a commercial interest, such as another business. It is harder, though certainly not impossible, to find defenses for defendants when the victim is a consumer or bystander.

A. CONTRACT (WARRANTY) THEORIES

As has already been indicated, product liability suits became possible largely because of the undermining of the legal theory of privity of contract, which continues to be the case with respect to the ordinary consumer of the product or a bystander and remains an issue with commercial plaintiffs. Recall that years ago, a consumer could only sue the business that actually sold the product to the consumer rather than also being able to sue the manufacturer. This privity of contract limitation to product liability cases no longer has the same strength. Courts continue to eliminate privity concerns vertically, which means that, it makes no difference to the injured party as to who among the chain of manufacturers is liable.

While privity is not much help these days, defendants can obtain some protection by restricting the time within which one can report a problem, which is an easier case to defend than trying to disclaim the adequate function of a product. . It is one thing to say that a new dishwasher won't wash dishes. It is hard to justify a seller disclaiming a warranty such as this. But it is not unreasonable for a seller to say that the warranty on the dishwasher ends in three or five years. After that, it is possible that a dishwasher might not wash dishes so well anymore. Limitations of warranty based on time may protect the seller and manufacturer. Furthermore, as seen in the case below, there may also be a statute of limitations for claims of breach of warranty.

Trans-Spec Truck Service, Inc. v. Caterpillar Inc.

524 F.3d 315 (1st Cir. 2008)

In March 1999, Trans-Spec and Sterling Truck Corporation prepared a "specification proposal" for twenty-two heavy-duty, custom-built trucks that Trans-Spec intended to purchase from Sterling for use in Trans-Spec's oil delivery and dump trailer operations. The proposal called for installation of Caterpillar's C-12 model engines in each of the trucks. Trans-Spec allegedly decided upon Caterpillar engines after extensive conversations with Caterpillar's employees and agents regarding engine specifications and performance, the terms of the warranty, and which engine manufacturer would "stand behind their warranty the best." After finalizing the agreement, Caterpillar shipped completely assembled engines to Sterling for installation in the trucks. In December 1999 and January 2000, Trans-Spec took delivery of the trucks and put them into service.

By late 2001, serious problems had begun to develop with the flywheel housing on the Caterpillar engines in several of Trans-Spec's trucks. The housings loosened and cracked, leading to disruptions in the use of the trucks and time-consuming repair efforts. Caterpillar reimbursed Trans-Spec for the cost of the repairs to the first six trucks that experienced these flywheel housing failures in 2001 and 2002. When a seventh truck became inoperable, Caterpillar refused to pay for additional repairs. Since that time, Trans-Spec avers that an average of six, and as many as ten, of the twenty-two trucks have been inoperable at any given time due to engine-related issues.

Trans-Spec claims that the flywheel housing failures were caused by a major design defect in the C-12 engine, and that Caterpillar knew or should have known of this defect. Trans-Spec contends that the housing failures fell under the Caterpillar warranty and that Caterpillar should have rectified the problems. Trans-Spec also avers that, at meetings in June and August 2004, Caterpillar acknowledged responsibility for the flywheel housing failures and promised to "make [Trans-Spec] whole." In August 2004, apparently unpersuaded by this promise, Trans-Spec filed this suit against Caterpillar.

Trans-Spec's initial complaint alleged breach of warranty (Count I) and violations of Massachusetts General Laws chapter 93A (Count II). Its second amended complaint added a negligence claim (Count III) as well. Caterpillar moved to dismiss the second amended complaint on the grounds that Counts I and II were time-barred and that Count III was barred by the economic loss doctrine.

We begin with the district court's determination that Counts I and II of Trans-Spec's complaint are time-barred. We review the grant of a motion to dismiss de novo, accepting as true the factual allegations of the complaint and drawing all reasonable inferences in favor of the plaintiff.

The Uniform Commercial Code ("U.C.C."), as adopted in Massachusetts, provides that an action for breach of warranty must be commenced within four years of the date when the cause of action accrues. The code section then specifies when the cause of action accrues:

A breach of warranty occurs when tender of delivery is made, except that where a warranty explicitly extends to future performance of the goods and discovery of the breach must await the time of such performance the cause of action accrues when the breach is or should have been discovered.

Thus, the default rule in § 2-725(2) is that the cause of action for breach of warranty is time-barred if brought more than four years after tender of delivery. However, if the warranty explicitly extends to future performance, "the four-year clock begins to tick when the breach is discovered or should have been discovered, or when the explicit time period expires, whichever occurs first."

Trans-Spec's complaint stated that Trans-Spec accepted delivery of the trucks containing Caterpillar's allegedly defective flywheel housing in December 1999 and January 2000. Trans-Spec filed suit for breach of warranty in August 2004. Thus, on its face, Trans-Spec's complaint is not timely unless the warranty on which its claims are based is one that "explicitly extend[s] to future performance of the goods" and the circumstances are such that the "'discovery of the breach must await'" the time of the promised future performance.

The Supreme Judicial Court of Massachusetts has not discussed the proper application of the future performance requirement in § 2-725(2) of the U.C.C. Thus we must make "an informed prophecy of what the court would do in the same situation." In making such a prophecy, we look to analogous cases decided by other courts in the forum state, persuasive reasoning in cases from other states, and learned treatises. To determine whether a warranty is one of future performance, we must look to the language of the warranty itself to determine whether it *explicitly* guarantees the future performance of the goods.

The only warranty language properly before us in considering Caterpillar's motion to dismiss is contained in the "On-Highway Vehicle Engine Extended Service Coverage" ("ESC") document, which was appended to Trans-Spec's complaint. The ESC states: "This service contract . . . provides full components and labor coverage for covered components failures due to defects in Caterpillar materials or workmanship under normal use." The ESC guarantees that "Caterpillar will pay 100% of the components and labor charges for covered failures, with no deductible charges" for failures occurring within the first 60 months or 500,000 miles. It specifies Caterpillar's responsibility to "restore the engine to its operating condition prior to failure by repairing/replacing only the defective components and consequential damaged components necessary to remove/repair/install the defective components."

The ESC thus never guaranteed that Caterpillar's engines would not fail; it merely warranted that Caterpillar would pay to repair them if they did fail. As such, the warranty provided in the ESC is not a warranty that explicitly extends to the

future performance of the goods, and the later accrual date specified in § 2-725(2) does not apply. Thus, Trans-Spec's claims are time-barred by the four-year statute of limitations that began to run on the date of delivery of the trucks . . . If Trans-Spec finds itself without an adequate remedy here, it is because, as we describe above, Trans-Spec did not assert its contract remedies in a timely fashion.

So too could a situation that arises if the buyer inspects the product prior to actually purchasing it. If this has happened, then an implied warranty of merchantability could be more successfully disclaimed unless, of course, the defect was latent and the buyer unable to ascertain whether or not there were any product defects.

B. TORT THEORIES

Historically, one defense a defendant had was contributory negligence. This was a harsh defense. As we saw in the chapter on torts, if the plaintiff was in any way negligent, that negligence eliminated defendant liability. This is an idea that runs contrary to the entire theory of products liability and can no longer be used successfully. A less draconian version of the idea is called comparative negligence, which is still very much in use. Under this defense, courts compare how negligent each party is, and then reduces the award received by the plaintiff to reflect his percentage of fault. So, if the judge or jury determined a plaintiff was 25% negligent and the award was for $10,000,000, then the amount actually going to the plaintiff would be $7,500,000 rather than $10,000,000. The $2,500,000 difference is accounted for by the plaintiff's negligence.

In the following case, the court found that though there was a design defect, the total award to the plaintiff should be reduced because the plaintiff was comparatively negligent.

General Motors Corporation v. Sanchez

997 S.W.2d 584 (Tex.1999)

Lee Sanchez, Jr. left his home to feed a pen of heifers in March 1993. The ranch foreman found his lifeless body the next morning and immediately called Sanchez's father. Apparently, Sanchez's 1990 Chevy pickup had rolled backward with the driver's side door open pinning Sanchez to the open corral gate in the angle between the open door and the cab of the truck. Sanchez suffered a broken right arm and damaged right knee where the gate crushed him against the door pillar, the vertical metal column to which the door is hinged. He bled to death from a deep laceration in his right upper arm.

The Sanchez family, his estate, and his wife sued General Motors Corporation and the dealership that sold the pickup for negligence, products liability, and gross negligence based on a defect in the truck's transmission and transmission-control linkage. The plaintiffs presented circumstantial evidence to support the following theory of how the accident happened. Sanchez drove his truck into the corral and stopped to close the gate. He mis-shifted into what he thought was Park, but what was actually an intermediate, "perched" position between Park and Reverse where the transmission was in "hydraulic neutral." Expert witnesses explained that hydraulic neutral exists at the intermediate positions between the denominated gears, Park, Reverse, Neutral, Drive, and Low, where no gear is actually engaged. Under this scenario, as Sanchez walked toward the gate, the gear shift slipped from the perched position of hydraulic neutral into Reverse and the truck started to roll backwards. It caught Sanchez at or near the gate and slammed him up against it, trapping his right arm and knee. He was pinned between the gate and the door pillar by the pressure the truck exerted while idling in Reverse. Struggling to free himself, Sanchez severed an artery in his right arm and bled to death after 45 to 75 minutes.

In the trial court, G.M. offered alternative theories explaining the cause of the accident, all of which directed blame at Sanchez. It suggested that Sanchez left his truck in Reverse either accidentally or in a conscious attempt to prevent cattle from escaping the corral. Alternatively, G.M. suggested that Sanchez simply left the truck in Neutral and it rolled down the five degree slope toward the gate. Finally, G.M. argued that even if the accident was caused by a mis-shift as alleged by the plaintiffs, the mis-shift was a result of operator error, and not a defect in design.

The jury rejected G.M.'s theories and found that G.M. was negligent, the transmission was defectively designed, and G.M.'s warning was so inadequate as to constitute a marketing defect. The jury also found that Sanchez was fifty percent responsible for the accident, but the trial court disregarded this finding. The trial court rendered judgment for actual and punitive damages of $8.5 million for the plaintiffs. A panel of the court of appeals affirmed the trial court's judgment with one justice dissenting.

G.M. argues that there is no evidence to support liability for negligence or strict liability. Alternatively, G.M. challenges the trial court's refusal to apply the comparative responsibility statute. The plaintiffs respond that evidence supports both the negligence and strict liability findings, and that Sanchez's negligence was nothing more than a failure to discover or guard against a product defect. Thus, they contend, comparative responsibility does not apply here as a defense to strict liability.

Here, G.M. does not dispute that Sanchez's fatal injury was caused when he mis-shifted the truck's transmission into hydraulic neutral, which then migrated into Reverse. The parties agree that all transmissions made today can mis-shift, that no design eliminates the possibility of a mis-shift, and that a mis-shifted car is dangerous. As G.M. puts it, a "[m]is-shift is just physics." G.M. contends that it has no liability, even if its product is defective, because the plaintiffs failed to present evidence of a safer alternative design.

* * *

Most of the plaintiff's design evidence came in through the testimony of the plaintiffs' expert, Simon Tamny, who testified about the operation of the 700R4 transmission in Sanchez's truck. He opined that the G.M. transmission and transmission-control linkage presented a particular risk. All transmissions have an intermediate position between Reverse and Park. It is impossible, under federal standardization guidelines, to design a gear shift without an intermediate position between Reverse and Park. However, Tamny testified that G.M.'s transmission has the added danger that internal forces tend to move the gear selector toward Reverse rather than Park when the driver inadvertently leaves the lever in this intermediate position. Tamny explained how G.M. could alter the design to make the operation of the 700R4 safer.

Tamny admitted that his design change would not totally eliminate the possibility of leaving the gearshift in the intermediate position of hydraulic neutral. However, according to Tamny, his design change would totally eliminate the possibility of slipping into Reverse from hydraulic neutral. Tamny described his design change as a "99% solution" to the mis-shift problem. While his design change would not eliminate the risk that the car might roll in hydraulic neutral, it would eliminate the most dangerous risk of migration to Reverse and powered movement without a driver.

* * *

The evidence supporting Tamny's conclusion that his design is safer raises a fact question that the jury resolved in favor of the plaintiffs. We conclude that the plaintiffs have presented more than a scintilla of evidence that Tamny's alternative design substantially reduced the risk of injury.

Having determined that the plaintiffs met their burden of proving some evidence of design defect, we need not consider G.M.'s challenge to the findings of a marketing defect or negligence. We next consider whether to give effect to the jury's comparative responsibility findings.

The jury found that Sanchez was fifty percent responsible for his accident. in negligence or strict liability. However, the plaintiffs argue that Sanchez's actions amounted to no more than a failure to discover or guard against a product defect and, because of our decision in *Keen v. Ashot Ashkelon, Ltd.*, such negligence does not constitute a defense to strict liability . . . Implicit in this Court's holding in *Keen* was that a consumer has no duty to discover or guard against a product defect. We believe that a duty to discover defects, and to take precautions in constant anticipation that a product might have a defect, would defeat the purposes of strict liability. Thus, we hold that a consumer has no duty to discover or guard against a product defect, but a consumer's conduct other than the mere failure to discover or guard against a product defect is subject to comparative responsibility. Public policy favors reasonable conduct by consumers regardless of whether a product is defective. A consumer is not relieved of the responsibility to act reasonably nor may a consumer fail to take reasonable precautions regardless of a known or unknown product defect . . . we next determine whether the decedent's conduct in this case was merely the failure to discover or guard against a product defect or some other negligence unrelated to a product defect.

The truck's owner's manual describes safety measures designed to ensure that the truck would not move when parked: (1) set the parking brake; (2) place the truck completely in Park; (3) turn off the engine; (4) remove the key from the ignition; and (5) check that Park is fully engaged by pulling down on the gear shift. Sanchez's father testified that his son probably read the entire owner's manual. The plaintiff's own experts agreed at trial that Sanchez failed to perform any of the safety measures described in the owner's manual and that performing any one of them would have prevented the accident. This evidence is sufficient to support the jury's negligence finding.

Regardless of any danger of a mis-shift, a driver has a duty to take reasonable precautions to secure his vehicle before getting out of it. The danger that it could roll, or move if the engine is running, exists independently of the possibility of a mis-shift. For instance, the driver could inadvertently leave a vehicle in gear or a mechanical problem unrelated to a product defect could prevent Park from fully engaging. A moving vehicle without a driver is a hazard to public safety. The state licenses drivers who have demonstrated the minimum knowledge and skill necessary to safely operate a motor vehicle. Many, perhaps most, consumer products may be operated without a license, including lawn and garden equipment, household appliances, and powered hand tools. It follows then that, because of this licensing requirement, as well as other special duties imposed on drivers, more is expected of an operator of a motor vehicle than of users of most other consumer products. Thus, although we do not expect the average driver to have the engineering background to discover defects in their car's transmission, we do expect the reasonably prudent driver to take safety precautions to prevent a runaway car. Sanchez had a responsibility to operate his truck in a safe manner. The fact that the precautions demanded of a driver generally would have prevented this accident does not make Sanchez's negligence a mere failure to discover or guard against a mis-shift. We hold as a matter of law that such conduct must be scrutinized under the duty to use ordinary care or other applicable duty. We conclude that there was legally sufficient evidence to support the jury's verdict that Sanchez breached the duty to use ordinary care and was fifty percent responsible for the accident.

In conclusion, we hold that (1) there is some evidence of a product defect; (2) comparative responsibility applies because there was evidence of negligence beyond the mere failure to discover or guard against a product defect; and (3) there is no evidence supporting the gross negligence finding. Accordingly, we reverse the court of appeals judgment and render judgment that the plaintiffs recover their actual damages reduced by the jury's finding of fifty percent comparative responsibility.

Another tort defense is assumption of risk, which holds that if the plaintiff discovers a defect and continues to use the product, she has assumed a risk that the defect may cause harm. The test for assumption of risk is whether 1) the plaintiff actually knew and understood the risk or danger from a product defect yet continued to use it; 2) the plaintiff voluntarily encountered the risk while realizing the danger, and 3) the plaintiff's decision to encounter the risk was unreasonable. The following case tests how knowledge and action by the plaintiff is sufficient to determine that the plaintiff did, in fact, accept the risk of injury.

Johnson v. Clark Equipment Co.

547 P.2d 132 (Or. 1976)

Plaintiff was employed as a forklift operator at the Warrenton Lumber Company in Warrenton. His job entailed moving bundles of lumber about the Warrenton plant. Because of his various responsibilities, the job was a rather hectic one. The accident occurred on June 24, 1971, shortly after plaintiff's shift began and while he was engaged in feeding the random planer. Plaintiff was in a hurry and was carrying two banded bundles of 2x4's which were to be placed on the chains leading into the planer. Before the bundles could be placed on the chains, it was necessary to cut the metal bands around them. Normally, these bands were cut either by the forklift driver himself or by another Warrenton employee. On the day of the accident, plaintiff had no one to help him by cutting the bands. Although he normally dismounted his machine and moved to the front to cut the bands on this occasion plaintiff remained in the cab of the forklift and reached through the uprights with the cutters. While he was cutting the bands, his body came in contact with the ascent/descent lever controlling the movement of the forks. The forklift carriage descended and severed his arms just below the elbows.

In his complaint, plaintiff alleged faulty design and manufacture of the forklift. He charged that the forklift was defective and unreasonably dangerous in that (a) the uprights and cross members were positioned in a manner which allowed them to sever plaintiff's arms; (b) no guard or screen was placed between the cab and the uprights; (c) the ascent/descent lever was located so as to permit the operator's body to unintentionally come in contact with it; (d) the lever was not designed to remain in a neutral position until manually released; and (e) no adequate signs were included to warn the operator of the dangers posed by the machine.

As a preliminary matter, we note defendants' contention that any error committed in the instructions given concerning the concept of strict liability and the defense of assumption of risk was harmless because defendants' motions for a directed verdict and for an involuntary nonsuit should have been granted . . . We believe that there was a jury question as to the existence of the alleged defects and as to whether such defects rendered the forklift dangerously defective.

The concept of assumption of risk in a products liability case differs somewhat from the traditional tort doctrine of assumption of risk. Accordingly, in *Findlay v. Copeland Lumber Co.*, we adopted the definition of assumption of risk for products liability cases which is contained in Comment N to § 402A of the Restatement of Torts 2d (1965). In contrast to the more traditional defense which includes only two elements—subjective knowledge and voluntary encounter—Comment N sets forth three elements which must be shown before the plaintiff can be barred from recovery. The defendant must show, first, that the plaintiff Himself actually knew and appreciated the particular risk or danger created by the defect; second, that plaintiff voluntarily encountered the risk while realizing the danger; and, third, that plaintiff's decision to voluntarily encounter the known risk was unreasonable. If the trier of fact finds that any one of these elements did not exist in a particular case, the defense cannot be sustained.

In this case, although the trial court properly began by distinguishing assumption of risk from contributory negligence, the court's definition of assumption of risk was not complete. There was no discussion of the element of unreasonableness as it relates to plaintiff's decision to encounter the risk. Although the court did not least mention the other two elements, proof of all three elements is essential to the assumption of the risk defense outlined in Comment N, and adopted by this court in *Findlay v. Copeland Lumber, supra.*

The reasonableness of any decision to encounter a known danger must depend upon the circumstances surrounding that decision as well as on the relative probability and gravity of the risk incurred. Whenever the jury attempts to ascertain whether a plaintiff's decision to encounter a known risk was reasonable, it will be necessary for them to consider the conditions which motivated the decision, the pressures which were operating on the plaintiff, and the amount of time which he had to make the decision.

It should be emphasized that this element of unreasonableness pertains only to the nature of plaintiff's decision to encounter the known danger. We are not concerned with the apparent reasonableness or unreasonableness of the physical conduct through which plaintiff encountered the danger, but rather the reasonableness of his decision to do so. This distinction, while seemingly theoretical, is significant.

"We feel that working conditions and related circumstances are a particularly relevant consideration in an inquiry into the reasonableness of a decision to encounter a job-related danger. Such factors often will have a strong influence on that decision, and, in some cases, they may represent the most important motivational factors."

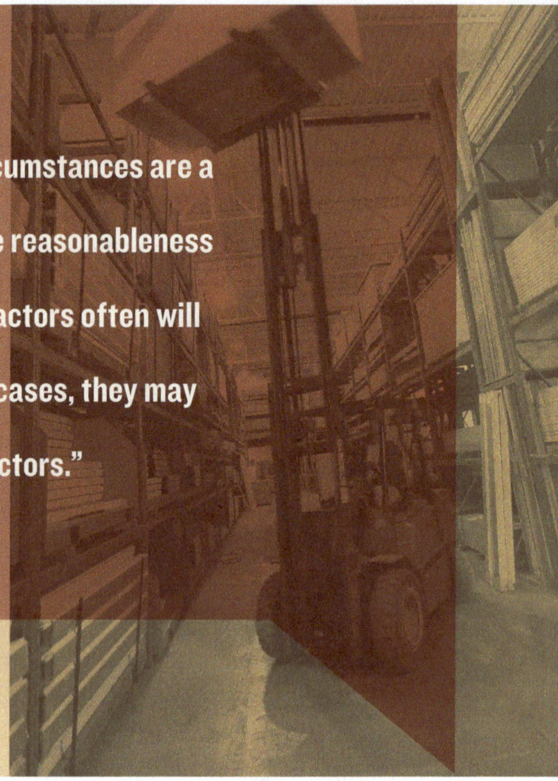

Image: thinkstock.com

The actions through which one encounters a known danger may appear unreasonable—such as reaching through the uprights of a forklift—and yet the decision to so act still could be found to be reasonable when the circumstances surrounding the incident are considered.

We feel that working conditions and related circumstances are a particularly relevant consideration in an inquiry into the reasonableness of a decision to encounter a job-related danger. Such factors often will have a strong influence on that decision, and, in some cases, they may represent the most important motivational factors. For example, a worker might fear that a slowdown in his individual production would slow down the entire production team and thereby draw the attention of his boss. If he has a history of such slow-downs, or of causing excessive spoilage or ruining machine parts, he may have good cause to fear dismissal. The job market could be tight, and he may have little hope of being able to find a new job. Moreover, the situation may demand an immediate, hurried decision. It is certainly possible that, under such circumstances, a reasonable jury could find that his decision to encounter a known risk was not unreasonable.

Hindsight is always better than foresight, and the reasonableness of a decision to encounter a risk should be determined as of the time that decision is made. In this case there was considerable testimony about the hectic nature of the forklift driver's job from both the plaintiff himself and from a former driver who had been doing the same work plaintiff was doing at the time of the injury, and who had asked for another position when he found that he was no longer able to keep up that job's demands. Plaintiff indicated that if his forklift had been able to keep up with the heavy loads and the fast pace which he was required to maintain, he would not have been in a rush, time would not have been so important, and he would have been able to get off the machine to cut the wire bands. Plaintiff testified that all he was thinking of at the time of the accident was '(t)he time that I had to do the job in, and the job I was doing.' He also stated that if he had had time to think about it he would not have reached through the uprights. Significantly, the defendants' brief concedes that plaintiff encountered the risk only because of his working conditions, and at trial defendants even argued that such factors were the sole cause of plaintiff's injury.

Therefore, even if the jury disbelieved plaintiff's testimony and concluded that he knew and appreciated the danger that the carriage might somehow start to descend while his arms were through the uprights, and, further, that his actions in reaching through the uprights were voluntary, there would still remain an issue for the jury's consideration—whether, under the evidence in this case, his decision to do so was unreasonable. The issue is not whether it might have been more reasonable to have selected another method of cutting the bands around the lumber but rather, whether it was unreasonable, under all the circumstances, for plaintiff to have selected the method he did. Thus, considering all these circumstances, we find that the requested instruction should have been given.

Reversed and remanded for a new trial.

Another defense that may be used is one of **product misuse**, which occurs when the plaintiff uses the product in a way unintended by the seller and in a way that the seller could not have reasonably anticipated, but where the plaintiff did not directly appreciate the risk itself (which would be more akin to assumption of risk). Related to this is the **defense of alteration of a product**, where the plaintiff is injured due to a subsequent alteration to a product that was otherwise without defect. These cases are very contentious. A seller has reason to complain that they should not be liable if a consumer uses the product in a way that it is not supposed to be used. The buyer's response is that a seller should reasonably foresee the uses a buyer may make of the product and should therefore protect the buyer in such instances. The following case explores these arguments.

Jones v. Ryobi, Ltd.

37 F.3d 423, 425 (8th Cir. 1994)

Jennifer Jones was employed at Business Cards Tomorrow (BCT) as the operator of a small printing press known as an offset duplicator. Jones seriously injured her left hand when she caught it in the moving parts of the press. The press involved in Jones's injury operates by passing blank paper through several moving parts, imprinting an image on the paper, and dispensing the printed paper through upper and lower "eject wheels." To avoid streaking the freshly printed image, on each job the operator must adjust the eject wheels to ensure the wheels do not touch the freshly printed area. The press was manufactured and sold to BCT equipped with both a plastic guard that prevented the operator from reaching into the moving parts to adjust the eject wheels, and an electric interlock switch that automatically shut off the press if the guard was opened. Sometime after the press was manufactured and delivered to BCT, the guard was removed and the interlock switch was disabled to allow the press to run without the guard. Because this modification increased production by saving the few seconds required to stop and to restart the press when the operator adjusted the eject wheels, the modification was a common practice in the printing industry.

Jones learned to operate the press by watching other BCT employees. Jones testified she knew the guard was missing and knew it was dangerous to have her hands near the unguarded moving parts, but her supervisor pressured her to save time by adjusting the eject wheels while the press was running. Jones feared she would be fired if she took the time to stop the press. While Jones was adjusting the eject wheels on the running press, a noise startled her. Jones jumped and her left hand was caught in the press's moving parts and crushed.

In granting the manufacturer's and the distributor's motions for judgment as a matter of law (JAML), the district court relied on the open and obvious nature of the asserted danger. *See* Restatement (Second) of Torts § 402A cmt. i (1965) (consumer expectation test). The district court did not reach the manufacturer's and the distributor's other grounds for JAML. We review the district court's grant of JAML de novo; thus, we may affirm on another ground.

To recover on a theory of strict liability for defective design under Missouri law, Jones must prove she was injured as a direct result of a defect that existed when the press was sold. *Jasinski v. Ford Motor Co.*, Jones had the burden to show the press had not been modified to create a defect that could have proximately caused her injury. *Id.* Jones failed to meet this burden because her evidence showed the press had been substantially modified by removing the safety guard and disabling the interlock switch, and showed the modification caused her injury. **When a third party's modification makes a safe product unsafe, the seller is relieved of liability even if the modification is foreseeable. Jones did not show who modified the press, but her**

evidence clearly showed that a third party, not the manufacturer or the distributor, was responsible for the modification. Although the manufacturer provided tools for general maintenance of the press that could also be used to remove the guard, we do not believe this made the manufacturer responsible for the guard's removal. Jones produced no evidence that any representative of the manufacturer or the distributor removed the guard or instructed BCT to remove the guard from the press involved in Jones's injury. Indeed, the distributor's service representative testified he told BCT's owner several times the guard should be replaced, but BCT's owner shrugged off the suggestion. Because BCT knew the guard was missing and the interlock switch was disabled, but did not follow the distributor's advice to repair the disabled safety features, the distributor's service work on the press did not extend the distributor's liability to defects that were not present when the press was sold. Because Jones's evidence showed a third party's modification, not a defect existing when the press was sold, was the sole cause of her injury, her strict product liability claim for defective design fails as a matter of law.

The district court thus properly granted the manufacturer's and the distributor's JAML motions.

Accordingly, we affirm.

Because the employer knew there was an alteration and disabled safety features but did not follow the distributor's advice to repair these alterations, the alteration of the press did not extend the distributor's liability for defective design to defects that were not present when the press was sold.

As we have already seen, courts do expect companies to foresee some degree of product misuse. That is why there are so many warning labels on ladders and lawn mowers. Potential misuse is particularly foreseeable when selling a product to the public. However, the more one is selling a product to another business, the more closely courts will look at the alleged misuses as they did in the above case.

Finally, as with limitations on warranties on the basis of time, so too will legislatures enact **statutes of repose** that provide a time frame within which one must bring a suit for a defective product. These time limitations force an injured party to file suit within a time specified by the statute or forfeit their rights to sue.

NOTES AND COMMENTS on the Legal Environment of Business

1. **ONE THING TO KEEP IN MIND** about product liability is that, perhaps more so than many other branches of the law, it continues to rapidly develop before our eyes. Some reform efforts now seek to make tests of times when products vary from design defects similar to strict liability standards, even if the manufacturer used all possible care. [1] At the same time, reformers have proposed that design defects themselves be treated more on a negligence standard. Other proposals pertain to the use of warnings and how they increase or decrease the safety of products.

2. **THE ATTEMPT TO REIGN IN DAMAGE AWARDS,** especially punitive damage awards, remains a hotly contested issue, and there is little reason to believe that it will be resolved soon. What do you think the proper mix of punitive and compensatory damage should be? Should there be limits on the amount of punitive damages? On the amount of pain and suffering? What kind of rules would you propose? Do you think damages should all go to the injured party or should some be paid to a public fund?

3. **DO YOU BELIEVE** that tort judgments reflect societal values as to how to assign fault and responsibility? Do you think such judgments assess such fault fairly?

NOTES AND COMMENTS on the Ethical Environment of Business

1. **WE HAVE ALREADY** seen that both contracts and torts are loaded with ethical questions. Thus, it is not surprising that products liability, a combination of the two, continue the questions we had in those chapters.

   Of all the issues associated with products liability, the one business students most want to debate seems to be the question of product misuse. It is one thing for an injured party to sue a manufacturer if the product blows up in their face or cuts their hand off through no fault of the injured party. It is another thing when the injured party used the product in a way that it was not intended to be used. For example, take another look at the *Wyda* case in this chapter. It is an example of a misuse of a product by the injured party.

The question for the case, as with other product misuses cases, is whether the misuse of the product undercuts any claim for recovery or, on the other hand, whether if a manufacturer can reasonably foresee that the product is being misused, should the manufacturer take steps to make sure that a person is not injured through additional safety devices. This question brings up questions of responsibility for one's actions. Shouldn't a person be responsible for their own actions? If I am reckless enough to stand on the very top of a ladder and fall off, isn't that the cause of my injuries? On the other hand, if a product is being produced that has a flaw in it so that it requires some jimmying in order to get it to work right, shouldn't the manufacturer be held liable? And, of course, the real debates occur in between these two fairly extreme cases.

2. **SO IN THE USUAL STEP** of going back through the cases in the chapter, keep an eye on this balance that essentially asks: who is in the best position to prevent an injury from happening? And once you determine who is in that position, then what laws should be enacted by a legislature (or decided by a court), to put the responsibility on that person.

3. **AS WITH TORTS,** issues of damages loom large in products liability cases and often times even more so because the setting for a products liability case is a company (which connotes, perhaps wrongly, that there are deep pockets involved) that caused injury to a person. Thus, is there money to be had from a suit and, in order to get the company to changes its ways so it produces a safer product, can punitive damages be a lever to get the company's attention?

4. **THE QUESTION OF** creating safe products and the costs of making the product safe, most often done in strict liability cases, also raise ethical questions too. What is that balance between safety and expense? If the law were not there to force companies to pay more attention to safe products, would companies still aim to spend money for safety? In other words, are market forces enough to create the duties for companies to attend sufficiently to safety? Why do you believe that? And if you don't—that is, if you think some external legal force is required for companies to attend to safety—then how far should the law go?

5. **FINALLY, AS YOU** go through the warranty-related cases, ask just how far should liability reach under each of the warranty theories, but especially through the implied warranty of merchantability. Should it apply to the seller of the product? The manufacturer? A middle-man? The courts, as we have seen, have made judgments about these, but how far do you think liability should extend.

6. **TURNING TO *ETHICS VIGNETTES*,** take a look at some more "in the weeds" issues. For example, Chapter 2's case on The Truck Accident, looks at some interesting accounting questions of how one goes about calculating damages. Especially with currency fluctuations, those calculations themselves often come with their own set of ethical questions.

7. **NEXT TAKE A** look at Chapter 10's essay by Professor Presser on how the law of Products Liability should be harmonized with that of other countries? This brings a comparative analysis to these kinds of cases. The U.S. approach to product liability has quite a few differences than that of other countries. Professor Presser provides an interesting set of questions of how to harmonized the U.S. approach with those.

8. **FINALLY, TAKE A** look at Chapter 5's article on DePuy's Dilemma. This is a student paper that was written for an ethics course. It sets out a very interesting dilemma on the balance between safety and being able to make enough money to be able to offer a hip replacement device.

1 see Restatement of Torts 3

CHAPTER

13

The Law of Agency

Agency, as a part of business law, is that body of law that determines when one person (the principal) is legally responsible for the acts of another (the agent). The law of agency also determines the duty which the agent owes to the principal. Without the law of Agency, complex business organizations would be impossible and we may regard it as a fundamental building block of business law, just as are the doctrines of property, torts and contracts, which we have previously explored. For our purposes, then, the two main questions in the first part of this chapter are: (1) when is the agency relationship created, and (2) what duties does the agent owe the principal? In the second part of this chapter, we will explore the ways in which the principal can be liable, contractually or through tort, to a third party for the actions of the agent. The final part of this chapter will look at some lingering issues, including the agent's own responsibility to a third party.

I. Relationship of Principal and Agent

Agency law is contract law. In order for there to be an agency relationship, the principal and the agent need to have some meeting of the minds where there is a proposal (and offer) and an acceptance to do something. There has to be consideration and the purpose needs to be lawful. After all, the courts will not enforce an agreement for the agent to do something illegal. As we will see later in the chapter, the capacity aspect is different. In a "regular" contract, both parties need to have capacity and so if one party does not—for example, if one party is a minor—then the contract may not be valid. However, with an agency relationship, the agent only needs to have the capacity necessary to understand the nature of the duties they are to carry out. This is one reason why high school students, who otherwise would not have capacity to contract, have summer and after-school jobs. (Legislatures also often step in to specify workplace hours, but that is a separate question.)

Thus, as you read this chapter, bear in mind those principles that you learned in common law contracts. The reason to remember common law principles, as opposed to the Uniform Commercial Code rules, is that principal-agent relationships are just that: relationships. They are service contracts rather than contracts involving the sale of goods, which are the kinds of contracts to which the UCC applies.

A. CREATION OF THE AGENCY RELATIONSHIP

According to § 1.01 of the Restatement of Agency (3rd) "Agency is the fiduciary relationship that arises when one person (a 'principal') manifests assent to another person (an 'agent') that the agent shall act on the principal's behalf and subject to the principal's control, and the agent manifests assent or otherwise consents so to act." We will soon explore what is meant by "fiduciary relationship," but let's first explore how the law determines whether the manifestation of assent to create the agency relationship is found. The principal will be liable to third parties for the acts of an agent, so long as the agent is acting within the scope of the authority the principal has granted the agent. This question, whether the principal gives the agent the proper "authority" to act on the principal's behalf, is not quite as straightforward as we might think. Consider the following intriguing agency case.

Croisant v. Watrud

248 Or. 234, 432 P.2d 799 (1967)

* * *

O'Connell, Justice, for the court

This is a [lawsuit] brought against [some] partners in a firm of certified public accountants and the [estate] of a deceased partner, LaVern Watrud. * * * The defendants engaged in the accounting practice with their principal office in Klamath Falls and their branch office in Medford. Watrud was in charge of the Medford office. Plaintiff was the owner of a sawmill, timberlands, and other property over which she exercised general control, delegating the details of management of the business to others.

In 1955 plaintiff employed the defendant partnership to advise her on tax matters and to prepare income tax returns for her business enterprises. All of these services were performed by Watrud * * * . In 1956 plaintiff sold her sawmill. Thereafter her business activities consisted almost entirely of making collections under the contract for the sale of the mill, collections on the sale of timber, collections of rents, and various disbursements from the moneys so collected.

In 1957 plaintiff moved to California. She made arrangements with Watrud to make the collections referred to above, to make certain disbursements, to keep her financial books and records, and to prepare her financial statements and tax returns. The moneys collected by Watrud were deposited in the account of the Lloyd Timber Company (plaintiff 's business name in Oregon) in a Grants Pass bank.

In 1957 plaintiff learned that her husband, Glenn Lloyd, had induced Watrud to make unauthorized payments out of the Lloyd Timber Company account to him. Plaintiff instructed Watrud not to make any further payments to her husband, but Watrud violated her instructions. Plaintiff was informed of these subsequent misappropriations by Watrud on behalf of Glenn Lloyd in 1958. She also learned that her husband was unfaithful to her. Plaintiff again excused Watrud's breach of trust and her husband's infidelity. After their reconciliation, plaintiff and her husband took a trip to Europe. When they returned, plaintiff discovered that her husband had forged checks on her California bank account and had also forged her signature upon a $75,000 note and negotiated it. Plaintiff also became aware of the fact that Watrud had continued to pay money to Glenn Lloyd out of plaintiff 's Oregon account. In addition, she learned that Watrud, without authorization, had drawn a check payable to himself. When Watrud was confronted with this evidence he finally acknowledged his abuse of his trust. Soon thereafter Watrud died from gunshot wounds while hunting.

Plaintiff then filed this suit . . . against [Watrud's] surviving partners [of the firm of accountants].

* * *

It is undisputed that plaintiff 's initial business arrangements for tax advice and the preparation of tax returns were with the partnership and not simply with Watrud individually. After the partnership was employed, Watrud individually performed all of the services sought by plaintiff. As time went on plaintiff called upon Watrud to perform additional services in connection with her business including the collection and disbursements of funds. The initial question is whether these subsequent services performed by Watrud are to be regarded as having been performed as a part of the partnership business or under a separate arrangement calling only for the services of Watrud personally.

The record suggests that plaintiff, Watrud, and defendants considered all of Watrud's services to the plaintiff as services performed by a member of a partnership on behalf of that firm. The partnership received a check each month for all of Watrud's services including the services involved in handling plaintiff 's business affairs. Had the parties viewed the services in making collections and disbursements for plaintiff as independent activities separate compensation would have been in order. Although the partnership's Medford office was geographically separated from the Klamath Falls office, both operations constituted one autonomous business enterprise and consequently defendants cannot insulate themselves from liability on the ground that the Medford office was a separate business operation. Defendants are liable, therefore, if Watrud can be regarded as the agent of the partnership in performing the fund-handling services for plaintiff.

It is clear that Watrud had no express authority from defendants to perform these services. And there was no evidence from which an authority implied in fact could be derived. If it were common knowledge that accountants frequently act as trustees in the collection and disbursement of funds, we would be in a position to take judicial notice of the common practice and thus find an implied authority or an apparent authority. But we have no basis for saying that accountants commonly or frequently perform fund-handling services. Thus we conclude that liability cannot be rested upon a manifestation by defendants that they assented to be bound for such services. However, an agent can impose liability upon his principal even where there is no actual or apparent authority or estoppel. An agent may have an "inherent agency power" to bind his principal. Such power is defined in Restatement (Second), Agency § 8A as "the power of an agent which is derived not from authority, apparent authority or estoppel, but solely from the agency relation and exists for the protection of persons harmed by or dealing with a servant or other agent." When an agent has acted improperly in entering into a contract the inherent agency power "is based neither upon the consent of the principal nor upon his manifestations."

* * *

It will be noted that Section 161 states that the principal is liable only for his agent's acts "which *usually accompany* or are *incidental* to transactions which the agent is authorized to conduct * * * ." (Emphasis added.) As we have previously observed, we have neither evidence nor judicial knowledge of the practice of accountancy from which to decide whether the collection and disbursement of accounts is commonly undertaken by accountants. We cannot say, therefore, that the fund-handling services performed by Watrud in this case were the type which "usually accompany" the transactions which accountants ordinarily conduct viewed from the standpoint of those engaged in accountancy. Upon similar reasoning we are unable to say that the services here were "incidental" to the transactions Watrud was authorized to conduct. But this does not conclude the matter. Assuming that accountants do not regard the collection and disbursement of funds as a part of the services usually offered by members of their profession, what significance should

this have if, in the particular circumstances, a person dealing with a member of an accounting partnership reasonably believes that accountants perform the kind of service which he seeks to have performed? * * *

If a third person reasonably believes that the services he has requested of a member of an accounting partnership is undertaken as a part of the partnership business, the partnership should be bound for a breach of trust incident to that employment even though those engaged in the practice of accountancy would regard as unusual the performance of such service by an accounting firm. The reasonableness of a third person's belief in assuming that a partner is acting within the scope of the partnership should not be tested by the profession's own description of the function of its members. Those who seek accounting services may not understand the refinements made by accountants in defining the services they offer to the public. Whether a third person's belief is reasonable in assuming that the service he seeks is within the domain of the profession is a question which must be answered upon the basis of the facts in the particular case.

We are of the opinion that the facts in the present case are sufficient to establish a reasonable belief on the part of plaintiff that Watrud had undertaken all of the work assigned to him by plaintiff as a continuation of the original employment of the partnership firm. The initial work for which defendants were engaged was the preparation of income tax returns. Thereafter plaintiff sought Watrud's advice on tax matters and continued to have him prepare income tax returns for her business ventures. Watrud did not do the actual bookkeeping for plaintiff 's business activities when the partnership was first employed, but eventually he prepared and kept in his own custody the financial books and records of plaintiff 's enterprises. This service was assumed by Watrud when plaintiff decided to move to California permanently. When plaintiff left Grants Pass she also arranged with Watrud to have him receive all the income from her Oregon and California properties and to make disbursements from the money so collected. Before she employed him to handle her funds she asked him if he was bonded and he assured her that he was. We think it is important to note that the increased responsibilities directed to Watrud coincided with plaintiff's departure for California.

Thereafter, Watrud was the only person who drew checks on the account set up pursuant to the arrangement with plaintiff, although the bank signature card included the names of plaintiff and others. Watrud handled a very substantial amount of plaintiff 's money during the course of his employment, drawing as many as 1500 checks per year. The bank statements and cancelled checks were sent directly to Watrud; he collected her business mail at her post office box in Grants Pass and in other respects acted in her behalf after her departure for California. As we have already mentioned, the partnership received compensation for these services at the rate of $800 per month. As plaintiff testified, nothing was ever said or done by Watrud which might have indicated to her that he was acting on his account as distinguished from acting for the partnership. It was reasonable for plaintiff to assume that the added assignment of collecting and disbursing funds delegated to Watrud was an integral part of the function of one employed to keep the accounts reflecting the income and disbursement of those funds. This assumption, we think, is even more likely in circumstances such as we have here where there is trust and confidence reposed in the person employed. * * *

This case serves many purposes for us, but the primary one is to introduce you to the doctrines of agency, and, indeed, those of partnership. To begin with the basics, as indicated earlier, an agent is someone who acts on behalf of and subject to the control of another, known as the principal. While acting on behalf of a principal, an agent possesses a fiduciary duty to the principal, which means that he or she must place the principal's financial interests above the agent's own. As this case makes clear, enunciating another basic principle of agency, the principal is bound by the acts of the agent. In other words, the principal is liable to third parties as a result of obligations created by the agent's interaction with the third party, if the agent was acting according to the directions of the principal within the scope of his employment, if, as the law puts it, the agent acted pursuant to sufficient authority given by the principal.

As you will have discerned from the case, there are several different kinds of authority the principal can grant the agent. These include, among others, **actual authority, apparent authority, agency by estoppel**, and, finally, the elusive kind of authority discussed in the *Croisant* case, **inherent authority**.

A principal is also liable for the acts of his or her agent even if no authority was present when the acts purportedly binding the principal occurred if the principal later **ratifies** the acts of the agent, that is, agrees to accept liability for them. As agency law is an important body of doctrines for both partnerships and corporations, it is worth going into a bit more detail about the agent's authority. As you may have discerned from the case above, in a partnership, absent a contrary agreement, all of the partners are regarded as agents of the partnership. This is why the other partners of the accounting partnership in the case were held liable for the results of Watrud's conduct. In a corporation or other forms of business organizations, various persons (officers, directors, employees) may, if given the proper authority, act as agents for those business organizations.

B. DUTIES OF AGENT TO PRINCIPAL

Surely one of the most remarkable things about the law of agency is the manner in which the law attempts to ensure that the agent (for whose actions the principal is liable) serves the interests of the principal. This is accomplished by the enforcement of the agent's fiduciary duty to the principal. Essentially, fiduciary duty means that the agent's responsibility is to place the interests of the principal ahead of the agent's own interests. With a little reflection, you can see that this is not an easy thing to do, yet the structure of agency law as well as modern business organizations greatly depend on agents exercising this duty. The extent to which this will be done is illustrated by the following case. Does it seem to you that the law of agency goes too far, not far enough, or just the right distance?

Tarnowski v. Resop

236 Minn. 33, 51 N.W.2d 801 (1952)

* * *

KNUTSON, J.

Plaintiff * * * engaged defendant as his agent to investigate and negotiate for the purchase of a route of coin-operated music machines. On June 2, 1947, relying upon the advice of defendant * * * plaintiff purchased such a business from Phillip Loechler and Lyle Mayer of Rochester, Minnesota, who will be referred to hereinafter as the sellers. The business was located at La Crosse, Wisconsin, and throughout the surrounding territory. Plaintiff alleges that defendant represented to him that he had made a thorough investigation of the route; that it had 75 locations in operation; that one or more machines were at each location; that the equipment at each location was not more than six months old; and that the gross income from all locations amounted to more than $3,000 per month. As a matter of fact, defendant had made only a superficial investigation and had investigated only five of the locations. Other than that, he had adopted false representations of the sellers as to the other locations and had passed them on to plaintiff as his own. Plaintiff was to pay $30,620 for the business. He paid $11,000 down. About six weeks after the purchase, plaintiff discovered that the representations made to him by defendant were false, in that there were not more than 47 locations; that at some of the locations there were no machines and at others there were machines more than six months old, some of them being seven years old; and that the gross income was far less than $3,000 per month. Upon discovering the falsity of defendant's representations and those of the sellers, plaintiff rescinded the sale. He offered to return what he had received, and he demanded the return of his money. The sellers refused to comply, and he brought suit against them in the district court of Olmsted county. The action was tried, resulting in a verdict of $10,000 for plaintiff. Thereafter, the sellers paid plaintiff $9,500, after which the action was dismissed with prejudice pursuant to a stipulation of the parties.

In this action, brought in Hennepin county, plaintiff alleges that defendant, while acting as agent for him, collected a secret commission from the sellers for consummating the sale, which plaintiff seeks to recover under his first cause of action. In his second cause of action, he seeks to recover damages [besides the side-payment to the agent, incidental to the case.] The case was tried to a jury, and plaintiff recovered a verdict of $5,200. This appeal is from the judgment entered pursuant thereto.

* * *

1. With respect to plaintiff 's first cause of action, the principle that all profits made by an agent in the course of an agency belong to the principal, whether they are the fruits of performance or the violation of an agent's duty, is firmly established and universally recognized. * * * It matters not that the principal has suffered no damage or even that the transaction has been profitable to him. * * *

"Fidelity in the agent is what is aimed at, and, as a means of securing it, the law will not permit him to place himself in a position in which he may be tempted by his own private interests to disregard those of his principal."

The rule and the basis therefor are well stated in *Lum v. McEwen*,, where, speaking through Mr. Justice Mitchell, we said: "Actual injury is not the principle the law proceeds on, in holding such transactions void. Fidelity in the agent is what is aimed at, and, as a means of securing it, the law will not permit him to place himself in a position in which he may be tempted by his own private interests to disregard those of his principal. * * * It is not material that no actual injury to the company [principal] resulted, or that the policy recommended may have been for its best interest. Courts will not inquire into these matters. It is enough to know that the agent in fact placed himself in such relations that he might be tempted by his own interests to disregard those of his principal. "The transaction was nothing more or less than the acceptance by the agent of a bribe to perform his duties in the manner desired by the person who gave the bribe. Such a contract is void.

* * *

It follows that, insofar as the secret commission of $2,000 received by the agent is concerned, plaintiff had an absolute right thereto, irrespective of any recovery resulting from the action against the sellers for rescission.

2. Plaintiff 's second cause of action is brought to recover damages for (1) losses suffered in the operation of the business prior to rescission; (2) loss of time devoted to operation; (3) expenses in connection with rescission of the sale and investigation therewith; (4) nontaxable expenses in connection with the prosecution of the suit against the sellers; and (5) attorneys' fees in connection with the suit.

* * * Our inquiry is limited to a consideration of the question whether a principal may recover [from] an agent who has breached his trust the items of damage mentioned after a successful prosecution of an action for rescission against the third parties with whom the agent dealt for his principal.

The general rule is stated in Restatement, Agency, § 407(1), as follows:

> "If an agent has received a benefit as a result of violating his duty of loyalty, the principal is entitled to recover from him what he has so received, its value, or its proceeds, and also the amount of damage thereby caused, except that if the violation consists of the wrongful disposal of the principal's property, the principal cannot recover its value and also what the agent received in exchange therefor."
>
> * * *.

The general rule is given in Restatement, Torts, § 910, as follows: "A person injured by the tort of another is entitled to recover damages from him for all harm, past, present and prospective, legally caused by the tort." ***Bergquist v. Kreidler*** **involved an action to recover attorneys' fees expended by plaintiffs in an action seeking to enforce and protect their right to the possession of real estate. Defendant, acting as the owner's agent, had falsely represented to plaintiffs that they could have possession on August 1, 1920. It developed after plaintiffs had purchased the premises that a tenant had a lease running to August 1, 1922, on a rental much lower than the actual value of the premises. Defendant (the agent) conceded that plaintiffs were entitled to recover the loss in rent, but contended that attorneys' fees and disbursements expended by plaintiffs in testing the validity of the tenant's lease were not recoverable. In affirming plaintiffs' right to recover we said (158 Minn. 132, 196 N.W. 966): " * * * the litigation in which plaintiffs became involved was the direct, legitimate and a to-be-expected result of appellant's misrepresentation. The loss sustained by plaintiffs in conducting that litigation 'is plainly traceable' to appellant's wrong and he should make compensation accordingly."**

So far as the right to recover attorneys' fees is concerned, the same may be said in this case. Plaintiff sought to return what had been received and demanded a return of his down payment. The sellers refused. He thereupon sued to accomplish this purpose, as he had a right to do, and was successful. His attorneys' fees and expenses of suit were directly traceable to the harm caused by defendant's wrongful act. As such, they are recoverable. * * * The same is true of the other elements of damage involved. ***See, generally,*** **15** ***Am. Jur., Damages,*** **§ 138.**

3. Defendant contends that plaintiff had an election of remedies and, having elected to proceed against the sellers to recover what he had paid, is now barred from proceeding against defendant. It is true that upon discovery of the fraud plaintiff had an election of remedies against the sellers. It is not true, however, that, having elected

to sue for recovery of that with which he had parted, he is barred from proceeding against his agent to recover damages for [the agent's] tortious conduct. While some of the allegations in plaintiff 's complaint against the sellers are similar to or identical with those in his complaint in this case, insofar as the fraud is concerned, the right of recovery here against the agent goes much further than the action against the sellers. Many of the elements of damage against the agent are not available to plaintiff against the sellers. For instance, he has no right to recover attorneys' fees and expenses of the litigation against the sellers. He has that right against the agent. * * *

Losses directly flowing from the agent's tortious conduct are not recoverable against the sellers in an action for rescission, but they may be recovered against the agent, whose breach of faith has caused such losses.

4. Nor is the settlement and dismissal of the action against the sellers a bar to an action against the agent, for the same reasons as stated above. The sellers and agent are not joint tortfeasors in the sense that their wrongful conduct necessarily grows out of the same wrong. Their individual torts may have been based on the same fraud, but their liabilities to plaintiff do not have the same limitations. In simple terms, the causes of action are not the same. * * *

One can summarize the duties of the agent to the principal as the fiduciary duty of care described above. This would include avoiding conflicts of interest, maintaining confidences, and not competing with the principal. In addition, the agent has the duty to obey reasonable instructions of the principal. If the principal directs the agent to undertake some illegal activity, then the agent of course, may (and should) refrain from doing so. In this sense, agency principles are like those of the military, where a subordinate is to carry out the orders of a commanding officer, but if that officer were to instruct a soldier to torture innocent civilians, the soldier could (and should) refuse. It is certainly possible, of course, that the agent might then be fired or disciplined by the principal, but the subordinate agent would have grounds for recovery and/or exoneration.

Finally, the agent has the duty to exercise reasonable care in the work they do on behalf of the principal. This requires a level of diligence that would typically be exercised by a person doing the kind of work done by the agent and to act in a way that protects the reputation of the principal. In some cases, the agent must maintain proper records as well.

C. DUTIES OF PRINCIPAL TO THE AGENT

The duties of the principal to the agent tend to be fewer and basically are to provide compensation for the work done by the agent and reasonable reimbursement for expenses incurred. There are many different kinds of ways a principal might compensate an agent, ranging from an hourly basis to a contingent fee or based on the accomplishment of a particular job. The reimbursement requirement is relatively straightforward, but also includes indemnifying the agent for any authorized actions the agent took on behalf of the principal that caused injury. We have already seen an example of how the principal is liable for the actions of an agent while on the job and we will explore this a bit more in materials to follow.

D. TERMINATION OF THE AGENCY RELATIONSHIP

There are five ways in which an agency relationship can be terminated. The most basic one is an action by either party that amounts to "I quit" or "You're fired." Because of the nature of the agency relationship, there are times when the relationship is terminated because of the operation of law. If the agent or principal dies, for example, then the relationship ends. Of course, the parties may have arranged for an immediate successor to step into the deceased party's role. Often when a person executes a power of attorney, which is a document that authorizes another person to transact business on one's behalf, the document contains a provision that in the event the agent dies, a successor immediately takes over. Even if that is the case, however, then the agency relationship has changed because a different party has entered the mix. Other ways in which an agency relationship can terminate because of the operation of law would be the loss of the contractual capacity of the principal or the requisite capacity of the agent, the bankruptcy of either party, or a legal authority making the activity of the relationship illegal.

Another way of terminating the relationship is if one of the parties breached their duty to the other party. We have already seen examples of this in the cases in this chapter. The fourth and fifth ways share a common element of time. Suppose the agency relationship is based on the occurrence of a specific event; for example, if a politician hires someone to be their campaign manager. When the campaign ends, the event for which the agent was hired is over and so might the agency relationship be as well unless the parties desire to continue it. Similarly, a lapse of time might end the agency relationship.

The following case looks at the termination of an agency relationship. In this particular case, the agent was forced out by others who did not the way the agent exercised authority, so the question became whether the principal had the capacity to terminate the relationship.

Gaddy v. Douglass

359 S.C. 329, 597 S.E.2d 12 (2004)

Ms. M was born in 1918 and grew up in Fairfield County. She moved to Greenville, where she majored in sociology at Furman University and later worked for the South Carolina Department of Social Services. After retiring, Ms. M returned to Fairfield where she lived on her family farm with her brother, a dentist, until his death in the early 1980s. Ms. M never married.

Dr. Gaddy was Ms. M's physician and a close family friend. Ms. M and Dr. Gaddy's family lived on nearby farms and visited each other frequently throughout the 1980s and 1990s. For many years Ms. M spent holidays and birthdays with the Gaddy family rather than her own family. She also attended the Gaddy family reunions and visited Dr. Gaddy's family in Aiken. Eventually, Ms. M grew to refer to Dr. Gaddy as her "son" and his children as her "grandchildren."

Conversely, Ms. M had little contact with many of her relatives, including Appellants.

In 1988, Ms. M asked Dr. Gaddy to accompany her to a meeting with Albert C. Todd, III, her estate-planning attorney. After Ms. M met privately with Todd, Dr. Gaddy was called into Todd's office, at which point Todd informed Dr. Gaddy that Ms. M desired for Dr. Gaddy to handle her affairs. Dr. Gaddy consented. Ms. M then executed a durable general power of attorney (1988 durable power of attorney) designating Dr. Gaddy as her attorney-in-fact. She also executed a will (1988 Will) leaving Dr. Gaddy her personal property and farm, and appointing him as trustee of a revocable trust she created to provide scholarships to the Medical University of South Carolina.

Dr. Gaddy did not immediately record the 1988 durable power of attorney, and Ms. M continued to manage her affairs. However, by 1994, Ms. M began showing signs of dementia. For example, she became forgetful, locked herself out of her home, and neglected her personal hygiene. She eventually stopped cooking and cleaning for herself. Concerns about Ms. M's progressively worsening mental condition prompted Dr. Gaddy to file the 1988 durable power of attorney in November 1995. Pursuant to the 1988 durable power of attorney, Dr. Gaddy began to act as Ms. M's attorney-in-fact and assumed control of her finances, farm, and health care. His responsibilities included paying her bills, tilling her garden, repairing fences, and hiring caregivers.

In March 1996, Dr. Gaddy discovered Ms. M had fallen in her home and fractured a vertebra. Ms. M was hospitalized for six weeks. During the hospitalization, Dr. Gaddy fumigated and cleaned her home, which had become flea-infested and unclean to the point where rat droppings were found in the house. Finding that Ms. M was not mentally competent to care for herself, he arranged for full-time caretakers to attend to her after she recovered from the injuries she sustained in her fall. He made improvements in her home, including replacing moth-eaten area rugs with new rugs and upgraded her kitchen to enable caretakers to prepare her meals. Dr. Gaddy also made plumbing repairs to the house, and took steps to adapt a bathroom to make it safer for caretakers to bathe Ms. M, who was incapable of doing so unassisted. During Ms. M's hospitalization, neither of the Appellants visited her in the hospital or sought to assist her in any manner.

Dr. Gaddy had Ms. M examined and evaluated by Dr. James E. Carnes, a neurologist, in December 1996. After examining Ms. M, Dr. Carnes found that she suffered from dementia and confirmed she was unable to handle her affairs.

As Ms. M's Alzheimer's disease progressed and her faculties deteriorated, Dr. Gaddy managed her financial affairs, oversaw maintenance of her properties, and ensured that she received constant care including food, clothing, bathing, and housekeeping. He also constructed a metal barn for multiple purposes, including the storing of Ms. M's personal property and farm equipment used to maintain the 200-acre farm. The barn also included small living accommodations that Dr. Gaddy planned to use to house a caretaker or someone to maintain the farm.

Ms. M's long-standing distant relationship with some members of her family, including Appellants, changed in March of 1999.

On March 12, 1999, Appellants visited Ms. M, and with the help of disgruntled caretaker Lil Heller, took her to an appointment with Columbia attorney Douglas N. Trulsow to "get rid of Dr. Gaddy." On the drive to Truslow's office, Heller had to remind Ms. M several times of their destination and purpose. At Truslow's office, Ms. M signed a document revoking the 1988 Will and the 1988 durable power of attorney. She also signed a new durable power of attorney (1999 durable power of attorney) naming Appellants as her attorneys-in-fact. Appellants failed to disclose Ms. M's dementia to Truslow. David Byrd, a witness to the execution of the March 12 documents, was likewise not informed of Ms. M's dementia.

Armed with the revocation of the 1988 power of attorney and recently executed power of attorney in their favor, Appellants prohibited Dr. Gaddy from contacting Ms. M. Dr. Gaddy was even threatened with arrest if he tried to visit Ms. M.

On March 15, 1999, three days after Ms. M purportedly revoked the 1988 documents and executed the 1999 durable power of attorney, Dr. Gaddy initiated the present action as her attorney-in-fact pursuant to the 1988 durable power of attorney. He alleged, among other things, that the purported revocation of the 1988 durable power of attorney and the execution of the 1999 durable power of attorney were invalid because "on March 12, 1999, the date on which Ms. M purportedly signed the 1999 power of attorney and the revocation, she was not mentally competent" due to "senile dementia of the Alzheimer's type." The action sought declaratory judgment to render the 1999 durable power of attorney invalid and declare the 1988 durable power of attorney valid.

* * *

[Based on multiple medical determinations Ms. M's inability to understand legal documents, t]he trial court concluded that Ms. M lacked contractual and testamentary capacity "from March 12, 1999 and continuously thereafter." As a result, he invalidated the 1999 revocation of the 1988 durable power of attorney and the 1988 Will. He also invalidated the 1999 durable power of attorney, and declared valid the 1988 durable power of attorney. Finally, he awarded Dr. Gaddy litigation expenses to be paid from Ms. M's assets.

DISCUSSION

Since 1986, the South Carolina Legislature has expressly authorized and sanctioned the use and efficacy of durable powers of attorneys. * * * Upon the execution of a durable power of attorney, the attorney-in-fact retains authority to act on the principal's behalf notwithstanding the subsequent physical disability or mental incompetence of the principal. To honor this unmistakable legislative intent, it is incumbent on courts to uphold a durable power of attorney unless the principal retains contractual capacity to revoke the then existing durable power of attorney or to execute a new power of attorney. Otherwise, the very purpose of section 62-5-501 would be undermined.

* * * "[I]n order to execute or revoke a valid power of attorney, the principal must possess contractual capacity." * * * Here, the credible medical and lay testimony presented compellingly indicates that Ms. M suffered from at least moderate to severe dementia caused by Alzheimer's Disease, a chronic and permanent organic disease, on March 12, 1999. We are firmly persuaded that Ms. M's dementia, chronic and progressive in nature, clearly rendered her incapable of possessing contractual capacity to revoke the 1988 durable power of attorney or execute the 1999 power of attorney. We find this conclusion inescapable based on the record before us.

Specifically, the evidence supplied by Doctors Carnes, Taylor and McClure established Ms. M's history of debilitating dementia dating back to 1996, as well as the progressive, chronic, organic, and irreversible nature of the disease. Although a patient suffering from such severe dementia may at times appear normal, they opined such a patient could not make rational decisions, understand the nature of his or her actions, or handle their business or legal affairs. The credible lay testimony of Judge Eppes, Earl Wilkes, and Rosemary Wade provides forceful evidence corroborating the testimony of these three neurologists.

In contrast, the only expert medical testimony supporting Appellants' position that Ms. M possessed sufficient capacity to execute or revoke a power of attorney came from their two medical experts, Drs. Campbell and Zamrini. As noted, Dr. Campbell, an internist, when asked if she claimed "to have any expertise in the area of Alzheimer's disease or dementia," replied, "I don't." Dr. Zamrini's testimony is similarly lacking, primarily as a result of the false medical history provided to him by Appellants.

Based on our view of the evidence, we conclude that by at least March 12, 1999, and at all times thereafter, Ms. M lacked contractual capacity because she suffered from severe dementia caused by Alzheimer's disease, a chronic illness involving the irreversible degeneration of brain cells.

* * *

The very idea of a durable power of attorney is to protect the principal should he or she become incapacitated. This case is precisely the type of situation for which the durable power of attorney is intended. On March 12, 1999, Ms. M, due to her chronic and severe dementia, lacked capacity to revoke the 1988 durable power of attorney and execute the 1999 power of attorney, and the evidence in this regard is overwhelming. In so holding, we return to Dr. Gaddy his fiduciary obligations to Ms. M, which he faithfully discharged prior to Appellants' regrettable involvement. The decision of the trial court is

AFFIRMED IN PART AND VACATED IN PART.

II. Liability to Third Parties from the Principal-Agent Relationship

AS WE HAVE SEEN, there are occasionally disputes between the principal and the agent. Perhaps one of them has not lived up to their duties, so a lawsuit results. On many other occasions, however, the legal question is not a dispute between the principal and agent *per se*, but whether a third party can hold the principal liable for the actions of the agent. There are both contractual and tort-based considerations and instances of these kinds of disputes.

A. CONTRACT

There are two main kinds of authority an agent can contractually hold. That is, if an agent has either of these kinds of authority, the principal can be held contractually liable for the actions of the agent. The first, actual authority, tests the reasonable belief of an agent that she had authority to act from the principal. The second, apparent authority, tests whether a third party had a reasonable belief that the agent was acting on behalf of the principal.

I. Actual Authority

An agent exercises *actual authority* if the agent reasonably believes from the principal's conduct or words that the principal has authorized him to act. Even when the principal's subjective intention may have been otherwise, if an agent reasonably understands that the principal intended to confer authority, then the agent has actual authority and the principal will be liable for the acts of the agent. Actual authority can be either **express**, when a principal specifies exactly what the agent is to do or not do, or **implied**, when a principal specifies what an agent is to do, but the power to choose the method or other acts incidental to the specified act can be reasonably inferred by the agent. A common type of implied actual authority is **incidental authority** in which the agent is authorized to do acts reasonably or usually necessary to accomplish the principal's desired objectives. Note that the determination of whether an agent has actual authority is made with reference to what the *agent* reasonably believed, and does not turn on what the third party knew regarding the agent's authority. Unless otherwise specified, actual authority terminates when either the agent or the principal provides notice to the other of his wish to terminate their relationship.

For example, P leaves a note on the desk of a stockbroker, A, saying, "I authorize you to purchase 100 shares of Intel for me today." When A acts on P's behalf in accordance with the note, A has *actual* authority to serve as a stockbroker for P, *express* authority to purchase the shares, perhaps *implied* authority to wait until the price drops in the afternoon before buying, and *incidental* authority to pay the transactional fees for purchasing the shares. Would A have been acting within a grant of authority from P if he sold the shares mid-day and repurchased them when the price dropped again? What if A used the profits from that transaction to purchase additional shares of Intel?

a. Express Authority

Express authority is the most straightforward kind of authority. This is where the principal explicitly states—in writing or verbally—that the agent has authority to do certain acts. A bit earlier, we considered powers of attorney, which are examples of a principal-agent relationship. Powers of attorney are typically very detailed, specifying exactly what the agent is permitted to do. Lawyers draft this but the forms for the powers of attorney are readily available online as well. For example, here is one from Wikihow:

DURABLE POWER OF ATTORNEY

KNOW ALL MEN BY THESE PRESENTS, that I, the undersigned ______________, over the age of eighteen years, of _____ County, _________, do hereby name, designate, constitute, and appoint, __________________________, as my true and lawful attorney in fact for me, in my name, place and stead to do either, any or all of the following:

To open accounts in my name at any bank, financial institution, or brokerage firm; to conduct any and all ordinary business at any bank, financial institution, or brokerage firm in which I might have an account of any kind or nature; to write or draw checks upon any of my accounts; to endorse checks, promissory notes, drafts, and/or bills of exchange for collection or deposit; to purchase or sell securities; to waive or to demand notice of protest of all such writings; to settle and adjust my accounts with any bank, financial institution, or brokerage firm; to open and have access to any safe deposit box standing in my name at any bank or financial institution; and to do whatsoever might be necessary and proper to conduct my business affairs with relation to any banking, lending institution, financial institution, or brokerage firm.

To borrow such sums of money, and upon such terms, as may be advisable or expedient in relation to any business venture on my behalf or that might be necessary or proper for the conduct of my business affairs, upon the security of any of my property, either real, personal, or otherwise, and for such purposes to give and execute, deliver, and acknowledge mortgages with such powers and provisions as my attorney might deem proper, including such notes or bonds as it is necessary or proper to use therewith.

To collect, ask, demand, sue for, levy, recover, and receive all such sums of money, debts, rents, goods, wares, dues, accounts, and other demands whatsoever, which are or shall be due, owing, payable, and belonging to me by any person or persons, partnership association, company or corporation whatsoever, and in my name, to give effectual and sufficient receipts, acquittances, or discharges.

To adjust, settle, compromise, or submit to arbitration any accounts, debts, claims, demands, disputes, and matters which may hereafter arise between me and any other person or persons, or between my said attorney on my behalf and any other person or persons.

To execute, acknowledge, deliver and cause to be recorded any and all deeds or other writings which may be necessary or desirable for me to execute, including contracts of sale or deeds, conveying title to real estate owned by me or in which I have any interest, present or contingent; and to do, execute and perform all and every other act or acts, thing or things, needful and necessary to be done in and about any premises which I might own or have an interest in, as fully and amply to all intents and purposes as I might or could do if I were personally present and acting. In my name and as my act and deed, to sign, seal, acknowledge, and deliver all such leases and agreements as shall be requisite or proper in the management of my real estate.

I hereby ratify and confirm as good and effectual, at law or in equity, all that my attorney in fact, and any agents and attorneys in fact appointed by my attorney in fact, and their agents, associates, and substitutes, may do by virtue hereof. However, despite the above provisions, nothing herein shall be construed as imposing a duty on my attorney in fact to act or assume responsibility for any matters referred to above or other matters, even though my attorney in fact may have the power or authority hereunder to do so.

My attorney is obliged and instructed to retain all assets of the principal separate and singular and the creation of any multi-party accounts shall be created only by the direction of the principal.

This power of attorney shall remain in full force and effect and shall not be affected by my incompetence, incapacity, or disability, it being my intent that the power granted herein shall continue without interruption until my death, unless revoked by me, or until such time as I am adjudged incompetent or a disabled person by a court of competent jurisdiction. Any person dealing with my attorney in fact may rely without inquiry upon his/her certification that this power of attorney has not been revoked. Further, in the event that it becomes necessary that a guardian or conservator be appointed over my person or estate, I request that the designated attorney-in-fact be first considered to serve as such conservator or guardian.

No person relying upon this power of attorney shall be required to see to the application or disposition of any monies, stocks, bonds, securities, or other property paid to or delivered to my attorney, or my attorney's substitute, pursuant to the provisions hereof.

Reproductions of this executed original (with reproduced signatures and the certificate of acknowledgment) shall be deemed to be original counterparts of this power of attorney.

My attorney-in-fact shall have all the powers and duties as set forth in the _______________(your state) code, and such powers and duties are incorporated by reference as though set forth herein.

IN WITNESS WHEREOF, I have signed this power of attorney this ______ day of ____________, 20_____.

____

Your Name

STATE OF __________ COUNTY OF __________ , SS: _________________

certify that ________________________, personally appeared before me this day and acknowledged execution of the foregoing as his/her free and voluntary act and deed.

WITNESS my hand and notarial seal this ______ day of ____, 20______.

____

Notary Public (signature)

This power of attorney is very explicit, though it is also rather simple. Other power of attorney forms can be far more detailed. They can also be general, authorizing the agent to essentially do everything the principal could do, and they could also be limited. For example, suppose you were buying a house but could not be present at the closing. You might authorize your real estate agent to sign documents on your behalf through a limited power of attorney.

Powers of attorney need not be limited to property. Health care powers of attorney authorize others to make decisions for a person who may not be able to make decisions because of illness. Thus, these authorizations, with names like Health Care Power of Attorneys, Living Wills, or Advanced Directives, create an agency relationship and often do so very specifically and, thus, create express authority.

b. Implied Authority

Sometimes the authorization to act on another party's behalf is not as detailed as what we have just described. Or perhaps the authorization is specific, but the nature of life is that you cannot anticipate everything. Either way, there are times when an agent reasonably believes he has the authority to act on behalf of the principal even though there has not been an express specification of that authority. There are three kinds of these implied authorities.

i. Incident to Express or Inherent Authority

According to Restatement (Second) of Agency and, as you saw in *Croisant v. Watrud*, even when an agent acts without actual authority or apparent authority, a principal can still be liable through the application of the doctrine of inherent authority. Somewhat similar to apparent authority, inherent authority turns on the beliefs of the particular involved third party. The difference between apparent and inherent authority has not always been easy for courts or commentators to discern. Inherent authority exists when a particular third party has an actual and reasonable belief that the agent possesses authority to act in a specified manner on behalf of the principal, even if that third party's belief is not based on particular manifestations by the principal (as is true for apparent authority). Inherent authority arises solely from the agency relationship itself, and, as the *Croisant* court indicates, is based on the theory that if a principal appoints an agent to conduct a series of transactions, it is only fair that the principal should bear losses that are incurred when the agent, although not authorized to do so, does something that is closely connected with the transactions he is employed to conduct. As in *Croisant*, a principal is liable for his agent's actions that "usually accompany or are incidental to transactions which the agent is authorized to conduct," even if no authority is given or implied. Because inherent agency imposes liability on a principal in an indefinite variety of circumstances, potentially beyond those when actual or apparent authority are present, the existence of the doctrine purportedly encourages principals to exercise more caution in selecting agents, thereby minimizing their potential liability and perhaps avoiding harm to third persons.

ii. Ratification

Another way in which the agent might reasonably believe that she has the authority to act for the principal is when she exceeds the express authority given to her and the principal does not object. Suppose the principal hired the agent to manage her apartment building. The principal does not specify that the agent is to collect rents or keep the units clean; the principal has simply made a general authorization to manage the units. The agent might reasonably believe that she has the authority, in fact, to collect rents and keep the units clean. Doing so would be inherent in the authorization, as described above, but in addition, if she did these things and the principal does not object to her doing these things, then the principal has ratified the agent's actions. The agent thus then has an additional reason to believe that she has this authority from the principal.

iii. Emergency

Suppose in managing the above-referenced apartment units, a natural disaster hits: an earthquake or hurricane. Or, perhaps the units catch on fire. The principal cannot be located and there is no specific authorization for the agent to take steps to protect the building, clean up afterwards or any other things that might result from such an emergency. The agent again might well have reasonable belief that he should undertake such actions for the benefit of the principal.

2. Apparent Authority

An agent acts with apparent authority if the principal's manifestations led the involved third party reasonably to conclude that the principal had authorized the agent to act in a specified manner. Here it is not the understanding of the agent that is at issue, but the understanding of the third party. Nevertheless, you can probably understand why apparent authority often coincides with actual authority. Note that apparent authority can be present even if a principal does not intend to authorize the agent to act. Frequently an officer's position within a corporation provides apparent authority if a third party reasonably believes the agent's authority to be consistent with his position. This is called authority by position.

For example, suppose A is the President, Chairman of the Board and Chief Executive Officer (CEO) of XYZ, Inc. In his position, A is the agent of corporation. T, a third party who signs a contract with A, could reasonably believe from the corporation's Board of Directors (which selects the officers) appointment of A to a high position within the corporation that the Board had implicitly or expressly authorized A to sign contracts on behalf of XYZ, especially if that is the usual practice for executives in his position. In this situation, A would have apparent authority to sign a contract with T, and XYZ, Inc. would be liable for A's actions, even if no one else involved in the corporation had wished for A to sign a contract with T.

a. Ratification

As with actual authority, an agent who acts on behalf of a principal but without actual or apparent authority can still bind the principal to third parties if the principal, who later acquires knowledge of the material facts regarding the agent's dealings with the third party, either objectively manifests his consent to being liable for the agent's conduct, or behaves in such a way that consent can be inferred. The legal consequence of the principal's ratification is that the agency relationship is treated as if the agent possessed actual authority at the time of the relevant acts.

b. Estoppel and Imposter

A would-be principal can be estopped [a technical term of art which means "prevented by the law," in order to promote justice] from denying an agency relationship and become liable to a third party if the third party relied to his detriment on his belief in an agent's authority. The third party's belief must have been caused either by intentional or careless behavior of the would-be principal, or a failure of the principal to take reasonable steps to notify the third party of the error of such belief.

Although agency by estoppel usually involves false representations by an actor purporting to be an agent, a would-be principal will still be found liable because it was his acts or his failure reasonably to act to deny authority which enabled the purported agent to misrepresent his or her authority to third parties. Agency by estoppel, like apparent authority, rests on the *third party's* understanding. Unlike apparent authority, in order to be invoked, agency by estoppel requires detrimental reliance on the part of the third party.

For example, T enters a store called "P's Stereos" and is approached by A, wearing a "P's Stereos" shirt and acting like a salesman. Although T doesn't know it, A had found the shirt and a P's Stereos receipt book on the sidewalk, where P had negligently left them the day before. A induces T to purchase a stereo, and, in exchange for cash, gives T an official-looking receipt and explains that the stereo will be delivered later in the day. T never receives his stereo, nor does P ever receive the cash from the transaction. A is neither an agent nor employee of P, and does not have actual or apparent authority to sell from P's inventory. Even so, P may be liable for T's detrimental reliance through the creation of agency by estoppel because P's carelessness with identifying materials and lack of surveillance over the store's sales force facilitated T's reasonable belief that A was authorized as an agent of P.

c. Lingering

A final kind of apparent authority is lingering. Suppose an agent worked for a company for years. In doing so, one of her tasks was to organize periodic retreats for the staff, which she held at her home. She made use of the company credit card to order food. Assume the agent no longer works for the company, but she decides to host one more retreat, this time just for fun and with no work related; in other words, she wanted to throw a party and charged the expenses to the company credit card number which she had memorized.

The (former) agent would certainly be liable to the company for these charges since she had no authorization to throw a party for herself. But the third party, from whom she purchased the supplies for the event, could hold the company liable for paying unless it had notice or reason to know that the former agent was no longer, in fact, an agent.

3. Disclosed and Undisclosed Principals

Sometimes a third party knows who the principal is and sometimes the third party does not. There are three kinds of Disclosed principals. When dealing with an agent, one may know that the agent has a principal and who that principal is. When dealing with an agent, one may not know that there is a principal at all. When dealing with an agent, one may know that the agent is acting on behalf of someone (i.e. that there is a principal), but not know who that principal is (i.e. the identity is unknown).

If there is a disclosed principal and the agent has actual or apparent authority, then the principal and not the agent is bound to the third party. If, however, the agent exceeds his actual or apparent authority, then the principal is not bound, but the agent might be. The agent can be personally liable if the principal is partially disclosed or if the principal is not disclosed at all. In both of these latter two cases, the theory is that a third party is dealing more on the basis of the credibility of the agent per se as opposed to the principal the agent represents.

a. Tort

Generally speaking, principals and agents are both liable for the injuries they cause third parties. An agent who sexually harasses a co-worker is liable for his actions. So too might be the principal as we shall see, but the principal's liability does not eliminate the agent's liability. If a principal specifically instructs an agent to do something injurious, such as to sell a defective product, then the principal is also directly liable.

i. Respondeat Superior

Many times, however, the principal does not specifically tell the agent to do something illegal, but an injury occurs nonetheless. It is in those cases where the idea of *respondeat superior* comes in. We have already seen this concept in the chapters on Tort and Product Liability. It means that the principal is liable for the actions of a subordinate—i.e. an agent—if the agent is acting within the scope of his employment. The following case provides an introduction to both scope of employment and *respondeat superior.*

Hayes v. Far West Services, Inc.

50 Wash.App. 505, 749 P.2d 178 (1988)

Frederick Hayes and Judy Frounfelter brought suit for damages against Thomas McGrath and his former law firm, Torbenson, Thatcher, McGrath, Treadwell & Schoonmaker, Inc., P.S., for injuries arising out of McGrath's shooting of Hayes. On motion for summary judgment, the trial court dismissed the firm as a defendant. Hayes appeals.

The facts are these: at approximately 4:30 p.m. on February 11, 1980, McGrath went to a restaurant/cocktail establishment in Kirkland. From then until about 11 o'clock, he imbibed considerable alcohol while socializing and discussing personal and firm-related business. After 11 o'clock, McGrath continued to socialize until approximately 1:45 a.m., when he and Hayes, another bar patron, exchanged words. Shortly thereafter, the two encountered each other outside, and after another exchange, McGrath shot Hayes in what he claims was self-defense. Frounfelter, who was in the company of Hayes, is alleged to have sustained emotional trauma.

The basic question is whether the law firm is liable on the theory of *respondeat superior* for damages arising out of McGrath's shooting of Hayes. The basic rule is stated in *Kuehn v. White* (1979):

> **"A master is responsible for the servant's acts under the doctrine of respondeat superior when the servant acts within the scope of his or her employment and in furtherance of the master's business. Where a servant steps aside from the master's business in order to effect some purpose of his own, the master is not liable.**

Under the traditional interpretation of respondeat superior, there is not sufficient evidence to establish liability on the part of the law firm. Viewing the evidence in a light most favorable to the nonmoving parties, Hayes and Frounfelter, as we must, there is nothing to indicate either directly or by inference that McGrath was acting in the scope of his employment when he shot Hayes. There is no evidence McGrath transacted firm business or engaged in any promotional activities anytime after 11 p.m.

But in *Dickinson v. Edwards*, (1986), the Supreme Court extended the doctrine of respondeat superior, allowing a plaintiff to recover from a banquet-hosting employer if the following prima facie case is proven:

1. The employee consumed alcohol at a party hosted by the employer which was held to further the employer's interest in some way and at which the employee's presence was requested or impliedly or expressly required by the employer.

2. The employee negligently consumed alcohol to the point of intoxication when he knew or should have known he would need to operate a vehicle on some public highway upon leaving the banquet.

3. The employee caused the accident while driving from the banquet.

4. The proximate cause of the accident, the intoxication, occurred at the time the employee negligently consumed the alcohol.

5. Since this banquet was beneficial to the employer who impliedly or expressly required the employee's attendance, the employee negligently consumed this alcohol during the scope of his employment. Appellants, citing *Dickinson v. Edwards, supra*, argue that McGrath's firm is liable under *respondeat superior* because McGrath negligently became intoxicated while acting within the scope of his employment, and his intoxication was the proximate cause of the shooting.

[1] The decision in *Dickinson v. Edwards, supra*, is based on *Chastain v. Litton Sys., Inc.*, (4th Cir. 1982). That case employed essentially a 3-prong analysis: (1) was the employee's consumption of alcohol within the scope of employment, (2) did the employee's consumption of alcohol while within the scope of employment constitute negligence, and (3) did the negligent intoxication continue until the time of the incident and constitute a proximate cause of the injuries. *Chastain*, at 962; *See also Childers v. Shasta Livestock Auction Yard, Inc.* (1987).

Under this formulation of the rule, there is sufficient evidence to present a jury question as to whether McGrath was acting within the scope of his employment when he consumed alcohol. Prior to 8:30 p.m., McGrath met with several acquaintances, including a friend from an insurance company he had been trying to secure as a client for the firm for some time; McGrath later submitted a charge slip marked "Entertainment" to his firm for bar purchases while with the friend. From about 8:30 p.m. to 11 p.m., McGrath discussed settlement possibilities with opposing counsel on a bankruptcy case he was handling for his firm; McGrath's firm subsequently billed their client in the bankruptcy for 2.7 hours for that settlement conference. Moreover, McGrath's activities appear consistent with his firm's policies; members were encouraged to engage in promotional activities, and the firm gave partners such as McGrath considerable discretion in billing for expenses, as evidenced by the numerous reimbursements made to McGrath for his business and entertainment expenditures.

There is also sufficient evidence to present a jury question as to whether McGrath consumed alcohol to the point of intoxication while within the scope of his employment. McGrath admitted to having several drinks prior to 11 p.m., and Hayes and several others said McGrath appeared intoxicated before the shooting.

But there is nothing in the record to show that McGrath's consumption of alcohol was negligent. Negligence necessarily involves a foreseeable risk; if an actor could not reasonably foresee any injury as the result of his act, there is no negligence and no liability. *Hunsley v. Giard* (1976). In *Dickinson v. Edwards, supra*, negligence was defined in terms of whether the employee knew or should have known he would be operating a motor vehicle on a public highway upon leaving the banquet. Because the employee had driven to the banquet, it was foreseeable that he would have to drive away, and the risks of driving while intoxicated are well recognized. Such a situation is far removed from the particulars of this case. There is no evidence to suggest McGrath knew or should have known that his drinking would lead to his becoming involved in an altercation that would result in his firing a gun at another bar patron; nothing in the record shows that the cocktail lounge was a frequent scene of such incidents or that its patrons were known to be confrontational, or that when intoxicated, McGrath became violent or had ever drawn a gun. Accordingly, there is not sufficient evidence to establish liability on the part of the law firm under the application of *respondeat superior* set forth in *Dickinson v. Edwards, supra.*

The remaining arguments are insubstantial. The notion of "enterprise liability" was specifically rejected by the court in *Kuehn v. White*, and no subsequent cases have indicated otherwise. Nothing in the record supports a finding of liability based on either a theory of negligent retention and supervision or a duty to control because of a "special relation" between McGrath and his firm. And finally, the court did not err in striking certain materials submitted by the appellants, nor was its denial of their motion for continuance an abuse of discretion.

Affirmed.

---

b. Employer-Employee vs. Independent Contractor

Two concepts are crucial in invoking *respondeat superior.* One is whether the agency relationship is an employer-employee relationship or that of a principal with an independent contractor.

The employer-employee relationship, historically often referred to as a master-servant relationship, is the one far more likely to trigger *respondeat superior.* It's one where the employer, the principal, has the ability to control the actions of the agent, also knows as the employee.

The independent contractor relationship is one where the agent has a separate identify from the principal, but works on the principal's behalf. A lawyer or an accountant, for example, would be an independent contractor, working on behalf of a principal.

Much depends on whether the principal-agent relationship in question is employer-employee or independent contractor. While there is no one definitive test the courts use, here are some factors courts to consider:

- Who pays social security taxes? If the independent contractor pays his own FICA taxes, it is an indication of being an independent contractor. If the principal pays FICA taxes, it is an indication of an employer-employee relationship.

- Who provides the tools for the work? If the principal supplies the tools or equipment for the job, it indicates an employer-employee relationship. If the independent contractor supplies the tools or equipment, it indicates an independent contractor relationship.

- How is the agent compensated and are there benefits associated with the job, such as health insurance or retirement plans? The more a principal-agent relationship looks like a typical employer-employee relationship, the more it will be treated as such. The same applies with respect to an independent contractor's relationship with the principal.

An employer-employee relationship is more likely to trigger *respondeat superior.* The logic is that since the principal has a greater capacity to control the employee's actions, the employer should be liable whereas the principal has less ability to control the actions of an independent contractor.

c. Frolicking and Detouring

Respondeat superior applies if the agent acts within the scope of his employment. If the employee drives to visit a prospective client and injures a third party on the way, the employer will usually be liable because the agent is doing something for the principal. What if the agent takes a "detour," stops at McDonald's to grab some lunch and while backing out of a parking space, injures someone? One might argue that grabbing lunch at McDonald's is not within the scope of employment, but courts generally hold that if an action is a detour—a slight variation of one's job requirements and one that could be reasonably expected to occur—then the detour does not abrogate the principal's liability.

A **frolic**, on the other hand, is a significant departure from one's employment. Frolicking will relieve the principal from liability of an employee's actions. Thus, rather than going to McDonald's for lunch for thirty minutes, the employee heads to a bar for two hours, and then hits someone while backing out of the parking lot to head on over to a client's place of business. Drawing the exact line of where detouring ends and frolicking begins is not always easy, but typically the consideration will be given to whether the excursion can be reasonably expected and if the employee generally remains in the process of doing something to benefit the employer. Stopping for a quick lunch is one thing; hanging out at a bar for a couple of hours is another.

NOTES AND QUESTIONS on the Legal Environment of Business

1. **SO FAR YOU HAVE LEARNED** that agents are authorized to conduct business for a principal and can enter into contracts which bind the principal, if they act with sufficient authority. The *Tarnowski* case is your introduction to an equally important aspect of agency law, the *fiduciary responsibility* of the agent to the principal. As indicated, the essence of this fiduciary responsibility is that the agent is required to put the principal's interests ahead of his own. Why should this be so? Because many business entities, particularly corporations, can only act through agents (can you understand why this is the case?) regulating their behavior is tremendously important. Can you understand why the fiduciary principle is necessary, given the enormous discretion that agents may have not only to make binding contracts for their principals, but also to negotiate and execute them?

2. **GIVEN HUMAN NATURE,** one will want to look out for one's own interests ahead of those of others. Agency law must come to grips with the fact that the inevitable agency relationship will require some mechanisms so that the principal can minimize the temptation of the agent to betray the principal's interests in favor of the agent's own. There is a vast economic literature on this problem, but for our purposes it is enough to note that without legal restraints on the agent, and even with them, principals will often expend **monitoring costs** to ensure that their agents act according to the principal's wishes. The principal might also require that the agent enter into some kind of security arrangement so that funds are forfeited if the agent acts in a manner contrary to the principal's interest. The costs of such an arrangement are known as **bonding costs**. Finally, as we have seen in *Tarnowski*, if the agent does fail to perform according to the wishes and interests of the principal, the principal may face some loss, either of lost opportunity, or of money expended for inferior goods. This is generally referred to as **residual loss.**

The economic literature explains that **agency costs**—the costs to all concerned of employing agents to carry out transactions—is the sum of the monitoring expenses expended by the principal, the bonding expenditures of the agent, and the residual loss faced by the principal. Can you understand how imposing a fiduciary duty on the agent serves to reduce agency costs?

3. **IN *TARNOWSKI*** the agent, Resop, took a bribe and bound his principal in a business deal that featured fraud on the part of the sellers (the third parties) and also on the part of the agent. The principal, Tarnowski, sued the sellers, and essentially recovered his losses from the fraudulent transaction, and then Tarnowski proceeded to bring a second lawsuit against his disloyal agent. Because he had previously been made virtually whole as a result of the favorable settlement of the lawsuit against the sellers, it might be said that Tarnowski was no longer financially harmed by his agent's taking of a bribe, yet the court rules that he is still entitled to that bribe, or "side payment" made by the sellers to the agent. Why? The court writes in its decision, "all profits made by an agent in the course of an agency belong to the principal, whether they are the fruits of performance or the violation of an agent's duty." The court continues, "it matters not that the principal has suffered no damage or even that the transaction has been profitable to him." How can this be? Is it wise policy? If side-payments from third parties to agents can be recovered by principals, will principals take less care to hire trustworthy agents?

4. **AS YOU MAY KNOW,** Courts rarely and reluctantly award attorney's fees, particularly in private disputes, unless such remedy is set forth in a statute. In *Tarnowski*, the court awarded attorneys fees expended by Tarnowski. In the logic of the court, "the attorneys' fees and expenses of suit were directly traceable to the harm caused by defendant's wrongful act." Does this decision seem fair to you, given the usual reluctance to award attorney's fees?

   Note that the court reaches this decision after consulting authorities regarding the law of torts. Is this a torts case or a contracts case? Should it make a difference?

   For further thoughts on the fiduciary duty as it applies to agents in a variety of contexts, *see* Victor Brudney, *Contract and Fiduciary Duty in Corporate Law,* 38 B.C.L. Rev. 595 (1997), and, for an analysis of the problem of agency from a literary perspective, *see* Allen D. Boyer, *Agents, Lovers, and Institutions: John Le Carre as Legal Critic*, 65 Notre Dame L. Rev. 78 (1989).

5. **WHAT DIFFERENCE DOES IT MAKE,** if any, that the purported principal in *Croisant* is a partnership? What can you infer about the nature of partnerships from the case? See if your inferences are borne out by the consideration of partnership law which follows this chapter on Agency.

6. **IN AN IMPORTANT LAW REVIEW ARTICLE,** one critic of the Third Restatement's elimination of inherent authority argues that apparent authority ought to be conceptualized as only a small subset of inherent authority, and thus it should not be expanded to replace inherent authority. This critic explains the distinction between the two kinds of authority by suggesting that inherent authority requires only that the third party's belief be actual and reasonable, whereas apparent authority requires that the third party's belief be actual, reasonable, and based on the principal's manifestations. Inherent authority thus becomes the most useful in cases, such as *Croisant*, where the third party's beliefs are reasonable but cannot be traced to manifestations by the principal. Because of this narrow but useful difference between inherent authority and actual authority, it is suggested that elimination of inherent authority breaks with precedent cases like *Croisant* and constitutes an inappropriate substantive change of the law.[1] Remember that Restatements are not supposed to change the law, just to reflect it. Having read a case in which apparent authority and inherent authority both play a large role, do you agree with the new Restatement's elimination of inherent authority? Do you think this change potentially makes the law clearer or does the new Restatement increase confusion?

7. **INHERENT AUTHORITY HAS RECENTLY** been eliminated in drafts of the Restatement (Third) of Agency. As the law develops, the Restatements have gone through subsequent drafts. The drafters of this Third Restatement removed the distinction between inherent authority and apparent authority by expanding the definition of the principal's manifestations to include situations without verbal communications by the principal, such as appointments of agents to certain positions. The confusion between apparent and inherent authority explains the suggestion in *Croisant* that "whether the theory is characterized as one of apparent authority . . . or as arising out of an inherent agency power is immaterial."

1 Matthew P. Ward, *Note: A Restatement or a Redefinition: Elimination of Inherent Agency in the Tentative Draft of the Restatement (Third) of Agency,* 59 Wash & Lee L. Rev. 1585, 1626 2002).

NOTES AND QUESTIONS on the Ethical Environment of Business

1. **ECONOMISTS AND ORGANIZATIONAL** theorists often worry about "the agency problem." It is an ethical problem of when those working for you don't do what they are supposed to do. They may "shirk," meaning that they goof off and don't work as diligently as they should or they may "shark," meaning that they take advantage of the opportunities presented to them as an agent and use them for their own benefit rather than for the benefit of the principal for whom they are working. And so a large literature looks at how to create incentives or monitoring that lessens the likelihood of either of these things from happening.

   We see these issues in this chapter, especially that of sharking, for instance in the *Tarnowski* case. The legal standard for these kinds of cases is that of fiduciary duty, which means that the agent should put the interests of the principal ahead of their own interests. Do you think this duty is fair? Does it restrict an agent's own opportunities? How do you assess *Tarnowski* ethically?

2. **WHAT ABOUT THE OTHER CASES** in the chapter? What are the ethical duties of someone acting as a power of attorney—or seeking to become a power of attorney—for another person? Do you agree with the principles of the times and instances where a third party can hold a principal liable, even via contracts or torts, liable for the actions of an agent?

3. **TURNING TO *ETHICS VIGNETTES*,** we can see these same issues arising in Chapter Two's attention to accounting issues. Do you think the *Barrington* case is rightly decided?

CHAPTER

14

Employment Law

The previous chapter on Agency Law provides the basis for Employment Law. Employees serve as agents of a principal. Because Agency Law itself is an aspect of Contract Law, principles of Contract Law also apply to the employer-employee relationship. As we saw in Agency Law, principals can hire independent contractors—lawyers, accountants, consultants, and others—to be their agents. Principals have a great deal of freedom in how they treat independent contractors, within limits of course. Typically, a principal has no obligation to withhold taxes from the compensation provided to the independent contractor. Usually, the principal is not liable for the tortious actions of the independent agent. Things change significantly with respect to an employee.

Employees have many more rights and protections than do independent contractors. Employers do have to withhold taxes, are often liable for the tortious actions of their employees, and have a series of other obligations in their treatment of employees. While it is true the American tradition is one of **employment-at-will**, employees also enjoy many regulatory protections.

In this chapter, we will focus on the foundational rules of employment law, which include both common law principles as well as collective bargaining rights. Then the chapter will look at a range of regulatory protections that have been enacted to protect employees. These include protection of income-related rights (pensions, unemployment compensation, wage rates, and benefits), health-related rights (health and safety standards, insurance, workers compensation and family and medical leave), anti-discrimination protections (race, gender, and age), and privacy rights. Finally the chapter will look at the issues of post-employment, including potential regulatory restrictions such as the limits of a government employee to work in the private sector after their public service ends and the private sector analogue: covenants not to compete.

I. Common Law Foundations

Because both the potential employer and employee have the freedom to decide to enter into an employment relationship, the basic rules of contracts apply, including terminating the contract. Of course, the employee can almost always decide to quit a job for any reason and usually not have obligations to pay the employer anything unless there are specific contractual agreements in place. For example, most universities will grant a tenured professor a sabbatical, but the agreement usually provides that if the professor leaves her position immediately after the sabbatical, then she must repay some or all the determined value of that leave of absence. More typically, however, an employee can simply decide to leave the job without consequences. Because requiring an employee to continue to work for a company if the employee does not want to smacks of "involuntary servitude" or even slavery, courts almost never force a person to continue to be employed against their will.

Generally speaking, an employer can also discharge an employee for any reason. Yet because there are so many protections of the employee, an employer firing an employee must be very careful to document that the reasons for the dismissal do not violate any of those legal protections. Unless the employer has records that establish the reasons for the firings—perhaps documentation of unsatisfactory work and warnings—the employer is open to claims that the discharge violated a law.

Sometimes an employer may guarantee a person a job for life, or at least the statements made by the employer suggest this might be the case. Those are less common than they were a few decades ago, but the arguments for why these promises existed continue with respect to other contractual provisions and promises. Statements in employee handbook or past practices or training programs that might suggest a commitment to work with the employee over an extended period of time might have been found to bind an employer to long-term employment years ago. Such standardized provisions can also be found to be part of the employment contract today. Let's look at an example of a long-term contract.

Toussaint v. Blue Cross & Blue Shield

408 Mich. 579, 292 N.W.2d 880

LEVIN, JUSTICE (for reversal in *Toussaint* and affirmance in *Ebling*).

Charles Toussaint was employed in a middle management position with Blue Cross and Walter Ebling was similarly employed by Masco. After being employed five and two years, respectively, each was discharged. They commenced actions against their former employers, claiming that the discharges violated their employment agreements which permitted discharge only for cause. A verdict of $72,835.52 was rendered for Toussaint and a verdict of $300,000 for Ebling whose discharge left him ineligible to exercise a stock option. Different panels of the Court of Appeals reversed Toussaint and affirmed Ebling.

* * *

Both Toussaint and Ebling inquired regarding job security when they were hired. Toussaint testified that he was told he would be with the company "as long as I did my job." Ebling testified that he was told that if he was "doing the job" he would not be discharged. Toussaint's testimony, like Ebling's, made submissible to the jury whether there was an agreement for a contract of employment terminable only for cause.

Toussaint's case is, if anything, stronger because he was handed a manual of Blue Cross personnel policies which reinforced the oral assurance of job security. It stated that the disciplinary procedures applied to all Blue Cross employees who had completed *598 their probationary period and that it was the "policy" of the company to release employees "for just cause only."

* * *

We hold that

1) a provision of an employment contract providing that an employee shall not be discharged except for cause is legally enforceable although the contract is not for a definite term the term is "indefinite," and

2) such a provision may become part of the contract either by express agreement, oral or written, or as a result of an employee's legitimate expectations grounded in an employer's policy statements.

3) In Toussaint, as in Ebling, there was sufficient evidence of an express agreement to justify submission to the jury.

4) A jury could also find for Toussaint based on legitimate expectations grounded in his employer's written policy statements set forth in the manual of personnel policies.

* * *

We do not, however, rest our conclusion that the jury could properly find that the Blue Cross policy manual created contractual rights solely on Toussaint's testimony concerning his conversation with the executive who interviewed and hired him.

While an employer need not establish personnel policies or practices, where an employer chooses to establish such policies and practices and makes them known to its employees, the employment relationship is presumably enhanced. The employer secures an orderly, cooperative and loyal work force, and the employee the peace of mind associated with job security and the conviction that he will be treated fairly. No pre-employment negotiations need take place and the parties' minds need not meet on the subject; nor does it matter that the employee knows nothing of the particulars of the employer's policies and practices or that the employer may change them unilaterally. It is enough that the employer chooses, presumably in its own interest, to create an environment in which the employee believes that, whatever the personnel policies and practices, they are established and official at any given time, purport to be fair, and are applied consistently and uniformly to each employee. The employer has then created a situation "instinct with an obligation."

Blue Cross offered no evidence that the manual and guidelines are not what they purport to be statements of company policy on the subjects there addressed, including discipline and termination.

The jury could properly conclude that the statements of policy on those subjects were applicable to Toussaint although the manual did not explicitly refer to him. The manual, by its terms, purports to apply to all employees who have completed a probationary period. The inference that the policies and procedures applied to Toussaint is supported by his testimony that he was handed the manual in the course of a conversation in which he inquired about job security.

Although Toussaint's employment was for an indefinite term, the jury could find that the relationship was not terminable at the will of Blue Cross. Blue Cross had established a company policy to discharge for just cause only, pursuant to certain procedures, had made that policy known to Toussaint, and thereby had committed itself to discharge him only for just cause in compliance with the procedures. There were, thus, on this separate basis alone, special circumstances sufficient to overcome the presumptive construction that the contract was terminable at will.

We hold that employer statements of policy, such as the Blue Cross Supervisory Manual and Guidelines, can give rise to contractual rights in employees without evidence that the parties mutually agreed that the policy statements would create contractual rights in the employee, and, hence, although the statement of policy is signed by neither party, can be unilaterally amended by the employer without notice to the employee, and contains no reference to a specific employee, his job description or compensation, and although no reference was made to the policy statement in pre-employment interviews and the employee does not learn of its existence until after his hiring.

* * *

The Blue Cross Manual, too, promised that the company would conduct itself in a certain way with the stated objective of achieving fairness. "The cooperation desired was to be mutual" both employer and employee were to adhere to stated procedures, and no doubt those policies contributed to a "spirit of cooperation and friendliness." Since Blue Cross published and distributed a 260-page manual establishing elaborate procedures promising "(t)o provide for the administration of fair, consistent and reasonable corrective discipline" and "to treat employees leaving Blue Cross in a fair and consistent manner and to release employees for just cause only," its employees could justifiably rely on those expressions and conduct themselves accordingly.

Recognition that contractual obligations can be implicit in employer policies and practices is not confined to cases where compensation is in issue. * * *

An employer who establishes no personnel policies instills no reasonable expectations of performance. Employers can make known to their employees that personnel policies are subject to unilateral changes by the employer. Employees would then have no legitimate expectation that any particular policy will continue to remain in force. Employees could, however, legitimately expect that policies in force at any given time will be uniformly applied to all. If there is in effect a policy to dismiss for cause only, the employer may not depart from that policy at whim simply because he was under no obligation to institute the policy in the first place. Having announced the policy, presumably with a view to obtaining the benefit of improved employee attitudes and behavior and improved quality of the work force, the employer may not treat its promise as illusory.

* * * We affirm Ebling and remand Toussaint to the trial court with instructions to reinstate the verdict.

Just as the expectation of lifetime employment is far less common than it might have been in the 1970s, so too labor union protection of workers is not as strong as it was at that time. Yet as the case above demonstrates, the protection of employees in the expectation of a long-term relationship does retain legal leverage. While less likely to pertain to career employment per se, employer guarantees can continue with respect to process steps. General language can become, at least potentially, part of the employment agreement. This is the same kind of contractual approach found in the basic issues of offer and acceptance.

Recall, for example the *Steinberg* case in the Contracts chapter, where statements in the Chicago Medical School's brochure were held to be contractual commitments as to how a person's application would be evaluated. Or in the *Lefkowitz* case, where statements in a newspaper advertisement were held to be an offer for the sale of a fur if a person was one of the first to stand in line at the store. What's important from the *Toussaint* case, then, is in part the question of whether generalized statements in a company brochure can bind (or not) an employer to lifetime contractual obligations to an employee, and also whether other provisions for how to evaluate an employee might be embedded in standardized language.

II. Labor Rights and Collective Bargaining

Labor rights are also not as strong as they were in the 1970s, both in the private sector, and especially with respect to governmental employees. As of 2015, approximately 11% of the U.S. workforce was unionized. While 35% of public sector employees were unionized, only about 7% of private sector employees were. New York had the highest percentage of union employees with 24% whereas South Carolina had the lowest with 2%.[1]

The right to unionize involved a hard-fought battle in the midst of abuses that occurred during the Industrial Revolution. Perhaps the high point for the protection of unions came in the 1935 passage of the National Labor Relations Act, which gave workers the right to unionize and select a union to bargain on their collective behalf. The employer was not allowed to interfere with the employees' decision to organize nor to refuse to deal with some unions over others, but instead was expected to negotiate in good faith with whatever union had been chosen.

The National Labor Relations Board adjudicates disputes regarding the process of organizing and to hear complaints about unfair labor practices. The NLRB also hears cases as to what parts of a company could organize; for example, does each company plant have the right to their own union or does the union represent all employees to the one employer they have. Determining the appropriateness of picketing and lockouts also fall within NLRB's scope of authority.

The following case demonstrates both the principles underlying the rights to **collective bargaining** and contemporary protection of labor rights in a public sector employer situation.

1 http://www.bls.gov/news.release/pdf/union2.pdf

United Public Workers, AFSCME Local 646, AFL-CIO v. Yogi

101 Hawai'i 26, 62 P.3d 189 (2002)

Opinion by RAMIL, J.

The main issue before us is whether Section 2 violates article XIII, section 2 of our state constitution. We hold that it does. Accordingly, we focus our analysis on Plaintiffs' collective bargaining rights. We affirm.

1. Background

During the 1999 legislative session, the Hawai'i State Legislature enacted Act 100. See 1999 Haw. Sess. L. Act 100, at 368–70. Section 2 of Act 100 amended Hawai'i Revised Statutes ("HRS") § 89-9(a) by adding the language underscored:

§ 89-9 Scope of negotiations.

> [Section effective until June 30, 2002 . . . .] (a) The employer and the exclusive representative shall meet at reasonable times, including meetings in advance of the employer's budget-making process, and shall negotiate in good faith with respect to wages, hours, the number of incremental and longevity steps and movement between steps within the salary range, the amounts of contributions by the State and respective counties to the Hawai'i public employees health fund to the extent allowed in subsection (e), and other terms and conditions of employment which are subject to negotiations under this chapter and which are to be embodied in a written agreement, or any question arising thereunder, but such obligation does not compel either party to agree to a proposal or make a concession; provided that the parties may not negotiate with respect to cost items as defined by section 89-2 for the biennium 1999 to 2001, and the cost items of employees in bargaining units under section 89-6 in effect on June 30, 1999, shall remain in effect until July 1, 2001.

HRS § 89-9(a) (2001) (underscoring added). "Cost items" include "wages, hours, amounts of contributions by the State and Counties to the Hawai'i public employees health fund, and other terms and conditions of employment, the implementation of which requires an appropriation by a legislative body." HRS § 89-2 (1993). In essence, Section 2 of Act 100 prohibited public employers and public employees' unions from collectively bargaining over cost items for the biennium 1999 to 2001.

* * *

Defendant Yogi * * * contends that article XIII, section 2 "recognize[s] a constitutional right to organize for the purpose of collective bargaining" but "does not create a right to collectively bargain." Yogi maintains that, by inserting the phrase as "provided by law", the framers intended for the legislature to retain the ultimate authority to govern the parameters of collective bargaining. * * * Defendants Kusaka and Yamashiro argue that (1) the legislature intended Section 2 to serve an important public interest; (2) HRS chapter 89 exhibits examples of the legislature's discretion to limit the right to bargain collectively; and (3) Plaintiffs suffered no irreparable injury.

Plaintiffs assert that (1) the words "collective bargaining as provided by law" in article XIII, section 2 had "a well-recognized meaning in pre-existing federal and state statutes[ ] and five state constitutions" by 1968, and the term "law" referred "not just to statutory 'law,' but also to constitutional and case 'law' which gave substance and meaning to the words 'collective bargaining' "; (2) "the object of the 1968 amendment was to extend to public employees rights enjoyed by private employees"; and (3) their position is supported by the legislative history of HRS chapter 89, "contemporary 'understanding' " of the meaning of "collective bargaining as provided by law," and case law from other states.

* * *

[Our state's] constitution " 'must be construed with due regard to the intent of the framers and the people adopting it, and the fundamental principle in interpreting a constitutional provision is to give effect to that intent.' " . . . "This intent is to be found in the instrument itself."

Based upon our careful review of the proceedings of the constitutional convention, we find that the framers of article XII, section 2 did not intend to grant our legislators complete and absolute discretion to determine the scope of "collective bargaining." There are evidence in the 1968 proceedings indicating that the framers were not in favor of granting the legislature the ultimate power to deny the right to organize for the purpose of collectively bargaining. For instance, the framers defeated an amendment in the committee of the whole to limit public employee rights to "procedures as established by law in the areas therein prescribed" by a vote of 62 to 13. * * *

In construing a constitutional provision, the court can also look to understanding of voters who ratified the constitutional provision, and legislative implementation of constitutional amendment. At the time the people voted, the word "collective bargaining as prescribed by law" had a well recognized meaning. Black's defined "collective bargaining" as follows:

> COLLECTIVE BARGAINING. As contemplated by National Labor Relations Act is a procedure looking toward making of collective agreements between employer and accredited representatives of employees concerning

> wages, hours, and other conditions of employment, and requires that parties deal with each other with open and fair minds and sincerely endeavor to overcome obstacles existing between them to the end that employment relations may be stabilized and obstruction to free flow of commerce prevented.

Black's Law Dictionary 328–29 (1968) (emphasis added). Webster's defines the phrase "collective bargaining" as:

> [A] negotiation for the settlement of terms of collective agreement between an employer or group of employers on one side and a union or number of unions on the other; broadly, any union-management negotiation.

"Collective agreement" is defined as:

> [A]n agreement between an employer and a union usually reached through collective bargaining and establishing wage rates, hours of labor, and working conditions.

Webster's Third New International Dictionary (1966) (emphasis added). Finally, Random House defines "collective bargaining" as follows:

> [T]he process by which wages, hours, rules, and working conditions are negotiated and agreed upon by a union with an employer for all the employees collectively whom it represents.

Random House Unabridged Dictionary (1967) (emphasis added).

In light of the foregoing definitions of "collective bargaining," it is clear that, when the people ratified article XII, section 2, they understood the phrase to entail the ability to engage in negotiations concerning core subjects such as wages, hours, and other conditions of employment. Section 2 of Act 100 violates article XII, section 2, because it withdraws from the bargaining process these core subjects of bargaining that the voters contemplated.

Granting the lawmakers absolute discretion to define the scope of collective bargaining would also produce the absurd result of nullifying the "right to organize for the purpose of collective bargaining." A constitutional provision must be construed "to avoid an absurd result" and to recognize the mischief the framers intended to remedy. * * * As a matter of policy, we do not blindly apply rules of construction to the point that we reach absurd conclusions that are inconsistent with the intent of our lawmakers. * * *

Here, the intent and object of the framers who adopted article XII, section 2 was to extend to public employees similar rights to collective bargaining previously adopted for private employees under article XII, section 1.[10] Defendants' construction

of article XII, section 2 would render that provision meaningless, because, if we follow the Defendants' reading of that provision to its logical conclusion, it would be possible for the legislature to establish a freeze in contractual terms on cost items not only for two years but for two decades. Surely, the framers did not contemplate such an absurd and unjust result, especially in light of the fact that their foremost intent in drafting this constitutional provision is to improve the standard of living of public employees. Accordingly, we reject Defendants' contention that the phrase "as provided by law" gave the legislature complete discretion to take away public employees' right to organize for the purpose of collective bargaining. Such reading is contrary to the underlying object and purpose of the constitutional provision.

Based on the foregoing, we hold that Section 2 of Act 100, 1999 Haw. Sess. L., violates the rights of public employees under article XIII, section 2 of the Hawai'i Constitution.

The circuit court's judgment is hereby affirmed.

The right of workers to organize with union representation was a difficult battle. Those rights were strengthened, both in law and with respect to the power of unions, through the middle of the twentieth century. Through globalization, technology and other factors, however, the leverage unionized workers had vis-à-vis corporations has dissipated in recent years. With the threat of closing plants and moving factories across borders and with increasing automation, it is often more typical now for workers not to have union membership and representation. That is a matter of the reality of **economic markets**. Yet the right to organize and to have representation retains strong **legal precedent**.

III. Government Protection of Employee Rights

A. INCOME, BENEFITS, HEALTH AND SAFETY

While employees prefer higher wages, employers prefer lower ones. Because employees need jobs, the people who have them to offer generally have more leverage. In a high growth, high employment market, employees certainly have more leverage than they would have had in a low growth, low employment market. To safeguard against those times and places where the principles of supply and demand may drive wages down and in those times when even in high employment markets, not everyone in the economy is necessarily doing well, Congress (as well as states and municipalities) enact minimum wage laws.

These laws had been held as an unconstitutional infringement on employer's rights until the 1930s, when the Supreme Court upheld New Deal legislation. The Fair Labor Standards Act of 1938 is the primary law that authorizes the setting of minimum wages and overtime pay. Even in doing so, however, there are many exceptions.

The New Deal also put into place a series of other "safety net" income protections such as retirement, disability, life insurance, medical insurance and welfare. Employers and employees each pay a portion of the costs of these programs. Self-employed persons pay the entire amount themselves, but can obtain a tax credit for a portion of the amount contributed.

At retirement, a person who has paid into the Social Security system receives a monthly payment. The age for retirement has changed over the years (and most likely will again), with smaller monthly benefits paid out if one retires sooner and larger monthly benefits if one retires later. Surviving spouses are able to rely upon the social security benefits of their deceased spouses if they remained unmarried and as long as they have minor children.

For those who have become disabled, Social Security also provides for additional benefits, though these are much harder to obtain. Unlike retirement benefits, which are fairly automatic, to receive disability payments one must be determined to have an actual disability, which requires medical evidence sufficient to persuade the Social Security Administration.

Social Security also provides for life insurance benefits, though these tend to be quite small, as well as medical insurance through Medicaid and Medicare for those who qualify. Medicare is for those who are retired whereas Medicaid is for those who do not have the means to provide for their own care. These programs have been augmented by President Obama's Affordable Care Act, which provides further guarantees for access to health insurance. Finally, Supplemental Security Income acts as an additional resource for the poor, with eligibility determined on the basis of the assets the person owns.

Except for certain small businesses, employers are also required to pay into a system that provides for unemployment insurance. If an employee loses his job, he can apply for unemployment benefits, which will last for a limited time, generally about six months. An employee who quits, however, is not eligible unless the reason he quit can be tied to harassing or dangerous job conditions. Employees fired for misconduct also cannot collect unemployment benefits. As one can imagine, much of the litigation on these issues involves what constitutes "dangerous or harassing conditions" or whether alleged "misconduct" is accurately labelled.

Two kinds of laws govern family-related situations. One pertains to child labor. While states can differ, persons under the age of fourteen are not allowed to work except in certain cases such as family farms and newspaper deliveries. Those who are fourteen to sixteen can work as long as it does not interfere with school; this provision often requires certification from the school itself and/or explicit parental approval. After sixteen years of age, more employment opportunities open, though work in dangerous or hazardous industries is still prohibited.

The other family-related situation involves family and medical leave. Employers are required to provide unpaid leave to an employee after the birth (or adoption) of a child and for medically-determined reasons. Both fathers and mothers are eligible to take medical leave after the birth or adoption of the child. A person taking such leave, however, is not guaranteed their exact same job upon return—though overwhelmingly, that is what happens—but they are assured of a comparable job.

While employees don't have a right to be covered by a retirement plan, standards do apply if a company has a program in place. Those standards attempt to make sure that all employees, subject to waiting periods and **vesting** that may take a few years to complete, can receive benefits. Such benefits are not just reserved for high-income individuals. There is also a difference between a **defined benefit program** and **defined contribution program.** The former guarantees that the employee will be covered by an applicable monthly plan the company promises to provide. While these are more prevalent in the public sector, they were once more prevalent in the private sector, but have increasingly been replaced with a defined contribution program. There is no provision that the company will provide benefits in defined contribution programs, but instead enable employees to make tax-deferred contributions to a savings account, often matched all or in part by the company.

Recall the case in chapter on the Common Law where the "fellow-servant rule" was struck down by the courts in the Lawrence case. One of the key reasons for that elimination of precedent was that programs such as workers compensation had developed to protect employees in the event of injury in the workplace without opening the door to extensive lawsuits against employers. These programs, administered by the states, specify a damage award if an injury is accidental, "arises out of work," and "arises out of the course of the job." When these conditions are met, the injury is compensated by a formula. Physical injuries are relatively straight-forward if all the conditions are met but mental damages, such as pain and suffering, as well as injuries from chronic conditions (rather than a suddenly occurring injury) tend to raise more uncertainty.

Employees are also protected through the Occupational Safety and Health Administration (OSHA), which establishes standards for workplace safety and fines violations found during inspections. Some companies will act with an eye toward providing health and safety provisions to their employees. As a general rule, this is a good thing, but there are times and places where these actions can compromise other rights individual employees possess. The following well-known case provides an example of the Supreme Court's striking down of a corporate action that claimed to protect health (and potential corporate liability for employees' illnesses), but undermined the rights of women to make decisions affecting their own health.

International Union v. Johnson Controls, Inc.

499 U.S. 187 (1991)

JUSTICE BLACKMUN delivered the opinion of the Court.

In this case we are concerned with an employer's gender-based fetal-protection policy. May an employer exclude a fertile female employee from certain jobs because of its concern for the health of the fetus the woman might conceive?

Respondent Johnson Controls, Inc., manufactures batteries. In the manufacturing process, the element lead is a primary ingredient. Occupational exposure to lead entails health risks, including the risk of harm to any fetus carried by a female employee.

Before the Civil Rights Act of 1964, 78 Stat. 241, became law, Johnson Controls did not employ any woman in a battery-manufacturing job. In June 1977, however, it announced its first official policy concerning its employment of women in lead-exposure work * * * Johnson Controls "stopped short of excluding women capable of bearing children from lead exposure," but emphasized that a woman who expected to have a child should not choose a job in which she would have such exposure. The company also required a woman who wished to be considered for employment to sign a statement that she had been advised of the risk of having a child while she was exposed to lead. The statement informed the woman that although there was evidence "that women exposed to lead have a higher rate of abortion," this evidence was "not as clear . . . as the relationship between cigarette smoking and cancer," but that it was, "medically speaking, just good sense not to run that risk if you want children and do not want to expose the unborn child to risk, however small . . . . "

Five years later, in 1982, Johnson Controls shifted from a policy of warning to a policy of exclusion. Between 1979 and 1983, eight employees became pregnant while maintaining blood lead levels in excess of 30 micrograms per deciliter. This appeared to be the critical level noted by the Occupational Safety and Health Administration (OSHA) for a worker who was planning to have a family. The company responded by announcing a broad exclusion of women from jobs that exposed them to lead. * * * The policy defined "women . . . capable of bearing children" as "[a]ll women except those whose inability to bear children is medically documented." It further stated that an unacceptable work station was one where, "over the past year," an employee had recorded a blood lead level of more than 30 micrograms per deciliter or the work site had yielded an air sample containing a lead level in excess of 30 micrograms per cubic meter.

* * *

The District Court granted summary judgment for defendant-respondent Johnson Controls. * * *

The Court of Appeals for the Seventh Circuit, sitting en banc, affirmed the summary judgment by a 7-to-4 vote. * * * With its ruling, the Seventh Circuit became the first Court of Appeals to hold that a fetal-protection policy directed exclusively at women could qualify as a BFOQ.

* * *

Under § 703(e)(1) of Title VII, an employer may discriminate on the basis of "religion, sex, or national origin in those certain instances where religion, sex, or national origin is a bona fide occupational qualification reasonably necessary to the normal operation of that particular business or enterprise." We therefore turn to the question whether Johnson Controls' fetal-protection policy is one of those "certain instances" that come within the BFOQ exception.

The BFOQ defense is written narrowly, and this Court has read it narrowly. * * *

The wording of the BFOQ defense contains several terms of restriction that indicate that the exception reaches only special situations. The statute thus limits the situations in which discrimination is permissible to "certain instances" where sex discrimination is "reasonably necessary" to the "normal operation" of the "particular" business. Each one of these terms-certain, normal, particular-prevents the use of general subjective standards and favors an objective, verifiable requirement. But the most telling term is "occupational"; this indicates that these objective, verifiable requirements must concern job-related skills and aptitudes.

* * *

Johnson Controls argues that its fetal-protection policy falls within the so-called safety exception to the BFOQ. Our cases have stressed that discrimination on the basis of sex because of safety concerns is allowed only in narrow circumstances. In Dothard v. Rawlinson, this Court indicated that danger to a woman herself does not justify discrimination. We there allowed the employer to hire only male guards in contact areas of maximum-security male penitentiaries only because more was at stake than the "individual woman's decision to weigh and accept the risks of employment." We found sex to be a BFOQ inasmuch as the employment of a female guard would create real risks of safety to others if violence broke out because the guard was a woman. Sex discrimination was tolerated because sex was related to the guard's ability to do the job-maintaining prison security. We also required in Dothard a high correlation between sex and ability to perform job functions and refused to allow employers to use sex as a proxy for strength although it might be a fairly accurate one.

* * *

We have no difficulty concluding that Johnson Controls cannot establish a BFOQ. Fertile women, as far as appears in the record, participate in the manufacture of batteries as efficiently as anyone else. Johnson Controls' professed moral and ethical concerns about the welfare of the next generation do not suffice to establish a BFOQ of female sterility. Decisions about the welfare of future children must be left to the parents who conceive, bear, support, and raise them rather than to the employers who hire those parents. Congress has mandated this choice through Title VII, as amended by the PDA. Johnson Controls has attempted to exclude women because of their reproductive capacity. Title VII and the PDA simply do not allow a woman's dismissal because of her failure to submit to sterilization.

* * *

It is no more appropriate for the courts than it is for individual employers to decide whether a woman's reproductive role is more important to herself and her family than her economic role. Congress has left this choice to the woman as hers to make.

The judgment of the Court of Appeals is reversed, and the case is remanded for further proceedings consistent with this opinion.

It is so ordered.

B. SEXUAL HARASSMENT

Title VII of the Civil Rights Act makes it illegal to discriminate against a person on the basis of sex as well as on the basis of race, religion, and national origin. This law governs issues of sexual harassment, and either through a quid pro quo demand or the creation of a hostile work environment, an employee can bring suit on the basis of civil rights discrimination.

One might think that these issues do not come up as much as they may have thirty years ago. While there has been a significant rise in awareness regarding issues of sexual harassment and increasing understanding of what constitutes inappropriate behavior, the issue has hardly gone away. During the 2016 campaign for the U.S. presidency, multiple allegations of sexual harassment (or assault) were made against the Republican nominee that also brought to mind past charges against a former Democratic President, while other, separate and contemporaneous allegations further implicated the head of a major news network. These high-profile cases are apart from day-in, day-out issues that occur throughout the country. Thus, while there is more guidance today as to what constitutes harassment and assault, it remains a pervasive issue.

The following case provides a contemporary example of a sexual harassment issue in a university setting.

Nelson v. University Of Hawai'i

97 Hawai'i 376, 38 P.3d 95 (2001)

Opinion of the Court by Moon, C.J.

Plaintiff-appellant Karyn Nelson brought an action against action against defendants-appellees the University of Hawai'i, Bart Buxton (Dr. Buxton), and Kwok W. Ho (Dr. Ho) [hereinafter, collectively, Defendants], involving numerous claims arising out of her employment as an assistant professor at the university. * * * In August 1992, Nelson was hired by the University of Hawai'i at Manoa (the University) as an assistant professor in the Department of Health, Physical Education, and Recreation (HPER) of the College of Education. Nelson alleged that she was subjected to discriminatory treatment and harassment based on her gender throughout her employment, but that problems with Dr. Ho, the chair of HPER, and Dr. Buxton, a fellow faculty member, escalated in 1994.

* * *

Sexual harassment is a form of sex discrimination prohibited by HRS § 378–2. "Quid pro quo" cases generally involve allegations that an employer conditioned employment benefits on sexual favors. "Hostile environment" sexual harassment (HESH) is defined as:

> Unwelcome sexual advances, requests for sexual favors, and other verbal or physical conduct or visual forms of harassment of a sexual nature constitute sexual harassment when . . . [t]hat conduct has the purpose or effect of unreasonably interfering with an individual's work performance or creating an intimidating, hostile, or offensive working environment.

The aforementioned definition of HESH is virtually identical to the corresponding federal regulations under Title VII of the Civil Rights Act, adopted by the EEOC. This court has held that a HESH claim exists when an employee can show:

1. That he or she was subjected to sexual advances, requests for sexual favors, or other verbal or physical conduct of a sexual nature,

2. That this conduct was unwelcome; and

3. That the conduct had the purpose or effect of either:

a. unreasonably interfering with an individual's work performance or

b. creating an intimidating, hostile, or offensive work environment.

* * *

In addition to the foregoing elements, a plaintiff is also required to establish that the harassing conduct was "severe or pervasive." However, in discussing this "severe or pervasive" requirement, state and federal courts and agencies have used somewhat inconsistent language. For example, based on federal case law interpreting Title VII, Steinberg discussed the perspectives to be used in evaluating a HESH claim as follows:

> [T]he perspective to be used is that of the victim. Thus, if the complainant is a woman, the objective standard is met if a reasonable woman would consider such conduct sufficiently severe or pervasive to alter the conditions of employment and either [(a)] unreasonably interfere with work performance or [(b)] create an intimidating, hostile, or offensive work environment.

The language in Steinberg, setting forth the "severe or pervasive" requirement (see underscored text above), although not incorrect, is different from the standard discussed in Ellison.

* * *

Based on the foregoing, we take this opportunity to clarify the elements of a HESH claim set forth in Steinberg and hold that, in order to establish a HESH claim, the claimant must show that: (1) he or she was subjected to sexual advances, requests for sexual favors, or other verbal or physical conduct or visual forms of harassment of a sexual nature; (2) the conduct was unwelcome; (3) the conduct was severe or pervasive; (4) the conduct had the purpose or effect of either: (a) unreasonably interfering with the claimant's work performance, or (b) creating an intimidating, hostile, or offensive work environment; (5) the claimant actually perceived the conduct as having such purpose or effect; and (6) the claimant's perception was objectively reasonable to a person of the claimant's gender in the same position as the claimant.

In addition, with regard to the third element of the claim, we observe that the required showing of severity or seriousness varies inversely with the pervasiveness or frequency of the conduct. For example, a single severe act can be enough to establish a claim, and multiple incidents, each of which may not be severe when considered individually, can be enough to establish a claim when evaluated collectively.

Moreover, we emphasize that, to establish the last two elements of a HESH claim, it is not necessary for the claimant to prove that he or she has suffered tangible

physical or psychological harm: the claimant's perception is the harm as long as the perception is objectively reasonable.

Finally, we emphasize that, in evaluating a HESH claim for purposes of dismissal, summary judgment or judgment as a matter of law, or in instructing juries, courts must "look at the record as a whole and at the totality of the circumstances, such as the nature of the sexual advances and the context in which the alleged incidents occurred." * * *

In this case, the court instructed the jury that the plaintiff must show that the employer

> engaged in harassing conduct directed toward the plaintiff; that sex was a motivating factor for the harassment; that this conduct was unwelcome and sufficiently severe or pervasive that it had the purpose or effect of altering the conditions of Plaintiff's employment and creating an intimidating, hostile, abusive, or offensive working environment; the environment created by the conduct would have been perceived as intimidating, hostile, abusive, or offensive by a reasonable person in the same position as Plaintiff; that Plaintiff did in fact perceive the environment as intimidating, hostile, abusive or offensive; and this environment caused plaintiff injury, damage, loss, or harm.
>
> * * *

Based on the foregoing, we hold that (1) the trial court abused its discretion in excluding Nelson's proffered rebuttal evidence of her publications, and the exclusion of such evidence resulted in substantial prejudice to Nelson's claims for employment discrimination and negligent and intentional infliction of emotional distress; (2) the trial court's jury instruction with respect to sexual harassment (instruction No. 9) was prejudicially erroneous and misleading; and (3) the trial court erred in granting Defendants' motion for judgment notwithstanding the verdict. Therefore, we vacate the judgment of the circuit court and remand this case for a new trial with respect to Nelson's claims of employment discrimination and negligent and intentional infliction of emotional distress only.

C. ANTI-DISCRIMINATION

While there may be employment-at-will, Congress and the Courts have recognized that there also have been many times in which employers have discriminated against employees. Not all differentiation is improper. Any employee evaluation requires comparisons and determinations of whether performance is acceptable. Hiring decisions discriminate when a smarter, more experienced or more personable employee is selected. Thus, it is incorrect to think that all discrimination is bad. But discrimination on the basis of certain categories is illegal.

It is easier for the Constitution to apply to public sector employees because the Constitution governs the actions of government. However, as we saw in the chapter on Constitutional Law, the Commerce Clause has also been a powerful tool for Congress to constitutionally regulate businesses so that the private sector cannot discriminate on the basis of certain categories. The commerce clause was the provision that authorized the 1964 Civil Rights Act, which is the foundational source for most of today's anti-discrimination rules.

As we have already seen, there is a major exception that permeates all discussion of anti-discrimination laws. It is called the **Bona Fide Occupational Qualification** (BFOQ). Employers can discriminate on the basis of religion, sex or national origin if there is a reasonable business necessity for doing so. So, if one is hiring for a professional women's basketball team, it would be a BFOQ for the employee to be a woman. If a church is hiring a minister, it would be a BFOQ that the minister be ordained by the faith tradition of the hiring church. BFOQ exemption generally does not apply to issues of race.

The easier cases for the Equal Employment Opportunity Commission, which oversees the enforcement of Title VII, is when there is **disparate treatment**, or when a specific individual is treated differently by an employer. The harder issue is when the job requirements are themselves silent as to qualifications, but the impact tends to discriminate against a particular group of people. The following case is a famous Supreme Court case that analyzes this issue.

Wards Cove Packing Co., Inc. v. Atonio

490 U.S. 642 (1989)

JUSTICE WHITE delivered the opinion of the Court.

Title VII of the Civil Rights Act of 1964, 78 Stat. 253 makes it an unfair employment practice for an employer to discriminate against any individual with respect to hiring or the terms and condition of employment because of such individual's race, color, religion, sex, or national origin; or to limit, segregate, or classify his employees in ways that would adversely affect any employee because of the employee's race, color, religion, sex, or national origin. * * *

The claims before us are disparate-impact claims, involving the employment practices of petitioners, two companies that operate salmon canneries in remote and widely separated areas of Alaska. The canneries operate only during the salmon runs in the summer months. They are inoperative and vacant for the rest of the year. In May or June of each year, a few weeks before the salmon runs begin, workers arrive and prepare the equipment and facilities for the canning operation. Most of these workers possess a variety of skills. When salmon runs are about to begin, the workers who will operate the cannery lines arrive, remain as long as there are fish to can, and then depart. The canneries are then closed down, winterized, and left vacant until the next spring. During the off-season, the companies employ only a small number of individuals at their headquarters in Seattle and Astoria, Oregon, plus some employees at the winter shipyard in Seattle.

The length and size of salmon runs vary from year to year, and hence the number of employees needed at each cannery also varies. Estimates are made as early in the winter as possible; the necessary employees are hired, and when the time comes, they are transported to the canneries. Salmon must be processed soon after they are caught, and the work during the canning season is therefore intense. For this reason, and because the canneries are located in remote regions, all workers are housed at the canneries and have their meals in company-owned mess halls.

Jobs at the canneries are of two general types: "cannery jobs" on the cannery line, which are unskilled positions; and "noncannery jobs," which fall into a variety of classifications. Most noncannery jobs are classified as skilled positions. Cannery jobs are filled predominantly by nonwhites: Filipinos and Alaska Natives. The Filipinos are hired through, and dispatched by, Local 37 of the International Longshoremen's and Warehousemen's Union pursuant to a hiring hall agreement with the local. The Alaska Natives primarily reside in villages near the remote cannery locations. Noncannery jobs are filled with predominantly white workers, who are hired during the winter months from the companies' offices in Washington and Oregon. Virtually all of the noncannery jobs pay more than cannery positions. The predominantly white noncannery workers and the predominantly nonwhite cannery employees live in separate dormitories and eat in separate mess halls.

In 1974, respondents, a class of nonwhite cannery workers who were (or had been) employed at the canneries, brought this Title VII action against petitioners. Respondents alleged that a variety of petitioners' hiring/promotion practices—e.g., nepotism, a rehire preference, a lack of objective hiring criteria, separate hiring channels, a practice of not promoting from within—were responsible for the racial stratification of the work force and had denied them and other nonwhites employment as noncannery workers on the basis of race. Respondents also complained of petitioners' racially segregated housing and dining facilities. All of respondents' claims were advanced under both the disparate-treatment and disparate-impact theories of Title VII liability.

* * *

[T]the cannery work force in no way reflected "the pool of qualified job applicants" or the "qualified population in the labor force." Measuring alleged discrimination in the selection of accountants, managers, boat captains, electricians, doctors, and engineers—and the long list of other "skilled" noncannery positions found to exist by the District Court, see 34 EPD ¶ 34,437, p. 33,832—by comparing the number of nonwhites occupying these jobs to the number of nonwhites filling cannery worker positions is nonsensical. If the absence of minorities holding such skilled positions is due to a dearth of qualified nonwhite applicants (for reasons that are not petitioners' fault), petitioners' selection methods or employment practices cannot be said to have had a "disparate impact" on nonwhites.

One example illustrates why this must be so. Respondents' own statistics concerning the noncannery work force at one of the canneries at issue here indicate that approximately 17% of the new hires for medical jobs, and 15% of the new hires for officer worker positions, were nonwhite. If it were the case that less than 15 to 17% of the applicants for these jobs were nonwhite and that nonwhites made up a lower percentage of the relevant qualified labor market, it is hard to see how respondents, without more, would have made out a prima facie case of disparate impact. Yet, under the Court of Appeals' theory, simply because nonwhites comprise 52% of the cannery workers at the cannery in question.

Such a result cannot be squared with our cases or with the goals behind the statute. **The Court of Appeals' theory, at the very least, would mean that any employer who had a segment of his work force that was—for some reason—racially imbalanced, could be haled into court and forced to engage in the expensive and time-consuming task of defending the "business necessity" of the methods used to select the other members of his work force. The only practicable option for many employers would be to adopt racial quotas, insuring that no portion of their work forces deviated in racial composition from the other portions thereof; this is a result that Congress expressly rejected in drafting Title VII. The Court of Appeals' theory would "leave the employer little choice . . . but to engage in a subjective quota system of employment selection. This, of course, is far from the intent of Title VII."**

The Court of Appeals also erred with respect to the unskilled noncannery positions. Racial imbalance in one segment of an employer's work force does not, without more, establish a prima facie case of disparate impact with respect to the selection of workers for the employer's other positions, even where workers for the different positions may have somewhat fungible skills (as is arguably the case for cannery and unskilled noncannery workers). As long as there are no barriers or practices deterring qualified nonwhites from applying for noncannery positions, if the percentage of selected applicants who are nonwhite is not significantly less than the percentage of qualified applicants who are nonwhite, the employer's selection mechanism probably does not operate with a disparate impact on minorities. Where this is the case, the percentage of nonwhite workers found in other positions in the employer's labor force is irrelevant to the question of a *prima facie* statistical case of disparate impact. As noted above, a contrary ruling on this point would almost inexorably lead to the use of numerical quotas in the workplace, a result that Congress and this Court have rejected repeatedly in the past.

Moreover, isolating the cannery workers as the potential "labor force" for unskilled noncannery positions is at once both too broad and too narrow in its focus. It is too broad because the vast majority of these cannery workers did not seek jobs in unskilled noncannery positions; there is no showing that many of them would have done so even if none of the arguably "deterring" practices existed. Thus, the pool of cannery workers cannot be used as a surrogate for the class of qualified job applicants because it contains many persons who have not (and would not) be noncannery job applicants. Conversely, if respondents propose to use the cannery workers for comparison purposes because they represent the "qualified labor population" generally, the group is too narrow because there are obviously many qualified persons in the labor market for noncannery jobs who are not cannery workers. * * *

Consequently, we reverse the Court of Appeals' ruling that a comparison between the percentage of cannery workers who are nonwhite and the percentage of noncannery workers who are nonwhite makes out a prima facie case of disparate impact. * * *

It is so ordered.

To what do anti-discrimination protections apply? This is an expanding area. Prohibitions against discrimination on the basis of race, religion, ethnic origin, and gender have been relatively long-standing. Age has received protection as well. Increasingly, protection has also been extended on the basis of sexual orientation and gender identity. Individual statutes have refined, clarified and extended these protections to different groups, as have interpretations of court decisions.

Each state's anti-discrimination laws are a little different. To summarize them in one place, a chart of all the states in the US plus the District of Columbia can be found in the Appendix.

D. PRIVACY

Courts try to strike a balance in the workplace between the right of employees to keep personal issues private and the property right of employers to make sure employees are working and performing as they should. This explains drug testing policies, for example, where courts have held that employers have a property interest in making sure that their employees are ready and able to work so can therefore test to see it the employee may be taking drugs. The more a company has a need for a high degree of security—a prison system, an airline, a bus company—the more the courts will defer to the business's plan for drug testing. The less security or safety is a concern, the more restrictive of drug testing the courts are likely to be.

A similar balancing test exists with respect to electronic spying. Companies do have a right to monitor employee movement on company-provided computers if for no other reasons than to (a) make sure the employee is working rather than keeping track of his March Madness Brackets during the NCAA Basketball Tournament or to (b) make sure the employee is not accessing sexually explicit websites and therefore both not working and contributing to a hostile work environment.

Requiring polygraphs is become more controversial because it intrudes even more into an employee's personal space. Along these lines, after the terrorist attacks of 9/11, there was a strong national consensus that some loss of privacy rights was justified in order to prevent the possibility of other such attacks. The following case looks at this kind of issue.

City of Ontario, Cal. v. Quon

560 U.S. 746 (2010)

JUSTICE KENNEDY delivered the opinion of the Court.

* * *

The City of Ontario (City) is a political subdivision of the State of California. The case arose out of incidents in 2001 and 2002 when respondent Jeff Quon was employed by the Ontario Police Department (OPD). * * * In October 2001, the City acquired 20 alphanumeric pagers capable of sending and receiving text messages. Arch Wireless Operating Company provided wireless service for the pagers. Under the City's service contract with Arch Wireless, each pager was allotted a limited number of characters sent or received each month. Usage in excess of that amount would result in an additional fee. The City issued pagers to Quon and other SWAT Team members in order to help the SWAT Team mobilize and respond to emergency situations.

Before acquiring the pagers, the City announced a "Computer Usage, Internet and E-Mail Policy" (Computer Policy) that applied to all employees. Among other provisions, it specified that the City "reserves the right to monitor and log all network activity including e-mail and Internet use, with or without notice. Users should have no expectation of privacy or confidentiality when using these resources." In March 2000, Quon signed a statement acknowledging that he had read and understood the Computer Policy.

* * * Although the Computer Policy did not cover text messages by its explicit terms, the City made clear to employees, including Quon, that the City would treat text messages the same way as it treated e-mails. At an April 18, 2002, staff meeting at which Quon was present, Lieutenant Steven Duke, the OPD officer responsible for the City's contract with Arch Wireless, told officers that messages sent on the pagers "are considered e-mail messages. This means that [text] messages would fall under the City's policy as public information and [would be] eligible for auditing." Duke's comments were put in writing in a memorandum sent on April 29, 2002, by Chief Scharf to Quon and other City personnel.

Within the first or second billing cycle after the pagers were distributed, Quon exceeded his monthly text message character allotment. Duke told Quon about the overage, and reminded him that messages sent on the pagers were "considered e-mail and could be audited." Duke said, however, that "it was not his intent to audit [an] employee's text messages to see if the overage [was] due to work related transmissions." Duke suggested that Quon could reimburse the City for the overage fee rather than have Duke audit the messages. Quon wrote a check to the City for the overage. Duke offered the same arrangement to other employees who incurred overage fees.

Over the next few months, Quon exceeded his character limit three or four times. Each time he reimbursed the City. Quon and another officer again incurred overage fees for their pager usage in August 2002. At a meeting in October, Duke told Scharf that he had become " 'tired of being a bill collector.' " Scharf decided to determine whether the existing character limit was too low—that is, whether officers such as Quon were having to pay fees for sending work-related messages—or if the overages were for personal messages. Scharf told Duke to request transcripts of text messages sent in August and September by Quon and the other employee who had exceeded the character allowance.

At Duke's request, an administrative assistant employed by OPD contacted Arch Wireless. After verifying that the City was the subscriber on the accounts, Arch Wireless provided the desired transcripts. Duke reviewed the transcripts and discovered that many of the messages sent and received on Quon's pager were not work related, and some were sexually explicit. Duke reported his findings to Scharf, who, along with Quon's immediate supervisor, reviewed the transcripts himself. After his review, Scharf referred the matter to OPD's internal affairs division for an investigation into whether Quon was violating OPD rules by pursuing personal matters while on duty.

The officer in charge of the internal affairs review was Sergeant Patrick McMahon. Before conducting a review, McMahon used Quon's work schedule to redact the transcripts in order to eliminate any messages Quon sent while off duty. He then reviewed the content of the messages Quon sent during work hours. McMahon's report noted that Quon sent or received 456 messages during work hours in the month of August 2002, of which no more than 57 were work related; he sent as many as 80 messages during a single day at work; and on an average workday, Quon sent or received 28 messages, of which only 3 were related to police business. The report concluded that Quon had violated OPD rules. Quon was allegedly disciplined.

* * *

The Fourth Amendment states: "The right of the people to be secure in their persons, houses, papers, and effects, against unreasonable searches and seizures, shall not be violated . . . . " It is well settled that the Fourth Amendment's protection extends beyond the sphere of criminal investigations. "The Amendment guarantees the privacy, dignity, and security of persons against certain arbitrary and invasive acts by officers of the Government," without regard to whether the government actor is investigating crime or performing another function. The Fourth Amendment applies as well when the Government acts in its capacity as an employer.

* * *

These matters would all bear on the legitimacy of an employee's privacy expectation. The Court must proceed with care when considering the whole concept of privacy expectations in communications made on electronic equipment owned by a government employer. The judiciary risks error by elaborating too fully on the Fourth Amendment implications of emerging technology before its role in society has become clear.

* * *

As for the scope of the search, reviewing the transcripts was reasonable because it was an efficient and expedient way to determine whether Quon's overages were the result of work-related messaging or personal use. The review was also not " 'excessively intrusive.' Although Quon had gone over his monthly allotment a number of times, OPD requested transcripts for only the months of August and September 2002. While it may have been reasonable as well for OPD to review transcripts of all the months in which Quon exceeded his allowance, it was certainly reasonable for OPD to review messages for just two months in order to obtain a large enough sample to decide whether the character limits were efficacious. * * * As a law enforcement officer, he would or should have known that his actions were likely to come under legal scrutiny, and that this might entail an analysis of his on-the-job communications. Under the circumstances, a reasonable employee would be aware that sound management principles might require the audit of messages to determine whether the pager was being appropriately used. Given that the City issued the pagers to Quon and other SWAT Team members in order to help them more quickly respond to crises—and given that Quon had received no assurances of privacy—Quon could have anticipated that it might be necessary for the City to audit pager messages to assess the SWAT Team's performance in particular emergency situations.

* * *

Because the search was motivated by a legitimate work-related purpose, and because it was not excessive in scope, the search was reasonable * * * . For these same reasons—that the employer had a legitimate reason for the search, and that the search was not excessively intrusive in light of that justification—the Court also concludes that the search would be "regarded as reasonable and normal in the private-employer context" and would satisfy the approach of Justice SCALIA's concurrence. The search was reasonable, and the Court of Appeals erred by holding to the contrary. Petitioners did not violate Quon's Fourth Amendment rights.

* * *

It is so ordered.

The interaction between privacy and both business and governmental interests in security and protection of property makes it an active area of regulation. A summary chart of the various privacy-related laws affecting the workplace can be found in the Appendix.

E. TORTIOUS INTERFERENCE AND COVENANTS NOT TO COMPETE

Especially early in your career, the possibility that you may have your freedom to move from job-to-job limited seems remote. What is important is getting a job and, perhaps after getting some experience, moving to a new, more attractive position. Yet at least two potential traps lurk. We have caught glimmers of each in previous chapters, but it worth revisiting them to conclude this chapter.

The first potential hindrance to job mobility is a covenant not to compete. In order to protect the investment they make in an employee's training and experience as well as to protect their own company secrets, companies may insert a clause in the employee agreement that restricts the employee's ability to work for a competing company or even within the same industry. Courts look at these clauses carefully because they do not want to restrict peoples' freedom of movement or their capacity to choose the direction of their careers. Thus, the covenant must be reasonable both in terms of duration and geographical scope.

The second potential pitfall comes on the other side of a recruitment. Namely, the company wooing another company's employee to leave their current position and come to work for them could be found to have committed a tort of interfering with a contractual relationship. Here again, recruitments happen all the time and, in the majority of cases, there are no objections or lawsuits. However, especially if the employee is important to a business, there can be grounds for a lawsuit for the **tortious interference** with a contractual relationship. We have already seen how covenants not to compete operate in the Contracts chapter but the following case deals with the second trap of tortious interference with a contractual relationship.

Greenville Automatic Gas Co. v. Automatic Propane Gas and Supp., LLC

465 S.W.3d 778 (Tex. App. Dallas 2015)

Opinion by CHIEF JUSTICE THOMAS, Retired

* * *

Greenville employed Anderson for approximately fifteen years as a route driver, delivering propane to Greenville's customers. The parties agree that, after working for Greenville for several months, Anderson signed an agreement involving his employment. Anderson contends he signed a three-page agreement that addressed only the company's method of calculating overtime pay. Greenville contends Anderson signed a nine-page employment agreement that contained—among other terms—a covenant not to compete with Greenville in certain Texas counties and a covenant not to solicit Greenville's customers after he left Greenville's employ. We will refer to the nine-page version of the contract—the only one in evidence below—as the Employment Agreement.

In 2011, Anderson resigned his position at Greenville and went to work for Automatic Propane, a competitor of Greenville. Counsel for Greenville sent letters to Anderson and to Automatic Propane invoking the covenants not to compete or solicit.

* * *

Greenville pleaded that Automatic Propane tortuously interfered with both Anderson's Employment Agreement and Greenville's contracts with its customers; it also pleaded that Anderson tortuously interfered with Greenville's contracts with its customers. To recover for tortious interference with a contract, Greenville would have to prove: (1) the existence of a contract subject to interference, (2) a willful and intentional act of interference, (3) the act was a proximate cause of damages, and (4) actual damages or loss. In their no-evidence motion, appellees asserted that Greenville had no evidence of each of those four required elements.

We first examine Automatic Propane's alleged interference with Anderson's Employment Agreement in light of the second element of the alleged tort. "To establish a willful and intentional act of interference, there must be evidence that the defendant was more than a willing participant—the defendant must have knowingly induced one of the contracting parties to breach its obligations under a contract." The willful act could not merely be Automatic Propane's hiring of Anderson: the parties agree Anderson was an at-will employee. Greenville contends Automatic Propane was aware—before it hired Anderson—that some of Greenville employees were bound by contractual covenants not to compete. But Greenville has failed to come forward with summary judgment evidence indicating Automatic Propane had knowledge of Anderson's covenant before he was hired. Instead, the first indication in the record that Automatic Propane knew of restrictions on Anderson's employment came when Greenville counsel advised the company of the Employment Agreement, at least a month after Anderson left Greenville and began working there. We discern no summary judgment evidence of a willful, intentional act of interference with Anderson's Employment Agreement on the part of Automatic Propane.

As to Greenville's claim that both appellees interfered with contracts between Greenville and its customers, we conclude Greenville again failed to carry its summary judgment burden. There is no summary judgment evidence of any Greenville customer contract, written or oral, that could be subject to interference by either Automatic Propane or Anderson. Instead, the summary judgment record includes testimony from Greenville's president that the only restriction it could enforce against its customers was to prohibit competitors from filling tanks that were rented from Greenville. He acknowledged that Greenville could not force any customer to purchase its propane. Nor could Greenville prevent any customer from obtaining a tank and propane from a competitor.

* * *

Greenville pleaded that Automatic Propane and Anderson used Anderson's confidential knowledge of Greenville's customers to damage Greenville. Under Texas law, a plaintiff can recover for misappropriation of trade secrets by establishing (1) the existence of proprietary information or a trade secret, (2) a breach of a confidential relationship or improper discovery of the information or secret, (3) a use of the information or secret without the plaintiff's authorization, and (4) resulting damages. In their no-evidence motion, appellees challenged Greenville's ability to bring forward evidence sufficient to raise an issue of material fact on each of these elements.

In its response, Greenville pointed to Anderson's knowledge of Greenville's "customer lists, customer addresses, customer phone numbers, customer creditworthiness, whether the customer owned [its] tank, [and] customer routes" as information that was taken from Greenville contrary to the Employment Agreement and without Greenville's permission. However, even if we assume—without deciding—that this list of materials is sufficiently proprietary to support a misappropriation tort, Greenville did not offer summary judgment evidence of either appellee's use of the confidential information. Greenville points to Anderson's testimony that he serviced some of the same customers for Automatic Propane that he had serviced for Greenville. Based on that statement alone, Greenville concludes Anderson "must have used the names and addresses of the customers, at a minimum." But Automatic Propane could have developed its own customer list in any number of ways—this is not evidence of use of confidential information sufficient to defeat appellees' no-evidence summary judgment motion.

We conclude the trial court did not err in granting summary judgment for appellees on Greenville's claim for misappropriation of proprietary information and trade secrets.

* * *

Greenville also pleaded that Automatic Propane and Anderson conspired to misappropriate Greenville's proprietary information and trade secrets. In this instance, we look to appellees' traditional motion for summary judgment for the most direct resolution of Greenville's claim. Both Greenville and appellees acknowledge that civil conspiracy is a derivative tort. Stated differently, conspiracy requires an underlying tort reflecting an unlawful means or purpose by the conspirators. Id. We have already concluded the trial court properly granted summary judgment on and dismissed Greenville's misappropriation claim. In the absence of that misappropriation claim, there can be no claim for a conspiracy to commit misappropriation.

We conclude the trial court did not err in granting summary judgment on Greenville's civil conspiracy claim.

* * *

Under the heading of Unfair Competition, Greenville pleaded that Automatic Propane and Anderson engaged in "conduct that is contrary to honest practice in industrial or commercial matters." Looking again to appellees' traditional motion, they argue that unfair competition is not an independent tort. Rather, they contend that—like conspiracy—unfair competition is a derivative tort that requires a viable underlying tort or other illegal conduct for liability to exist. We agree. We have concluded that the trial court did not err in granting summary judgment in appellees' favor on each of Greenville's tort counterclaims that are before us. In the absence of any underlying tort or illegal conduct, the trial court did not err in granting summary judgment on the unfair competition claim as well.

We overrule Greenville's third issue.

CONCLUSION

We affirm the trial court's judgment insofar as it ordered that Greenville take nothing on its counterclaims for business disparagement, tortious interference with contract, misappropriation of proprietary information and trade secrets, conspiracy to misappropriate proprietary information and trade secrets, and unfair competition. In all other respects, we reverse the trial court's judgment. We remand the case to the trial court for further proceedings consistent with this opinion.

Because employment involves relationships between human beings, there are legal and ethical issues involved in adjudicating the balances of authority and power. Often new laws are couched quite specifically in ethical terms, such as the entire notion of civil rights. Thus, it is worth considering both some additional legal questions as well as some ethical questions to see the interaction between the two.

NOTES AND COMMENTS on the Legal Environment of Business

1. **IN YOUR VIEW,** what are legitimate and illegitimate reasons to discriminate? Our nation's laws have (often slowly) evolved to protect an increasing number of classes of individuals from discrimination. At the same time, we tend not to worry about other discriminations, for example, in the form of a graduated income tax where those earning more money pay taxes at a higher rate than those who earn less. Is that fair? Or have the courts struck the right balance of permitting discrimination on the basis of income-based situations, such as the tax code, while extending protection to those discriminated on the basis of race, gender, ethnic origin, religion, age, and sexual orientation? What are the reasons you offer for your view?

2. **DO YOU THINK** that covenants not to compete and lawsuits that allow companies to sue others on the basis of tortious interference with a contractual relationship should be allowed? Are these unfair restrictions to an employee's ability to have a career? How would you balance the need for freedom of movement and career with a company's interest to protect the investment they make in an employee?

3. **HOW WILLING ARE** you to have your employer track your emails? Texts? Website movement? Keystrokes? Phone calls? Where do you think the line should be drawn?

NOTES AND COMMENTS on the Ethical Environment of Business

1. **NEARLY EVERYONE IS** either an employer or an employee. There may be a few individuals who completely encapsulate their own business so they neither need someone else to employ them nor do they need to have help from employees to get their work done. Because most people interact with others at work, there are bound to be ethical issues that arise at work that have to be addressed.

2. **THIS CHAPTER ON** employment law deals with many kinds of cases, most of them related to some kind of discriminatory issues. Did an employer discriminate intentionally or via impact against others because of race, gender, national origins, etc. How do you come out on these issues? Do you think these cases were decidedly fairly? Why? If not, what modifications do you think would make the law fairer?

3. **WHAT ABOUT ISSUES** surrounding collective bargaining? Given the reduction of unionization, especially outside of the public sector, are unions whose time as passed? If so, then what are the levers to protect workers from employers whose conduct is problematic? If you think that unions still should play a strong role, then do you think the current laws have union rights basically correct? What did you think of the two collective bargaining cases in this chapter?

4. **TURNING TO *ETHICS VIGNETTES***, Chapter Nine has three interesting ethics-related employment questions. The first revisits this book's chapter on contracts where it looks at non-competition covenants. Do you think these are fair? What lines would you draw? Are there differences now because of the Internet? In other words, it may have been one thing to preclude an insurance agent from quitting his job, moving across the street with some of his former firm's clients and competing against the former firm. Restrictions of how a person could do that were exactly what non-compete covenants addressed. But if one is working for a company that has a significant online component, how do you draw those lines? How restrictive can a covenant be when location can be so global?

5. **ONE MIGHT THINK THAT,** today and especially in law firms where knowledge of the law should be at its highest, we would not see many sexual harassment cases. Yet, some of the highest profile sexual harassment cases come directly from some of the world's largest and most prestigious law firms. How does this happen? Why would there continue to be such cases even in a place that pays attention to the law every working hour? What does this say about human beings? What does it say about the law's ability to direct behavior?

6. **FINALLY, CHAPTER NINE** provides an account of the concussion issue the National Football League is dealing with. Do you think the NFL has done enough to protect its players? What more, if anything should be done? Or, as some have argued, making the game safer simply detracts from what is a violent, even according to some players, barbaric sport? On the other hand, if the NFL doesn't get its hands around this issue, is the existence of the NFL in question? Or, is it possible that its popularity will significantly diminish? Would that be a good thing or a bad thing? What duty does the NFL have to protect its employees?

CHAPTER

15

Introduction to Business Organizations

In a follow-up book, we address issues of business organizations in great detail. In this, concluding chapter, we provide an introductory overview of sole proprietorships, partnerships, and corporations with a particular eye toward the debates about the history and purpose of corporations and the arguments surrounding the nature, if any, of their social responsibilities.

I. Choice of Entity

ALTHOUGH MOST OF OUR TIME in this chapter will be spent studying aspects of the corporation, it is still important to understand the basics of the other business associations, how they differ from corporations, and why a business might choose one form over another. Although each state has authorized different forms of business associations, the same types of organizations exist throughout the nation, and the laws governing them are similar. Three basic business forms were widely used in Britain and pre-Revolutionary America—the general partnership, the limited partnership, and the corporation.[1] The other business forms available to modern enterprises include a variety of hybrid forms in which some benefits of partnerships

1 Robert W. Hamilton, *Entity Proliferation*, 37 Suffolk U. L. Rev. 859, 862 (2004).

are combined with some characteristics of corporations. The following is an outline of the currently most-popular business organizations.

A. SOLE PROPRIETORSHIP

A **sole proprietorship,** the simplest business organization to start and maintain, is an unincorporated business owned by one individual. There is no separate existence of the business apart from the owner, so all liabilities of the proprietorship are personal liabilities, and all income or expenses of the business must be included on the owner's personal tax return.

Advantages of the sole proprietorship include ease of creation and termination—states do not require any organizational documents to be filed—and operational flexibility, as the business is operated entirely at the discretion of the owner, without required formalities such as shareholder meetings. The principal disadvantage is the unlimited liability that results because there is no separate existence of the business apart from the owner.[2]

B. GENERAL PARTNERSHIP

A **general partnership** is the simplest business organization for two or more people jointly carrying on a trade or business. General partnerships can be formed by nothing more than a verbal agreement among the partners that each party will contribute and expects to share in the profits and losses of the business. Frequently, however, written agreements and contracts will be drafted by lawyers to ensure that the organization is precisely as the partners want it. Until very recently, in most jurisdictions, a partnership was not actually a legally separate entity, so the partnership could not hold property, sue or be sued, and (as is still true) was not taxed as a separate entity.

Advantages of general partnerships include the ease of formation and, as indicated earlier, avoidance of the "double tax" corporations and their shareholders must pay. This feature is sometimes referred to as "flow-through" taxation. Income and expenses of the partnership are taxed only once, on individual partners' personal tax returns. The disadvantages of partnerships include joint and several liability on the part of individual partners for the entirety of the partnership's obligations and the fact that each partner is potentially an agent of the partnership able to bind all the others. In addition, ownership of a partnership is generally not transferable and

---

2 Small Business Opportunity Clinic, Northwestern University School of Law. "Comparison of Business Entities Overview," (privately distributed paper prepared by David Gaffin, used by permission of the author).

partnerships are not perpetual, dissolving when one partner dies or withdraws from the business.[3]

C. LIMITED PARTNERSHIP

While the general partnership emerged from the common law, the **limited partnership** is a creature of statute. Still, a limited partnership is in many respects similar to a general partnership, the primary difference being that a limited partnership involves limited liability for one or more of the partners. A limited partnership must have at least one **general partner**, which general partner will be personally liable for the limited partnership's debts and obligations and will actively manage the business. This general partner can be an individual or a corporation. The other partners, called, not surprisingly, **limited partners**, are not liable for partnership obligations, do not control the day-to-day operations of the partnership, and are not authorized to act as agents of the limited partnership. When limited partners withdraw or transfer their interest in the business, the limited partnership does not dissolve.

As in general partnerships, the partner's share of the income and expenses of the limited partnership are reported on each partner's personal tax returns. Another advantage of limited partnerships is that the law of limited partnerships is well established and well settled, unlike that of other more recently-developed business associations. The law governing limited partnerships is more complex than that of general partnerships, however, and several state and federal requirements must be fulfilled to set up this type of partnership. Another disadvantage of limited partnership is the fragility of a limited partner's liability shield. In the past, a limited partner could be personally liable for the partnership's debts if he participated in the control and management of the business. This "control rule" was eliminated in the Uniform Limited Partnership Act of 2001, which made it easier for a limited partner to participate in business as a limited partner, and allowed for a limited partner to become a general partner with the implied consent of the other partners, instead of requiring written consent.[4]

D. LIMITED LIABILITY PARTNERSHIP (LLP)

A **limited liability partnership** is organized as a general partnership but allows for all partners to avoid personal liability for firm obligations, whether or not they

3 Id.

4 Carter G. Bishop, *The New Limited Partner Liability Shield: Has the Vanquished Control Rule Unwittingly Resurrected Lingering Limited Partner Estoppel Liability as well as Full General Partner Liability?*, 37 Suffolk U. L. Rev. 667, 668 (2004).

are active in the management of the business. This is a relatively new business form, authorized first in Texas in the late 1980s, and now adopted in virtually all states.[5] LLPs are popular business organizations for law and accounting firms, but not widely used in commercial businesses. LLPs are essentially hybrids of the general partnership and corporate forms, including the tax and control advantages of a partnership and the limited liability advantage of a corporation. One disadvantage of the LLP is that, as in a partnership, ownership is not transferable. Another disadvantage of the LLP form is increased formalities—LLPs must register with the permitting state, and many states require that a minimum amount of liability insurance be carried by the firm or that the firm segregate client funds from its own.

E. LIMITED LIABILITY LIMITED PARTNERSHIP (LLLP)

A **limited liability limited partnership** is permitted by statute in something less than half of the states. This business organization applies the limited liability partnership concept of limited personal liability to the limited partnership concept of general and limited partners. In an LLLP, there is still a distinction between general and limited partners' roles in the organization, as in a limited partnership, but all general partners have the protection of an LLP—no personal liability. Because the name serves as a beacon to third parties that they may not rely upon the credit and personal liability of any partner in the firm, this organization theoretically eliminates liability through estoppel against partners, as may have been a problem in limited partnerships.[6] As with all other partnerships, the business is not a separate legal entity, and individual partners must report their share of the firm's expenses and income on their personal tax returns.

F. CORPORATION

The most significant features of a **corporation** include (1) limited liability for shareholders, (2) free transferability of ownership interest, (3) perpetual existence, (4) separation of ownership and management ("centralized control"), and (5) legal status of the corporation as a separate entity ("artificial personality"). As a legally separate entity, a corporation can sue and be sued, can own property, and can generally exercise rights as a person would, including enjoying the benefits of some Constitutional protections. A corporation must generally pay income taxes as a separate entity, and shareholders must pay taxes on the dividends or distributions they

5 Hamilton, 37 Suffolk U. L. Rev. at 863.

6 Bishop, supra, 37 Suffolk U. L. Rev. at 716.

receive from their corporations (this is the so-called "double taxation" applicable to corporations and their shareholders).

Corporations were originally permitted only if the King granted a charter, and after American independence the state legislatures took the place of the King in making the decision whether corporations would be permitted to exist. During the course of the Nineteenth century, instead of requiring a separate legislative act, incorporation became routinely available if certain state requirements were met and certain information was filed with a state official, usually the Secretary of State. Each of the fifty states has its own separate corporations though there are increasing similarities. Generally speaking, corporations are statutorily required to have a three-tiered structure, including shareholders, directors and officers.

Shareholders are the owners of the corporation, but they have limited managerial control. Their primary power is to elect and remove directors, although they must also vote on major decisions of the corporation, such as the amendment of the corporate charter, mergers or sale of substantially all of the assets of the corporation.

Directors have general management power, and depending on the size of the corporation, the directors either monitor the management or act as managers themselves. Large corporations often have professional managers to conduct the day-to-day business operations, and the Board of Directors, who are legally required to meet at least once a year, are responsible for voting on major decisions, and for conducting votes by shareholders when those are required. Directors may be paid for their services, or may be compensated by stock or stock options in the corporation. Directors, like partners, are fiduciaries, who must place the interests of the corporation above their own. Directors are agents of the **corporation**, not of its shareholders. More, as has been held in some cases, they are bound to exercise their independent judgment and cannot simply take orders from shareholders.

Officers of the corporation are selected and terminated by the board of directors. Typical officers might include a Chairman of the Board, a President, a Secretary, a Treasurer, a Comptroller, and assorted Vice Presidents. Generally officers and their responsibilities are not spelled out in statutes, but will vary with the individual corporate charter or bylaws The precise nature of the officers' duties and powers will thus vary across corporations, but an officer's position may carry with it certain generally understood powers, giving rise to apparent or inherent authority. For example, Presidents can usually enter into contracts on behalf of the corporation, treasurers and comptrollers have broad power to monitor the financial activity of the corporation, and secretaries will have custody over the shareholder lists and the books and records of the corporation. In theory, at least, the officers carry out the directors' decisions, rather than setting policy for the corporation.

There are two main types of corporations we will be considering. One is the "publicly-held" corporation, so-called because share ownership is widely dispersed among members of the public. A second is the "closely-held" or "close" corporation, the most notable feature of which is that ownership is in a smaller number of shareholders. In close corporations, the divisions between shareholders, directors, and officers may not be as distinct as in larger, publicly traded, publicly held corporations, and some states, most notably Delaware, permit close corporations entirely to dispense with the three-tiered structure of publicly-held corporations, and have shareholders manage the corporation as if they were partners. When they choose to do so, they assume a fiduciary liability akin to that of partners. In all the states, close corporations generally are operated more informally, although they must still meet some formal statutory requirements. Other significant characteristics of close corporations are that they are often family-run businesses, there is generally not a significant public market for their shares, and the transferability of those shares is often limited by shareholders' agreements. A third type of corporation, the charitable corporation, is not, strictly speaking, a business organization, and is beyond the scope of this book.

Corporations are similarly divided into two types under the United States Internal Revenue Code, called subchapter "S" and subchapter "C" corporations.

In Subchapter "S" corporations (sometimes called "S-corps") the shareholders are treated like partners for tax purposes, and profits or losses of the S-corp are taxed directly to shareholders. Small corporations may elect subchapter S status only if they meet certain requirements: the corporation must have no more than 75 shareholders, only one class of stock is permitted, all shareholders must be US residents, and all shareholders must be individuals and not other corporate entities. The number of shareholders allowed in an S corporation changed from 35 to 75 in 1996,[7] and that maximum was increased to 100 shareholders in 2004. The basic advantage of S corporation election is to avoid double taxation. An S corporation is generally exempt from federal income tax, so shareholders include on their personal tax returns their share of the corporation's income, deductions and losses.

A "C corporation," on the other hand, is any corporation which does not meet the criteria for S corporation election or has not chosen to become an S corporation. A C corporation can have an unlimited number of shareholders, non-US resident shareholders, and can be owned by S or C corporations or any other business form. A C corporation, is, of course, subject to "double" taxation.

It is likely that the primary advantage of the corporate form is shareholder limited liability. A corporation is also the entity through which shares can most easily be marketed to the public (except for close corporations), which market availability is often essential for raising large amounts of capital. Other advantages of the corporate form include free transferability of interest, and potentially perpetual existence. This is to be contrasted with the partnership form, where ownership interests cannot change hands without the agreement of all the partners, and where the business ends if any partner wishes to end it.[8]

---

7 26 USCS § 1361 (2004).

8 Comparison of Business Entities Overview, Small Business Opportunity Clinic, Northwestern University School of Law.

The process of incorporation is also more formalized, regulated and expensive than the process required of partnerships or sole practitioners, where normally nothing must be filed with the state. All states require a filing procedure for corporations, require a filing fee that may amount to several hundred dollars or more, and often require regular reports as well as the filing of corporate tax returns. An important feature of corporate law is that the internal affairs of the corporation (the relationship among officers, directors, and shareholders) will be governed by the state of incorporation, and one can choose to incorporate in any state, even if corporate headquarters will be in another state, and business will be conducted in still other states. Some states require that any corporations operating in their jurisdiction must make certain filings or pay certain fees, but all states recognize that when they deal with corporations it is the law of the state of incorporation that governs internal matters, the so-called "internal affairs" doctrine.

A closely held corporation will generally choose to incorporate in the state in which it expects to do business. As a corporation must pay taxes on both its income and a franchise tax to the state for the privilege of conducting business in the state, limiting the number of states in which a small corporation must pay taxes is seen as an advantage. For larger, publicly held corporations, on the other hand, state taxes and filings are frequently inconsequential compared to overall revenues. Considerations for choosing where to incorporate publicly-held companies often include how state laws affect business organization or shareholder voting. States generally wish to encourage incorporation, because of the revenue from filing fees, and some states have crafted their corporate law governing internal affairs to encourage such incorporation. As we will see, of all the states, Delaware has been so successful in crafting its corporate law, that most large publicly-held United States corporations now choose to incorporate in Delaware.

After choosing a state of incorporation, a corporation must file a "certificate of incorporation," "articles of incorporation" or a "charter" with the state (the three terms refer to the same document), which charter contains provisions meeting statutory requirements. The certificate of incorporation designates the classes of stock and the number of shares that the corporation is authorized to issue, as well as other important corporate specifications, including such matters as the number of Board Members, the kinds of officers, the corporation's purpose, and the location of its headquarters. The "bylaws" of the corporation, which specify the manner in which the corporation will conduct its ongoing operations, including such matters as how vacancies in the board are to be filled, how many members of the board constitute a quorum, which officers can perform which functions, etc., must generally also be filed with the state of incorporation.

G. LIMITED LIABILITY COMPANY (LLC)

A **limited liability company** is a relatively new business form, developed since the late 1970s, which provides the limited liability and tax benefits of an S corporation, commonly called "partnership-tax status," without the restrictions placed on S corporation ownership.[9] Like a corporation and unlike a partnership, an LLC is treated as a legally separate entity, distinct from its members. As such, the LLC members are shielded from personal liability for the business's obligations, whether or not they are active in management. Another benefit of an LLC is the breadth of flexibility in management—it can be managed as if it were a sole proprietorship, partnership or corporation. The manner in which the LLC will be managed will be set out in a "Members Agreement" which might be regarded as analogous to the Corporate Charter, or the Partnership Agreement. Members can also transfer their interest in an LLC without causing dissolution, an advantage over partnerships and LLPs.

LLCs are becoming the most popular form for new small businesses; over 697,000 were formed in 2002, as compared to 63,000 partnerships.[10] LLCs are primarily replacing general and limited partnerships, although they provide a good alternative to closely-held corporations as well. The law governing LLCs is not yet well established, and can vary greatly between states. In Florida and Texas, for example, LLCs are taxed as corporations for purposes of the state corporate franchise tax, eliminating some incentive for forming this type of organization in those states. In Illinois and some other states LLCs are more expensive to form than corporations due to higher initial filing fees and annual report filing fees.[11] We will occasionally refer to the LLC in what follows, but, again, our primary interest is in the corporation. While LLC case law is still in its infancy, it does appear that for many matters, most prominently shareholder liability for entity debts when shareholders abuse their power to the detriment of third parties ("piercing the corporate veil"), the law of LLC's tracks that of corporations.

---

9 Hamilton, *supra*, 37 Suffolk U. L. Rev. at 863.

10 2002 Report of International Association of Commercial Administrators (IACA), *www.iaca.org*, as cited by Daniel S. Kleinberger, *A User's Guide to the New Uniform Limited Partnership Act*, 37 Suffolk U. L. Rev. 583, 588 n31–32. (Fall, 2004).

11 Small Business Opportunity Clinic, Northwestern University School of Law. "Comparison of Business Entities Overview," supra note 2.

II. A Short History of the Corporation

AS WE HAVE CONSIDERED throughout this book and consistent with our efforts to integrate ethical considerations into the discussion of business law, it is important to recognize that there is now and has been for some time considerable debate about the social responsibility of American corporations. At one time it might have been said that there was a burden of proof that incorporators had to meet before the monarch, or the legislature, as a matter of discretion, would confer what was then regarded as the **privilege** of incorporation. That privilege was only to be granted if incorporation served the public good, and that notion is not completely absent from the law even today. Still, it is more common to view incorporation as a ministerial act, one to which any incorporators meeting simple and formal registration requirements can claim a right. The view of incorporation as a privilege granted to serve the public interest, however, was central to corporate existence through many centuries, and a full understanding of the law of corporations and the policies it seeks to implement is impossible without some consideration of this history.

The corporate form dates back to the early Roman Empire, but its use for private commercial enterprise is considerably more recent. Blackstone attributed the idea for the corporate form to Numa Pompilius, a Roman who helped the warring factions of Sabines and Romans incorporate as separate municipal entities, believing that if the groups could govern and view themselves as independent, it would reduce bloodshed.[12]

The life of the corporation as a creature of English law began in England during the twelfth and thirteenth centuries, as towns sought independence from feudal and ecclesiastical control and were incorporated as self-governing municipalities. During the same era, general merchant or crafts guilds were the most important form of commercial organization, and in exchange for substantial fees to the crown, enjoyed a monopoly of their trade within a city's walls.[13] These merchant guilds were perhaps more like trade unions than modern corporations, as they were principally concerned with supervising apprenticeships, determining who ought to be admitted to the trade, and taking other steps to protect guild members' interests and their exclusive right to carry on trade. In the manner in which they functioned, however, the guilds can properly be viewed as prototypical corporate forms. The Guilds were governed by a council, similar to the modern corporate board of directors, and as early as 1437, the guilds had to be registered with and approved by the town where they were established.[14] Beginning in the fifteenth century, the crafts guild and the municipal

---

12 Douglas Arner, *Article in Tribute: Development of the American Law of Corporations to 1832*, 55 SMU L. Rev. 23, 25 (2002).

13 John Micklethwait & Adrian Wooldridge, *The Company: A Short History of a Revolutionary Idea* 23 (Weidenfeld and Nicolson 2003).

14 Arner, *supra* n. 12 at 26

borough were viewed as distinct in function, with the municipal corporation acting as a governing body while the crafts guild served as an economic tool only for its members, although the corporate forms of the two types of entities were identical and both ensured survival of the institutions themselves, even though the governing persons and the individual members would eventually pass on. Both types of corporations could include either natural members or "bodies incorporate and political," indicating that corporations could be part of other corporations.[15]

Nineteenth century American legal scholars Joseph K. Angell and Samuel Ames and English economist Adam Smith divided early economic corporations into two classes: regulated companies and joint stock companies.[16] Regulated companies were state-chartered monopolies authorized to pursue interests beneficial to the state and were dependent on the state for their continued power and success. The most successful of the regulated companies was the Staple of London, founded in 1248 to control wool exports and granted power in 1357 to collect taxes on wool exports in return for helping finance Edward III's French wars.[17] Joint stock companies, which emerged during the sixteenth and seventeenth centuries, more closely resemble the modern business corporation, as they involved owners who left the management of the business entirely to a body of directors.[18] Joint stock companies did not invent the selling of shares on the open market—an idea that dates back to at least the thirteenth century when shares in mines and ships were commonly sold—but they did substantially advance the technique of selling shares as a means of raising large amounts of corporate capital.[19]

Shareholders in joint stock companies also enjoyed some limited liability, enhanced by the fact that the company itself usually held substantial assets in land, and exposure to tort liability during this period was rare. Generally, shareholders would agree to be responsible for the contribution of a certain amount of total capital, even though they would customarily not pay the entire amount as an initial investment. The result was that even though the shareholder could be liable for more than his initial investment, his liability was capped at that agreed-upon amount.[20] Joint stock companies appear to have gradually developed due to the activities of wealthy merchants, property owners, and successful tradesmen who combined their resources to undertake ventures beyond their individual means or tolerance for risk, and utilizing the now available corporate form in a manner very different from that of the early incorporated towns and guilds. This development reflects the general expansion of

15 *Id.* at 29–30, citing Coke 5. Co. Rep. 23, 29b (1526–1616).

16 *Id.* at 26 and 38.

17 Micklethwait and Wooldridge, *supra* n. 13 at 24.

18 Arner, *supra* n. 12 at 26, citing Joseph K. Angell and Samuel Ames, *Treatise on the Law of Private Corporations Aggregate* 32 (reprint N.Y. Arno Press 1972) (1832).

19 Micklethwait and Wooldridge, *supra* n. 13 at 26.

20 Arner, *supra* n. 12 at 39.

markets and private capital investment, which became as important to commerce as the specialized skills of merchant craftsmen had been earlier.[21]

In the first two decades of the seventeenth century, forty joint stock "colonizing" companies were granted charters and trading monopolies in exchange for the crown's rights to the land discovered or settled by the corporations. The trade monopolies granted to these corporations encouraged shareholders to invest in these high risk ventures, even though their liability was not fully limited.[22] In addition, the shares held in these corporations were not fully protected as an individual property right, since the monarch retained the prerogative to refuse to renew or to withdraw the corporate charter. Nevertheless, interests in those corporations were widely traded on a stock exchange, much in the manner they are now.[23] As with earlier regulated corporations, the division between those that ought to be regarded as purely private and those that might be classified as "public" was often difficult to determine—directors of the British East India Company, for example, a concern that made many of its individual investors wealthy men, reported that "the Company traded more for the benefit of the nation [England] than for itself."[24]

The English "Bubble Act" of 1720 marks a definitive point in the history of modern business corporations. When the South Sea Company took over the British national debt in an attempt to retire it by selling shares on the open market to individuals, other corporations fought to participate in this emerging public debt market. The South Sea Company lobbied for the Bubble Act to be passed, in an attempt to restrict competing enterprises. The act, among other things, made it clearly illegal for any joint stock company to operate without a charter from parliament or the king.[25] As formalized charters were relatively difficult to obtain for most businesses, the act essentially cut off the growth of the private corporation in England until the nineteenth century, leaving contract-formed partnerships to emerge as the preferred vehicle of business in England.[26] The Bubble Act was extended to the colonies in 1741 and, along with the general political unrest that characterized the colonies in the eighteenth century, slowed the development of the corporation there. To circumvent the Bubble Act, many colonial businesses were formed according to private articles of agreement, and although legally partnerships, these businesses were able to approximate the joint stock form.[27]

---

21 *Id.* at 27.

22 Janet McLean, *The Transnational Corporation in History: Lessons for Today?*, 79 Ind. L.J. 363, 365–66 (2004).

23 *Id.* at 370 n.43.

24 *Id.* at 369 n, 33, citing K.N Chaudhuri, *The Trading World of Asia and the English East India Company, 1660–1760* 121 (1978).

25 Micklethwait and Wooldridge, *supra* n. 13 at 40–41.

26 *Supra* n. 12 at 33–34.

27 *Id.* at 43, citing Shaw Livermore, Unlimited Liability in Early American Corporations, 43 J. of Pol. Econ. 674,

After the American Revolution, it was commonly understood that the power to grant corporate charters, which in England had eventually come to be shared by the king and parliament, was possessed in America solely by the state legislatures.[28] Colonial legislatures had made frequent use of the corporate form to organize religious congregations and units of local government, and general incorporation statutes for creating these organizations were passed in many states shortly after the Revolution.[29] Forming a private business corporation, however, required more formalities. State legislatures had to pass a special act of incorporation for each new entity, which was required first to demonstrate that its operation would confer a public benefit. A charter might then be granted, which gave legal standing to the corporation and might also confer special franchise rights such as monopolies. As a result, the majority of early American corporations might be characterized as close to "public utilities," and included banks, insurance companies, universities, and companies engaged in constructing turnpikes, bridges and canals.[30] These early American corporations were usually limited to 5 to 30-year terms, with perpetual duration of corporations remaining rare until after the Civil War.[31]

In the nineteenth century, four important developments in American business and politics combined to produce changes that led to the form of business corporation we have today, which entity does, perhaps, represent American law's greatest contribution to world commerce.

The first important event was a clarification of the Constitutional status of the American corporation, through one of the most important decisions ever rendered by the United States Supreme Court. In *Dartmouth College v. Woodward*, 17 U.S. (4 Wheat.) 518, 4 L.Ed. 629 (1819), the Court held that the charter of Dartmouth College (organized as a corporation) was a contract conferring private rights on the incorporators and their successors. The charter, then, was understood to be the valuable private property of the corporation, rather than property held in trust for the state, as had previously been the more commonly accepted view. Prior to *Dartmouth College*, it was understood that the granting of a corporate charter by a state legislature was no different from any other legislative act, and that as was true for any other law, the grant of a charter might be amended or repealed if the operation of the corporation was deemed by the legislature no longer to be in the public interest.[32]

---

674 n.2 (1935).

28 E. Dodd, *American Business Corporations Until 1860* 196 (1954).

29 Ronald E. Seavoy, *The Origins of the American Business Corporation, 1784–1855: Broadening the Concept of Public Service During Industrialization* 4–5 (1982).

30 James Willard Hurst, *The Legitimacy of the Business Corporation in the Law of the United States 1780–1970* 18 (U. Press of Va. 1970).

31 Lawrence Friedman, *A History of American Law* 188–192 (2d ed. 1985).

32 See, for the leading case expressing this view, *Currie's Administrators v. The Mutual Assurance Society*, 14 Va. 315 (1809).

Because the corporate charter was held to be a contract in *Dartmouth College*, this brought into play Article I, Section 10, clause 1 of the United States Constitution, which provides in pertinent part that "No State [legislature] shall . . . pass any . . . Law impairing the Obligation of Contracts." This meant, then, that no state legislature could alter any corporate charter unless it had reserved the right to do so in the original grant. Writing for the Court in *Dartmouth College*, Chief Justice John Marshall observed that private colleges were essential in America, and that no one would ever found or invest in a college or other corporation while "believing that it is immediately to be deemed a public institution, whose funds are to be governed and applied, not by the will of the donor, but by the will of the legislature."[33] Justice Story, in his concurrence in the case, suggested that private colleges were like privately-funded banks, and that while both performed functions that were beneficial to the public, neither should be regarded as "public corporations," but rather as private entities, the private property of which required insulation from legislative interference. As Story put it, "the mere act of incorporation will not change the charity from a private to a public one."[34]

The second important development was the rise of the railroads, the first national-scale businesses. Administering these enterprises required the creation of a complex hierarchy of managers who, although they did not own the businesses with which they were involved, came to stake their professional careers on enabling enterprise to grow and prosper. This separation of management and ownership also further accelerated the development of large-scale public markets for the sale of shares, since it was now possible for investors passively to reap the rewards of investment in corporations without participating in management. By 1898, railroads accounted for over 60% of the publicly-issued stock in the US.[35]

The third development was the formation of large-scale manufacturing, mining and other industrial concerns which created a rapid increase in the number of charters granted to businesses that did not directly perform a public benefit. As requests for such charters became more frequent and were granted, the understanding that corporate charters were a privilege granted only to those who served the public began to erode. As corporations became more common and legislators became more familiar with the corporation as an instrument of private business, political, legal and structural changes followed. In what, as you will see, has been characterized as a "race to the bottom" that began in the 1820s and purportedly continues today, states began to loosen their regulation of corporations and to make it easier to incorporate. This occurred not only because the economic operations of corporations might be beneficial to the state of incorporation, but also because incorporators began to understand that they had some choice in determining in which state they

33 17 U.S. (4 Wheat.) at 647.

34 *Id.* at 671.

35 Micklethwait and Wooldridge, *supra* n. 13 at 66.

might incorporate, and states found that incorporation and franchise fees could be an important source of state income.[36]

These changes led to the passage of general incorporation laws that removed the requirement of the legislature's individual approval for each entity and, eventually, evolved into a system that made incorporation an option for almost any enterprise. The standard general incorporation acts of the 1880s made corporate status available through simple administrative procedures, but required very strict compliance with limits on capitalization, corporate organization and share structure.[37] By the1930s, a more liberalized type of general incorporation had been put in place throughout the country, providing a standard corporate structure but allowing variations as the drafters of individual corporate bylaws desired.[38] Throughout the twentieth century, general incorporation statutes came to grant expansive power for incorporators to vary, through contracts, charter or bylaws, the terms that the law might otherwise impose for corporate organization and governance.[39]

Finally, in what may have been the most important of these developments, limited shareholder liability became commonplace during the nineteenth century. Some firms chartered in the eighteenth and early nineteenth centuries were granted a form of limited liability, perhaps in exchange for the firms' building of public improvements without the expenditure of public funds.[40] Although limited liability was thus not unknown in the eighteenth century, there is at least one instance of a corporate charter's dictating that shareholders had **unlimited** liability for the enterprise's debts.[41] Unlimited liability became even more common in the first part of the nineteenth century, as a legislative policy of protecting corporate creditors took hold in many American jurisdictions.[42] This policy was based, at least in part, on the belief that corporations could more easily amass the necessary capital from creditors' loans if creditors knew that there was recourse against the individuals involved. Making capital more easily available from creditors, so the argument ran, would itself benefit fledgling entrepreneurs, and this would ultimately benefit the public. By 1840, however, perhaps as private equity investment became a preferred means of raising capital, many states' legislators amended their corporate laws to provide for limited shareholder liability. This legislative change was supported not only by the economic argument that lowering liability would lead to additional investment in the state's businesses, but also by the notion that by removing the threat of unlimited

---

36 Hurst, *supra* n. 30 at 18.

37 *Id.* at 69.

38 *Id.* at 70.

39 *Id.* at 120.

40 Seavoy, *supra* n. 29 at 257–58.

41 Dodd, *supra* n. 28 at 227.

42 *E.g.*, Handlin and Handlin, *Origins of the American Business Corporation*, 5 J. Econ. Hist. 1, 10 (1945).

liability, shareholders of modest means would be able to invest in corporations, thus democratizing corporate ownership.[43]

The notion of limited liability is not without controversy today.[44] Critics claim that limited liability encourages corporations to make risky and dangerous investments; because their potential losses are limited to the amount of their investments, owners have the incentive to skimp on precautions and prudent safeguards while overinvesting in hazardous industries. Thus society, rather than the offending corporation, pays the cost for massive torts whose damages exceed corporate equity. Proponents of unlimited liability believe that corporations would become more responsible without the shield of limited liability. As you might imagine, criticisms of this view abound. Perhaps the most obvious objection is that a regime of unlimited liability would have a severe chilling effect on investment in equity, making it extremely difficult for companies to raise money. Secondly, critics charge that unlimited liability would make securities markets illiquid: it would be many times more difficult to sell a security when a buyer knows she would be personally liable for the torts of a corporation over which she may exert minimal influence. Recently, there have been some calls to institute unlimited corporate liability in certain cases, often concerning environmental damage. However, large-scale changes to the doctrine of corporate limited liability are unlikely to come to pass in the foreseeable future. There is one long-standing exception to the doctrine of corporate limited liability, known as "piercing the corporate veil."

One of most recent and most important developments in the operations of private corporations, one that has led to an explosion of corporate development in the twentieth and on into the twenty-first century, is the increasing prevalence of subsidiary and affiliated corporations. These are corporations owned by each other, or sister corporations for whom ownership is identical, often in another corporation. Giant global business entities, many incorporated in the state of Delaware, now function all over the world through separately-incorporated subsidiaries and affiliates. It is now universally accepted that absent an abuse of the corporate form, a corporate shareholder has the same limited liability for the debts of its subsidiaries and affiliates as does an individual investing in a corporation. The rise of operation through subsidiaries and affiliates appears to have come about in tandem with the wide dispersal of passive shareholder investors, and the rise of professional managers. The number of individuals owning shares in corporations rose from two million in 1920 to over ten million in 1930. Current estimates suggest that approximately sixty percent of American households can be regarded as investors in corporations, and, during the

43 Seavoy, *supra* n. 29 at 115.

44 For a modern criticism of limited liability for corporate shareholders (including a proposed model for unlimited liability), see Henry Hansmann & Reinier Kraakman, "Toward Unlimited Shareholder Liability for Corporate Torts," 100 Yale L.J. 1879 (1991).

2004 Presidential election, some commentators suggested that "investor interests" were important in the reelection of the Republican candidate, George W. Bush.

In the 1960s, diversified conglomerate corporate entities emerged and grew to be a powerful economic force by taking over divisions of other corporations, either through friendly negotiated buyouts or hostile "takeovers." By 1973, fifteen of the top 200 American manufacturing corporations were conglomerates, but by then this particular wave of mergers and acquisitions was ending, as the conglomerates failed to deliver expected returns and the stock value of these huge businesses declined.[45]

Even so, the urge to merge grew again as financing became more generally available in the 1980s. Large corporations grew even larger and more diverse through the "merger boom" of the 1980s, but all was not well.[46] From 1970 to 1990, the rate at which large American companies left the Fortune 500 increased four times, and many large conglomerates found it more profitable to slim down and focus on core businesses.[47] The business of many American corporations also changed radically toward the turn of the Century. By 1999, the most valuable American export was probably intellectual capital, as old-style manufacturing gave way to the "information age" and the "service economy" and new groups of entrepreneurs found success in small, flexible upstart corporations.[48]

By the end of the twentieth century, there seemed to be a discernable trend for state and national governments to set the corporation free by deregulating markets, simplifying general incorporation procedures, and loosening trade barriers. At the same time, however, and somewhat paradoxically, the state legislatures and Congress increasingly regulated the ongoing operations of corporations through laws governing accounting procedures, the health and safety of workers, the environment, affirmative action, and the protection of employee, consumer and even investor rights.[49] Although general incorporation statutes had been simplified and streamlined such that the act of incorporation seemed little more than a formality, modern corporations still needed some form of government authorization to exist, and the corporate laws and other regulatory measures of particular states continued to have great influence on where businesses chose to incorporate. In 1999, most of the largest American companies were incorporated in Delaware, a state whose laws favored the discretion of managers and majority shareholders over the purported corporate governance rights of minority shareholders.

We will explore several of the implications of this brief history of corporations, but this whistle-stop tour should give you enough information to reach some preliminary

45 *Id.* at 120.

46 *Id.* at 138.

47 *Id.* at 125.

48 *Id.* at 139.

49 *Id.* at 146.

conclusions. Are you comfortable with the ubiquity of the corporation (and other similar business vehicles such as the limited liability company (LLC))? Is the history of the development of the corporation, and the emergence of the modern American business corporation (the model for the rest of the world) an unqualifiedly noble human achievement? How should the corporation be regulated in the public interest?

III. The Purpose of the Corporation

CONSIDER THE IMPLICATIONS of *Ford v. Dodge* and *Wrigley v. Shlensky* excerpted in Chapter One.

It centers on the fiduciary duties of corporate managers and whether such duties allow for the consideration of the interests of non-shareholders, such as workers or consumers. By 1919, when the case arose, Henry Ford had become the Bill Gates of his era; he was a phenomenally-successful businessman, and as the Court observes, he had increased the wealth of his investors, including the plaintiffs in this case, the Dodge brothers many times over. Ford wants to reinvest in the company, lower the production price of his cars, and ultimately pass the savings on to the buyers of Fords. The Dodge brothers believe the amount of money Ford is reinvesting is excessive and that the money should be distributed to the investors in the form of a special dividend. To whom do you think Ford owes the greater duty, the consumers whose expenditures have allowed him to build his fortune, and increase the wealth of the corporation, or the investors who have originally financed his enterprise? The court rules in favor of the Dodge brothers, holding that Ford should distribute the earnings in the form of a special dividend. One reason is that "[t]he purpose of any [corporate] organization under the law is earnings." Should corporations be guided by anything other than making profits for their investors? If so, what outside concerns should be considered? Is the Court's view of the limited purposes of corporations persuasive?

Note that the court begins by indicating the rule of the common law that it is inappropriate to interfere with directors' discretion to declare a dividend "unless they are guilty of a willful abuse of their discretionary powers, or of bad faith or of a neglect of duty." Furthermore there must be "a very strong case to induce a court of equity to order the directors to declare a dividend." In your view, was *Dodge v. Ford* such a case? If the same factual situation arose today, would it be appropriate for a court to intervene? To determine whether this situation merits intervention, the court looks to the profit history of the company. Ford had been making large profits and was in the habit of declaring large dividends. Furthermore, Ford's business plan which would ultimately reduce production costs had the immediate effect of "diminish[ing] the value of shares and the returns to shareholders." Is it fair to help non-shareholders at the expense of corporate investors? If you are an investor, do you want Ford as a CEO? If you are a CEO, should you consider non-shareholder interests at all?

Ford says his ambition "is to employ still more men, to spread the benefits of this industrial system to the greatest possible number, to help them build up their lives and their homes." In 1918, Ford's workers were paid $6 for an eight hour day, which at the time was quite a substantial wage, one almost unheard of for laborers. Ford also allowed his employees to enter into an innovative profit-sharing program. Is there an extra-legal obligation among managers to enable more people than shareholders to reap the benefits of the industrial system? Even if there is not an implicit obligation, should the courts allow or encourage this type of benefit sharing? Did the court's decision help or harm capitalism?

Professor Stephen M. Bainbridge writes in the *Northwestern Law Review* that "Dodge's theory of shareholder wealth maximization has widely been accepted by the courts." Professor Bainbridge continues "shareholder wealth maximization is not only the law, but also is a basic feature of corporate ideology."50 Is this an ideology to which you subscribe? Is there an alternative? Given that such a high percentage of Americans have portions of their earnings, or retirement or pension funds invested in the stock market, either directly through their purchase of stocks or mutual funds, or indirectly through the purchase of insurance underwritten by entities invested in the market, or through their participation as students attending endowed universities, is the Dodge theory of shareholder primacy with regards to the distribution of corporate assets the fairest method to the largest group of people? To what extent should corporate officers and directors be able to act on the basis of the interests of other constituencies or stakeholders such as creditors, employees, workers, consumers or the community generally? As the economy is increasingly global, do American corporations owe any obligations to their overseas workers? Do corporations have a duty to be ambassadors for capitalism? Should American corporations be more considerate of how Americans will be perceived in the era of a war on terrorism? Remember these issues as you read through the next case.

In a very provocative piece, law Professor Lynn A. Stout, Professor Bainbridge's colleague at UCLA, has argued that it is a mistake to continue to teach *Dodge v. Ford Motor Co.*, because, she asserts, it is now no longer true (if it ever was) that the legally-sanctioned purpose of corporations is to make money for shareholders. Lynn A. Stout, "Why We Should Stop Teaching *Dodge v. Ford*," Chapter 1 of Jonathan R. Macey, ed., *The Iconic Cases in Corporate Law* 1 (2008). Is this correct? Turning to *Wrigley*, what do you make of the Chicago Cubs' consideration of night games on the well-being of the surrounding community, of building a family-friendly brand, and of even maintaining a tradition of playing baseball only during the daytime as a strategy for running a corporation?

---

50 Stephen M. Bainbridge, *Director Primacy: The Means and Ends of Corporate Governance,* 97 Nw. U.L. Rev. 547, 575–576 (2003).

As we saw in Ford v. Dodge, the issue of the social responsibilities and duties of corporations is a complicated one. Debates over to whom corporations owe obligations have no doubt existed since the first corporation, but one important debate in American legal circles, alluded to by the court in Smith v. Barlow, took place in the pages of the *Harvard Law Review* between A.A. Berle and E. Merrick Dodd in 1932.

Writing in 2002, Professor C.A. Harwell Wells[51] argued that all subsequent debates over corporate responsibility "shar[e] conceptual foundations" with the debate between Berle and Dodd.[52] Professor Wells indicates that like the controversy between Berle and Dodd, all subsequent controversies share four characteristic premises. The first is that corporate "social responsibility is about big business" and that legal scholars writing about corporate responsibility always "really mean the responsibility of giant corporations." The second premise is that the goal is "to reform corporate power, not eliminate it," and because of this goal, no "proponents of corporate social responsibility were genuinely radical." Third, the general form of the debate, regardless of the period when it took place, always remains "duty to owners alone versus duties to many constituencies." The final premise, according to Wells, is that "each decade supplies its own reason why corporations should assume greater responsibility," which Wells calls "an unchanging solution to an ever-new problem."[53]

The publication of E. Merrick Dodd's "For Whom Are Corporate Managers Trustees?"[54] helped to begin the still-ongoing modern debate regarding corporate social responsibility. Dodd saw the 1920s, before the crash of 1929, as "a moment in time when corporations had finally begun to take responsibility for their employees and communities."[55] Both Dodd and his principal adversary, A.A. Berle, were responding to the fact, noted earlier, that by the first third of the twentieth century, at least with regard to large publicly-held corporations, there had come to be an increasing separation between ownership and management, as corporations were controlled by their officers and directors, and shareholders had become, essentially, passive investors.

A.A. Berle saw this separation as something that should be reflected by changes in the law, that the law had formerly given too much deference to corporate owners, and that since they were now removed from control, managers should be regulated, to make them act more like responsible owners, and, in particular, to get them to assume responsibility not just to line the pockets of their passive shareholders, but

---

51 C.A. Harwell Wells, "The Cycles of Corporate Social Responsibility: An Historical Retrospective for the Twenty-first century," 51 Kan L.Rev. 77 (2002).

52 *Id.*, at 79.

53 *Id.*, at 80–81.

54 E. Merrick Dodd, Jr., *For Whom Are Corporate Managers Trustees?*, 45 Harv. L. Rev. 1145 (1932).

55 Wells, *supra* note 50, at 92.

also to assume some of the social burdens of the time.[56] Dodd, while sympathizing somewhat with Berle's desire for social responsibility, saw Berle's solution—increased regulation—as too radical.

Dodd argued that appropriate rules were already in place, and that added regulation would probably halt or, at best, slow economic progress. Dodd wanted managers, instead of being subject to regulation, to have the flexibility to respond to the times as they saw fit. He wrote "many conservatives . . . believe that capitalism is worth saving but that it can not permanently survive under modern conditions unless it treats the economic security of the worker as one of its obligations and is intelligently directed so as to attain that object."[57] Dodd argued, however, that regulations passed in the interests of employees and consumers "may increasingly limit the methods which managers of incorporated business enterprises may employ in seeking profits for their stockholders without in any way affecting the proposition that the sole function of such managers is to work for the best interests of the stockholders."

Dodd saw business as "a profession of public service, not primarily because the law had made it such but because a public opinion shared by business men themselves had brought about a professional attitude."[58] Dodd believed that if corporate managers were to be left to their own devices, they would come up with solutions to problems more efficiently than if government regulations mandated charitable contributions or safe workplaces—that public outcry would direct the actions of those at the top of corporations more efficiently than federal regulation. Dodd wrote "power over the lives of others tends to create on the part of those most worthy to exercise it a sense of responsibility."[59] Do you agree? Are those in charge often those most "worthy"?

A.A. Berle was much less sanguine. As did many American academics, he believed that the Great Depression and the stock market crash came about because of widespread misconduct. He saw the 1920s as a time rife with corporate wrongdoing and stock market fraud. Writing in response to Dodd, Berle suggested that leaving management unfettered by outside regulation "might be unsafe" and was "an invitation not to law or orderly government, but to a process of economic civil war."[60] Berle believed that corporate management had accomplished a "seizure of power without recognition of responsibility-ambition without courage."[61] According to Professor Wells, Berle's "problem with Dodd's proposal was not that it replaced

56 This argument was most fully elaborated in A.A. Berle and Gardner Means, *The Corporation and Private Property* (1932), a modern classic.

57 Dodd, *For Whom Are Corporate Managers Trustees?,* 45 Harv. L. Rev 1145.

58 Dodd, *supra* note 56, at 1154.

59 *Id.*, at 1157.

60 A.A. Berle, Jr., *For Whom Corporate Managers Are Trustees: A Note*, 45 Harv. L. Rev. 1365, 1369 (1932).

61 Ibid.

shareholder primacy with broader responsibilities, but that it replaced shareholder primacy with nothing at all."[62]

Professor Cynthia A. Williams nicely suggests that what Dodd and Berle were arguing about was "the extent to which the corporation should be thought of primarily as an economic entity, versus the extent to which it should be thought of primarily as a social entity."63 Professor Williams argues that globalization "undermines sovereigns' power to regulate corporate activity . . . companies can, and do, move their productive processes to different countries or 'outsource' to independent producers in other countries to take advantage of competitive opportunities."64 Williams wonders whether the principle of shareholder primacy with its attendant lack of regulation in the interest of non-shareholder constituencies is appropriate for our age of globalization. She suggests that we should require greater "transparency" in the international activities of our corporations, primarily through mandating increased disclosure of corporate activities. One could, of course, go further, and suggests that American courts, realizing the problem of there being no appropriate international body to regulate corporations, should, once they shake off the purportedly archaic notions of shareholder primacy, offer themselves as a forum to aid non-shareholder plaintiffs from all over the world in getting corporations to operate in their interests. Would this sort of a change in the common law be appropriate? Would the judges in Smith v. Barlow have approved? Is the notion of "shareholder primacy" archaic, or is there still much to be said for it? And what of Delaware, the state that has done more than any other to facilitate the operation of and the investment in the management-run modern American corporation?

IV. A Note on Delaware Incorporation

OVER FIFTY PERCENT of all publicly-traded American corporations and 58% of Fortune 500 corporations are incorporated in Delaware. According to the state's webpage, "[b]usinesses choose Delaware because we provide a complete package of incorporation services including modern and flexible corporate laws, our highly-respected Court of Chancery, a business-friendly State Government, and the customer service oriented Staff of the Delaware Division of Corporations."

At first blush, it seems surprising that a tiny state on the Eastern Seaboard should be the nominal home to so many great American corporations. How did this come about? As already indicated, towards the end of the 19th century, many states began

62 Wells, *supra*, note 50, at 95.

63 Cynthia A. Williams "Symposium: Corporations Theory and Corporate Governance Law: Corporate Social Responsibility in an Era of Economic Globalization." 35 U.C. Davis L. Rev. 705. 707 (2002).

64 *Id.* at 726.

to relax their general incorporation laws in an attempt to attract more corporations and acquire more revenue from franchise taxes and fees associated with incorporation. Initially, it was Delaware's neighbor, New Jersey, which won this battle. In 1896, New Jersey enacted the most liberal general incorporation law in the nation. Soon, however, Woodrow Wilson, then governor of New Jersey, spearheaded an effort to change the policies of the state, and New Jersey passed the "Seven Sisters Act" in 1913, effectively outlawing trusts (a device by which a very small number of persons could control a large number of corporations) and holding companies (corporations that owned other corporations). Soon after, Delaware, which still permitted such devices, found itself the nation's leading haven for incorporation.

After the stock market crash of 1929, and the passage of significant federal legislation to regulate the issuance and trading in the stock of corporations, the wave of incorporations in Delaware subsided somewhat, and after the close of World War II, many states revised their laws to compete more effectively with Delaware. In 1967 the Delaware Bar Association, with the aid of many leading corporate law experts, substantially revised Delaware's General Corporation Law in order once again to make the state the most attractive for incorporation. One of the most important changes to come out of that revision is a speedy amendment process for the Delaware Corporations statutes, which "allows the Delaware General Assembly to keep ahead of legal developments, fix ambiguities in the law, and correct problems noted by judicial decisions."

Delaware's Corporate legislation, and the process whereby the state seeks to be the premier site for incorporation, are not without their critics. Over the years, many scholars, politicians and even some judges have blasted Delaware and other states that have purportedly loosened restrictions on corporations. One of the most famous such critiques came from Supreme Court Associate Justice Louis Brandeis writing in dissent in *Louis K. Liggett Co. v. Lee.* Said the great Justice and former prototype of the public interest lawyer,

> "[t]he removal by the leading industrial states of the limitations upon the size and powers of business corporations appears to have been due, not to their conviction that maintenance of the restrictions was undesirable in itself, but to the conviction that it was futile to insist upon them; because local restriction would be circumvented by foreign incorporation. Indeed, local restriction seemed worse than futile. Lesser states, eager for the revenue derived from the traffic in charters, had removed safeguards from their own incorporation laws. Companies were early formed to provide charters for corporations in states where the cost was lowest and the laws least restrictive. The states joined in advertising their wares. **The race was one not of diligence but of laxity.** Incorporation under such laws was possible; and the great industrial States yielded in order not to lose wholly the prospect of

> the revenue and the control incident to domestic incorporation." [Emphasis supplied][65]

Brandeis thus regarded Delaware's attempts to liberalize corporate law as a cynical ploy by the state to raise and protect revenue associated with incorporation. Was Brandeis correct, or are there more benign explanations for Delaware's success as a haven for incorporation?

In a manner similar to the assertions of Brandeis, after the 1967 revisions of Delaware's Corporations Law, in a seminal piece for the Yale Law Journal,[66] Professor William L. Cary stated that "Delaware is both the sponsor and the victim of a system contributing to the deterioration of corporation standards." Professor Cary argued that the competition among the states to attract incorporation was "a race to the bottom," in which the states tried to outdo each other in creating the most lenient business laws, to attract incorporations in order to raise funds through fees, while failing to protect shareholders, workers and consumers.

Professor Cary did not level all of his fire on Delaware for the race to the bottom phenomenon, noting that "other states would have joined in to attract the lucrative business of incorporating." Still, Cary challenged Delaware's claim to be acting in the best interests of its corporations, as he observed that at the time his article was published, Delaware derived approximately a quarter of its state revenue from incorporations and franchise taxes. In Delaware, Cary stated, "both the courts and the legislature may be said to lack the neutrality and detachment 'to hold the balance nice, clear, and true' required in passing upon the complaints of shareholders." Cary thought that Delaware's corporate law unduly favored management and thus posed a danger to shareholders. He thought it wrong that one tiny state should possess such power to "set social policy in the corporate field." His solution was to advocate federal chartering of corporations, with more stringent regulatory standards.

Consider Professor Cary's thesis. Do you think that because Delaware raises large amounts of revenue through incorporations that the state has lost its impartiality, and cannot be trusted to come up with a system that is fair to shareholders, managers, and the rest of the corporate constituencies or stakeholders? Do you think if Delaware's laws were dangerous to shareholders that shareholders would invest in Delaware corporations, instead of corporations incorporated in states with laws that may be more favorable? Professor Cary argues that management decisions "should be disclosed and monitored by outside groups" to protect investors. Cary favors a federally supervised plan requiring frequent shareholder approval of corporate transactions, the abolition of nonvoting shares and federal fiduciary standards. Do you agree with Professor Cary as to the extent of the threat states like Delaware pose to shareholders' rights? Do you think that increased federal regulation would better

---

65 *Louis K. Liggett Co. v. Lee*, 288 U.S. 517, 557–560, 53 S.Ct. 481, 77 L.Ed. 929 (1933).

66 William L. Cary, Federalism and Corporate Law: Reflections upon Delaware, 83 Yale L.J. 663 (1974).

protect shareholders' rights? As we will soon see, ever since Cary's piece there has been substantial federal intervention further to regulate corporations, on the theory that state law does not adequately protect shareholders. The solution endorsed by many critics of the current system of corporate management continues to be to give shareholders more explicitly-protected rights and more opportunities for corporate control. Do you think investors desire this level of involvement or do more investors prefer a passive role in the management of corporate affairs? Would changes such as those Cary advocates (changes, by the way, that seem to be the thrust of modern federal legislation) solve the problem that Berle perceived because of the separation of corporate ownership from management?

Professor Cary's "race to the bottom" thesis was attacked by equally passionate defenders of Delaware. They argued that Delaware and other states were engaged not in a "race to the bottom," but rather in a "race to the top" to find the optimal form of corporate regulation. According to this view Delaware's success in attracting incorporators is the result of Delaware's success in crafting legislation which permitted more profitable corporate operation, thus benefiting shareholders, who otherwise would not stand for incorporation or reincorporation (moving one's state of incorporation) in Delaware. The fact that the traffic in reincorporation seemed to run virtually only one way (into Delaware) is often cited as evidence of Delaware's positive achievement, as is the fact that the stock market prices shares higher once corporations reincorporate in Delaware. Nevertheless, although no general federal incorporation statute, along the lines advocated by Cary was ever passed, his "race to the bottom thesis" still survives, especially in some parts of the legal academy. Professor John C. Coffee, Jr. wrote in a response to critics of Cary that Cary's article, among other effects, "embarrassed and infuriated the Delaware bench and bar, may have been responsible for a surprising string of pro-shareholder decisions in Delaware over the next decade, provoked the then adolescent 'law and economics' movement to argue that the race was to the top, not the bottom, and motivated Ralph Nader and similar corporate reformers to join Cary in recommending federal chartering of corporations."[67]

Catherine Holst has pointed out that "the American debate over the 'race to the bottom' thesis assumes as a starting point that regulatory competition has beneficial effects."[68] Holst believes that federal minimum standards could be designed to place limits on the extent to which states could favor management over shareholders. Holst concludes that while Professor Cary's article has advanced the debate over the nature of competition for corporate charters, "his conclusions are arguably not self-evident and indeed, his call for federal regulatory intervention has gone unheeded in the

67 John C. Coffee, Jr., Commentary on William L. Cary, Federalism and Corporate Law: Reflections Upon Delaware, 83 YALE L.J. 663 (1974), 100 Yale L.J. 1449 (1991) (Part of commentary on the most-cited law review articles from the Yale Law Journal. Cary's article was number fourteen).

68 *European Company Law after Centros: Is the EU on the Road to Delaware?*, 8 Colum. J. Eur. L. 323 (2002).

U.S." See if you agree with Ms. Holst after considering the federal law to which will soon turn.

It may still be true, however, that state law is still the primary regulator of corporations. Why do you suppose, then, that Cary's call for federal regulation has been unsuccessful? Who gets it right, Cary or his critics? Cary singled out several purportedly pernicious provisions of the Delaware Corporate law, some of which we will return to later, but which might be quickly summarized.

(1) Cary observed that it was easier to accomplish organic change (mergers, sale of substantially all of the assets, amending of the corporate charter, etc.) in Delaware than in any other state, since all that was required was a vote of the majority of the board followed by a vote of the majority of the shareholders. Other states often required super-majority votes to accomplish such matters. (2) Cary suggested that it was easier to declare dividends in Delaware than in any other state, and (3) Cary observed that Delaware did not require cumulative voting for shareholders (which procedure made it easier for shareholder minorities to be represented on the Board), that (4) Delaware did not require that all members of the Board be subject to election each year, that (5) Delaware did not require pre-emptive rights (allowing shareholders the first option of purchasing an aliquot share of new issues of corporate stock), and that (6) Delaware went further than any other state in allowing corporations to hold officers and directors harmless for action taken in good faith, but which later proved deleterious to the corporation. Looking at all of this, in a famous metaphor, Cary stated that Delaware "waters down the rights of shareholders to a thin gruel." Do you agree?

One way of trying to understand whether Delaware law is good or bad for shareholders is to try to discern how Delaware law orders the relationship among shareholders, directors, and officers. A fine vehicle for seeking to achieve this understanding is the great case of *Campbell v. Loews*, which follows. Would you say that the opinion of Judge Seitz in that case seeks admirably to protect shareholders or not?

V. The Players in the Corporation: Shareholders, Directors, and Officers

RECALL THE THREE CATEGORIES of participants in the ownership and management of a corporation: stockholders, officers, and directors. Stockholders are the owners of the corporation, and vote on major corporate actions and to fill the board of directors. Officers are high-ranking employees of the corporation who direct its day-to-day business activity. Finally, directors have control of the business and determine its strategy. While directors are under no obligation to follow the wishes of stockholders, they can be voted out of office, and always owe fiduciary duties to the stockholders.

Shareholders: Shareholders own the corporation. They invest their resources in order to obtain stock in the company. Frequently, stock ownership carries with it rights to vote for issues that arise for the corporation. These may include resolutions that are brought before a shareholders' meeting as well as voting for the directors of the company. Voting rights are most often associated with common stock, but they can also be part of a preferred stock. Preferred stock generally stands in a superior position to common stock in terms of dividend rights and to the a right to assets of a company upon liquidation that are ahead of common stockholders; the tradeoff is that the value of preferred stockholders generally does not increase if the market value increases.

Shareholders also have rights to call meetings and a specified quorum is necessary in order to have a meeting of the shareholders. Typically a shareholder has a right to cast a vote for each share of stock they own, but if the by-laws permit, the shareholder might be able to bundle all their votes to vote for one particular director. This increases the power of minority shareholders because they don't have to spread their votes around, where they might always be defeated by majority interests. Shareholders can also designate others – known as proxies – to vote their shares on their behalf. A proxy can be just about anyone –a proxy is another example of an agency relationship – and often the "person" receiving the proxy authorization is the board of directors. As we have seen in the *Dodge v Ford* case, majority shareholders (such as Henry Ford) may own fiduciary duties to minority shareholders.

Finally, shareholders have rights to sue the company. If the suite is something that concerns mismanagement of the company as a whole, it is called a derivative suit. If instead, the suit is about a complaint the individual shareholder has against the company (such as a refusal to share the books of the company upon a reasonable request), then the suite is one of an individual nature.

Directors: Directors are the governing authority of the corporation. Directors owe fiduciary duties to the shareholders. Often times, a director is recruited to a board because they have knowledge of the industry in which the company operates. If so, there could be a conflict of interest if that director's personal interests conflict with those of the companies. This highlights the duty of the director to exercise loyalty to the company on whose board he sits and, in the event of a conflict, the director may have to recuse himself. The director also owes the shareholders a duty of care so that they are spend sufficient time and effort to make informed decisions and to attend board meetings.

Officers: Like directors, officers have a duty to look our for the wellbeing of the company ahead of their own personal interests. While directors are the governing body of the company, officers (such as the President or Chief Financial Officer) manage the company.

Bear in mind that these descriptions provide bare minimum statements of each of these categories. Our accompanying book provides much more detail about the activities and disputes that occur among these participants in the corporation.

NOTES AND QUESTIONS

1. **GIVEN WHAT YOU HAVE READ** throughout this book and especially in this chapter, what do you think the purpose of the corporation is? Why does it seem to change? Does the fact that the purpose of the corporation not only seems to have been debated for centuries but that the law has actually possessed different standards change your notions of exactly what the purpose of a corporation is or may become in the future?

2. **THINK OF WHAT BUSINESSES** you might like to start as an entrepreneur. What business organization do you think would be most appropriate for them? How might your choice change over time as the business matures? What goals would you have for your business when it starts? John Mackey, who founded Whole Foods, says that he has never met an entrepreneur who started a business solely to make money; he says there has always been an additional purpose. That purpose might be some social good. Or, he says, it may be simply to show your parents that you can start a business just as well as your sibling. Or it may be because you can't work with anyone else and need to run your own business. If you were starting a business, would you have any other purpose beside profit? What would that be? How would you sustain that purpose over time?

3. **KNOWING WHAT YOU KNOW** about Delaware, would you incorporate there or somewhere else? Why?

Appendix A: Characteristics of Common Law and Civil Law Countries

G 20 MEMBER	GENERAL ORIENTATION	NOTABLE CHARACTERISTICS
ARGENTINA	Civil	• No jury trials in Argentina. • Government structure and court system are similar to that of the U.S.
AUSTRALIA	Common	• Australia is a federation of six states, each with their own constitution and three branches of government: the executive, the legislature and the judiciary. • Systems of law of the six states are influential on each other but not binding.
BRAZIL	Civil	• Federation of 26 states, each with their own constitution and laws. • State constitutions and laws must follow principles established in the Federal Constitution. • Moving towards a trend of incorporating *stare decisis* into legal system.
CANADA	Common	• All provinces of Canada follow the common law system, with the exception of Quebec. • Quebec follows a civil law tradition in private law and follows a common law system in matters of public law. • All legal systems are subject to the Constitution of Canada.
CHINA	Other	• The current constitution of the People's Republic of China was enacted in 1982 and has been revised many times since. • Judiciary lacks transparency because there is no technical separation between the judiciary and the government. • Courts do not review legislation for constitutionality.
FRANCE	Civil	• Dual legal system made up of: Droit Public (public law) and Droit Privé (private law). • Inquisitorial rather than adversarial legal system. • Judges are trained at a national postgraduate school called *"École Nationale de la Magistrature."*

G 20 MEMBER	GENERAL ORIENTATION	NOTABLE CHARACTERISTICS
GERMANY	Civil	• Strong influences from the French legal tradition. • Has trial courts, specialized courts, and constitutional courts. • The constitution is also known as the Basic Law.
INDIA	Common	• Strong influences from the British legal system. • Constitution of India was adopted in 1949 and amended many times. • Civil courts, District courts, State High Courts, and the Supreme Court of India. • Muslim personal law is applied in regular courts. • Customary law may be applied in issues of succession.
INDONESIA	Civil	• Legal system is a mix of customary law and colonial Dutch-Roman law. • Constitutional Court created in 2001. • Predominantly Muslim country with a specialized Religious Court.
ITALY	Civil	• Fixed constitution, meaning it cannot be amended by ordinary laws. • jurisdiction: constitutional courts, ordinary courts, and specialized courts. • Special courts for administrative, auditing, military and fiscal issues.
JAPAN	Civil	• Constitution of Japan was adopted in 1946, following WWII. • Constitution provides 31 articles relating to human rights. • Though a civil law system, judges look heavily to precedent to guide decisions. • Civil law in Japan is highly influenced by German and French civil law. • Oral contracts carry a great deal of weight in Japan.
MEXICO	Civil	• Constitution provides for three branches of government: the judiciary, the executive and the legislature. • Sources of the law in Mexico according to legal hierarchy are: the Federal Constitution of 1917; International treaties and conventions; federal statutes; codes; doctrine; custom; and, general principles of law.

G 20 MEMBER	GENERAL ORIENTATION	NOTABLE CHARACTERISTICS
RUSSIA	Civil	• Current constitution was adopted in 1993. • Three separate court systems: constitutional courts, commercial courts, and courts of general jurisdiction. • Judiciary is autonomous from the legislature and the executive. • Many current judges were educated under the old legal system of the Soviet Union.
SAUDI ARABIA	Other	• Absolute monarchy with no binding written constitution. • Supreme law of the land is Sharia, Islamic law. • While most Islamic states codify parts of Sharia law, Saudi Arabia regards uncodified Sharia law in its entirety as the law of the land. • Sharia court system. • No jury trials. • Lawyers and judges are also part of the country's religious leadership. • The Specialized Criminal Court (non-Sharia) was founded in 2008 for terrorism related offenses.
SOUTH AFRICA	Civil and Common	• Constitution came into force in 1997. • Follows English common law in civil procedure and criminal law and Dutch common law in substantive issues such as contracts, family law, torts. • Has a constitutional court.
SOUTH KOREA	Civil	• Limited jury system for criminal and environmental cases. • Private law is based upon Japan's civil code. • Has a constitutional court.
TURKEY	Civil	• Judiciary is independent from the executive and the legislature. • Separate jurisdiction over civilian and military matters. • Military court can exercise jurisdiction over civilians during times of martial law. • No juries.

G 20 MEMBER	GENERAL ORIENTATION	NOTABLE CHARACTERISTICS
UNITED KINGDOM	Common	• Three legal systems: English law, North Ireland law, and Scots law. • English law and North Ireland law follow common law tradition. • Scots law follows civil law tradition. • Supreme Court of the U.K. is the highest court.
UNITED STATES	Common	• Strongly reinforced separation of powers between the judiciary, the legislature and the executive. • Supreme Court hears constitutional matters.
EUROPEAN UNION	Civil	• Common legislation and regulations are binding on all members of the EU. • Directives from the EU are binding but member states have flexibility to draft their own legislation to put the directive into force nationally.

Appendix B: National Conference of State Legislatures
State Employment-Related Discrimination Statutes, July 2015

State	Statute	Covered Employers	Factors On Which Employment Discrimination is Prohibited	Compensatory Damages	Punitive Damages	Attorney Fees	Other Relief
AL	No general anti-discrimination statute Age discrimination statute: Ala. Code § 25-1-20, *et. seq.* EEOC	Age discrimination: employers with 20 or more employees, employment agencies, labor organizations, prints and advertisements	Age 40 and above, retaliation			X	Age discrimination: equitable relief
AK	Alaska Stat. Ann. § 18.80, *et. seq.* Administrative Order 195 (2002) Alaska State Commission for Human Rights	Employers with 1 or more employees, public and private employers, employment agencies, labor organizations, communications and advertisements, media Does not include exclusively social clubs, fraternal, educational, charitable, or religious associations or corporations that are not organized for private profit	Race, color, national origin, religion, age, physical or mental disability, sex, marital status, pregnancy or parenthood, retaliation For public employers, sexual orientation by Executive Order	X Limited to actual damages	X	X	Back pay, reinstatement, promotion, hiring, front pay, equitable relief
AZ	Ariz. Rev. Stat. Ann. § 41-1461, *et. seq.* Ariz. Rev. Stat. Ann. § 36-2813 Executive Order 2003-22 (2003) Attorney General's Civil Rights Division	Employers with 1 or more employees, employment agencies, labor organizations, communications and advertisements Does not include the US or any department or agency of the US, or government corporations, or private membership clubs that are tax exempt	Race, color, religion, gender, age 40 and over, physical or mental disability, national origin, pregnancy, genetic information, retaliation, medical marijuana* Does not include illegal drug use For public employers, sexual orientation by Executive Order	X Restrictions apply	X	X	Actual damages, preventative relief Medical marijuana: no relief provided
AR	Ark. Code Ann. § 16-123-101, *et. seq.* EEOC	Employers who employ 9 or more employees in each of twenty or more calendar weeks in the previous year Sovereign immunity not waived Does not include private clubs or religious organizations	Race, religion, national origin, gender. pregnancy, sensory/mental/physical disability, retaliation Disability does not include compulsive behavior, illegal drug use, or alcoholism	X Fewer than 15 employees: $15,000, 14 to 100 employees: $ 50,000 101 to 200 employees: $100,000, 201 to 500 employees: $ 200,000, Over 500 employees: $300,000	X Included in compensatory damages	X	Back pay, injunctive relief, cease and desist

State	Statute	Covered Employers	Factors On Which Employment Discrimination is Prohibited	Compensatory Damages	Punitive Damages	Attorney Fees	Other Relief
CA	West's Ann. Cal. Gov. Code § 12900, *et. seq.* Department of Fair Employment and Housing	Employers with 5 or more employees, both public and private, employment agencies, labor organizations Does not include religious organizations or non-profits Employers with 1 or more employees for purposes of employer liability	Race, religious creed, color, national origin, ancestry, physical or mental disability, medical condition, genetic information, marital status, sex, pregnancy, childbirth, and related medical conditions, breastfeeding, sex, gender identity, gender expression, age 40 and above, sexual orientation, military or veteran status, retaliation Does not include compulsive behavior or illegal drug use	X Not limited by statute	X Reasonable	X	Reinstatement, back pay, reimbursement, injunctive relief
CO	Colo. Rev. Stat. § 24-34-401, et. seq. Colorado Civil Rights Commission	Public and private employers, employment agencies, labor organizations, communications and advertisements Does not include religious organizations or non-profits	Race, creed, color, sex, sexual orientation, gender identity, age 40 and over, disability, religion, national origin, ancestry, engaging in any lawful activity off the premises of the employer during nonworking hours, victims of domestic violence, stalking, sexual assault	X 1 to 4 employees: $10,000, 5 to 14 employees: $25,000, 15 to 100 employees: $50,000, 101 to 200 employees: $100,000, 201 to 500 employees: $200,000, More than 500 employees: $300,000	X Private, not public employers, included in compensatory damages	X	Reinstatement, back pay, front pay, other equitable relief deemed appropriate
CT	Conn. Gen. Stat. Ann. § 46a-60, *et. seq.* Conn. Gen. Stat. Ann. § 21a-408p Commission on Human Rights and Opportunities	Employers with 3 or more employees, public and private employers, employment agencies, labor organizations Does not include religious organizations	Race, color, religious creed, age, sex, gender identity or expression, marital status, national origin, ancestry, present or past history of mental disability, intellectual disability, learning disability or physical disability, including, but not limited to, blindness, sexual orientation (actual or perceived), civil union status, pregnancy, criminal conviction alone, medical marijuana*	Not expressly provided for in statute – Conn. Supreme Court ruled the statute did not provide for this in 1995	X Not expressly in statute – litigated in court	X	Injunctive relief, back pay Medical Marijuana: no relief provided
DE	19 Del. Code Ann. § 710, *et. seq.* 19 Del. Code Ann. § 720, *et. seq.* 16 Del. Code Ann. § 4903A 16 Del. Code Ann. § 4905A Delaware Department of Labor	Employers with 4 or more employees within the state, public and private employers, employment agencies, labor organizations Does not include religious organizations for sexual orientation or gender identity	Race, marital status, genetic information, color, age 40 and above, religion, sex, pregnancy, sexual orientation, gender identity, or national origin, credit score (pre-hiring), criminal record (pre-hiring), disability, retaliation, medical marijuana* Does not include drug or alcohol abuse	X 1 to 100 employees: $50,000, 101 to 200 employees: $100,000, 201 to 500 employees: $200,000, More than 500 employees: $300,000	X	X	Reinstatement, hiring, promotion, cease and desist discriminatory practices Medical Marijuana: no relief provided

State	Statute	Covered Employers	Factors On Which Employment Discrimination is Prohibited	Compensatory Damages	Punitive Damages	Attorney Fees	Other Relief
DC	D.C. Code Ann. § 2-1402, et. seq. Office of Human Rights	Employers with 1 or more employees, government, public and private employers, employment agencies, labor organizations Does not include religious organizations or non-profits	Race, color, religion, national origin, sex, pregnancy, childbirth, breastfeeding, reproductive health decisions, age 18 to 65 (with exceptions), marital status, personal appearance, sexual orientation, gender identity or expression, family responsibilities, matriculation, political affiliation, genetic information, disability, retaliation	X Not limited by statute	X	X	Injunctive relief, hiring, reinstatement, promotion, back pay
FL	Fla. Stat. Ann. § 760.01, *et. seq.* Fla. Stat. Ann. § 448.075-.076 Fla. S.B. No. 982 Florida Commission on Human Relations	Employers with 15 or more employees for each working day in each of 20 or more calendar weeks Does not apply to religious organizations for religious discrimination	Race, color, religion, sex, national origin, age, handicap, marital status, sickle-cell trait, pregnancy	X Private: not limited State: up to $200,000 or $300,000 under Fla. Stat. Ann. § 768.28(5)	X Private: up to $100,000 State: none	X	Other relief deemed appropriate, back pay
GA	No general anti-discrimination statute for private employers State employers: Ga. Code Ann. § 45-19-20, et. seq. Sex Equal pay: Ga. Code Ann. § 34-5-1, et. seq. Disability: Ga. Code Ann. § 34-6a-1, *et. seq.* Age: Ga. Code Ann. § 31-4-2, *et. seq.* EEOC	State employers: employers with 15 or more employees within the state for each working day in each of 20 or more calendar weeks in the current or preceding calendar year, notice or advertisement Equal pay: public and private employers with 10 or more employees, engaged in interstate commerce	State employers: race, color, religion, national origin, sex, physical or mental disability, age 40 and above, retaliation Private employers in interstate commerce: discrimination in pay based on gender and discrimination based on disability			X	Hiring, reinstatement, promotion, back pay
HI	Haw. Rev. Stat. §378.1, *et. seq.* Hawaii Civil Rights Commission	Employers with 1 or more employees, public and private employers, employment agencies, labor organizations Does not include religious organizations and charitable or educational organizations	Race, sex, gender identity or expression, sexual orientation, age, religion, color, ancestry, physical or mental disability, marital status, domestic or sexual violence victim status, pregnancy, childbirth, retaliation, required submission to lie detector tests, credit history or credit report, conviction record	X Not limited by statute	X	X	Reinstatement, back pay, hiring, promotion, injunction, any other orders deemed appropriate

State	Statute	Covered Employers	Factors On Which Employment Discrimination is Prohibited	Compensatory Damages	Punitive Damages	Attorney Fees	Other Relief
ID	Idaho Code §67-5909, et. seq. Idaho Human Rights Commission	Employers with 5 or more employees for each working day in each of twenty (20) or more calendar weeks in the current or preceding calendar year, public and private employers, employment agencies, labor organizations, prints or publications, Does not include religious organizations and private clubs	Race, religion, color, sex, national origin, disability, age 40 and above, retaliation	X Not limited by statute	X	X	Cease and desist order, back pay, reinstatement, hiring, promotion, any other orders deemed appropriate
IL	775 Ill. Comp. Stat. 5/1-101, *et. seq.* 410 Ill. Comp. Stat. 513/, *et. seq.* 410 Ill. Comp. Stat. 130/40 Illinois Department of Human Rights	Employers with 15 or more employees within Illinois during 20 or more calendar weeks within the calendar year of or preceding the alleged violation, employees with 1 or more employees for physical or mental disability, pregnancy, or sexual harassment cases The state regardless of number of employees, employment agencies, labor organizations Does not include religious organizations	Race, color, religion, sex, pregnancy, childbirth or related medical conditions, national origin, sexual orientation, gender identity, age 40 and above, ancestry, marital status, citizenship status, physical or mental handicap, military duty status or discharge status (with exceptions), genetic testing (under Genetic Information Privacy Act), retaliation, medical marijuana*, expunged or sealed criminal history	X Not limited by statute	X	X	Cease and desist, hiring, reinstatement, promotion, back pay, equitable relief Medical Marijuana: no relief provided
IN	Ind. Code Ann. § 22-9-1-1, et. seq. Ind. Code Ann. § 22-9-2-1, et. seq. Governor's Policy Statement, April 26, 2005 Indiana Civil Rights Commission	Employers with 6 or more employees, public and private employers, employment agencies, labor organizations Does not include religious organizations, non-profits, or exclusive social clubs For age discrimination, employers with 1 or more employees	Race, religion, color, sex, disability, national origin, ancestry, age 40 to 75, retaliation, veteran status For public employers, sexual orientation and gender identity by Executive Order			X	Cease and desist, restore losses incurred, employer's potential loss of license
IO	Iowa Code Ann. § 216.1, *et. seq.* Iowa Civil Rights Commission	Employers with 4 or more employees, public and private employers, employment agencies, labor organizations Does not include religious organizations for purposes of religious, sexual orientation, or gender identity discrimination	Race, creed, color, sex, sexual orientation, gender identity, national origin, religion, physical or mental disability, pregnancy, childbirth, age, genetic information, HIV testing, polygraph testing (excludes police or corrections officers)	X Not limited by statute		X	Back pay, reinstatement, hiring, promotion, other remedial action
KS	Kan. Stat. Ann. § 44-1001, et. seq. Kansas Human Rights Commission	Employers with 4 or more employees, public and private employers, employment agencies, labor organizations, nonsectarian corporations, and organizations engaged in social service work Does not include non-profits or social clubs	Race, religion, color, sex, national origin, ancestry, physical or mental disability, age, genetic testing, retaliation Public employer: height (exception for fire department, law enforcement, and security officers)	X Up to $2000		X	Back pay, hiring, reinstatement, promotion, cease and desist

State	Statute	Covered Employers	Factors On Which Employment Discrimination is Prohibited	Compensatory Damages	Punitive Damages	Attorney Fees	Other Relief
KY	Ky. Rev. Stat. §344.040, et. seq. Ky. Rev. Stat. §207.135 Ky. Rev. Stat. §342.197 Executive Order 2003-533 (2008) Kentucky Commission on Human Rights	Employers with 8 or more employees within the state in each of 20 or more calendar weeks in the current or preceding calendar year, public and private employers, employment agencies, labor organizations For disability discrimination, an employer with 15 or more employees	Race, color, religion, national origin, sex, pregnancy, childbirth, age over 40, disability, HIV status, black lung disease, smoking, disability, retaliation For public employers, sexual orientation and gender identity by Executive Order	X Not limited by statute		X	Back pay, front pay, hiring, reinstatement, promotion, any other appropriate relief
LA	La. Rev. Stat. Ann. § 23:301, *et. seq.* Louisiana Commission on Human Rights	Employers with 20 or more employees, employers with 25 or more employees for pregnancy, childbirth, or related medical condition cases, public and private employers, employment agencies, labor organizations	Race, color, religion, sex, national origin, sickle-cell disease traits, pregnancy, childbirth, and related conditions, age 40 and above, disability, veteran status, genetic information	X Not limited by statute		X	Back pay, benefits, reinstatement, front pay
ME	Me. Rev. Stat. Ann. Tit. 5, §4572, *et. seq.* Me. Rev. Stat. Ann. Tit. 22, §2423-E(2)	Public and private employers with any amount of employees, employment agencies, labor organizations	Race, color, sex, sexual orientation, gender identity, physical or mental disability, religion, age, ancestry, national origin, retaliation, genetic information, pregnancy,	X 14 to 100 employees: $50,000, 101-200: $100,000,	X	X	Cease and desist, reinstatement, hiring, promotion, back pay
	Maine Human Rights Commission	Does not include religious organizations, non-profits, fraternal organizations	breastfeeding, medical marijuana* Does not apply to illegal drug use or alcohol use during working hours	201-500: $300,000, 500 or more employees: $500,000			Medical Marijuana: no relief provided
MD	Md. State Government Code Ann. § 20-601, *et. seq.* Maryland Commission on Human Relations *City and county laws vary	Employer with 15 or more employees for each working day in each of 20 or more calendar weeks in the current or preceding calendar year, public and private employers, employment agencies, labor organizations, publications or advertisements Baltimore County: employers with fewer than 15 employees Does not include private membership, tax exempt clubs, or religious organizations	Race, color, religion, national origin, ancestry, sex, age, marital status, sexual orientation, gender identity, physical or mental disability, genetic information, retaliation, pregnancy	X In Baltimore County only		X In Howard, Montgomery, and Prince George's County, and Baltimore County	Baltimore County: injunctive relief, back pay

State	Statute	Covered Employers	Factors On Which Employment Discrimination is Prohibited	Compensatory Damages	Punitive Damages	Attorney Fees	Other Relief
MA	Ann. Laws of Mass. Gen. Laws, ch. 151B, § 1, *et. seq.* Massachusetts Commission Against Discrimination	Employers with 6 or more employees, public and private employers, employment agencies, labor organizations Does not include exclusively social organizations if not-for- profit or religious organizations	Race, religious creed, color, national origin, ancestry, sex, gender identity, sexual orientation, disability, genetic information, age 40 and above, pregnancy, criminal record, lie- detector test, victim of sex offense or domestic violence	X Not limited by statute	X	X	Reinstatement, promotion, hiring, back pay, front pay, cease and desist
MI	Mich. Comp. Laws §37-2202, *et. seq.* Mich. Comp. Laws §37.1202, *et. seq.* Executive Directive 2003-24 (2003, 2007) Michigan Department of Civil Rights	Employers with 1 or more employees, public and private employers, employment agencies, labor organizations	Race, color, religion, sex, national origin, marital status, height, weight, age, pregnancy, childbirth, or related medical condition, disability, retaliation For public employers, sexual orientation and gender identity by Executive Order	X Not limited by statute		X	Injunctive relief, reinstatement, hiring, promotion, other relief deemed appropriate
MN	Minn. Stat. Ann. § 363A.08, et. seq. Minn. Stat. Ann. § 152.32 Minnesota Department of Human Rights	Employers with 1 or more employees, public and private employers, employment agencies, labor organizations Does not include religious or fraternal organizations for purposes of religious or sexual orientation discrimination, or nonpublic service organizations for purposes of sexual orientation discrimination	Race, color, creed, religion, national origin, sex, sexual orientation, gender identity, marital status, acceptance of public assistance benefits or housing, physical/sensory/mental disability, age, pregnancy, childbirth, and related medical conditions, familial status, medical marijuana*	X Not limited by statute	X	X	Injunctive relief, back pay Medical Marijuana: no relief provided
MS	No general state anti- discrimination statute for public employers Miss. Code Ann. §§ 25-9- 103; 149 Miss. Code Ann. § 71-1-55 EEOC	State employers Breastfeeding accommodation: public and private employers	Political affiliation, race, national origin, sex, religion, age, disability Accommodation for breastfeeding				
MO	Mo. Ann. Stat. §213.010, et. seq. Executive Order 10-24 (2010) Missouri Commission on Human Rights	Employers with 6 or more employees, public and private employers, employment agencies, labor organizations Does not include religious corporations or sectarian corporations	Race, color, religion, national origin, sex, ancestry, age 40 to 70 (exception for high policy- making positions and executives), physical or mental disability, pregnancy, retaliation For the executive branch, sexual orientation by Executive Order	X Not limited by statute	X	X	Injunctive relief, temporary restraining order, other orders

State	Statute	Covered Employers	Factors On Which Employment Discrimination is Prohibited	Compensatory Damages	Punitive Damages	Attorney Fees	Other Relief
Mt	Mont. Code Ann. §49-2- 101, *et. seq.* Nondiscrimination-EEO Policy 3-0630 (2000) Human Rights Bureau	Employers with 1 or more employees, public and private employers, employment agencies, labor organizations, prints and advertisements Does not include fraternal, charitable, or religious non- profit organizations, or Indian tribes	Race, creed, religion, color, national origin, age, physical or mental disability, marital status, sex, pregnancy, retaliation For public employers, sexual orientation by Executive Order			X	Cease and desist, injunction, order to rectify the harm (pecuniary or otherwise) Sexual Orientation:
NE	Neb. Rev. Stat. Ann. §48-1101, *et. seq.* Neb. Rev. Stat. Ann. §48-1001, *et. seq.* Nebraska Equal Opportunity Commission	Employers with 15 or more employees, public and private employers, employment agencies, labor organizations For age discrimination, employers with 20 or more employees Does not include religious corporations, associations, or societies with respect to religious discrimination	Race, color, religion, sex, disability, marital status, national origin, age 40 and above, pregnancy, childbirth, and related medical conditions, retaliation Does not apply to members of the Communist Party, or include illegal drug use	X Not limited by statute		X	Injunctive relief, cease and desist, reinstatement, hiring, back pay
NV	Nev. Rev. Stat. Ann. §613.310, *et. seq.* Nev. Rev. Stat. Ann. § 453A.800 Nevada Equal Rights Commission	Employers with 15 or more employees, public and private employers, employment agencies, labor organizations, prints and advertisements Does not include Indian tribes, religious corporations, associations, or societies for purposes of religious, sexual orientation, or gender identity discrimination	Race, color, religion, sex, sexual orientation, age, physical or mental disability, national origin, genetic testing, pregnancy, retaliation, gender expression, gender identity, pregnancy, use of lawful products off premises of employer, medical marijuana*	Not specifically allowed for in statute		X	Back pay, reinstatement, cease and desist, injunctive relief Medical Marijuana: no relief provided
NH	N.H. Rev. Stat. Ann. §354-A:1, *et. seq.* New Hampshire Commission for Human Rights	Employers with 6 or more employees, public and private employers, employment agencies, labor organizations Does not include religious organizations or exclusive social clubs	Age, sex, race, creed, color, marital status, national origin, physical or mental disability, sexual orientation, pregnancy, and medical conditions, retaliation	X Not limited by statute		X	Back pay, front pay, reinstatement, cease and desist, hiring, reinstatement, promotion
NJ	N.J. Stat. Ann. §10:5-12, et. seq. New Jersey Division on Civil Rights	Employers with 1 or more employees, public and private employers, employment agencies, labor organizations, prints and advertisements Does not include religious organizations, social clubs, or fraternal clubs	Race, creed, color, national origin, ancestry, age, marital status, civil union status, domestic partnership status, affectional or sexual orientation, genetic information, pregnancy, sex, gender identity or expression, disability or atypical hereditary cellular or blood trait of any individual, nationality, military service, genetic testing, retaliation	X Not limited by statute	X	X	Hiring, reinstatement, promotion, back pay

State	Statute	Covered Employers	Factors On Which Employment Discrimination is Prohibited	Compensatory Damages	Punitive Damages	Attorney Fees	Other Relief
NM	N.M. Stat. Ann. §28-1-7, *et. seq.* New Mexico Human Rights Division	Employers with 4 or more employees, public and private employers, employment agencies, labor organizations For sexual orientation and gender identity, employers with 15 or more employees For spousal affiliation, employers with 50 or more employees Does not include religious organizations for purposes of sexual orientation or gender identity discrimination	Race, age, religion, color, national origin, ancestry, sex, physical or mental handicap or serious medical condition, retaliation, sexual orientation, gender identity, spousal affiliation	X Not limited by statute		X	Reinstatement, hiring, promotion, cease and desist, back pay
NY	N.Y. Exec. Law § 290, *et. seq.* N.Y. Laws H. B. No. A06357 Executive Order No. 33 (2009) New York Division of Human Rights	Employers with 4 or more employees, public and private employers, licensing agencies, employment agencies, and labor organizations, employers employing 1 or more domestic worker Does not include distinctly private clubs or religious corporations and non-profits	Age, race, creed, color, national origin, sexual orientation, military status, sex, disability, predisposing genetic characteristics, marital status, domestic violence victim status, pregnancy, sealed arrest or conviction record, retaliation, medical marijuana* (starting July 1, 2015) For public employers, gender identity by Executive Order	X Not limited by statute		X	Injunctive relief, back pay, reinstatement, hiring, promotion Medical Marijuana: treated the same as disability under Art. 15 of Exec. Law, but no specific relief provided in statute
NC	N.C. Gen. Stat. § 143-422.1, et. seq. N.C. Gen. Stat. § 95-28.1, et. seq. N.C. Gen. Stat. § 130A-148, et. seq. N.C. Gen. Stat. § 168a, *et. seq.* EEOC	Employers with 15 or more employees, public and private employers, employment agencies, labor organizations Employers with 3 or more regularly employed employees for use of lawful products off the job	Race, religion, color, national origin, age, sex, disability, sickle-cell trait or hemoglobin C, AIDS/HIV (with restrictions), retaliation			X	Hiring, reinstatement, back pay
ND	N.D. Laws § 14-02.4, *et. seq.* N.D Laws H. B. No. 1463; West's No. 219 Human Rights Division of the North Dakota Department of Labor	Employers with 1 or more employees, employment agencies, and labor organizations, advertisements Does not include private clubs	Race, color, religion, sex, national origin, age 40 and above, physical or mental disability, status with respect to marriage or assistance, participation in lawful activities during non-work hours, pregnancy, retaliation			X	Injunctive relief, equitable relief, back pay
OH	Ohio Rev. Code §4112.01, et. seq. Executive Order 2007-10S (2007) Ohio Civil Rights Commission	Employers with 4 or more employees, public and private employers, employment agencies, labor organizations Does not include religious organizations	Race, color, religion, sex, national origin, disability, age, ancestry, pregnancy, childbirth, and related medical conditions, retaliation For public employers, sexual orientation and gender identity by executive order	X Not limited by statute	X	X	Cease and desist, injunctive relief, back pay, reinstatement, hiring, promotion

State	Statute	Covered Employers	Factors On Which Employment Discrimination is Prohibited	Compensatory Damages	Punitive Damages	Attorney Fees	Other Relief
OK	25 Okla. Stat. Ann. §§1301, *et. seq.* Oklahoma Human Rights Commission	Employers with 1 or more employees, public and private employers, employment agencies, labor organizations Does not include Indian tribes or bona fide tax-exempt membership clubs, or religious organizations	Race, color, religion, sex, national origin, age, disability, genetic information, pregnancy, childbirth, and related medical conditions			X	Back pay, reinstatement, hiring, injunctive relief
OR	Or. Rev. Stat. § 659a.001, et. seq. Or. Rev. Stat. § 174.100 Civil Rights Division	Employers with 1 or more employees, public and private employers, employment agencies, labor organizations Federal law exempts private clubs and religious organizations for race and sex discrimination and religious organizations for religious discrimination	Race, religion, color, sex, sexual orientation, gender identity, national origin, marital and familial status, age 18 and above, disability, expunged juvenile record, pregnancy, childbirth, and related medical conditions, injured workers, retaliation, requiring submission to breathalyzer test, lie detector, genetic testing, psychological stress test, use of legal tobacco during non-working hours, person with a degree in theology or religious occupations, victims of domestic violence or sexual crimes, credit history, testifying at unemployment compensation hearings, leave to attend a criminal proceeding, military service Does not include illegal drug use	X Not limited by statute	X	X	Reinstatement, hiring, promotion, back pay, injunctive or equitable relief deemed appropriate
PA	Pa. Stat. Ann. tit. 43, § 951, *et. seq.* Executive Order 1975-5 (2003) Pennsylvania Human Relations Commission	Employers with 4 or more employees, public and private employers, employment agencies, labor organizations Does not include religious organizations for purposes of religion-based sex discrimination, fraternal organizations, charitable organizations	Race, color, familial status, religious creed, ancestry, age 40 and above, sex, pregnancy, national origin, disability, use of service animal, refusal to perform abortion or sterilization, retaliation For public employers, sexual orientation and gender identity by executive order	X Not limited by statute		X	Reinstatement, hiring, promotion, back pay, other legal or equitable relief deemed appropriate
PR	29 Laws of P.R. Ann. § 146, *et. seq.* Anti- Discrimination Unit, Department of Human Resources	Employers with 1 or more employees, public and private employers, labor unions, publications and advertisements Federal law exempts private clubs and religious organizations for race and sex discrimination and religious organizations for religious discrimination	Age from which minors can work, race, color, sex, social or national origin or social condition, political affiliation, political or religious ideology, or for being a victim or perceived as a victim of domestic violence, sexual aggression or stalking, sexual orientation, gender identity, retaliation, military status			X	Reinstatement, cease and desist, back pay, actual damages
RI	R.I. Gen.Laws Ann. § 28-5-1, *et. seq.* Rhode Island Commission for Human Rights	Employers with 4 or more employees, public and private employers, employment agencies, labor organizations Does not include religious organizations for purposes of religious discrimination	Race, color, religion, sex, sexual orientation, gender identity, gender expression, disability, age 40 and above, country of ancestral origin, retaliation, pregnancy, childbirth, and related medical conditions	X Not limited by statute	X Private only	X	Cease and desist, reinstatement, hiring, promotion, back pay

State	Statute	Covered Employers	Factors On Which Employment Discrimination is Prohibited	Compensatory Damages	Punitive Damages	Attorney Fees	Other Relief
SC	S.C. Code § 1- 13-30, *et. seq.* South Carolina Human Affairs Commission	Employers with 15 or more employees, public and private employers, employment agencies, labor organizations Does not include Indian tribes, private clubs, or religious organizations for religions discrimination	Race, religion, color, sex, age 40 and above, national origin, pregnancy, childbirth, and related medical conditions, physical or mental disability, medical examinations				Hiring, reinstatement, promotion, back pay
SD	S.D. Code.Law § 20-13-1, et. seq. State Commission of Human Rights	Employers with 1 or more employees, public and private employers, employment agencies, labor organizations, advertisements Does not include religious organizations for religious discrimination	Race, color, creed, religion, sex, ancestry, disability, national origin, retaliation			X	Hiring, reinstatement, promotion, back pay, injunctive relief, equitable relief
TN	Tenn. Code Ann. § 4-21-201, *et. seq.* Tenn. Code Ann. §8-50-103 Tennessee Human Rights Commission	Employers with 8 or more employees, public and private employers, employment agencies, labor organizations Does not apply to religious organizations for purposes of religious discrimination	Race, color, creed, religion, sex, age 40 and above, national origin, mental, visual, or physical disability, retaliation	X Not limited by statute		X	Hiring, reinstatement, promotion, back pay, appropriate relief
TX	Tex. Lab. Code § 21.001, et. seq. Texas Workforce Commission Civil Rights Division	Employers with 15 or more employees engaged in industry affecting commerce, public and private employers, employment agencies, labor organizations Does not apply to religious organizations for purposes of religious discrimination	Race, color, disability, religion, sex, national origin, age, pregnancy, childbirth, and related medical conditions, retaliation, genetic information	X Fewer than 101 employees: $50,000 101 to 200 employees: $100,000 201 to 500 employees: $300,000 501 or more employees: $300,000	X	X Court may include expert fees	Back pay, reinstatement, hiring, promotion, injunctive relief, equitable relief
UT	Utah Code Ann. § 34a-5-101, et. seq. Utah Code S. B. No. 296 (legislation adding gender identity and sexual orientation and gender identity) Utah Anti- discrimination and Labor Division	Employers with 15 or more employees, public and private employers, employment agencies, labor organizations Does not include religious organizations	Race, color, sex, pregnancy, childbirth, and related medical conditions, age 40 and above, religion, national origin, disability, retaliation, sexual orientation, gender identity			X	Cease and desist, reinstatement, back pay
VT	Vt. Stat. Ann. tit. 21, § 495, *et. seq.* Civil Rights Unit of the Vermont Attorney General's Office	Employers with 1 or more employees, public and private employers, employment agencies, labor organizations Does not include religious organizations for purposes of religious, sexual orientation, or gender identity discrimination	Race, color, religion, sex, sexual orientation, gender identity, national origin, age, disability, ancestry, place of birth, HIV status, retaliation, genetic testing, pregnancy, credit history	X Not limited by statute	X	X	Injunctive relief, back pay, front pay, reinstatement, other appropriate relief, class action restitution

State	Statute	Covered Employers	Factors On Which Employment Discrimination is Prohibited	Compensatory Damages	Punitive Damages	Attorney Fees	Other Relief
VA	Va. Code Ann. 2.1-714, *et. seq.* Executive Order No. 1 (2014) Virginia Council on Human Rights	Employers with more than 5 but less than 15 employees For purposes of age discrimination, employers with more than 5 and less than 20 employees	Race, color, religion, national origin, sex, pregnancy, childbirth, and related medical conditions, age 40 and above, marital status, disability For public employers, sexual orientation and gender identity by Executive Order			X 25% of back pay	Back pay
VI	24 V.I. Code § 451, *et. seq.* 10 V.I. Code § 64, *et. seq.* Virgin Islands Civil Rights Commission	Employers with 1 or more employees, public and private employers, other legal entities Does not include religious organizations for the purposes of religious discrimination	Age, race, creed, color, national origin, sex, political affiliation, pregnancy, childbirth, and related medical	X Not limited by statute	X	X	Reinstatement, hiring, promotion, back pay
WA	Wash. Rev. Code Ann. §49.60.010, et. seq. Washington State Human Rights Commission	Employers with 8 or more employees, public and private employers, employment agencies, labor organizations Does not include religious organizations organized not for profit	Age, sex, marital status, sexual orientation, gender identity, race, creed, color, national origin, honorably discharged veteran or military status, or the presence of any sensory, mental, or physical disability or the use of a trained dog guide or service animal by a person with a disability, breastfeeding, pregnancy, retaliation	X Not limited by statute		X	Back pay, front pay, hiring, reinstatement, promotion, cease and desist
WV	W. Va. Code §5-11-1, *et. seq.* West Virginia Human Rights Commission	Employers with 1 or more employees, public and private employers, employment agencies, labor organizations, prints and advertisements Does not include private clubs	Race, color, religion, sex, national origin, age 40 and above, disability, ancestry, retaliation, pregnancy, childbirth, and related medical conditions	X Not limited by statute	X	X	Equitable relief, civil penalties, injunctive relief, reinstatement, hiring, promotion, back pay
WI	Wis. Stat. Ann. §111.31, *et. seq.* Wisconsin Equal Rights Division	Employers with 1 or more employees, public and private employers, employment agencies, labor organizations Does not include religious organizations for purposes of religious discrimination	Age, race, color, religion, creed, gender, disability, marital status, national origin, ancestry, arrest record, conviction record, sexual orientation, military status, use or nonuse of lawful products off premises during nonworking hours, retaliation, pregnancy, childbirth, maternity leave, and related medical conditions, lie detector test, genetic test, declining to attend a meeting or to participate in any communication about religious matters or political matters	X Not limited by statute	X	X	Back pay, other appropriate relief

State	Statute	Covered Employers	Factors On Which Employment Discrimination is Prohibited	Compensatory Damages	Punitive Damages	Attorney Fees	Other Relief
WY	Wyo. Stat. § 27-9-101, et. seq. Labor Standards Division of the Wyoming Department of Employment	Employers with 2 or more employees, public and private employers, employment agencies, labor organizations Does not include religious organizations	Race, color, creed, sex, national origin, age 40 or above, disability, ancestry, pregnancy, off-the-job use of tobacco, retaliation			X	Cease and desist, reinstatement, hiring, promotion, back pay, front pay

Sources: Guide to Employment Law and Regulation; annual year-end StateNet bill tracking searches, 2009-2014, Westlaw 50-state statute searches, July 2015.

**Arizona, Connecticut, Delaware, Illinois, Maine, Nevada, New York, and Minnesota all have medical marijuana laws with anti-discrimination provisions addressed to employers, prohibiting adverse employment action against an employee solely for participating in the state's medical marijuana program, unless doing so would violate federal law or regulations. However, the laws do not necessarily preclude adverse employment action based on drug test results. States often have laws other than their anti-discrimination statues that influence their treatment of drug testing in employment discrimination claims. http://www.huntonlaborblog.com/2015/01/articles/employment-policies/antidiscrimination-provisions-in-state-medical-marijuana-laws-raise-additional-considerations-for-workplace-drug-testing/*

Note: Executive Orders prohibiting discrimination based on sexual orientation for state employers do not provide relief.

Appendix C: Summary of Selected Federal Laws and Regulations Addressing Confidentiality, Privacy and Security

Federal Law	Citation	General Description	Applicability	Information Covered	Summary
The Privacy Act of 1974	5 U.S.C. § 552a; 45 C.F.R. Part 5b; OMB Circular No. A-108 (1975)	The Privacy Act of 1974 is a withholding statute.	Any Executive department, military department, Government corporation, Government controlled corporation, or other establishment in the executive branch of the [federal] Government (including the Executive Office of the President), or any independent regulatory agency	The Privacy Act applies when the federal government maintains a system of records by which information about individuals is retrieved by use of the individuals' personal identifiers (names, social security numbers, or any other codes or identifiers that are assigned to the individual). A "record" for purposes of the Privacy Act means any item, collection, or grouping of information about an individual that is maintained by the agency and that contains the individual's name or other personal identifier.	The Privacy Act of 1974 and its implementing regulations: 1) Prohibits the disclosure of personally identifiable information maintained by agencies is a system of records without the consent of the subject individual, subject to twelve codified exceptions (2) Grants individuals increased rights of access to agency records maintained on themselves. (3) Grant individuals the right to seek amendment of agency records maintained on themselves upon a showing that the records are not accurate, relevant, timely, or complete. (4) Establishes a code of "fair information practices" which requires agencies to comply with statutory norms for collection, maintenance, and dissemination of records.

Federal Law	Citation	General Description	Applicability	Information Covered	Summary
The Freedom of Information Act (FOIA) 5 U.S.C. § 552 (2006), amended by OPEN Government Act of 2007, Pub. L. No. 110-175, 121Stat. 2524.	5 U.S.C. § 552; 45 C.F.R. Part 5	The Freedom of Information Act is a disclosure statute.	Agencies within the Executive Branch of the federal government, including independent regulatory agencies and some components within the Executive Office of the President, are subject to the provisions of the FOIA.	Records that are (1) either created or obtained by an agency, and (2) under agency control at the time of the FOIA request.	When an agency receives a proper FOIA request for records it must make the records "promptly available" unless the records or portions of the records are exempt from mandatory disclosure under subsection (b), or excluded under subsection (c). Subsection (b) of the FOIA establishes nine exemptions from disclosure, which were created by Congress to permit agencies to protect from disclosure certain specific types of information. Exemption 6 of subsection (b) allows for the withholding of personnel, medical, or similar files, the release of which would constitute a clearly unwarranted invasion of personal privacy. Exemption 7(C) provides protection for law enforcement information, the disclosure of which could reasonably be expected to constitute an unwarranted invasion of personal privacy. Subsection (c) of the FOIA establishes three special categories of law enforcement- related records that are entirely excluded from the coverage of the FOIA in order tosafeguard against specific types of harm. The extraordinary protection embodied in subsection (c) permits an agency to respond to a request for such records as if the records in fact did not exist.
Health Insurance Portability and Accountability Act (HIPAA), Privacy Rule (2000)	See generally, Pub. L. No. 104-191 (42 U.S.C. § 1320d-2 note) 45 C.F.R. Part 160 and Subparts A and E of Part 164 *See generally http:// www.hhs.gov/ ocr/ privacy/index.ht ml*	Establishes national standards regarding health information privacy	Covered health entities; indirectly, business associates (who will become directly covered in 2010 pursuant to the American Recovery and Reinvestment Act of 2009)	Protected health information (certain individually identifiable health information)	Provides a federal floor of health information privacy protection; more protective state laws remain in force. The Rule assures certain individual rights in health information, imposes restrictions on uses and disclosures of protected health information, and provides for civil and criminal penalties for violations.
Health Insurance Portability and Accountability Act (HIPAA) Security Rule	42 U.S.C. § 1320d-2(d) 45 C.F.R. Part 160 and Subparts A and C of Part 164 *See Generally http:// www.cms.hhs.gov/ SecurityStand ard/ Downloads/sec urityfinalrule.*pdf	Establishes national required and addressable security standards.	Covered health entities; indirectly business associates (who will become directly covered in 2010 pursuant to the American Recovery and Reinvestment Act of 2009)	Electronic protected health information (certain electronic individually identifiable information)	Works in tandem with HIPAA Privacy Rule and lays out three types of security safeguards required for compliance: administrative, physical, and technical.

Federal Law	Citation	General Description	Applicability	Information Covered	Summary
Health Breach Notification Rule (Federal Trade Commission Rule)	16 C.F.R. Part 318 *http://www.ftc.gov/os/2009/04/R911002healthbreach.pdf*	This proposed rule requires vendors of personal health records (PHRs) and related entities to notify individuals when their individually identifiable health information is breached	Vendors of PHRs, their related entities, and and other third party service providers who do not qualify as entities covered under HIPAA	Unsecured identifiable health information of an individual in a personal health record	These proposed rule requires vendors of personal health records (PHRs) and related entities to provide notice to consumers following a security breach. Stipulates that if a service provider of a PHR vendor experiences a breach, it must notify the PHR vendor. The PHR vendor, in turn, must notify consumers of the breach. The proposed rule contains additional requirements governing the standard for what triggers the notice, as well as the timing, method, and content of notice.
Health Breach Notification Rule (Health and Human Services)	45 C.F.R. Parts 160 and Subparts A and D of Part 164 *http://www.hhs.gov/ocr/privacy/hipaa/understanding/coveredentities/federalregisterbreachrfi.pdf*	Requires notification from HIPAA covered entities, upon discovery of a breach of security	HIPAA covered entities; business associates	HIPAA protected health information	Requires covered entities to provide notice to patients, HHS, and in some cases, the media following a breach of unsecured protected health information. Aso requires business associates to notify covered entities following the discovery of such a breach.
SAMHSA: Confidentiality of Substance Abuse Patient Records	42 U.S.C. § 290dd-2, 42 C.F.R. Part 2	Confidentiality of substance abuse patient records (alcohol and drug abuse patient records)	Federally assisted alcohol and drug abuse programs that provide diagnosis, treatment or referral for treatment	Substance abuse patient records; information that identifies a person as an alcohol or drug abuser	It is prohibited to disclose substance abuse patient records and information that identifies an individual as an alcohol or drug abuser without obtaining the written consent of the individual. The regulations establish limited circumstances permitting disclosures without consent for medical emergencies, audit/evaluation activities, and research. Other disclosures without patient consent are permitted with an authorizing court order issued by a court of competent jurisdiction.
Medicaid Privacy Requirements	42 U.S.C. 1396a(a)(7) 42 C.F.R. §§ 431.300-307	Administrative privacy requirements for Medicaid State agencies	States holding data related to Medicaid beneficiaries	Information concerning applicants for and recipients of Medicaid	A State plan must provide, under a State statute that imposes legal sanctions, safeguards meeting the requirements of this subpart that restrict the use or disclosure of information concerning Medicaid applicants and recipients to purposes directly connected with the administration of the plan and, at the option of the States, the exchange of information necessary to verify the certification of eligibility of children for free or reduced school meals.

Federal Law	Citation	General Description	Applicability	Information Covered	Summary
Genetic Information Nondiscrimination Act of 2008 (GINA)	Pub. L. No. 110- 233 *http://www.gpo.gov/fdsys/pkg/PLAW-110publ233/content-detail.html* HHS Office for Civil Rights Proposed Rule *http://www.hhs.gov/ocr/privacy/hipaa/understanding/special/genetic/ginanprm.pdf* Equal Employment Opportunity Commission regulation 74 Fed. Reg. 9056 Proposed Rule 29 C.F.R. Part 1635 *http://edocket.access.gpo.gov/2009/E9- 4221.htm* HHS, Labor, and Treasury Final Rule *http://www.hhs.gov/ocr/privacy/hipaa/understanding/speci al/genetic/ginaifr.pdf*	Protections for genetic information in health insurance and employment	Group health plans and employers (amends ERISA)	Genetic test results, family history, or use of genetic services in the individual or family members	Generally, prohibits discrimination by group health plans and employers on the basis of genetic information. Prohibits a group health plan from adjusting premium or contribution amounts for a group on the basis of genetic information, requesting or requiring an individual or family member to undergo a genetic test, or from using or disclosing genetic information for underwriting or enrollment determination. Allows plans to request but not require genetic testing for research. Prohibits employers from using genetic information for terminating, not hiring, refusing to include in special programs and training, or affecting employment status in any way. Requires genetic information held by employers to be maintained in separate files and prohibits disclosure of such information except under extremely limited circumstances. Agencies with regulatory authority include the Departments of Labor, Health and Human Services and Treasury.
Clinical Laboratory Improvement Amendments (CLIA) (1988)	42 U.S.C. § 263a 42 C.F.R. §493.1291 *http://wwwn.cdc.gov/clia/regs/toc.aspx*	Regulates laboratories conducting testing on human specimens for medical purposes	Any facility which performs laboratory testing on human specimens for medical purposes	Identifiable lab specimens and test results	Assures quality standards for all laboratory testing to ensure the accuracy, reliability and timeliness of patient test results. Certified labs may disclose test results or reports only to authorized people, those responsible for using (i.e. those treating the patient) the results, and the referring lab in a reference lab scenario; State laws define who is authorized, which may or may not include the patient.
Federal Food, Drug, and Cosmetic Act (FDCA)	21 U.S.C. § 301, et.seq. See generally 21 C.F.R. Part 50	Assures the safety of food and drug products	Any product or activity that falls within its jurisdiction	Confidential information that may identify human subjects	Generally, no investigator may involve a human being as a subject in research covered by these regulations unless the investigator has obtained the legally effective informed consent of the subject or the subject's legally authorized representative. An investigator must seek such consent only under circumstances that provide the prospective subject or the representative sufficient opportunity to consider whether or not to participate and that minimize the possibility of coercion or undue influence. In seeking informed consent, a statement must be provided to the each subject describing the extent, if any, to which confidentiality of records identifying the subject will be maintained and that notes the possibility that the Food and Drug Administration may inspect the records.
Controlled Substances Act (CSA)	21 U.S.C. § 801, et. seq. 21 C.F.R. § 1316.23	Allows researchers to petition the U.S. Attorney General for a grant of confidentiality to protect the identify of human subjects	Bona fide research projects directly related to the enforcement of the laws under the jurisdiction of the U.S. Attorney General	Identity of persons involved in research of drugs and substances covered under the Controlled Substances Act	Protects identifiable research information from forced or compelled disclosure. Allows for refusal to disclose identifying information regarding research participants in civil, criminal, administrative, legislative, or other proceedings

Federal Law	Citation	General Description	Applicability	Information Covered	Summary
Federal Policy for the Protection of Human Subjects (Common Rule)	45 C.F.R. §§ 46.111(a)(7), 46.116(a)(5) *http://www.hhs.gov/ ohrp/humansubject s/guidance/45cfr46. htm* *See http://www.hhs. gov/ ohrp/policy/ commo n.html for codifications of the Common Rule into various agency regulations*	Procedures and protections for human subjects participating in research funded by Federal agencies which adopted the Common Rule	Institutions, institutional review boards (IRBs), investigators conducting research	Research records identifying the subject and research data, which both can include health information	Governs Institutional Review Boards (IRBs) which exercise oversight of human subject research. As a prerequisite for IRB approval of research is that, when appropriate, the research must include adequate provisions protecting the privacy of subjects and maintaining confidentiality of data. Requires obtaining informed consent from research subjects, which includes providing subjects with information about the extent, if any, to which confidentiality of records identifying the subject will be maintained.
Statutory Authority for Certificates of Confidentiality	42 U.S.C. 241(d)	Allows the Secretary of HHS to issue a certificate to protect information from disclosure	Researchers	Identity of persons involved in biomedical, behavioral, clinical, or other research (including research on mental health, and on the use and effect of alcohol and other psychoactive drugs	Certificates of confidentiality may be Issued by the National Institutes of Health (NIH) and other HHS agencies to protect identifiable research information from forced or compelled disclosure. They allow for refusal to disclose identifying information on research participants in civil, criminal, administrative, legislative, or other proceedings.
AHRQ Confidentiality Provisions	42 U.S.C. §§ 299c-3(c), (d)	Requires AHRQ to get consent from subjects or suppliers of data before releasing identifiable data	Identifiable data collected by AHRQ	Data collected for health care improvement research or patient safety research by AHRQ	Data collected by AHRQ cannot be used for any purpose other than the purpose for which it was supplied unless the identifiable establishment, person, or other supplier of the data has consented to its use for such other purpose. Provides a civil penalty of up to $10,000 for individuals who violate this provision.
CDC Confidentiality Provisions	42 U.S.C. § 242m(d)	Requires CDC to get consent before releasing identifiable information	Data collected by CDC	Data collected for research, evaluations, and demonstrations in health statistics, health services, and health care technology	Data collected by CDC cannot be used for any purpose other than the purpose for which it was supplied unless such establishment or person has consented (as determined under regulations of the Secretary) to its use for such other purpose.
SAMHSA: Confidentiality Provisions for Data Collection and Survey Information	42 U.S.C. § 290aa(n)	Requires the consent of the person or establishment prior to use or release of identifiable information	Data obtained in the course of activities undertaken or supported by collected by SAMHSA	Data on mental health and substance abuse	Identifiable information obtained in the course of activities undertaken or supported by SAMHSA pursuant to data collection activities authorized under 42 U.S.C. §290aa-4 may not be used for any purpose other than the purpose for which it was supplied unless such establishment or person has consented (as determined under regulations of the Secretary) to its use for such other purpose.
Patient Safety and Quality Improvement Act of 2005 (Patient Safety Act)	42 U.S.C. 299b-21 to 299b-26; 42 C.F.R. Part 3 http:// edocket.acces s.gpo.gov/2008/ E8- 27475.htm	Allows providers to voluntarily report information to Patient Safety Organizations (PSOs), on a privileged and confidential basis, for aggregation and analysis of patient safety events.	PSOs and providers that voluntarily participate	Data related to patient safety events	Establishes a framework by which hospitals, doctors, and other health care providers may voluntarily report information related to patient safety events (termed "patient safety work product") to Patient Safety Organizations (PSOs), on a privileged and confidential basis, for aggregation and analysis of patient safety events. Does not shield providers from having to comply with other Federal, state, or local laws pertaining to medical errors. PSO is a statutorily defined term of art and, by statute, the organizations must be listed by ARHQ, acting on behalf of the HHS Secretary.

Federal Law	Citation	General Description	Applicability	Information Covered	Summary
Employee Retirement Income Security Act of 1974 (ERISA)	29 U.S.C. § 1132	Provision of consumer information by certain health plans	Private industry pension and health plans	Personal health information	Requires pension and health benefits plans to provide information about plan features and funding to consumers; provides fiduciary responsibilities for management and control of plan assets; establish a plan grievance and appeals process; and gives plan members the right to sue for benefits and breaches of fiduciary duty, including breaches of privacy. Responsibility for the interpretation and enforcement of ERISA is divided among the Department of Labor, the Department of the Treasury, and the Pension Benefit Guaranty Corporation.
Individuals with Disabilities Education Improvement Act (2004)	20 U.S.C. § 1400, *et seq.* 34 C.F.R. Parts 300 and 301 *http://frwebgate4.ac cess.gpo.gov/cgi-bin/waisgate.cgi?WAISdocID=81055712322+1+0+0&WAISaction=retrieve*	Ensure services to children with disabilities	All public and private schools receiving federal funds	Educational records	Governs how states and public agencies provide early intervention, special education and related services to children with disabilities; infants, toddlers, children and youth with disabilities. Includes requirements regarding surrogate parents, notice and parental consent regarding disability information.
Family Educational Rights and Privacy Act (1974)	20 U.S.C. § 1232g 34 C.F.R. Part 99 *http://www.ed.gov/policy/gen/reg/ferpa/index.html*	Privacy of student education records	Educational agencies and institutions that receive funds under any program administered by the Secretary of Education	Educational records maintained by the institution that relate directly to the student	Limits disclosure of educational records maintained by agencies and institutions that receive federal funding. Protects the confidentiality of student records to some extent, while also giving students the right to review their own records. "Directory information" is not protected.
Protection of Pupil Rights Amendment (2002)	20 U.S.C. § 1232h 34 C.F.R. Part 98 *http://www4.law.cornell.edu/uscode/20/1232h.html*	Protects rights of parents and students	Programs with funding from the U.S. Department of Education	Personal information, including some health related information	Protects the rights of parents and students by 1) making instructional materials used in Department of Education funded surveys and analyses available to parents, and 2) ensuring that written parental consent is obtained before minor students participate in such surveys and analyses. Topics emphasized are: mental and psychological problems; sex behavior and attitudes; illegal, anti-social, self- incriminating and demeaning behavior; and income. Parents or students who believe their rights under PPRA may have been violated may file a complaint with the Department of Education.
Right to Financial Privacy Act (1978)	12 U.S.C. § 3401, *et seq.*	Protects the confidentiality of personal financial records	Federal agencies	Personal financial records	Protects the confidentiality of personal financial records by requiring that federal government agencies provide individuals with a notice and an opportunity to object before a bank or other specified institution can disclose personal financial information to a federal government agency.

Federal Law	Citation	General Description	Applicability	Information Covered	Summary
Financial Modernization Act (Gramm-Leach-Bliley Act 1999) and Privacy of Consumer Financial Information Regulations	15 U.S.C. §§ 6801-6809 16 C.F.R. Part 313 *http://ecfr.gpoacces s.gov/cgi/t/text/text-idx?c=ecfr&tpl=/ecfr browse/Title16/16cf r313_main_02.tpl*	Protects non-public personal information collected by financial institutions	Any institution engaged in financial activities	Personal non-public information	Financial institutions must protect information collected about individuals; it does not apply to information collected in business or commercial activities. Financial institutions must issue privacy notices to their customers, with the opportunity to opt- out of some sharing of personally identifiable financial information with outside companies. Consumers have no right to stop sharing among affiliates, any company that controls, is controlled by, or is under common control with another company. Agencies with regulatory authority include the National Credit Union Administration, the Secretary of the Treasury, the Securities and Exchange Commission, and the Federal Trade Commission
Fair and Accurate Credit Transaction Act (FACTA) (2003)	Various provisions located throughout the Fair Credit Reporting Act, 15 U.S.C. § 1681, *et seq.*	Combats identity theft and allows consumers to exercise greater control over their personal information Adds a new section 604(g)(1) to the Fair Credit Reporting Act	Credit reporting agencies	Consumer information	Allows consumers to request and obtain a free credit report once every twelve months; individuals can place alerts on their credit histories if identity theft is suspected, or if deploying overseas in the military to deter fraudulent credit applications; requires secure disposal of consumer information.
Fair Credit Reporting Act (FCRA) (1970)	15 U.S.C. § 1681, *et seq.*	Protects consumers from certain disclosures by consumer reporting agencies	Credit reporting agencies	Personal information	Provides important protections for credit reports, consumer investigatory reports, and employment background checks. Requires credit reporting agencies to protect the confidentiality, accuracy, and relevance of credit information. Establishes a framework of Fair Information Practices for personal information: rights of data quality (access and correct), data security, use limitations, requirements for data destruction, notice, user participation (consent), and accountability. FCRA was re- visited in the Fair and Accurate Credit Transactions Act of 2003 (FACTA).
Fair Credit Reporting Medical Information Regulations (2005)	12 C.F.R. Part 717 *http://www.access.g po.gov/nara/cfr/wai sidx_06/12cfr717_0 6.html*	Allows creditors to obtain or use consumer medical information for any credit eligibility determination	Credit reporting agencies	Personal information	A creditor may not obtain or use medical information in connection with any determination of a consumer's eligibility, or continued eligibility, for credit except as permitted by regulations or FACTA. Creditors can obtain or use medical information for credit eligibility determinations where necessary for legitimate purposes, and may permit affiliates to share medical information with each other without becoming consumer reporting agencies.
Fair Debt Collection Practices Act (Revised 2006)	15 U.S.C. § 1692	Addresses abusive debt collection practices	Debt collectors	Personal information	Promotes fair debt collection and provides consumers the right to dispute the accuracy of debt information. Creates guidelines under which debt collectors may conduct business, defines rights of consumers involved with debt collectors, and prescribes penalties and remedies for violations. The debt collector may only contact the debtor's through his/her attorney; if no attorney, then the collector may contact other people, but only to obtain an address, phone number, and work location. Collectors usually are prohibited from contacting such third parties more than once.

Federal Law	Citation	General Description	Applicability	Information Covered	Summary
Children's Online Privacy Protection Act (1998) and accompanying rule	15 U.S.C. S§ 6501–6506 16 C.F.R. Part 312 *http://www.ftc.gov/os/1999/10/64fr59888.htm*	Protects children's personal information online	Commercial web sites and other online services directed at children under 13, or which collect users' age	Personal information	Protects the privacy of children under the age of 13 by requesting parental consent for the collection or use of any personal information of the users.
Cable Communications Policy Act (1984)	47 U.S.C. § 551	Cable service privacy	Cable service providers	Personally identifiable information	Generally, cable service providers must obtain consent from the subscriber before collecting or disclosing any personal information and provide a written notice of privacy practices annually.
Telephone Consumer Protection Act (1991)	47 U.S.C. § 227	Restricts the use of automated telephone systems for telemarketing	Any business that solicits consumers by phone or other electronic media (fax, voice messages, text messaging)	Personal information	Governs the conduct of telephone solicitations or telemarketing. Requires the Federal Communications Commission to promulgate rules to protect residential telephone subscribers' privacy rights. Established the do not call list for consumers to opt out of telemarketing calls.
Video Privacy Protection Act (1988)	18 U.S.C. § 2710	Prevents disclosure of personally identifiable records of video rentals or purchases by consumers	Video service providers	Personal information and video preferences	Prohibits disclosure of customer records without consumer consent. Requires destruction of personally identifiable customer information when no longer necessary.
Drivers Privacy Protection Act (1994)	18 U.S.C. § 2721	Limits disclosures of personal drivers license information	Departments of motor vehicles	Personal information	Release of information for official functions requires the express consent of the individual. There are, however, a large number of exceptions, and disclosure is permitted for agency functions, civil/judicial proceedings, etc.
REAL ID Act (2005)	H.R. 1268, 109 P.L. 13	Requires states to implement new requirements for drivers licenses and identification cards	State governments	Personal information	Imposes specific federal driver's license standards. The standards govern what information must be collected for and on the license, and in what format. Requires use of enhanced data collection, automation and security protections. States must meet requirements related to: • information and security features for the cards • proof of identity and U.S. legal status • verification of the source documents provided Also requires each state to share its motor vehicle database with all other states.
Employee Polygraph Protection Act (1988)	29 U.S.C §§ 2001-2009 29 C.F.R. Part 801 *http://finduslaw.com/employee_polygraph_protection_epp_29_u_s_code_chap ter_22*	Prevents employers from requiring lie detector tests for employees or job applicants, with certain exceptions	Employers	Personal information	Prevents employers from using lie detector tests, either for pre-employment screening or during the course of employment, with certain exemptions. Employers generally may not require any employee or job applicant to take a lie detector test, or discharge, discipline, or discriminate against an employee or job applicant for refusing to take a test.
Federal Trade Commission Act (FTCA) (1914)	15 U.S.C. § 41, et seq.	Established the Federal Trade Commission (FTC) and its roles; governs consumer protection and business competition in the United States	Trade and commerce activities	Information related to any questionable business practices	Maintains a competitive marketplace for both consumers and businesses by policing anticompetitive practices. Monitors unfair and deceptive acts or practices including the Telemarketing Sales Rule, the Pay-Per-Call Rule and the Equal Credit Opportunity Act. The FTC has the authority to adopt trade regulation rules that define unfair or deceptive acts in particular industries.

Federal Law	Citation	General Description	Applicability	Information Covered	Summary
Federal Information Security Management Act (FISMA) (2002)	44 U.S.C. § 3541(a)(1)(A)	Ensures that federal government information systems and information have security protections commensurate with the risk and magnitude of the harm resulting from unauthorized access, use, disclosure, disruption, modification, or destruction	Executive branch of the federal government and to outside entities acting on behalf of the federal government, including government contractors	Any. System risks are determined by classifying the types of information in it	Requires a mandatory set of IT system security processes that must be followed for all federal information systems. Compliance is monitored through yearly audits. As of 2008, annual reports must include: 1) by agency, the number of each type of privacy review conducted that year; 2) information about the privacy advice provided by the Senior Agency Official for Privacy; 3) the number of written complaints for each type of privacy issue allegation received, and 4) the number of complaints the agency referred to another agency
Electronic Signatures in Global and National Commerce Act (2000)	15 U.S.C. § 7001, *et seq.*	Guarantees the same legal validity for electronic contracts and signatures as for those executed by hand	Applies to any transaction relating to the conduct of business, consumer or commercial affairs between two or more persons	Any information contained in contracts; individual signatures	A contract or signature may not be denied legal effect, validity, or enforceability solely because it is in electronic form. Facilitates the use of electronic records and signatures in interstate and foreign commerce by ensuring the validity and legal effect of contracts entered into electronically. Consumers have the right to be aware of and consent to the use of an electronic record/signature. However, the legal effectiveness of the record may be affected by the lack of informed consent. Addresses retention of contracts and records.
Telecommunications Act (1996)	104 P.L. 104-104, 110 Stat. 56 *http://frwebgate.acc ess.gpo.gov/cgi-bin/getdoc.cgi?dbname=104_cong_public_laws&docid=f:p ubl104.104*	Governs telecommunications licensure and activities	Telecommunication s companies	Personal information	Requires telephone companies to give customers explicit notice of their right to control the use of their personal information and obtain express written, oral or electronic approval for its use. Certain provisions relate to prevention of unfair billing practices for information or services provided over toll-free telephone calls, privacy of consumer information, and a report on the use of advance telecommunications services for medical purposes.
Stored Communications Act	18 U.S.C. § 2701, *et seq.*	Prohibits unauthorized access of electronic communications	Everyone	Wire or electronic communications	Prohibits unauthorized access of electronic communications and provides civil and criminal remedies for violations, including a private right of action for aggrieved individuals. Also requires notice in the event of unauthorized access to a consumer's electronic records.
Electronic Communications Privacy Act (1986)	18 U.S.C §§ 2510-22, 2701-11, 3121-26.	Protections for electronic communications	Federal agencies	Privileged communications	Protects wire, oral, and electronic communications while in transit, and communication held in electronic storage. It sets requirements for search warrants under some circumstances that are more stringent than in other settings. It also prohibits the use of devices to record dialing, routing, addressing, and signaling information used in transmitting wire or electronic communications without a search warrant. Exceptions include: No protection for employee using employers equipment and it is not unlawful to capture info if at least one person in conversation knows about activities

Federal Law	Citation	General Description	Applicability	Information Covered	Summary
The PATRIOT Act (2001)	109 P.L. 177 (2005 reauthorization) *http://frwebgate.acc ess.gpo.gov/cgi-bin/getdoc.cgi?dbn ame=109_cong_pu blic_laws&do-cid=f:p ubl177.109.pdf*	Expands the authority of US law enforcement agencies to fight terrorism in the United States and abroad.	Federal enforcement agencies	Restricts, reduces or eliminates many federal privacy law protections	Significantly increased the surveillance and investigative powers of law enforcement agencies in the United States to monitor private communications and access personal information for the purpose of locating terrorists and preventing terrorist acts. Amends a number of federal laws that contain privacy protections.
Foreign Intelligence Surveillance Act (FISA) (1978)	50 U.S.C. §§1801–1811, 1821–29, 1841–46, and 1861–62	Provides procedures for the surveillance and collection of foreign intelligence	Federal agencies	Personal information obtained without warrants or knowledge of the individual	Created a court which meets in secret, and approves or denies requests for search warrants. The 2001 Patriot Act included provisions to bypass the FISA Court and conduct surveillance without a warrant.
Privacy Protection Act (1980)	42 U.S.C. § 2000aa, *et seq.*	Requires law enforcement use of subpoenas or voluntary cooperation to obtain evidence from those engaged in First Amendment activities	Government officers and employees	Personal information and personal privacy	Protects journalists and publishers from being required to turn over to law enforcement any work product and documentary materials, including sources, before it is disseminated to the public.
Communications Assistance for Law Enforcement Act (1994)	47 U.S.C. § 1001, *et seq.*	Defines telecommunications carriers' duty to cooperate in intercepting communications for law enforcement and other purposes	Telecommunication s carriers and manufacturers of telecommunication s equipment	Customer personal information	Telecommunications carriers must assist law enforcement in executing electronic surveillance pursuant to lawful authorization. Requires telecommunications carriers and manufacturers of telecommunications equipment to modify and design their equipment, facilities, and services to ensure the necessary surveillance capabilities. Preserves law enforcement's ability to conduct lawfully-authorized electronic surveillance while preserving public safety and the public's right to privacy. Includes some privacy enhancements, such as raising the standard for government access to transactional data.
Confidential Information Protection and Statistical Efficiency Act of 2002	Pub. L. 107-347, 116 Stat. 2962 (44 U.S.C. 3501	Protects the confidentiality of identifiable information acquired by federal agencies	Government agencies	Data supplied by Individuals and organizations to federal agencies under a pledge of confidentiality for statistical purposes	Data or information acquired by an agency under a pledge of confidentiality for exclusively statistical purposes shall not be disclosed by an agency in identifiable form, for any use other than an exclusively statistical purpose, except with the informed consent of the respondent.
Computer Fraud and Abuse Act	18 U.S.C. §1030	Protects computers used in Federal government, certain financial institutions or computers used in interstate and foreign commerce	Federal government, financial institutions, computers used in interstate commerce	Information stored in computers of the federal government or certain financial institutions or computers used in interstate and foreign commerce	Protects computers used in Federal government, certain financial institutions or computers unused in interstate and foreign commerce from unauthorized access. Imposes fines and imprisonment for violations.
Federal Trade Commission Identify Theft Rule	16 C.F.R. Part 681 *See http://www.ftc.gov/o s/fedreg/2007/nove mber/071109redfla gs.pdf*	Require individuals and entities to develop processes that detect identity theft.	Financial institutions and creditors with covered accounts	Information stored by Financial Institutions and Creditors with Covered Accounts	Requires financial Institutions and creditors with covered accounts to develop a written program that identifies and detects the relevant warning signs—or "red flags"—of identity theft. The program must describe appropriate responses that would prevent and mitigate the crime and detail a plan to update the program.

This glossary provides basic definitions of many of the legal terms you will encounter in this book. A number of our entries are modifications to the definitions found in the glossary provided by the federal judiciary (which is available online at *http://www.uscourts.gov/Common/Glossary.aspx*). For more detail on any of the terms, please consult *Black's Law Dictionary* or another legal reference book.

Abstract of title. A condensed history of the title to a piece of land listing all conveyances, liens, and liabilities on it.

Advance directives. Individuals will often create a document that specifies what medical treatment they wish to have – or not have – to inform health care professionals of their wishes when they (the patient) are no longer able to convey that information themselves.

Adverse possession. Method of acquiring title to real property by openly occupying land for a continuous period of time set by statute. Occupancy must be hostile, that is, occupying party does not recognize title of actual holder, and he uses property without permission of the title holder. Occupant should visibly display his intent to claim and hold property.

Affirmative defense. A defendant's answer to a complaint that does not deny the facts of the charge or the plaintiff's complaint, but which presents evidence or arguments in favor of the defendant that mitigate or excuse the defendant's actions (e.g., insanity, self-defense, and duress are pleas used in criminal cases which are affirmative defenses).

Agency. 1. A fiduciary relationship in which one party represents another by the latter's authority. The relationship can be between an agent and a principal, in which case the agent acts for the principal by, for example, handling his finances; between a master and a servant, that is, between an employer and an employee; or between an employer and an independent contractor. 2. The place where an agent operates. 3. A branch of government (e.g., a police department).

Agent. A person who is authorized to act on behalf of another.

Answers. 1. A reply, response. 2. The first response or pleading made by a defendant to the charges leveled against him in a lawsuit. It must contain a denial of the allegations, and may also contain affirmative defenses, and any permissive or compulsory counterclaims.

Assault. 1. The attempt or threat, accompanied by the apparent present ability, to inflict bodily harm on another. 2. The display of force as to cause fear of bodily harm. Cf. battery. In many states, the crime of assault may include common law battery as well as assault.

Assumption of risk. An affirmative defense used by a defendant in a negligence suit in which he asserts plaintiff knew of a danger and voluntarily exposed himself to it. Assumption of risk by plaintiff would relieve defendant of legal responsibility for any resulting injury.

Attractive nuisances. Dangerous piece of property that may be attractive to children; the doctrine which states that a person who has such a possibly dangerous property or condition on his premises has the duty to take reasonable precautions to guard against injury to children attracted to it. The fact that a child is a trespasser does not relieve owner of responsibility for injuries (e.g., a swimming pool is an attractive yet potentially dangerous condition, and its owner has a responsibility to put a fence around it).

Authority. 1. The right, permission, or power to act, as in the permission a principal gives to his agent to act in his behalf, or the power a police officer has in the lawful exercise of his duties. Authority can be "express" (i.e., that which is explicitly given as in a document of Power of Attorney); it can be "implied," as in that which can be inferred from a person's conduct or from circumstances; and it can be "apparent," as when a principal permits an agent to act. 2. Judicial precedent (i.e., higher court decisions have authority over those of lower courts). 3. A body with power to act.

Battery. The unlawful, undesired, and unprovoked use of force on another person with the intention to harm or create fear of harm in that person; harmful touching. In tort law, all parts of a person's body and anything closely attached to it (such as clothes or a car being driven) are protected. Assault is the threat to use force; its actual use in an offensive way, even though slight, is battery.

Bona fide occupational qualification. A provision that allows employers to discriminate against potential employees on the basis of sex, religion, or national origin, provided employers can show that those qualifications relate to an essential duty of the job and are reasonably necessary for normal operation of the employer. Such a qualification is, thus, a B.F.O.Q.

Capacity. The mental ability to comprehend the nature and effect of one's acts, especially in the making of a will or contract or in the commission of a crime. Regarding wills, capacity includes one's ability to understand the nature and extent of one's property and the claims made upon it. Regarding contracts, capacity requires one to be of legal age, of sound mind and sobriety to make a contract. Regarding criminal acts, capacity means one is able to understand the criminality of an act and be able to conform to the law.

Capias ad respondendum. (CAP-ee-as" or "CAPE-ee-as) Lat. That you take. General term for various writs issued by a judge to the police to take someone into custody, (e.g., a "capias pro fine" is a writ authorizing the taking into custody and detention of someone until a fine is paid).

Collective bargaining. A procedure by which employers and representatives of their employees negotiate a bargain regarding conditions of their employment such as wages, working hours, benefits and working conditions. The procedure is used to settle labor disputes, and must be conducted in "good faith" (i.e., with an open and honest desire to solve the differences between them).

Commerce clause. Article I, section 8, clause 3, of the U.S. Constitution, which states, "Congress shall have the power to regulate commerce with foreign nations, and among the several states and with the Indian tribes."

Comparative negligence. A doctrine that compares the relative degree of fault attributed to a defendant and a plaintiff in a negligence suit; it states that a plaintiff may recover damages from a defendant in a negligence suit even though the plaintiff may be guilty of some negligence himself, provided that the negligence of the defendant was greater. In states with pure comparative negligence, a plaintiff may recover even if his negligence is greater than that of the defendant. The damages awarded the plaintiff will be diminished in proportion to the degree of negligence attributed to him.

Compensatory damages. Those recoverable for the precise injury sustained; damages that make an injured party whole as opposed to punitive, nominal, or exemplary damages. Compensatory damages include medical expenses, pain, mental suffering, and injury to one's reputation.

Consideration. The thing of value each party to a contract agrees to give in exchange for what he receives; the reason a contract is made. Consideration is necessary to make a contract binding. The term includes both the benefit gained by one party and the corresponding responsibility undertaken by the other (e.g., if a builder makes a contract with a homeowner to build an addition to the homeowner's house, he undertakes the responsibility to do the job in exchange for the promise he will be paid an agreed-to amount; the homeowner's promise to pay for the addition is consideration for the builder's promise to do the work, and vice versa).

Contingent fee arrangement. When a person is injured, they may not have funds to pay a lawyer's rate. Instead, the lawyer may promise that that plaintiff need not expend any money, but if the lawyer wins the case for the plaintiff, then the lawyer gets a percentage of the damages, an amount that would be higher than the lawyer's usual rate. Of course, if the plaintiff loses, the lawyer gets nothing. Trial attorneys may also vary the percentage so that they may receive 25% of the damages if the case is settled before trial, 33% if the case goes to trial, and 40% if the case goes onto appeal.

Contract. An agreement between two or more parties which creates legally binding obligations. A valid contract must involve competent parties, proper subject matter, consideration (see consideration), and mutuality of agreement and of obligation. The Uniform Commercial Code defines contract as "the total legal obligation which results from the parties' agreement." Contracts are classified in many ways, some of which follow:

Bilateral or unilateral. A bilateral contract is one involving mutual promises between parties. A unilateral contract is a one-sided promise where one party undertakes an obligation without a reciprocal promise or obligation being made or undertaken.

Executed or executory. An executed contract is one which has been carried out (i.e., where both parties have met their obligations). An executory contract is one where an obligation is to be carried out in the future.

Express or implied. An express contract is openly expressed in writing or orally. An implied contract is one inferred by law to exist because the parties' conduct or surrounding circumstances indicate a contractual relationship exists.

Contributory negligence. Lack of ordinary care for one's safety on the part of an injured plaintiff that, when added to the negligence of another, contributes to the cause of an injury. It is an affirmative defense to a negligence charge, but it has often been replaced by the doctrine of comparative negligence. See comparative negligence.

Copyrights. Statutory protection of work such as a literary work, musical composition, or film or other audiovisual creation giving the creator (or the holder of the copyright) the right to regulate the publication, reproduction, distribution, performance, or use of the copyrighted material for a certain period of time. It is an incorporeal right (i.e., a right to something intangible as opposed to tangible, such as a right to land).

Corporate constituency statutes. Based on the legal version of stakeholder theory, a constituent is a stakeholder. In many states, companies can (and at least in one state must) take into account the actions of the company on its constituents in making corporate decisions.

Co-tenancy. Ownership of property by two or more persons who have unity of possession (i.e., a right to possess the entire property). Term includes joint tenancy, tenancy in common, and tenancy by the entirety (see joint tenancy, tenancy in common, and tenancy by the entirety).

Counterclaim. A counter demand made by a defendant against a plaintiff (i.e., between opposing parties in the original action) in a civil suit. It is not a defense, answer or denial, but an independent cause of action made to diminish or defeat the plaintiff's claim. A counterclaim may be compulsory, arising out of the subject matter of the claim against the defendant, or permissive, not arising out of that subject matter. See set-off; compare cross-claim.

Covenants not to compete. A contractual agreement in which the parties consent not to compete against each other; generally invoked in the sale of a business or as a part of an employment contract.

Deed. A written instrument which transfers real property or the right to real property. A "bargain and sale deed" is a conveyance with a consideration regarding its use attached. A "quitclaim deed" releases and conveys only the interest the grantor has in the property involved. A "warranty deed" insures the validity of the title. The covenants of title are warranty of seisin, quiet enjoyment, and right to convey, freedom from encumbrances, and defense of title as to all claims.

Deed in lieu of foreclosure. If a property owner is unable to pay their mortgage, the financial institution holding the mortgage may accept a deed for ownership of the property rather than going through the process of foreclosing on the property.

Defamation. The publication of material injurious to a person's good name and reputation. Includes both libel and slander.

Denial. In pleading, a refuting of the charges made against one; a contradiction; a traverse. Denials can be general and refute all allegations made in a complaint, or specific and address a particular allegation.

Design patent. A patent granted for the ornamentation attached to a functional item.

Detrimental reliance. A way for there to be consideration in a contract, this notion is that if one party relied on the promises of another to that party's detriment, then they have given up something of legal value that satisfies the consideration requirement for a binding contract. For example, if Party A promises to B that A will give a million dollars to B if B will give up their job and home and move across the country to care for A and A does not live up to the promise even after B makes the move, then B has detrimentally relied on A's promise and the court would find that consideration exists.

Disparate impact. The effect of an employment practice that is non-discriminatory on its face, but that has the effect of discriminating based on age, race, sex, national origin, or disability.

Diversity jurisdiction. A ground used to invoke the jurisdiction of the federal courts when parties on different sides of a controversy involving more than $75,000 live in different states, or when one party is an alien. See the judicial powers granted the United States under Article III, section 2 of the U.S. Constitution.

Doctrine of incapacity/infancy doctrine. 1. The inability to enter into a legally binding transaction; incompetency. An infant has no capacity to enter into a contract. 2. In Workers' Compensation: Inability to work due either to physical inability to perform or inability to find employment.

Due process clause. A flexible term for the fair and orderly administration of justice in the courts. Essential to the concept is the right a person has to be notified of legal proceedings against him, the opportunity to be heard and to defend himself in an orderly proceeding, and the right to have counsel represent him. Basically, due process is the fundamental fairness principle at the core of the Anglo-American system of jurisprudence. Due process also refers to the actual legal proceedings which serve to protect and enforce individual rights and liberties.

The phrase is expressed in the Fifth Amendment to the U.S. Constitution: ". . . nor [shall any person] be deprived of life, liberty, or property, without due process of law," and also in the Fourteenth Amendment which applied the principle to the states.

Durational residency requirement. This is a law some states enact that requires that a person live in the jurisdiction for a period of time before qualifying for benefits, such as welfare or unemployment. The length of these requirements have become litigated.

Easement by necessity. Any real estate has a right to some form of transportation (such as a road). If landlocked, there can be an easement by necessity over property that would allow for such access.

Easement by prescription. The process of acquiring an easement (the right to use part of another's property, water, or light) by continuous use, rather than by asking the owner of the property. "Prescription" applies to easements as "adverse possession" applies to real property.

Eminent domain. A government's power to take, or authorize others to take, private property for a public purpose provided that just compensation is paid for it. In theory, the sovereign has superior dominion over all land, and its "owner" holds it mediately or immediately and must surrender it when the sovereign reasserts its dominion over it. The process of so taking land is called "expropriation" or "condemnation."

Employment. The duties or conduct of an employee that fall within the parameters of his job or position.

Enterprise liability theory. A product may cause damages, but it may be unclear which company's product actually did cause the damage. For example, a person may take a drug sold by three different companies. The court can determine that the drug caused damages to a patient, but it cannot tell which company the patient bought the drug from. The court may then divide up liability according to the market share of each company in the geographic region determined to be the location where the injury occurred.

Equal protection clause of the fourteenth amendment. Constitutional guarantee (Fourteenth Amendment), applicable only to the states, that law shall equally protect all persons under the same circumstances. This does not imply that the law cannot classify persons for specific reasons (e.g., taxation), but only that the classification cannot be arbitrary. Principles of equal protection are enforced against the federal government by application of the Fifth Amendment Due Process Clause (e.g., racial discrimination violates due process).

Estate. 1. The interest a person has in real property. This interest varies from absolute ownership to naked possession (actual possession without color of tide). 2. All the property, whether real or personal, in which one has an interest (e.g., a decedent's estate).

Executed contract. An executed contract is one which has been carried out (i.e., where both parties have met their obligations). An executory contract is one where an obligation is to be carried out in the future.

Executive branch. The branch of government entrusted with executing and enforcing the country's laws and headed by the President of the United States.

Executory contract. An executed contract is one which has been carried out (i.e., where both parties have met their obligations). An executory contract is one where an obligation is to be carried out in the future.

Exemplary damages. Damages awarded in excess of actual damages (i.e., more than is required to compensate plaintiff for injuries sustained). Such damages are awarded to punish defendant, to discourage him and others from committing acts similar to the one for which he is being punished, and to provide some solace to plaintiff for mental anguish and shame. Same as "punitive damages" and "vindictive damages."

Express warranty. Clear, definite, or actual; conveyed in explicit terms (e.g., an express contract, an express warranty). Contrasted with "implied."

Fair use. Principle which allows a person other than the owner of a copyright to use the copyrighted material in a reasonable manner and for certain purposes without the consent of the copyright owner.

Federalism. Federalism can have multiple meanings, depending on the time in which it was used. At the time of the framing of the Constitution, Federalism emphasized the need to strengthen the central government. Today, it is more used to describe the fact that there are state as well as federal governments, each with a range of authority.

The Federalist Papers. Alexander Hamilton, James Madison, and John Jay wrote these philosophical essays anonymously in explaining the proposed U.S. Constitution.

Fee simple/fee simple absolute. An estate in land without any limitations on it which gives the owner the absolute power of disposition. Today there is a presumption that an estate is given in fee simple unless there is a clear intention to give a more limited estate. Also called "fee" or "fee simple absolute."

Firm offer. Written offer which will be held open by a merchant for a certain length of time to buy or sell goods. A firm offer requires no consideration in order to be valid and if no length of time is stated then the offer is irrevocable for a reasonable time, not to exceed three months. U.C.C. § 2–205.

Fraud. Deception, deceit; trickery. An act using deceit such as intentional distortion of the truth or misrepresentation or concealment of a material fact to gain an unfair advantage over another in order to secure something of value or deprive another of a right. Fraud is grounds for setting aside a transaction at the option of the party prejudiced by it or for recovery of damages. "Actual fraud" involves a deliberate misrepresentation or concealment. A court may infer "constructive" or "legal fraud" either from the nature of a contract or from the relationship of the parties.

Freehold estate. The interest a person has in real property. This interest varies from absolute ownership to naked possession (actual possession without color of tide).

Frolic. When an agent or employee performs acts outside the scope of his employment, he is "on a frolic of his own" (e.g., a truck driver who drives off the delivery route for personal activities is on a frolic). See dual purpose doctrine.

Grantor. A person who makes a grant of real property.

Implied authority. The actual authority of an agent implied from circumstances though not expressly granted by the principal.

Implied warranty of merchantability. Under the U.C.C., a guarantee implied from the circumstances of a sale of goods that applies unless disclaimed. Implied warranty of merchantability: Goods sold by a merchant must, among other things, be fit for ordinary purposes. U.C.C. § 2–314. Implied warranty of fitness for a particular purpose: Where the seller knows of a particular purpose for which goods are to be used and the buyer relies on the seller's skill or judgment to furnish suitable goods, the goods must be fit for such purposes. U.C.C. § 2–315.

Incorporation doctrine. The doctrine that a will may incorporate into itself another document which is in existence at the time the will is executed and is sufficiently identified in the will.

Incorporeal interests. Intangible; lacking physical substance or material form. One may have an incorporeal right to intellectual property, for example.

Infringement. 1. The breach of any law. 2. An interference with the legal rights of another. 3. In copyright law: The unauthorized reproduction, performance, distribution, public display, transmission by webcast, or creation of a work derivative of a work protected by copyright. 4. In trademark law: The unlicensed use of a mark in a way that is likely to cause consumer confusion as to the source or origin of goods. 5. In patent law: Manufacturing or using a patented invention or improvement without the permission of the owner of the patent.

Injunction. An equitable remedy in which the court orders a party to perform or to desist from a particular act.

Mandatory injunction commands the defendant to take a positive action to accomplish a specific purpose (e.g., the court may order a school to admit a particular student).

Restrictive injunction forbids the defendant or his agents from attempting or continuing some activity that is injurious to the plaintiff (e.g., the court may prohibit a school from suspending or expelling a student).

Interlocutory injunction is any injunction issued prior to trial to prevent irreparable injury to the plaintiff while the court considers whether to grant permanent relief. Granted for a limited time only. Two types: 1. A "preliminary injunction," which is granted after the defendant has received notice and has had an opportunity to participate in a hearing on the issue, and 2. A "temporary restraining order," which is granted without notice to the defendant in situations where the plaintiff will suffer irreparably if immediate relief is not granted.

A permanent or perpetual injunction is a final disposition in the suit and is indefinite in length of time.

In personam. (in per-SONE-am) Lat. Against the person. In procedure: An action taken against a person which involves his personal rights and is based on jurisdiction over him as opposed to seeking a judgment against property (in rem). Equity courts are said to give "in personam" decisions, meaning that their judgments usually command a person to do or refrain from doing something.

An action for a judgment "in personam" is initiated by giving notice to the affected party either by serving him personally or by substitute service. An example of an action in personam is a lawsuit against an individual who intentionally hit the plaintiff, because the judgment would be against the aggressor himself.

Intangible property. "Intangible property" is not physical (e.g., a copyright, an easement, goodwill, or rights under a contract).

Intentional torts. An intentional tort requires that the actor desired to cause the consequences of his act or recognizes that these consequences are substantially certain to result from his act.

Issue. 1. (v.) To send forth; to put into circulation; to promulgate. 2. To send out officially, as in writs or services of process. 3. (n.) A legal point of dispute between two or more parties to the litigation which, if it is a matter of law, should be resolved by the court or, if it is a matter of fact, should be resolved by the jury. 4. All who are descended from a common ancestor. In wills, this meaning is usually narrowed to include children alone, depending on the intention of the testator. Most states allow an illegitimate child to inherit from his mother but not from his father. Many states consider an adopted child to be the "issue" of his/her adoptive parents. 5. In securities: The offering for sale of a corporation's stock. The securities, themselves, which are being offered for sale. 6. A series or group of bonds or stock which is put into circulation at the same time.

Invitee. One who is invited onto the property of another, either expressly or impliedly, to conduct business for their mutual benefit or for the benefit of the occupier, or to engage in an activity which the occupier permits to be conducted on his property (e.g., a customer who enters a store is an invitee regardless of whether he makes a purchase). In tort law, a property owner has an affirmative duty to protect the invitee not only against known dangers but also against those dangers which the owner may discover by exercising reasonable care.

Joint tenancy. Ownership of real property, created under a single deed or instrument, whereby two or more persons have an undivided interest in the whole of the property, an equal right to share in the use and benefits of the property, and attached to which is the right of survivorship.

Judicial branch. The branch of government entrusted with judicial power and the administration of the courts in the federal system.

Judicial review. 1. Review of a government action by a court. 2. Appellate court review of trial court decisions.

Judicial sale. The sale of property made under the authority or supervision of a court, such as the sale of property ordered by a court to satisfy a tax lien.

Judgment. 1. The decision of a court. 2. The final determination of a court on a matter submitted to it.

Jury instruction. Before a jury decides a case, the judge must provide instructions to the jury that summarizes the applicable law they are to follow. Thus, the court may instruct a jury that if they find that x and y are true, then they must find that the defendant has violated law z. The lawyers, of course, argue as to the exact summary of the law and the losing party will often use a "flawed" jury instruction as grounds for an appeal.

Landlord-tenant relationship. The person who owns real property, and leases it to a tenant. A landlord is often referred to as a lessor.

Lease. Agreement between two parties whereby one party, the lessor, yields his right of possession and use of some real or personal property for a specified period of time to a lessee in return for consideration. Leases of personal property in most states are governed by U.C.C. Article 2A.

Legal precedent. 1. A previously decided case which is used as an example or authority for similar cases which subsequently arise. (See stare decisis.) 2. A rule of law established for a certain type of case. 3. A "precedent condition" or "condition precedent" is a condition that must exist before something, such as a contract or an estate, can take effect.

Legal value. For there to be consideration, each party has to give up something of legal value. The exchange of value does not have to be equal; it can be lopsided, but there needs to be something of tangible legal value that the courts can look to in order to find there is consideration present.

Legislative branch. The branch of government that passes laws, comprised of two houses: The House of Representatives and the Senate.

Licensee. 1. One who enters on another's land with the possessor's permission, express or implied, for her own purpose (e.g., social guest). 2. The person who receives or acquires a license.

Life estates. An ownership interest in property granted to a person for as long as he or another person lives; upon the end of the measuring life, the land will either revert to the grantor of the life estate or will go to a person holding a remainder interest in the property.

Lobby. 1. The act of seeking to sway, influence, or manipulate the beliefs and opinions of legislators. 2. Any attempt to influence the status of proposed or existing legislation.

Long-arm statutes. State legislative acts which allow local courts to obtain jurisdiction over nonresident defendants to a lawsuit where the cause of action is local in origin or has an effect in the state (e.g., a nonresident corporation could be a party to a lawsuit in a jurisdiction other than its own if its goods injured residents of that jurisdiction).

Mailbox rule. Common law contracts doctrine providing that acceptance of an offer is effective when it is deposited in mail, if it is properly addressed and unless another acceptance method is otherwise agreed to.

Mandate. 1. Order of a court directing some specific action or enforcement of a judgment. 2. Bailment of property, when the bailee agrees to do some act without pay.

Mandatory authority. Having an obligation or command which must be obeyed.

Marital deduction. A tax deduction wherein a married person may deduct the value of the property that has been transferred to his or her spouse, or from one spouse to another. This deduction takes the form of an estate or gift tax deduction. I.R.C. §§ 2056, 2523.

Materially alter. Any change in the terms of a written instrument which gives it a legal meaning or effect that is different from its original state.

Measuring life. An ownership interest in property granted to a person for as long as he or another person lives; upon the end of the measuring life, the land will either revert to the grantor of the life estate or will go to a person holding a remainder interest in the property.

Meeting of the minds. 1. A meeting of the minds on a specific matter. 2. In contracts, agreeing to the same bargain at the same time.

Mens rea. (menz RAY-a) Lat. A guilty mind. Criminal intent; the mental state of a person committing an act which constitutes a crime.

Mutual assent. Mutually agreed upon.

The necessary and proper clause. Clause 18 of Section 8 of Article 1 of the U.S. Constitution, which grants to Congress the power to make all laws which are "necessary and proper" to carry out the specific Congressional powers enumerated in the preceding clauses of Section 8.

Negligence per se. An unexcused act or omission that automatically establishes the existence of a duty and breach thereof. Often results from violation of certain statutes (e.g., failure to stop for red traffic signal).

Non-compete clause. An example of a contract that courts often do not enforce because it violates public policy. Companies may require an employee to promise that they will not work for a competitor after leaving their current company. Courts are sympathetic to the rights of companies who have spent money developing individual talent as well as protecting their own company information. On the other hand, courts do not wish to restrict freedom of movement of employees. So the courts will uphold these only if the restrictions are reasonable both with respect to their proposed time limits and geographic constraints.

Opening statements. Presentation made by counsel at beginning of trial in which she summarizes her client's case and the evidence which she will present on the client's behalf.

Output contracts. A contract in which one party agrees to purchase all that the other party is able to produce, in good faith.

Parol evidence rule. Rule of substantive law which states that once an agreement is reduced to writing and both parties have acknowledged this writing as the final expression of their agreement, then parol (oral) evidence of any prior or present understanding of the parties as to the terms of the agreement is inadmissible if it alters or contradicts the meaning of the written document. The basis of the rule is that a clear and unambiguous writing is the best evidence of the intent of the parties and the terms of the agreement. Agreements made subsequent to the writing, whether written or oral, are not subject to the rule. Furthermore, all evidence (whether written or oral) concerning the finality of the agreement is admissible as is evidence of fraud, duress, mistake, misrepresentation, or illegality or evidence offered to rescind or reform the contract.

Patents. A grant issued by the government to an inventor, giving him the exclusive right to make, use, or sell the invention for a specified number of years, constituting a legitimate monopoly.

Personal property. All property not real estate. The two categories of personal property are "corporeal," consisting of movable objects such as furniture or jewelry, and "incorporeal," consisting of the interest one has in something, such as in a corporation by the ownership of stock. See chose in action, personalty.

Persuasive authority. Not all court decisions must be followed, especially when the court is not within the same jurisdiction. For example, a Montana court does not need to follow the law decided by the Supreme Court of Florida. Yet, the Florida court may analyze a case so well, that its views may have persuasive authority that becomes important to the Montana court.

Power of attorney. Document by which a person (principal) grants authority to another (agent) to perform specified acts on the principal's behalf. Also called "letter of attorney" and "warrant of attorney."

Preliminary injunction. A "preliminary injunction," which is granted after the defendant has received notice and has had an opportunity to participate in a hearing on the issue, and 2. A "temporary restraining order," which is granted without notice to the defendant in situations where the plaintiff will suffer irreparably if immediate relief is not granted.

Prima facie. (PRIME-a FAY-shee) Lat. On its face. Describing a fact convincing on its face, without any further proof of validity.

Principal. 1. Most important or highest in rank. 2. In agency law: one who directs or allows another to act for his benefit, subject to his direction and control. The principal may be "disclosed" (known to third parties); "partially disclosed" (when third parties know only that the agent is acting for some principal); or "undisclosed" (when third parties do not know that the agent is acting for any principal). 3. In criminal law: one who commits a crime, as opposed to an "accessory," who may aid the crime but is not present at the commission of the crime. 4. In commercial law: the amount of the loan or investment, not including any interest. 5. In trust law: the money and property in the trust, not including any profit. 6. In the law of guaranty and surety: the one who is obligated to perform a contract which the surety guarantees.

Privity. A relationship of common interests or common legal rights (e.g., a privity of contract is required in a breach of contract action; the defendant must be a party in interest to the plaintiffs contract).

Privity of contract. A relationship of common interests or common legal rights (e.g., a privity of contract is required in a breach of contract action; the defendant must be a party in interest to the plaintiffs contract).

Procedural due process. Constitutional guarantee that a person whose right to life, liberty or property is to be affected is entitled to reasonable notice and an opportunity to he heard and present a defense to the proposed action before a fair and impartial decision-maker. See due process of law.

Puffing. Statement made by a seller which is not a representation of fact, but rather an exaggeration concerning the quality of goods; generally bragging about the product rather than a legally binding representation.

Punitive damages. Award of damages not related to actual harm caused to plaintiff, but instead intended to punish the defendant and deter future wrongdoing. Usually awarded when a tort is aggravated by evil motives, actual malice, deliberate violence, or oppression. Also called "exemplary damages" or "vindictive damages."

Quitclaim deed. Deed by which the grantor releases all his interest in property by passing any interest, claim, or title in the property which he has. The grantor makes no warranties or covenants for title in a quitclaim deed. The deed only purports to convey such title as the grantor has.

Ratification. 1. The acceptance or confirmation of a prior act done by oneself or another for one's benefit, which authorizes the prior act as if it had been originally authorized. 2. The approval by state legislatures or popular conventions of proposed constitutional amendments. 3. Subsequent approval by a principal of an agent's unauthorized act.

Rational basis test. Method by which courts determine the constitutionality of a law. Under this test, the legislature must have had a rational basis for enacting a law, and the law must reasonably relate to a legitimate governmental objective, for it to be constitutional. This is the most permissive of tests used by courts for constitutional questions.

Real property. Land (including buildings and other permanent attachments to the land) and the rights arising out of land. Real property is distinguished from "personal property," which is temporary and movable in nature. A "leasehold interest," the right to rent land for a particular time, is characterized as personal property because it is thought to be temporary.

Rebuttal. Evidence that defeats, refutes, or proves the contrary of facts or presumptions offered in evidence by the opposing party. Rebuttal evidence may be offered at the close of the opponent's case.

Remainder interest. In property, an interest or estate in land that will take effect when the immediately preceding estate terminates. Thus, if A grants Greenacre to B for 10 years with the "remainder" to C, C's estate will begin 10 years after the original grant, on the condition that C is existing and ascertained at the time her estate is due to commence. A remainder can only be valid when the previous estate is less than a "fee simple," when the previous estate terminates regularly, when the remainder is created in the same grant as the previous estate, and when the remainder "vests" (or becomes ascertained) during the previous estate.

Remaindermen. One who is entitled, by grant of the original owner, to a future estate in a remainder of land at the termination of the previous estate.

Reply. In modern civil procedure, the plaintiff's pleading following the defendant's answer. The reply may respond only to the defendant's counterclaims unless the court orders the plaintiff to respond to the defendant's answer or a third-party answer. See Federal Rule of Civil Procedure 7(a).

Res ipsa loquitur. (race IP-sa LO-kwi-tur) Lat. The thing speaks for itself. Doctrine in tort cases which creates a permissible inference of negligence unless the defendant can prove otherwise when (a) the defendant had exclusive control of the thing producing injury and (b) the injury would not normally occur without negligence (e.g., a baby exhibits clear dog bite marks and the defendant owns the only dog in the neighborhood).

Respondeat superior. (ray-spon-day-AT soo-PEER-ee-or) Lat. Let the superior answer. Doctrine that a principal (master or employer) is liable for injuries proximately resulting from the negligent acts of his agent (servant or employee) when the acts are committed within the scope of the agent's authority or apparent authority of employment. The principal, who is deemed to act through his agents, maintains a duty to conduct his affairs so as not to injure others, and is thus liable for the negligent acts of his agents.

Restitution damages/quantum meruit. (KWAN-tum MARE-oo-it) Lat. As much as he deserves. An equitable doctrine that allows a party to recover for the value of his labor and materials furnished to another even though there was no actual contract so that the other party will not be unjustly enriched. The suit is based on an implied promise to pay.

Restrictive covenants. 1. In a deed, a promise to restrict the use of real property, which is a covenant said to "run with the land." Restrictive covenants that prohibit selling property to a person of a certain race are unenforceable by the courts under the due process clause of the Fourteenth Amendment. 2. In a contract, a promise by the employee or partner to refrain from performing similar work after the contract terminates, which is valid if limited to a reasonable geographical area and period of time.

Right of privacy. Those rights expressly granted by the U.S. Constitution, (e.g., right to vote), or those which are necessarily implied from those provisions (e.g., right of privacy).

Ripeness. Constitutional law principle in which federal courts may not hear an action unless it is an actual, present controversy which is neither speculative nor hypothetical in nature. Generally, the case will not be heard unless the plaintiff has been harmed or is threatened with immediate harm.

The rule against perpetuities. In property law, the ancient rule that a future (or contingent) interest which, by any possibility, may not vest within 21 years after a life or lives in being at the time of its creation is void from the time it is created. The rule was introduced to promote the free transfer of land and to restrict tying up the land indefinitely for some unknown claimant.

Sampling. In copyright law, incorporating a small portion of a sound recording into another recording. The portion taken may be manipulated or edited. Sampling may constitute copyright infringement.

Scienter. (sigh-EN-ter) Lat. Knowingly; intentionally; purposely; with knowledge.

Seasonable notice. In a reasonable amount of time; timely; in due season or time.

Secured creditor. A creditor who holds security that ensures the payment of his or her debt, should the debtor default.

The separation of powers. Division of authority between the three branches of government (judicial, legislative, executive). One branch of government is not permitted to impinge on the duties of another (e.g., the judiciary is not permitted to legislate and enact laws, which is the domain of the legislature).

Servient dominant. A tenement or estate whose owner benefits from an easement on another estate (servient estate). For example, A, the owner of a piece of land, sells half of it to B, his neighbor, yet retains the right to build a driveway across the land to get to the street. A holds the dominant estate, B the servient estate.

Servient tenement. The property over which a servient dominant runs. See the following definition of the servient dominant.

Sheriff's deed. Once a property has been foreclosed on, including with a court judgment, the property may be auctioned by an official, such as a sheriff with the winning bidder receiving a deed from the sheriff conveying the property. Usually, the winning bidder is the financial institution itself.

Sheriff's sale. The sale by a sheriff or court official of a party's property, pursuant to a court-ordered decree of execution or foreclosure (e.g., sale of attached property in order to satisfy an unpaid judgment).

Short sale. A sale of shares of stock which the seller does not own or control at the time the sale is negotiated but which she acquires at a lower price prior to the time the delivery of the shares to the buyer is required.

Sovereign immunity. Doctrine that holds that a government or sovereign is immune or exempt from tort liability because of its status in society. Most jurisdictions have waived tort immunity to a certain extent.

Special warranty deed. A deed in which the grantor of real property only agrees to defend and protect the grantee's interest in and title to the property against all claims that arise out or the grantor's interest in the property.

Specific performance. 1. Equitable remedy granted by a court where there has been a breach of contract and where damages would be inadequate to compensate the injured party so that the court requires the breaching party to fulfill his obligations under the contract. 2. The fulfillment or achievement of one's obligations under a contract.

Stakeholder theory. Usually associated with the field of business ethics, a stakeholder is defined as anyone affected by an organizational act. Most typically, the organization is a corporation, but the term can be applied to any organization. Descriptively, organizations do have stakeholders (customers, employees, community, environment, etc.). Instrumentally, organizations need to determine how to interact with stakeholders to be successful. Normatively, stakeholders are individuals with dignity and therefore should be treated as ends not as means to an end.

Standard of care. A standard of behavior used in negligence law, which takes into consideration the degree of care that a reasonable person of ordinary prudence would exercise in similar circumstances.

Standing. 1. To have the right to bring a suit or other legal action before a court of justice (i.e., having a stake in the outcome); to be eligible to bring a cause of action against another party in a court of justice. 2. A person's status, rank, or position within society, an organization, or government.

Statute of frauds. Law that holds that certain contracts may not be enforced unless there is some writing signed by the defendant to the dispute indicating that there was an agreement.

Statutes of repose. Law that prohibits bringing a lawsuit after a specified time since the defendant acted, even if the cause of action has not accrued.

Straw man. A person who secretly acts on behalf of others while at the same time he represents himself to third parties as acting in his own behalf (e.g., a person who buys a building in his own name from a third party but who is in fact purchasing the building on behalf of someone else).

Strict liability. Legal doctrine that holds a manufacturer or a seller liable for all the defects and injuries caused by his products regardless of the degree of care that it exercised.

Strict liability/absolute duty. Legal doctrine that holds a manufacturer or a seller liable for all the defects and injuries caused by his products regardless of the degree of care that it exercised.

Strict scrutiny. Method by which courts determine the constitutionality of a law, when a law affects a fundamental right (e.g., the right to equal protection). Under the strict scrutiny test, the legislature must have a compelling interest to enact the law, and the measures prescribed by the law must be the least restrictive means possible to accomplish the legislature's goal.

Substantive due process. The essence of due process requires that no person be deprived of life, liberty, or property by unreasonable and arbitrary laws.

The supremacy clause. Clause in Article VI, section 2 of the U.S. Constitution which establishes that the laws, treaties and actions of the federal government pursuant to the Constitution are superior to those of the states. Thus, if a federal and state law conflict, federal law governs.

Suretyship. A person who agrees to fulfill a financial obligation of another person upon that person's default of his obligation.

Tacking. 1. In property law, the joining of periods of possession of consecutive adverse possessors, for purposes of establishing title by adverse possession. 2. Generally, any joining or adding together of elements.

Takings clause. Associated with the following entry, eminent domain, this provision of the Fifth Amendment to the Constitution, addresses the times when government attempts to "take" private property, the need to do so only for a public purpose, and the need for the government to provide adequate compensation to the property owner.

Tangible property. In property law, referring to things with a definite physical existence (e.g., an object, a building, a bank account). "Intangible property" is not physical (e.g., a copyright, an easement, goodwill, or rights under a contract).

Taxing and spending. Under the Article I of the Constitution, Congress has the authority to raise taxes for the support of the government and also to spend federal money. These powers are given great deference by the courts so that laws passed by Congress pursuant to these powers have a very good chance to be upheld.

Tenancy by the entirety. Ownership of property by a husband and wife together so that upon the death of either spouse the other will take full and complete ownership of the entire property. Neither spouse can sell the property without the consent of the other. A divorce terminates the tenancy by the entirety and creates a "tenancy in common."

Tenancy in common. Undivided ownership in property by two or more persons, each having the same right to the use and possession of the property. Thus, each owner may separately partition, convey, sell, or dispose by will his share of the property.

Title opinion. Prior to a financial institution issuing a mortgage and often times prior a new owner closing on property, a lawyer may research the history of the property to make sure the property is not encumbered with any liens or other financially burdensome items.

Tortfeasor/defendant. The person who commits a tort.

Tortious interference. Describing action or conduct that results from a breach of a legal duty which may subject the actor to liability.

Torts. A wrongful injury; a private or civil wrong which is not a breach of contract. A tort is some action or conduct by the defendant which results from a breach of a legal duty owed by the defendant to the plaintiff, which proximately causes injury or damage to the plaintiff. Torts may be "intentional" (when the defendant intends to violate a legal duty) or "negligent" (when the defendant fails to exercise the proper degree of care established by law).

Trademarks. Any mark, picture, symbol, or stamp used to designate a certain product of a certain manufacturer and to distinguish it from other manufacturers' similar products. The trademark must be adopted by the manufacturer or merchant and affixed to the product. Generic names are not valid trademarks. Personal names, place names, and common adjectives are valid trademarks only if they have acquired a secondary meaning identifying them with a product. The federal government gives trademark holders exclusive rights to use the trademark for a period of years that may be renewed indefinitely; actions for infringement of trademark may be brought in federal court.

Trespass. 1. Wrongful interference with or damage to another's real or personal property, including entering onto land, physical assault, or destruction of legal rights. 2. In common law pleading, any type of broad civil wrong or tort.

Unconscionable contracts. These are contracts that a court may not enforce because they violate public policy. The components are when there are grossly unequal bargaining positions and the terms of the contract are so one-side so as to shock the conscience. The unequal positions generally take the form of the vulnerable party being unable to read or write or understand the language of the contract. In other words, an MBA student may be in an unequal bargaining position vis-à-vis Apple Computer, but an agreement between the two is not likely to be considered an unconscionable contract.

Undivided interest. An interest or right in property, in which the tenant has an equal right to use and enjoy the entire property (i.e., joint tenancy, tenancy in common, and tenancy by the entirety).

Unity of interest. The condition that cotenants' shares in a joint tenancy be equal and that they be acquired in the same transaction.

Unity of possession. One of the essential properties of a joint estate, which requires that each joint tenant hold the same undivided possession of the whole.

Unity of title. Phrase that recognizes that cotenants in a joint tenancy own their property under the same legal title.

Utility patents. In patent law, the capacity to perform a function or achieve a result.

Vest. To give an immediate, fixed right of present or future enjoyment.

Void. Defective, but capable of confirmation or ratification, such as a minor's contract. A minor does not have the capacity to enter into a contract; therefore, any contract he makes is voidable. However, the contract is not void, and, therefore, it is binding on the competent party unless the minor repudiates it. A voidable transaction is one that can be affirmed by a party entitled to void it.

Voidable. Defective, but capable of confirmation or ratification, such as a minor's contract. A minor does not have the capacity to enter into a contract; therefore, any contract he makes is voidable. However, the contract is not void, and, therefore, it is binding on the competent party unless the minor repudiates it. A voidable transaction is one that can be affirmed by a party entitled to void it.

Voir dire. (vwar or vore deer) Lat. To speak the truth. 1. An examination of a person as a prospective juror to test her competency and prejudice. 2. Preliminary examination of a witness in order to determine her competency to speak the truth.

Waivers of liability. An example of a contract that courts often do not enforce because it violates the public policy. Courts take a very hard look at agreements where one person waives their right to sue the other party for negligence, though these are commonly signed by participants in charitable contests and even childhood play activities. To enforce, the courts will want to determine if (a) the person signing the agreement was aware of the legal consequences of giving away their rights and (b) were fully aware of the risks of engaging in the activity.

Warranty deed. Deed in which the grantor warrants that the title is free of encumbrances (unless noted in the instrument). The usual warranties included are seisin, right to convey, quiet enjoyment, freedom from encumbrances and defense of title against all claims.